Rereading America

*Cultural Contexts for Critical
Thinking and Writing*

Rereading America

Cultural Contexts for Critical Thinking and Writing

Eighth Edition

Edited by

Gary Colombo
LOS ANGELES COMMUNITY COLLEGE DISTRICT

Robert Cullen
SAN JOSE STATE UNIVERSITY

Bonnie Lisle
UNIVERSITY OF CALIFORNIA, LOS ANGELES

Bedford/St. Martin's   Boston   •   New York

For Bedford/St. Martin's
Senior Developmental Editor: Ellen Darion
Senior Production Editor: Karen S. Baart
Production Supervisor: Andrew Ensor
Marketing Manager: Molly Parke
Editorial Assistant: Melissa L. Cook
Production Assistant: David Ayers
Copyeditor: Karen Stocz
Senior Art Director: Anna Palchik
Cover Design: Sara Gates
Cover Art: Jasper Johns, © VAGA, NY. *Flags II*. 1970. Lithograph, printed in color. Gift of the Celeste and Armand Barrios Foundation. The Museum of Modern Art, New York, NY. Digital image © The Museum of Modern Art/Licensed by SCALA/Art Resource, NY
Composition: Achorn International, Inc.
Printing and Binding: Haddon Craftsmen, Inc., an RR Donnelley & Sons Company

President: Joan E. Feinberg
Editorial Director: Denise B. Wydra
Editor in Chief: Karen S. Henry
Director of Marketing: Karen R. Soeltz
Director of Editing, Design, and Production: Marcia Cohen
Assistant Director of Editing, Design, and Production: Elise S. Kaiser
Managing Editor: Elizabeth M. Schaaf

Library of Congress Control Number: 2010920324

Manufactured in the United States of America.

5   4   3   2
i   h   g

For information, write: Bedford/St. Martin's, 75 Arlington Street, Boston, MA 02116 (617-399-4000)

ISBN-10: 0–312–54854–0
ISBN-13: 978–0–312–54854–4

Acknowledgments

Preface for Instructors

About *Rereading America*

Designed for first-year writing and critical thinking courses, *Rereading America* anthologizes a diverse set of readings focused on the myths that dominate U.S. culture. This central theme brings together thought-provoking selections on a broad range of topics—family, education, success, race, gender roles, and nature and the environment—topics that raise controversial issues meaningful to college students of all backgrounds. We've drawn these readings from many sources, both within the academy and outside of it; the selections are both multicultural and cross-curricular and thus represent an unusual variety of voices, styles, and subjects.

The readings in this book speak directly to students' experiences and concerns. Every college student has had some brush with prejudice, and most have something to say about education, the family, or the gender stereotypes they see in films and on television. The issues raised here help students link their personal experiences with broader cultural perspectives and lead them to analyze, or "read," the cultural forces that have shaped and continue to shape their lives. By linking the personal and the cultural, students begin to recognize that they are not academic outsiders—they too have knowledge, assumptions, and intellectual frameworks that give them authority in academic culture. Connecting personal knowledge and academic discourse helps students see that they are able to think, speak, and write academically and that they don't have to absorb passively what the "experts" say.

Features of the Eighth Edition

A Cultural Approach to Critical Thinking Like its predecessors, the eighth edition of *Rereading America* is committed to the premise that learning to think critically means learning to identify and see beyond dominant cultural myths—collective and often unconsciously held beliefs that influence our thinking, reading, and writing. Instead of treating cultural diversity as just another topic to be studied or "appreciated," *Rereading America* encourages students to grapple with the real differences in perspective that arise in a pluralistic society like ours. This method helps students to break through conventional assumptions and patterns of thought that hinder fresh critical responses and inhibit dialogue. It helps them recognize that even the most apparently "natural" fact or obvious idea results from a process of social construction. And it helps them to develop the intellectual independence essential to critical thinking, reading, and writing.

Classic and Conservative Perspectives   To provide students with the historical context they often need, each chapter in this edition of *Rereading America* includes a "classic" expression of the myth under examination. Approaching the myth of success, for example, by way of Horatio Alger's *Ragged Dick* — or the myth of racial superiority by way of Thomas Jefferson's infamous diatribe against "race mixing" — gives students a better sense of the myth's origins and impact. We've also included at least one contemporary conservative revision of the myth in each chapter, so you'll find in this edition readings by cultural critics who stand to the right of center, writers like Patrick J. Buchanan, Jennifer Roback Morse, and John Berlau.

New Issues   Over the past decade, rising concern about global warming has reinvigorated the American environmental movement. On campuses across the nation, students are mobilizing behind causes that promote a healthy planet and enrolling in courses focused on sustainability and "green studies." This edition of *Rereading America* offers a new, final chapter that invites students to explore American attitudes toward nature and some of the most urgent questions associated with the climate change crisis. In "Ah Wilderness! American Myths of Nature and the Environment," selections by Henry David Thoreau, Annie Dillard, Richard Louv, and Charles Siebert challenge students to consider the power of nature and the role that the natural world plays in American lives. Environmental writers like Joy Williams, Bill McKibben, and Graeme Wood raise questions about what we can and can't do to save the planet from extinction. Critical perspectives offered by John (Fire) Lame Deer, Nydia M. Velázquez, and John Berlau question mainstream American thinking about nature and the aims of the contemporary environmental movement. The chapter's Visual Portfolio includes R. Crumb's famous "A Short History of America" and a gallery of images documenting past and present examples of American environmental abuse. "Ah Wilderness!" also offers a generous helping of eco-friendly cartoons and an excerpt from Derrick Jensen and Stephanie McMillan's graphic novel *As the World Burns.*

Timely New Readings   To keep *Rereading America* up to date, we've worked hard to bring you the best new voices speaking on issues of race, gender, class, family, education, and the environment. As in past editions, we've retained old favorites like Malcolm X, Richard Rodriguez, Studs Terkel, Jamaica Kincaid, Jonathan Kozol, Jean Anyon, Toni Cade Bambara, Gary Soto, Judith Ortiz Cofer, and Mike Rose. But you'll also find a host of new selections by authors such as Andrew Sullivan, Reihan Salam, Michael Kimmel, Hua Hsu, Annie Dillard, and Bill McKibben. And like earlier versions, this edition of *Rereading America* includes a healthy mix of personal and academic writing, representing a wide variety of genres, styles, and rhetorical strategies.

Visual Portfolios In addition to frontispieces and cartoons, we've included a Visual Portfolio of myth-related images in every chapter of *Rereading America*. These collections of photographs and reproductions of famous paintings invite students to examine how visual "texts" are constructed and how, like written texts, they are susceptible to multiple readings and rereadings. Each portfolio is accompanied by a series of questions that encourage critical analysis and connect portfolio images to ideas and themes in chapter reading selections. As in earlier editions, the visual frontispieces that open each chapter are integrated into the prereading assignments found in the chapter introductions. The cartoons, offered as a bit of comic relief and as opportunities for visual thinking, are paired with appropriate readings thoughout the text.

Focus on Media We've continued the practice of including selections focusing on the media. Chapter Three includes a selection by Diana Kendall on the media's role in disseminating myths of material success. Chapter Five offers analyses of gender issues in the media, including Jean Kilbourne on images of women in advertising and Joan Morgan on black feminism and hip-hop culture. In Chapter Six, Charles Siebert explores the way animals are presented on television and raises questions about what TV nature programming says about American culture and our relationship to the natural world.

Focus on Struggle and Resistance Most multicultural readers approach diversity in one of two ways: either they adopt a pluralist approach and conceive of American society as a kind of salad bowl of cultures, or, in response to worries about the lack of "objectivity" in the multicultural curriculum, they take what might be called the "talk show" approach and present American culture as a series of pro-and-con debates on a number of social issues. The eighth edition of *Rereading America,* like its predecessors, follows neither of these approaches. Pluralist readers, we feel, make a promise that's impossible to keep: no single text, and no single course, can do justice to the many complex cultures that inhabit the United States. Thus, the materials selected for *Rereading America* aren't meant to offer a taste of what "family" means for Native Americans, or the flavor of gender relations among immigrants. Instead, we've included selections like Melvin Dixon's "Aunt Ida Pieces a Quilt" or Harlon Dalton's "Horatio Alger" because they offer us fresh critical perspectives on the common myths that shape our ideas, values, and beliefs. Rather than seeing this anthology as a mosaic or kaleidoscope of cultural fragments that combine to form a beautiful picture, it's more accurate to think of *Rereading America* as a handbook that helps students explore the ways that the dominant culture shapes their ideas, values, and beliefs.

This notion of cultural dominance is studiously avoided in most recent multicultural anthologies. "Salad bowl" readers generally sidestep the issue of cultural dynamics: intent on celebrating America's cultural diversity, they offer a relatively static picture of a nation fragmented into a kind of cultural archipelago. "Talk show" readers admit the idea of conflict, but they distort the reality of cultural dynamics by presenting cultural conflicts as a matter of rational—and equally balanced—debate. All of the materials anthologized in *Rereading America* address the cultural struggles that animate American society—the tensions that result from the expectations established by our dominant cultural myths and the diverse realities that these myths often contradict.

Extensive Apparatus   *Rereading America* offers a wealth of features to help students hone their analytic abilities and to aid instructors as they plan class discussions, critical thinking activities, and writing assignments. These include:

- *A Comprehensive Introductory Essay*   The book begins with a comprehensive essay, "Thinking Critically, Challenging Cultural Myths," that introduces students to the relationships between thinking, cultural diversity, and the notion of dominant cultural myths, and shows how such myths can influence their academic performance. We've also included a section devoted to active reading, which offers suggestions for prereading, prewriting, note taking, text marking, and keeping a reading journal. Another section helps students work with the many visual images included in the book.

- *"Fast Facts" Begin Each Chapter*   Several provocative statistics before each chapter introduction provide context for students and prompt discussion. For example, "Roughly 10% of white Americans, 21% of Latinos, and 25% of blacks are below the official poverty line."

- *Detailed Chapter Introductions*   An introductory essay at the beginning of each chapter offers students a thorough overview of each cultural myth, placing it in historical context, raising some of the chapter's central questions, and orienting students to the chapter's internal structure.

- *Prereading Activities*   Following each chapter introduction you'll find prereading activities designed to encourage students to reflect on what they already know about the cultural myth in question. Often connected to the images that open every chapter, these prereading activities help students to engage the topic even before they begin to read.

- *Questions to Stimulate Critical Thinking*   Three groups of questions following each selection encourage students to consider the reading carefully in several contexts: "Engaging the Text" focuses on close reading of the selection itself; "Exploring Connections" puts the selection into dialogue with other selections throughout the book; "Extending the Critical Context" invites students to connect the ideas they read about here with sources of knowledge outside the anthology, including library and Internet research, personal experience, interviews, ethnographic-style observations, and so forth. As in past editions, we've included a number of questions linking readings with contemporary television shows and feature films for instructors who want to address the interplay of cultural myths and the mass media.

- *"Further Connections" Close Each Chapter*   These questions and assignments help students make additional connections among readings. They also provide suggestions for exploring issues through research and include ideas for community projects.

Acknowledgments

Critical thinking is always a collaborative activity, and the kind of critical thinking involved in the creation of a text like *Rereading America* represents collegial collaboration at its very best. Since publication of the last edition, we've heard from instructors across the country who have generously offered suggestions for new classroom activities and comments for further refinements and improvements. Among the many instructors who shared their insights with us as we reworked this edition, we'd particularly like to thank the following: Lysbeth Benkert-Rasmussen, Northern State University; Harilaos Costarides, City College of San Francisco; Sharon Delmendo, St. John Fisher College; Deanne Fernandez, San Diego State University; Art Goldman, East L.A. College; Kim Greenfield, Lorain County Community College; Tim Gustafson, University of Minnesota; Adam Heidenreich, Joliet Junior College; Jeffrey Hillard, College of Mount St. Joseph; Robert S. Imbur, The University of Toledo; Deveryle James, University at Buffalo; Kerry J. Lane, Joliet Junior College; Kristin LaTour, Joliet Junior College; Scott A. Leonard, Youngstown State University; Carol Nowotny-Young, University of Arizona; Laura Patterson, Seton Hill University; Michael Ronan, Houston Community College; Carolyn E. Rubin-Trimble, University of Houston–Downtown; Steven Wolfe, Houston Community College.

For their help with the seventh edition, we'd like to thank José Amaya, Iowa State University; Michael A. Arnzen, Seton Hill University; Alvin Clarke, Iowa State University; Scott DeShong, Quinebaug Valley Community College; Stephen Evans, University of Kansas; Irene Faass, Iowa State University; Eileen Ferretti, Kingsborough Community College; Susan E. Howard, University of Houston, Downtown; Emily Isaacs, Montclair State University; Laureen Katana, Community College of Philadelphia; Misty Krueger, University of Tennessee; Robb Kunz, Utah State University; Mark Lidman, Maple Woods Community College; Seri Luangphinith, University of Hawai'i at Hilo; Michael Morris, Eastfield College; Roxanne Munch, Joliet Junior College; Beverly Neiderman, Kent State University; Carol Nowotny-Young, University of Arizona; Ellen O'Brien, Roosevelt University; Ildiko Olasz, Michigan State University; Cecilia Ornelas, California State University, Fullerton; Ted Otteson, University of Missouri, Kansas City; Carol Perdue, Green River Community College; Evelyn Pezzulich, Bridgewater State College; Mary Anne Quick, Bristol Community College; Elizabeth Rich, Saginaw Valley State University; Therese Rizzo, University of Delaware; Carolyn Rubin-Trimble, University of Houston–Downtown; Lori Taylor, SUNY University at Buffalo; Linda Tucker, Southern Arkansas University; Phoebe Wiley, Frostburg State University; Malcolm Williams, University of Houston, Downtown; Elizabeth Wright, Pennsylvania State University, Hazleton.

For their help with the sixth edition, we'd like to thank Andrea Beaudin, Southern Connecticut State University; Nancy C. Botkin, Indiana University South Bend; Deborah Brink, Lower Columbia College; Blythe Creamer, University of California, Davis; Stephen F. Evans, University of Kansas; Kathy A. Fedorko, Middlesex County College; Julie Hirsch, University of Arizona, Tucson; Jennifer Lynn Holley, Southern Connecticut State University; Deborah Kirkman, University of Kentucky; Anna Leahy, Missouri Western State College; Kelly Mayhew, San Diego City College; Julie Nash, Merrimack College; Deirdre Neilen, SUNY Upstate Medical University; Hector Perez, University of the Incarnate Word; Josephine Perry, Los Medanos College; Margaret B. Racin, West Virginia University; Daniela Ragusa, University of Rhode Island; Marguerite Regan, Southwestern College; Elizabeth Rich, Saginaw Valley State University; Kim Robeson, MiraCosta Community College; Renée Ruderman, Metropolitan State College of Denver; Tereza M. Szeghi, University of Arizona; Karen Toloui, Diablo Valley College; Lisa Toner, University of Kentucky; Alberto S. Vitale, Indiana University South Bend; James Ray Watkins, Jr., Eastern Illinois University; James M. Welch, Wittenberg University; and Terry Williams, San Diego State University.

For their help with the fifth edition of *Rereading America,* we'd like to thank the following: Etta C. Abrahams, Michigan State University; Richard L. Arthur, Miami University of Ohio; Scott E. Ash, Nassau Community College; Michael Augsperger, University of Iowa; Larry Cain, Chabot College; Rosann M. Cook, Purdue University at Calumet; Mary Jean Corbett, Miami University of Ohio; Stephen Curley, Texas A&M University at Galveston; Ann M. DeDad, Cannon University; Florence Emch, California State University, Los Angeles; Juan F. Flores, Del Mar College; Nancy Gonchar, The College of New Rochelle; Tara Hart, Howard Community College; Sue Ellen Holbrook, Southern Connecticut State University; Stephen Horvath, Howard Community College; Irwin J. Koplik, Hofstra University; Michael Lewis, University of Iowa; Linda Maitland, University of Houston; Doug Merrell, University of Washington; Robert Murray, St. Thomas Aquinas College; Kathleen O'Brien, Boston University; Renée Ruderman, Metropolitan State College of Denver; Karen Ryan-Engel, Gannon University;

Amy Sileven, Southern Illinois University at Carbondale; Jane E. Simonsen, University of Iowa; Juliet Sloger, University of Rochester; Ken Smith, Indiana University South Bend; Judith A. Stainbrook, Gannon University; Douglas Steward, University of Kansas.

We are also grateful to those reviewers who helped shape previous editions.

As always, we'd also like to thank all the kind folks at Bedford/St. Martin's, who do their best to make the effort of producing a book like this a genuine pleasure. Our publishers, former president Charles Christensen and president Joan Feinberg, deserve special praise for the support they've shown us over the years and for the wise counsel they've offered in the occasional hour of need. We're delighted to have worked once again with our editor, Ellen Darion, who also edited the first edition of *Rereading America*; her patience, professionalism, and sense of humor have helped us immensely throughout the process of producing this new edition of the book. We also want to thank Karen Baart, who served as production editor on this edition; Karen Stocz, who expertly copyedited the manuscript; Sara Gates, who produced our new cover; Sandy Schechter, for clearing text permissions; Linda Finnegan, for researching and tracking down art; and editorial assistant Melissa Cook, who helped out with many of the hundreds of details that go into a project such as this. Finally, we'd like to acknowledge our spouses, Elena Barcia, Liz Silver, and Roy Weitz.

Gary Colombo
Robert Cullen
Bonnie Lisle

Online Resources for Students and Instructors

Rereading America doesn't stop with a book. Online, Bedford/St. Martin's also offers both free and affordable premium resources to students and instructors; see complete descriptions below. To learn more or to order any of the products below, contact your Bedford/St. Martin's sales representative, e-mail sales support (sales_support@bfwpub.com), or visit the Web site at bedfordstmartins.com/rereadingamerica/catalog.

Student Resources

Send students to free and open resources, upgrade to an expanding collection of innovative digital content, or package a stand-alone CD-ROM for free with *Rereading America*.

Re:Writing, the best free collection of online resources for the writing class, offers clear advice on citing sources, thirty sample papers and designed documents, and over nine thousand writing and grammar exercises with immediate feedback and reporting in *Exercise Central*. Updated and re-designed, *Re:Writing* also features five free videos from *VideoCentral* and three new visual tutorials from our popular *ix: visualizing composition*. *Re:Writing* is completely free and open (no codes required) to ensure access to all students. Visit bedfordstmartins.com/rewriting.

VideoCentral is a growing collection of videos for the writing class that captures real-world, academic, and student writers talking about how and why they write. *VideoCentral* can be packaged with *Rereading America* at a significant discount. An activation code is required. To learn more, visit bedfordstmartins.com/videocentral. To order *VideoCentral* packaged with the print book, use ISBN 0–312–64904–5 or 978–0–312–64904–3.

Re:Writing Plus gathers all of Bedford/St. Martin's premium online content for composition into one online collection. It includes hundreds of model documents, the first ever peer review game, and *VideoCentral*. *Re:Writing Plus* can be purchased separately or packaged with the print book at a significant discount. An activation code is required. To learn more, visit bedfordstmartins.com/rewriting. To order *Re:Writing Plus* packaged with the print book, use ISBN 0–312–62481–6 or 978–0–312–62481–1.

i-series on CD-ROM presents multimedia tutorials in a flexible for-mat—because there are things you can't do in a book. To learn more, visit bedfordstmartins.com/rereadingamerica/catalog.

- *ix: visual exercises* helps students put key rhetorical and visual concepts into practice. To order *ix: visual exercises* packaged with the print book, use ISBN 0–312–62479–4 or 978–0–312–62479–8.

- *i-claim: visualizing argument* offers a new way to see argument—with six tutorials, an illustrated glossary, and over seventy multimedia argu-ments. To order *i-claim: visualizing argument* packaged with the print book, use ISBN 0–312–62478–6 or 978–0–312–62478–1.

- *i-cite: visualizing sources* brings research to life through an animated introduction, four tutorials, and hands-on source practice. To order *i-cite: visualizing sources* packaged with the print book, use ISBN 0–312–62476–X or 978–0–312–62476–7.

Instructor Resources

You have a lot to do in your course. Bedford/St. Martin's wants to make it easy for you to find the support you need—and get it quickly. To find everything available with *Rereading America*, visit bedfordstmartins.com/rereadingamerica/catalog.

The Instructor's Manual, *Resources for Teaching Rereading America,* is available in a downloadable PDF from the Bedford/St. Martin's online catalog. In addition to chapter overviews and teaching tips, the Instructor's Manual provides detailed advice about ways to make the most of both the readings and the questions and includes suggestions for putting together syllabi. It also offers further ideas for discussion, class activities, and writing assignments, garnered from classroom experiences.

Teaching Central offers the entire list of Bedford/St. Martin's print and online professional resources in one place. You'll find landmark reference works, sourcebooks on pedagogical issues, award-winning collections, and practical advice for the classroom—all free for instructors.

Bits collects creative ideas for teaching a range of composition topics in an easily searchable blog. A community of teachers—leading scholars, authors, and editors—discuss revision, research, grammar and style, technology, peer review, and much more. Take, use, adapt, and pass the ideas around. Then, come back to the site to comment or share your own suggestions.

Content cartridges for the most common course management systems—Blackboard, WebCT, Angel, and Desire2Learn—allow you to easily download digital materials from Bedford/St. Martin's for your course.

Contents

1

Harmony at Home:
The Myth of the Model Family   *17*

3

Money and Success:
The Myth of Individual Opportunity   253

> "The poor do not fare well on television entertainment shows, where writers typically represent them with one-dimensional, bedraggled characters standing on a street corner holding cardboard signs that read 'Need money for food.'"

> "The fate of Missing Class families is a test for this country of what it can offer to those citizens—immigrants and native-born alike—who have pulled themselves off the floor that poverty represents."

> "We're homeless and being evicted? Now I've heard everything."

> "Welfare and workfare indicate bare survival—recipients are not meant to rise even to lower-middle-class status."

> "The American Dream, I see now, is governed not by education, opportunity, and hard work, but by power and fear."

4

Created Equal: *The Myth of the Melting Pot*   373

> "I advance it, therefore, as a suspicion only, that the blacks . . . are inferior to the whites in the endowments both of body and mind."

5

True Women and Real Men: *Myths of Gender*   *515*

6

Ah Wilderness!
American Myths of Nature
and the Environment   **639**

> "For environmentalists, there will always be too many people and too few species! All statements coming from environmentalists must be evaluated by looking through the anti-human lens that much of them hold."

Rereading America

*Cultural Contexts for Critical
Thinking and Writing*

Thinking Critically, Challenging Cultural Myths

Becoming a College Student

Beginning college can be a disconcerting experience. It may be the first time you've lived away from home and had to deal with the stresses and pleasures of independence. There's increased academic competition, increased temptation, and a whole new set of peer pressures. In the dorms you may find yourself among people whose backgrounds make them seem foreign and unapproachable. If you commute, you may be struggling against a feeling of isolation that you've never faced before. And then there are increased expectations. For an introductory history class you may read as many books as you covered in a year of high school coursework. In anthropology, you might be asked to conduct ethnographic research — when you've barely heard of an ethnography before, much less written one. In English you may tackle more formal analytic writing in a single semester than you've ever done in your life.

College typically imposes fewer rules than high school, but also gives you less guidance and makes greater demands — demands that affect the quality as well as the quantity of your work. By your first midterm exam, you may suspect that your previous academic experience is irrelevant, that nothing you've done in school has prepared you to think, read, or write in the ways your professors expect. Your sociology instructor says she doesn't care whether you can remember all the examples in the textbook as long as you can apply the theoretical concepts to real situations. In your composition class, the perfect five-paragraph essay you turn in for your first assignment is dismissed as "superficial, mechanical, and dull." Meanwhile, the lecturer in your political science or psychology course is rejecting ideas about country, religion, family, and self that have always been a part of your deepest beliefs. How can you cope with these new expectations and challenges?

There is no simple solution, no infallible five-step method that works for everyone. As you meet the personal challenges of college, you'll grow as a human being. You'll begin to look critically at your old habits, beliefs, and values, to see them in relation to the new world you're entering. You may have to re-examine your relationships to family, friends, neighborhood, and heritage. You'll have to sort out your strengths from your weaknesses and make tough choices about who you are and who you want to become. Your

1

academic work demands the same process of serious self-examination. To excel in college work you need to grow intellectually — to become a critical thinker.

What Is Critical Thinking?

What do instructors mean when they tell you to think critically? Most would say that it involves asking questions rather than memorizing information. Instead of simply collecting the "facts," a critical thinker probes them, looking for underlying assumptions and ideas. Instead of focusing on dates and events in history or symptoms in psychology, she probes for motives, causes — an explanation of how these things came to be. A critical thinker cultivates the ability to imagine and value points of view different from her own — then strengthens, refines, enlarges, or reshapes her ideas in light of those other perspectives. She is at once open and skeptical: receptive to new ideas yet careful to test them against previous experience and knowledge. In short, a critical thinker is an active learner, someone with the ability to shape, not merely absorb, knowledge.

All this is difficult to put into practice, because it requires getting outside your own skin and seeing the world from multiple perspectives. To see why critical thinking doesn't come naturally, take another look at the cover of this book. Many would scan the title, *Rereading America,* take in the surface meaning — to reconsider America — and go on to page one. There isn't much to question here; it just "makes sense." But what happens with the student who brings a different perspective? For example, a student from El Salvador might justly complain that the title reflects an ethnocentric view of what it means to be an American. After all, since America encompasses all the countries of North, South, and Central America, he lived in "America" long before arriving in the United States. When this student reads the title, then, he actually does *reread* it; he reads it once in the "commonsense" way but also from the perspective of someone who has lived in a country dominated by U.S. intervention and interests. This double vision or double perspective frees him to look beyond the "obvious" meaning of the book and to question its assumptions.

Of course, you don't have to be bicultural to become a proficient critical thinker. You can develop a genuine sensitivity to alternative perspectives even if you've never lived outside your hometown. But to do so you need to recognize that there are no "obvious meanings." The automatic equation that the native-born student makes between "America" and the United States seems to make sense only because our culture has traditionally endorsed the idea that the United States *is* America and, by implication, that other countries in this hemisphere are somehow inferior — not the genuine article. We tend to accept this equation and its unfortunate implications because we are products of our culture.

The Power of Cultural Myths

Culture shapes the way we think; it tells us what "makes sense." It holds people together by providing us with a shared set of customs, values, ideas, and beliefs, as well as a common language. We live enmeshed in this cultural web: it influences the way we relate to others, the way we look, our tastes, our habits; it enters our dreams and desires. But as culture binds us together it also selectively blinds us. As we grow up, we accept ways of looking at the world, ways of thinking and being that might best be characterized as cultural frames of reference or cultural myths. These myths help us understand our place in the world — our place as prescribed by our culture. They define our relationships to friends and lovers, to the past and future, to nature, to power, and to nation. Becoming a critical thinker means learning how to look beyond these cultural myths and the assumptions embedded in them.

You may associate the word "myth" primarily with the myths of the ancient Greeks. The legends of gods and heroes like Athena, Zeus, and Oedipus embodied the central ideals and values of Greek civilization — notions like civic responsibility, the primacy of male authority, and humility before the gods. The stories were "true" not in a literal sense but as reflections of important cultural beliefs. These myths assured the Greeks of the nobility of their origins; they provided models for the roles that Greeks would play in their public and private lives; they justified inequities in Greek society; they helped the Greeks understand human life and destiny in terms that "made sense" within the framework of that culture.

Our cultural myths do much the same. Take, for example, the American dream of success. Since the first European colonists came to the "New World" some four centuries ago, America has been synonymous with the idea of individual opportunity. For generations, immigrants have been lured across the ocean to make their fortunes in a land where the streets were said to be paved with gold. Of course, we don't always agree on what success means or how it should be measured. Some calculate the meaning of success in terms of six-figure salaries or the acreage of their country estates. Others discover success in the attainment of a dream — whether it's graduating from college, achieving excellence on the playing field, or winning new rights and opportunities for less fortunate fellow citizens. For some Americans, the dream of success is the very foundation of everything that's right about life in the United States. For others, the American dream is a cultural mirage that keeps workers happy in low-paying jobs while their bosses pocket the profits of an unfair system. But whether you embrace or reject the dream of success, you can't escape its influence. As Americans, we are steeped in a culture that prizes individual achievement; growing up in the United States, we are told again and again by parents, teachers, advertisers, Hollywood writers, politicians, and opinion makers that we, too, can achieve our dream — that we, too, can "Just Do It" if we try. You might aspire to become an Internet tycoon, or you might rebel and opt for a simple life, but you can't ignore the impact of the myth. We each define success in our own way, but, ultimately, the myth of success defines who we are and what we think, feel, and believe.

Cultural myths gain such enormous power over us by insinuating themselves into our thinking before we're aware of them. Most are learned at a deep, even unconscious level. Gender roles are a good example. As children we get gender role models from our families, our schools, our churches, and other important institutions. We see them acted out in the relationships between family members or portrayed on television, in the movies, or in song lyrics. Before long, the culturally determined roles we see for women and men appear to us as "self-evident": it seems "natural" for a man to be strong, responsible, competitive, and heterosexual, just as it may seem "unnatural" for a man to shun competitive activity or to take a romantic interest in other men. Our most dominant cultural myths shape the way we perceive the world and blind us to alternative ways of seeing and being. When something violates the expectations that such myths create, it may even be called unnatural, immoral, or perverse.

Cultural Myths as Obstacles to Critical Thinking

Cultural myths can have more subtle effects as well. In academic work they can reduce the complexity of our reading and thinking. A few years ago, for example, a professor at Los Angeles City College noted that he and his students couldn't agree in their interpretations of the following poem by Theodore Roethke:

My Papa's Waltz

The whiskey on your breath
Could make a small boy dizzy;
But I hung on like death:
Such waltzing was not easy.

We romped until the pans
Slid from the kitchen shelf;
My mother's countenance
Could not unfrown itself.

The hand that held my wrist
Was battered on one knuckle;
At every step you missed
My right ear scraped a buckle.

You beat time on my head
With a palm caked hard by dirt,
Then waltzed me off to bed
Still clinging to your shirt.

The instructor read this poem as a clear expression of a child's love for his blue-collar father, a rough-and-tumble man who had worked hard all his life ("a palm caked hard by dirt"), who was not above taking a drink of whiskey to ease his mind, but who also found the time to "waltz" his son off to bed. The students didn't see this at all. They saw the poem as a story about an abusive father and heavy drinker. They seemed unwilling to look beyond the father's roughness and the whiskey on his breath, equating these with drunken violence. Although the poem does suggest an element of fear mingled with the boy's excitement ("I hung on like death"), the class ignored its complexity — the mixture of fear, love, and boisterous fun that colors the son's memory of his father. It's possible that some students might overlook the positive traits in the father in this poem because they have suffered child abuse themselves. But this couldn't be true for all the students in the class. The difference between these interpretations lies, instead, in the influence of cultural myths. After all, in a culture now dominated by images of the family that emphasize "positive" parenting, middle-class values, and sensitive fathers, it's no wonder that students refused to see this father sympathetically. Our culture simply doesn't associate good, loving families with drinking or with even the suggestion of physical roughness.

Years of acculturation — the process of internalizing cultural values — leave us with a set of rigid categories for "good" and "bad" parents, narrow conceptions of how parents should look, talk, and behave toward their children. These cultural categories work like mental pigeonholes: they help us sort out and evaluate our experiences rapidly, almost before we're consciously aware of them. They give us a helpful shorthand for interpreting the world; after all, we can't stop to ponder every new situation we meet as if it were a puzzle or a philosophical problem. But while cultural categories help us make practical decisions in everyday life, they also impose their inherent rigidity on our thinking and thus limit our ability to understand the complexity of our experience. They reduce the world to dichotomies — simplified either/or choices: either women or men, either heterosexuals or homosexuals, either nature or culture, either animal or human, either "alien" or American, either them or us.

Rigid cultural beliefs can present serious obstacles to success for first-year college students. In a psychology class, for example, students' cultural myths may so color their thinking that they find it nearly impossible to comprehend Freud's ideas about infant sexuality. Ingrained assumptions about childhood innocence and sexual guilt may make it impossible for them to see children as sexual beings — a concept absolutely basic to an understanding of the history of psychoanalytic theory. Yet college-level critical inquiry thrives on exactly this kind of revision of common sense: academics prize the unusual, the subtle, the ambiguous, the complex — and expect students to appreciate them as well. Good critical thinkers in all academic disciplines welcome the opportunity to challenge conventional ways of seeing the world;

they seem to take delight in questioning everything that appears clear and self-evident.

Questioning: The Basis of Critical Thinking

By questioning the myths that dominate our culture, we can begin to resist the limits they impose on our vision. In fact, they invite such questioning. Often our personal experience fails to fit the images the myths project: a young woman's ambition to be a test pilot may clash with the ideal of femininity our culture promotes; a Cambodian immigrant who has suffered from racism in the United States may question our professed commitment to equality; a student in the vocational track may not see education as the road to success that we assume it is; and few of our families these days fit the mythic model of husband, wife, two kids, a dog, and a house in the suburbs.

Moreover, because cultural myths serve such large and varied needs, they're not always coherent or consistent. Powerful contradictory myths coexist in our society and our own minds. For example, while the myth of "the melting pot" celebrates equality, the myth of individual success pushes us to strive for inequality — to "get ahead" of everyone else. Likewise, our attitudes toward education are deeply paradoxical: on one level Americans tend to see schooling as a valuable experience that unites us in a common culture and helps us bring out the best in ourselves; yet at the same time we suspect that formal classroom instruction stifles creativity and chokes off natural intelligence and enthusiasm. These contradictions infuse our history, literature, and popular culture; they're so much a part of our thinking that we tend to take them for granted, unaware of their inconsistencies.

Learning to recognize contradictions lies at the very heart of critical thinking, for intellectual conflict inevitably generates questions. Can both (or all) perspectives be true? What evidence do I have for the validity of each? Is there some way to reconcile them? Are there still other alternatives? Questions like these represent the beginning of serious academic analysis. They stimulate the reflection, discussion, and research that are the essence of good scholarship. Thus, whether we find contradictions between myth and lived experience, or between opposing myths, the wealth of powerful, conflicting material generated by our cultural mythology offers a particularly rich context for critical inquiry.

The Structure of *Rereading America*

We've designed this book to help you develop the habits of mind you'll need to become a critical thinker — someone who recognizes the way that cultural myths shape thinking and can move beyond them to evaluate issues from multiple perspectives. Each of the book's six chapters addresses one of the dominant myths of American culture. We begin with the myth that's literally closest to home — the myth of the model family. In "Harmony at Home" we look at the impact that the idea of the nuclear family has had on generations of Americans, then develop a broader perspective by considering how cultural traditions and economic realities can make the mythic nuclear family undesirable or unattainable for many families. The chapter also includes several short readings and visual images from the raging cultural debate over same-sex marriage equality. Next we turn to a topic that every student should have a lot to say about — the myth of educational empowerment. "Learning Power" gives you the chance to reflect on how the "hidden curriculum" of schooling has shaped your own attitudes toward learning. We begin our exploration of American cultural myths by focusing on home and education because most students find it easy to make personal connections with these topics and because they both involve institutions — families and schools — that are surrounded by a rich legacy of cultural stories and myths. These two introductory chapters are followed by consideration of what is perhaps the most famous of all American myths, the American Dream. Chapter Three, "Money and Success," addresses the idea of unlimited personal opportunity that brought millions of immigrants to our shores and set the story of America in motion. It invites you to weigh some of the human costs of the dream and to reconsider your own definition of a successful life.

The second portion of the book focuses on three cultural myths that offer greater intellectual and emotional challenges because they touch on highly charged social issues. The book's fourth chapter, "Created Equal," examines two myths that have powerfully shaped racial and ethnic relations in the United States: the myth of the melting pot, which celebrates cultural homogenization, and the myth of racial and ethnic superiority, which promotes separateness and inequality. This chapter probes the nature of prejudice, explores the ways that prejudicial attitudes are created, and examines ethnic identities within a race-divided society. Chapter Five, "True Women and Real Men," considers the socially constructed categories of gender — the traditional roles that enforce differences between women and men. This chapter also explores the perspectives of Americans who defy conventional gender boundaries. Each of these two chapters questions how our culture divides and defines our world, how it artificially channels our experience into oppositions like black and white, male and female, straight and gay. The book's sixth and final chapter — "Ah Wilderness!" — addresses American attitudes toward nature and the environment. This new chapter invites you to explore how Americans have viewed nature and wilderness since the landing of the Pilgrims. It also offers you the opportunity to engage some of the most pressing environmental challenges involved with climate change and global warming. Today, as we struggle to find solutions that will literally save the planet, the ability to examine the impact of our cultural assumptions about the natural world is more important than ever.

The Selections

Our identities — who we are and how we relate to others — are deeply entangled with the cultural values we have internalized since infancy. Cultural myths become so closely identified with our personal beliefs that rereading them actually means rereading ourselves, rethinking the way we see the world. Questioning long-held assumptions can be an exhilarating experience, but it can be distressing too. Thus, you may find certain selections in *Rereading America* difficult, controversial, or even downright offensive. They are meant to challenge you and to provoke classroom debate. But as you discuss the ideas you encounter in this book, remind yourself that your classmates may bring with them very different, and equally profound, beliefs. Keep an open mind, listen carefully, and treat other perspectives with the same respect you'd expect other people to show for your own. It's by encountering new ideas and engaging with others in open dialogue that we learn to grow.

Because *Rereading America* explores cultural myths that shape our think-ing, it doesn't focus on the kind of well-defined public issues you might expect to find in a traditional composition anthology. You won't be reading argu-ments for and against affirmative action, bilingual education, or the death penalty here. Although we do include conservative as well as liberal — and even radical — perspectives, we've deliberately avoided the traditional pro-and-con approach because we want you to aim deeper than that; we want you to focus on the subtle cultural beliefs that underlie, and frequently determine, the debates that are waged on public issues. We've also steered clear of the "issues approach" because we feel it reinforces simplistic either/or thinking. Polarizing American culture into a series of debates doesn't encourage you to examine your own beliefs or explore how they've been shaped by the cultures you're part of. To begin to appreciate the influence of your own cultural myths, you need new perspectives: you need to stand out-side the ideological machinery that makes American culture run to begin to appreciate its power. That's why we've included many strongly dissenting views: there are works by community activists, gay-rights activists, socialists, libertarians, and more. You may find that their views confirm your own expe-rience of what it means to be an American, or you may find that you bitterly disagree with them. We only hope that you will use the materials here to gain some insight into the values and beliefs that shape our thinking and our national identity. This book is meant to complicate the mental categories that our cultural myths have established for us. Our intention is not to pre-sent a new "truth" to replace the old but to expand the range of ideas you bring to all your reading and writing in college. We believe that learning to see and value other perspectives will enable you to think more critically — to question, for yourself, the truth of any statement.

You may also note that several selections in *Rereading America* chal-lenge the way you think writing is supposed to look or sound. You won't find many "classic" essays in this book, the finely crafted reflective essays on gen-eral topics that are often held up as models of "good writing." It's not that we reject this type of essay in principle. It's just that most writers who stand outside mainstream culture seem to have little use for it.

Our selections, instead, come from a wide variety of sources: professional books and journals from many disciplines, popular magazines, college text-books, autobiographies, oral histories, and literary works. We've included this variety partly for the very practical reason that you're likely to encounter texts like these in your college coursework. But we also see textual diversity, like ethnic and political diversity, as a way to multiply perspectives and stimulate critical analysis. For example, an academic article like Jean Anyon's study of social class and school curriculum might give you a new way of understanding Mike Rose's personal narrative about his classroom experiences. On the other hand, you may find that some of the teachers Rose encounters don't neatly fit Anyon's theoretical model. Do such discrepancies mean that Anyon's argu-ment is invalid? That her analysis needs to be modified to account for these teachers? That the teachers are simply exceptions to the rule? You'll probably want to consider your own classroom experience as you wrestle with such questions. Throughout the book, we've chosen readings that "talk to each other" in this way and that draw on the cultural knowledge you bring with you. These readings invite you to join the conversation; we hope they raise difficult questions, prompt lively discussion, and stimulate critical inquiry.

The Power of Dialogue

Good thinking, like good writing and good reading, is an intensely social activity. Thinking, reading, and writing are all forms of relationship — when you read, you enter into dialogue with an author about the subject at hand; when you write, you address an imaginary reader, testing your ideas against probable responses, reservations, and arguments. Thus, you can't become an accomplished writer simply by declaring your right to speak or by criticizing as an act of principle: real authority comes when you enter into the discipline of an active exchange of opinions and interpretations. Critical thinking, then, is always a matter of dialogue and debate — discovering relationships between apparently unrelated ideas, finding parallels between your own experiences and the ideas you read about, exploring points of agreement and conflict between yourself and other people.

We've designed the readings and questions in this text to encourage you to make just these kinds of connections. You'll notice, for example, that we often ask you to divide into small groups to discuss readings, and we frequently sug-gest that you take part in projects that require you to collaborate with your class-mates. We're convinced that the only way you can learn critical reading, think-ing, and writing is by actively engaging others in an intellectual exchange. So we've built into the text many opportunities for listening, discussion, and debate.

The questions that follow each selection should guide you in critical thinking. Like the readings, they're intended to get you started, not to set limits; we strongly recommend that you also devise your own questions and pursue them either individually or in study groups. We've divided our questions into three categories. Here's what to expect from each:

- Those labeled "Engaging the Text" focus on the individual selection they follow. They're designed to highlight important issues in the reading, to help you begin questioning and evaluating what you've read, and sometimes to remind you to consider the author's choices of language, evidence, structure, and style.

- The questions labeled "Exploring Connections" will lead you from the selection you've just finished to one or more other readings in this book. It's hard to make sparks fly from just one stone; if you think hard about these connecting questions, though, you'll see some real collisions of ideas and perspectives, not just polite and predictable "differences of opinion."

- The final questions for each reading, "Extending the Critical Context," invite you to extend your thinking beyond the book — to your family, your community, your college, the media, or the more traditional research environment of the library. The emphasis here is on creating new knowledge by applying ideas from this book to the world around you and by testing these ideas in your world.

Active Reading

You've undoubtedly read many textbooks, but it's unlikely that you've had to deal with the kind of analytic, argumentative, and scholarly writing you'll find in college and in *Rereading America.* These different writing styles require a different approach to reading as well. In high school you probably read to "take in" information, often for the sole purpose of reproducing it later on a test. In college you'll also be expected to recognize larger issues, such as the author's theoretical slant, her goals and methods, her assumptions, and her relationship to other writers and researchers. These expectations can be especially difficult in the first two years of college, when you take introductory courses that survey large, complex fields of knowledge. With all these demands on your attention, you'll need to read actively to keep your bearings. Think of active reading as a conversation between you and the text: instead of listening passively as the writer talks, respond to what she says with questions and comments of your own. Here are some specific techniques you can practice to become a more active reader.

Prereading and Prewriting

It's best with most college reading to "preread" the text. In prereading, you briefly look over whatever information you have on the author and the selection itself. Reading chapter introductions and headnotes like those provided in this book can save you time and effort by giving you information about the author's background and concerns, the subject or thesis of the selection, and its place in the chapter as a whole. Also take a look at the title and at any headings or subheadings in the piece. These will give you further clues about an article's general scope and organization. Next, quickly skim the entire selection, paying a bit more attention to the first few paragraphs and the conclusion. Now you should have a pretty good sense of the author's position — what she's trying to say in this piece of writing.

At this point you may do one of several things before you settle down to in-depth reading. You may want to jot down in a few lines what you think the author is doing. Or you may want to make a list of questions you can ask about this topic based on your prereading. Or you may want to freewrite a page or so on the subject. Informally writing out your own ideas will prepare you for more in-depth reading by recalling what you already know about the topic.

We emphasize writing about what you've read because reading and writing are complementary activities: being an avid reader will help you as a writer by familiarizing you with a wide range of ideas and styles to draw on; likewise, writing about what you've read will give you a deeper understanding of your reading. In fact, the more actively you "process" or reshape what you've read, the better you'll comprehend and remember it. So you'll learn more effectively by marking a text as you read than by simply reading; taking notes as you read is even more effective than marking, and writing about the material for your own purposes (putting it in your own words and connecting it with what you already know) is better still.

Marking the Text and Taking Notes

After prereading and prewriting, you're ready to begin critical reading in earnest. As you read, be sure to highlight ideas and phrases that strike you as especially significant — those that seem to capture the gist of a particular paragraph or section, or those that relate directly to the author's purpose or argument. While prereading can help you identify central ideas, you may find that you need to reread difficult sections or flip back and skim an earlier passage if you feel yourself getting lost. Many students think of themselves as poor readers if they can't whip through an article at high speed without pausing. However, the best readers read recursively — that is, they shuttle back and forth, browsing, skimming, and rereading as necessary, depending on their interest, their familiarity with the subject, and the difficulty of the material. This shuttling actually parallels what goes on in your mind when you read actively, as you alternately recall prior knowledge or experience and predict or look for clues about where the writer is going next.

Keep a record of your mental shuttling by writing comments in the margins as you read. It's often useful to gloss the contents of each paragraph or section, to summarize it in a word or two written alongside the text. This note will serve as a reminder or key to the section when you return to it for further thinking, discussion, or writing. You may also want to note passages that puzzled you. Or you may want to write down personal reactions or questions stimulated by the reading. Take time to ponder why you felt confused or annoyed or affirmed by a particular passage. Let yourself wonder "out loud" in the margins as you read.

The following section illustrates one student's notes on a few stanzas of Inés Hernández-Ávila's "Para Teresa" (p. 207). In this example, you can see that the reader puts glosses or summary comments to the left of the poem and questions or personal responses to the right. You should experiment and create your own system of note taking, one that works best for the way you read. Just remember that your main goals in taking notes are to help you understand the author's overall position, to deepen and refine your responses to the selection, and to create a permanent record of those responses.

Para Teresa[1]

INÉS HERNÁNDEZ-ÁVILA

This poem explores and attempts to resolve an old conflict between its speaker and her schoolmate, two Chicanas at "Alamo which-had-to-be-its-name" Elementary School who have radically different ideas about what education means and does. Inés Hernández-Ávila (b. 1947) is an associate professor of Native American Studies at the University of California, Davis. This poem appeared in her collection Con Razón, Corazón *(1987).*

Writes **to Teresa**	A tí-Teresa — **Why in Spanish?** Te dedico las palabras estás que ⟨explotan⟩ de mi corazón[2] **Why do her words explode?**
The day **of their** **confron-** **tation**	That day during lunch hour at Alamo which-had-to-be-its-name **!Why?** Elementary my dear raza — **Feels close to T. (?)** That day in the bathroom Door guarded Myself cornered I was accused by you, Teresa Tú y las demás de tus amigas Pachucas todas Eran Uds. cinco.[3]

[1]*Para Teresa:* For Teresa. [All notes are Hernández-Ávila's.]
[2]*A . . . corazón:* To you, Teresa, I dedicate these words that explode from my heart.
[3]*Tú . . . cinco:* You and the rest of your friends, all Pachucas, there were five of you.

> **T.'s accusation**
>
> Me gritaban que porque me creía tan grande[4]
> What was I trying to do, you growled
> Show you up?
> Make the teachers like me, pet me,
> Tell me what a credit to my people I was?
> I was playing right into their hands, you challenged
> And you would have none of it.
> I was to stop.

Teachers must be white / Anglo.

Speaker is a "good student."

Keeping a Reading Journal

You may also want (or be required) to keep a reading journal in response to the selections you cover in *Rereading America*. In such a journal you'd keep all the freewriting that you do either before or after reading. Some students find it helpful to keep a double-entry journal, writing initial responses on the left side of the page and adding later reflections and reconsiderations on the right. You may want to use your journal as a place to explore personal reactions to your reading. You can do this by writing out imaginary dialogues — between two writers who address the same subject, between yourself and the writer of the selection, or between two parts of yourself. You can use the journal as a place to rewrite passages from a poem or essay in your own voice and from your own point of view. You can write letters to an author you particularly like or dislike or to a character in a story or poem. You might even draw a cartoon that comments on one of the reading selections.

Many students don't write as well as they could because they're afraid to take risks. They may have been repeatedly penalized for breaking "rules" of grammar or essay form; their main concern in writing becomes avoiding trouble rather than exploring ideas or experimenting with style. But without risk and experimentation, there's little possibility of growth. One of the benefits of journal writing is that it gives you a place to experiment with ideas, free from worries about "correctness." Here are two examples of student journal entries, in response to "Para Teresa" (we reprint the entries as they were written):

Entry 1: Internal Dialogue

Me 1: I agree with Inés Hernández-Ávila's speaker. Her actions were justifiable in a way that if you can't fight 'em, join 'em. After all, Teresa is just making the situation worse for her because not only is she sabotaging the teacher-student relationship, she's also destroying her chance for a good education.

Me 2: Hey, Teresa's action was justifiable. Why else would the speaker admit at the end of the poem that what Teresa did was fine thus she respects Teresa more?

Me 1: The reason the speaker respected Teresa was because she (Teresa) was still keeping her culture alive, although through

---

[4]*Me . . . grande:* You were screaming at me, asking me why I thought I was so hot.

different means. It wasn't her action that the speaker respected, it was the representation of it.

Me 2: The reason I think Teresa acted the way she did was because she felt she had something to prove to society. She wanted to show that no one could push her people around; that her people were tough.

Entry 2: Personal Response

"Con cố gắng học gioi, cho Bá Má,
Rỗi sau nây dời sống cua con sẽ thõai mái lắm."[5]
What if I don't want to?
What if I can't?
Sometimes I feel my parents don't understand what
I'm going through.
To them, education is money.
And money is success.
They don't see beyond that.
Sometimes I want to fail my classes purposely to
See their reaction, but that is too cruel.
They have taught me to value education.
Education makes you a person, makes you somebody, they say.
I agree.
They are proud I am going to UCLA.
They brag to their friends, our Vietnamese community, people
I don't even know.

. . .

They believe in me, but I doubt myself. . . .

You'll notice that neither of these students talks directly about "Para Teresa" as a poem. Instead, each uses it as a point of departure for her own reflections on ethnicity, identity, and education. Although we've included a number of literary works in *Rereading America,* we don't expect you to do literary analysis. We want you to use these pieces to stimulate your own thinking about the cultural myths they address. So don't feel you have to discuss imagery in Inés Hernández-Ávila's "Para Teresa" or characterization in Toni Cade Bambara's "The Lesson" in order to understand and appreciate them.

Working with Visual Images

The myths we examine in *Rereading America* make their presence felt not only in the world of print — essays, stories, poems, memoirs — but in every aspect of our culture. Consider, for example, the myth of "the American family." If you want to design a minivan, a restaurant, a cineplex, a park, a synagogue, a personal computer, or a tax code, you had better have some idea of what families are like and how they behave. Most

---

[5]"*Con . . . lám*": "Daughter, study hard (for us, your Mom and Dad), so your future will be bright and easy."

important, you need a good grasp of what Americans *believe* about families, about the mythology of the American family. The Visual Portfolio in each chapter, while it maintains our focus on myths, also carries you beyond the medium of print and thus lets you practice your analytic skills in a different arena.

Although we are all surrounded by visual stimuli, we don't always think critically about what we see. Perhaps we are numbed by constant exposure to a barrage of images on TV, in magazines and newspapers, in video games and films. In any case, here are a few tips on how to get the most out of the images we have collected for this book. Take the time to look at the images carefully; first impressions are important, but many of the photographs contain details that might not strike you immediately. Once you have noted the immediate impact of an image, try focusing on separate elements such as background, foreground, facial expressions, and body language. Read any text that appears in the photograph, even if it's on a T-shirt or a belt buckle. Remember that many photographs are carefully *constructed,* no matter how "natural" they may look. In a photo for a magazine advertisement, for example, everything is meticulously chosen and arranged: certain actors or models are cast for their roles; they wear makeup; their clothes are really costumes; the location or setting of the ad is designed to reinforce its message; lighting is artificial; and someone is trying to sell you something.

Also be sure to consider the visual images contextually, not in isolation. How does each resemble or differ from its neighbors in the portfolio? How does it reinforce or challenge cultural beliefs or stereotypes? Put another way, how can it be understood in the context of the myths examined in *Rereading America*? Each portfolio is accompanied by a few questions to help you begin this type of analysis. You can also build a broader context for our visual images by collecting your own, then working in small groups to create a portfolio or collage.

Finally, remember that both readings and visual images are just starting points for discussion. You have access to a wealth of other perspectives and ideas among your family, friends, classmates; in your college library; in your personal experience; and in your imagination. We urge you to consult them all as you grapple with the perspectives you encounter in this text.

1

Harmony at Home

The Myth of the Model Family

The Donna Reed Show.

FAST FACTS

1. Experts estimate that 40% to 50% of existing marriages will end in divorce.
2. Nearly 14 million American households are headed by women with no husband present. Nearly 70% of American households are childless.
3. About 14% of American men over age 65 are widowed; 44% of women over 65 are widowed.
4. As of June, 2009, same-sex marriage was legal in six states: Connecticut, Iowa, Maine, Massachusetts, New Hampshire, and Vermont.
5. Roughly 80% of mothers aged 25 to 54 are in the labor force.

Sources: (1, 2, 3) U.S. Census Bureau; (5) U.S. Current Population Survey.

THE NEED TO REREAD COMMONPLACE IDEAS is nowhere more apparent than in the ongoing culture war over the American family. Everyone is in favor of "family," but our definitions differ. Most obviously, legal and political battles over same-sex marriage are being fought or planned in every state, but the new century has brought many other developments as well. We've seen a pregnant man, for example, and many couples are embracing cutting-edge medical technologies to help them have a family or to control its size or makeup; at the same time, a conservative Christian movement is using ancient biblical authority to promote prolific childbearing — eight or ten or twelve children per family.

Amidst such changes, the traditional vision of the ideal nuclear family — Dad, Mom, a couple of kids, maybe a dog, and a spacious suburban home — remains surprisingly strong. The cliché is also a potent myth, a dream that millions of Americans work to fulfill. The image is so compelling that it's easy to forget what a short time it's been around, especially compared with the long history of the family itself.

In fact, what we call the "traditional" family, headed by a breadwinner-father and a housewife-mother, has existed for little more than two hundred years, and the suburbs only came into being in the 1950s. But the family as a social institution was legally recognized in Western culture at least as far back as the Code of Hammurabi, created in ancient Mesopotamia some four thousand years ago. To appreciate how profoundly concepts of family life have changed, consider the absolute power of the Mesopotamian father, the patriarch: the law allowed him to use any of his dependents, including his wife, as collateral for loans or even to sell family members outright to pay his debts.

Although patriarchal authority was less absolute in Puritan America, fathers remained the undisputed heads of families. Seventeenth-century Connecticut, Massachusetts, and New Hampshire enacted laws condemning rebellious children to severe punishment and, in extreme cases, to death. In the early years of the American colonies, as in Western culture stretching back to Hammurabi's time, unquestioned authority within the family served as both the model for and the basis of state authority. Just as family members owed complete obedience to the father, so all citizens owed unquestioned loyalty to the king and his legal representatives. In his influential volume *Democracy in America* (1835), French aristocrat Alexis de Tocqueville describes the relationship between the traditional European family and the old political order:

> Among aristocratic nations, social institutions recognize, in truth, no one in the family but the father; children are received by society at his hands; society governs him, he governs them. Thus, the parent not only has a natural right, but acquires a political right to command them; he is the author and the support of his family; but he is also its constituted ruler.

By the mid-eighteenth century, however, new ideas about individual freedom and democracy were stirring the colonies. And by the time Tocqueville visited the United States in 1831, they had evidently worked a revolution in the family as well as in the nation's political structure: he observes, "When the condition of society becomes democratic, and men adopt as their general principle that it is good and lawful to judge of all things for one's self, . . . the power which the opinions of a father exercise over those of his sons diminishes, as well as his legal power." To Tocqueville, this shift away from strict patriarchal rule signaled a change in the emotional climate of families: "as manners and laws become more democratic, the relation of father and son becomes more intimate and more affectionate; rules and authority are less talked of, confidence and tenderness are oftentimes increased, and it would seem that the natural bond is drawn closer." In his view, the American family heralded a new era in human relations. Freed from the rigid hierarchy of the past, parents and children could meet as near equals, joined by "filial love and fraternal affection."

This vision of the democratic family — a harmonious association of parents and children united by love and trust — has mesmerized popular culture in the United States. From the nineteenth century to the present, popular novels, magazines, music, and advertising images have glorified the comforts of loving domesticity. In recent years, we've probably absorbed our strongest impressions of the ideal family from television situation comedies. In the 1950s we had the Andersons on *Father Knows Best,* the Stones on *The Donna Reed Show,* and the real-life Nelson family on *The Adventures of Ozzie & Harriet.* Over the next three decades, the model stretched to include single parents, second marriages, and inter-racial adoptions on *My Three Sons, The Brady Bunch,* and *Diff'rent Strokes,* but the underlying ideal of wise, loving parents and harmonious, happy families remained unchanged. But today, America has begun to worry about the health of its families: even the families on TV no longer reflect the domestic tranquility of the Anderson clan. America is becoming increasingly ambivalent about the future of family life, and perhaps with good reason. The myth of the family scarcely reflects the complexities of modern American life. High divorce rates, the rise of the single-parent household, the national debate about same-sex marriage, and a growing frankness about domestic violence are transforming the way we see family life.

This chapter examines the myth of the model family and explores alternative visions of family life, including marriage equality for gay and lesbian couples. It opens with three paintings by Norman Rockwell that express the meaning of "family values" circa 1950, an era some consider the heyday of American family life. The subsequent readings immediately challenge the ideal of the harmonious nuclear family. In "Looking for Work," Gary Soto recalls his boyhood desire to live the myth and recounts his humorous attempts to transform his working-class Chicano family into a facsimile of the Cleavers on *Leave It to Beaver.* Stephanie Coontz then takes a close analytical look at the 1950s family, explaining its lasting appeal to some Americans but also documenting its dark side.

The next selections blend narrative, analytical, and visual approaches to understanding the meanings of family. "Aunt Ida Pieces a Quilt," a short poem by Melvin Dixon, tells the story of an extended African American family helping one another cope with the loss of Ida's nephew to AIDS. In "An Indian Story," Roger Jack paints a warm, magical portrait of the bond between a Native American boy and his caretaker aunt. "The Color of Family Ties," by Naomi Gerstel and Natalia Sarkisian, moves us from individual experience to sociological analysis, as the authors challenge common misconceptions by carefully examining how ethnicity and social class shape the behaviors of American families. Next, the chapter's Visual Portfolio offers you a chance to practice interpreting images; the photographs in this collection suggest some of the complex ways the contemporary American family intersects with gender, ethnicity, and social class.

The chapter concludes with a collection of short readings on same-sex marriage, looking briefly at developments in California as a kind of case study and then broadening to a national perspective. We begin with a pair of conservative readings. The first is "Proposition 8," a ballot measure which amended California's Constitution to define marriage as valid only between a man and a woman; next, Jennifer Roback Morse's "8 Is Not Hate" explains that her support of Proposition 8 is not grounded in any animosity toward gays and lesbians. In stark contrast to Morse, "Prop 8 Hurt My Family — Ask Me How," a report from Marriage Equality USA, describes the harassment that Prop 8 opponents and their families were subjected to during the 2008 campaign, including homophobic slurs and threats of physical violence. In the following essay, Evan Wolfson, a prominent marriage-equality advocate, explains why marriage matters even when states have instituted "domestic partnerships" or other legal provisions for lesbians and gays; he argues forcefully that lesbian and gay Americans deserve the same rights to civil marriages that other citizens — including felons — enjoy. Finally, in "My Big Fat Straight Wedding," Andrew Sullivan describes the complete normalcy of his "gay" marriage and suggests that such unions will inevitably become routine.

Sources

Lerner, Gerda. *The Creation of Patriarchy*. New York: Oxford University Press, 1986. Print.

Mintz, Steven, and Susan Kellogg. *Domestic Revolutions: A Social History of American Life*. New York: Free Press, 1988. Print.

Tocqueville, Alexis de. *Democracy in America*. 1835. New York: Vintage Books, 1990. Print.

Before Reading

- Spend ten minutes or so jotting down every word, phrase, or image you associate with the idea of "family." Write as freely as possible, without censoring your thoughts or worrying about grammatical correctness. Working in small groups, compare lists and try to categorize your responses. What assumptions about families do they reveal?

- Draw a visual representation of your family. This could take the form of a graph, chart, diagram, map, cartoon, symbolic picture, or literal portrait. Don't worry if you're not a skillful artist: the main point is to convey an idea, and even stick figures can speak eloquently. When you're finished, write a journal entry about your drawing. Was it easier to depict some feelings or ideas visually than it would have been to describe them in words? Did you find some things about your family difficult or impossible to convey visually? Does your drawing "say" anything that surprises you?

- Do a brief freewrite about the television family — from *The Donna Reed Show* — pictured on the title page of this chapter (p. 17). What can you tell about their relationship? What does this image suggest to you about the ideals and realities of American family life?

A *Family Tree, Freedom from Want,* and *Freedom from Fear*

NORMAN ROCKWELL

The first "reading" for this book consists of three paintings by Norman Rockwell (1894–1978), one of America's most prolific and popular artists. Together they capture what the idea of family meant to the nation half a century ago, a time some consider the golden age of American family life. A Family Tree (1959) is an oil painting that, like hundreds of Rockwell's images, became cover art for the Saturday Evening Post. Freedom from Want *and* Freedom from Fear *are part of Rockwell's Four Freedoms series (1943). Their appearance in the* Saturday Evening Post, *along with* Freedom of Speech *and* Freedom of Worship, *generated millions of requests for reprints.*

A Family Tree, by Norman Rockwell.

Freedom from Want, by Norman Rockwell.

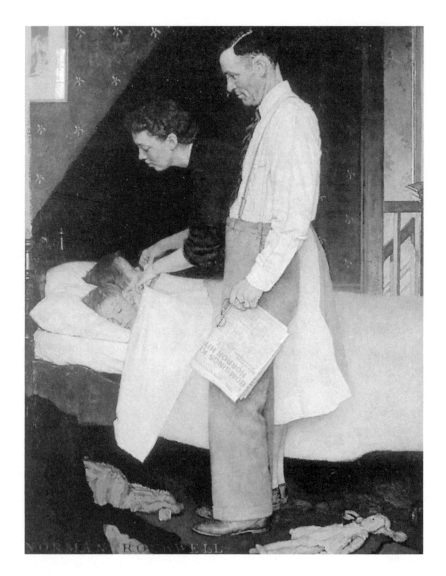

Freedom from Fear, by Norman Rockwell.

Engaging the Text

1. What is the usual purpose of family trees? Why do you think they are important to many Americans? How significant is a family tree to you or others in your family?

2. Discuss the details of *A Family Tree* and their significance. For example, identify each figure and explain what it contributes to Rockwell's composite picture of America.

3. How does Rockwell's painting differ from a typical family tree? What are its basic messages about American families and marriages? What does it "say" about U.S. history, race relations, and occupations?

4. What is the appeal of *Freedom from Want?* What ideas about family does it assume or promote? What is your own reaction to Rockwell's image? Support your answers with reference to details of the painting.

5. Rockwell's Four Freedoms paintings allude to Franklin D. Roosevelt's 1941 State of the Union address, which described "four essential human freedoms." Roosevelt defined freedom from want as "economic understandings which will secure to every nation a healthy peacetime life for its inhabitants — everywhere in the world." To what extent does Rockwell's *Freedom from Want* reflect FDR's definition, and what meanings does it add or alter?

6. In *Freedom from Fear,* why did Rockwell choose this moment to paint? What can you guess about the relationships within the family? What about its relationship to the rest of the world?

7. In his speech before Congress, Roosevelt said that freedom from fear, "translated into world terms, means a worldwide reduction of armaments to such a point and in such a thorough fashion that no nation will be in a position to commit an act of physical aggression against any neighbor — anywhere in the world." Compare FDR's ideas to those expressed in Rockwell's *Freedom from Fear.* To what extent can the differences be explained by the shift from Roosevelt's preparing the nation for war in early 1941 to our full engagement in World War II when Rockwell's paintings appeared?

Exploring Connections

8. Compare Rockwell's paintings to the frontispiece photo for this chapter (p. 17). How does Rockwell's vision of family life differ from that depicted by the photo?

9. Rockwell's art is sometimes thought to present an overly optimistic view of American life. Look for counterevidence: study the three paintings here for undercurrents of conflict and then compare them to the photographs in the Visual Portfolio on pages 71–77. Given this slightly broader context, is it fair to say that Rockwell's work is naïve?

10. How are women and girls portrayed in these three paintings and in the photograph on page 72, which was art-directed by Rockwell? Look through *Rereading America* to find several images that challenge or complicate Rockwell's portrayals of femininity, and explain the differences you see. Can you find any images that closely resemble Rockwell's?

11. Write a paragraph about what "freedom from fear" or "freedom from want" might mean to one of the people in a photograph from the Visual Portfolio on pages 71–77.

EXTENDING THE CRITICAL CONTEXT

12. Research your family tree and make your own drawing of it. How does it compare to the family tree Rockwell has created? Write a journal entry or short essay about your family tree.

13. Discuss how well the idea of a tree can represent what you know about families. Are there ways in which the tree image or metaphor might be misleading or inaccurate? What other analogies or metaphors can you suggest for depicting family histories? Draw either an updated version of Rockwell's family tree or an image based on a fresh metaphor or analogy.

14. What might pictures entitled *Freedom from Want* and *Freedom from Fear* look like if they were painted today? Describe in detail a scene or image to fit each of these titles; if possible, draw, paint, or photograph your image.

15. Millions of Americans "consumed" the images Rockwell produced for the *Saturday Evening Post*. What images are we consuming today? What ideas about family and marriage appear in today's mass culture — advertisements, song lyrics, cereal boxes, sitcoms, reality shows, talk radio, junk mail, and similar cultural products?

Looking for Work

GARY SOTO

"Looking for Work" is the narrative of a nine-year-old Mexican Ameri-can boy who wants his family to imitate the "perfect families" he sees on TV. Much of the humor in this essay comes from the author's perspective as an adult looking back at his childhood self, but Soto also respects the child's point of view. In the marvelous details of this midsummer day, Soto cap-tures the interplay of seductive myth and complex reality. Gary Soto (b. 1952) grew up "on the industrial side of Fresno, right smack against a junkyard and the junkyard's cross-eyed German shepherd." Having discov-ered poetry almost by chance in a city college library, he has now published

eleven volumes of his own for adult readers, in addition to many volumes of fiction, nonfiction, and poetry for children and young adult readers. His New and Selected Poems *(1995) was a finalist for both the* Los Angeles Times Book Award *and the* National Book Award. *Recent publications include* Facts of Life: Stories *(2008),* The Skirt *(2008), and* Partly Cloudy: Poems of Love and Longing *(2009).*

One July, while killing ants on the kitchen sink with a rolled newspaper, I had a nine-year-old's vision of wealth that would save us from ourselves. For weeks I had drunk Kool-Aid and watched morning reruns of *Father Knows Best*, whose family was so uncomplicated in its routine that I very much wanted to imitate it. The first step was to get my brother and sister to wear shoes at dinner.

"Come on, Rick — come on, Deb," I whined. But Rick mimicked me and the same day that I asked him to wear shoes he came to the dinner table in only his swim trunks. My mother didn't notice, nor did my sister, as we sat to eat our beans and tortillas in the stifling heat of our kitchen. We all gleamed like cellophane, wiping the sweat from our brows with the backs of our hands as we talked about the day: Frankie our neighbor was beat up by Faustino; the swimming pool at the playground would be closed for a day because the pump was broken.

Such was our life. So that morning, while doing-in the train of ants which arrived each day, I decided to become wealthy, and right away! After downing a bowl of cereal, I took a rake from the garage and started up the block to look for work.

We lived on an ordinary block of mostly working class people: ware-housemen, egg candlers,[1] welders, mechanics, and a union plumber. And there were many retired people who kept their lawns green and the gutters uncluttered of the chewing gum wrappers we dropped as we rode by on our bikes. They bent down to gather our litter, muttering at our evilness.

At the corner house I rapped the screen door and a very large woman   5 in a muu-muu answered. She sized me up and then asked what I could do.

"Rake leaves," I answered smiling.

"It's summer, and there ain't no leaves," she countered. Her face was pinched with lines; fat jiggled under her chin. She pointed to the lawn, then the flower bed, and said: "You see any leaves there — or there?" I followed her pointing arm, stupidly. But she had a job for me and that was to get her a Coke at the liquor store. She gave me twenty cents, and after ditching my rake in a bush, off I ran. I returned with an unbagged Pepsi, for which she thanked me and gave me a nickel from her apron.

---

[1]*egg candler:* One who inspects eggs by holding them up to a light.

I skipped off her porch, fetched my rake, and crossed the street to the next block where Mrs. Moore, mother of Earl the retarded man, let me weed a flower bed. She handed me a trowel and for a good part of the morning my fingers dipped into the moist dirt, ripping up runners of Bermuda grass. Worms surfaced in my search for deep roots, and I cut them in halves, tossing them to Mrs. Moore's cat who pawed them playfully as they dried in the sun. I made out Earl whose face was pressed to the back window of the house, and although he was calling to me I couldn't understand what he was trying to say. Embarrassed, I worked without looking up, but I imagined his contorted mouth and the ring of keys attached to his belt — keys that jingled with each palsied step. He scared me and I worked quickly to finish the flower bed. When I did finish Mrs. Moore gave me a quarter and two peaches from her tree, which I washed there but ate in the alley behind my house.

I was sucking on the second one, a bit of juice staining the front of my T-shirt, when Little John, my best friend, came walking down the alley with a baseball bat over his shoulder, knocking over trash cans as he made his way toward me.

Little John and I went to St. John's Catholic School, where we sat   10 among the "stupids." Miss Marino, our teacher, alternated the rows of good students with the bad, hoping that by sitting side-by-side with the bright students the stupids might become more intelligent, as though intelligence were contagious. But we didn't progress as she had hoped. She grew frustrated when one day, while dismissing class for recess, Little John couldn't get up because his arms were stuck in the slats of the chair's backrest. She scolded us with a shaking finger when we knocked over the globe, denting the already troubled Africa. She muttered curses when Leroy White, a real stupid but a great softball player with the gift to hit to all fields, openly chewed his host[2] when he made his First Communion; his hands swung at his sides as he returned to the pew looking around with a big smile.

Little John asked what I was doing, and I told him that I was taking a break from work, as I sat comfortably among high weeds. He wanted to join me, but I reminded him that the last time he'd gone door-to-door asking for work his mother had whipped him. I was with him when his mother, a New Jersey Italian who could rise up in anger one moment and love the next, told me in a polite but matter-of-fact voice that I had to leave because she was going to beat her son. She gave me a homemade popsicle, ushered me to the door, and said that I could see Little John the next day. But it was sooner than that. I went around to his bedroom window to suck my popsicle and watch Little John dodge his mother's blows, a few hitting their mark but many whirring air.

It was midday when Little John and I converged in the alley, the sun blazing in the high nineties, and he suggested that we go to Roosevelt High School to swim. He needed five cents to make fifteen, the cost of admission,

[2]*his host:* The wafer that embodies, in the Catholic sacrament of Communion, the bread of the Last Supper and the body of Christ.

and I lent him a nickel. We ran home for my bike and when my sister found out that we were going swimming, she started to cry because she didn't have the fifteen cents but only an empty Coke bottle. I waved for her to come and three of us mounted the bike — Debra on the cross bar, Little John on the handle bars and holding the Coke bottle which we would cash for a nickel and make up the difference that would allow all of us to get in, and me pumping up the crooked streets, dodging cars and pot holes. We spent the day swimming under the afternoon sun, so that when we got home our mom asked us what was darker, the floor or us? She feigned a stern posture, her hands on her hips and her mouth puckered. We played along. Looking down, Debbie and I said in unison, "Us."

That evening at dinner we all sat down in our bathing suits to eat our beans, laughing and chewing loudly. Our mom was in a good mood, so I took a risk and asked her if sometime we could have turtle soup. A few days before I had watched a television program in which a Polynesian tribe killed a large turtle, gutted it, and then stewed it over an open fire. The turtle, basted in a sugary sauce, looked delicious as I ate an afternoon bowl of cereal, but my sister, who was watching the program with a glass of Kool-Aid between her knees, said, "Caca."

My mother looked at me in bewilderment. "Boy, are you a crazy Mexican. Where did you get the idea that people eat turtles?"

"On television," I said, explaining the program. Then I took it a step further. "Mom, do you think we could get dressed up for dinner one of these days? David King does."   15

"*Ay, Dios,*" my mother laughed. She started collecting the dinner plates, but my brother wouldn't let go of his. He was still drawing a picture in the bean sauce. Giggling, he said it was me, but I didn't want to listen because I wanted an answer from Mom. This was the summer when I spent the mornings in front of the television that showed the comfortable lives of white kids. There were no beatings, no rifts in the family. They wore bright clothes; toys tumbled from their closets. They hopped into bed with kisses and woke to glasses of fresh orange juice, and to a father sitting before his morning coffee while the mother buttered his toast. They hurried through the day making friends and gobs of money, returning home to a warmly lit living room, and then dinner. *Leave It to Beaver* was the program I replayed in my mind:

"May I have the mashed potatoes?" asks Beaver with a smile.

"Sure, Beav," replies Wally as he taps the corners of his mouth with a starched napkin.

The father looks on in his suit. The mother, decked out in earrings and a pearl necklace, cuts into her steak and blushes. Their conversation is politely clipped.

"Swell," says Beaver, his cheeks puffed with food.   20

Our own talk at dinner was loud with belly laughs and marked by our pointing forks at one another. The subjects were commonplace.

"Gary, let's go to the ditch tomorrow," my brother suggests. He explains that he has made a life preserver out of four empty detergent bottles strung together with twine and that he will make me one if I can find more bottles. "No way are we going to drown."

"Yeah, then we could have a dirt clod fight," I reply, so happy to be alive.

Whereas the Beaver's family enjoyed dessert in dishes at the table, our mom sent us outside, and more often than not I went into the alley to peek over the neighbor's fences and spy out fruit, apricots or peaches.

I had asked my mom and again she laughed that I was a crazy *chavalo*[3] as she stood in front of the sink, her arms rising and falling with suds, face glistening from the heat. She sent me outside where my brother and sister were sitting in the shade that the fence threw out like a blanket. They were talking about me when I plopped down next to them. They looked at one another and then Debbie, my eight-year-old sister, started in.

"What's this crap about getting dressed up?"

She had entered her *profanity* stage. A year later she would give up such words and slip into her Catholic uniform, and into squealing on my brother and me when we "cussed this" and "cussed that."

I tried to convince them that if we improved the way we looked we might get along better in life. White people would like us more. They might invite us to places, like their homes or front yards. They might not hate us so much.

My sister called me a "craphead," and got up to leave with a stalk of grass dangling from her mouth. "They'll never like us."

My brother's mood lightened as he talked about the ditch — the white water, the broken pieces of glass, and the rusted car fenders that awaited our knees. There would be toads, and rocks to smash them.

David King, the only person we knew who resembled the middle class, called from over the fence. David was Catholic, of Armenian and French descent, and his closet was filled with toys. A bear-shaped cookie jar, like the ones on television, sat on the kitchen counter. His mother was remarkably kind while she put up with the racket we made on the street. Evenings, she often watered the front yard and it must have upset her to see us — my brother and I and others — jump from trees laughing, the unkillable kids of the very poor, who got up unshaken, brushed off, and climbed into another one to try again.

David called again. Rick got up and slapped grass from his pants. When I asked if I could come along he said no. David said no. They were two years older so their affairs were different from mine. They greeted one another with foul names and took off down the alley to look for trouble.

I went inside the house, turned on the television, and was about to sit down with a glass of Kool-Aid when Mom shooed me outside.

"It's still light," she said. "Later you'll bug me to let you stay out longer. So go on."

[3]*chavalo:* Kid.

I downed my Kool-Aid and went outside to the front yard. No one was   35
around. The day had cooled and a breeze rustled the trees. Mr. Jackson, the
plumber, was watering his lawn and when he saw me he turned away to
wash off his front steps. There was more than an hour of light left, so I took
advantage of it and decided to look for work. I felt suddenly alive as I
skipped down the block in search of an overgrown flower bed and the dime
that would end the day right.

ENGAGING THE TEXT

1. Why is the narrator attracted to the kind of family life depicted on TV?
   What, if anything, does he think is wrong with his life? Why do his desires
   apparently have so little impact on his family?

2. Why does the narrator first go looking for work? How has the meaning of
   work changed by the end of the story, when he goes out again "in search of an
   overgrown flower bed and the dime that would end the day right"? Explain.

3. As Soto looks back on his nine-year-old self, he has a different perspective
   on things than he had as a child. How would you characterize the mature
   Soto's thoughts about his childhood family life? (Was it "a good family"?
   What was wrong with Soto's thinking as a nine-year-old?) Back up your
   remarks with specific references to the narrative.

4. Review the story to find each mention of food or drink. Explain the role
   these references play.

5. Review the cast of "supporting characters" in this narrative — the mother,
   sister, brother, friends, and neighbors. What does each contribute to the
   story and in particular to the meaning of family within the story?

EXPLORING CONNECTIONS

6. Read Roger Jack's "An Indian Story" (p. 52) and compare Soto's family to the
   one Roger Jack describes. In particular, consider gender roles, the household
   atmosphere, and the expectations placed on children and parents.

7. Compare and contrast the relationship of school and family in this narrative
   to that described by Mike Rose (p. 157), Richard Rodriguez (p. 194), or
   Inés Hernández-Ávila (p. 207).

8. Like Soto's story, the cartoon on page 35 attests to the power of the media
   to shape our ideas about family. Write a journal entry describing the media
   family that most accurately reflects your image of family life. Discuss these
   entries, and the impact of media on your image of the family, with your
   classmates.

EXTENDING THE CRITICAL CONTEXT

9. Write a journal entry about a time when you wished your family were
   somehow different. What caused your dissatisfaction? What did you want
   your family to be like? Was your dissatisfaction ever resolved?

10. "Looking for Work" is essentially the story of a single day. Write a narrative of one day when you were eight or nine or ten; use details as Soto does to give the events of the day broader significance.

What We Really Miss About the 1950s

STEPHANIE COONTZ

Popular myth has it that the 1950s were the ideal decade for the American family. In this example of academic writing at its best, Stephanie Coontz provides a clear, well-documented, and insightful analysis of what was really going on and suggests that our nostalgia for the 1950s could mislead us today. Stephanie Coontz is Professor of Family History at the Evergreen State College in Olympia, Washington. An award-winning writer and nationally recognized expert on the family, she has testified before a House Select Committee on families, appeared in several television documentaries, and published widely. Her books include Marriage, A History: From Obedience to Intimacy, or How Love Conquered Marriage *(2005) and* The Way We Really Are: Coming to Terms with America's Changing Families *(1997), from which this selection is excerpted.*

In a 1996 poll by the Knight-Ridder news agency, more Americans chose the 1950s than any other single decade as the best time for children to grow up.[1] And despite the research I've done on the underside of 1950s families, I don't think it's crazy for people to feel nostalgic about the period. For one thing, it's easy to see why people might look back fondly to a decade when real wages grew more in any single year than in the entire ten years of the 1980s combined, a time when the average 30-year-old man could buy a median-priced home on only 15–18 percent of his salary.[2]

---

[1]Steven Thomma, "Nostalgia for '50s Surfaces," *Philadelphia Inquirer,* Feb. 4, 1996. [All notes are Coontz's.]

[2]Frank Levy, *Dollars and Dreams: The Changing American Income Distribution* (New York: Russell Sage, 1987), p. 6; Frank Levy, "Incomes and Income Inequality," in Reynolds Farley, ed., *State of the Union: America in the 1990s,* vol. 1 (New York: Russell Sage, 1995), pp. 1–57; Richard May and Kathryn Porter, "Poverty and Income Trends, 1994," Washington, D.C.: Center on Budget and Policy Priorities, March 1996; Rob Nelson and Jon Cowan, "Buster Power," *USA Weekend,* October 14–16, 1994, p. 10.

But it's more than just a financial issue. When I talk with modern parents, even ones who grew up in unhappy families, they associate the 1950s with a yearning they feel for a time when there were fewer complicated choices for kids or parents to grapple with, when there was more predictability in how people formed and maintained families, and when there was a coherent "moral order" in their community to serve as a reference point for family norms. Even people who found that moral order grossly unfair or repressive often say that its presence provided them with something concrete to push against.

I can sympathize entirely. One of my most empowering moments occurred the summer I turned 12, when my mother marched down to the library with me to confront a librarian who'd curtly refused to let me check out a book that was "not appropriate" for my age. "Don't you *ever* tell my daughter what she can and can't read," fumed my mom. "She's a mature young lady and she can make her own choices." In recent years I've often thought back to the gratitude I felt toward my mother for that act of trust in me. I wish I had some way of earning similar points from my own son. But much as I've always respected his values, I certainly wouldn't have walked into my local video store when he was 12 and demanded that he be allowed to check out absolutely anything he wanted!

Still, I have no illusions that I'd actually like to go back to the 1950s, and neither do most people who express such occasional nostalgia. For example, although the 1950s got more votes than any other decade in the Knight-Ridder poll, it did not win an outright majority: 38 percent of respondents picked the 1950s; 27 percent picked the 1960s or the 1970s. Voters between the ages of 50 and 64 were most likely to choose the 1950s, the decade in which they themselves came of age, as the best time for kids; voters under 30 were more likely to choose the 1970s. African Americans differed over whether the 1960s, 1970s, or 1980s were best, but all age groups of blacks agreed that later decades were definitely preferable to the 1950s.

Nostalgia for the 1950s is real and deserves to be taken seriously, but it usually shouldn't be taken literally. Even people who *do* pick the 1950s as the best decade generally end up saying, once they start discussing their feelings in depth, that it's not the family arrangements in and of themselves that they want to revive. They don't miss the way women used to be treated, they sure wouldn't want to live with most of the fathers they knew in their neighborhoods, and "come to think of it" — I don't know how many times I've recorded these exact words — "I communicate with my kids *much* better than my parents or grandparents did." When Judith Wallerstein recently interviewed 100 spouses in "happy" marriages, she found that only five "wanted a marriage like their parents'." The husbands "consciously rejected the role models provided by their fathers. The women said they could never be happy living as their mothers did."[3]

5

[3]Judith Wallerstein and Sandra Blakeslee, *The Good Marriage: How and Why Love Lasts* (Boston: Houghton Mifflin, 1995), p. 15.

People today understandably feel that their lives are out of balance, but they yearn for something totally *new* — a more equal distribution of work, family, and community time for both men and women, children and adults. If the 1990s are lopsided in one direction, the 1950s were equally lopsided in the opposite direction.

What most people really feel nostalgic about has little to do with the internal structure of 1950s families. It is the belief that the 1950s provided a more family-friendly economic and social environment, an easier climate in which to keep kids on the straight and narrow, and above all, a greater feeling of hope for a family's long-term future, especially for its young. The contrast between the perceived hopefulness of the fifties and our own misgivings about the future is key to contemporary nostalgia for the period. Greater optimism *did* exist then, even among many individuals and groups who were in terrible circumstances. But if we are to take people's sense of loss seriously, rather than merely to capitalize on it for a hidden political agenda, we need to develop a historical perspective on where that hope came from.

Part of it came from families comparing their prospects in the 1950s to their unstable, often grindingly uncomfortable pasts, especially the two horrible decades just before. In the 1920s, after two centuries of child labor and income insecurity, and for the first time in American history, a bare majority of children had come to live in a family with a male breadwinner, a female homemaker, and a chance at a high school education. Yet no sooner did the ideals associated with such a family begin to blossom than they were buried by the stock market crash of 1929 and the Great Depression of the 1930s. During the 1930s domestic violence soared; divorce rates fell, but informal separations jumped; fertility plummeted. Murder rates were higher in 1933 than they were in the 1980s. Families were uprooted or torn apart. Thousands of young people left home to seek work, often riding the rails across the country.[4]

World War II brought the beginning of economic recovery, and people's renewed interest in forming families resulted in a marriage and childbearing boom, but stability was still beyond most people's grasp. Postwar communities were rocked by racial tensions, labor strife, and a right-wing backlash against the radical union movement of the 1930s. Many women resented being fired from wartime jobs they had grown to enjoy. Veterans often came home to find that they had to elbow their way back into their families, with wives and children resisting their attempts to reassert domestic authority. In

---

[4]Donald Hernandez, *America's Children: Resources from Family, Government and the Economy* (New York: Russell Sage, 1993), pp. 99, 102; James Morone, "The Corrosive Politics of Virtue," *American Prospect* 26 (May–June 1996), p. 37; "Study Finds U.S. No. 1 in Violence," *Olympian*, November 13, 1992. See also Stephen Mintz and Susan Kellogg, *Domestic Revolutions: A Social History of American Family Life* (New York: The Free Press, 1988).

ROGER REALIZES A CHERISHED CHILDHOOD
MEMORY IS ACTUALLY A SCENE FROM AN
OLD MOVIE.

one recent study of fathers who returned from the war, four times as many
reported painful, even traumatic, reunions as remembered happy ones.[5]

By 1946 one in every three marriages was ending in divorce. Even   10
couples who stayed together went through rough times, as an acute housing

[5]William Tuttle, Jr., *"Daddy's Gone to War": The Second World War in the Lives of
America's Children* (New York: Oxford University Press, 1993).

shortage forced families to double up with relatives or friends. Tempers frayed and generational relations grew strained. "No home is big enough to house two families, particularly two of different generations, with opposite theories on child training," warned a 1948 film on the problems of modern marriage.[6]

So after the widespread domestic strife, family disruptions, and violence of the 1930s and the instability of the World War II period, people were ready to try something new. The postwar economic boom gave them the chance. The 1950s was the first time that a majority of Americans could even *dream* of creating a secure oasis in their immediate nuclear families. There they could focus their emotional and financial investments, reduce obligations to others that might keep them from seizing their own chance at a new start, and escape the interference of an older generation of neighbors or relatives who tried to tell them how to run their lives and raise their kids. Oral histories of the postwar period resound with the theme of escaping from in-laws, maiden aunts, older parents, even needy siblings.

The private family also provided a refuge from the anxieties of the new nuclear age and the cold war, as well as a place to get away from the political witch hunts led by Senator Joe McCarthy and his allies. When having the wrong friends at the wrong time or belonging to any "suspicious" organization could ruin your career and reputation, it was safer to pull out of groups you might have joined earlier and to focus on your family. On a more positive note, the nuclear family was where people could try to satisfy their long-pent-up desires for a more stable marriage, a decent home, and the chance to really enjoy their children.

The 1950s Family Experiment

The key to understanding the successes, failures, and comparatively short life of 1950s family forms and values is to understand the period as one of *experimentation* with the possibilities of a new kind of family, not as the expression of some longstanding tradition. At the end of the 1940s, the divorce rate, which had been rising steadily since the 1890s, dropped sharply; the age of marriage fell to a 100-year low; and the birth rate soared. Women who had worked during the Depression or World War II quit their jobs as soon as they became pregnant, which meant quite a few women were specializing in child raising; fewer women remained childless during the 1950s than in any decade since the late nineteenth century. The timing and spacing of childbearing became far more compressed, so that young mothers were likely to have two or more children in diapers at once, with no older sibling to help in their care. At the same time, again for the first time in 100 years, the educational gap between young middle-class women and men increased, while job segregation for working men and women seems to

[6]"Marriage and Divorce," *March of Time*, film series 14 (1948).

have peaked. These demographic changes increased the dependence of women on marriage, in contrast to gradual trends in the opposite direction since the early twentieth century.[7]

The result was that family life and gender roles became much more predictable, orderly, and settled in the 1950s than they were either twenty years earlier or would be twenty years later. Only slightly more than one in four marriages ended in divorce during the 1950s. Very few young people spent any extended period of time in a nonfamily setting: They moved from their parents' family into their own family, after just a brief experience with independent living, and they started having children soon after marriage. Whereas two-thirds of women aged 20 to 24 were not yet married in 1990, only 28 percent of women this age were still single in 1960.[8]

Ninety percent of all the households in the country were families in the 1950s, in comparison with only 71 percent by 1990. Eighty-six percent of all children lived in two-parent homes in 1950, as opposed to just 72 percent in 1990. And the percentage living with both biological parents — rather than, say, a parent and stepparent — was dramatically higher than it had been at the turn of the century or is today: seventy percent in 1950, compared with only 50 percent in 1990. Nearly 60 percent of kids — an all-time high — were born into male breadwinner–female homemaker families; only a minority of the rest had mothers who worked in the paid labor force.[9]

If the organization and uniformity of family life in the 1950s were new, so were the values, especially the emphasis on putting all one's emotional and financial eggs in the small basket of the immediate nuclear family. Right up through the 1940s, ties of work, friendship, neighborhood, ethnicity, extended kin, and voluntary organizations were as important a source of identity for most Americans, and sometimes a *more* important source of obligation, than marriage and the nuclear family. All this changed in the postwar era. The spread of suburbs and automobiles, combined with the destruction of older ethnic neighborhoods in many cities, led to the decline

15

---

[7]Arlene Skolnick and Stacey Rosencrantz, "The New Crusade for the Old Family," *American Prospect,* Summer 1994, p. 65; Hernandez, *America's Children,* pp. 128–32; Andrew Cherlin, "Changing Family and Household: Contemporary Lessons from Historical Research," *Annual Review of Sociology* 9 (1983), pp. 54–58; Sam Roberts, *Who We Are: A Portrait of America Based on the Latest Census* (New York: Times Books, 1995), p. 45.

[8]Levy, "Incomes and Income Inequality," p. 20; Arthur Norton and Louisa Miller, *Marriage, Divorce, and Remarriage in the 1990s,* Current Population Reports Series P23-180 (Washington, D.C.: Bureau of the Census, October 1992); Roberts, *Who We Are* (1995 ed.), pp. 50–53.

[9]Dennis Hogan and Daniel Lichter, "Children and Youth: Living Arrangements and Welfare," in Farley, ed., *State of the Union,* vol. 2, p. 99; Richard Gelles, *Contemporary Families: A Sociological View* (Thousand Oaks, Calif.: Sage, 1995), p. 115; Hernandez, *America's Children,* p. 102. The fact that only a small percentage of children had mothers in the paid labor force, though a full 40 percent did not live in male breadwinner–female homemaker families, was because some children had mothers who worked, unpaid, in farms or family businesses, or fathers who were unemployed, or the children were not living with both parents.

of the neighborhood social club. Young couples moved away from parents and kin, cutting ties with traditional extrafamilial networks that might compete for their attention. A critical factor in this trend was the emergence of a group of family sociologists and marriage counselors who followed Talcott Parsons in claiming that the nuclear family, built on a sharp division of labor between husband and wife, was the cornerstone of modern society.

The new family experts tended to advocate views such as those first raised in a 1946 book, *Their Mothers' Sons,* by psychiatrist Edward Strecker. Strecker and his followers argued that American boys were infantilized and emasculated by women who were old-fashioned "moms" instead of modern "mothers." One sign that you might be that dreaded "mom," Strecker warned women, was if you felt you should take your aging parents into your own home, rather than putting them in "a good institution . . . where they will receive adequate care and comfort." Modern "mothers" placed their parents in nursing homes and poured all their energies into their nuclear family. They were discouraged from diluting their wifely and maternal commitments by maintaining "competing" interests in friends, jobs, or extended family networks, yet they were also supposed to cheerfully grant early independence to their (male) children — an emotional double bind that may explain why so many women who took this advice to heart ended up abusing alcohol or tranquilizers over the course of the decade.[10]

The call for young couples to break from their parents and youthful friends was a consistent theme in 1950s popular culture. In *Marty,* one of the most highly praised TV plays and movies of the 1950s, the hero almost loses his chance at love by listening to the carping of his mother and aunt and letting himself be influenced by old friends who resent the time he spends with his new girlfriend. In the end, he turns his back on mother, aunt, and friends to get his new marriage and a little business of his own off to a good start. Other movies, novels, and popular psychology tracts portrayed the dreadful things that happened when women became more interested in careers than marriage or men resisted domestic conformity.

Yet many people felt guilty about moving away from older parents and relatives; "modern mothers" worried that fostering independence in their kids could lead to defiance or even juvenile delinquency (the recurring nightmare of the age); there was considerable confusion about how men and women could maintain clear breadwinner-homemaker distinctions in a period of expanding education, job openings, and consumer aspirations. People clamored for advice. They got it from the new family education specialists and marriage counselors, from columns in women's magazines, from government pamphlets, and above all from television. While 1950s TV melodramas warned against letting anything dilute the commitment to getting married and having kids, the new family sitcoms gave people nightly

[10]Edward Strecker, *Their Mothers' Sons: The Psychiatrist Examines an American Problem* (Philadelphia: J. B. Lippincott, 1946), p. 209.

lessons on how to make their marriage or rapidly expanding family work —
or, in the case of *I Love Lucy,* probably the most popular show of the era,
how *not* to make their marriage and family work. Lucy and Ricky gave
weekly comic reminders of how much trouble a woman could get into by
wanting a career or hatching some hare-brained scheme behind her husband's back.

At the time, everyone knew that shows such as *Donna Reed, Ozzie and*   20
Harriet, Leave It to Beaver, and *Father Knows Best* were not the way families really were. People didn't watch those shows to see their own lives
reflected back at them. They watched them to see how families were *supposed* to live — and also to get a little reassurance that they were headed in
the right direction. The sitcoms were simultaneously advertisements, etiquette manuals, and how-to lessons for a new way of organizing marriage
and child raising. I have studied the scripts of these shows for years, since I
often use them in my classes on family history, but it wasn't until I became a
parent that I felt their extraordinary pull. The secret of their appeal, I suddenly realized, was that they offered 1950s viewers, wracked with the same
feelings of parental inadequacy as was I, the promise that there were easy
answers and surefire techniques for raising kids.

Ever since, I have found it useful to think of the sitcoms as the 1950s
equivalent of today's beer ads. As most people know, beer ads are consciously aimed at men who *aren't* as strong and sexy as the models in the
commercials, guys who are uneasily aware of the gap between the ideal
masculine pursuits and their own achievements. The promise is that if the
viewers on the couch will just drink brand X, they too will be able to run
10 miles without gasping for breath. Their bodies will firm up, their complexions will clear up, and maybe the Swedish bikini team will come over
and hang out at their place.

Similarly, the 1950s sitcoms were aimed at young couples who had married in haste, women who had tasted new freedoms during World War II
and given up their jobs with regret, veterans whose children resented their
attempts to reassert paternal authority, and individuals disturbed by the
changing racial and ethnic mix of postwar America. The message was clear:
Buy these ranch houses, Hotpoint appliances, and child-raising ideals; relate
to your spouse like this; get a new car to wash with your kids on Sunday
afternoons; organize your dinners like that — and you too can escape from
the conflicts of race, class, and political witch hunts into harmonious families
where father knows best, mothers are never bored or irritated, and teenagers
rush to the dinner table each night, eager to get their latest dose of parental
wisdom.

Many families found it possible to put together a good imitation of this
way of living during the 1950s and 1960s. Couples were often able to construct marriages that were much more harmonious than those in which they
had grown up, and to devote far more time to their children. Even when
marriages were deeply unhappy, as many were, the new stability, economic

security, and educational advantages parents were able to offer their kids counted for a lot in people's assessment of their life satisfaction. And in some matters, ignorance could be bliss: The lack of media coverage of problems such as abuse or incest was terribly hard on the casualties, but it protected more fortunate families from knowledge and fear of many social ills.[11]

There was tremendous hostility to people who could be defined as "others": Jews, African Americans, Puerto Ricans, the poor, gays or lesbians, and "the red menace." Yet on a day-to-day basis, the civility that prevailed in homogeneous neighborhoods allowed people to ignore larger patterns of racial and political repression. Racial clashes were ever-present in the 1950s, sometimes escalating into full-scale antiblack riots, but individual homicide rates fell to almost half the levels of the 1930s. As nuclear families moved into the suburbs, they retreated from social activism but entered voluntary relationships with people who had children the same age; they became involved in PTAs together, joined bridge clubs, went bowling. There does seem to have been a stronger sense of neighborly commonalities than many of us feel today. Even though this local community was often the product of exclusion or repression, it sometimes looks attractive to modern Americans whose commutes are getting longer and whose family or work patterns give them little in common with their neighbors.[12]

The optimism that allowed many families to rise above their internal   25
difficulties and to put limits on their individualistic values during the 1950s came from the sense that America was on a dramatically different trajectory than it had been in the past, an upward and expansionary path that had already taken people to better places than they had ever seen before and would certainly take their children even further. This confidence that almost everyone could look forward to a better future stands in sharp contrast to how most contemporary Americans feel, and it explains why a period in which many people were much worse off than today sometimes still looks like a better period for families than our own.

[11]For discussion of the discontents, and often searing misery, that were considered normal in a "good-enough" marriage in the 1950s and 1960s, see Lillian Rubin, *Worlds of Pain: Life in the Working-Class Family* (New York: Basic Books, 1976); Mirra Komarovsky, *Blue Collar Marriage* (New Haven, Conn.: Vintage, 1962); Elaine Tyler May, *Homeward Bound: American Families in the Cold War Era* (New York: Basic Books, 1988).

[12]See Robert Putnam, "The Strange Disappearance of Civic America," *American Prospect,* Winter 1996. For a glowing if somewhat lopsided picture of 1950s community solidarities, see Alan Ehrenhalt, *The Lost City: Discovering the Forgotten Virtues of Community in the Chicago of the 1950s* (New York: Basic Books, 1995). For a chilling account of communities uniting against perceived outsiders, in the same city, see Arnold Hirsch, *Making the Second Ghetto: Race and Housing in Chicago, 1940–1960* (Cambridge, Mass.: Harvard University Press, 1983). On homicide rates, see "Study Finds United States No. 1 in Violence," *Olympian,* November 13, 1992; *New York Times,* November 13, 1992, p. A9; and Douglas Lee Eckberg, "Estimates of Early Twentieth-Century U.S. Homicide Rates: An Econometric Forecasting Approach," *Demography* 32 (1995), p. 14. On lengthening commutes, see "It's Taking Longer to Get to Work," *Olympian,* December 6, 1995.

Throughout the 1950s, poverty was higher than it is today, but it was less concentrated in pockets of blight existing side-by-side with extremes of wealth, and, unlike today, it was falling rather than rising. At the end of the 1930s, almost two-thirds of the population had incomes below the poverty standards of the day, while only one in eight had a middle-class income (defined as two to five times the poverty line). By 1960, a majority of the population had climbed into the middle-income range.[13]

Unmarried people were hardly sexually abstinent in the 1950s, but the age of first intercourse was somewhat higher than it is now, and despite a tripling of nonmarital birth rates between 1940 and 1958, more than 70 percent of nonmarital pregnancies led to weddings before the child was born. Teenage birth rates were almost twice as high in 1957 as in the 1990s, but most teen births were to married couples, and the effect of teen pregnancy in reducing further schooling for young people did not hurt their life prospects the way it does today. High school graduation rates were lower in the 1950s than they are today, and minority students had far worse test scores, but there were jobs for people who dropped out of high school or graduated without good reading skills — jobs that actually had a future. People entering the job market in the 1950s had no way of knowing that they would be the last generation to have a good shot at reaching middle-class status without the benefit of postsecondary schooling.

Millions of men from impoverished, rural, unemployed, or poorly educated family backgrounds found steady jobs in the steel, auto, appliance, construction, and shipping industries. Lower-middle-class men went further on in college during the 1950s than they would have been able to expect in earlier decades, enabling them to make the transition to secure white-collar work. The experience of shared sacrifices in the Depression and war, reinforced by a New Deal–inspired belief in the ability of government to make life better, gave people a sense of hope for the future. Confidence in government, business, education, and other institutions was on the rise. This general optimism affected people's experience and assessment of family life. It is no wonder modern Americans yearn for a similar sense of hope.

But before we sign on to any attempts to turn the family clock back to the 1950s we should note that the family successes and community solidarities of the 1950s rested on a totally different set of political and economic conditions than we have today. Contrary to widespread belief, the 1950s was not an age of laissez-faire government and free market competition. A

---

[13]The figures in this and the following paragraph come from Levy, "Incomes and Income Inequality," pp. 1–57; May and Porter, "Poverty and Income Trends, 1994"; Reynolds Farley, *The New American Reality: Who We Are, How We Got Here, Where We Are Going* (New York: Russell Sage, 1996), pp. 83–85; Gelles, *Contemporary Families*, p. 115; David Grissmer, Sheila Nataraj Kirby, Mark Bender, and Stephanie Williamson, *Student Achievement and the Changing American Family*, Rand Institute on Education and Training (Santa Monica, Calif.: Rand, 1994), p. 106.

major cause of the social mobility of young families in the 1950s was that
federal assistance programs were much more generous and widespread
than they are today.

In the most ambitious and successful affirmative action program ever   30
adopted in America, 40 percent of young men were eligible for veterans'
benefits, and these benefits were far more extensive than those available to
Vietnam-era vets. Financed in part by a federal income tax on the rich that
went up to 87 percent and a corporate tax rate of 52 percent, such benefits
provided quite a jump start for a generation of young families. The GI bill
paid most tuition costs for vets who attended college, doubling the percentage of college students from prewar levels. At the other end of the life span,
Social Security began to build up a significant safety net for the elderly, formerly the poorest segment of the population. Starting in 1950, the federal
government regularly mandated raises in the minimum wage to keep pace
with inflation. The minimum wage may have been only $1.40 as late as
1968, but a person who worked for that amount full-time, year-round,
earned 118 percent of the poverty figure for a family of three. By 1995, a
full-time minimum-wage worker could earn only 72 percent of the poverty
level.[14]

An important source of the economic expansion of the 1950s was that
public works spending at all levels of government comprised nearly 20 percent of total expenditures in 1950, as compared to less than 7 percent in
1984. Between 1950 and 1960, nonmilitary, nonresidential public construction rose by 58 percent. Construction expenditures for new schools (in dollar amounts adjusted for inflation) rose by 72 percent; funding on sewers
and waterworks rose by 46 percent. Government paid 90 percent of the
costs of building the new Interstate Highway System. These programs
opened up suburbia to growing numbers of middle-class Americans and
created secure, well-paying jobs for blue-collar workers.[15]

Government also reorganized home financing, underwriting low down
payments and long-term mortgages that had been rejected as bad business
by private industry. To do this, government put public assets behind housing lending programs, created two new national financial institutions to
facilitate home loans, allowed veterans to put down payments as low as a

[14]William Chafe, *The Unfinished Journey: America Since World War II* (New York: Oxford
University Press, 1986), pp. 113, 143; Marc Linder, "Eisenhower-Era Marxist-Confiscatory
Taxation: Requiem for the Rhetoric of Rate Reduction for the Rich," *Tulane Law Review* 70
(1996), p. 917; Barry Bluestone and Teresa Ghilarducci, "Rewarding Work: Feasible Antipoverty
Policy," *American Prospect* 28 (1996), p. 42; Theda Skocpol, "Delivering for Young Families,"
American Prospect 28 (1996), p. 67.

[15]Joel Tarr, "The Evolution of the Urban Infrastructure in the Nineteenth and Twentieth
Centuries," in Royce Hanson, ed., *Perspectives on Urban Infrastructure* (Washington, D.C.:
National Academy Press, 1984); Mark Aldrich, *A History of Public Works Investment in the
United States,* report prepared by the CPNSAD Research Corporation for the U.S. Depart-
ment of Commerce, April 1980.

dollar on a house, and offered tax breaks to people who bought homes. The National Education Defense Act funded the socioeconomic mobility of thousands of young men who trained themselves for well-paying jobs in such fields as engineering.[16]

Unlike contemporary welfare programs, government investment in 1950s families was not just for immediate subsistence but encouraged long-term asset development, rewarding people for increasing their investment in homes and education. Thus it was far less likely that such families or individuals would ever fall back to where they started, even after a string of bad luck. Subsidies for higher education were greater the longer people stayed in school and the more expensive the school they selected. Mortgage deductions got bigger as people traded up to better houses.[17]

These social and political support systems magnified the impact of the postwar economic boom. "In the years between 1947 and 1973," reports economist Robert Kuttner, "the median paycheck more than doubled, and the bottom 20 percent enjoyed the greatest gains." High rates of unionization meant that blue-collar workers were making much more financial progress than most of their counterparts today. In 1952, when eager home buyers flocked to the opening of Levittown, Pennsylvania, the largest planned community yet constructed, "it took a factory worker one day to earn enough money to pay the closing costs on a new Levittown house, then selling for $10,000." By 1991, such a home was selling for $100,000 or more, and it took a factory worker *eighteen weeks* to earn enough money for just the closing costs.[18]

The legacy of the union struggle of the 1930s and 1940s, combined with government support for raising people's living standards, set limits on corporations that have disappeared in recent decades. Corporations paid 23 percent of federal income taxes in the 1950s, as compared to just 9.2 percent in 1991. Big companies earned higher profit margins than smaller firms, partly due to their dominance of the market, partly to America's postwar economic advantage. They chose (or were forced) to share these extra earnings, which economists call "rents," with employees. Economists at the Brookings Institution and Harvard University estimate that 70 percent of such corporate rents were passed on to workers at all levels of the firm, benefiting secretaries and janitors as well as CEOs. Corporations routinely retained workers even in slack periods, as a way of ensuring workplace

35

[16]For more information on this government financing, see Kenneth Jackson, *Crabgrass Frontier: The Suburbanization of the United States* (New York: Oxford University Press, 1985); and *The Way We Never Were*, chapter 4.

[17]John Cook and Laura Sherman, "Economic Security Among America's Poor: The Impact of State Welfare Waivers on Asset Accumulation," Center on Hunger, Poverty, and Nutrition Policy, Tufts University, May 1996.

[18]Robert Kuttner, "The Incredible Shrinking American Paycheck," *Washington Post National Weekly Edition*, November 6–12, 1995, p. 23; Donald Bartlett and James Steele, *America: What Went Wrong?* (Kansas City: Andrews McMeel, 1992), p. 20.

stability. Although they often received more generous tax breaks from communities than they gave back in investment, at least they kept their plants and employment offices in the same place. AT&T, for example, received much of the technology it used to finance its postwar expansion from publicly funded communications research conducted as part of the war effort, and, as current AT&T Chairman Robert Allen puts it, there "used to be a lifelong commitment on the employee's part and on our part." Today, however, he admits, "the contract doesn't exist anymore."[19]

Television trivia experts still argue over exactly what the fathers in many 1950s sitcoms did for a living. Whatever it was, though, they obviously didn't have to worry about downsizing. If most married people stayed in long-term relationships during the 1950s, so did most corporations, sticking with the communities they grew up in and the employees they originally hired. Corporations were not constantly relocating in search of cheap labor during the 1950s; unlike today, increases in worker productivity usually led to increases in wages. The number of workers covered by corporate pension plans and health benefits increased steadily. So did limits on the work week. There is good reason that people look back to the 1950s as a less hurried age: The average American was working a shorter workday in the 1950s than his or her counterpart today, when a quarter of the workforce puts in 49 or more hours a week.[20]

So politicians are practicing quite a double standard when they tell us to return to the family forms of the 1950s while they do nothing to restore the job programs and family subsidies of that era, the limits on corporate relocation and financial wheeling-dealing, the much higher share of taxes paid by corporations then, the availability of union jobs for noncollege youth, and the subsidies for higher education such as the National Defense Education Act loans. Furthermore, they're not telling the whole story when they claim that the 1950s was the most prosperous time for families and the most secure decade for children. Instead, playing to our understandable nostalgia for a time when things seemed to be getting better, not worse, they engage in a tricky chronological shell game with their figures, diverting our attention from two important points. First, many individuals, families, and groups were excluded from the economic prosperity, family optimism,

---

[19]Richard Barnet, "Lords of the Global Economy," *Nation*, December 19, 1994, p. 756; Clay Chandler, "U.S. Corporations: Good Citizens or Bad?" *Washington Post National Weekly Edition*, May 20–26, 1996, p. 16; Steven Pearlstein, "No More Mr. Nice Guy: Corporate America Has Done an About-Face in How It Pays and Treats Employees," *Washington Post National Weekly Edition*, December 18–24, 1995, p. 10; Robert Kuttner, "Ducking Class Warfare," *Washington Post National Weekly Edition*, March 11–17, 1996, p. 5; Henry Allen, "Ha! So Much for Loyalty," *Washington Post National Weekly Edition*, March 4–10, 1996, p. 11.

[20]Ehrenhalt, *The Lost City*, pp. 11–12; Jeremy Rifken, *The End of Work: The Decline of the Global Labor Force and the Dawn of the Post-Market Era* (New York: G. P. Putnam's Sons, 1995), pp. 169, 170, 231; Juliet Schorr, *The Overworked American: The Unexpected Decline of Leisure* (New York: Basic Books, 1991).

and social civility of the 1950s. Second, the all-time high point of child well-being and family economic security came not during the 1950s but *at the end of the 1960s.*

We now know that 1950s family culture was not only nontraditional; it was also not idyllic. In important ways, the stability of family and community life during the 1950s rested on pervasive discrimination against women, gays, political dissidents, non-Christians, and racial or ethnic minorities, as well as on a systematic cover-up of the underside of many families. Families that were harmonious and fair of their own free will may have been able to function more easily in the fifties, but few alternatives existed for members of discordant or oppressive families. Victims of child abuse, incest, alcoholism, spousal rape, and wife battering had no recourse, no place to go, until well into the 1960s.[21]

At the end of the 1950s, despite ten years of economic growth, 27.3 percent of the nation's children were poor, including those in white "underclass" communities such as Appalachia. Almost 50 percent of married-couple African American families were impoverished — a figure far higher than today. It's no wonder African Americans are not likely to pick the 1950s as a golden age, even in comparison with the setbacks they experienced in the 1980s. When blacks moved north to find jobs in the postwar urban manufacturing boom they met vicious harassment and violence, first to prevent them from moving out of the central cities, then to exclude them from public space such as parks or beaches.

In Philadelphia, for example, the City of Brotherly Love, there were   40
more than 200 racial incidents over housing in the first six months of 1955 alone. The Federal Housing Authority, such a boon to white working-class families, refused to insure homes in all-black or in racially mixed neighborhoods. Two-thirds of the city dwellers evicted by the urban renewal projects of the decade were African Americans and Latinos; government did almost nothing to help such displaced families find substitute housing.[22]

Women were unable to take out loans or even credit cards in their own names. They were excluded from juries in many states. A lack of options outside marriage led some women to remain in desperately unhappy unions that were often not in the best interests of their children or themselves. Even women in happy marriages often felt humiliated by the constant messages they received that their whole lives had to revolve around a man. "You are not ready when he calls — miss one turn," was a rule in the Barbie game marketed to 1950s girls; "he criticizes your hairdo — go to the beauty shop."

---

[21]For documentation that these problems existed, see chapter 2 of *The Way We Never Were.*

[22]The poverty figures come from census data collected in *The State of America's Children Yearbook, 1996* (Washington, D.C.: Children's Defense Fund, 1996), p. 77. See also Hirsch, *Making the Second Ghetto;* Raymond Mohl, "Making the Second Ghetto in Metropolitan Miami, 1940–1960," *Journal of Urban History* 25 (1995), p. 396; Micaela di Leonardo, "Boys on the Hood," *Nation,* August 17–24, 1992, p. 180; Jackson, *Crabgrass Frontier,* pp. 226–227.

Episodes of *Father Knows Best* advised young women: "The worst thing you can do is to try to beat a man at his own game. You just beat the women at theirs." One character on the show told women to always ask themselves, "Are you after a job or a man? You can't have both."[23]

The Fifties Experiment Comes to an End

The social stability of the 1950s, then, was a response to the stick of racism, sexism, and repression as well as to the carrot of economic opportunity and government aid. Because social protest mounted in the 1960s and unsettling challenges were posed to the gender roles and sexual mores of the previous decade, many people forget that families continued to make gains throughout the 1960s and into the first few years of the 1970s. By 1969, child poverty was down to 14 percent, its lowest level ever; it hovered just above that marker until 1975, when it began its steady climb up to contemporary figures (22 percent in 1993; 21.2 percent in 1994). The high point of health and nutrition for poor children was reached in the early 1970s.[24]

So commentators are being misleading when they claim that the 1950s was the golden age of American families. They are disregarding the number of people who were excluded during that decade and ignoring the socioeconomic gains that continued to be made through the 1960s. But they are quite right to note that the improvements of the 1950s and 1960s came to an end at some point in the 1970s (though not for the elderly, who continued to make progress).

Ironically, it was the children of those stable, enduring, supposedly idyllic 1950s families, the recipients of so much maternal time and attention, that pioneered the sharp break with their parents' family forms and gender roles in the 1970s. This was not because they were led astray by some youthful Murphy Brown in her student rebel days or inadvertently spoiled by parents who read too many of Dr. Spock's child-raising manuals.

Partly, the departure from 1950s family arrangements was a logical   45 extension of trends and beliefs pioneered in the 1950s, or of inherent contradictions in those patterns. For example, early and close-spaced childbearing freed more wives up to join the labor force, and married women began to flock to work. By 1960, more than 40 percent of women over the age of 16 held a job, and working mothers were the fastest growing component of the labor force. The educational aspirations and opportunities that opened up for kids of the baby boom could not be confined to males, and

---

[23]Susan Douglas, *Where the Girls Are: Growing Up Female with the Mass Media* (New York: Times Books, 1994), pp. 25, 37.

[24]*The State of America's Children Yearbook, 1966,* p. 77; May and Porter, "Poverty and Income Trends: 1994," p. 23; Sara McLanahan et al., *Losing Ground: A Critique,* University of Wisconsin Institute for Research on Poverty, Special Report No. 38, 1985.

many tight-knit, male-breadwinner, nuclear families in the 1950s instilled in their daughters the ambition to be something other than a homemaker.[25]

Another part of the transformation was a shift in values. Most people would probably agree that some changes in values were urgently needed: the extension of civil rights to racial minorities and to women; a rejection of property rights in children by parents and in women by husbands; a reaction against the political intolerance and the wasteful materialism of 1950s culture. Other changes in values remain more controversial: opposition to American intervention abroad; repudiation of the traditional sexual double standard; rebellion against what many young people saw as the hypocrisy of parents who preached sexual morality but ignored social immorality such as racism and militarism.

Still other developments, such as the growth of me-first individualism, are widely regarded as problematic by people on all points along the political spectrum. It's worth noting, though, that the origins of antisocial individualism and self-indulgent consumerism lay at least as much in the family values of the 1950s as in the youth rebellion of the 1960s. The marketing experts who never allowed the kids in *Ozzie and Harriet* sitcoms to be shown drinking milk, for fear of offending soft-drink companies that might sponsor the show in syndication, were ultimately the same people who slightly later invested billions of dollars to channel sexual rebelliousness and a depoliticized individualism into mainstream culture.

There were big cultural changes brewing by the beginning of the 1970s, and tremendous upheavals in social, sexual, and family values. And yes, there were sometimes reckless or simply laughable excesses in some of the early experiments with new gender roles, family forms, and personal expression. But the excesses of 1950s gender roles and family forms were every bit as repellent and stupid as the excesses of the sixties: Just watch a dating etiquette film of the time period, or recall that therapists of the day often told victims of incest that they were merely having unconscious oedipal fantasies.

Ultimately, though, changes in values were not what brought the 1950s family experiment to an end. The postwar family compacts between husbands and wives, parents and children, young and old, were based on the postwar social compact between government, corporations, and workers. While there was some discontent with those family bargains among women and youth, the old relations did not really start to unravel until people began to face the erosion of the corporate wage bargain and government broke its tacit societal bargain that it would continue to invest in jobs and education for the younger generation.

---

[25]For studies of how both middle-class and working-class women in the 1950s quickly departed from, or never quite accepted, the predominant image of women, see Joanne Meyerowitz, ed., *Not June Cleaver: Women and Gender in Postwar America, 1945–1960* (Philadelphia: Temple University Press, 1994).

In the 1970s, new economic trends began to clash with all the social   50
expectations that 1950s families had instilled in their children. That clash,
not the willful abandonment of responsibility and commitment, has been
the primary cause of both family rearrangements and the growing social
problems that are usually attributed to such family changes, but in fact have
separate origins.

ENGAGING THE TEXT

1. According to Coontz, what do we really miss about the 1950s? In addition,
   what *don't* we miss?
2. In Coontz's view, what was the role of the government in making the 1950s
   in America what they were? What part did broader historical forces or
   other circumstances play?
3. Although she concentrates on the 1950s, Coontz also describes the other
   decades from the 1920s to the 1990s, when she wrote this piece. Use her
   information to create a brief chart naming the key characteristics of each
   decade. Then consider your own family history and see how well it fits the
   pattern Coontz outlines. Discuss the results with classmates or write a journal entry reflecting on what you learn.
4. Consider the most recent ten years of American history. What events or
   trends (for example, the 9/11 attacks, same-sex marriage legislation) do you
   think a sociologist or cultural historian might consider important for understanding our current mythologies of family? How do you think our ideas
   about family have changed in this decade?

EXPLORING CONNECTIONS

5. Compare Norman Rockwell's enormously popular portrayals of family life
   (pp. 22–24) with the account provided by Coontz. Do you think she would
   call Rockwell's paintings "nostalgic"? What do we mean by this word?
6. Review "Looking for Work" by Gary Soto (p. 26). How does this narrative
   evoke nostalgia for a simpler, better era for families? Does it reveal any of
   the problems with the 1950s that Coontz describes?

EXTENDING THE CRITICAL CONTEXT

7. Coontz suggests that an uninformed nostalgia for the 1950s could promote
   harmful political agendas. (See, for example, paras. 7 and 37.) Do you see
   any evidence in contemporary media of nostalgia for the 1950s? Do you
   agree with Coontz that such nostalgia can be dangerous? Why or why not?
8. Watch an episode of a 1950s sitcom (if possible, record it) such as *Father
   Knows Best*, *The Donna Reed Show*, *Leave It to Beaver*, or *I Love Lucy*. Analyze the extent to which it reveals both positive and negative aspects of the
   1950s that Coontz discusses (for example, an authoritarian father figure, limited roles for wives, economic prosperity, or a sense of a secure community).

Aunt Ida Pieces a Quilt

MELVIN DIXON

*This is an extraordinary poem about AIDS, love, and family life. Its
author, Melvin Dixon (1950–1992), received his Ph.D. from Brown University; in addition to teaching English at Queens College in New York, he published poetry, literary criticism, translations, and two novels. "Aunt Ida"
appeared in* Brother to Brother: New Writings by Black Gay Men *(1991).
Dixon died of complications from AIDS in 1992.*

> You are right, but your patch isn't big enough.
> — JESSE JACKSON
>
> *When a cure is found and the last panel is
> sewn into place, the Quilt will be displayed
> in a permanent home as a national monument
> to the individual, irreplaceable people lost to AIDS —
> and the people who knew and loved them most.*
> — CLEVE JONES, *founder,* THE NAMES *Project*

They brought me some of his clothes. The hospital gown,
those too-tight dungarees, his blue choir robe
with the gold sash. How that boy could sing!
His favorite color in a necktie. A Sunday shirt.
What I'm gonna do with all this stuff?   5
I can remember Junie without this business.
My niece Francine say they quilting all over the country.
So many good boys like her boy, gone.

At my age I ain't studying no needle and thread.
My eyes ain't so good now and my fingers lock in a fist,   10
they so eaten up with arthritis. This old back
don't take kindly to bending over a frame no more.
Francine say ain't I a mess carrying on like this.
I could make two quilts the time I spend running my mouth.

Just cut his name out the cloths, stitch something nice   15
about him. Something to bring him back. You can do it,
Francine say. Best sewing our family ever had.
Quilting ain't that easy, I say. Never was easy.
Y'all got to help me remember him good.

Most of my quilts was made down South. My mama   20
And my mama's mama taught me. Popped me on the tail

if I missed a stitch or threw the pattern out of line.
I did "Bright Star" and "Lonesome Square" and "Rally Round,"
what many folks don't bother with nowadays. Then Elmo and me
married and came North where the cold in Connecticut   25
cuts you like a knife. We was warm, though.
We had sackcloth and calico and cotton, 100% pure.
What they got now but polyester rayon. Factory made.

Let me tell you something. In all my quilts there's a secret
nobody knows. Every last one of them got my name Ida   30
stitched on the back side in red thread.
That's where Junie got his flair. Don't let nobody fool you.
When he got the Youth Choir standing up and singing
the whole church would rock. He'd throw up his hands
from them wide blue sleeves and the church would hush   35
right down to the funeral parlor fans whisking the air.
He'd toss his head back and holler and we'd all cry holy.

And nevermind his too-tight dungarees.
I caught him switching down the street one Saturday night,
and I seen him more than once. I said, Junie,   40
you ain't got to let the world know all your business.
Who cared where he went when he wanted to have fun.
He'd be singing his heart out come Sunday morning.

When Francine say she gonna hang this quilt in the church
I like to fall out. A quilt ain't no showpiece,   45
it's to keep you warm. Francine say it can do both.
Now I ain't so old-fashioned I can't change,
but I made Francine come over and bring her daughter
Belinda. We cut and tacked his name, *JUNIE.*
Just plain and simple, *"JUNIE, our boy."*   50
Cut the *J* in blue, the *U* in gold. *N* in dungarees
just as tight as you please. The *I* from the hospital gown
and the white shirt he wore First Sunday. Belinda
put the necktie in *E* in the cross stitch I showed her.

Wouldn't you know we got to talking about Junie.   55
We could smell him in the cloth.
Underarm. Afro Sheen pomade.[1] Gravy stains.
I forgot all about my arthritis.
When Francine left me to finish up, I swear
I heard Junie giggling right along with me   60
as I stitched Ida on the back side in red thread.

---

[1]*Afro Sheen pomade:* Hair-care product for African Americans.

Francine say she gonna send this quilt to Washington
like folks doing from all 'cross the country,
so many good people gone. Babies, mothers, fathers
and boys like our Junie. Francine say   65
they gonna piece this quilt to another one,
another name and another patch
all in a larger quilt getting larger and larger.

Maybe we all like that, patches waiting to be pieced.
Well, I don't know about Washington.   70
We need Junie here with us. And Maxine,
she cousin May's husband's sister's people,
she having a baby and here comes winter already.
The cold cutting like knives. Now where did I put that needle?

Engaging the Text

1. Identify all of the characters and their relationships in the poem. Then retell the story of the poem in your own words.
2. Discuss the movement of Aunt Ida's mind and her emotions as we move from stanza to stanza. What happens to Aunt Ida in the poem? What is the dominant feeling at the end of the poem?
3. Junie's clothes take on symbolic weight in the quilt and, of course, in the poem as well. What do the hospital gown, the dungarees, the choir robe, and the white shirt and necktie represent?
4. What is Aunt Ida about to make at the end of the poem, and what is its significance?

Exploring Connections

5. Look at the paintings by Norman Rockwell (pp. 22–24) and the photographs in this chapter's Visual Portfolio (p. 71). Discuss how you might tell the story of "Aunt Ida Pieces a Quilt" visually instead of verbally — for example, as a painting, a mural, a photograph, or a photo essay. Sketch or draw an image based on the poem and share it with classmates.
6. What roles do women play in "Aunt Ida Pieces a Quilt"? Compare these roles to those played by women in the Rockwell paintings (pp. 22–24), Gary Soto's "Looking for Work" (p. 26), and "What We Really Miss About the 1950s" by Stephanie Coontz (p. 32). Based on these examples, would it be fair to conclude that Americans see "the family" as predominantly a woman's responsibility?

Extending the Critical Context

7. Write a screenplay or dramatic script to "translate" the story of "Aunt Ida Pieces a Quilt" into dramatic form. Time permitting, organize a group to read or perform the piece for the class.

8. Watch the documentary *Common Threads: Stories from the Quilt* and write a poem based on the life of one of the people profiled in this film.

An Indian Story

ROGER JACK

This narrative concerns growing up away from one's father in one of the Indian cultures of the Pacific Northwest. It's also an intimate view of a non-nuclear family; the author is interested in the family not as a static set of defined relationships but as a social network that adapts to the ever-changing circumstances and needs of its members. Roger Jack worked as a counselor and instructor for the American Indian Studies Program at Eastern Washington University. His work has been published in several journals and anthologies, including Spawning the Medicine River, Earth Power Coming, *and* The Clouds Threw This Light. *"An Indian Story" appeared in* Dancing on the Rim of the World: An Anthology of Contemporary Northwest Native American Writing *(1990), edited by Andrea Lerner.*

Aunt Greta was always a slow person. Grandpa used to say she was like an old lady out of the old days who never hurried herself for anything, no matter what. She was only forty-five, heavyset, dark-complexioned, and very knowledgeable of the old ways, which made her seem even older. Most of the time she wore her hair straight up or in a ponytail that hung below her beltline. At home she wore pants and big, baggy shirts, but at ritual gatherings she wore her light blue calico dress, beaded moccasins, hair braided and clasped with beaded barrettes. Sometimes she wore a scarf on her head like ladies older than she. She said we emulate those we love and care for. I liked seeing her dressed for ceremonials. Even more, I liked seeing her stand before crowds of tribal members and guests translating the old language to the new for our elders, or speaking on behalf of the younger people who had no understanding of the Indian language. It made me proud to be her nephew and her son.

My mom died when I was little. Dad took care of me as best he could after that. He worked hard and earned good money as an accountant at the agency. But about a year after Mom died he married a half-breed Indian and this made me feel very uncomfortable. Besides, she had a child of her own who was white. We fought a lot — me and Jeffrey Pine — and then I'd get into trouble because I was older and was supposed to know better than to misbehave.

I ran away from home one day when everyone was gone — actually, I walked to Aunt Greta's and asked if I could move in with her since I had already spent so much time with her anyway. Then after I had gone to bed that night, Dad came looking for me and Aunt Greta told him what I had told her about my wanting to move in with her. He said it would be all right for a while, then we would decide what to do about it later. That was a long time ago. Now I am out of high school and going to college. Meanwhile, Jeffrey Pine is a high-school dropout and living with the folks.

Aunt Greta was married a long time ago. She married a guy named Mathew who made her very happy. They never had children, but when persistent people asked either of them what was wrong, they would simply reply they were working on it. Then Mathew died during their fifth year of marriage. No children. No legacy. After that Aunt Greta took care of Grandpa, who had moved in with them earlier when Grandma died. Grandpa wasn't too old, but sometimes he acted like it. I guess it came from that long, drawn-out transition from horse riding and breeding out in the wild country to reservation life in buggies, dirt roads, and cars. He walked slowly everywhere he went; he and Aunt Greta complemented each other that way.

Eventually, Aunt Greta became interested in tribal politics and threatened to run for tribal council, so Grandpa changed her Indian name from Little Girl Heart to Old Woman Walking, which he had called Grandma when she was alive. Aunt Greta didn't mind. In fact, she was proud of her new name. Little Girl Heart was her baby name, she said. When Grandpa died a couple of years later she was all alone. She decided tribal politics wasn't for her but began teaching Indian culture and language classes. That's when I walked into her life like a newborn Mathew or Grandpa or the baby she never had. She had so much love and knowledge to share, which she passed on to me naturally and freely; she received wages for teaching others. But that was gesticulation, she said.

My home and academic life improved a lot after I had moved in with Aunt Greta. Dad and his wife had a baby boy, and then a girl, but I didn't see too much of them. It was like we were strangers living a quarter mile from one another. Aunt Greta and I went on vacations together from the time I graduated from the eighth grade. We were trailblazers, she said, because our ancestors never traveled very far from the homeland.

The first year we went to Maryhill, Washington, which is about a ten-hour drive from our reservation home in Park City, and saw the imitation Stonehenge Monument. We arrived there late in the evening because we had to stop off in every other town along the road to eat, whether or not we were hungry, because that was Aunt Greta's way and Grandma's and all the other old ladies of the tribe. You have to eat to survive, they would say. It was almost dark when we arrived at the park. We saw the huge outlines of the massive hewn stones placed in a circular position and towering well over our heads. We stood small and in awe of their magnificence, especially seeing darkness fall upon us. Stars grew brighter and we saw them more keenly as time passed. Then they started falling, dropping out of the sky to meet us where we stood. I could see the power of Aunt Greta protruding through her eyes; if I had power I wouldn't have to explore, physically, the sensation I imagined her feeling. She said nothing for a long time. Then, barely audible, she murmured something like, "I have no teepee. I need no cover. This moment has been waiting for me here all this time." She paused. Then, "I wasn't sure what I would find here, but I'm glad we came. I was going to say something goofy like 'we should have brought the teepee and we could call upon Coyote to come and knock over these poles so we could drape our canvas over the skeleton and camp!' But I won't. I'm just glad we came here."

"Oh no, you aren't flipping out on me, are you?" I ribbed her. She always said good Indians remember two things: their humor and their history. These are the elements that dictate our culture and our survival in this crazy world. If these are somehow destroyed or forgotten, we would be doomed to extinction. Our power gone. And she had the biggest, silliest grin on her face. She said, "I want to camp right here!" and I knew she was serious.

We camped in the car, in the parking lot, that night. But neither of us slept until nearly daybreak. She told me Coyote stories and Indian stories and asked me what I planned to do with my life. "I want to be like you," I told her. Then she reminded me that I had a Dad to think about, too, and that maybe I should think about taking up his trade. I thought about a lot of stories I had heard about boys following in their father's footsteps — good or bad — and I told Aunt Greta that I wasn't too sure about living on the reservation and working at the agency all my life. Then I tried to sleep, keeping in mind everything we had talked about. I was young, but my Indian memory was good and strong.

On our way home from Maryhill we stopped off at Coyote's Sweat-   10
house down by Soap Lake. I crawled inside the small cavernous stone structure and Aunt Greta said to make a wish for something good. She tossed a coin inside before we left the site. Then we drove through miles of desert country and basalt cliffs and canyons, but we knew we were getting closer to home when the pine trees started weeding out the sagebrush, and the mountains overrode the flatland.

Our annual treks after that brought us to the Olympic Peninsula on the coast and the Redwood Forest in northern California; Yellowstone National Park in Wyoming and Glacier Park in Montana; and the Crazy Horse/ Mount Rushmore Monuments in South Dakota. We were careful in coordinating our trips with pow-wows too. Then we talked about going all the way to Washington, D.C., and New York City to see the sights and how the other half lived, but we never did.

After high-school graduation we went to Calgary for a pow-wow and I got into trouble for drinking and fighting with some local Indians I had met.

They talked me into it. The fight occurred when a girlfriend of one of the guys started acting very friendly toward me. Her boyfriend got jealous and started pushing me around and calling me names; only after I defended myself did the others join in the fight. Three of us were thrown into the tribe's makeshift jail. Aunt Greta was not happy when she came to pay my bail. As a matter of fact, I had never seen her angry before. Our neighbors at the campground thought it was funny that I had been arrested and thrown into jail and treated the incident as an everyday occurrence. I sat in the car imagining my own untimely death. I was so sick.

After dropping the ear poles, I watched Aunt Greta take down the rest of the teepee with the same meticulousness with which we had set it up. She went around the radius of the teepee removing wooden stakes from the ground that held fast the teepee's body to the earth. Then she stood on a folding chair to reach the pins that held the face of the teepee together. She folded the teepee into halves as it hung, still, on the center pole. She folded it again and again until it grew clumsy and uneven, then she motioned for me to come and drop the pole so she could untie the fastener that made the teepee our home. Meanwhile, I had to drop all skeletal poles from the sky and all that remained were a few holes in the ground and flattened patches of grass that said we had been there. I stood looking over the crowd. Lots of people had come from throughout Canada and the northern states for the pow-wow. Hundreds of people sat watching the war dance. Other people watched the stick-games and card games. But what caught my attention were the obvious drunks in the crowd. I was "one of them" now.

Aunt Greta didn't talk much while we drove home. It was a long, lonely drive. We stopped only twice to eat cold, tasteless meals. Once in Canada and once stateside. When we finally got home, Aunt Greta said, "Good night," and went to bed. It was only eight o'clock in the evening. I felt a heavy calling to go talk to Dad about what had happened. So I did.

He was alone when I arrived at his house. As usual I walked through the front door without knocking, but immediately heard him call out, "Son?"   15

"Yeah," I said as I went to sit on a couch facing him. "How did you know it was me?"

He smiled, said hello, and told me a father is always tuned in to his son. Then he sensed my hesitation to speak and asked, "What's wrong?"

"I got drunk in Calgary." My voice cracked. "I got into a fight and thrown in jail too. Aunt Greta had to bail me out. Now she's mad at me. She hasn't said much since we packed to come home."

"Did you tell her you were sorry for screwing up?" Dad asked.

"Yeah. I tried to tell her. But she clammed up on me."   20

"I wouldn't worry about it," Dad said. "This was bound to happen sooner or later. You really feel guilty when you take that first drink and get caught doing it. Hell, when I got drunk the first time, my Mom and Dad took turns preaching to me about the evils of drinking, fornication, and loose living. It didn't stop me though. I was one of those smart asses who had to have his own way. What you have to do is come up with some sort of reparation. Something that will get you back on Greta's good side."

"I guess that's what got to me. She didn't holler or preach to me. All the while I was driving I could feel her staring at me." My voice strengthened, "But she wouldn't say anything."

"Well, Son. You have to try to imagine what's going through her mind too. As much as I love you, you have been Greta's boy since you were knee-high to a grasshopper. She has done nothing but try to provide all the love and proper caring that she can for you. Maybe she thinks she has done something wrong in your upbringing. She probably feels more guilty about what happened than you. Maybe she hasn't said anything because she isn't handling this very well either." Dad became a little less serious before adding, "Of course, Greta's been around the block a time or two herself."

Stunned, I asked, "What do you mean?"

"Son, as much as Greta's life has changed, there are some of us who 25
remember her younger days. She liked drinking, partying, and loud music along with war dancing, stick-games, and pow-wows. She got along wherever she went looking for a good time. She was one of the few who could do that. The rest of us either took to drinking all the time, or we hit the pow-wow circuit all straight-faced and sober, never mixing up the two. Another good thing about Greta was that when she found her mate and decided to settle down, she did it right. After she married Mathew she quit running around." Dad smiled, "Of course, Mathew may have had some influence on her behavior, since he worked for the alcohol program."

"I wonder why she never remarried?" I asked.

"Some women just don't," Dad said authoritatively. "But she never had a shortage of men to take care of. She had your Grandpa — and YOU!" We laughed. Then he continued, "Greta could have had her pick of any man on the reservation. A lot of men chased after her before she married, and a lot of them chased after her after Mathew died. But she never had time for them."

"I wonder if she would have gotten married again if I hadn't moved in on her?"

"That's a question only Greta can answer. You know, she may work in tribal programs and college programs, but if she had to give it all up for one reason in the world, it would be you." Dad became intent, "You are her bloodline. You know that? Otherwise I wouldn't have let you stay with her all these years. The way her family believes is that two sisters coming from the same mother and father are the same. Especially blood. After your Mother died and you asked to go and live with your Aunt, that was all right. As a matter of fact, according to her way, we were supposed to have gotten married after our period of mourning was over."

"You — married to Aunt Greta!" I half-bellowed and again we laughed. 30

"Yeah. We could have made a hell of a family, don't you think?" Dad tried steadying his mood. "But, you know, maybe Greta's afraid of losing you too. Maybe she's afraid that you're entering manhood and that you'll be leaving her. Like when you go away to college. You are still going to college, aren't you?"

"Yeah. But I never thought of it as leaving her. I thought it more like going out and doing what's expected of me. Ain't I supposed to strike out on my own one day?"

"Yeah. Your leaving your family and friends behind may be expected, but like I said, 'you are everything to Greta,' and maybe she has other plans for you." Dad looked down to the floor and I caught a glimpse of graying streaks of hair on top of his head. Then he asked me which college I planned on attending.

"One in Spokane," I answered. "I ain't decided which one yet."

Then we talked about other things and before we knew it his missus   35
and the kids were home. Junior was nine, Anna Lee eight; they had gone to the last day of the tribe's celebration and carnival in Nespelem, which was what Aunt Greta and I had gone to Calgary to get away from for once. I sat quietly and wondered what Aunt Greta must have felt for my wrongdoing. The kids got louder as they told Dad about their carnival rides and games and prizes they had won. They shared their goodies with him and he looked to be having a good time eating popcorn and cotton candy.

I remembered a time when Mom and Dad brought me to the carnival. Grandpa and Grandma were with us. Mom and Dad stuck me on a big, black merry-go-round horse with flaming red nostrils and fiery eyes. Its long, dangling tongue hung out of its mouth. I didn't really want to ride that horse, but I felt I had to because Grandpa kept telling Mom and Dad that I belonged on a real horse and not some wooden thing. I didn't like the horse, when it hit certain angles it jolted and scared me even more. Mom and Dad offered me another ride on it, but I refused.

"Want some cotton candy?" Junior brought me back to reality. "We had fun going on the rides and trying to win some prizes. Here, you can have this one." He handed me one of his prizes. And, "Are you gonna stay with us tonight?"

I didn't realize it was after eleven o'clock.

"You can sleep in my bed," Junior offered.

"Yeah. Maybe I will, Little Brother." Junior smiled. I bade everyone   40
good night and went to his room and pulled back his top blanket revealing his Star Wars sheets. I chuckled at the sight of them before lying down and trying to sleep on them. This would be my first time sleeping away from Aunt Greta in a long time. I still felt tired from my drinking and the long drive home, but I was glad to have talked to Dad. I smiled in thinking that he said he loved me, because Indian men hardly ever verbalize their emotions. I went to sleep thinking how alone Aunt Greta must have felt

after I had left home and promised myself to return there as early as I could.

I ate breakfast with the family before leaving. Dad told me one last thing that he and Aunt Greta had talked about sometime before. "You know, she talked about giving you an Indian name. She asked me if you had one and I said 'no.' She talked about it and I thought maybe she would go ahead and do it too, but her way of doing this is: boys are named for their father's side and girls are named for their mother's. Maybe she's still waiting for me to give you a name. I don't know."

"I remember when Grandpa named her, but I never thought of having a name myself. What was the name?" I asked.

"I don't remember. Something about stars."

Aunt Greta was sitting at the kitchen table drinking coffee and listening to an Elvis album when I got home. Elvis always made her lonesome for the old days or it cheered her up when she felt down. I didn't know what to say, but showed her the toy totem pole Junior had given me.

"That's cute," she said. "So you spent the night at the carnival?"   45

"No. Junior gave it to me," I explained. "I camped at Dad's."

"Are you hungry?" she was about to get up from the table.

"No. I've eaten." I saw a stack of pancakes on the stove. I hesitated another moment before asking, "What's with Elvis?"

"He's dead!" she said and smiled, because that's what I usually said to her. "Oh well, I just needed a little cheering up, I guess."

I remember hearing a story about Aunt Greta that happened a long time   50 ago. She was a teenager when the Elvis craze hit the reservation. Back then hardly any families had television sets, so they couldn't see Elvis. But when his songs hit the airwaves on the radio the girls went crazy. The guys went kind of crazy too — but they were pissed off crazy. A guy can't be that good looking and talented too, they claimed. They were jealous of Elvis. Elvis had a concert in Seattle and my Mom and Aunt Greta and a couple other girls went to it. Legend said that Elvis kissed Aunt Greta on the cheek during his performance and she took to heart the old "ain't never going to wash that cheek again" promissory and never washed her cheek for a long time and it got chapped and cracked until Grandpa and Grandma finally had to order her to go to the clinic to get some medicine to clean up her face. She hated them for a while, still swearing Elvis would be her number one man forever.

"How's your Dad?"

"He's all right. The kids were at the carnival when I got to his house, so we had a nice, long visit." I paused momentarily before adding, "And he told me some stories about you too."

"Oh?" she acted concerned even though her crow's feet showed.

"Yeah. He said you were quite a fox when you were young. And he said you probably could have had any man you wanted before you married Uncle Mathew, and you could have had any man after Uncle Mathew died. So, how come you never snagged yourself another husband?"

Aunt Greta sat quietly for a moment. I could see her slumping into the   55
old way of doing things which said you thought things through before saying
them. "I suppose I could have had my pick of the litter. It's just that after
my old man died I didn't want anyone else. He was so good to me that I
didn't think I could find any better. Besides, I had you and Grandpa to care
for, didn't I? Have I ever complained about that?"

"Yeah," I persisted, "but haven't you ever thought about what might
have happened if you had gotten married again? You might have done like
Dad and started a whole new family. Babies, even!"

Aunt Greta was truly embarrassed. "Will you get away from here with
talk like that. I don't need babies. Probably won't be long now and you'll be
bringing them home for me to take care of anyhow."

Now I was embarrassed. We got along great after that initial conversation. It was like we had never gone to Calgary and I had never gotten on to
her wrong side at all. We were like kids rediscovering what it was worth to
have a real good friend go away for a while and then come back. To be
appreciative of each other, I imagined Aunt Greta might have said.

Our trip to Calgary happened in July. August and September found me
dumbfounded as to what to do with myself college-wise. I felt grateful that
Indian parents don't throw out their offspring when they reach a certain
age. Aunt Greta said it was too late for fall term and that I should rest my
brain for a while and think about going to college after Christmas. So I
explored different schools in the area and talked to people who had gone to
them. Meanwhile, some of my friends were going to Haskell Indian Junior
College in Kansas. Aunt Greta frowned upon my going there. She said it
was too far away from home, people die of malaria there, and if you're not
drunk, you're just crazy. So I stuck with the Spokane plan.

That fall Aunt Greta was invited to attend a language seminar in Port-   60
land. She taught Indian language classes when asked to. So we decided to
take a side trip to our old campsite at Stonehenge. This time we arrived
early in the morning and it was foggy and drizzling rain. The sight of the
stones didn't provide the feeling we had experienced earlier. To us, the
sight seemed to be just a bunch of rocks standing, overlooking the Columbia River, a lot of sagebrush, and two state highways. It didn't offer us feelings of mysticism and power anymore. Unhappy with the mood, Aunt Greta
said we might as well leave; her words hung heavy on the air.

We stayed in Portland for a week and then made it a special point to
leave late in the afternoon so we could stop by Stonehenge again at dusk. So
with careful planning we arrived with just enough light to take a couple pictures and then darkness began settling in. We sat in the car eating baloney
sandwiches and potato chips and drinking pop because we were tired of
restaurant food and we didn't want people staring at us when we ate. That's
where we were when an early evening star fell. Aunt Greta's mouth fell
open, potato chip crumbs clung to the sides of her mouth. "This is it!" she
squealed in English, Indian, and English again. "Get out of the car, Son,"

and she half pushed me out the door. "Go and stand in the middle of the circle and pray for something good to happen to you." I ran out and stood waiting and wondering what was supposed to happen. I knew better than to doubt Aunt Greta's wishes or superstitions. Then the moment came to pass.

"Did you feel it?" she asked as she led me back to the car.

"I don't know," I told her because I didn't think anything had happened.

"I guess it just takes some people a little longer to realize," she said.

I never quite understood what was supposed to have happened that   65 day. A couple months later I was packing up to move to Spokane. I decided to go into the accounting business, like Dad. Aunt Greta quizzed me hourly before I was to leave whether I was all right and if I would be all right in the city. "Yeah, yeah," I heard myself repeating. So by the time I really was to leave she clued me in on her new philosophy: it wasn't that I was leaving her, it was just that she wouldn't be around to take care of me much anymore. She told me, "Good Indians stick together," and that I should search out our people who were already there, but not forget those who were still at home.

After I arrived in Spokane and settled down I went home all too frequently to actually experience what Aunt Greta and everyone told me. Then my studies got so intense that I didn't think I could travel home as much anymore. So I stayed in Spokane a lot more than before. Finally it got so I didn't worry as much about the folks at home. I would be out walking in the evening and know someone's presence was with me. I never bothered telephoning Dad at his office at the agency; and I never knew where or when Aunt Greta worked. She might have been at the agency or school. Then one day Dad telephoned me at school. After asking how I was doing, he told me why he was calling. "Your Aunt Greta is sick. The doctors don't know what's wrong with her yet. They just told me to advise her family of the possibility that it could be serious." I only half heard what he was saying, "Son, are you there?"

"Yeah."

"Did you hear me? Did you hear what I said?"

"Yeah. I don't think you have to worry about Aunt Greta though. She'll be all right. Like the old timers used to say, 'she might go away for a while, but she'll be back,'" and I hung up the telephone unalarmed.

Engaging the Text

1. Give specific examples of how the narrator's extended family or kinship structure works to solve family problems. What problems does it seem to create or make worse?

2. What key choices does the narrator make in this story? How are these choices influenced by family members or family considerations?

3. Is the family portrayed here matriarchal, patriarchal, egalitarian, or something else? Explain. To what extent is parenting influenced by gender roles?

4. What events narrated in this story might threaten the survival of a nuclear family? How well does the extended family manage these crises?
5. How strong an influence does the narrator's father have on him? How can you explain the father's influence given how rarely the two see each other?
6. How do you interpret the narrator's reaction when he hears about Aunt Greta's failing health? What is implied in the story's closing lines?

EXPLORING CONNECTIONS

7. Compare and contrast "Looking for Work" (p. 26) and "An Indian Story" in terms of what each narrator learns about family and how they learn it. Do they learn the same things they would likely learn in a traditional nuclear family headed by a father? Explain.
8. Compare the family dynamics in "Aunt Ida Pieces a Quilt" (p. 49) and "An Indian Story." In each case, how does the family seem to define itself? Who makes the decisions? How — and how well — does each family handle the crises it faces?

EXTENDING THE CRITICAL CONTEXT

9. This story celebrates the power of stories to connect people and to shape or affirm one's identity. Throughout, the narrator relates family stories about his father and his aunt that give him a clearer sense of himself and his relationship to those he loves. In a journal entry or essay, relate one or two family stories that are important to you and explain how they help you define who you are.

The Color of Family Ties: Race, Class, Gender, and Extended Family Involvement

NAOMI GERSTEL AND NATALIA SARKISIAN

The myth of the nuclear family is not just a harmless cliché; rather, it can lock us into fundamental misunderstandings of how American families live, misunderstandings that can divide groups and promote simplistic public policy. In this study, sociologists Naomi Gerstel and Natalia Sarkisian examine data on black, white, and Latino/Latina families to challenge the popular notion that minority families have weaker ties and are more fragmented than white families. They find that social class is more important than ethnicity; moreover, while differences between ethnic groups do exist, each group has

*developed ways to cope with the practical, emotional, and financial chal-
lenges they face and to maintain family solidarity. Gerstel and Sarkisian are
professors of sociology, Gerstel at the University of Massachusetts, Amherst,
and Sarkisian at Boston College. Their coauthored article on gender, employment, and help given to parents (in* Journal of Marriage and the Family,
*2004) won the 2005 Rosabeth Moss Kanter International Award for
Research Excellence in Families and Work. "The Color of Family Ties"
appeared in* American Families: A Multicultural Reader, *edited by Stephanie
Coontz (see p. 32) with Maya Parson and Gabrielle Raley (2008).*

    When talking about family obligations and solidarities, politicians and
social commentators typically focus on the ties between married couples
and their children. We often hear that Black and Latino/a, especially
Puerto Rican, families are more disorganized than White families, and that
their family ties are weaker, because rates of non-marriage and single parenthood are higher among these minority groups. But this focus on the
nuclear family ignores extended family solidarities and caregiving activities.
Here we examine these often overlooked extended kinship ties.[1]

    Taking this broader perspective on family relations refutes the myth
that Blacks and Latinos/as lack strong families. Minority individuals are
more likely to live in extended family homes than Whites and in many ways

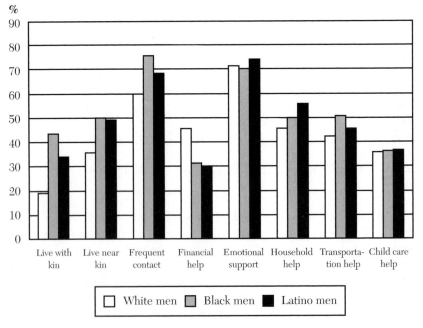

Figure 1   Ethnicity and extended kin involvement among men.
Source: National Survey of Families and Households, 1992–94.

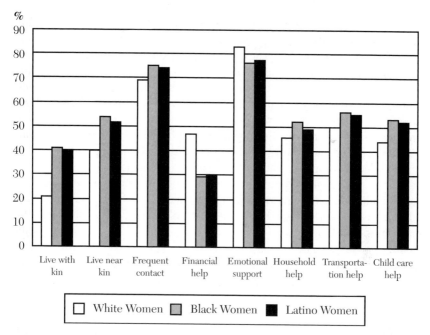

Figure 2   Ethnicity and extended kin involvement among women.
Source: National Survey of Families and Households, 1992–94.

more likely to help out their aging parents, grandparents, adult children, brothers, sisters, cousins, aunts, uncles, and other kin.

According to our research using the second wave of the National Survey of Families and Households, as Figures 1 and 2 show, Blacks and Latinos/as, both women and men, are much more likely than Whites to share a home with extended kin: 42 percent of Blacks and 37 percent of Latinos/as, but only 20 percent of Whites, live with relatives. Similar patterns exist for living near relatives: 54 percent of Blacks and 51 percent of Latinos/as, but only 37 percent of Whites, live within two miles of kin. Blacks and Latinos/as are also more likely than Whites to frequently visit kin. For example, 76 percent of Blacks, 71 percent of Latinos/as, but just 63 percent of Whites see their relatives once a week or more.

Even if they don't live together, Blacks and Latinos/as are as likely as Whites — and in some ways more likely — to be supportive family members. But there are important racial and ethnic differences in the type of support family members give each other. Whites are more likely than ethnic minorities to give and receive large sums of money, and White women are more likely than minority women to give and receive emotional support, such as discussing personal problems and giving each other advice. When it comes to help with practical tasks, however, we find that Black and Latino/a relatives are more likely than Whites to be supportive: they are more likely to give each other help with household work and child care, as

well as with providing rides and running errands. These differences are especially pronounced among women.

 This is not to say that Black and Latino men are not involved with kin, 5
as is implied in popular images of minority men hanging out on street corners rather than attending to family ties. In fact, Black and Latino men are
more likely than White men to live near relatives and to stay in touch with
them. White men, however, are more likely to give and receive large-scale
financial help. Moreover, the three groups of men are very similar when it
comes to giving and getting practical help and emotional support.

 These data suggest that if we only consider married couples or parents
and their young children, we are missing much of what families in general
and families of color in particular do for each other. A focus on nuclear families in discussions of race differences in family life creates a biased portrait
of families of color.

Explaining Race Differences: Is It Culture or Class?

 When discussing differences in family experiences of various racial and
ethnic groups, commentators often assume that these differences can be
traced to cultural differences or competing "family values." Sometimes
these are expressed in a positive way, as in the stereotype that Latino families have more extended ties because of their historical traditions and religious values. Other times these are expressed in a negative way, as when
Blacks are said to lack family values because of the cultural legacy of slavery
and subsequent years of oppression. Either way, differences in family
behaviors are often explained by differences in cultural heritage.

 In contrast, in our research, we find that social class rather than culture
is the key to understanding the differences in extended family ties and
behaviors between Whites and ethnic minorities. To be sure, differences in
cultural values do exist. Blacks and Latinos/as are more likely than Whites
to say they believe that extended family is important; both groups are also
more likely to attend religious services. Blacks tend to hold more egalitarian
beliefs about gender than Whites, while Latinos/as, especially Mexican
Americans, tend to hold more "traditional" views. But these differences in
values do not explain racial differences in actual involvement with relatives.
It is, instead, social class that matters most in explaining these differences.

 It is widely known (and confirmed by U.S. Census data presented in
Table 1) that Blacks and Latinos/as tend to have far less income and education than Whites. Families of color are also much more likely than White
families to be below the official poverty line. In our research, we find that
the differences in extended family ties and behaviors between Whites and
ethnic minorities are primarily the result of these social class disparities.

 Simply put, White, Black, and Latino/a individuals with the same 10
amount of income and education have similar patterns of involvement with
their extended families. Just like poor minorities, impoverished Whites are
more likely to exchange practical aid and visit with extended kin than are

Table 1   Education, Income, and Poverty Rates by Race

	WHITES	BLACKS	LATINOS/AS
Median household income	$50,784	$30,858	$35,967
Percentage below poverty line	8.4%	24.7%	22.0%
Education:			
Less than high school	14.5%	27.6%	47.6%
High school graduate	58.5%	58.1%	42.0%
Bachelor's degree or higher	27.0%	14.3%	10.4%

Source: U.S. Census Bureau, 2005.

their wealthier counterparts. Just like middle-class Whites, middle-class Blacks and Latinos/as are more likely to talk about their personal concerns or share money with relatives than are their poorer counterparts.

More specifically, it is because Whites tend to have more income than Blacks and Latinos/as that they are more likely to give money to their relatives or get it from them. And the higher levels of emotional support among White women can be at least in part traced to their higher levels of education, perhaps because schooling encourages women to talk out their problems and makes them more likely to give (and get) advice.

Conversely, we find that the relative economic deprivation of racial/ethnic minorities leads in many ways to higher levels of extended family involvement. Individuals' lack of economic resources increases their need for help from kin and boosts their willingness to give help in return. Because Blacks and Latinos/as typically have less income and education than Whites, they come to rely more on their relatives for daily needs such as child care, household tasks, or rides. The tendency of Blacks and Latinos/as to live with or near kin may also reflect their greater need for kin cooperation, as well as their decreased opportunities and pressures to move away, including moving for college.

Social Class and Familial Trade-Offs

How do our findings on race, social class, and familial involvement challenge common understandings of minority families? They show that poor minority families do not necessarily lead lives of social isolation or lack strong family solidarities. The lower rates of marriage among impoverished groups may reflect not a rejection of family values but a realistic assessment of how little a woman (and her children) may be able to depend upon marriage. Sociologists Kathryn Edin and Maria Kefalas (2007) recently found that because disadvantaged men are often unable to offer women the kind of economic security that advantaged men provide, poor women are less likely to marry. Instead, these women create support

"Me? I thought you were raising them."

networks beyond the nuclear family, regularly turning to extended kin for practical support.

Reliance on extended kin and lack of marital ties are linked. In another analysis of the National Survey of Families and Households, we found that, contrary to much rhetoric about marriage as a key source of adult social ties, marriage actually diminishes ties to kin. Married people — women as well as men — are less involved with their parents and siblings than those never married or previously married. These findings indicate a trade-off between commitments to nuclear and extended family ties. Marriage, we have found, is a "greedy" institution: it has a tendency to consume the bulk of people's energies and emotions and to dilute their commitments beyond the nuclear family.

On the one hand, then, support given to spouses and intimate partners sometimes comes at the expense of broader kin and community ties. Indeed, married adult children take care of elderly parents less often than their unmarried siblings. Marriage can also cut people off from networks of mutual aid. Married mothers, for example, whether Black, Latina, or White, are often unable to obtain help from kin in the way that their single counterparts can. Although the "greedy" nature of marriage may pose a problem across social class, it is especially problematic for those less well off economically, as these individuals most need to cultivate wider circles of obligation, mutual aid, and reciprocity.

On the other hand, support to relatives sometimes comes at the expense of care for partners, and can interfere with nuclear family formation or stability. Indeed, individuals who are deeply immersed in relationships with extended families may be less likely to get married or, if they marry, may be less likely to put the marital ties first in their loyalties. Several decades ago in her observations of a poor Black community, anthropologist Carol Stack (1974) found that the reciprocal patterns of sharing with kin and "fictive kin" forged in order to survive hardship often made it difficult for poor Blacks either to move up economically or to marry. To prevent the dilution of their social support networks, some extended families may even discourage their members from getting married, or unconsciously sabotage relationships that threaten to pull someone out of the family orbit. As sociologists Domínguez and Watkins (2003) argue, the ties of mutual aid that help impoverished individuals survive on a day-to-day basis may also prevent them from saying "no" to requests that sap their ability to get ahead or pursue individual opportunities.

Overall, we should avoid either denigrating or glorifying the survival strategies of the poor. Although social class disparities are key to understanding racial and ethnic variation in familial involvement, it is too simple to say that class differences create "more" involvement with relatives in one group and "less" in another. In some ways economic deprivation increases ties to kin (e.g., in terms of living nearby or exchanging practical help) and in other ways it reduces them (e.g., in terms of financial help or emotional support). These findings remind us that love and family connections are expressed both through talk and action. Equally important, focusing solely on the positive or on the negative aspects of either minority or White families is problematic. Instead, we need to think in terms of trade-offs — among different kinds of care and between the bonds of kinship and the bonds of marriage. Both trade-offs are linked to social class.

Why Do These Differences in Family Life Matter?

Commentators often emphasize the disorganization and dysfunction of Black and Latino/a family life. They suggest that if we could "fix" family values in minority communities and get them to form married-couple households, all their problems would be solved. This argument misunderstands causal connections by focusing on the family as the source of problems. Specifically, it ignores the link between race and class and attributes racial or ethnic differences to cultural values. Instead, we argue, it is important to understand that family strategies and behaviors often emerge in response to the challenges of living in economic deprivation or constant economic insecurity. Therefore, social policies should not focus on changing family behaviors, but rather aim to support a range of existing family arrangements and improve economic conditions for the poor.

Social policies that overlook extended family obligations may introduce, reproduce, or even increase ethnic inequalities. For example, the relatives of Blacks and Latinos/as are more likely than those of Whites to provide various kinds of support that policymakers tend to assume is only provided by husbands and wives. Such relatives may need the rights and support systems that we usually reserve for spouses. For instance, the Family and Medical Leave Act is an important social policy, but it only guarantees unpaid leave from jobs to provide care to spouses, children, or elderly parents requiring medical attention. Our findings suggest that, if we really want to support families, such policies must be broadened to include adult children, needy grown-up brothers and sisters, cousins, aunts and uncles. Similarly, Medicaid regulations that only pay for non-familial care of ill, injured, or disabled individuals implicitly discriminate against Blacks and Latinos/as who provide significant amounts of care to extended kin. "Pro-marriage" policies that give special incentives to impoverished women for getting married may penalize other women who turn down marriage to a risky mate and rely instead on grandparents or other relatives to help raise their children.

Extended family obligations should be recognized and accommodated   20 where possible. But they should not be counted on as a substitute for anti-poverty measures, nor should marriage promotion be used in this way. Policymakers must recognize that support from family — whether extended or nuclear — cannot fully compensate for the disadvantages of being poor, or minority, or both. Neither marital ties nor extended family ties can substitute for educational opportunities, jobs with decent wages, health insurance, and affordable child care. Instead of hoping that poor families pull themselves out of poverty by their own bootstraps, social policy should explicitly aim to rectify economic disadvantages. In turn, improvements in economic opportunities and resources will likely shape families.

Note

1. For the extensive analysis underlying this discussion, see: (1) Natalia Sarkisian, Mariana Gerena, and Naomi Gerstel, "Extended Family Integration among Mexican and Euro Americans: Ethnicity, Gender, and Class," *Journal of Marriage and Family*, 69 (2007), 1 (February), 40–54. (2) Natalia Sarkisian, Mariana Gerena, and Naomi Gerstel, "Extended Family Ties among Mexicans, Puerto Ricans and Whites: Superintegration or Disintegration?," *Family Relations*, 55 (2006), 3 (July), 331–344. (3) Natalia Sarkisian and Naomi Gerstel, "Kin Support Among Blacks and Whites: Race and Family Organization," *American Sociological Review*, 69 (2004), 4 (December), 812–837. (4) Amy Armenia and Naomi Gerstel, "Family Leaves, The FMLA, and Gender Neutrality: The Intersection of Race and Gender," *Social Science Research*, 35 (2006), 871–891. (5) Naomi Gerstel and Natalia Sarkisian, "A Sociological Perspective on Families and Work: The Import of Gender, Class, and Race," in Marcie Pitt Catsouphes, Ellen Kossek, and Steven Sweet (eds.), *The Work and Family Handbook: Multi-disciplinary Perspectives, Methods, and Approaches* (Mahwah, NJ: Lawrence Erlbaum, 2006), pp. 237–266. (6) Naomi Gerstel and Natalia Sarkisian, "Marriage: The Good, the Bad, and the Greedy," *Contexts*, 5 (2006) 4 (November), 16–21. (7) Naomi Gerstel and Natalia Sarkisian, "Inter-

generational Care and the Greediness of Adult Children's Marriages," in J. Suitor and T. Owens (eds.), *Interpersonal Relations across the Life Course. Advances in the Life Course Research*, Volume 12. (Greenwich, CT: Elsevier / JAI Press, 2007). [Gerstel and Sarkisian's note.]

References

Domínguez, Silvia, and Celeste Watkins. "Creating Networks for Survival and Mobility: Examining Social Capital Amongst Low-Income African-American and Latin-American Mothers." *Social Problems*, 50 (2003), 1 (February), 111–135.

Edin, Kathryn, and Kefalas, Maria. *Promises I Can Keep: Why Poor Women Put Motherhood Before Marriage.* (Berkeley, CA: University of California Press, 2007).

Stack, Carol B. *All Our Kin: Strategies for Survival in a Black Community.* (New York: Harper and Row, 1974).

ENGAGING THE TEXT

1. In paragraph 1, what might politicians and social commentators mean when they describe black and Latino/Latina families as "more disorganized" than white families? How accurate is this label in Gerstel and Sarkisian's view? Why might a politician find the term "disorganized" useful?

2. What evidence do Gerstel and Sarkisian give that social class is even more important than ethnicity in understanding differences between families? Why is this a critical distinction to the authors?

3. What examples of "extended family solidarities and caretaking activities" (para. 1) do the authors provide? How common or uncommon are these in your own family or community? Do your personal experiences and those of your classmates tend to support, refute, or complicate Gerstel and Sarkisian's analysis?

4. Explain why you agree or disagree with the claim that "social policy should explicitly aim to rectify economic disadvantages" (para. 20). What would this abstract language mean in practice?

EXPLORING CONNECTIONS

5. Review the selections listed below. To what extent could these families be described as "disorganized" (para. 1) and to what extent do they exhibit "extended family solidarities and caretaking activities" (para. 1)?

> Gary Soto, "Looking for Work" (p. 26)
> Roger Jack, "An Indian Story" (p. 52)
> Melvin Dixon, "Aunt Ida Pieces a Quilt" (p. 49)

6. Carefully study the frontispiece to Chapter Three on page 253. What symbols of affluence does the photograph contain? How might Gerstel and Sarkisian read the importance of family background in the man's level of economic achievement?

7. How might Gerstel and Sarkisian read the cartoon on page 66?

EXTENDING THE CRITICAL CONTEXT

8. In this article, Gerstel and Sarkisian focus on just three groups — blacks, Latinos, and whites. What do you think the data would look like for other groups such as Asian Americans, Pacific Islanders, Native Americans, or recent immigrants? Find data to support or refute your guesses.

9. Study the footnote on pages 68–69, which lists seven articles by Gerstel, Sarkisian, and others. Based on the journal and article titles in the footnote, what can you say about the scope, purpose, and methodologies of Gerstel and Sarkisian's research? To extend the assignment, read one of the articles and report its key findings to the class.

Visual Portfolio

Reading Images of American Families

Closing a Summer Cottage, Quogue, New York, a 1957 Norman Rockwell art-directed Colorama by Ralph Amdursky and Charles Baker. © 2009 Kodak, Courtesy of George Eastman House, International Museum of Photography and Film.

Visual Portfolio
READING IMAGES OF AMERICAN FAMILIES

1. The first image in the portfolio (p. 71) shows a family posing for a group photograph. What might be the occasion? Who do you think the people are, and what are their relationships? What impressions do you get about them from their facial expressions, their clothing, and the room and its furnishings? In terms of its messages about family, how closely does this image resemble those by Norman Rockwell on pages 22–24?

2. What indications of time and place can you find in the photograph of the summer cottage (p. 72)? This image was art-directed by Norman Rockwell (see caption p. 72); analyze his arrangement of the photo. In discussion with classmates, "read" the image in terms of some of the themes of *Rereading America* — family, social class, race, gender, and nature/environment.

3. The photograph of Thomas Jefferson's descendants (p. 73) is clearly posed. Explain in detail why you think photographer Erica Burger organized the image as she did. What events in American history can you link to specific details in the photo, and what does the photo say to you about the next century of American history?

4. What is your first reaction to the photograph of the mother and her eight children (p. 74)? How old do you think the mother and the kids are? What is the tone of the image, and what does it tell us about motherhood? How would the meaning of the image change if the father were included? How does it compare to the next picture, the mother washing her child in a basin (p. 75)?

5. What is the emotional impact of the photograph of a woman bathing her child in a washtub in the kitchen (p. 75)? Why does the photographer consider this moment worthy of our attention? How might sociologists Gerstel and Sarkisian (p. 61) interpret the image?

6. First describe your initial reaction to the photograph of the lesbian brides (p. 76); for example, did it surprise you or work against your expectations? Next, tell the story of this picture: discuss what's happening and find out if your classmates read the photo in the same way you do. Explain the significance of as many details in the image as possible — for example, gowns, facial expressions, setting, and background. This photo was published with the caption "Love and Marriage"; explain why you think this is or is not a good title for the image.

7. What do you think is the setting for the photograph of the boy who loves his two dads (p. 77)? Does the image seem posed or natural? What are its logical and emotional appeals? How old do you think the boy is? How would the message be different in a photograph of a gay couple with a sign "Our son loves us both"?

Proposition 8: The California Marriage Protection Act

The movement to secure equal marriage rights for gay and lesbian citizens, which has been gaining momentum for many years, has now moved same-sex marriage to the foreground in American political, legal, and cultural debate. Marriage laws differ by state, but the recent battles in California offer insight into the debate nationwide. The most critical developments in the California saga are as follows:

- *In May 2008, a state Supreme Court ruling made same-sex marriages legal in California under the state Constitution as it then existed.*
- *Opponents of same-sex marriage gathered enough signatures to put Proposition 8 on the ballot, and in November 2008 voters passed the measure, thus changing the state Constitution and making same-sex marriage invalid.*
- *In May 2009, the state Supreme Court upheld the constitutionality of Proposition 8, but also held that some 18,000 marriages performed between May 2008 and the passage of Proposition 8 were valid.*
- *Activists for marriage equality have vowed to continue their fight. Their strategies include grass-roots organization, advertising campaigns, and the use of social networking tools such as Facebook and Twitter. A proposition that would repeal Prop 8 may appear on a California ballot in 2010 or 2012.*

This initiative measure is submitted to the people in accordance with the provisions of Article II, Section 8, of the California Constitution.

This initiative measure expressly amends the California Constitution by adding a section thereto; therefore, new provisions proposed to be added are printed in *italic type* to indicate that they are new.

SECTION 1.   Title

This measure shall be known and may be cited as the "California Marriage Protection Act."

SECTION 2.   Section 7.5 is added to Article I of the California Constitution, to read:

SEC. 7.5.   *Only marriage between a man and a woman is valid or recognized in California.*

ENGAGING THE TEXT

1. The title of the ballot initiative measure is the "California Marriage Protection Act." What is the title's intended rhetorical impact? How might Prop 8 opponents critique this title, and what titles might they suggest for Prop 8?

2. The heart of Prop 8 is one apparently simple sentence — "Only marriage between a man and a woman is valid or recognized in California." Closely consider each key word here — marriage, man, woman, valid, recognized, California — and discuss whether there is any chance of ambiguity, interpretation, or disagreement in the meanings of these terms or of the sentence as a whole.

3. To what extent would the word "marriage" remain significant if lesbian and gay couples everywhere could live together, raise children, file joint tax returns, and so on under the protection of a different term, such as "joint partnership" or "civil union"?

4. Founding Father and fourth President James Madison warned in *Federalist Paper No. 10* that "measures are too often decided, not according to the rules of justice and the rights of the minor party, but by the superior force of an interested and overbearing majority." What, if anything, limits the power of a majority in a case like Prop 8? Can Prop 8 reasonably be seen as the "tyranny of the majority"?

5. Write a one-sentence proposition which would have the opposite effect of Proposition 8 — that is, to guarantee equal marriage rights to same-sex partners.

6. In upholding the constitutionality of Prop 8 in its May 2009 decision, the California Supreme Court also specifically designated as valid the marriages of approximately 18,000 gay and lesbian couples that took place between the court's May 2008 ruling and the passage of Prop 8 in November 2008. Discuss the reasonableness of this compromise and the relative legal and social status of couples who did and did not wed during this period.

Exploring Connections

7. Are the women pictured on page 76 married? Is it possible to tell without knowing the time and place of the photograph? What does this exercise suggest about the relationship of personal experience to the law?

8. Read Andrew Sullivan's "My Big Fat Straight Wedding" on page 102. Imagine it is the day after Prop 8 passed and write a brief blog from Sullivan's point of view.

9. Review the paintings by Norman Rockwell on pages 22–24. Then design a "Freedom to Marry" poster.

Extending the Critical Context

10. Establish small teams to research current marriage/domestic partnership law in your state and several others. (Also pay attention to any pending legislation, ballot initiatives, or court cases.) How substantially do the laws vary from state to state? What scenarios can you imagine in which crossing a border might cause legal problems or ambiguities? You may want to begin your search at a marriage-equality Web site such as www.freedomtomarry.org or www.marriageequality.org.

11. Prop 8 is an example of "direct democracy" in the sense that voters estab-
    lished the law themselves, without the legislature, governor, or courts.
    Research the procedures for direct democracy in your state (for example,
    ballot initiatives, referendums, recalls), the kinds of issues they have been
    used to address, and the advantages and disadvantages of your state's system.
    Do you think direct democracy is working well in your state, or do you think
    that state legislators would usually make better decisions than the voters?

8 Is Not Hate: The Meaning of a Proposition

JENNIFER ROBACK MORSE

This short editorial appeared in National Review Online *in November 2008, at the height of the Proposition 8 campaign. (If you haven't read "Proposition 8: The California Marriage Protection Act" on p. 79, take a minute to do so now.) Morse writes that gay rights activists misunderstand the motives of Proposition 8 supporters: the Proposition is not an expression of hatred toward gays, but a way of restraining an overzealous state Supreme Court which had attempted to redefine marriage. Morse (b. 1953) has taught economics at Yale and George Mason Universities. She is a regular contributor to the* National Catholic Register *and is the author of* Love and Economics: Why the Laissez-Faire Family Doesn't Work *(2001) and* Smart Sex: Finding Life-Long Love in a Hook-up World *(2005).*

In Fresno, a Catholic priest who recently came out to his parishioners asked them to imagine they have just discovered they are gay: "How would you feel when you saw a car with a 'Yes on 8' bumper sticker?" In San Diego, a group opposing Proposition 8 calls itself "Californians Against Hate." In San Jose, two women parked in front of a house that had a large "Yes on 8" banner. They spray painted their own car to turn it into a billboard saying "Bigots Live Here."

Given all these episodes, I would like for the gays and lesbians of California to know what I mean by the "Yes on Proposition 8" sign in my yard. I want you to know what I am saying, and what I'm not saying, by driving around with a "Yes on Prop 8" sticker. Some opponents of Proposition 8 seem to view it as a referendum on whether we like gay people. I do not share this view. From my perspective, it would be tragic for the gays and

MORE NONTRADITIONAL FAMILY UNITS

Guy, Chair, Three-Way Lamp

A Woman, Her Daughter, Forty-four
My Little Ponies

The Troy Triplets and Their
Personal Trainer

Two Guys, Two Gals, Two Phones,
a Fax, and a Blender

R. Chast

lesbians of California to believe that every house with a Yes on 8 sign in the yard is inhabited by someone who hates them.

I'm voting "yes" on 8, not because of my views of gays and lesbians, but because of my views about marriage. I view marriage as a gender-based institution that attaches mothers and fathers to each other and to their children. Those of us who support Proposition 8 believe that children deserve at least the chance to have a relationship with a mom and a dad. That isn't hateful toward anyone.

We have watched as the small children of Massachusetts were taught about homosexuality in their public schools. We believe parents should decide when and what to teach their children about homosexuality, in accordance with their values and their perception of their child's maturity. We have trouble believing that the well-being of gays and lesbians really depends on children reading *King & King*[1] in kindergarten.

We believe the California Supreme Court greatly overstepped its   5 bounds. Their decision did more than legalize same-sex marriage. The Court declared that requiring spouses to be of the opposite sex counts as discrimination. Religious groups that act on the belief that marriage is between a man and a woman are henceforth engaged in unlawful discrimination.

The Court also changed the jurisprudence of sexual-orientation discrimination cases, giving same-sex couples the highest possible level of protection. This means that in contests between religious liberty and sexual-orientation discrimination, religious liberty would almost always lose. The Court's ruling gave gays and lesbians new grounds on which to sue religious people and a higher probability of winning than before. Fair-minded Californians of all political persuasions don't want every church-related activity threatened with legal harassment. Every marriage-preparation class, every preschool, every adoption agency, every high school, every teen youth group is potentially covered by the Court's ruling. Voting Yes on Proposition 8 is one of the few ways ordinary citizens can protest. They are not saying they hate gay people: they are saying the Court is out of control.

Millions of people are going to vote Yes on Prop 8. People of every religion and no religion are going to vote Yes on Prop 8. People with gay loved ones are going to vote Yes on Prop 8. It would be tragic, and completely unwarranted, for gay men and lesbians to conclude that all these people hate them.

ENGAGING THE TEXT

1. What is Morse's thesis in this editorial? To what extent does she rely on logos, pathos, or ethos to back up her thesis — that is, how does she appeal to the reader's sense of logic, emotion, or confidence in her trustworthiness as a writer?

2. Discuss Morse's definition of marriage as a "gender-based institution that attaches mothers and fathers to each other and to their children" (para. 3). For example, in what sense are mothers, fathers, and children "attached" by marriage in ways that same-sex marriage would not allow? What alternative definitions of marriage can you come up with? Can the class reach a consensus on any of these?

[1]*King & King*: A 2002 children's book by Linda de Haan and Stern Nijland in which a prince discovers that his true love is not a princess, but another prince.

3. Explain why you think it is likely or unlikely that recognition of same-sex marriage might lead to frequent lawsuits against religious people or threats of legal harassment against "every church-related activity" (para. 6)?

EXPLORING CONNECTIONS

4. Look ahead to the next reading, "Prop 8 Hurt My Family — Ask Me How" (below). What might Morse say about the expressions of hatred cited in that report?
5. Look at the images in the chapter's Visual Portfolio of the lesbian brides (p. 76) and the boy holding the sign (p. 77). Would these people be safe from verbal or physical harassment in your community?
6. Read or review "An Indian Story" by Roger Jack (p. 52) or "Looking for Work" by Gary Soto (p. 26). Discuss what would change in these narratives if one or more of the important adults were lesbian or gay.

EXTENDING THE CRITICAL CONTEXT

7. Morse writes that some Prop 8 opponents treated it as if it were "a referendum on whether we like gay people" (para. 2). Review a few marriage-equality Web sites such as www.marriageequality.org or www.freedomtomarry.org. What evidence do you see to support or refute Morse's characterization of Prop 8 opponents?
8. In paragraph 4, Morse voices her opposition to "small children in Massachusetts being taught about homosexuality in the public schools." She is apparently referring to a case brought by David Parker and others against the Lexington School District. Chief Judge Mark L. Wolf of the U.S. District Court of Massachusetts wrote the legal opinion that dismissed Parker's suit and upheld school policies concerning diversity education. Find Judge Wolf's opinion through the District Court Web site (www.mad.uscourts .gov) and summarize his main arguments. On what issues do Judge Wolf and Morse have basic disagreements?

Prop 8 Hurt My Family — Ask Me How
MARRIAGE EQUALITY USA

Marriage Equality USA is a national organization whose mission is "to secure legally recognized civil marriage equality for all, at the federal and state level, without regard to gender identity or sexual orientation." The 2009 report excerpted here documents the physical and emotional toll that anti same-sex amendments take on lesbian, gay, bisexual, transgender, and

*intersex (LGBTI) individuals and their allies. Problems include vandalism,
name-calling, threats, bullying of children, and more. We reprint here the
report's introduction and first section, which together offer a broad overview
of the problem and several short accounts of harassment.*

Introduction

In January 2009, the American Psychological Association (APA) released
three separate studies that described the psychological distress associated
with anti same-sex marriage amendments. One study using national survey
responses of LGBTI[1] individuals found that those who live in states that
have passed marriage amendments experienced increased psychological
stress not due to other pre-existing conditions but as "a direct result of the
negative images and messages associated with the ballot campaign and the
passage of the amendment." Furthermore, participants reported feeling
"alienated from their community, fearful they would lose their children, and
concerned they would become victims of anti-gay violence." These studies
also reported that this harm extends to Lesbian, Gay, Bisexual, Transgender,
and Intersex (LGBTI) family members and straight allies who experience a
form of "secondary minority stress." Finally, "although many participants displayed resiliency and effective coping with this stress, some experienced
strong negative consequences to their mental and physical health."

Marriage Equality USA, through a series of town halls held across California and a national on-line survey of over 3,100 respondents, collected
community input regarding the homophobia and other harm experienced
through initiative campaigns, like Proposition 8,[2] and received personal
stories that mirror these APA findings. In our report "Prop 8 Hurt My Family — Ask Me How," we collected almost 1,200 individual experiences
which illustrate how:

- LGBTI people experience increased verbal abuse, homophobia, physical
  harm, and other discrimination associated with or resulting from the
  Prop 8 campaign;
- Children of same-sex couples express fear due to direct exposure to
  homophobia and hate and concerns that the passage of Prop 8 means
  they could be taken from their families and targeted for further violence;
- LGBTI youth and their supporters experience increased bullying at
  schools as Prop 8's passage fosters a supportive environment for homophobic acts of physical and emotional violence;

---

[1]*LGBTI:* Lesbian, gay, bisexual, transsexual, intersex. "Intersex" refers to a number of
medical conditions in which an individual's sex anatomy is not considered standard. Like "her-
maphrodite," the term is problematic; a 2006 "Consensus Statement on Intersex Disorders"
published by the American Academy of Pediatrics recommended instead the term Disorders
of Sex Development (DSD) to refer to "congenital conditions in which development of chro-
mosomal, gonadal, or anatomic sex is atypical."

[2]*Proposition 8:* See "Proposition 8: The California Marriage Protection Act" (p. 79).

- Straight allies experience the impact of homophobia firsthand and express shock and fear for their LGBTI family members and friends and the danger they may experience if they were perceived as gay or an ally;
- Families are torn apart as relatives divide on Prop 8; and
- Communities are destroyed from the aftermath of abusive behavior toward them during local street demonstrations, neighborhood divisions, and the impact of "knowing your neighbor" voted against your family.

Despite the harm and discrimination that opponents of Prop 8 experienced, LGBTI people, their families and friends, and supportive community members stated that they are more resolved and determined to fight until every family receives the same dignity and protection that only marriage can provide. But the report also documents the inherent unfairness and strife that comes from putting the fundamental rights of some of the community up for a popular vote and points out the lasting harm and fear that is generated from these campaigns.

We conclude this report with stories that describe why some believe it is important for the California Supreme Court to overturn Prop 8. Our hope in sharing these stories is that all Californians, including those who voted Yes on 8, can reflect on the harm that has resulted from this initiative campaign and come to the conclusion that we don't want to repeat this experience. We hope California lives up to our ideals and that our Constitution remains intact and continues to serve its role in protecting the minority from the tyranny of the majority. In the words of President and Chief Justice William Howard Taft, "Constitutions are checks upon the hasty action of the majority. They are self-imposed restraints of a whole people upon a majority of them to secure sober action and a respect for the rights of the minority."

Prop 8 Hurt Real People

> I think the LGBTI community has been under constant stress for the last eight years. We have been used as a political punching bag. The anxiety affects all of us and most of us just want to live our lives quietly with the same rights and responsibilities as everyone else. We are a tiny minority, but our well-being is at the mercy of a still homophobic majority.
> — Contra Costa County

Not only did LGBTI people lose their right to marry, but they were verbally assaulted, had property vandalized and destroyed, received death threats, and several people reported being terminated from their jobs because they were gay and / or due to their opposition to Prop 8.

Anti-gay initiative campaigns promote an environment that fosters discrimination, rejection, and homophobia. Marriage Equality USA's on-line survey found that over 40 percent of all respondents, the majority being LGBTI individuals, indicated they faced homophobia, hate speech, violence, or threats resulting from California's Prop 8 campaign. Many town hall participants and survey respondents described the whole ballot initiative process as homophobic, starting with the failed effort to encourage Californians to decline to sign the proposed initiative followed by being forced to endure Yes on 8 advertisements, media coverage and letters to the editor that reinforced negative stereotypes, prejudice and discrimination, and finally suffering the brutal realization that California voters would not support their right to be treated as equal citizens.

LGBTI community members expressed pride and felt empowered through participating in rallies, phone banking, wearing No on 8 buttons or having No on 8 bumper stickers or lawn signs; however this involvement also increased their exposure to glares, obscenities, harassment, threats, and violence as demonstrated by the following examples:

- "One day, I was called a faggot four times in Oakland while wearing my No on 8 button."— Alameda County
- "We put up a No on 8 lawn sign and people would drive by our house just to give us dirty looks and flip us off, even in front of our daughter."— Fresno County
- "While in my car at a red light, four men came up to my window and started yelling threats because of my No on 8 bumper sticker. One man yelled, 'I will kill you bitch. I will follow you home.' I had to call the police and they escorted me home."— Sacramento County
- "Every rally included a day long barrage of classic slurs being shouted from passing cars. One man drove by several times with four boys in the car shouting 'fuck you faggots' and flashing their middle fingers. It was like the adult was modeling, teaching, and celebrating gay bashing behavior."— San Diego County
- "My employer received anonymous threats about me and implying personal risk for the children I teach. I was suspended with pay while the school district assessed the threat. My home was vandalized with anti-gay slogans and slurs. Our car was destroyed when someone put sugar in the tank. All this because of an article about our marriage."— San Bernardino County

Prop 8 was not a school bond or redistricting initiative, it was an effort to eliminate the fundamental right of marriage for same-sex couples. As one San Luis Obispo respondent described, "Marriage never was hugely important to me, so it came as quite a shock when I read the [California Supreme Court marriage decision] and started to sob. Someone had finally said I was a decent human being and deserved equal protection under the laws." Marriage matters and for those personally affected, Prop 8 was a personal attack on our lives and families. Living through this campaign exerted a high toll on the sense of well-being and connection within the larger community that affected everyone. As one Santa Clara County respondent stated, "It is frustrating and exhausting to go through the course of each day feeling like we somehow have to defend our marriage. It weighs on a person and on a couple." Another resident from San Francisco described, "The psychological trauma of having my civil rights debated by people who do not even know me has been astounding. I didn't realize the effect this vote would have on me until after it happened."

For same-sex couples who were unable to marry before November 4th, they expressed despair over the passage of Prop 8. As one Alameda County respondent described, "I don't want to wait until I have gray hair to marry my girlfriend. I deeply regret not having the money to do it while I had the chance. I never thought Prop 8 would pass." Many same-sex couples who were married also expressed concerns their marriages were at risk, and their fears were validated when Prop 8 proponents filed papers to have their marriage licenses take away.

For other LGBTI community members, the passage of Prop 8 has resulted   10
in increased anxiety and fear. As one Sonoma County resident described, "There's a quiet rift between my friends, family, and I now — gay and straight. This is painful. I wonder who hates me. Am I in danger in this situation? How about this one? Who voted against my rights?" Another Santa Clara County resident shared, "Since Prop 8 passed, my wife had developed significant anxiety. She feels like at any moment we will be hate-crime victims. When she heard about the lesbian in Richmond who was gang raped, it was as if they were coming for us next. I think a lot of the LGBTI community feels that way." And a Sonoma County resident summed up, "Every time an anti-gay measure passes, it makes the LGBTI community more vulnerable. I have been physically threatened before because I am gay, and that fear is always in the back of my mind, particularly when there is a general feeling that the majority of the people in my state (or country) are systematically stripping us of rights."

Despite all the homophobia and hate that LGBTI community members faced, we received many comments that demonstrate the courage and resolve to continue our fight for marriage equality, including this one from San Joaquin County, "This election has been very emotional and hurtful for me. Although at the same time, it has made me stronger to fight for what I believe in."

ENGAGING THE TEXT

1. The Marriage Equality USA report cites three recent studies by the American Psychological Association and presents findings from Marriage Equality USA's own town hall meetings and national online survey. Does this body of evidence fully persuade you that the campaigns for anti same-sex marriage amendments have caused real and serious harm to many Americans? Explain why or why not.

2. How persuasive or instructive do you find the embedded personal comments and stories? How many of the people quoted in the report would you say have been victims of criminal acts?

3. Most readers of a Marriage Equality USA report are probably already in favor of the full legality of same-sex marriage. What might be the purpose of a report like this if it is not to persuade such readers?

EXPLORING CONNECTIONS

4. Write or role-play a brief debate between a Marriage Equality USA spokesperson and Jennifer Roback Morse (p. 81) over the importance of homophobia and hatred in the Proposition 8 battle.

5. Look at the Visual Portfolio photograph in which a boy holds a sign reading "I love my dads" (p. 77). How does reading the Marriage Equality USA report affect your interpretation of that image? (For your information, the photograph appeared on the title page of the report.)

EXTENDING THE CRITICAL CONTEXT

6. Consult the full report through www.marriageequalityusa.org. Summarize the findings of one or more of the other sections (e.g. "Prop 8 Promoted Bullying in Schools") and report to the class.

7. Find one of the 2009 American Psychological Association studies mentioned in paragraph 1 of the report and summarize its methods and conclusions for the class.

What Is Marriage?

EVAN WOLFSON

Marriage involves a legally binding contract, a moral commitment, a change in familial ties, and in some cases, a religious rite. Evan Wolfson explores the nature of this complex yet familiar state in the following selection. Wolfson, named by Time *magazine in 2004 as among the 100 most powerful and influential people in the world, has had a distinguished and diverse career. Educated at Yale College and Harvard Law School, he spent two years in the Peace Corps, participated in the investigation of the Iran-Contra scandal that rocked the Reagan presidency, and appeared before the U.S. Supreme Court in* Boy Scouts *of* America v. James Dale. *He is currently executive director of Freedom to Marry, a gay and nongay partnership seeking equal marriage rights for all Americans. The excerpt reprinted here is from his book* Why Marriage Matters: America, Equality, and Gay People's Right to Marry *(2004).*

> Civil marriage is at once a deeply personal commitment to another
> human being and a highly public celebration of the ideals of mutuality,
> companionship, intimacy, fidelity, and family.
>> — MASSACHUSETTS SUPREME JUDICIAL COURT,
>> *Goodridge v. Department of Public Health* (2003)[1]

>> How the world can change,
>> It can change like that,
>> Due to one little word:
>> "Married."
>> — JOHN KANDER AND FRED EBB,
>> "Married," *Cabaret* (1966)

Depending on which linguistic expert you ask, there are anywhere from
two thousand to seven thousand different languages spoken in the world
today. That's a huge number to put your mind around — even for someone
who lives in Manhattan, where seemingly hundreds of those languages can
be heard on the subway on any given day. Still, I'm willing to bet that each
of these languages has something in common with the others: a word that
means marriage.

No matter what language people speak — from Arabic to Yiddish, from
Chinook to Chinese — marriage is what we use to describe a specific relationship of love and dedication to another person. It is how we explain the
families that are united because of that love. And it universally signifies a
level of self-sacrifice and responsibility and a stage of life unlike any other.

Now of course, different cultures and times have had many different
conceptions of marriage, different rules and different ways of regarding
those who are married — not to mention different treatment for married
men and married women. . . . But with all this variety and all the changes
that have occurred in marriage over time and in different places, including
our country and within our lifetime, it is clear that marriage has been a
defining institution in virtually every society throughout history. Given its
variety and omnipresence, it is not surprising that when people talk about
marriage, they often mean different things.

Consider all the different dimensions of marriage in the United States
alone. First, marriage is a personal commitment and an important choice
that belongs to couples in love. In fact, many people consider their choice of

---

[1]*Goodridge v. Department of Public Health*, 440 Mass. 309 (Massachusetts Supreme
Judicial Court, 2003). [Editors' note: This is the case that effectively legalized same-sex marriage in Massachusetts; the Court ruled that "barring an individual from the protections, benefits, and obligations of civil marriage solely because that person would marry a person of the
same sex violates the Massachusetts Constitution."] [All notes are Wolfson's unless otherwise
indicated.]

partner the most significant choice they will ever make. It is a relationship between people who are, hopefully, in love and an undertaking that most couples hope will endure.

Marriage is also a social statement, preeminently describing and defin- 5 ing a person's relationships and place in society. Marital status, along with what we do for a living, is often one of the first pieces of information we give to others about ourselves. It's so important, in fact, that most married people wear a symbol of their marriage on their hand.

Marriage is also a relationship between a couple and the government. Couples need the government's participation to get into and out of a marriage. Because it is a legal or "civil" institution, marriage is the legal gateway to a vast array of protections, responsibilities, and benefits — most of which cannot be replicated in any other way, no matter how much forethought you show or how much you are able to spend on attorneys' fees and assembling proxies and papers.

The tangible legal and economic protections and responsibilities that come with marriage include access to health care and medical decision making for your partner and your children; parenting and immigration rights; inheritance, taxation, Social Security, and other government benefits; rules for ending a relationship while protecting both parties; and the simple ability to pool resources to buy or transfer property without adverse tax treatment. In 1996, the federal government cataloged more than 1,049 ways in which married people are accorded special status under federal law; in a 2004 report, the General Accounting Office bumped up those federal effects of marriage to at least 1,138. Add in the state-level protections and the intangible as well as tangible privileges marriage brings in private life, and it's clear that the legal institution of marriage is one of the major safety nets in life, both in times of crisis and in day-to-day living.

Marriage uniquely permits couples to travel and deal with others in business or across borders without playing a game of "now you're legally next of kin; now you're legally not." It is a known commodity; no matter how people in fact conduct their marriages, there is a clarity, security, and automatic level of respect and legal status when someone gets to say, "That's my husband" or "I love my wife."

Marriage has spiritual significance for many of us and familial significance for nearly all of us. Family members inquire when one is going to get married, often to the point of nagging. Many religions perform marriage ceremonies, many consider marriage holy or a sacrament within their faith, and the majority of American couples get married in a religious setting — although the percentage of those having a purely civil ceremony is at nearly 40 percent and growing. As far as the law is concerned, however, what counts is not what you do at the altar or whether you march down the aisle, but that you get a civil marriage license from the government and sign a legal document in the vestibule of the church, synagogue, temple, or mosque — or at city hall, a court, or a clerk's office. As a legal matter, what the priest, minister, rabbi, or other clergy member does is *witness* the couple's commitment and attest to their conformity with the requirements for a civil marriage license.

As ubiquitous and varied as the institution is, the word *marriage* and its myriad translations throughout the world also have a unique meaning that children often use in making a joke. Who doesn't remember taunting friends with a question like this: "If you love candy so much, why don't you marry it?" Of course we know now — and I suppose we must have known then — that the punch line was in the question itself. The joke shows that though they may well "go together like a horse and carriage," *marriage* is different from *love*. *Love* is a word that can be applied to anything from your favorite song and your best-fitting pair of Levi's to your parents, your roommate, or your boyfriend, while *marriage* signifies an unequaled commitment. And, as the childhood taunt illustrates, that's a distinction most of us have understood since we were kids.

Still, marriage is now the vocabulary we use to talk of love, family, dedication, self-sacrifice, and stages of life. Marriage is a language of love, equality, and inclusion. While recognizing that marriage should not be the sole criterion for benefits and support — nor the only family form worthy of respect — most of us take marriage seriously and most of us do marry.

None of this is to say that marriage is the right choice for everybody. One need only meet a happy single or divorced person to know that many people are pleased with their decision to avoid matrimony. And, of course, we've all been to weddings where we wonder how *she* could marry *him*. As splendid as the institution is in the abstract, and as revered as marriage is in virtually every society, one need only look at the divorce rate to know that there are bad marriages and marriages that, without fault, have ceased to work.

There is clearly a difference between *marriage* and *marriages,* between the institution and the choices and conduct of real couples in their commitment. For better or for worse, marriage is about choice, whether it be the choice to "make it official" with your beloved and to accept the protections and the responsibilities that accompany that decision; the choice to work at your marriage and make it rewarding and good; the choice to betray or divorce a spouse; or the choice to avoid the institution of marriage altogether.

But marriage hasn't always been about choice. In fact, ... it has historically been a battlefield, the site of collisions within and between governments and religions over who should regulate it. But marriage has weathered centuries of skirmishes and change. It has evolved from an institution that was imposed on some people and denied to others, to the loving union of companionship, commitment, and caring between equal partners that we think of today.[2]

---

[2]Hendrik Hartog, "What Gay Marriage Teaches About the History of Marriage," *History News Network,* April 5, 2004, http://hnn.us/articles/4400.html (lecture by author of *Man and Wife in America: A History* to Organization of American Historians tracing evolution of marriage and past battles).

In ancient Rome, for example, a man was not considered a citizen until   15
he was married, and in many countries today, people, no matter how old, live
under the roof, and remain under the control, of their parents until they
wed — often a powerful incentive to marry (and a far cry from our idea of
marriage as a choice made out of love). And you might be surprised to learn
that, for example, the Catholic Church had nothing to do with marriage during the church's first one thousand years; marriage was not yet recognized
officially as a Catholic sacrament, nor were weddings then performed in
churches. Rather, marriage was understood as a dynastic or property
arrangement for families and the basic social unit, *households* (then often
extended families or kin, often including servants and even slaves). Family
life and law in past centuries, let alone marriage, were very different from
anything we'd recognize in the United States today.

Battles over marriage have taken place in America, too. . . . There was a
time when our country excluded African-Americans from marriage altogether, prohibited people from marrying a partner of the "wrong" race,
denied married people the use of contraception, and stripped women of
their rights and even personhood — essentially making them chattel — at
the altar. It took decades and decades of fighting to change these injustices.
And change still needs to take place in the hearts of many, not to mention
the law. As recently as 1998 in South Carolina and 2000 in Alabama, 40 percent of the voters in each state voted to keep offensive language barring
interracial marriage in their respective state constitutions.

But fortunately, the general story of our country is movement toward inclusion and equality. The majority of Americans are fair. They realize that exclusionary conceptions of marriage fly in the face of our national commitment to freedom as well as the personal commitment made by loving couples. Americans have been ready again and again to make the changes needed to ensure that the institution of marriage reflects the values of love, inclusion, interdependence, and support.

Such a change came about as recently as 1987, when a group of Americans who had been denied the freedom to marry came before the U.S. Supreme Court. Before the justices issued an opinion in the case, *Turner v. Safley,* they had to determine what role marriage plays in American society. Or, more precisely, what role marriage plays in American law.

After careful consideration, the justices outlined four "important attributes" of marriage: First, they said, marriage represents an opportunity to make a public statement of commitment and love to another person, and an opportunity to receive public support for that commitment. Second, the justices said, marriage has for many people an important spiritual or religious dimension. Third, marriage offers the prospect of physical "consummation," which of course most of us call something else. And fourth, the justices said, marriage in the United States is the unique and indispensable gateway, the "precondition," for a vast array of protections, responsibilities, and benefits — public and private, tangible and intangible, legal and economic — that have real importance for real people.

The Supreme Court of course understood, as we discussed above, that   20
marriage has other purposes and aspects in the religious sphere, in business, and in people's personal lives. The justices knew, for example, that for many people, marriage is also important as a structure in which they can have and raise children. But when examined with the U.S. Constitution in mind, these four attributes or interests identified by the Court are the ones that have the legal weight. And after weighing these attributes, the justices ruled — in a unanimous decision — that marriage is such an important choice that it may not be arbitrarily denied by the government. Accordingly, they ordered that the government stop refusing marriage licenses to the group of Americans who had brought the case.

That group of Americans was prisoners.

Seventeen years after the Supreme Court recognized that the choice to marry is so important that it cannot be arbitrarily denied to convicted felons, one group of Americans is still denied the freedom to marry. No matter how long they have been together as a couple, no matter how committed and loving their relationship, and no matter how much they need the basic tools and support that come with marriage, lesbian and gay Americans in this country are excluded from the legal right to obtain a civil marriage license and marry the person they love.

Who are these same-sex couples and how does the exclusion from marriage harm them and their families?

They include Maureen Kilian and Cindy Meneghin of Butler, New Jersey, a committed couple ever since they met more than thirty years ago during their junior year in high school. Maureen works part-time as a parish administrator for Christ Church in nearby Pompton Lakes, where her job includes entering the names of married couples into the church registry. Cindy, meanwhile, is the director of Web services at Montclair State University. The women wish that one of them could stay at home full-time to help care for their two children, Josh and Sarah. But because they aren't married, neither of them is eligible for family health insurance through her employer, so both of them have to leave the kids in order to stay insured.

"We are good citizens, we pay our taxes, and we are caring parents — but we don't have the same equality as other Americans," Maureen told the *New York Times.* "We're tired of having to explain our relationship. When you say you're married, everyone understands that." More than anything, Maureen and Cindy told the *Times,* they want spousal inheritance rights, so that if one of them dies, the other one can stay in their home without having to pay crippling estate taxes to the Internal Revenue Service. That security comes with marriage.[3]

Alicia Heath-Toby and Saundra Toby-Heath also live in New Jersey and have been a couple for more than fifteen years. Alicia is a deacon and Saundra an usher in the Liberation in Truth Unity Fellowship Church, an African-American congregation, and they regularly participate in church cookouts, picnics, dances, and family activities as well as services. The women have children and grandchildren, bought a home together in Newark, and pay taxes. When Alicia had surgery, Saundra took weeks off from her work as a FedEx dispatcher to take care of her. Denied access to family health insurance and required to pay two deductibles instead of one because they are not married, Saundra and Alicia want to enter a legal commitment to match the religious one they already celebrated in their church.

"If two complete strangers met each other last week and got legally married today, they would have more rights under the law than our relationship has after fifteen years of being together. That's not fair," Saundra and Alicia told their lawyers at Lambda Legal Defense & Education Fund. "We pay first-class taxes, but we're treated like second-class citizens."[4] They worry about their kids and each other, and they want the best legal and economic protection they can get for their family. That protection comes with marriage.

Tony Eitnier and Thomas Arnold have been life partners for more than ten years, but until recently they were faced every day with the fear that it would be their last together. That's because Tony is from the United States and Thomas is from Germany. Unlike most of America's close allies, such as Canada and the United Kingdom, our country discriminates with policies

25

---

[3]Andrew Jacobs, "More Than Mere Partners," *New York Times,* December 19, 2003, p. B1.
[4]"New Black Group to Fight for Marriage Equality," *Blacklight,* National Black Justice Coalition, March 24, 2004, http://www.blacklightonline.com/fma.html.

that do not allow gay citizens to remain together with committed partners from other countries under the family unification principles that normally apply in immigration. "It [is] a mental battle not to go crazy, never knowing if your partner is going to have to leave tomorrow," Tony told the Associated Press. "You become paranoid."[5]

Because Germany is one of more than fifteen countries with an immigration policy that treats binational same-sex couples equally, Tony and Thomas moved to Berlin, where they can live together without fear of a forced separation. That's little comfort for Tony's family in San Diego, California, though. "I'm very close to my family, and it was extremely traumatic to have to leave," Tony said. "My parents are bitter at the government."[6] The couple holds on to the hope that they can return to the U.S. and live openly and legally as a couple in Tony's own country, America, the land of the free. That right comes with marriage.

Chris Lodewyks and Craig Hutchison of Pompton Lakes, New Jersey, 30 have been committed partners since they met when they were freshmen in college, more than thirty years ago. As is the case for many middle-aged couples, Chris and Craig have spent a good part of the past decade looking after their aging parents. When Chris's mom was battling cancer at the end of her life, Craig took time off from work to help care for her. And now that Chris is retired, he can spend time helping Craig's elderly mother. The men also are active in the community. Chris has spearheaded a town cleanup day, with businesses donating prizes to hundreds of volunteers, and Craig serves on the board of a YMCA camp. "Gay and lesbian topics are in the news every day," Chris told New Jersey's *Bergen County Record*. "This is an emotional time, and some people may be looking at this like it's going too fast. But it's not going too fast. It's time for us to have the same civil rights as everyone else."[7]

Chris and Craig have shown the personal commitment to each other, have done the work, and have undertaken on their own many of the family responsibilities of a married couple, including caring for each other's parents. Now they want the full legal responsibilities and protections that the government bestows on married couples. "After thirty years of commitment and responsibility the government treats our accomplishments together as worthless," Craig said.[8] Full protections and legal responsibility come with marriage.

Julie and Hillary Goodridge of Jamaica Plain, Massachusetts, have been in a committed relationship for sixteen years and are raising a young daughter

[5]David Cray, "Painful Choices Face Many Same-sex Couples When One Is American, the Other Foreign," Associated Press, November 23, 2003.

[6]Cray, "Painful Choices."

[7]John Chadwick, "White House Working on Law to Block Gay Marriage," *Bergen County (N.J.) Record*, July 31, 2003, p. A1.

[8]Lambda Legal, "New Jersey Family Profiles," March 24, 2004, http://www.lambdalegal.org/cgibin/iowa/documents/record?record=1068.

together. One day the women played the Beatles song "All You Need Is Love" for their daughter, Annie, who was five years old at the time. When Hillary asked Annie if she knew any people who loved each other, Annie named several of her mothers' married friends. "What about Mommy and Ma?" Hillary asked. "Well," Annie replied, "if you loved each other you'd get married." At that point, Hillary later told *Newsweek* magazine, "My heart just dropped."[9]

It wasn't the first time that the freedom to marry would have helped clarify the Goodridges' family relationship for the people around them. The most dramatic illustration of how exclusion from marriage harms their family took place after Julie's caesarean delivery of Annie, when Hillary was denied entry into the ICU to see her newborn daughter. "They said, 'Only immediate family,' and I had a fit," Hillary told *People* magazine.[10]

Who wouldn't have a fit? And who should have to go through an ordeal like that, especially at such an important, trying, and hopefully joyous time as the birth of a child? The Goodridges want assurance that they won't encounter similar obstacles the next time Julie, Hillary, or Annie is hospitalized or in need. That assurance comes with marriage.

In fact, exclusion from the freedom to marry unfairly punishes commit-   35
ted same-sex couples and their families by depriving them of critical assistance, security, and obligations in virtually every area of life, including, yes, even death and taxes:

- Death: If a couple is not married and one partner dies, the other partner is not entitled to get bereavement leave from work, to file wrongful death claims, to draw the Social Security payments of the deceased partner, or to automatically inherit a shared home, assets, or personal items in the absence of a will.
- Debts: Unmarried partners do not generally have responsibility for each other's debt.
- Divorce: Unmarried couples do not have access to the courts or to the legal and financial guidelines in times of breakup, including rules for how to handle shared property, child support, and alimony, or to protect the weaker party and the kids.
- Family leave: Unmarried couples are often not covered by laws and policies that permit people to take medical leave to care for a sick spouse or for the kids.
- Health: Unlike spouses, unmarried partners are usually not considered next of kin for the purposes of hospital visitation and emergency medical decisions. In addition, they can't cover their families on their health plans without paying taxes on the coverage, nor are they eligible for Medicare and Medicaid coverage.

[9]Evan Thomas, "The War Over Gay Marriage," *Newsweek,* July 7, 2003, p. 38.
[10]Richard Jerome, "State of the Union," *People,* August 18, 2003, p. 100.

- Housing: Denied marriage, couples of lesser means are not recognized as a family and thus can be denied or disfavored in their applications for public housing.

- Immigration: U.S. residency and family unification are not available to an unmarried partner from another country.

- Inheritance: Unmarried surviving partners do not automatically inherit property should their loved one die without a will, nor do they get legal protection for inheritance rights such as elective share or to bypass the hassles and expenses of probate court.

- Insurance: Unmarried partners can't always sign up for joint home and auto insurance. In addition, many employers don't cover domestic partners or their biological or nonbiological children in their health insurance plans.

- Parenting: Unmarried couples are denied the automatic right to joint parenting, joint adoption, joint foster care, and visitation for nonbiological parents. In addition, the children of unmarried couples are denied the guarantee of child support and an automatic legal relationship to both parents, and are sometimes sent a wrongheaded but real negative message about their own status and family.

- Portability: Unlike marriages, which are honored in all states and countries, domestic partnerships and other alternative mechanisms only exist in a few states and countries, are not given any legal acknowledgment in most, and leave families without the clarity and security of knowing what their legal status and rights will be.

- Privilege: Unmarried couples are not shielded against having to testify against each other in judicial proceedings, and are also usually denied the coverage in crime-victims counseling and protection programs afforded married couples.

- Property: Unmarried couples are excluded from special rules that permit married couples to buy and own property together under favorable terms, rules that protect married couples in their shared homes, and rules regarding the distribution of property in the event of death or divorce.

- Retirement: In addition to being denied access to shared or spousal benefits through Social Security as well as coverage under Medicare and other programs, unmarried couples are denied withdrawal rights and protective tax treatment given to spouses with regard to IRAs and other retirement plans.

- Taxes: Unmarried couples cannot file joint tax returns and are excluded from tax benefits and claims specific to marriage. In addition, they are denied the right to transfer property to each other and pool the family's resources without adverse tax consequences.

And, again, virtually all of these critical, concrete legal incidents of marriage cannot be arranged by shelling out money for an attorney or writing up private agreements, even if the couple has lots of forethought to discuss all the issues in advance and then a bunch of extra cash to throw at lawyers.

It's not just same-sex couples who are harmed by society's refusal to respect their personal commitment and human desire for the protections and statement of marriage. Going back to that juvenile quip, "If you love it, why don't you marry it," let me tell you one of my earliest memories of when I realized I was gay.

I am lucky to have a very close and loving family, and grew up living with my parents, sister, and two brothers. One night — I couldn't have been more than eleven or twelve — my mother and I were watching something on TV and talking. Dad was out on his weekly bowling night and the other kids must have already gone off to sleep. I remember saying to my mom, in what must have seemed an out-of-the-blue declaration, "I don't think I'll get married." I don't remember if, or how, my mom responded. But I do remember that I realized I might be excluded from the joys of married life, and felt there was something in the picture society showed me that I didn't fit into, before I could tell my mom or even fully understand that I was gay.

Many gay kids, even before they hear the word *gay* and associate it with themselves, and even before they fully understand how their own lives will take shape, do understand that they are different from their friends. For the most part, of course, gay kids grow up in the nongay world — raised by nongay parents; surrounded by mostly nongay siblings, friends, relatives, and teachers; exposed to nongay images and expectations everywhere, from church, television, and popular music. And yet, until now our society has also sent those kids the message that the dream of romantic love, of commitment, of family, of marriage is not for them. America tells its children that the dream of "first comes love, then comes marriage" is not for you if you're gay.

This is wrong and has to change.

Unlike the members of most other minority groups, we gay people are not usually born into our own identity or community, or into families that share or understand our sense of self; we have to find our way largely on our own, often after working through negative messages about homosexuality, or a lack of understanding from family members, peers, churches, and the other institutions that people rely on for self-identification, solidarity, and support. 40

When I told my mother I didn't think I'd get married, I was not rejecting marriage; I was working out my own sense of difference in a world that said I could not have what marriage signifies — life as a couple with the person you choose, legal recognition, acceptance — given the restrictions placed both on marriage and on people like me.

Again, I was lucky. I never doubted that my parents loved me and would love me, even if and when they found out I was gay. That doesn't mean it was easy for my parents. When, years later, I told them I am gay, it meant there were some differences in the life they imagined for me, differences they in turn had to accept as part of their unconditional love for me.

Even with loving parents and personal self-confidence, as a young child not even knowing the word *gay,* I was led to believe that I had to reject a pattern of life that didn't seem to be available for me with the kind of partner I could truly love, someone of the same sex. In a childish way, I thought it was "marriage" I didn't fit into, when, in fact, the love and commitment marriage signifies were perfectly appropriate dreams for me. It was exclusion, rejection, and the denial of the freedom to marry that were and are unnecessary, harsh, harmful, and wrong.

Notice here that I'm not using terms like "gay marriage" or "same-sex marriage." That's because these terms imply that same-sex couples are asking for rights and privileges that married couples do not have, or for rights that are something lesser or different than what nongay couples have. In fact, we don't want "gay marriage," we want marriage — the same freedom to marry, with the same duties, dignity, security, and expression of love and equality as our nongay brothers and sisters have.

Gay people have the same mix of reasons for wanting the freedom to marry as nongay people: emotional and economic, practical and personal, social and spiritual. The inequities and the legal and cultural second-class status that exclusion from marriage reinforces affect all gay people, but the denial of marriage's safety net falls hardest on the poor, the less educated, and the otherwise vulnerable. And the denial of the freedom to marry undermines young gay people's sense of self and their dreams of a life together with a partner.

Of course our country needs to find ways other than marriage to support and welcome all kids, all families, and all communities. Marriage is not, need not, and should not be the only means of protecting oneself and a loving partner or family. But like other Americans, same-sex couples need the responsibilities and support marriage offers legally and economically to families dealing with parenting, property, Social Security, finances, and the like, especially in times of crisis, health emergency, divorce, and death. And gay people, like all human beings, love and want to declare love, want inclusion in the community and the equal choices and possibilities that belong to us all as Americans.

Marriage equality is the precondition for these rights, these protections, this inclusion, this full citizenship. The freedom to marry is important in building strong families and strong communities. What sense does it make to deny that freedom to Maureen and Cindy, Alicia and Saundra, Tony and Thomas, Chris and Craig, or Julie and Hillary?

How many more young people have to grow up believing that they are alone, that they are not welcome, that they are unequal and second-class, that their society does not value their love or expect them to find permanence and commitment?

How many nongay parents and family members have to worry or feel pain for their gay loved ones? What mother doesn't want the best for all her kids, or want to be able to dance at her lesbian daughter's wedding just as she did at her other child's?

As Americans have done so many times in the past, it's time we learn 50 from our mistakes and acknowledge that lesbian and gay Americans — like people the world around — speak the vocabulary of marriage, live the personal commitment of marriage, do the hard work of marriage, and share the responsibilities we associate with marriage. It's time to allow them the same freedom every other American has — the freedom to marry.

ENGAGING THE TEXT

1. Banning legally recognized marriage for lesbian and gay couples does not mean they are not establishing families and raising children in countless American communities. Why is the formal legal recognition of marriage for same-sex couples a crucial issue for Wolfson? Why is there such strong opposition to his views?

2. Wolfson begins this reading (and thus Chapter One of his book) with an extended definition of marriage (paras. 2–13). Why does he make this his first task, and what are the key elements of his definition? Do you find his definition fair and sensible, or is it somehow slanted, incomplete, or illogical? Explain.

3. Review the examples of real-life couples Wolfson describes in paragraphs 24–34. For each couple, explain why Wolfson chose to include them in his book. How does each example contribute to his argument?

4. Wolfson is writing for a broad audience, but he hasn't set aside his legal expertise. Discuss how both the "content" and the form of "What Is Marriage?" reflect his background in the law.

5. Review how Wolfson uses the court case *Turner v. Safley* (paras. 18–21), which ruled that Missouri could not arbitrarily deny marriage rights to prisoners. What is his rhetorical strategy in this section, and how effective do you judge it? Discuss whether *Turner v. Safley* is relevant to the issue of same-sex marriage.

EXPLORING CONNECTIONS

6. Write or role-play a discussion between Wolfson and Jennifer Roback Morse (p. 81).

7. Re-examine the image of the lesbian brides in the Visual Portfolio (p. 76). How has your own understanding of the image developed through your reading of Wolfson?

EXTENDING THE CRITICAL CONTEXT

8. The Massachusetts Supreme Judicial Court did not reach a unanimous decision in *Goodridge v. Department of Public Health,* the 2003 case that legalized same-sex marriages in Massachusetts. Debate the following two key points made in dissenting opinions:

[The issue of gay marriage] is one deeply rooted in social policy [and the] decision must be made by the Legislature, not the court.

— Dissent filed by JUSTICE ROBERT J. CORDY

It is rational for the Legislature to postpone any redefinition of marriage that would include same-sex couples until such time as it is certain that redefinition will not have unintended and undesirable social consequences.

— Dissent filed by JUSTICE MARTHA B. SOSMAN

How do you think Wolfson might respond to these arguments?

9. Research and report on the status of same-sex marriage and civil unions in your state. Start by finding out what the law currently says; to extend the research you may wish to learn about relevant court cases, proposed legislation, ballot measures, and political action on either side of the debate.

10. Throughout this chapter, families have been portrayed through a variety of metaphors: they have appeared as a nuclear unit, a family tree, a network of relationships, and a quilt with many parts. What are the implications of each of these metaphors? How do they affect our view of family? What other metaphors might capture your vision of American family life?

My Big Fat Straight Wedding

ANDREW SULLIVAN

The most surprising thing about Andrew Sullivan's same-sex wedding was its normalcy: in the attendant rituals, emotions, and conversations, Sullivan found himself to be just like his heterosexual friends and family. Sullivan (b. 1963) is among the nation's most accomplished journalists and editors, having written for such publications as the Wall Street Journal, *the* Washington Post, Esquire, *and in particular* The New Republic, *where he was editor for more than 250 issues of the magazine in the 1990s. He is author of* Virtually Normal: An Argument about Homosexuality *(1995) and* Love Undetectable: Notes on Friendship, Sex, and Survival *(1998). Sullivan is currently a senior editor at* The Atlantic; *the following selection appeared in that magazine in September 2008.*

What if gays were straight?

The question is absurd — gays are defined as not straight, right? — yet increasingly central to the debate over civil-marriage rights. Here is how

California's Supreme Court put it in a key passage in its now-famous May 15 ruling that gay couples in California must be granted the right to marry, with no qualifications or euphemisms:

> These core substantive rights include, most fundamentally, the opportunity of an individual to establish — with the person with whom the individual has chosen to share his or her life — an *officially recognized and protected family* possessing mutual rights and responsibilities and entitled to the same respect and dignity accorded a union traditionally designated as marriage.

What's notable here is the starting point of the discussion: an "individual." The individual citizen posited by the court is defined as prior to his or her sexual orientation. He or she exists as a person before he or she exists as straight or gay. And the right under discussion is defined as "the opportunity of an individual" to choose another "person" to "establish a family" in which reproduction and children are not necessary. And so the distinction between gay and straight is essentially abolished. For all the debate about the law in this decision, the debate about the terms under discussion has been close to nonexistent. And yet in many ways, these terms are at the core of the decision, and are the reason why it is such a watershed. The ruling, and the language it uses, represents the removal of the premise of the last generation in favor of a premise accepted as a given by the next.

The premise used to be that homosexuality was an activity, that gays were people who chose to behave badly; or, if they weren't choosing to behave badly, were nonetheless suffering from a form of sickness or, in the words of the Vatican, an "objective disorder." And so the question of whether to permit the acts and activities of such disordered individuals was a legitimate area of legislation and regulation.

But when gays are seen as the same as straights — as individuals; as   5
normal, well-adjusted, human individuals — the argument changes altogether. The question becomes a matter of how we treat a minority with an involuntary, defining characteristic along the lines of gender or race. And when a generation came of age that did not merely grasp this intellectually, but knew it from their own lives and friends and family members, then the logic for full equality became irresistible.

This transformation in understanding happened organically. It began with the sexual revolution in the 1970s, and then came crashing into countless previously unaware families, as their sons and uncles and fathers died in vast numbers from AIDS in the 1980s and 1990s. It emerged as younger generations came out earlier and earlier, and as their peers came to see gay people as fellows and siblings, rather than as denizens of some distant and alien subculture. It happened as lesbian couples became parents and as gay soldiers challenged the discrimination against them. And it percolated up through the popular culture — from *Will & Grace* and *Ellen* to almost every reality show since *The Real World*.

What California's court did, then, was not to recognize a new right to same-sex marriage. It was to acknowledge an emergent cultural consensus. And once that consensus had been accepted, the denial of the right to marry became, for many, a constitutional outrage. The right to marry, after all, is, as the court put it, "one of the basic, inalienable civil rights guaranteed to an individual." Its denial was necessarily an outrage — and not merely an anomaly — because the right to marry has such deep and inalienable status in American constitutional law.

The political theorist Hannah Arendt, addressing the debate over miscegenation laws during the civil-rights movement of the 1950s, put it clearly enough:

> The right to marry whoever one wishes is an elementary human right compared to which 'the right to attend an integrated school, the right to sit where one pleases on a bus, the right to go into any hotel or recreation area or place of amusement, regardless of one's skin or color or race' are minor indeed. Even political rights, like the right to vote, and nearly all other rights enumerated in the Constitution, are secondary to the inalienable human rights to 'life, liberty and the pursuit of happiness' proclaimed in the Declaration of Independence; and to this category the right to home and marriage unquestionably belongs.

Note that Arendt put the right to marry before even the right to vote. And this is how many gay people of the next generation see it. Born into straight families and reared to see homosexuality as a form of difference, not disability, they naturally wonder why they would be excluded from the integral institution of their own families' lives and history. They see this exclusion as unimaginable — as unimaginable as straight people would if they were told that they could not legally marry someone of their choosing. No other institution has an equivalent power to include people in their own familial narrative or civic history as deeply or as powerfully as civil marriage does. And the next generation see themselves as people first and gay second.

Born in a different era, I reached that conclusion through more pain   10
and fear and self-loathing than my twenty-something fellow homosexuals do today. But it was always clear to me nonetheless. It just never fully came home to me until I too got married.

It happened first when we told our families and friends of our intentions. Suddenly, they had a vocabulary to describe and understand our relationship. I was no longer my partner's "friend" or "boyfriend"; I was his fiancé. Suddenly, everyone involved themselves in our love. They asked how I had proposed; they inquired when the wedding would be; my straight friends made jokes about marriage that simply included me as one of them. At that first post-engagement Christmas with my in-laws, I felt something shift. They had always been welcoming and supportive. But now I was family. I felt an end —

a sudden, fateful end — to an emotional displacement I had experienced since childhood.

The wedding occurred last August in Massachusetts in front of a small group of family and close friends. And in that group, I suddenly realized, it was the heterosexuals who knew what to do, who guided the gay couple and our friends into the rituals and rites of family. Ours was not, we realized, a different institution, after all, and we were not different kinds of people. In the doing of it, it was the same as my sister's wedding and we were the same as my sister and brother-in-law. The strange, bewildering emotions of the moment, the cake and reception, the distracted children and weeping mothers, the morning's butterflies and the night's drunkenness: this was not a gay marriage; it was a marriage.

And our families instantly and for the first time since our early childhood became not just institutions in which we were included, but institutions that we too owned and perpetuated. My sister spoke of her marriage as if it were interchangeable with my own, and my niece and nephew had no qualms in referring to my husband as their new uncle. The embossed invitations and the floral bouquets and the fear of fluffing our vows: in these tiny, bonding gestures of integration, we all came to see an alienating distinction become a unifying difference.

It was a moment that shifted a sense of our own identity within our psyches and even our souls. Once this happens, the law eventually follows. In California this spring, it did.

Engaging the Text

1. Sullivan writes that views of gays have evolved since the 1970s so that they are seen not as "denizens of some distant and alien subculture" (para. 6) but as "normal, well-adjusted, human individuals" (para. 5). To what does he attribute this transformation, and do you see evidence of it in your family, school, church, or community? Similarly, do you see evidence of the generational shift in views of homosexuality that Sullivan describes in paragraphs 5 and 6?

2. "My Big Fat Straight Wedding" is both a personal essay and an argument. Analyze the mix of personal and argumentative writing and assess how well they fit together in this essay. Stated in your own words, what is Sullivan's thesis?

3. Sullivan celebrates the May 2008 court decision that temporarily legalized same-sex marriage in California. In November of that year, however, Proposition 8 (p. 79) changed California's Constitution and restricted marriage to a union "between a man and a woman." Does this turn of events overthrow or substantially weaken Sullivan's claims in this essay? Explain.

4. The California Supreme Court called the right to marry "one of the basic, inalienable civil rights guaranteed to an individual" (para. 7). If this statement is taken as true, can the right to marry be limited by law? Would

an inalienable civil right to marry imply a right to marry multiple partners?

Exploring Connections

5. How does Sullivan use the quotation from Hannah Arendt to position same-sex marriage? How does his definition of the institution clash with Morse's in "8 Is Not Hate" (p. 81)?

6. Evan Wolfson, author of "What Is Marriage?" (p. 89), and Andrew Sullivan are on the same side of the marriage-equality debate, but Sullivan's approach here is much more personal, less analytical and argumentative, than Wolfson's. Which reading do you find more persuasive, and which approach do you think is more likely to sway public opinion nationally?

Extending the Critical Context

7. Write a journal entry or personal essay about a time you found yourself in a new relationship to friends and family, or about a time when you strongly felt their support.

8. If you know someone living in a civil union, domestic partnership, or similar same-sex relationship, interview her or him about the differences between full civil marriage and his or her situation. Write up your observations about the importance or unimportance of marriage equality to your interviewee.

9. Stephanie Coontz, a writer whose work appears earlier in this chapter (p. 32), is also an editor of *American Families: A Multicultural Reader*, which contains nearly three dozen scholarly articles about the family. Write a short research paper, using *American Families* to help define a topic and to provide your first sources.

FURTHER CONNECTIONS

1. Family relationships are a frequent subject for novels and films, perhaps because these extended forms can take the time to explore the complexities of family dynamics. Making substantial use of at least one reading in this chapter, write an essay analyzing the portrayal of family in a single novel or film.

2. Writers and analysts routinely use data from the U.S. Census Bureau to get a "snapshot" of the American population as a whole or to track national trends over time. However, the bureau also provides a wealth of information at the state and county levels. Choose two counties in your state that you think are substantially different demographically; explore the Census Bureau Web site (www.census.gov) and gather statistical data on items like size of households, their median income, the number of households headed by women, and so on. Report your findings to the class, or collaborate with classmates to build an overview of your state.

3. Tolstoy wrote that all happy families are alike, but that each unhappy family is unhappy in its own way. Taking into account your own experience and the readings in this chapter, write a journal entry or an essay articulating your views of what makes families happy or unhappy, and assessing your own experiences of family up to this point in your life.

2

Learning Power

The Myth of Education and Empowerment

Skeptical Student, photo by Charles Agel.

FAST FACTS

1. The median annual earnings of workers with a high school diploma, a bachelor's degree, and an advanced degree in 2007 were, respectively, $26,712, $46,277, and $61,014.

2. Students who do not complete high school can expect to earn $19,089 per year and have a 15.5% unemployment rate.

3. Only 71% of U.S. students earn a high school diploma, with fewer than six in ten minority students graduating with their peers.

4. Nearly 40% of all African American students nationwide attend "apartheid schools" — institutions that have virtually no white student populations.

5. The percentage of white, Asian, Mexican American, and African American college students who graduate in four years or less is, respectively, 37.6%, 38.8%, 21.3%, and 28.9%.

6. In 2007, American eighth graders ranked in the top 10 in terms of mathematics achievement, coming in behind their peers in Chinese Taipei, Republic of Korea, Singapore, Hong Kong SAR, and Japan.

Sources: (1) U.S. Census Bureau; (2) U.S. Census Bureau and U.S. Bureau of Labor Statistics; (3) The Bill and Melinda Gates Foundation; (4) The Civil Rights Project/Proyecto Derechos Civiles at UCLA; (5) UCLA Higher Education Research Institute; (6) National Center for Education Statistics.

Broke out of Chester gaol,[1] last night, one James Rockett, a very short well set fellow, pretends to be a schoolmaster, of a fair complexion, and smooth fac'd; Had on when he went away, a light colored camblet coat, a blue cloth jacket, without sleeves, a check shirt, a pair of old dy'd leather breaches, gray worsted stockings, a pair of half worn pumps, and an almost new beaver hat; his hair is cut off, and wears a cap; he is a great taker of snuff, and very apt to get drunk; he has with him two certificates, one from some inhabitants in Burlington county, Jersey, which he will no doubt produce as a pass. Who ever takes up and secures said Rockett in any gaol, shall have two Pistoles reward, paid by October 27, 1756. — SAMUEL SMITH, Gaoler

> — Advertisement for a "runaway schoolmaster"
> *Pennsylvania Gazette*, November 25, 1756

[1]*gaol:* Jail.

AMERICANS HAVE ALWAYS HAD mixed feelings about schooling. Today, most Americans tend to see education as something intrinsically valuable or important. After all, education is the engine that drives the American Dream. The chance to learn, better oneself, and gain the skills that pay off in upward mobility has sustained the hope of millions of Americans. As a nation we look up to figures like Abraham Lincoln and Frederick Douglass, who learned to see beyond poverty and slavery by learning to read. Education tells us that the American Dream can work for everyone. It reassures us that we are, in fact, "created equal" and that the path to achievement lies through individual effort and hard work, not blind luck or birth.

But as the advertisement quoted above suggests, American attitudes toward teachers and teaching haven't always been overwhelmingly positive. The Puritans who established the Massachusetts Bay Colony viewed education with respectful skepticism. Schooling in Puritan society was a force for spiritual rather than worldly advancement. Lessons were designed to reinforce moral and religious training and to teach children to read the Bible for themselves. Education was important to the Puritan "Divines" because it was a source of order, control, and discipline. But when education aimed at more worldly goals or was undertaken for self-improvement, it was seen as a menacing, sinful luxury. Little wonder, then, that the Puritans often viewed teaching as something less than an ennobling profession. In fact, teachers in the early colonies were commonly treated as menial employees by the families and communities they served. The following list of the "Duties of a Schoolmaster" gives you some idea of the status of American educators in the year 1661:

1. Act as court-messenger
2. Serve summonses
3. Conduct certain ceremonial church services
4. Lead Sunday choir
5. Ring bell for public worship
6. Dig graves
7. Take charge of school
8. Perform other occasional duties

Colonial American teachers were frequently indentured servants who had sold themselves for five to ten years, often for the price of passage to the New World. Once here, they drilled their masters' children in spiritual exercises until they earned their freedom — or escaped.

The reputation of education in America began to improve with the onset of the Revolutionary War. Following the overthrow of British rule, leaders sought to create a spirit of nationalism that would unify the former colonies. Differences were to be set aside, for, as George Washington pointed out, "the more homogeneous our citizens can be made ... the greater will be our prospect of permanent union." The goal of schooling became the creation of uniformly loyal, patriotic Americans. In the words of Benjamin Rush, one of the signers of the Declaration of Independence, "Our schools of learning, by producing one general and uniform system of education, will render the mass of people more homogeneous and thereby fit them more easily for uniform and peaceable government."

Thomas Jefferson saw school as a training ground for citizenship and democratic leadership. Recognizing that an illiterate and ill-informed population would be unable to assume the responsibilities of self-government, Jefferson laid out a comprehensive plan in 1781 for public education in the state of Virginia. According to Jefferson's blueprint, all children would be eligible for three years of free public instruction. Of those who could not afford further schooling, one promising "genius" from each school was to be "raked from the rubbish" and given six more years of free education. At the end of that time, ten boys would be selected to attend college at public expense. Jeffersonian Virginia may have been the first place in the United States where education so clearly offered the penniless boy a path to self-improvement. However, this path was open to very few, and Jefferson, like Washington and Rush, was more concerned with benefiting the state than serving the individual student: "We hope to avail the state of those talents which nature has sown as liberally among the poor as the rich, but which perish without use, if not sought for and cultivated." For leaders of the American Revolution, education was seen as a tool for nation-building, not personal development.

Perhaps that's why Native American leaders remained lukewarm to the idea of formal education despite its growing popularity with their colonial neighbors. When, according to Ben Franklin's report, the government of Virginia offered to provide six American Indian youths with the best college education it could afford in 1744, the tribal leaders of the Six Nations politely declined, pointing out that

> our ideas of this kind of education happen not to be the same with yours. We have had some experience of it; several of our young people were formerly brought up at the colleges of the northern provinces; they were instructed in all your sciences; but when they came back to us, they were bad runners; ignorant of every means of living in the woods; unable to bear either cold or hunger; knew neither how to build a cabin, take a deer, or kill an enemy; spoke our language imperfectly; were therefore neither fit for hunters, warriors, or counselors: they were totally good for nothing.

It's not surprising that these tribal leaders saw American education as useless. Education works to socialize young people — to teach them the values, beliefs, and skills central to their society; the same schooling that prepared students for life in Anglo-American culture made them singularly unfit for tribal life. As people who stood outside the dominant society, Native Americans were quick to realize education's potential as a tool for enforcing cultural conformity. But despite their resistance, by the 1880s the U.S. government had established special "Indian schools" dedicated to assimilating Indian children into Anglo-American culture and destroying tribal knowledge and tribal ways.

In the nineteenth century two great historical forces — industrialization and immigration — combined to exert even greater pressure for the "homogenization" of young Americans. Massive immigration from Ireland and Eastern and Central Europe led to fears that "non-native" peoples would undermine the cultural identity of the United States. Many saw school as the first line of defense against this perceived threat, a place where the children of "foreigners" could become Americanized. In a meeting of educators in 1836, one college professor stated the problem as bluntly as possible:

> Let us now be reminded, that unless we educate our immigrants, they will be our ruin. It is no longer a mere question of benevolence, of duty, or of enlightened self-interest, but the intellectual and religious training of our foreign population has become essential to our own safety; we are prompted to it by the instinct of self-preservation.

Industrialization gave rise to another kind of uniformity in nineteenth-century public education. Factory work didn't require the kind of educational preparation needed to transform a child into a craftsman or merchant. So, for the first time in American history, school systems began to categorize students into different educational "tracks" that offered qualitatively different kinds of education to different groups. Some — typically students from well-to-do homes — were prepared for professional and managerial positions. But most were consigned to education for life "on the line." Increasing demand for factory workers put a premium on young people who were obedient and able to work in large groups according to fixed schedules. As a result, leading educators in 1874 proposed a system of schooling that would meet the needs of the "modern industrial community" by stressing "punctuality, regularity, attention, and silence, as habits necessary through life." History complicates the myth of education as a source of personal empowerment. School can bind as effectively as it can liberate; it can enforce conformity and limit life chances as well as foster individual talent.

But history also supplies examples of education serving the idealistic goals of democracy, equality, and self-improvement. Nineteenth-century educator and reformer Horace Mann worked to expand educational opportunity to all Americans. Mann believed that genuine democratic self-government would become a reality only if every citizen were sufficiently educated to make reasoned judgments about even the thorniest public issues. "Education," according to Mann, "must prepare our citizens to become municipal officers, intelligent jurors, honest witnesses, legislators, or competent judges of legislation — in fine, to fill all the manifold relations of life." In Mann's conception, the "common school," offering educational opportunity to anyone with the will to learn, would make good on the central promise of American democracy; it would become "the great equalizer of the conditions of men."

At the turn of the century, philosopher and educational theorist John Dewey made even greater claims for educational empowerment. A fierce opponent of the kind of "tracking" associated with industrial education, Dewey proposed that schools should strive to produce thinking citizens rather than obedient workers. As members of a democracy, all men and women, according to Dewey, are entitled to an education that helps them make the best of their natural talents and enables them to participate as fully as possible in the life of their community: "only by being true to the full growth of the individuals who make it up, can society by any chance be true to itself." Most of our current myths of education echo the optimism of Mann and Dewey. Guided by their ideas, most Americans still believe that education leads to self-improvement and can help us empower ourselves — and perhaps even transform our society.

Does education empower us? Or does it stifle personal growth by squeezing us into prefabricated cultural molds? This chapter takes a critical look at American education: what it can do and how it shapes or enhances our identities. The first set of readings provides a starting point for exploring the myth of educational empowerment. We begin with a classic statement of the goals of American education — Horace Mann's 1848 "Report of the Massachusetts Board of Education." Mann's optimistic view of education as a means of social mobility in a democratic state provides a clear statement of the myth of personal empowerment through education. For a quick update on where we stand a century and a half later, we turn to documentary filmmaker Michael Moore's scathing assessment of the current state of American education in "Idiot Nation."

Next, in "Against School," veteran teacher and libertarian John Taylor Gatto offers his own provocative analysis of how public education "cripples our kids." In "'I Just Wanna Be Average,'" Mike Rose provides a moving personal account of the dream of educational success and pays tribute to an inner-city teacher who never loses sight of what can be achieved in a classroom. An excerpt from Jean Anyon's "Social Class and the Hidden Curriculum of Work" rounds off the section by suggesting that schools virtually program students for success or failure according to their socioeconomic status.

Following these initial readings, the chapter's Visual Portfolio presents three paintings by Norman Rockwell that reflect some of America's most hallowed cultural memories of the classroom experience. The reproductions include *The Spirit of Education, The Graduate,* and Rockwell's famous civil-rights-movement portrait of Ruby Bridges as she was escorted to the schoolhouse door. They offer you the chance to consider the place of education in America's cultural mythology and to imagine how a contemporary artist might update the story of educational success for the twenty-first century.

The next group of readings offers a closer look at the tensions experienced by so-called nontraditional students as they struggle with the complexities — and prejudices — of a deeply traditional educational system. The section begins with a classic autobiographical selection by Richard Rodriguez, which raises questions about the ambivalent role schooling plays in the lives of many Americans who come from families new to the world of higher education. In her dramatic narrative poem "Para Teresa," Inés Hernández-Ávila asks whether academic achievement demands cultural conformity or whether it can become a form of protest against oppression and racism. "Learning to Read" closes the section with the moving story of Malcolm X's spiritual and political rebirth through his self-made and highly untraditional education in prison.

We end our examination of American education with two readings that raise questions about the current state of education in the United States. In "Still Separate, Still Unequal," education activist Jonathan Kozol issues a stern warning about the "resegregation" of schools across the nation and the negative impact of recent education reforms. The anonymous "Professor X" closes the chapter by challenging us to consider whether higher education really does more harm than good for students who find themselves "In the Basement of the Ivory Tower."

Sources

Best, John Hardin, and Robert T. Sidwell, eds. *The American Legacy of Learning: Readings in the History of Education.* Philadelphia: J. B. Lippincott Co., 1966. Print.

Cohen, Sol, ed. *Education in the United States: A Documentary History.* 5 vols. New York: Random House, 1974. Print.

Dewey, John. "The School and Society" (1899) and "My Pedagogic Creed" (1897). *John Dewey on Education.* New York: Modern Library, 1964. Print.

Franklin, Benjamin. "Remarks Concerning the Savages of North America." *The Works of Dr. Benjamin Franklin.* Hartford: S. Andrus and Son, 1849. Print.

Jefferson, Thomas. *Notes on the State of Virginia.* Chapel Hill: University of North Carolina Press, 1955. Print.

Pangle, Lorraine Smith and Thomas L. *The Learning of Liberty: The Educational Ideas of the American Founders.* Lawrence: University Press of Kansas, 1993. Print.

Pitt, Leonard. *We Americans.* 3rd ed. Vol. 2. Dubuque: Kendall/Hunt, 1987. Print.

Stevens, Edward, and George H. Wood. *Justice, Ideology, and Education: An Introduction to the Social Foundations of Education.* New York: Random House, 1987. Print.

Vallance, Elizabeth. "Hiding the Hidden Curriculum: An Interpretation of the Language of Justification in Nineteenth-Century Educational Reform." *Curriculum Theory Network*, Vol. 4. No. 1. Toronto: Ontario Institute for Studies in Education, 1973–1974. 5–21. Print.

Westbrook, Robert B. "Public Schooling and American Democracy." *Democracy, Education, and the Schools.* Ed. Roger Soder. San Francisco: Jossey-Bass Publishers, 1996. Print.

BEFORE READING

- Freewrite for fifteen or twenty minutes about your best and worst educational experiences. Then, working in groups, compare notes to see if you can find recurring themes or ideas in what you've written. What aspects of school seem to stand out most clearly in your memories? Do the best experiences have anything in common? How about the worst? What aspects of your school experience didn't show up in the freewriting?

- Work in small groups to draw a collective picture that expresses your experience of high school or college. Don't worry about your drawing skill — just load the page with imagery, feelings, and ideas. Then show your work to other class members and let them try to interpret it.

- Write a journal entry from the point of view of the girl pictured on the title page of this chapter (p. 109). Try to capture the thoughts that are going through her head. What has her day in school been like? What is she looking forward to? What is she dreading? Share your entries with your classmates and discuss your responses.

From *Report of the Massachusetts Board of Education, 1848*

HORACE MANN

If you check a list of schools in your home state, you'll probably discover at least a few dedicated to the memory of Horace Mann. We memorialize Mann today in school systems across the country because he may have done more than any other American to codify the myth of empowerment through education. Born on a farm in Franklin, Massachusetts, in 1796, Mann raised himself out of rural poverty to a position of national eminence through hard work and study. His first personal educational experiences, however, were far from pleasurable: the ill-trained and often brutal school-masters he first encountered in rural Massachusetts made rote memoriza-tion and the power of the rod the focus of their educational approach. After graduating from Brown University in 1819, Mann pursued a career in law and politics and eventually served as president of the Massachusetts State Senate. Discouraged by the condition of the state's public schools, Mann abandoned his political career to become secretary of the Massachusetts Board of Education in 1837. Mann's vision of "the common school," the centerpiece of his approach to democratic education, grew out of research he conducted on the Prussian school system during his tour of Europe in 1843. Presented originally as an address to the Massachusetts State Legisla-ture, the report of 1848 has had a lasting impact on the goals and content of American education.

Without undervaluing any other human agency, it may be safely affirmed that the common school, improved and energized as it can easily be, may become the most effective and benignant of all the forces of civiliza-tion. Two reasons sustain this position. In the first place, there is a universal-ity in its operation, which can be affirmed of no other institution whatever. If administered in the spirit of justice and conciliation, all the rising generation may be brought within the circle of its reformatory and elevating influences. And, in the second place, the materials upon which it operates are so pliant and ductile as to be susceptible of assuming a greater variety of forms than any other earthly work of the Creator. The inflexibility and ruggedness of the oak, when compared with the lithe sapling or the tender germ, are but feeble emblems to typify the docility of childhood when contrasted with the obdu-racy and intractableness of man. It is these inherent advantages of the com-mon school, which, in our own State, have produced results so striking, from a system so imperfect, and an administration so feeble. In teaching the blind and the deaf and dumb, in kindling the latent spark of intelligence that lurks in an idiot's mind, and in the more holy work of reforming abandoned and outcast children, education has proved what it can do by glorious experi-ments. These wonders it has done in its infancy, and with the lights of a limited experience; but when its faculties shall be fully developed, when it shall be trained to wield its mighty energies for the protection of society against the giant vices which now invade and torment it, — against intem-perance, avarice, war, slavery, bigotry, the woes of want, and the wicked-ness of waste, — then there will not be a height to which these enemies of the race can escape which it will not scale, nor a Titan among them all whom it will not slay.

I proceed, then, in endeavoring to show how the true business of the schoolroom connects itself, and becomes identical, with the great interests of society. The former is the infant, immature state of those interests; the latter their developed, adult state. As "the child is father to the man," so may the training of the schoolroom expand into the institutions and fortunes of the State.

Physical Education

In the worldly prosperity of mankind, health and strength are indispensable ingredients. . . .

Leaving out, then, for the present purpose, all consideration of the pains of sickness and the anguish of bereavement, the momentous truth still remains, that sickness and premature death are positive evils for the statesman and political economist to cope with. The earth, as a hospital for the diseased, would soon wear out the love of life; and, if but the half of mankind were sick, famine, from non-production, would speedily threaten the whole.

Now, modern science has made nothing more certain than that both good and ill health are the direct result of causes mainly within our own control. In other words, the health of the race is dependent upon the conduct of the race. The health of the individual is determined primarily by his parents, secondarily by himself. The vigorous growth of the body, its strength and its activity, its powers of endurance, and its length of life, on the one hand; and dwarfishness, sluggishness, infirmity, and premature death on the other, — are all the subjects of unchangeable laws. These laws are ordained of God; but the knowledge of them is left to our diligence, and the observance of them to our free agency. . . .

My general conclusion, then, under this head, is, that it is the duty of all the governing minds in society — whether in office or out of it — to diffuse a knowledge of these beautiful and beneficent laws of health and life throughout the length and breadth of the State; to popularize them; to make them, in the first place, the common acquisition of all, and, through education and custom, the common inheritance of all, so that the healthful habits naturally growing out of their observance shall be inbred in the people, exemplified in the personal regimen of each individual, incorporated into the economy of every household, observable in all private dwellings, and in all public edifices, especially in those buildings which are erected by capitalists for the residence of their work-people, or for renting to the poorer classes; obeyed, by supplying cities with pure water; by providing public baths, public walks, and public squares; by rural cemeteries; by the drainage and sewerage of populous towns, and by whatever else may promote the general salubrity of the atmosphere: in fine, by a religious observance of all those sanitary regulations with which modern science has blessed the world.

For this thorough diffusion of sanitary intelligence, the common school is the only agency. It is, however, an adequate agency. . . .

Intellectual Education as a Means of Removing Poverty, and Securing Abundance

. . . According to the European theory, men are divided into classes, — some to toil and earn, others to seize and enjoy. According to the Massachusetts theory, all are to have an equal chance for earning, and equal security in the enjoyment of what they earn. The latter tends to equality of condition; the former, to the grossest inequalities. . . .

But is it not true that Massachusetts, in some respects, instead of adhering more and more closely to her own theory, is becoming emulous of the baneful examples of Europe? The distance between the two extremes of society is lengthening, instead of being abridged. With every generation, fortunes increase on the one hand, and some new privation is added to poverty on the other. We are verging towards those extremes of opulence and of penury, each of which unhumanizes the human mind. A perpetual struggle for the bare necessaries of life, without the ability to obtain them, makes men wolfish. Avarice, on the other hand, sees, in all the victims of misery around it, not objects for pity and succor, but only crude materials to be worked up into more money.

I suppose it to be the universal sentiment of all those who mingle any   10
ingredient of benevolence with their notions on political economy, that vast and overshadowing private fortunes are among the greatest dangers to which the happiness of the people in a republic can be subjected. Such fortunes would create a feudalism of a new kind, but one more oppressive and unrelenting than that of the middle ages. The feudal lords in England and on the Continent never held their retainers in a more abject condition of servitude than the great majority of foreign manufacturers and capitalists hold their operatives and laborers at the present day. The means employed are different; but the similarity in results is striking. What force did then, money does now. The villein of the middle ages had no spot of earth on which he could live, unless one were granted to him by his lord. The operative or laborer of the present day has no employment, and therefore no bread, unless the capitalist will accept his services. The vassal had no shelter but such as his master provided for him. Not one in five thousand of English operatives or farm-laborers is able to build or own even a hovel; and therefore they must accept such shelter as capital offers them. The baron prescribed his own terms to his retainers: those terms were peremptory, and the serf must submit or perish. The British manufacturer or farmer prescribes the rate of wages he will give to his work-people; he reduces these wages under whatever pretext he pleases; and they, too, have no alternative but submission or starvation. In some respects, indeed, the condition of the modern dependant is more forlorn than that of the

corresponding serf class in former times. Some attributes of the patriarchal relation did spring up between the lord and his lieges to soften the harsh relations subsisting between them. Hence came some oversight of the condition of children, some relief in sickness, some protection and support in the decrepitude of age. But only in instances comparatively few have kindly offices smoothed the rugged relation between British capital and British labor. The children of the work-people are abandoned to their fate; and notwithstanding the privations they suffer, and the dangers they threaten, no power in the realm has yet been able to secure them an education; and when the adult laborer is prostrated by sickness, or eventually worn out by toil and age, the poorhouse, which has all along been his destination, becomes his destiny. . . .

Now, surely nothing but universal education can counterwork this tendency to the domination of capital and servility of labor. If one class possesses all the wealth and the education, while the residue of society is ignorant and poor, it matters not by what name the relation between them may be called: the latter, in fact and in truth, will be the servile dependants and subjects of the former. But, if education be equably diffused, it will draw property after it by the strongest of all attractions, for such a thing never did happen, and never can happen, as that an intelligent and practical body of men should be permanently poor. Property and labor in different classes are essentially antagonistic; but property and labor in the same class are essentially fraternal. The people of Massachusetts have, in some degree, appreciated the truth, that the unexampled prosperity of the State — its comfort, its competence, its general intelligence and virtue — is attributable to the education, more or less perfect, which all its people have received: but are they sensible of a fact equally important; namely, that it is to this same education that two-thirds of the people are indebted for not being today the vassals of as severe a tyranny, in the form of capital, as the lower classes of Europe are bound to in the form of brute force?

Education, then, beyond all other devices of human origin, is the great equalizer of the conditions of men, — the balance-wheel of the social machinery. I do not here mean that it so elevates the moral nature as to make men disdain and abhor the oppression of their fellow-men. This idea pertains to another of its attributes. But I mean that it gives each man the independence and the means by which he can resist the selfishness of other men. It does better than to disarm the poor of their hostility towards the rich: it prevents being poor. Agrarianism is the revenge of poverty against wealth. The wanton destruction of the property of others — the burning of hay-ricks and corn-ricks, the demolition of machinery because it supersedes hand-labor, the sprinkling of vitriol on rich dresses — is only agrarianism run mad. Education prevents both the revenge and the madness. On the other hand, a fellow-feeling for one's class or caste is the common instinct of hearts not wholly sunk in selfish regards for person or for family. The spread of education, by enlarging the cultivated class or caste, will open a wider area over which the social feelings will expand; and, if this education should be universal and complete, it would do more than all things else to obliterate factitious distinctions in society. . . .

For the creation of wealth, then, — for the existence of a wealthy people and a wealthy nation, — intelligence is the grand condition. The number of improvers will increase as the intellectual constituency, if I may call it, increases. In former times, and in most parts of the world even at the present day, not one man in a million has ever had such a development of mind as made it possible for him to become a contributor to art or science. Let this development precede, and contributions, numberless, and of inestimable value, will be sure to follow. That political economy, therefore, which busies itself about capital and labor, supply and demand, interest and rents, favorable and unfavorable balances of trade, but leaves out of account the element of a widespread mental development, is nought but stupendous folly. The greatest of all the arts in political economy is to change a consumer into a producer; and the next greatest is to increase the producer's producing power, — an end to be directly attained by increasing his intelligence. For mere delving, an ignorant man is but little better than a swine, whom he so much resembles in his appetites, and surpasses in his powers of mischief. . . .

Political Education

The necessity of general intelligence, — that is, of education (for I use the terms as substantially synonymous, because general intelligence can never exist without general education, and general education will be sure to produce general intelligence), — the necessity of general intelligence under a republican form of government, like most other very important truths, has become a very trite one. It is so trite, indeed, as to have lost much of its force by its familiarity. Almost all the champions of education seize upon this argument first of all, because it is so simple as to be understood by the ignorant, and so strong as to convince the sceptical. Nothing would be easier than to follow in the train of so many writers, and to demonstrate by logic, by history, and by the nature of the case, that a republican form of government, without intelligence in the people, must be, on a vast scale, what a madhouse, without superintendent or keepers, would be on a small one, — the despotism of a few succeeded by universal anarchy, and anarchy by despotism, with no change but from bad to worse. . . .

However elevated the moral character of a constituency may be, however well informed in matters of general science or history, yet they must, if citizens of a republic, understand something of the true nature and functions of the government under which they live. That any one, who is to participate in the government of a country when he becomes a man, should receive no

15

instruction respecting the nature and functions of the government he is afterwards to administer, is a political solecism. In all nations, hardly excepting the most rude and barbarous, the future sovereign receives some training which is supposed to fit him for the exercise of the powers and duties of his anticipated station. Where, by force of law, the government devolves upon the heir while yet in a state of legal infancy, some regency, or other substitute, is appointed to act in his stead until his arrival at mature age; and, in the mean time, he is subjected to such a course of study and discipline as will tend to prepare him, according to the political theory of the time and the place, to assume the reins of authority at the appointed age. If in England, or in the most enlightened European monarchies, it would be a proof of restored barbarism to permit the future sovereign to grow up without any knowledge of his duties, — and who can doubt that it would be such a proof? — then, surely, it would be not less a proof of restored or of never-removed barbarism amongst us to empower any individual to use the elective franchise without preparing him for so momentous a trust. Hence the Constitution of the United States, and of our own State, should be made a study in our public schools. The partition of the powers of government into the three co-ordinate branches, — legislative, judicial, and executive — with the duties appropriately devolving upon each; the mode of electing or of appointing all officers, with the reasons on which it was founded; and, especially, the duty of every citizen, in a government of laws, to appeal to the courts for redress in all cases of alleged wrong, instead of undertaking to vindicate his own rights by his own arm; and, in a government where the people are the acknowledged sources of power, the duty of changing laws and rulers by an appeal to the ballot, and not by rebellion, — should be taught to all the children until they are fully understood.

Had the obligations of the future citizen been sedulously inculcated upon all the children of this Republic, would the patriot have had to mourn over so many instances where the voter, not being able to accomplish his purpose by voting, has proceeded to accomplish it by violence; where, agreeing with his fellow-citizens to use the machinery of the ballot, he makes a tacit reservation, that, if that machinery does not move according to his pleasure, he will wrest or break it? If the responsibleness and value of the elective franchise were duly appreciated, the day of our state and national elections would be among the most solemn and religious days in the calendar. Men would approach them, not only with preparation and solicitude, but with the sobriety and solemnity with which discreet and religious-minded men meet the great crises of life. No man would throw away his vote through caprice or wantonness, any more than he would throw away his estate, or sell his family into bondage. No man would cast his vote through malice or revenge, any more than a good surgeon would amputate a limb, or a good navigator sail through perilous straits, under the same criminal passions.

But perhaps it will be objected, that the Constitution is subject to different readings, or that the policy of different administrations has become the subject of party strife; and, therefore, if any thing of constitutional or political law is introduced into our schools, there is danger that teachers will be chosen on account of their affinities to this or that political party, or that teachers will feign affinities which they do not feel in order that they may be chosen; and so each schoolroom will at length become a miniature political club-room, exploding with political resolves, or flaming out with political addresses, prepared by beardless boys in scarcely legible hand-writing and in worse grammar.

With the most limited exercise of discretion, all apprehensions of this kind are wholly groundless. There are different readings of the Constitution, it is true; and there are partisan topics which agitate the country from side to side: but the controverted points, compared with those about which there is no dispute, do not bear the proportion of one to a hundred. And, what is more, no man is qualified, or can be qualified, to discuss the disputable questions, unless previously and thoroughly versed in those questions about which there is no dispute. In the terms and principles common to all, and recognized by all, is to be found the only common medium of language and of idea by which the parties can become intelligible to each other; and there, too, is the only common ground whence the arguments of the disputants can be drawn. . . .

. . . Thus may all the children of the Commonwealth receive instruction in all the great essentials of political knowledge, — in those elementary ideas without which they will never be able to investigate more recondite and debatable questions; thus will the only practicable method be adopted for discovering new truths, and for discarding, instead of perpetuating, old errors; and thus, too, will that pernicious race of intolerant zealots, whose whole faith may be summed up in two articles, — that they themselves are always infallibly right, and that all dissenters are certainly wrong, — be extinguished, — extinguished, not by violence, nor by proscription, but by the more copious inflowing of the light of truth.

Moral Education

Moral education is a primal necessity of social existence. The unre-   20
strained passions of men are not only homicidal, but suicidal; and a community without a conscience would soon extinguish itself. Even with a natural conscience, how often has evil triumphed over good! From the beginning of time, wrong has followed right, as the shadow the substance. . . .

But to all doubters, disbelievers, or despairers in human progress, it may still be said, there is one experiment which has never yet been tried. It is an experiment, which, even before its inception, offers the highest authority for its ultimate success. Its formula is intelligible to all; and it is as legible as though written in starry letters on an azure sky. It is expressed in these few and simple words: *"Train up a child in the way he should go; and, when he is old, he will not depart from it."* This declaration is positive. If the conditions are complied with, it makes no provision for a failure. Though pertaining to morals, yet, if the terms of the direction are observed, there is no more reason to doubt the result than there would be in an optical or a chemical experiment.

But this experiment has never yet been tried. Education has never yet been brought to bear with one-hundredth part of its potential force upon the natures of children, and, through them, upon the character of men and of the race. In all the attempts to reform mankind which have hitherto been made, whether by changing the frame of government, by aggravating or softening the severity of the penal code, or by substituting a government-created for a God-created religion, — in all these attempts, the infantile and youthful mind, its amenability to influences, and the enduring and self-operating character of the influences it receives, have been almost wholly unrecognized. Here, then, is a new agency, whose powers are but just beginning to be understood, and whose mighty energies hitherto have been but feebly invoked; and yet, from our experience, limited and imperfect as it is, we do know, that, far beyond any other earthly instrumentality, it is comprehensive and decisive. . . .

. . . So far as human instrumentalities are concerned, we have abundant means for surrounding every child in the State with preservative and moral influences as extensive and as efficient as those under which the present industrious, worthy, and virtuous members of the community were reared. And as to all those things in regard to which we are directly dependent upon the divine favor, have we not the promise, explicit and unconditional, that the men SHALL NOT depart from the way in which they should go, if the children are trained up in it? It has been overlooked that this promise is not restricted to parents, but seems to be addressed indiscriminately to all, whether parents, communities, states, or mankind. . . .

Religious Education

But it will be said that this grand result in practical morals is a consummation of blessedness that can never be attained without religion, and that no community will ever be religious without a religious education. Both these propositions I regard as eternal and immutable truths. Devoid of religious principles and religious affections, the race can never fall so low but that it may sink still lower; animated and sanctified by them, it can never rise so high but that it may ascend still higher. And is it not at least as presumptuous to expect that mankind will attain to the knowledge of truth, without being instructed in truth, and without that general expansion and development of faculty which will enable them to recognize and comprehend truth in any other department of human interest as in the department of religion? . . .

. . . That our public schools are not theological seminaries, is admitted. That they are debarred by law from inculcating the peculiar and distinctive doctrines of any one religious denomination amongst us, is claimed; and that they are also prohibited from ever teaching that what they do teach is the whole of religion, or all that is essential to religion or to salvation, is equally certain. But our system earnestly inculcates all Christian morals; it founds its morals on the basis of religion; it welcomes the religion of the Bible; and, in receiving the Bible, it allows it to do what it is allowed to do in no other system, — *to speak for itself.* But here it stops, not because it claims to have compassed all truth, but because it disclaims to act as an umpire between hostile religious opinions.

The very terms "public school" and "common school" bear upon their face that they are schools which the children of the entire community may attend. Every man not on the pauper-list is taxed for their support; but he is not taxed to support them as special religious institutions: if he were, it would satisfy at once the largest definition of a religious establishment. But he is taxed to support them as a *preventive* means against dishonesty, against fraud, and against violence, on the same principle that he is taxed to support criminal courts as a *punitive* means against the same offences. He is taxed to support schools, on the same principle that he is taxed to support paupers, — because a child without education is poorer and more wretched than a man without bread. He is taxed to support schools, on the same principle that he would be taxed to defend the nation against foreign invasion, or against rapine committed by a foreign foe, — because the general prevalence of ignorance, superstition, and vice, will breed Goth and Vandal at home more fatal to the public well-being than any Goth or Vandal from abroad. And, finally, he is taxed to support schools, because they are the most effective means of developing and training those powers and faculties in a child, by which, when he becomes a man, he may understand what his highest interests and his highest duties are, and may be in fact, and not in name only, a free agent. The elements of a political education are not bestowed upon any school child for the purpose of making him vote with this or that political party when he becomes of age, but for the purpose of enabling him to choose for himself with which party he will vote. So the religious education which a child receives at school is not imparted to him for the purpose of making him join this or that denomination when he arrives at years of discretion, but for the purpose of enabling him to judge for himself, according to the dictates of his own reason and conscience, what his religious obligations are, and whither they lead. . . .

Such, then, in a religious point of view, is the Massachusetts system of common schools. Reverently it recognizes and affirms the sovereign rights of

the Creator, sedulously and sacredly it guards the religious rights of the creature; while it seeks to remove all hinderances, and to supply all furtherances,
to a filial and paternal communion between man and his Maker. In a social
and political sense, it is a *free* school-system. It knows no distinction of rich
and poor, of bond and free, or between those, who, in the imperfect light of
this world, are seeking, through different avenues, to reach the gate of
heaven. Without money and without price, it throws open its doors, and
spreads the table of its bounty, for all the children of the State. Like the sun, it
shines not only upon the good, but upon the evil, that they may become good;
and, like the rain, its blessings descend not only upon the just, but upon the
unjust, that their injustice may depart from them, and be known no more.

ENGAGING THE TEXT

1. What is Mann's view of the powers of education? What does he see as
   education's role in society? To what extent would you agree that education
   successfully carries out these functions today?

2. What does Mann mean by "sanitary intelligence" (para. 7)? Why did he feel
   that the development of this kind of intelligence was such an important
   aspect of schooling? In what ways has your own education stressed the
   development of sanitary intelligence? How valuable has this nonacademic
   instruction been?

3. How does Mann view the role of education in relation to wealth and
   poverty? How do you think such views would be received today if advocated
   by a school-board candidate or contender for the presidency? In your estimation, how effective has education been in addressing economic differences in American society?

4. Mann suggests that education plays a special role in preparing citizens to
   become active participants in a republican form of government. In what
   ways has your education prepared you to participate in democratic decision
   making? How effective has this preparation been? What could be done to
   improve the way that schools currently prepare students for their role as
   citizens?

5. What, according to Mann, is the proper relationship of public education to
   issues of morality and religion? What specific moral or ethical principles
   should public schools attempt to teach?

EXPLORING CONNECTIONS

6. Read "Class in America — 2006" by Gregory Mantsios (p. 304), and
   "Stephen Cruz" by Studs Terkel (p. 366), and write an essay in which you
   discuss how class differences in American society complicate the educational program outlined by Mann.

7. Review the cartoon "If All the 'Education Reforms' Happened at Once,"
   which appears at the top of the next page. As a class, debate whether or not
   American education is trying to do too much today.

IF ALL THE "EDUCATION REFORMS" HAPPENED AT ONCE,

EXTENDING THE CRITICAL CONTEXT

8. Research recent court decisions and legislative initiatives on the issue of prayer in school. How do prevailing views of the separation of church and state compare with the ideas presented in Mann's assessment of the goals of public education in 1848? Then, as a class, debate the proper role of moral and religious instruction in public education.

9. Working in small groups, draft a list of what you think the proper goals of public education in a democracy should be. Exchange these lists, then compare and discuss your results. How does your class's view of the powers of education differ from that offered by Mann?

Idiot Nation

MICHAEL MOORE

When Michael Moore (b. 1954) held up his Oscar for best documentary during the 2002 Academy Awards show and shouted "Shame on you, Mr. Bush" to a chorus of boos from the audience, no one who knew his work would have been shocked. A social gadfly and cinematic activist without equal for the past two decades, Moore isn't the type to shy away from telling the president what he thinks of him on national TV; nor is he the type to disguise his contempt for the general level of idiocy he sees in American society. In this selection from Stupid White Men . . . and Other Sorry Excuses for the State of the Nation!, *his best-selling 2002 diatribe against our collective cluelessness, Moore zeroes in on the sorry state of American education. Serving up generous examples from his own less-than-stellar educational career, Moore takes us on a tour of the failings of America's schoolrooms — from libraries without books to commanders in chief who can't distinguish between countries and continents. Along the way, he touches on topics like the cultural illiteracy of television talk show hosts, the growing movement for educational "accountability," and the corporate takeover of America's classrooms. He even offers a list of things every student can do to fight back against educational subservience. Before winning the Oscar in 2002 for his* Bowling for Columbine, *Moore directed* Roger and Me *(1989), which chronicled his attempts to question then-General-Motors-chairman Roger Smith about a series of factory closures that devastated the economy of Flint, Michigan, Moore's hometown. His recent films include* Fahrenheit 9/11 *(2005), a controversial but highly successful documentary exploring the Bush administration's response to the 9/11 terrorist attacks;* Sicko, *an indictment of the American health-care system, which was nominated for an Academy Award in 2007; and* Capitalism: A Love Story *(2009).*

Do you feel like you live in a nation of idiots?

I used to console myself about the state of stupidity in this country by repeating this to myself: *Even if there are two hundred million stone-cold idiots in this country, that leaves at least eighty million who'll get what I'm saying — and that's still more than the populations of the United Kingdom and Iceland combined!*

Then came the day I found myself sharing an office with the ESPN game show *Two-Minute Drill*. This is the show that tests your knowledge of not only who plays what position for which team, but who hit what where in a 1925 game between Boston and New York, who was rookie of the year in 1965 in the old American Basketball Association, and what Jake Wood had for breakfast the morning of May 12, 1967.

I don't know the answer to any of those questions — but for some reason I do remember Jake Wood's uniform number: 2. Why on earth am I retaining that useless fact?

I don't know, but after watching scores of guys waiting to audition for that ESPN show, I think I do know something about intelligence and the American mind. Hordes of these jocks and lunkheads hang out in our hallway awaiting their big moment, going over hundreds of facts and statistics in their heads and challenging each other with questions I can't see why anyone would be able to answer other than God Almighty Himself. To look at these testosterone-loaded bruisers you would guess that they were a bunch of illiterates who would be lucky if they could read the label on a Bud.

In fact, they are geniuses. They can answer all thirty obscure trivia questions in less than 120 seconds. That's four seconds a question — including the time used by the slow-reading celebrity athletes who ask the questions.

I once heard the linguist and political writer Noam Chomsky say that if you want proof the American people aren't stupid, just turn on any sports talk radio show and listen to the incredible retention of facts. It is amazing — and it's proof that the American mind is alive and well. It just isn't challenged with anything interesting or exciting. *Our* challenge, Chomsky said, was to find a way to make politics as gripping and engaging as sports. When we do that, watch how Americans will do nothing but talk about who did what to whom at the WTO.[1]

But first, they have to be able to read the letters *WTO*.

There are forty-four million Americans who cannot read and write above a fourth-grade level — in other words, who are functional illiterates.

How did I learn this statistic? Well, I *read* it. And now you've read it. So we've already eaten into the mere 99 hours a *year* an average American adult spends reading a book — compared with 1,460 hours watching television.

I've also read that only 11 percent of the American public bothers to *read* a daily newspaper, beyond the funny pages or the used car ads.

So if you live in a country where forty-four million can't read — and perhaps close to another two hundred million can read but usually don't — well, friends, you and I are living in one very scary place. A nation that not only churns out illiterate students BUT GOES OUT OF ITS WAY TO REMAIN IGNORANT AND STUPID is a nation that should not be running the world — at least not until a majority of its citizens can locate Kosovo[2] (or any other country it has bombed) on the map.

---

[1]*WTO:* World Trade Organization.

[2]*Kosovo:* Province that precipitated the 1999 NATO invasion of Serbia after it demanded increased autonomy.

It comes as no surprise to foreigners that Americans, who love to revel in their stupidity, would "elect" a president who rarely reads *anything* — including his own briefing papers — and thinks Africa is a nation, not a continent. An idiot leader of an idiot nation. In our glorious land of plenty, less is always more when it comes to taxing any lobe of the brain with the intake of facts and numbers, critical thinking, or the comprehension of anything that isn't . . . well, sports.

Our Idiot-in-Chief does nothing to hide his ignorance — he even brags about it. During his commencement address to the Yale Class of 2001, George W. Bush spoke proudly of having been a mediocre student at Yale. "And to the C students, I say you, too, can be President of the United States!" The part where you also need an ex-President father, a brother as governor of a state with missing ballots, and a Supreme Court full of your dad's buddies must have been too complicated to bother with in a short speech.

As Americans, we have quite a proud tradition of being represented by   15
ignorant high-ranking officials. In 1956 President Dwight D. Eisenhower's nominee as ambassador to Ceylon (now Sri Lanka) was unable to identify either the country's prime minister or its capital during his Senate confirmation hearing. Not a problem — Maxwell Gluck was confirmed anyway. In 1981 President Ronald Reagan's nominee for deputy secretary of state, William Clark, admitted to a wide-ranging lack of knowledge about foreign affairs at his confirmation hearing. Clark had no idea how our allies in Western Europe felt about having American nuclear missiles based there, and didn't know the names of the prime ministers of South Africa or Zimbabwe. Not to worry — he was confirmed, too. All this just paved the way for Baby Bush, who hadn't quite absorbed the names of the leaders of India or Pakistan, two of the seven nations that possess the atomic bomb.

And Bush went to Yale *and* Harvard.

Recently a group of 556 seniors at fifty-five prestigious American universities (e.g., Harvard, Yale, Stanford) were given a multiple-choice test consisting of questions that were described as "high school level." Thirty-four questions were asked. These top students could only answer 53 percent of them correctly. And only one student got them all right.

A whopping 40 percent of these students did not know when the Civil War took place — even when given a wide range of choices: A. 1750–1800; B. 1800–1850; C. 1850–1900; D. 1900–1950; or E. after 1950. (*The answer is C, guys.*) The two questions the college seniors scored highest on were (1) Who is Snoop Doggy Dog? (98 percent got that one right), and (2) Who are Beavis and Butt-head? (99 percent knew). For my money, Beavis and Butt-head represented some of the best American satire of the nineties, and Snoop and his fellow rappers have much to say about America's social ills, so I'm not going down the road of blaming MTV.

What I *am* concerned with is why politicians like Senators Joe Lieberman of Connecticut and Herbert Kohl of Wisconsin want to go after MTV when *they* are the ones responsible for the massive failure of American education. Walk into any public school, and the odds are good that you'll find overflowing classrooms, leaking ceilings, and demoralized teachers. In one out of four schools, you'll find students "learning" from textbooks published in the 1980s — or earlier.

Why is this? Because the political leaders — and the people who vote   20
for them — have decided it's a bigger priority to build another bomber than to educate our children. They would rather hold hearings about the depravity of a television show called *Jackass* than about their own depravity in neglecting our schools and children and maintaining our title as Dumbest Country on Earth.

I hate writing these words. I *love* this big lug of a country and the crazy people in it. But when I can travel to some backwater village in Central America, as I did back in the eighties, and listen to a bunch of twelve-year-olds tell me their concerns about the World Bank, I get the feeling that *something* is lacking in the United States of America.

Our problem isn't just that our kids don't know nothin' but that the adults who pay their tuition are no better. I wonder what would happen if we tested the U.S. Congress to see just how much our representatives know. What if we were to give a pop quiz to the commentators who cram our TVs and radios with all their nonstop nonsense? How many would *they* get right?

A while back, I decided to find out. It was one of those Sunday mornings when the choice on TV was the *Parade of Homes* real estate show or *The McLaughlin Group.* If you like the sound of hyenas on Dexedrine, of course, you go with *McLaughlin.* On this particular Sunday morning, perhaps as my punishment for not being at Mass, I was forced to listen to magazine columnist Fred Barnes (now an editor at the right-wing *Weekly Standard* and co-host of the Fox News show *The Beltway Boys*) whine on and on about the sorry state of American education, blaming the teachers and their evil union for why students are doing so poorly.

"These kids don't even know what *The Iliad* and *The Odyssey* are!" he bellowed, as the other panelists nodded in admiration at Fred's noble lament.

The next morning I called Fred Barnes at his Washington office.   25
"Fred," I said, "tell me what *The Iliad* and *The Odyssey* are."

He started hemming and hawing. "Well, they're . . . uh . . . you know . . . uh . . . okay, fine, you got me — I don't know what they're about. Happy now?"

No, not really. You're one of the top TV pundits in America, seen every week on your own show and plenty of others. You gladly hawk your "wisdom" to hundreds of thousands of unsuspecting citizens, gleefully scorning others for their ignorance. Yet you and your guests know little or nothing yourselves. Grow up, get some books, and go to your room.

Yale and Harvard. Princeton and Dartmouth. Stanford and Berkeley. Get a degree from one of those universities, and you're set for life. So what if, on that test of the college seniors I previously mentioned, 70 percent of the students at those fine schools had never heard of the Voting Rights Act[3] or President Lyndon Johnson's Great Society initiatives?[4] Who needs to know stuff like that as you sit in your Tuscan villa watching the sunset and checking how well your portfolio did today?

So what if *not one* of these top universities that the ignorant students attend requires that they take even one course in American history to graduate? Who needs history when you are going to be tomorrow's master of the universe?

Who cares if 70 percent of those who graduate from America's colleges   30
are not required to learn a foreign language? Isn't the rest of the world speaking English now? And if they aren't, hadn't all those damn foreigners better GET WITH THE PROGRAM?

And who gives a rat's ass if, out of the seventy English Literature programs at seventy major American universities, only twenty-three now require English majors to take a course in Shakespeare? Can somebody please explain to me what Shakespeare and English have to do with each other? What good are some moldy old plays going to be in the business world, anyway?

Maybe I'm just jealous because I don't have a college degree. Yes, I, Michael Moore, am a college dropout.

Well, I never *officially* dropped out. One day in my sophomore year, I drove around and around the various parking lots of our commuter campus in Flint, searching desperately for a parking space. There simply was no place to park — every spot was full, and no one was leaving. After a frustrating hour spent circling around in my '69 Chevy Impala, I shouted out the window, "That's it, I'm dropping out!" I drove home and told my parents I was no longer in college.

"Why?" they asked.

"Couldn't find a parking spot," I replied, grabbing a Redpop and mov-   35
ing on with the rest of my life. I haven't sat at a school desk since.

My dislike of school started somewhere around the second month of first grade. My parents — and God Bless Them Forever for doing this — had taught me to read and write by the time I was four. So when I entered St. John's Elementary School, I had to sit and feign interest while the other kids, like robots, sang, "A-B-C-D-E-F-G . . . Now I know my ABCs, tell me what you think of me!" Every time I heard that line, I wanted to scream out,

---

[3]*Voting Rights Act:* 1965 legislation that guaranteed equal voting rights for African Americans.

[4]*Lyndon Johnson's Great Society initiatives:* 1964–65 program of economic and social welfare legislation designed by Lyndon Johnson, thirty-sixth president of the United States, to eradicate poverty.

"Here's what I think of you — quit singing that damn song! Somebody get me a Twinkie!"

I was bored beyond belief. The nuns, to their credit, recognized this, and one day Sister John Catherine took me aside and said that they had decided to skip me up to second grade, effective immediately. I was thrilled. When I got home I excitedly announced to my parents that I had already advanced a grade in my first month of school. They seemed under-whelmed by this new evidence of my genius. Instead they let out a "WHAT THE — ," then went into the kitchen and closed the door. I could hear my mother on the phone explaining to the Mother Superior that there was *no way* her little Michael was going to be attending class with kids bigger and older than him, so please, Sister, put him back in first grade.

I was crushed. My mother explained to me that if I skipped first grade I'd always be the youngest and littlest kid in class all through my school years (well, inertia and fast food eventually proved her wrong on that count). There would be no appeals to my father, who left most education decisions to my mother, the valedictorian of her high school class. I tried to explain that if I was sent back to first grade it would appear that I'd *flunked* second grade on my first day — putting myself at risk of having the crap beaten out of me by the first graders I'd left behind with a rousing "See ya, suckers!" But Mom wasn't falling for it; it was then I learned that the only person with higher authority than Mother Superior was Mother Moore.

The next day I decided to ignore all instructions from my parents to go back to first grade. In the morning, before the opening bell, all the students had to line up outside the school with their classmates and then march into the building in single file. Quietly, but defiantly, I went and stood in the sec-ond graders' line, praying that God would strike the nuns blind so they wouldn't see which line I was in. The bell rang — and no one had spotted me! The second grade line started to move, and I went with it. *Yes!* I thought. *If I can pull this off, if I can just get into that second grade class-room and take my seat, then nobody will be able to get me out of there.* Just as I was about to enter the door of the school, I felt a hand grab me by the collar of my coat. It was Sister John Catherine.

"I think you're in the wrong line, Michael," she said firmly. "You are now in first grade again." I began to protest: my parents had it "all wrong," or "those weren't *really* my parents," or . . .   40

For the next twelve years I sat in class, did my work, and remained con-stantly preoccupied, looking for ways to bust out. I started an underground school paper in fourth grade. It was shut down. I started it again in sixth. It was shut down. In eighth grade I not only started the paper again, I con-vinced the good sisters to let me write a play for our class to perform at the Christmas pageant. The play had something to do with how many rats occu-pied the parish hall and how all the rats in the country had descended on St. John's Parish Hall to have their annual "rat convention." The priest put a stop to that one — and shut down the paper again. Instead, my friends and I were told to go up on stage and sing three Christmas carols and then leave the stage without uttering a word. I organized half the class to go up there and utter nothing. So we stood there and refused to sing the carols, our silent protest against censorship. By the second song, intimidated by the stern looks from their parents in the audience, most of the protesters joined in on the singing — and by the third song, I too, had capitulated, joining in on "O Holy Night," and promising myself to live to fight another day.

High school, as we all know, is some sort of sick, sadistic punishment of kids by adults seeking vengeance because they can no longer lead the responsibility-free, screwing-around-24/7 lives young people enjoy. What other explanation could there be for those four brutal years of degrading comments, physical abuse, and the belief that you're the only one not having sex?

As soon as I entered high school — and the public school system — all the grousing I'd done about the repression of the Sisters of St. Joseph was forgotten; suddenly they all looked like scholars and saints. I was now walking the halls of a two-thousand-plus-inmate holding pen. Where the nuns had devoted their lives to teaching for no earthly reward, those running the public high school had one simple mission: "Hunt these little pricks down like dogs, then cage them until we can either break their will or ship them off to the glue factory!" Do this, don't do that, tuck your shirt in, wipe that smile off your face, where's your hall pass, THAT'S THE WRONG PASS! YOU — DETENTION!!

One day I came home from school and picked up the paper. The headline read: "26th Amendment Passes — Voting Age Lowered to 18." Below that was another headline: "School Board President to Retire, Seat Up for Election."

Hmm. I called the county clerk.   45

"Uh, I'm gonna be eighteen in a few weeks. If I can vote, does that mean I can also run for office?"

"Let me see," the lady replied. "That's a new question!"

She ruffled through some papers and came back on the phone. "Yes," she said, "you can run. All you need to do is gather twenty signatures to place your name on the ballot."

Twenty signatures? That's it? I had no idea running for elective office required so little work. I got the twenty signatures, submitted my petition, and started campaigning. My platform? "Fire the high school principal and the assistant principal!"

Alarmed at the idea that a high school student might actually find a   50
legal means to remove the very administrators he was being paddled by, five local "adults" took out petitions and got themselves added to the ballot, too.

Of course, they ended up splitting the older adult vote five ways — and I won, getting the vote of every single stoner between the ages of eighteen and twenty-five (who, though many would probably never vote again, relished the thought of sending their high school wardens to the gallows).

The day after I won, I was walking down the hall at school (I had one more week to serve out as a student), and I passed the assistant principal, my shirt tail proudly untucked.

"Good morning, Mr. Moore," he said tersely. The day before, my name had been "Hey-You!" Now I was his boss.

Within nine months after I took my seat on the school board, the principal and assistant principal had submitted their "letters of resignation," a face-saving device employed when one is "asked" to step down. A couple of years later the principal suffered a heart attack and died.

I had known this man, the principal, for many years. When I was eight   55
years old, he used to let me and my friends skate and play hockey on this little pond beside his house. He was kind and generous, and always left the door to his house open in case any of us needed to change into our skates or if we got cold and just wanted to get warm. Years later, I was asked to play bass in a band that was forming, but I didn't own a bass. He let me borrow his son's.

I offer this to remind myself that all people are actually good at their core, and to remember that someone with whom I grew to have serious disputes was also someone with a free cup of hot chocolate for us shivering little brats from the neighborhood.

Teachers are now the politicians' favorite punching bag. To listen to the likes of Chester Finn, a former assistant secretary of education in Bush the Elder's administration, you'd think all that has crumbled in our society can be traced back to lax, lazy, and incompetent teachers. "If you put out a Ten-Most-Wanted list of who's killing American education, I'm not sure who you would have higher on the list: the teachers' union or the education school faculties," Finn said.

Sure, there are a lot of teachers who suck, and they'd be better suited to making telemarketing calls for Amway. But the vast majority are dedicated educators who have chosen a profession that pays them less than what some of their students earn selling Ecstasy, and for that sacrifice we seek to punish them. I don't know about you, but I want the people who have the direct attention of my child more hours a day than I do treated with tender loving care. Those are my kids they're "preparing" for this world, so why on earth would I want to piss them off?

You would think society's attitude would be something like this:

Teachers, thank you so much for devoting your life to my child. Is there ANYTHING I can do to help you? Is there ANYTHING you need? I am here for you. Why? Because you are helping my child — MY BABY — learn and grow. Not only will you be largely responsible for her ability to make a living, but your influence will greatly affect how she views the world, what she knows about other people in this world, and how she will feel about herself. I want her to believe she can attempt anything — that no doors are closed and that no dreams are too distant. I am entrusting the most valuable person in my life to you for seven hours each day. You are thus one of the most important people in my life! Thank you.

No, instead, this is what teachers hear: 60

- "You've got to wonder about teachers who claim to put the interests of children first — and then look to milk the system dry through wage hikes." (*New York Post*, 12/26/00)
- "Estimates of the number of bad teachers range from 5 percent to 18 percent of the 2.6 million total." (Michael Chapman, *Investor's Business Daily*, 9/21/98)
- "Most education professionals belong to a closed community of devotees . . . who follow popular philosophies rather than research on what works." (Douglas Carminen, quoted in the *Montreal Gazette*, 1/6/01)
- "Teachers unions have gone to bat for felons and teachers who have had sex with students, as well as those who simply couldn't teach." (Peter Schweizen, *National Review*, 8/17/98)

What kind of priority do we place on education in America? Oh, it's on the funding list — somewhere down between OSHA[5] and meat inspectors. The person who cares for our child every day receives an average of $41,351 annually. A Congressman who cares only about which tobacco lobbyist is taking him to dinner tonight receives $145,100.

Considering the face-slapping society gives our teachers on a daily basis, is it any wonder so few choose the profession? The national teacher shortage is so big that some school systems are recruiting teachers outside the United States. Chicago recently recruited and hired teachers from twenty-eight foreign countries, including China, France, and Hungary. By the time the new term begins in New York City, seven thousand veteran teachers will have retired — and 60 percent of the new teachers hired to replace them are uncertified.

But here's the kicker for me: 163 New York City schools opened the 2000–2001 school year *without a principal!* You heard right — school, with *no one in charge.* Apparently the mayor and the school board are experimenting with chaos theory — throw five hundred poor kids into a crumbling building, and watch nature take its course! In the city from which most of the wealth in the world is controlled, where there are more millionaires per square foot than there is gum on the sidewalk, we somehow can't find the money to pay a starting teacher more than $31,900 a year. And we act surprised when we can't get results.

And it's not just teachers who have been neglected — American schools are *literally* falling apart. In 1999 one-quarter of U.S. public schools reported that the condition of at least one of their buildings was inadequate. In 1997 the entire Washington, D.C., school system had to delay the start of

---

[5]*OSHA:* Occupational Safety and Health Administration.

school for three weeks because nearly *one-third* of the schools were found
to be unsafe.

Almost 10 percent of U.S. public schools have enrollments that are   65
more than 25 percent greater than the capacity of their permanent buildings. Classes have to be held in the hallways, outdoors, in the gym, in the
cafeteria; one school I visited even held classes in a janitor's closet. It's not
as if the janitor's closets are being used for anything related to cleaning,
anyway — in New York almost 15 percent of the eleven hundred public
schools are without full-time custodians, forcing teachers to mop their own
floors and students to do without toilet paper. We already send our kids
out into the street to hawk candy bars so their schools can buy band
instruments — what's next? Car washes to raise money for toilet paper?

Further proof of just how special our little offspring are is the number
of public and even school libraries that have been shut down or had their
hours cut back. The last thing we need is a bunch of kids hanging out
around a bunch of books!

Apparently "President" Bush agrees: in his first budget he proposed cutting federal spending on libraries by $39 million, down to $168 million — a
nearly 19 percent reduction. Just the week before, his wife, former school
librarian Laura Bush, kicked off a national campaign for America's libraries,
calling them "community treasure chests, loaded with a wealth of information available to everyone, equally." The President's mother, Barbara Bush,
heads the Foundation for Family Literacy. Well, there's nothing like having
firsthand experience with illiteracy in the family to motivate one into acts
of charity.

For kids who are exposed to books at home, the loss of a library is sad.
But for kids who come from environments where people don't read, the loss
of a library is a tragedy that might keep them from ever discovering the joys
of reading — or from gathering the kind of information that will decide
their lot in life. Jonathan Kozol, for decades an advocate for disadvantaged
children, has observed that school libraries "remain the clearest window to a
world of noncommercial satisfactions and enticements that most children in
poor neighborhoods will ever know."

Kids deprived of access to good libraries are also being kept from developing the information skills they need to keep up in workplaces that are
increasingly dependent on rapidly changing information. The ability to conduct research is "probably the most essential skill [today's students] can have,"
says Julie Walker, executive director of the American Association of School
Librarians. "The knowledge [students] acquire in school is not going to serve
them throughout their lifetimes. Many of them will have four to five careers
in a lifetime. It will be their ability to navigate information that will matter."

Who's to blame for the decline in libraries? Well, when it comes to   70
school libraries, you can start by pointing the finger (yes, *that* finger) at
Richard Nixon. From the 1960s until 1974, school libraries received specific funding from the government. But in 1974 the Nixon administration

changed the rules, stipulating that federal education money be doled out in "block grants" to be spent by states however they chose. Few states chose to spend the money on libraries, and the downslide began. This is one reason that materials in many school libraries today date from the 1960s and early 1970s, before funding was diverted. ("No, Sally, the Soviet Union isn't our enemy. The Soviet Union has been kaput for ten years. . . .")

This 1999 account by an *Education Week* reporter about the "library" at a Philadelphia elementary school could apply to any number of similarly neglected schools:

> Even the best books in the library at T. M. Pierce Elementary School are dated, tattered, and discolored. The worst — many in a latter state of disintegration — are dirty and fetid and leave a moldy residue on hands and clothing. Chairs and tables are old, mismatched, or broken. There isn't a computer in sight. . . . Outdated facts and theories and offensive stereotypes leap from the authoritative pages of encyclopedias and biographies, fiction and nonfiction tomes. Among the volumes on these shelves a student would find it all but impossible to locate accurate information on AIDS or other contemporary diseases, explorations of the moon and Mars, or the past five U.S. presidents.

The ultimate irony in all of this is that the very politicians who refuse to fund education in America adequately are the same ones who go ballistic over how our kids have fallen behind the Germans, the Japanese, and just about every other country with running water and an economy not based on the sale of Chiclets. Suddenly they want "accountability." They want the teachers held responsible and to be tested. And they want the kids to be tested — over and over and over.

There's nothing terribly wrong with the concept of using standardized testing to determine whether kids are learning to read and write and do math. But too many politicians and education bureaucrats have created a national obsession with testing, as if everything that's wrong with the educational system in this country would be magically fixed if we could just raise those scores.

The people who really should be tested (besides the yammering pundits) are the so-called political leaders. Next time you see your state representative or congressman, give him this pop quiz — and remind him that any future pay raises will be based on how well he scores:

1. What is the annual pay of your average constituent?
2. What percent of welfare recipients are children?
3. How many known species of plants and animals are on the brink of extinction?
4. How big is the hole in the ozone layer?
5. Which African countries have a lower infant mortality rate than Detroit?

6. How many American cities still have two competing newspapers?

7. How many ounces in a gallon?

8. Which do I stand a greater chance of being killed by: a gun shot in school or a bolt of lightning?

9. What's the only state capital without a McDonald's?

10. Describe the story of either *The Iliad* or *The Odyssey*.

ANSWERS

1. $28,548

2. 67 percent

3. 11,046

4. 10.5 million square miles

5. Libya, Mauritius, Seychelles

6. 34

7. 128 ounces

8. You're twice as likely to be killed by lightning as by a gun shot in school.

9. Montpelier, Vermont

10. *The Iliad* is an ancient Greek epic poem by Homer about the Trojan War. *The Odyssey* is another epic poem by Homer recounting the ten-year journey home from the Trojan War made by Odysseus, the king of Ithaca.

Chances are, the genius representing you in the legislature won't score   75
50 percent on the above test. The good news is that you get to flunk him within a year or two.

There is one group in the country that isn't just sitting around carping about all them lamebrain teachers — a group that cares deeply about what kinds of students will enter the adult world. You could say they have a vested interest in this captive audience of millions of young people . . . or in the billions of dollars they spend each year. (Teenagers alone spent more than $150 billion last year.) Yes, it's Corporate America, whose generosity to our nation's schools is just one more example of their continuing patriotic service.

Just how committed are these companies to our children's schools?

According to numbers collected by the Center for the Analysis of Commercialism in Education (CACE), their selfless charity has seen a tremendous boom since 1990. Over the past ten years, school programs and activities have seen corporate sponsorship increase by 248 percent. In exchange for this sponsorship, schools allow the corporation to associate its name with the events.

For example, Eddie Bauer sponsors the final round of the National Geography Bee. Book covers featuring Calvin Klein and Nike ads are distributed to students. Nike and other shoemakers, looking for early access to tomorrow's stars, sponsor inner-city high school basketball teams.

Pizza Hut set up its "Book-It!" program to encourage children to read.   80
When students meet the monthly reading goal, they are rewarded with a
certificate for a Pizza Hut personal pan pizza. At the restaurant, the store
manager personally congratulates the children and gives them each a sticker
and a certificate. Pizza Hut suggests school principals place a "Pizza Hut
Book-It!" honor roll list in the school for everyone to see.

General Mills and Campbell's Soup thought up a better plan. Instead
of giving free rewards, they both have programs rewarding schools for getting parents to buy their products. Under General Mills's "Box Tops for
Education" program, schools get ten cents for each box top logo they send
in, and can earn up to $10,000 a year. That's 100,000 General Mills prod-
ucts sold. Campbell's Soup's "Labels for Education" program is no better. It
touts itself as "Providing America's children with FREE school equipment!"
Schools can earn one "free" Apple iMac computer for only 94,950 soup
labels. Campbell's suggests setting a goal of a label a day from each student.
With Campbell's conservative estimate of five labels per week per child, all
you need is a school of 528 kids to get that free computer.

It's not just this kind of sponsorship that brings these schools and corporations together. The 1990s saw a phenomenal 1,384 percent increase in
exclusive agreements between schools and soft-drink bottlers. Two hundred
and forty school districts in thirty-one states have sold exclusive rights to
one of the big three soda companies (Coca-Cola, Pepsi, Dr. Pepper) to push
their products in schools. Anybody wonder why there are more overweight
kids than ever before? Or more young women with calcium deficiencies
because they're drinking less milk? And even though federal law prohibits
the sale of soft drinks in schools until lunch periods begin, in some overcrowded schools "lunch" begins in midmorning. Artificially flavored carbonated sugar water — the breakfast of champions! (In March 2001 Coke
responded to public pressure, announcing that it would add water, juice,
and other sugar-free, caffeine-free, and calcium-rich alternatives to soda to
its school vending machines.)

I guess they can afford such concessions when you consider their deal
with the Colorado Springs school district. Colorado has been a trailblazer
when it comes to tie-ins between the schools and soft drink companies. In
Colorado Springs, the district will receive $8.4 million over ten years from
its deal with Coca-Cola — and more if it exceeds its "requirement" of selling
seventy thousand cases of Coke products a year. To ensure the levels are
met, school district officials urged principals to allow students unlimited
access to Coke machines and allow students to drink Coke in the classroom.

But Coke isn't alone. In the Jefferson County, Colorado, school district
(home of Columbine High School), Pepsi contributed $1.5 million to help
build a new sports stadium. Some county schools tested a science course,
developed in part by Pepsi, called "The Carbonated Beverage Company."
Students taste-tested colas, analyzed cola samples, watched a video tour of a
Pepsi bottling plant, and visited a local plant.

The school district in Wylie, Texas, signed a deal in 1996 that shared   85
the rights to sell soft drinks in the schools between Coke and Dr. Pepper.
Each company paid $31,000 a year. Then, in 1998, the county changed its
mind and signed a deal with Coke worth $1.2 million over fifteen years.
Dr. Pepper sued the county for breach of contract. The school district
bought out Dr. Pepper's contract, costing them $160,000 — plus another
$20,000 in legal fees.

It's not just the companies that sometimes get sent packing. Students
who lack the proper corporate school spirit do so at considerable risk. When
Mike Cameron wore a Pepsi shirt on "Coke Day" at Greenbrier High School
in Evans, Georgia, he was suspended for a day. "Coke Day" was part of the
school's entry in a national "Team Up With Coca-Cola" contest, which
awards $10,000 to the high school that comes up with the best plan for dis-
tributing Coke discount cards. Greenbrier school officials said Cameron was
suspended for "being disruptive and trying to destroy the school picture"
when he removed an outer shirt and revealed the Pepsi shirt as a photograph
was being taken of students posed to spell out the word *Coke.* Cameron said
the shirt was visible all day, but he didn't get in trouble until posing for the
picture. No slouch in the marketing department, Pepsi quickly sent the high
school senior a box of Pepsi shirts and hats.

If turning the students into billboards isn't enough, schools and corporations sometimes turn the school itself into one giant neon sign for corporate
America. Appropriation of school space, including scoreboards, rooftops,
walls, and textbooks, for corporate logos and advertising is up 539 percent.

Colorado Springs, not satisfied to sell its soul only to Coca-Cola, has
plastered its school buses with advertisements for Burger King, Wendy's,
and other big companies. Free book covers and school planners with ads for
Kellogg's Pop-Tarts and pictures of FOX TV personalities were also handed
out to the students.

After members of the Grapevine-Colleyville Independent School District in Texas decided they didn't want advertisements in the classrooms,
they allowed Dr. Pepper and 7-Up logos to be painted on the rooftops of
two high schools. The two high schools, not coincidentally, lie under the
Dallas airport flight path.

The schools aren't just looking for ways to advertise; they're also con-   90
cerned with the students' perceptions of various products. That's why, in some
schools, companies conduct market research in classrooms during school
hours. Education Market Resources of Kansas reports that "children respond
openly and easily to questions and stimuli" in the classroom setting. (Of
course, that's what they're *supposed* to be doing in a classroom — but for their
own benefit, not that of some corporate pollsters.) Filling out marketing surveys instead of learning, however, is probably *not* what they should be doing.

Companies have also learned they can reach this confined audience
by "sponsoring" educational materials. This practice, like the others, has
exploded as well, increasing 1,875 percent since 1990.

Teachers have shown a Shell Oil video that teaches students that the way to experience nature is by driving there — after filling your Jeep's gas tank at a Shell station. ExxonMobil prepared lesson plans about the flourishing wildlife in Prince William Sound, site of the ecological disaster caused by the oil spill from the Exxon *Valdez*. A third-grade math book features exercises involving counting Tootsie Rolls. A Hershey's-sponsored curriculum used in many schools features "The Chocolate Dream Machine," including lessons in math, science, geography — and nutrition.

In a number of high schools, the economics course is supplied by General Motors. GM writes and provides the textbooks and the course outline. Students learn from GM's example the benefits of capitalism and how to operate a company — like GM.

And what better way to imprint a corporate logo on the country's children than through television and the Internet beamed directly into the classroom. Electronic marketing, where a company provides programming or equipment to schools for the right to advertise to their students, is up 139 percent.

One example is the ZapMe! Corporation, which provides schools with a   95
free computer lab and access to pre-selected Web sites. In return, schools must promise that the lab will be in use at least four hours a day. The catch? The ZapMe! Web browser has constantly scrolling advertisements — and the company gets to collect information on students' browsing habits, information they can then sell to other companies.

Perhaps the worst of the electronic marketers is Channel One Television. Eight million students in 12,000 classrooms watch Channel One, an in-school news *and advertising* program, every day. (That's right: EVERY day.) Kids are spending the equivalent of six full school days a year watching Channel One in almost 40 percent of U.S. middle and high schools. Instructional time lost to the ads alone? One entire day per year. That translates into an annual cost to taxpayers of more than $1.8 billion.

Sure, doctors and educators agree that our kids can never watch enough TV. And there's probably a place in school for some television programs — I have fond memories of watching astronauts blasting off on the television rolled into my grade school auditorium. But out of the daily twelve-minute Channel One broadcasts, only 20 percent of the airtime is devoted to stories about politics, the economy, and cultural and social issues. That leaves a whopping 80 percent for advertising, sports, weather, features, and Channel One promotions.

Channel One is disproportionately shown in schools in low income communities with large minority populations, where the least money is available for education, and where the least amount is spent on textbooks and other academic materials. Once these districts receive corporate handouts, government's failure to provide adequate school funding tends to remain unaddressed.

For most of us, the only time we enter an American high school is to vote at our local precinct. (There's an irony if there ever was one — going to participate in democracy's sacred ritual while two thousand students in the same building live under some sort of totalitarian dictatorship.) The halls are packed with burned-out teenagers shuffling from class to class, dazed and confused, wondering what the hell they're doing there. They learn how to regurgitate answers the state wants them to give, and any attempt to be an individual is now grounds for being suspected to be a member of the trench coat mafia.[6] I visited a school recently, and some students asked me if I noticed that they and the other students in the school were all wearing white or some neutral color. Nobody dares wear black, or anything else wild and distinct. That's a sure ticket to the principal's office — where the school psychologist will be waiting to ascertain whether that Limp Bizkit shirt you have on means that you intend to shoot up Miss Nelson's fourth hour geometry class.

So the kids learn to submerge any personal expression. They learn that   100
it's better to go along so that you get along. They learn that to rock the boat could get them rocked right out of the school. Don't question authority. Do as you're told. Don't think, just do as I say.

Oh, and have a good and productive life as an active, well-adjusted participant in our thriving democracy!

Are You a Potential School Shooter?

The following is a list of traits the FBI has identified as "risk factors" among students who may commit violent acts. Stay away from any student showing signs of:

- Poor coping skills
- Access to weapons
- Depression
- Drug and alcohol abuse
- Alienation
- Narcissism
- Inappropriate humor
- Unlimited, unmonitored television and Internet use

Since this includes all of you, drop out of school immediately. Home schooling is not a viable option, because you must also stay away from yourself.

---

[6]*trench coat mafia:* Name of a self-styled group of students that included Columbine High School shooters Eric Harris and Dylan Klebold; hence, any potentially violent group of students.

How to Be a Student Subversive Instead of a Student Subservient

There are many ways you can fight back at your high school — and have fun while doing it. The key thing is to learn what all the rules are, and what your rights are by law and by school district policy. This will help to prevent you getting in the kinds of trouble you don't need.

It may also get you some cool perks. David Schankula, a college student who has helped me on this book, recalls that when he was in high school in Kentucky, he and his buddies found some obscure state law that said any student who requests a day off to go to the state fair must be given the day off. The state legislature probably passed this law years ago to help some farm kid take his prize hog to the fair without being penalized at school. But the law was still on the books, and it gave any student the right to request the state fair day off — regardless of the reason. So you can imagine the look on the principal's face when David and his city friends submitted their request for their free day off from school — and there was nothing the principal could do.

Here's a few more things you can do:

1. *Mock the Vote.*

Student council and class elections are the biggest smokescreen the school throws up, fostering the illusion that you actually have any say in the running of the school. Most students who run for these offices either take the charade too seriously — or they just think it'll look good on their college applications.

So why not run yourself? Run just to ridicule the whole ridiculous exercise. Form your own party, with its own stupid name. Campaign on wild promises: *If elected, I'll change the school mascot to an amoeba,* or *If elected, I'll insist that the principal must first eat the school lunch each day before it is fed to the students.* Put up banners with cool slogans: "Vote for me — a real loser!"

If you get elected, you can devote your energies to accomplishing things that will drive the administration crazy, but help out your fellow students (demands for free condoms, student evaluations of teachers, less homework so you can get to bed by midnight, etc).

2. *Start a School Club.*

You have a right to do this. Find a sympathetic teacher to sponsor it. The Pro-Choice Club. The Free Speech Club. The Integrate Our Town Club. Make every member a "president" of the club, so they all can claim it on their college applications. One student I know tried to start a Feminist Club, but the principal wouldn't allow it because then they'd be obliged to give equal time to a Male Chauvinist Club. That's the kind of idiot thinking you'll encounter, but don't give up. (Heck, if you find yourself in that situation, just say *fine* — and suggest that the principal could sponsor the Chauvinist Club.)

3. Launch Your Own Newspaper or Webzine.

You have a constitutionally protected right to do this. If you take care not to be obscene, or libelous, or give them any reason to shut you down, this can be a great way to get the truth out about what's happening at your school. Use humor. The students will love it.

4. Get Involved in the Community.

Go to the school board meetings and inform them what's going on in 110 the school. Petition them to change things. They will try to ignore you or make you sit through a long, boring meeting before they let you speak, but they have to let you speak. Write letters to the editor of your local paper. Adults don't have a clue about what goes on in your high school. Fill them in. More than likely you'll find someone there who'll support you.

Any or all of this will raise quite a ruckus, but there's help out there if you need it. Contact the local American Civil Liberties Union if the school retaliates. Threaten lawsuits — school administrators HATE to hear that word. Just remember: there's no greater satisfaction than seeing the look on your principal's face when you have the upper hand. Use it.

And Never Forget This:

There Is No Permanent Record!

ENGAGING THE TEXT

1. What evidence does Moore offer to support his contention that America is a nation of idiots? To what extent would you agree with this blunt assessment of American intelligence? Why? What limitations, if any, do you see in the "question/answer" approach that Moore takes to gauging intelligence?

2. Moore shares a number of personal experiences in this selection to dramatize his disgust with formal education. How do your own elementary and high school memories compare with Moore's school experiences? Overall, how would you characterize his attitude toward schools and schooling? To what extent would you agree with him?

3. How accurate is the grim picture of American schools that Moore offers in this selection? Would you agree with his assessment of the typical class room, the quality of the average school library, and the general ability of American teachers and of the staff who support them?

4. Who, in Moore's view, is responsible for the sorry state of America's schools? To what extent would you agree? What reforms do you think Moore would like to see, and what changes, if any, would you recommend?

5. How does Moore feel about corporate involvement in public education? Why? What possible conflicts of interest or ethical questions do you see arising in relation to the following kinds of corporate/school collaboration:

- Sponsorship of sports teams and clubs
- Exclusive contracts for soda and snack vending machines
- Fast-food franchise "food courts"
- Sponsorship of libraries, computer labs, etc.
- Commercial instruction via cable TV
- Free books with inserted advertising
- Free courses on history or economics with business or corporate content
- Volunteer "teachers" and tutors from corporate ranks

What role, if any, do you think corporations should play in support of American public schools? Why?

6. What does Moore suggest that individual students do to "fight back" against the deadening effects of the educational system? What did you do when you were in elementary and secondary school to make your own experience more meaningful? Now that you're in college, what can you do to be a "student subversive instead of a student subservient"?

EXPLORING CONNECTIONS

7. How does Moore's portrayal of the current state of American education compare with the image of the American school as described by Horace Mann (p. 116)? What seems to be the mission or goal of public schooling, according to Moore? How would you expect him to react to the goals that Mann envisions for the school? Why? Would you agree with Moore?

8. To what extent does Moore's depiction of the idiocy of schools support or challenge John Taylor Gatto's critique of American public education in "Against School" (p. 148)? Do you think that Moore would agree with Gatto's claim that mandatory public schooling has turned us into a nation of children?

EXTENDING THE CRITICAL CONTEXT

9. Test Moore's central thesis about the idiocy of the average American by working in groups to devise and administer your own general information test. You can borrow questions from the many bits of information that Moore offers throughout this selection, or simply pool your own knowledge supplemented with additional library research. Administer your questionnaire to groups of fellow students, professors, family, friends, or members of the community at large. Then compare your results to see if Americans really are as uninformed as Moore suggests.

10. As Moore suggests, even some top American universities no longer require students to take basic courses in subjects like history or foreign language. How comprehensive are the general education requirements at your college? Do you think that they provide the average student with a well-rounded education? What additional courses or requirements, if any, would you include? Why?

From *School Is Hell.* Copyright © 1987 Matt Groening. All rights reserved. Reprinted by permission of Pantheon Books, a division of Random House, Inc., New York. Courtesy of Acme Features Syndicate.

Against School

JOHN TAYLOR GATTO

The official mission statements of most American schools brim with good intentions. On paper, schools exist to help students realize their full potential, to equip them with the skills they'll need to achieve success and contribute to society, or to foster the development of independence, critical thinking, and strong ethical values. But as John Taylor Gatto (b. 1935) sees it, public schools actually exist to fulfill six covert functions meant to "cripple our kids." The frightening thing is that Gatto might know what he's talking about. An award-winning educator and ardent libertarian, Gatto has taught in New York public schools for more than two decades. In 1989, 1990, and 1991, he was named New York City Teacher of the Year, and in 1991 he was also honored as New York State Teacher of the Year. His publications include Dumbing Us Down: The Hidden Curriculum of Compulsory Schooling *(1992),* A Different Kind of Teacher *(2000),* The Underground History of American Education *(2001), and* Weapons of Mass Instruction: A Schoolteacher's Journey through the Dark World of Compulsory School-ing *(2008). This selection originally appeared in* Harper's *magazine in 2003.*

I taught for thirty years in some of the worst schools in Manhattan, and in some of the best, and during that time I became an expert in boredom. Boredom was everywhere in my world, and if you asked the kids, as I often did, *why* they felt so bored, they always gave the same answers: They said the work was stupid, that it made no sense, that they already knew it. They said they wanted to be doing something real, not just sitting around. They said teachers didn't seem to know much about their subjects and clearly weren't interested in learning more. And the kids were right: their teachers were every bit as bored as they were.

Boredom is the common condition of schoolteachers, and anyone who has spent time in a teachers' lounge can vouch for the low energy, the whining, the dispirited attitudes, to be found there. When asked why *they* feel bored, the teachers tend to blame the kids, as you might expect. Who wouldn't get bored teaching students who are rude and interested only in grades? If even that. Of course, teachers are themselves products of the same twelve-year compulsory school programs that so thoroughly bore their students, and as school personnel they are trapped inside structures even more rigid than those imposed upon the children. Who, then, is to blame?

We all are. My grandfather taught me that. One afternoon when I was seven I complained to him of boredom, and he batted me hard on the head. He told me that I was never to use that term in his presence again, that if I was bored it was my fault and no one else's. The obligation to amuse and instruct myself was entirely my own, and people who didn't know that were childish people, to be avoided if possible. Certainly not to be trusted. That episode cured me of boredom forever, and here and there over the years I was able to pass on the lesson to some remarkable student. For the most part, however, I found it futile to challenge the official notion that boredom and childishness were the natural state of affairs in the classroom. Often I had to defy custom, and even bend the law, to help kids break out of this trap.

The empire struck back, of course; childish adults regularly conflate opposition with disloyalty. I once returned from a medical leave to discover that all evidence of my having been granted the leave had been purposely destroyed, that my job had been terminated, and that I no longer possessed even a teaching license. After nine months of tormented effort I was able to retrieve the license when a school secretary testified to witnessing the plot unfold. In the meantime my family suffered more than I care to remember. By the time I finally retired in 1991, I had more than enough reason to think of our schools — with their long-term, cell-block-style, forced confinement of both students and teachers — as virtual factories of childishness. Yet I honestly could not see *why* they had to be that way. My own experience had revealed to me what many other teachers must learn along the way, too, yet keep to themselves for fear of reprisal: if we wanted to we could easily and inexpensively jettison the old, stupid structures and help kids *take* an education rather than merely *receive* a schooling. We could encourage the best qualities of youthfulness — curiosity, adventure, resilience, the capacity for surprising insight — simply by being more flexible about time, texts, and tests, by introducing kids to truly competent adults, and by giving each student what autonomy he or she needs in order to take a risk every now and then.

But we don't do that. And the more I asked why not, and persisted in   5
thinking about the "problem" of schooling as an engineer might, the more I missed the point: What if there is no "problem" with our schools? What if they are the way they are, so expensively flying in the face of common sense and long experience in how children learn things, not because they are doing something wrong but because they are doing something right? Is it possible that George W. Bush accidentally spoke the truth when he said we would "leave no child behind"? Could it be that our schools are designed to make sure not one of them ever really grows up?

Do we really need school? I don't mean education, just forced schooling: six classes a day, five days a week, nine months a year, for twelve years. Is this deadly routine really necessary? And if so, for what? Don't hide behind reading, writing, and arithmetic as a rationale, because 2 million happy homeschoolers have surely put that banal justification to rest. Even if they hadn't, a considerable number of well-known Americans never went through the twelve-year wringer our kids currently go through, and they turned out all right. George Washington, Benjamin Franklin, Thomas Jefferson, Abraham Lincoln? Someone taught them, to be sure, but they were not products of a school *system,* and not one of them was ever "graduated" from a secondary school. Throughout most of American history, kids generally didn't go to high school, yet the unschooled rose to be admirals, like Farragut;[1] inventors, like Edison; captains of industry, like Carnegie[2] and Rockefeller;[3] writers, like Melville and Twain and Conrad;[4] and even scholars, like Margaret Mead.[5] In fact, until pretty recently people who reached the age of thirteen weren't looked upon as children at all. Ariel Durant, who cowrote an enormous, and very good, multivolume history of the world with her husband, Will, was happily married at fifteen, and who could reasonably claim that Ariel Durant[6] was an uneducated person? Unschooled, perhaps, but not uneducated.

We have been taught (that is, schooled) in this country to think of "success" as synonymous with, or at least dependent upon, "schooling," but historically that isn't true in either an intellectual or a financial sense. And plenty of people throughout the world today find a way to educate themselves without resorting to a system of compulsory secondary schools that all too often resemble prisons. Why, then, do Americans confuse education with just such a system? What exactly is the purpose of our public schools?

Mass schooling of a compulsory nature really got its teeth into the United States between 1905 and 1915, though it was conceived of much earlier and pushed for throughout most of the nineteenth century. The reason given for this enormous upheaval of family life and cultural traditions was, roughly speaking, threefold:

1. To make good people.
2. To make good citizens.
3. To make each person his or her personal best.

[1]*Farragut:* Admiral David Glasgow Farragut (1801–1870), American naval officer who won several important victories for the North in the Civil War, including the capture of the port of New Orleans in 1862.

[2]*Carnegie:* Andrew Carnegie (1835–1919), American businessman and philanthropist who made his enormous fortune in the steel industry.

[3]*Rockefeller:* John D. Rockefeller (1839–1937), American industrialist who founded Standard Oil and who was for a time the richest man in the world.

[4]*Melville and Twain and Conrad:* Herman Melville (1819–1891), American novelist best known as the author of *Moby-Dick* (1851); Mark Twain, the pen name of American writer Samuel Langhorne Clemens (1835–1910), author of *Adventures of Huckleberry Finn* (1884); and Polish-born writer Joseph Conrad (1857–1924), best known for the novella "Heart of Darkness" (1899).

[5]*Margaret Mead:* American anthropologist (1901–1978) and author of the groundbreaking book *Coming of Age in Samoa* (1928).

[6]*Ariel Durant:* With husband Will (1885–1981), Ariel (1898–1981) won the Pulitzer Prize for literature for volume ten of their eleven-volume *The Story of Civilization,* published from 1935 to 1975.

These goals are still trotted out today on a regular basis, and most of us accept them in one form or another as a decent definition of public education's mission, however short schools actually fall in achieving them. But we are dead wrong. Compounding our error is the fact that the national literature holds numerous and surprisingly consistent statements of compulsory schooling's true purpose. We have, for example, the great H. L. Mencken,[7] who wrote in *The American Mercury* for April 1924 that the aim of public education is not

> to fill the young of the species with knowledge and awaken their intelligence.... Nothing could be further from the truth. The aim ... is simply to reduce as many individuals as possible to the same safe level, to breed and train a standardized citizenry, to put down dissent and originality. That is its aim in the United States ... and that is its aim everywhere else.

Because of Mencken's reputation as a satirist, we might be tempted to dismiss this passage as a bit of hyperbolic sarcasm. His article, however, goes on to trace the template for our own educational system back to the now vanished, though never to be forgotten, military state of Prussia. And although he was certainly aware of the irony that we had recently been at war with Germany, the heir to Prussian thought and culture, Mencken was being perfectly serious here. Our educational system really is Prussian in origin, and that really is cause for concern.

The odd fact of a Prussian provenance for our schools pops up again and   10 again once you know to look for it. William James[8] alluded to it many times at the turn of the century. Orestes Brownson,[9] the hero of Christopher Lasch's[10] 1991 book, *The True and Only Heaven*, was publicly denouncing the Prussianization of American schools back in the 1840s. Horace Mann's[11] "Seventh Annual Report" to the Massachusetts State Board of Education in 1843 is essentially a paean to the land of Frederick the Great[12] and a call for its schooling to be brought here. That Prussian culture loomed large in America is hardly surprising given our early association with that utopian state. A Prussian served as Washington's aide during the Revolutionary War, and so many German-speaking people had settled here by 1795 that Congress considered publishing a German-language edition of the federal laws.

[7]*H. L. Mencken:* American social critic and commentator known for his satiric wit (1880–1956).

[8]*William James:* American psychologist and philosopher (1842–1910).

[9]*Orestes Brownson:* American philosopher and essayist (1803–1876).

[10]*Christopher Lasch:* American historian and social critic (1932–1994), probably best known for *The Culture of Narcissism: American Life in an Age of Diminished Expectations* (1979) and *The Revolt of the Elites: And the Betrayal of Democracy* (1994).

[11]*Horace Mann:* Secretary of the State Board of Education in Massachusetts. See the excerpt from *Report of the Massachusetts Board of Education, 1848* (p. 116).

[12]*Frederick the Great:* King of Prussia (now part of present-day Germany), who reigned from 1740 to 1786.

But what shocks is that we should so eagerly have adopted one of the very worst aspects of Prussian culture: an educational system deliberately designed to produce mediocre intellects, to hamstring the inner life, to deny students appreciable leadership skills, and to ensure docile and incomplete citizens — all in order to render the populace "manageable."

It was from James Bryant Conant — president of Harvard for twenty years, World War I poison-gas specialist, World War II executive on the atomic-bomb project, high commissioner of the American zone in Germany after World War II, and truly one of the most influential figures of the twentieth century — that I first got wind of the real purposes of American schooling. Without Conant, we would probably not have the same style and degree of standardized testing that we enjoy today, nor would we be blessed with gargantuan high schools that warehouse 2,000 to 4,000 students at a time, like the famous Columbine High[13] in Littleton, Colorado. Shortly after I retired from teaching I picked up Conant's 1959 book-length essay, *The Child, the Parent, and the State,* and was more than a little intrigued to see him mention in passing that the modern schools we attend were the result of a "revolution" engineered between 1905 and 1930. A revolution? He declines to elaborate, but he does direct the curious and the uninformed to Alexander Inglis's 1918 book, *Principles of Secondary Education,* in which "one saw this revolution through the eyes of a revolutionary."

Inglis, for whom a lecture in education at Harvard is named, makes it perfectly clear that compulsory schooling on this continent was intended to be just what it had been for Prussia in the 1820s: a fifth column[14] into the burgeoning democratic movement that threatened to give the peasants and the proletarians a voice at the bargaining table. Modern, industrialized, compulsory schooling was to make a sort of surgical incision into the prospective unity of these underclasses. Divide children by subject, by age-grading, by constant rankings on tests, and by many other more subtle means, and it was unlikely that the ignorant mass of mankind, separated in childhood, would ever re-integrate into a dangerous whole.

Inglis breaks down the purpose — the *actual* purpose — of modern schooling into six basic functions, any one of which is enough to curl the hair of those innocent enough to believe the three traditional goals listed earlier:

1. The *adjustive* or *adaptive* function. Schools are to establish fixed habits of reaction to authority. This, of course, precludes critical judgment completely. It also pretty much destroys the idea that useful or interesting material should be taught, because you can't test for *reflexive* obedience until you know whether you can make kids learn, and do, foolish and boring things.

[13]*Columbine High:* Site of April 20, 1999, massacre by students Eric Harris and Dylan Klebold, who killed twelve and wounded twenty-four others before killing themselves.

[14]*a fifth column:* Secret group of infiltrators who undermine a nation's defenses.

2. The *integrating* function. This might well be called "the conformity function," because its intention is to make children as alike as possible. People who conform are predictable, and this is of great use to those who wish to harness and manipulate a large labor force.

3. The *diagnostic and directive* function. School is meant to determine each student's proper social role. This is done by logging evidence mathematically and anecdotally on cumulative records. As in "your permanent record." Yes, you do have one.

4. The *differentiating* function. Once their social role has been "diagnosed," children are to be sorted by role and trained only so far as their destination in the social machine merits — and not one step further. So much for making kids their personal best.

5. The *selective* function. This refers not to human choice at all but to Darwin's theory of natural selection as applied to what he called "the favored races." In short, the idea is to help things along by consciously attempting to improve the breeding stock. Schools are meant to tag the unfit — with poor grades, remedial placement, and other punishments — clearly enough that their peers will accept them as inferior and effectively bar them from the reproductive sweepstakes. That's what all those little humiliations from first grade onward were intended to do: wash the dirt down the drain.

6. The *propaedeutic* function. The societal system implied by these rules will require an elite group of caretakers. To that end, a small fraction of the kids will quietly be taught how to manage this continuing project, how to watch over and control a population deliberately dumbed down and declawed in order that government might proceed unchallenged and corporations might never want for obedient labor.

That, unfortunately, is the purpose of mandatory public education in this country. And lest you take Inglis for an isolated crank with a rather too cynical take on the educational enterprise, you should know that he was hardly alone in championing these ideas. Conant himself, building on the ideas of Horace Mann and others, campaigned tirelessly for an American school system designed along the same lines. Men like George Peabody, who funded the cause of mandatory schooling throughout the South, surely understood that the Prussian system was useful in creating not only a harmless electorate and a servile labor force but also a virtual herd of mindless consumers. In time a great number of industrial titans came to recognize the enormous profits to be had by cultivating and tending just such a herd via public education, among them Andrew Carnegie and John D. Rockefeller.

There you have it. Now you know. We don't need Karl Marx's conception of a grand warfare between the classes to see that it is in the interest of complex management, economic or political, to dumb people down, to   15 demoralize them, to divide them from one another, and to discard them if they don't conform. Class may frame the proposition, as when Woodrow Wilson, then president of Princeton University, said the following to the New York City School Teachers Association in 1909: "We want one class of persons to have a liberal education, and we want another class of persons, a very much larger class, of necessity, in every society, to forgo the privileges of a liberal education and fit themselves to perform specific difficult manual tasks." But the motives behind the disgusting decisions that bring about these ends need not be class-based at all. They can stem purely from fear, or from the by now familiar belief that "efficiency" is the paramount virtue, rather than love, liberty, laughter, or hope. Above all, they can stem from simple greed.

There were vast fortunes to be made, after all, in an economy based on mass production and organized to favor the large corporation rather than the small business or the family farm. But mass production required mass consumption, and at the turn of the twentieth century most Americans considered it both unnatural and unwise to buy things they didn't actually need. Mandatory schooling was a godsend on that count. School didn't have to train kids in any direct sense to think they should consume nonstop, because it did something even better: it encouraged them not to think at all. And that left them sitting ducks for another great invention of the modern era — marketing.

Now, you needn't have studied marketing to know that there are two groups of people who can always be convinced to consume more than they need to: addicts and children. School has done a pretty good job of turning our children into addicts, but it has done a spectacular job of turning our children into children. Again, this is no accident. Theorists from Plato to Rousseau[15] to our own Dr. Inglis knew that if children could be cloistered with other children, stripped of responsibility and independence, encouraged to develop only the trivializing emotions of greed, envy, jealousy, and fear, they would grow older but never truly grow up. In the 1934 edition of his once well-known book *Public Education in the United States*, Ellwood P. Cubberley detailed and praised the way the strategy of successive school enlargements had extended childhood by two to six years, and forced schooling was at that point still quite new. This same Cubberley — who was dean of Stanford's School of Education, a textbook editor at Houghton Mifflin, and Conant's friend and correspondent at Harvard — had written the following in the 1922 edition of his book *Public School Administration*: "Our schools are . . . factories in which the raw products (children) are to be shaped and fashioned. . . . And it is the business of the school to build its pupils according to the specifications laid down."

It's perfectly obvious from our society today what those specifications were. Maturity has by now been banished from nearly every aspect of our

---

[15]*Plato to Rousseau:* Plato (c. 427–c. 347 B.C.E.), extraordinarily influential Greek philosopher. Jean-Jacques Rousseau, Swiss philosopher and writer (1712–1778).

lives. Easy divorce laws have removed the need to work at relationships; easy credit has removed the need for fiscal self-control; easy entertainment has removed the need to learn to entertain oneself; easy answers have removed the need to ask questions. We have become a nation of children, happy to surrender our judgments and our wills to political exhortations and commercial blandishments that would insult actual adults. We buy televisions, and then we buy the things we see on the television. We buy computers, and then we buy the things we see on the computer. We buy $150 sneakers whether we need them or not, and when they fall apart too soon we buy another pair. We drive SUVs and believe the lie that they constitute a kind of life insurance, even when we're upside-down in them. And, worst of all, we don't bat an eye when Ari Fleischer[16] tells us to "be careful what you say," even if we remember having been told somewhere back in school that America is the land of the free. We simply buy that one too. Our schooling, as intended, has seen to it.

Now for the good news. Once you understand the logic behind modern schooling, its tricks and traps are fairly easy to avoid. School trains children to be employees and consumers; teach your own to be leaders and adventurers. School trains children to obey reflexively; teach your own to think critically and independently. Well-schooled kids have a low threshold for boredom; help your own to develop an inner life so that they'll never be bored. Urge them to take on the serious material, the *grown-up* material, in history, literature, philosophy, music, art, economics, theology — all the stuff schoolteachers know well enough to avoid. Challenge your kids with plenty of solitude so that they can learn to enjoy their own company, to conduct inner dialogues. Well-schooled people are conditioned to dread being alone, and they seek constant companionship through the TV, the computer, the cell phone, and through shallow friendships quickly acquired and quickly abandoned. Your children should have a more meaningful life, and they can.

First, though, we must wake up to what our schools really are: laborato-   20
ries of experimentation on young minds, drill centers for the habits and attitudes that corporate society demands. Mandatory education serves children only incidentally; its real purpose is to turn them into servants. Don't let your own have their childhoods extended, not even for a day. If David Farragut could take command of a captured British warship as a preteen, if Thomas Edison could publish a broadsheet at the age of twelve, if Ben Franklin could apprentice himself to a printer at the same age (then put himself through a course of study that would choke a Yale senior today), there's no telling what your own kids could do. After a long life, and thirty years in the public school trenches, I've concluded that genius is as common as dirt. We suppress our genius only because we haven't yet figured out how to manage a population of educated men and women. The solution, I think, is simple and glorious. Let them manage themselves.

[16]*Ari Fleischer:* Press secretary for George W. Bush from 2001 to 2003 (b. 1960).

Engaging the Text

1. Why does Gatto think that school is boring and childish? How does Gatto's depiction of school compare with your own elementary and secondary school experience?

2. What, according to Gatto, are the six unstated purposes of public schooling? To what extent does your own prior educational experience support this bleak view of American education?

From *Love Is Hell.* Copyright © 1986 Matt Groening. All rights reserved. Reprinted by permission of Pantheon Books, a division of Random House, Inc., New York. Courtesy of Acme Features Syndicate.

3. To what extent would you agree that we really don't need to go to school? Given the current state of technology and a globalizing economy, do you think most people would gain the abilities they need to survive and thrive through homeschooling?

4. How would you go about teaching your own children to be "leaders and adventurers," to think "critically and independently," and to "develop an inner life so that they'll never be bored"? How many parents, in your estimation, have the time, experience, and resources to make Gatto's ideal education a reality?

EXPLORING CONNECTIONS

5. Compare Horace Mann's view of the purpose of public education (p. 116) with Gatto's analysis of the hidden purposes of compulsory schooling. Which of these depictions of public education does your own experience of schooling support?

6. Look ahead to Jean Anyon's excerpt from *Social Class and the Hidden Curriculum of Work* (p. 169) and compare Anyon's analysis of the real agenda of American public education with that described by Gatto. To what extent does Anyon's class-based analysis of education in America support Gatto's description of the unspoken purposes of public schooling?

EXTENDING THE CRITICAL CONTEXT

7. Working in groups, write a proposal for a school that wouldn't be boring or childish and that would create the kind of independent, critical, active thinkers that Gatto prizes. What would a day in such a school be like? What would the students do? What would they learn? Who would teach them?

8. Research the state of Prussia and Frederick the Great to learn more about Prussian history and culture. How might your findings change your response to Gatto's argument? Would you agree that the Prussian influence on American schooling is really a "cause for concern"? Why? What other nineteenth-century nation might have offered a better model?

"I Just Wanna Be Average"

MIKE ROSE

Mike Rose is anything but average: he has published poetry, scholarly research, a textbook, and several widely praised books on education in America. A professor in the School of Education at UCLA, Rose (b. 1944) has won awards from the National Academy of Education, the National Council of Teachers of English, and the John Simon Guggenheim Memorial Foundation.

Below you'll read the story of how this highly successful teacher and writer started high school in the vocational education track, learning dead-end skills from teachers who were often underprepared or incompetent. Rose shows that students whom the system has written off can have tremendous unrealized potential, and his critique of the school system specifies several reasons for the failure of students who go through high school belligerent, fearful, stoned, frustrated, or just plain bored. This selection comes from Lives on the Boundary *(1989), Rose's exploration of America's educationally underprivileged. His publications also include* Possible Lives *(1996), an explanation of nationwide educational innovation;* The Mind at Work *(2006), a study of the complex thinking involved in common labor; and, most recently,* Why School? *(2009). Rose is currently a professor at the UCLA Graduate School of Education and Information Studies.*

It took two buses to get to Our Lady of Mercy. The first started deep in South Los Angeles and caught me at midpoint. The second drifted through neighborhoods with trees, parks, big lawns, and lots of flowers. The rides were long but were livened up by a group of South L.A. veterans whose parents also thought that Hope had set up shop in the west end of the county. There was Christy Biggars, who, at sixteen, was dealing and was, according to rumor, a pimp as well. There were Bill Cobb and Johnny Gonzales, grease-pencil artists extraordinaire, who left Nembutal-enhanced[1] swirls of "Cobb" and "Johnny" on the corrugated walls of the bus. And then there was Tyrrell Wilson. Tyrrell was the coolest kid I knew. He ran the dozens[2] like a metric halfback, laid down a rap that outrhymed and outpointed Cobb, whose rap was good but not great — the curse of a moderately soulful kid trapped in white skin. But it was Cobb who would sneak a radio onto the bus, and thus underwrote his patter with Little Richard, Fats Domino, Chuck Berry, the Coasters, and Ernie K. Doe's[3] mother-in-law, an awful woman who was "sent from down below." And so it was that Christy and Cobb and Johnny G. and Tyrrell and I and assorted others picked up along the way passed our days in the back of the bus, a funny mix brought together by geography and parental desire.

Entrance to school brings with it forms and releases and assessments. Mercy relied on a series of tests, mostly the Stanford-Binet,[4] for placement, and somehow the results of my tests got confused with those of another stu-

---

[1]*Nembutal:* Trade name for pentobarbital, a sedative drug.

[2]*the dozens:* A verbal game of African origin in which competitors try to top each other's insults.

[3]*Little Richard, Fats Domino, Chuck Berry, the Coasters, and Ernie K. Doe:* Popular black musicians of the 1950s.

[4]*Stanford-Binet:* An IQ test.

dent named Rose. The other Rose apparently didn't do very well, for I was placed in the vocational track, a euphemism for the bottom level. Neither I nor my parents realized what this meant. We had no sense that Business Math, Typing, and English-Level D were dead ends. The current spate of reports on the schools criticizes parents for not involving themselves in the education of their children. But how would someone like Tommy Rose, with his two years of Italian schooling, know what to ask? And what sort of pressure could an exhausted waitress apply? The error went undetected, and I remained in the vocational track for two years. What a place.

My homeroom was supervised by Brother Dill, a troubled and unstable man who also taught freshman English. When his class drifted away from him, which was often, his voice would rise in paranoid accusations, and occasionally he would lose control and shake or smack us. I hadn't been there two months when one of his brisk, face-turning slaps had my glasses sliding down the aisle. Physical education was also pretty harsh. Our teacher was a stubby ex-lineman who had played old-time pro ball in the Midwest. He routinely had us grabbing our ankles to receive his stinging paddle across our butts. He did that, he said, to make men of us. "Rose," he bellowed on our first encounter; me standing geeky in line in my baggy shorts. "'Rose'? What the hell kind of name is that?"

"Italian, sir," I squeaked.

"Italian! Ho. Rose, do you know the sound a bag of shit makes when it   5
hits the wall?"

"No, sir."

"Wop!"[5]

Sophomore English was taught by Mr. Mitropetros. He was a large, bejeweled man who managed the parking lot at the Shrine Auditorium. He would crow and preen and list for us the stars he'd brushed against. We'd ask questions and glance knowingly and snicker, and all that fueled the poor guy to brag some more. Parking cars was his night job. He had little training in English, so his lesson plan for his day work had us reading the district's required text, *Julius Caesar,* aloud for the semester. We'd finished the play way before the twenty weeks was up, so he'd have us switch parts again and again and start again: Dave Snyder, the fastest guy at Mercy, muscling through Caesar to the breathless squeals of Calpurnia, as interpreted by Steve Fusco, a surfer who owned the school's most envied paneled wagon. Week ten and Dave and Steve would take on new roles, as would we all, and render a water-logged Cassius and a Brutus that are beyond my powers of description.

Spanish I — taken in the second year — fell into the hands of a new recruit. Mr. Montez was a tiny man, slight, five foot six at the most, soft-spoken and delicate. Spanish was a particularly rowdy class, and Mr. Montez was as prepared for it as a doily maker at a hammer throw. He would tap his

[5]*Wop:* Derogatory term for Italian.

pencil to a room in which Steve Fusco was propelling spitballs from his heavy lips, in which Mike Dweetz was taunting Billy Hawk, a half-Indian, half-Spanish, reed-thin, quietly explosive boy. The vocational track at Our Lady of Mercy mixed kids traveling in from South L.A. with South Bay surfers and a few Slavs and Chicanos from the harbors of San Pedro. This was a dangerous miscellany: surfers and hodads[6] and South-Central blacks all ablaze to the metronomic tapping of Hector Montez's pencil.

One day Billy lost it. Out of the corner of my eye I saw him strike   10 out with his right arm and catch Dweetz across the neck. Quick as a spasm, Dweetz was out of his seat, scattering desks, cracking Billy on the side of the head, right behind the eye. Snyder and Fusco and others broke it up, but the room felt hot and close and naked. Mr. Montez's tenuous authority was finally ripped to shreds, and I think everyone felt a little strange about that. The charade was over, and when it came down to it, I don't think any of the kids really wanted it to end this way. They had pushed and pushed and bullied their way into a freedom that both scared and embarrassed them.

Students will float to the mark you set. I and the others in the vocational classes were bobbing in pretty shallow water. Vocational education has aimed at increasing the economic opportunities of students who do not do well in our schools. Some serious programs succeed in doing that, and through exceptional teachers — like Mr. Gross in *Horace's Compromise*[7] — students learn to develop hypotheses and troubleshoot, reason through a problem, and communicate effectively — the true job skills. The vocational track, however, is most often a place for those who are just not making it, a dumping ground for the disaffected. There were a few teachers who worked hard at education; young Brother Slattery, for example, combined a stern voice with weekly quizzes to try to pass along to us a skeletal outline of world history. But mostly the teachers had no idea of how to engage the imaginations of us kids who were scuttling along at the bottom of the pond.

And the teachers would have needed some inventiveness, for none of us was groomed for the classroom. It wasn't just that I didn't know things — didn't know how to simplify algebraic fractions, couldn't identify different kinds of clauses, bungled Spanish translations — but that I had developed various faulty and inadequate ways of doing algebra and making sense of Spanish. Worse yet, the years of defensive tuning out in elementary school had given me a way to escape quickly while seeming at least half alert. During my time in Voc. Ed., I developed further into a mediocre student and a somnambulant problem solver, and that affected the subjects I did have the wherewithal to handle: I detested Shakespeare; I got bored with history. My attention flitted here and there. I fooled around in class and read my books indifferently — the intellectual equivalent of playing with your food. I did what I had to do to get by, and I did it with half a mind.

---

[6]*hodads:* Nonsurfers.
[7]*Horace's Compromise:* A book on American education by Theodore Sizer.

But I did learn things about people and eventually came into my own socially. I liked the guys in Voc. Ed. Growing up where I did, I understood and admired physical prowess, and there was an abundance of muscle here. There was Dave Snyder, a sprinter and halfback of true quality. Dave's ability and his quick wit gave him a natural appeal, and he was welcome in any clique, though he always kept a little independent. He enjoyed acting the fool and could care less about studies, but he possessed a certain maturity and never caused the faculty much trouble. It was a testament to his independence that he included me among his friends — I eventually went out for track, but I was no jock. Owing to the Latin alphabet and a dearth of *R*s and *S*s, Snyder sat behind Rose, and we started exchanging one-liners and became friends.

There was Ted Richard, a much-touted Little League pitcher. He was chunky and had a baby face and came to Our Lady of Mercy as a seasoned street fighter. Ted was quick to laugh and he had a loud, jolly laugh, but when he got angry he'd smile a little smile, the kind that simply raises the corner of the mouth a quarter of an inch. For those who knew, it was an eerie signal. Those who didn't found themselves in big trouble, for Ted was very quick. He loved to carry on what we would come to call philosophical discussions: What is courage? Does God exist? He also loved words, enjoyed picking up big ones like *salubrious* and *equivocal* and using them in our conversations — laughing at himself as the word hit a chuckhole rolling off his tongue. Ted didn't do all that well in school — baseball and parties and testing the courage he'd speculated about took up his time. His textbooks were *Argosy* and *Field and Stream*, whatever newspapers he'd find on the bus stop — from the *Daily Worker* to pornography — conversations with uncles or hobos or businessmen he'd meet in a coffee shop, *The Old Man and the Sea.* With hindsight, I can see that Ted was developing into one of those rough-hewn intellectuals whose sources are a mix of the learned and the apocryphal, whose discussions are both assured and sad.

And then there was Ken Harvey. Ken was good-looking in a puffy way and had a full and oily ducktail and was a car enthusiast . . . a hodad. One day in religion class, he said the sentence that turned out to be one of the most memorable of the hundreds of thousands I heard in those Voc. Ed. years. We were talking about the parable of the talents, about achievement, working hard, doing the best you can do, blah-blah-blah, when the teacher called on the restive Ken Harvey for an opinion. Ken thought about it, but just for a second, and said (with studied, minimal affect), "I just wanna be average." That woke me up. Average? Who wants to be average? Then the athletes chimed in with the clichés that make you want to laryngectomize them, and the exchange became a platitudinous melee. At the time, I thought Ken's assertion was stupid, and I wrote him off. But his sentence has stayed with me all these years, and I think I am finally coming to understand it. 15

Ken Harvey was gasping for air. School can be a tremendously disorienting place. No matter how bad the school, you're going to encounter notions that don't fit with the assumptions and beliefs that you grew up with — maybe you'll hear these dissonant notions from teachers, maybe from the other students, and maybe you'll read them. You'll also be thrown in with all kinds of kids from all kinds of backgrounds, and that can be unsettling — this is especially true in places of rich ethnic and linguistic mix, like the L.A. basin. You'll see a handful of students far excel you in courses that sound exotic and that are only in the curriculum of the elite: French, physics, trigonometry. And all this is happening while you're trying to shape an identity, your body is changing, and your emotions are running wild. If you're a working-class kid in the vocational track, the options you'll have to deal with this will be constrained in certain ways: you're defined by your school as "slow"; you're placed in a curriculum that isn't designed to liberate you but to occupy you, or, if you're lucky, train you, though the training is for work the society does not esteem; other students are picking up the cues from your school and your curriculum and interacting with you in particular ways. If you're a kid like Ted Richard, you turn your back on all this and let your mind roam where it may. But youngsters like Ted are rare. What Ken and so many others do is protect themselves from such suffocating madness by taking on with a vengeance the identity implied in the vocational track. Reject the confusion and frustration by openly defining yourself as the Common Joe. Champion the average. Rely on your own good sense. Fuck this bullshit. Bullshit, of course, is everything you — and the others — fear is beyond you: books, essays, tests, academic scrambling, complexity, scientific reasoning, philosophical inquiry.

The tragedy is that you have to twist the knife in your own gray matter to make this defense work. You'll have to shut down, have to reject intellectual stimuli or diffuse them with sarcasm, have to cultivate stupidity, have to convert boredom from a malady into a way of confronting the world. Keep your vocabulary simple, act stoned when you're not or act more stoned than you are, flaunt ignorance, materialize your dreams. It is a powerful and effective defense — it neutralizes the insult and the frustration of being a vocational kid and, when perfected, it drives teachers up the wall, a delightful secondary effect. But like all strong magic, it exacts a price.

My own deliverance from the Voc. Ed. world began with sophomore biology. Every student, college prep to vocational, had to take biology, and unlike the other courses, the same person taught all sections. When teaching the vocational group, Brother Clint probably slowed down a bit or omitted a little of the fundamental biochemistry, but he used the same book and more or less the same syllabus across the board. If one class got tough, he could get tougher. He was young and powerful and very handsome, and looks and physical strength were high currency. No one gave him any trouble.

I was pretty bad at the dissecting table, but the lectures and the textbook were interesting: plastic overlays that, with each turned page, peeled away skin, then veins and muscle, then organs, down to the very bones that Brother Clint, pointer in hand, would tap out on our hanging skeleton. Dave Snyder was in big trouble, for the study of life — versus the living of it — was sticking in his craw. We worked out a code for our multiple-choice exams. He'd poke me in the back: once for the answer under *A*, twice for *B*, and so on; and when he'd hit the right one, I'd look up to the ceiling as though I were lost in thought. Poke: cytoplasm. Poke, poke: methane. Poke, poke, poke: William Harvey. Poke, poke, poke, poke: islets of Langerhans. This didn't work out perfectly, but Dave passed the course, and I mastered the dreamy look of a guy on a record jacket. And something else happened. Brother Clint puzzled over this Voc. Ed. kid who was racking up 98s and 99s on his tests. He checked the school's records and discovered the error. He recommended that I begin my junior year in the College Prep program. According to all I've read since, such a shift, as one report put it, is virtually impossible. Kids at that level rarely cross tracks. The telling thing is how chancy both my placement into and exit from Voc. Ed. was; neither I nor my parents had anything to do with it. I lived in one world during spring semester, and when I came back to school in the fall, I was living in another.

Switching to College Prep was a mixed blessing. I was an erratic student. 20
I was undisciplined. And I hadn't caught onto the rules of the game: why work hard in a class that didn't grab my fancy? I was also hopelessly behind in math. Chemistry was hard; toying with my chemistry set years before hadn't prepared me for the chemist's equations. Fortunately, the priest who taught both chemistry and second-year algebra was also the school's athletic director. Membership on the track team covered me; I knew I wouldn't get lower than a C. U.S. history was taught pretty well, and I did okay. But civics was taken over by a football coach who had trouble reading the textbook aloud — and reading aloud was the centerpiece of his pedagogy. College Prep at Mercy was certainly an improvement over the vocational program — at least it carried some status — but the social science curriculum was weak, and the mathematics and physical sciences were simply beyond me. I had a miserable quantitative background and ended up copying some assignments and finessing the rest as best I could. Let me try to explain how it feels to see again and again material you should once have learned but didn't.

You are given a problem. It requires you to simplify algebraic fractions or to multiply expressions containing square roots. You know this is pretty basic material because you've seen it for years. Once a teacher took some time with you, and you learned how to carry out these operations. Simple versions, anyway. But that was a year or two or more in the past, and these are more complex versions, and now you're not sure. And this, you keep telling yourself, is ninth- or even eighth-grade stuff.

Next it's a word problem. This is also old hat. The basic elements are as familiar as story characters: trains speeding so many miles per hour or shadows of buildings angling so many degrees. Maybe you know enough, have sat through enough explanations, to be able to begin setting up the problem: "If one train is going this fast . . ." or "This shadow is really one line of a triangle . . ." Then: "Let's see . . ." "How did Jones do this?" "Hmmmm." "No." "No, that won't work." Your attention wavers. You wonder about other things: a football game, a dance, that cute new checker at the market. You try to focus on the problem again. You scribble on paper for a while, but the tension wins out and your attention flits elsewhere. You crumple the paper and begin daydreaming to ease the frustration.

The particulars will vary, but in essence this is what a number of students go through, especially those in so-called remedial classes. They open their textbooks and see once again the familiar and impenetrable formulas and diagrams and terms that have stumped them for years. There is no excitement here. *No* excitement. Regardless of what the teacher says, this is not a new challenge. There is, rather, embarrassment and frustration and, not surprisingly, some anger in being reminded once again of long-standing inadequacies. No wonder so many students finally attribute their difficulties to something inborn, organic: "That part of my brain just doesn't work." Given the troubling histories many of these students have, it's miraculous that any of them can lift the shroud of hopelessness sufficiently to make deliverance from these classes possible.

Through this entire period, my father's health was deteriorating with cruel momentum. His arteriosclerosis progressed to the point where a simple nick on his shin wouldn't heal. Eventually it ulcerated and widened. Lou Minton would come by daily to change the dressing. We tried renting an oscillating bed — which we placed in the front room — to force blood through the constricted arteries in my father's legs. The bed hummed through the night, moving in place to ward off the inevitable. The ulcer continued to spread, and the doctors finally had to amputate. My grandfather had lost his leg in a stockyard accident. Now my father too was crippled. His convalescence was slow but steady, and the doctors placed him in the Santa Monica Rehabilitation Center, a sun-bleached building that opened out onto the warm spray of the Pacific. The place gave him some strength and some color and some training in walking with an artificial leg. He did pretty well for a year or so until he slipped and broke his hip. He was confined to a wheelchair after that, and the confinement contributed to the diminishing of his body and spirit.

I am holding a picture of him. He is sitting in his wheelchair and smil- 25
ing at the camera. The smile appears forced, unsteady, seems to quaver, though it is frozen in silver nitrate. He is in his mid-sixties and looks eighty. Late in my junior year, he had a stroke and never came out of the resulting coma. After that, I would see him only in dreams, and to this day that is how I join him. Sometimes the dreams are sad and grisly and primal: my father lying in a bed soaked with his suppuration,[8] holding me, rocking me. But sometimes the dreams bring him back to me healthy: him talking to me on an empty street, or buying some pictures to decorate our old house, or transformed somehow into someone strong and adept with tools and the physical.

---

[8]*suppuration:* Discharge from wounds.

Jack MacFarland couldn't have come into my life at a better time. My father was dead, and I had logged up too many years of scholastic indifference. Mr. MacFarland had a master's degree from Columbia and decided, at twenty-six, to find a little school and teach his heart out. He never took any credentialing courses, couldn't bear to, he said, so he had to find employment in a private system. He ended up at Our Lady of Mercy teaching five sections of senior English. He was a beatnik who was born too late. His teeth were stained, he tucked his sorry tie in between the third and fourth buttons of his shirt, and his pants were chronically wrinkled. At first, we couldn't believe this guy, thought he slept in his car. But within no time, he had us so startled with work that we didn't much worry about where he slept or if he slept at all. We wrote three or four essays a month. We read a book every two to three weeks, starting with the *Iliad* and ending up with Hemingway. He gave us a quiz on the reading every other day. He brought a prep school curriculum to Mercy High.

MacFarland's lectures were crafted, and as he delivered them he would pace the room jiggling a piece of chalk in his cupped hand, using it to scribble on the board the names of all the writers and philosophers and plays and novels he was weaving into his discussion. He asked questions often, raised everything from Zeno's paradox to the repeated last line of Frost's "Stopping by Woods on a Snowy Evening." He slowly and carefully built up our knowledge of Western intellectual history — with facts, with connections, with speculations. We learned about Greek philosophy, about Dante, the Elizabethan world view, the Age of Reason, existentialism. He analyzed poems with us, had us reading sections from John Ciardi's *How Does a Poem Mean?*, making a potentially difficult book accessible with his own explanations. We gave oral reports on poems Ciardi didn't cover. We imitated the styles of Conrad, Hemingway, and *Time* magazine. We wrote and talked, wrote and talked. The man immersed us in language.

Even MacFarland's barbs were literary. If Jim Fitzsimmons, hung over and irritable, tried to smart-ass him, he'd rejoin with a flourish that would spark the indomitable Skip Madison — who'd lost his front teeth in a hapless tackle — to flick his tongue through the gap and opine, "good chop," drawing out the single "o" in stinging indictment. Jack MacFarland, this tobacco-stained intellectual, brandished linguistic weapons of a kind I hadn't encountered before. Here was this *egghead*, for God's sake, keeping some pretty difficult people in line. And from what I heard, Mike Dweetz and Steve Fusco and all the notorious Voc. Ed. crowd settled down as well when MacFarland took the podium. Though a lot of guys groused in the schoolyard, it just seemed that giving trouble to this particular teacher was a silly thing to do. Tomfoolery, not to mention assault, had no place in the world he was trying to create for us, and instinctively everyone knew that. If nothing else, we all recognized MacFarland's considerable intelligence and respected the hours he put into his work. It came to this: the troublemaker would look foolish rather than daring. Even Jim Fitzsimmons was reading *On the Road* and turning his incipient alcoholism to literary ends.

There were some lives that were already beyond Jack MacFarland's ministrations, but mine was not. I started reading again as I hadn't since elementary school. I would go into our gloomy little bedroom or sit at the dinner table while, on the television, Danny McShane was paralyzing Mr. Moto with the atomic drop, and work slowly back through *Heart of Darkness,* trying to catch the words in Conrad's sentences. I certainly was not MacFarland's best student; most of the other guys in College Prep, even my fellow slackers, had better backgrounds than I did. But I worked very hard, for MacFarland had hooked me. He tapped my old interest in reading and creating stories. He gave me a way to feel special by using my mind. And he provided a role model that wasn't shaped on physical prowess alone, and something inside me that I wasn't quite aware of responded to that. Jack MacFarland established a literacy club, to borrow a phrase of Frank Smith's, and invited me — invited all of us — to join.

There's been a good deal of research and speculation suggesting that the   30 acknowledgment of school performance with extrinsic rewards — smiling faces, stars, numbers, grades — diminishes the intrinsic satisfaction children experience by engaging in reading or writing or problem solving. While it's certainly true that we've created an educational system that encourages our best and brightest to become cynical grade collectors and, in general, have developed an obsession with evaluation and assessment, I must tell you that venal though it may have been, I loved getting good grades from MacFarland. I now know how subjective grades can be, but then they came tucked in the back of essays like bits of scientific data, some sort of spectroscopic readout that said, objectively and publicly, that I had made something of value. I suppose I'd been mediocre for too long and enjoyed a public redefinition. And I suppose the workings of my mind, such as they were, had been private for too long. My linguistic play moved into the world; . . . these papers with their circled, red B-pluses and A-minuses linked my mind to something outside it. I carried them around like a club emblem.

One day in the December of my senior year, Mr. MacFarland asked me where I was going to go to college. I hadn't thought much about it. Many of the students I teach today spent their last year in high school with a physics text in one hand and the Stanford catalog in the other, but I wasn't even aware of what "entrance requirements" were. My folks would say that they wanted me to go to college and be a doctor, but I don't know how seriously I ever took that; it seemed a sweet thing to say, a bit of supportive family chatter, like telling a gangly daughter she's graceful. The reality of higher education wasn't in my scheme of things: no one in the family had gone to college; only two of my uncles had completed high school. I figured I'd get a night job and go to the local junior college because I knew that Snyder and Company were going there to play ball. But I hadn't even prepared for that. When I finally said, "I don't know," MacFarland looked down at me — I was seated in his office — and said, "Listen, you can write."

My grades stank. I had A's in biology and a handful of B's in a few English and social science classes. All the rest were C's — or worse. MacFarland said I would do well in his class and laid down the law about doing well in the others. Still, the record for my first three years wouldn't have been acceptable to any four-year school. To nobody's surprise, I was turned down flat by USC and UCLA. But Jack MacFarland was on the case. He had received his bachelor's degree from Loyola University, so he made calls to old professors and talked to somebody in admissions and wrote me a strong letter. Loyola finally accepted me as a probationary student. I would be on trial for the first year, and if I did okay, I would be granted regular status. MacFarland also intervened to get me a loan, for I could never have afforded a private college without it. Four more years of religion classes and four more years of boys at one school, girls at another. But at least I was going to college. Amazing.

In my last semester of high school, I elected a special English course fashioned by Mr. MacFarland, and it was through this elective that there arose at Mercy a fledgling literati. Art Mitz, the editor of the school newspaper and a very smart guy, was the kingpin. He was joined by me and by Mark Dever, a quiet boy who wrote beautifully and who would die before he was forty. MacFarland occasionally invited us to his apartment, and those visits became the high point of our apprenticeship: we'd clamp on our training wheels and drive to his salon.

He lived in a cramped and cluttered place near the airport, tucked away in the kind of building that architectural critic Reyner Banham calls a *dingbat.* Books were all over: stacked, piled, tossed, and crated, underlined and dog eared, well worn and new. Cigarette ashes crusted with coffee in saucers or spilling over the sides of motel ashtrays. The little bedroom had, along two of its walls, bricks and boards loaded with notes, magazines, and oversized books. The kitchen joined the living room, and there was a stack of German newspapers under the sink. I had never seen anything like it: a great flophouse of language furnished by City Lights and Café le Metro. I read every title. I flipped through paperbacks and scanned jackets and memorized names: Gogol, *Finnegans Wake,* Djuna Barnes, Jackson Pollock, *A Coney Island of the Mind,* F. O. Matthiessen's *American Renaissance,* all sorts of Freud, *Troubled Sleep,* Man Ray, *The Education of Henry Adams,* Richard Wright, *Film as Art,* William Butler Yeats, Marguerite Duras, *Redburn, A Season in Hell, Kapital.* On the cover of Alain-Fournier's *The Wanderer* was an Edward Gorey drawing of a young man on a road winding into dark trees. By the hotplate sat a strange Kafka novel called *Amerika,* in which an adolescent hero crosses the Atlantic to find the Nature Theater of Oklahoma. Art and Mark would be talking about a movie or the school newspaper, and I would be consuming my English teacher's library. It was heady stuff. I felt like a Pop Warner[9] athlete on steroids.

---

[9]*Pop Warner:* A nationwide youth athletics organization.

Art, Mark, and I would buy stogies and triangulate from MacFarland's 35
apartment to the Cinema, which now shows X-rated films but was then L.A.'s
premier art theater, and then to the musty Cherokee Bookstore in Hollywood to hobnob with beatnik homosexuals — smoking, drinking bourbon
and coffee, and trying out awkward phrases we'd gleaned from our mentor's
bookshelves. I was happy and precocious and a little scared as well, for
Hollywood Boulevard was thick with a kind of decadence that was foreign to
the South Side. After the Cherokee, we would head back to the security of
MacFarland's apartment, slaphappy with hipness.

Let me be the first to admit that there was a good deal of adolescent
passion in this embrace of the avant-garde: self-absorption, sexually charged
pedantry, an elevation of the odd and abandoned. Still it was a time during
which I absorbed an awful lot of information: long lists of titles, images
from expressionist paintings, new wave shibboleths,[10] snippets of philosophy, and names that read like Steve Fusco's misspellings — Goethe, Nietzsche, Kierkegaard. Now this is hardly the stuff of deep understanding. But
it was an introduction, a phrase book, a Baedeker[11] to a vocabulary of ideas,
and it felt good at the time to know all these words. With hindsight I realize
how layered and important that knowledge was.

It enabled me to do things in the world. I could browse bohemian
bookstores in far-off, mysterious Hollywood; I could go to the Cinema and
see events through the lenses of European directors; and, most of all, I
could share an evening, talk that talk, with Jack MacFarland, the man I
most admired at the time. Knowledge was becoming a bonding agent.
Within a year or two, the persona of the disaffected hipster would prove too
cynical, too alienated to last. But for a time it was new and exciting: it provided a critical perspective on society, and it allowed me to act as though I
were living beyond the limiting boundaries of South Vermont.[12]

ENGAGING THE TEXT

1. Describe Rose's life in Voc. Ed. What were his teachers like? Have you
   ever had experience with teachers like these?
2. What did Voc. Ed. do to Rose and his fellow students? How did it affect
   them intellectually, emotionally, and socially? Why was it subsequently so
   hard for Rose to catch up in math?
3. Why is high school so disorienting to students like Ken Harvey? How does
   he cope with it? What other strategies do students use to cope with the
   pressures and judgments they encounter in school?
4. What does Jack MacFarland offer Rose that finally helps him learn? Do
   you think it was inevitable that someone with Rose's intelligence would
   eventually succeed?

---

[10]*new wave shibboleths:* Trendy phrases or jargon.
[11]*Baedeker:* Travel guide.
[12]*South Vermont:* A street in an economically depressed area of Los Angeles.

EXPLORING CONNECTIONS

5. To what extent do Rose's experiences challenge or confirm John Taylor Gatto's critique of public education in "Against School" (p. 148)? How might Gatto account for the existence of truly remarkable teachers like Rose's Jack MacFarland?

6. How does Michael Moore's assessment of the general state of intelligence in America in "Idiot Nation" (p. 128) help to explain the attitudes of Rose's friends toward education? How would you account for the fact that many American teens seem to feel it's OK to be "average" intellectually even as they strive for other kinds of excellence?

7. Draw a Groening-style cartoon (see pp. 147 and 156) or comic strip of Rose in the vocational track, or of Rose before and after his liberation from Voc. Ed.

8. Read Gregory Mantsios's "Class in America — 2006" (p. 304) and write an imaginary dialogue between Rose and Mantsios about why some students, like Rose, seem to be able to break through social class barriers and others, like Dave Snyder, Ted Richard, and Ken Harvey, do not.

EXTENDING THE CRITICAL CONTEXT

9. Rose explains that high school can be a "tremendously disorienting place" (para. 16). What, if anything, do you find disorienting about college? What steps can students at your school take to lessen feelings of disorientation? What could the college do to help them?

10. Review one or more of Rose's descriptions of his high school classmates; then write a description of one of your own high school classmates, trying to capture in a nutshell how that person coped or failed to cope with the educational system.

11. Watch any one of the many films that have been made about charismatic teachers (for example, *Dangerous Minds, Renaissance Man, Stand and Deliver,* or *Dead Poets Society*) and compare Hollywood's depiction of a dynamic teacher to Rose's portrayal of Jack MacFarland. What do such charismatic teachers offer their students personally and intellectually? Do you see any disadvantages to classes taught by teachers like these?

From *Social Class and the Hidden Curriculum of Work*

JEAN ANYON

It's no surprise that schools in wealthy communities are better than those in poor communities, or that they better prepare their students for desirable jobs. It may be shocking, however, to learn how vast the differences in schools are—not so much in resources as in teaching methods and philosophies of education. Jean Anyon observed five elementary schools over the course of a full school year and concluded that fifth graders of different economic backgrounds are already being prepared to occupy particular rungs on the social ladder. In a sense, some whole schools are on the vocational education track, while others are geared to produce future doctors, lawyers, and business leaders. Anyon's main audience is professional educators, so you may find her style and vocabulary challenging, but, once you've read her descriptions of specific classroom activities, the more analytic parts of the essay should prove easier to understand. Anyon is professor of educational policy in the Graduate Center of the City University of New York. Her publications include Radical Possibilities: Public Policy, Urban Education and a New Social Movement *(2005) and* Theory and Educational Research: Toward Critical Social Explanation *(2009). This essay first appeared in the* Journal of Education *in 1980.*

Scholars in political economy and the sociology of knowledge have recently argued that public schools in complex industrial societies like our own make available different types of educational experience and curriculum knowledge to students in different social classes. Bowles and Gintis,[1] for example, have argued that students in different social-class backgrounds are rewarded for classroom behaviors that correspond to personality traits allegedly rewarded in the different occupational strata — the working classes for docility and obedience, the managerial classes for initiative and personal assertiveness. Basil Bernstein, Pierre Bourdieu, and Michael W. Apple,[2] focusing on school knowledge, have argued that knowledge and skills leading to social power and regard (medical, legal, managerial) are made available to the advantaged social groups but are withheld from the working classes, to whom a more "practical" curriculum is offered (manual skills, clerical knowledge). While there has been considerable argumentation of these points regarding education in England, France, and North America, there has been little or no attempt to investigate these ideas empirically in elementary or secondary schools and classrooms in this country.[3]

---

[1]S. Bowles and H. Gintis, *Schooling in Capitalist America: Educational Reform and the Contradictions of Economic Life* (New York: Basic Books, 1976). [All notes are the author's unless otherwise indicated.]

[2]B. Bernstein, *Class, Codes and Control*, Vol. 3. *Towards a Theory of Educational Transmission*, 2d ed. (London: Routledge & Kegan Paul, 1977); P. Bourdieu and J. Passeron, *Reproduction in Education, Society and Culture* (Beverly Hills, Calif.: Sage, 1977); M. W. Apple, *Ideology and Curriculum* (Boston: Routledge & Kegan Paul, 1979).

[3]But see, in a related vein, M. W. Apple and N. King, "What Do Schools Teach?" *Curriculum Inquiry* 6 (1977): 341-58; R. C. Rist, *The Urban School: A Factory for Failure* (Cambridge, Mass.: MIT Press, 1973).

WE DO NOT DISCRIMINATE ON THE BASIS OF RACE, AGE, SEX, OR RELIGION. STUDENTS SIMPLY MUST BE ABLE TO AFFORD $20,000 TUITION PER YEAR.

SCHWADR

Copyright © Harley Schwadron. Courtesy of CartoonStock.com.

This article offers tentative empirical support (and qualification) of the above arguments by providing illustrative examples of differences in student *work* in classrooms in contrasting social-class communities. The examples were gathered as part of an ethnographical[4] study of curricular, pedagogical, and pupil evaluation practices in five elementary schools. The article attempts a theoretical contribution as well and assesses student work in the light of a theoretical approach to social-class analysis. . . . It will be suggested that there is a "hidden curriculum" in schoolwork that has profound implications for the theory — and consequence — of everyday activity in education. . . .

The Sample of Schools

. . . The social-class designation of each of the five schools will be identified, and the income, occupation, and other relevant available social characteristics of the students and their parents will be described. The first three schools are in a medium-sized city district in northern New Jersey, and the other two are in a nearby New Jersey suburb.

---

[4]*ethnographical:* Based on an anthropological study of cultures or subcultures — the "cultures" in this case being the five schools observed. [Eds.]

The first two schools I will call *working-class schools.* Most of the parents have blue-collar jobs. Less than a third of the fathers are skilled, while the majority are in unskilled or semiskilled jobs. During the period of the study (1978–1979), approximately 15 percent of the fathers were unemployed. The large majority (85 percent) of the families are white. The following occupations are typical: platform, storeroom, and stockroom workers; foundrymen, pipe welders, and boilermakers; semiskilled and unskilled assemblyline operatives; gas station attendants, auto mechanics, maintenance workers, and security guards. Less than 30 percent of the women work, some part-time and some full-time, on assembly lines, in storerooms and stockrooms, as waitresses, barmaids, or sales clerks. Of the fifth-grade parents, none of the wives of the skilled workers had jobs. Approximately 15 percent of the families in each school are at or below the federal "poverty" level;[5] most of the rest of the family incomes are at or below $12,000, except some of the skilled workers whose incomes are higher. The incomes of the majority of the families in these two schools (at or below $12,000) are typical of 38.6 percent of the families in the United States.[6]

The third school is called the *middle-class school,* although because of   5
neighborhood residence patterns, the population is a mixture of several social classes. The parents' occupations can be divided into three groups: a small group of blue-collar "rich," who are skilled, well-paid workers such as printers, carpenters, plumbers, and construction workers. The second group is composed of parents in working-class and middle-class white-collar jobs: women in office jobs, technicians, supervisors in industry, and parents employed by the city (such as firemen, policemen, and several of the school's teachers). The third group is composed of occupations such as personnel directors in local firms, accountants, "middle management," and a few small capitalists (owners of shops in the area). The children of several local doctors attend this school. Most family incomes are between $13,000 and $25,000, with a few higher. This income range is typical of 38.9 percent of the families in the United States.[7]

The fourth school has a parent population that is at the upper income level of the upper middle class and is predominantly professional. This school will be called the *affluent professional school.* Typical jobs are: cardiologist, interior designer, corporate lawyer or engineer, executive in advertising or television. There are some families who are not as affluent as the majority (the family of the superintendent of the district's schools, and the one or two families in which the fathers are skilled workers). In addition, a

---

[5]The U.S. Bureau of the Census defines *poverty* for a nonfarm family of four as a yearly income of $6,191 a year or less. U.S. Bureau of the Census, *Statistical Abstract of the United States: 1978* (Washington, D.C.: U.S. Government Printing Office, 1978), 465, table 754.

[6]U.S. Bureau of the Census, "Money Income in 1977 of Families and Persons in the United States," *Current Population Reports* Series P-60, no. 118 (Washington, D.C.: U.S. Government Printing Office, 1979), p. 2, table A.

[7]Ibid.

few of the families are more affluent than the majority and can be classified in the capitalist class (a partner in a prestigious Wall Street stock brokerage firm). Approximately 90 percent of the children in this school are white. Most family incomes are between $40,000 and $80,000. This income span represents approximately 7 percent of the families in the United States.[8]

In the fifth school the majority of the families belong to the capitalist class. This school will be called the *executive elite school* because most of the fathers are top executives (for example, presidents and vice-presidents) in major United States–based multinational corporations — for example, AT&T, RCA, Citibank, American Express, U.S. Steel. A sizable group of fathers are top executives in financial firms on Wall Street. There are also a number of fathers who list their occupations as "general counsel" to a particular corporation, and these corporations are also among the large multinationals. Many of the mothers do volunteer work in the Junior League, Junior Fortnightly, or other service groups; some are intricately involved in town politics; and some are themselves in well-paid occupations. There are no minority children in the school. Almost all the family incomes are over $100,000, with some in the $500,000 range. The incomes in this school represent less than 1 percent of the families in the United States.[9]

Since each of the five schools is only one instance of elementary education in a particular social-class context, I will not generalize beyond the sample. However, the examples of schoolwork which follow will suggest characteristics of education in each social setting that appear to have theoretical and social significance and to be worth investigation in a larger number of schools. . . .

The Working-Class Schools

In the two working-class schools, work is following the steps of a procedure. The procedure is usually mechanical, involving rote behavior and very little decision making or choice. The teachers rarely explain why the work is being assigned, how it might connect to other assignments, or what the idea is that lies behind the procedure or gives it coherence and perhaps meaning or significance. Available textbooks are not always used, and the teachers often prepare their own dittos or put work examples on the board. Most of the rules regarding work are designations of what the children are to do; the rules are steps to follow. These steps are told to the children by the teachers and are often written on the board. The children are usually told to copy the steps as notes. These notes are to be studied. Work is often evaluated not according to whether it is right or wrong but according to whether the children followed the right steps.

---

[8]This figure is an estimate. According to the Bureau of the Census, only 2.6 percent of families in the United States have money income of $50,000 or over. U.S. Bureau of the Census, *Current Population Reports* Series P-60. For figures on income at these higher levels, see J. D. Smith and S. Franklin, "The Concentration of Personal Wealth, 1922–1969," *American Economic Review* 64 (1974): 162–67.

[9]Smith and Franklin, "The Concentration of Personal Wealth."

The following examples illustrate these points. In math, when two-digit   10
division was introduced, the teacher in one school gave a four-minute lecture on what the terms are called (which number is the divisor, dividend,
quotient, and remainder). The children were told to copy these names in
their notebooks. Then the teacher told them the steps to follow to do the
problems, saying, "This is how you do them." The teacher listed the steps
on the board, and they appeared several days later as a chart hung in the
middle of the front wall: "Divide, Multiply, Subtract, Bring Down." The
children often did examples of two-digit division. When the teacher went
over the examples with them, he told them what the procedure was for each
problem, rarely asking them to conceptualize or explain it themselves:
"Three into twenty-two is seven; do your subtraction and one is left over."
During the week that two-digit division was introduced (or at any other
time), the investigator did not observe any discussion of the idea of grouping involved in division, any use of manipulables, or any attempt to relate
two-digit division to any other mathematical process. Nor was there any
attempt to relate the steps to an actual or possible thought process of the
children. The observer did not hear the terms *dividend, quotient,* and so on,
used again. The math teacher in the other working-class school followed
similar procedures regarding two-digit division and at one point her class
seemed confused. She said, "You're confusing yourselves. You're tensing
up. Remember, when you do this, it's the same steps over and over again —
and that's the way division always is." Several weeks later, after a test, a
group of her children "still didn't get it," and she made no attempt to
explain the concept of dividing things into groups or to give them manipulables for their own investigation. Rather, she went over the steps with them
again and told them that they "needed more practice."

In other areas of math, work is also carrying out often unexplained fragmented procedures. For example, one of the teachers led the children
through a series of steps to make a 1-inch grid on their paper *without* telling
them that they were making a 1-inch grid or that it would be used to study
scale. She said, "Take your ruler. Put it across the top. Make a mark at every
number. Then move your ruler down to the bottom. No, put it across the
bottom. Now make a mark on top of every number. Now draw a line
from . . ." At this point a girl said that she had a faster way to do it and the
teacher said, "No, you don't; you don't even know what I'm making yet. Do
it this way or it's wrong." After they had made the lines up and down and
across, the teacher told them she wanted them to make a figure by connecting some dots and to measure that, using the scale of 1 inch equals 1 mile.
Then they were to cut it out. She said, "Don't cut it until I check it."

In both working-class schools, work in language arts is mechanics of
punctuation (commas, periods, question marks, exclamation points), capi-
talization, and the four kinds of sentences. One teacher explained to me,
"Simple punctuation is all they'll ever use." Regarding punctuation, either a
teacher or a ditto stated the rules for where, for example, to put commas. The

investigator heard no classroom discussion of the aural context of punctuation (which, of course, is what gives each mark its meaning). Nor did the investigator hear any statement or inference that placing a punctuation mark could be a decision-making process, depending, for example, on one's intended meaning. Rather, the children were told to follow the rules. Language arts did not involve creative writing. There were several writing assignments throughout the year, but in each instance the children were given a ditto, and they wrote answers to questions on the sheet. For example, they wrote their "autobiography" by answering such questions as "Where were you born?" "What is your favorite animal?" on a sheet entitled "All About Me."

In one of the working-class schools, the class had a science period several times a week. On the three occasions observed, the children were not called upon to set up experiments or to give explanations for facts or concepts. Rather, on each occasion the teacher told them in his own words what the book said. The children copied the teacher's sentences from the board. Each day that preceded the day they were to do a science experiment, the teacher told them to copy the directions from the book for the procedure they would carry out the next day and to study the list at home that night. The day after each experiment, the teacher went over what they had "found" (they did the experiments as a class, and each was actually a class demonstration led by the teacher). Then the teacher wrote what they "found" on the board, and the children copied that in their notebooks. Once or twice a year there are science projects. The project is chosen and assigned by the teacher from a box of 3-by-5-inch cards. On the card the teacher has written the question to be answered, the books to use, and how much to write. Explaining the cards to the observer, the teacher said, "It tells them exactly what to do, or they couldn't do it."

Social studies in the working-class schools is also largely mechanical, rote work that was given little explanation or connection to larger contexts. In one school, for example, although there was a book available, social studies work was to copy the teacher's notes from the board. Several times a week for a period of several months the children copied these notes. The fifth grades in the district were to study United States history. The teacher used a booklet she had purchased called "The Fabulous Fifty States." Each day she put information from the booklet in outline form on the board and the children copied it. The type of information did not vary: the name of the state, its abbreviation, state capital, nickname of the state, its main products, main business, and a "Fabulous Fact" ("Idaho grew twenty-seven billion potatoes in one year. That's enough potatoes for each man, woman, and . . ."). As the children finished copying the sentences, the teacher erased them and wrote more. Children would occasionally go to the front to pull down the wall map in order to locate the states they were copying, and the teacher did not dissuade them. But the observer never saw her refer to the map; nor did the observer ever hear her make other than perfunctory remarks concerning the information the children were copying. Occasionally the children colored in a ditto and cut it out to make a stand-up figure (representing, for example, a man roping a cow in the Southwest). These were referred to by the teacher as their social studies "projects."

Rote behavior was often called for in classroom work. When going over   15
math and language arts skills sheets, for example, as the teacher asked for the answer to each problem, he fired the questions rapidly, staccato, and the scene reminded the observer of a sergeant drilling recruits: above all, the questions demanded that you stay at attention: "The next one? What do I put here? . . . Here? Give us the next." Or "How many commas in this sentence? Where do I put them . . . The next one?"

The four fifth-grade teachers observed in the working-class schools attempted to control classroom time and space by making decisions without consulting the children and without explaining the basis for their decisions. The teacher's control thus often seemed capricious. Teachers, for instance, very often ignored the bells to switch classes — deciding among themselves to keep the children after the period was officially over to continue with the work or for disciplinary reasons or so they (the teachers) could stand in the hall and talk. There were no clocks in the rooms in either school, and the children often asked, "What period is this?" "When do we go to gym?" The children had no access to materials. These were handed out by teachers and closely guarded. Things in the room "belonged" to the teacher: "Bob, bring me my garbage can." The teachers continually gave the children orders. Only three times did the investigator hear a teacher in either working-class school preface a directive with an unsarcastic "please," or "let's," or "would you." Instead, the teachers said, "Shut up," "Shut your mouth," "Open your books," "Throw your gum away — if you want to rot your teeth, do it on your own time." Teachers made every effort to control the movement of the children, and often shouted, "Why are you out of your seat??!!" If the children got permission to leave the room, they had to take a written pass with the date and time. . . .

Middle-Class School

In the middle-class school, work is getting the right answer. If one accumulates enough right answers, one gets a good grade. One must follow the directions in order to get the right answers, but the directions often call for some figuring, some choice, some decision making. For example, the children must often figure out by themselves what the directions ask them to do and how to get the answer: what do you do first, second, and perhaps third? Answers are usually found in books or by listening to the teacher. Answers are usually words, sentences, numbers, or facts and dates; one writes them on paper, and one should be neat. Answers must be given in the right order, and one cannot make them up.

The following activities are illustrative. Math involves some choice: one may do two-digit division the long way or the short way, and there are some math problems that can be done "in your head." When the teacher explains how to do two-digit division, there is recognition that a cognitive process is involved; she gives you several ways and says, "I want to make sure you understand what you're doing — so you get it right"; and, when they go over the homework, she asks the *children* to tell how they did the problem and what answer they got.

In social studies the daily work is to read the assigned pages in the text-book and to answer the teacher's questions. The questions are almost always designed to check on whether the students have read the assignment and understood it: who did so-and-so; what happened after that; when did it happen, where, and sometimes, why did it happen? The answers are in the book and in one's understanding of the book; the teacher's hints when one doesn't know the answers are to "read it again" or to look at the picture or at the rest of the paragraph. One is to search for the answer in the "context," in what is given.

Language arts is "simple grammar, what they need for everyday life." 20 The language arts teacher says, "They should learn to speak properly, to write business letters and thank-you letters, and to understand what nouns and verbs and simple subjects are." Here, as well, actual work is to choose the right answers, to understand what is given. The teacher often says, "Please read the next sentence and then I'll question you about it." One teacher said in some exasperation to a boy who was fooling around in class, "If you don't know the answers to the questions I ask, then you can't stay in this *class!* [pause] You *never* know the answers to the questions I ask, and it's not fair to me — and certainly not to you!"

Most lessons are based on the textbook. This does not involve a critical perspective on what is given there. For example, a critical perspective in social studies is perceived as dangerous by these teachers because it may lead to controversial topics; the parents might complain. The children, how-ever, are often curious, especially in social studies. Their questions are tol-erated and usually answered perfunctorily. But after a few minutes the teacher will say, "All right, we're not going any farther. Please open your social studies workbook." While the teachers spend a lot of time explaining and expanding on what the textbooks say, there is little attempt to analyze how or why things happen, or to give thought to how pieces of a culture, or, say, a system of numbers or elements of a language fit together or can be analyzed. What has happened in the past and what exists now may not be equitable or fair, but (shrug) that is the way things are and one does not confront such matters in school. For example, in social studies after a child is called on to read a passage about the pilgrims, the teacher summarizes the paragraph and then says, "So you can see how strict they were about everything." A child asks, "Why?" "Well, because they felt that if you weren't busy you'd get into trouble." Another child asks, "Is it true that they burned women at the stake?" The teacher says, "Yes, if a woman did any-thing strange, they hanged them. [*sic*] What would a woman do, do you think, to make them burn them? [*sic*] See if you can come up with better

answers than my other [social studies] class." Several children offer suggestions, to which the teacher nods but does not comment. Then she says,
"Okay, good," and calls on the next child to read.

Work tasks do not usually request creativity. Serious attention is rarely
given in school work on *how* the children develop or express their own feelings and ideas, either linguistically or in graphic form. On the occasions
when creativity or self-expression is requested, it is peripheral to the main
activity or it is "enrichment" or "for fun." During a lesson on what similes
are, for example, the teacher explains what they are, puts several on the
board, gives some other examples herself, and then asks the children if they
can "make some up." She calls on three children who give similes, two of
which are actually in the book they have open before them. The teacher
does not comment on this and then asks several others to choose similes
from the list of phrases in the book. Several do so correctly, and she says,
"Oh good! You're picking them out! See how good we are?" Their homework is to pick out the rest of the similes from the list.

Creativity is not often requested in social studies and science projects,
either. Social studies projects, for example, are given with directions to "find
information on your topic" and write it up. The children are not supposed to
copy but to "put it in your own words." Although a number of the projects
subsequently went beyond the teacher's direction to find information and
had quite expressive covers and inside illustrations, the teacher's evaluative
comments had to do with the amount of information, whether they had
"copied," and if their work was neat.

The style of control of the three fifth-grade teachers observed in this
school varied from somewhat easygoing to strict, but in contrast to the
working-class schools, the teachers' decisions were usually based on external rules and regulations—for example, on criteria that were known or
available to the children. Thus, the teachers always honor the bells for
changing classes, and they usually evaluate children's work by what is in the
textbooks and answer booklets.

There is little excitement in schoolwork for the children, and the
assignments are perceived as having little to do with their interests and feelings. As one child said, what you do is "store facts up in your head like cold
storage—until you need it later for a test or your job." Thus, doing well is
important because there are thought to be *other*, likely rewards: a good job
or college.[10]

Affluent Professional School

In the affluent professional school, work is creative activity carried out
independently. The students are continually asked to express and apply

[10]A dominant feeling, expressed directly and indirectly by teachers in this school, was
boredom with their work. They did, however, in contrast to the working-class schools, almost
always carry out lessons during class times.

ideas and concepts. Work involves individual thought and expressiveness, expansion and illustration of ideas, and choice of appropriate method and material. (The class is not considered an open classroom, and the principal explained that because of the large number of discipline problems in the fifth grade this year they did not departmentalize. The teacher who agreed to take part in the study said she is "more structured" this year than she usually is.) The products of work in this class are often written stories, editorials and essays, or representations of ideas in mural, graph, or craft form. The products of work should not be like everybody else's and should show individuality. They should exhibit good design, and (this is important) they must also fit empirical reality. Moreover, one's work should attempt to interpret or "make sense" of reality. The relatively few rules to be followed regarding work are usually criteria for, or limits on, individual activity. One's product is usually evaluated for the quality of its expression and for the appropriateness of its conception to the task. In many cases, one's own satisfaction with the product is an important criterion for its evaluation. When right answers are called for, as in commercial materials like SRA (Science Research Associates) and math, it is important that the children decide on an answer as a result of thinking about the idea involved in what they're being asked to do. Teacher's hints are to "think about it some more."

The following activities are illustrative. The class takes home a sheet requesting each child's parents to fill in the number of cars they have, the number of television sets, refrigerators, games, or rooms in the house, and so on. Each child is to figure the average number of a type of possession owned by the fifth grade. Each child must compile the "data" from all the sheets. A calculator is available in the classroom to do the mechanics of finding the average. Some children decide to send sheets to the fourth-grade families for comparison. Their work should be "verified" by a classmate before it is handed in.

Each child and his or her family has made a geoboard. The teacher asks the class to get their geoboards from the side cabinet, to take a handful of rubber bands, and then to listen to what she would like them to do. She says, "I would like you to design a figure and then find the perimeter and area. When you have it, check with your neighbor. After you've done that, please transfer it to graph paper and tomorrow I'll ask you to make up a question about it for someone. When you hand it in, please let me know whose it is and who verified it. Then I have something else for you to do that's really fun. [pause] Find the average number of chocolate chips in three cookies. I'll give you three cookies, and you'll have to *eat* your way through, I'm afraid!" Then she goes around the room and gives help, suggestions, praise, and admonitions that they are getting noisy. They work sitting, or standing up at their desks, at benches in the back, or on the floor. A child hands the teacher his paper and she comments, "I'm not accepting this paper. Do a better design." To another child she says, "That's fantastic! But you'll never find the area. Why don't you draw a figure inside [the big one] and subtract to get the area?"

The school district requires the fifth grade to study ancient civilization (in particular, Egypt, Athens, and Sumer). In this classroom, the emphasis is on illustrating and re-creating the culture of the people of ancient times. The following are typical activities: the children made an 8mm film on Egypt, which one of the parents edited. A girl in the class wrote the script, and the class acted it out. They put the sound on themselves. They read stories of those days. They wrote essays and stories depicting the lives of the people and the societal and occupational divisions. They chose from a list of projects, all of which involved graphic representations of ideas: for example, "Make a mural depicting the division of labor in Egyptian society."

Each child wrote and exchanged a letter in hieroglyphics with a fifth grader in another class, and they also exchanged stories they wrote in cuneiform. They made a scroll and singed the edges so it looked authentic. They each chose an occupation and made an Egyptian plaque representing that occupation, simulating the appropriate Egyptian design. They carved their design on a cylinder of wax, pressed the wax into clay, and then baked the clay. Although one girl did not choose an occupation but carved instead a series of gods and slaves, the teacher said, "That's all right, Amber, it's beautiful." As they were working the teacher said, "Don't cut into your clay until you're satisfied with your design."

Social studies also involves almost daily presentation by the children of some event from the news. The teacher's questions ask the children to expand what they say, to give more details, and to be more specific. Occasionally she adds some remarks to help them see connections between events.

The emphasis on expressing and illustrating ideas in social studies is accompanied in language arts by an emphasis on creative writing. Each child wrote a rebus story for a first grader whom they had interviewed to see what kind of story the child liked best. They wrote editorials on pending decisions by the school board and radio plays, some of which were read over the school intercom from the office and one of which was performed in the auditorium. There is no language arts textbook because, the teacher said, "The principal wants us to be creative." There is not much grammar, but there is punctuation. One morning when the observer arrived, the class was doing a punctuation ditto. The teacher later apologized for using the ditto. "It's just for review," she said. "I don't teach punctuation that way. We use their language." The ditto had three unambiguous rules for where to put commas in a sentence. As the teacher was going around to help the children with the ditto, she repeated several times, "Where you put commas depends on how you say the sentence; it depends on the situation and what you want to say." Several weeks later the observer saw another punctuation activity. The teacher had printed a five-paragraph story on an oak tag and then cut it into phrases. She read the whole story to the class from the book, then passed out the phrases. The group had to decide how the phrases could best be put together again. (They arranged the phrases on the floor.) The point was not to replicate the story, although that was not irrelevant, but to "decide what you think the best way is." Punctuation marks on cardboard pieces were then handed out, and the children discussed and then decided what mark was best at each place they thought one was needed. At the end of each paragraph the teacher asked, "Are you satisfied with the way the paragraphs are now? Read it to yourself and see how it sounds." Then she read the original story again, and they compared the two.

Describing her goals in science to the investigator, the teacher said, "We use ESS (Elementary Science Study). It's very good because it gives a hands-on experience — so they can make *sense* out of it. It doesn't matter whether it [what they find] is right or wrong. I bring them together and there's value in discussing their ideas."

The products of work in this class are often highly valued by the children and the teacher. In fact, this was the only school in which the investigator was not allowed to take original pieces of the children's work for her files. If the work was small enough, however, and was on paper, the investigator could duplicate it on the copying machine in the office.

The teacher's attempt to control the class involves constant negotiation. 35 She does not give direct orders unless she is angry because the children have been too noisy. Normally, she tries to get them to foresee the consequences of their actions and to decide accordingly. For example, lining them up to go see a play written by the sixth graders, she says, "I presume you're lined up by someone with whom you want to sit. I hope you're lined up by someone you won't get in trouble with." . . .

One of the few rules governing the children's movement is that no more than three children may be out of the room at once. There is a school rule that anyone can go to the library at any time to get a book. In the fifth grade I observed, they sign their name on the chalkboard and leave. There are no passes. Finally, the children have a fair amount of officially sanctioned say over what happens in the class. For example, they often negotiate what work is to be done. If the teacher wants to move on to the next subject, but the children say they are not ready, they want to work on their present projects some more, she very often lets them do it.

Executive Elite School

In the executive elite school, work is developing one's analytical intellectual powers. Children are continually asked to reason through a problem, to produce intellectual products that are both logically sound and of top academic quality. A primary goal of thought is to conceptualize rules by which elements may fit together in systems and then to apply these rules in solving a problem. Schoolwork helps one to achieve, to excel, to prepare for life.

The following are illustrative. The math teacher teaches area and perimeter by having the children derive formulas for each. First she helps them, through discussion at the board, to arrive at $A = W \times L$ as a formula (not *the* formula) for area. After discussing several, she says, "Can anyone make up a formula for perimeter? Can you figure that out yourselves? [pause] Knowing what we know, can we think of a formula?" She works out three children's suggestions at the board, saying to two, "Yes, that's a good one," and then asks the class if they can think of any more. No one volunteers. To prod them, she says, "If you use rules and good reasoning, you get many ways. Chris, can you think up a formula?"

She discusses two-digit division with the children as a decision-making process. Presenting a new type of problem to them, she asks, "What's the *first* decision you'd make if presented with this kind of example? What is the first thing you'd *think?* Craig?" Craig says, "To find my first partial quotient." She responds, "Yes, that would be your first decision. How would you do that?" Craig explains, and then the teacher says, "OK, we'll see how that works for you." The class tries his way. Subsequently, she comments on the merits and shortcomings of several other children's decisions. Later, she tells the investigator that her goals in math are to develop their reasoning and mathematical thinking and that, unfortunately, "there's no *time* for manipulables."

While right answers are important in math, they are not "given" by the book or by the teacher but may be challenged by the children. Going over some problems in late September the teacher says, "Raise your hand if you do not agree." A child says, "I don't agree with sixty-four." The teacher responds, "OK, there's a question about sixty-four. [to class] Please check it. Owen, they're disagreeing with you. Kristen, they're checking yours." The teacher emphasized this repeatedly during September and October with statements like "Don't be afraid to say you disagree. In the last [math] class, somebody disagreed, and they were right. Before you disagree, check yours, and if you still think we're wrong, then we'll check it out." By Thanksgiving, the children did not often speak in terms of right and wrong math problems but of whether they agreed with the answer that had been given.

There are complicated math mimeos with many word problems. Whenever they go over the examples, they discuss how each child has set up the problem. The children must explain it precisely. On one occasion the teacher said, "I'm more — just as interested in *how* you set up the problem as in what answer you find. If you set up a problem in a good way, the answer is *easy* to find."

Social studies work is most often reading and discussion of concepts and independent research. There are only occasional artistic, expressive, or illustrative projects. Ancient Athens and Sumer are, rather, societies to analyze. The following questions are typical of those that guide the children's independent research. "What mistakes did Pericles make after the war?" "What mistakes did the citizens of Athens make?" "What are the elements of a civilization?" "How did Greece build an economic empire?" "Compare the way Athens chose its leaders with the way we choose ours." Occasionally the children are asked to make up sample questions for their social studies tests. On an occasion when the investigator was present, the social studies teacher rejected a child's question by saying, "That's just fact. If I asked you that question on a test, you'd complain it was just memory! Good questions ask for concepts."

In social studies — but also in reading, science, and health — the teachers initiate classroom discussions of current social issues and problems. These discussions occurred on every one of the investigator's visits, and a teacher told me, "These children's opinions are important — it's important that they learn to reason things through." The classroom discussions always struck the observer as quite realistic and analytical, dealing with concrete social issues like the following: "Why do workers strike?" "Is that right or wrong?" "Why do we have inflation, and what can be done to stop it?" "Why do companies put chemicals in food when the natural ingredients are available?" and so on. Usually the children did not have to be prodded to give their opinions. In fact, their statements and the interchanges between them struck the observer as quite sophisticated conceptually and verbally, and well-informed. Occasionally the teachers would prod with statements such as, "Even if you don't know [the answers], if you think logically about it, you can figure it out." And "I'm asking you [these] questions to help you think this through."

Language arts emphasizes language as a complex system, one that should be mastered. The children are asked to diagram sentences of complex grammatical construction, to memorize irregular verb conjugations (he lay, he has lain, and so on . . .), and to use the proper participles, conjunctions, and interjections in their speech. The teacher (the same one who teaches social studies) told them, "It is not enough to get these right on tests; you must use what you learn [in grammar classes] in your written and oral work. I will grade you on that."

Most writing assignments are either research reports and essays for 45
social studies or experiment analyses and write-ups for science. There is only an occasional story or other "creative writing" assignment. On the occasion observed by the investigator (the writing of a Halloween story), the points the teacher stressed in preparing the children to write involved the structural aspects of a story rather than the expression of feelings or other ideas. The teacher showed them a filmstrip, "The Seven Parts of a Story," and lectured them on plot development, mood setting, character development, consistency, and the use of a logical or appropriate ending. The stories they subsequently wrote were, in fact, well-structured, but many were also personal and expressive. The teacher's evaluative comments, however, did not refer to the expressiveness or artistry but were all directed toward whether they had "developed" the story well.

Language arts work also involved a large amount of practice in presentation of the self and in managing situations where the child was expected to be in charge. For example, there was a series of assignments in which each child had to be a "student teacher." The child had to plan a lesson in grammar, outlining, punctuation, or other language arts topic and explain the concept to the class. Each child was to prepare a worksheet or game and a homework assignment as well. After each presentation, the teacher and other children gave a critical appraisal of the "student teacher's" performance. Their criteria were: whether the student spoke clearly, whether the lesson was interesting, whether the student made any mistakes, and whether he or she kept control of the class. On an occasion when a child did not maintain control, the teacher said, "When you're up there, you have authority and you have to use it. I'll back you up." . . .

The executive elite school is the only school where bells do not demarcate the periods of time. The two fifth-grade teachers were very strict about changing classes on schedule, however, as specific plans for each session had been made. The teachers attempted to keep tight control over the children during lessons, and the children were sometimes flippant, boisterous, and occasionally rude. However, the children may be brought into line by reminding them that "It is up to you," "You must control yourself," "You are responsible for your work," you must "set your own priorities." One teacher told a child, "You are the only driver of your car — and only you can regulate your speed." A new teacher complained to the observer that she had thought "these children" would have more control.

While strict attention to the lesson at hand is required, the teachers make relatively little attempt to regulate the movement of the children at other times. For example, except for the kindergartners the children in this school do not have to wait for the bell to ring in the morning; they may go to their classroom when they arrive at school. Fifth graders often came early to read, to finish work, or to catch up. After the first two months of school, the fifth-grade teachers did not line the children up to change classes or to go to gym, and so on, but, when the children were ready and quiet, they were told they could go — sometimes without the teachers.

In the classroom, the children could get materials when they needed them and took what they needed from closets and from the teacher's desk. They were in charge of the office at lunchtime. During class they did not have to sign out or ask permission to leave the room; they just got up and left. Because of the pressure to get work done, however, they did not leave the room very often. The teachers were very polite to the children, and the investigator heard no sarcasm, no nasty remarks, and few direct orders. The teachers never called the children "honey" or "dear" but always called them by name. The teachers were expected to be available before school, after school, and for part of their lunchtime to provide extra help if needed. . . .

The foregoing analysis of differences in schoolwork in contrasting social- 50
class contexts suggests the following conclusion: the "hidden curriculum" of schoolwork is tacit preparation for relating to the process of production in a particular way. Differing curricular, pedagogical, and pupil evaluation practices emphasize different cognitive and behavioral skills in each social setting and thus contribute to the development in the children of certain potential

relationships to physical and symbolic capital,[11] to authority, and to the process of work. School experience, in the sample of schools discussed here, differed qualitatively by social class. These differences may not only contribute to the development in the children in each social class of certain types of economically significant relationships and not others but would thereby help to *reproduce* this system of relations in society. In the contribution to the reproduction of unequal social relations lies a theoretical meaning and social consequence of classroom practice.

The identification of different emphases in classrooms in a sample of contrasting social-class contexts implies that further research should be conducted in a large number of schools to investigate the types of work tasks and interactions in each to see if they differ in the ways discussed here and to see if similar potential relationships are uncovered. Such research could have as a product the further elucidation of complex but not readily apparent connections between everyday activity in schools and classrooms and the unequal structure of economic relationships in which we work and live.

ENGAGING THE TEXT

1. Examine the ways any single subject is taught in the four types of schools Anyon describes. What differences in teaching methods and in the student-teacher relationship do they reflect? What other differences do you note in the schools? What schools in your geographic region would closely approximate the working-class, middle-class, affluent professional, and executive elite schools of her article?

2. What attitudes toward knowledge and work are the four types of schools teaching their students? What kinds of jobs are students being prepared to do? Do you see any evidence that the schools in your community are producing particular kinds of workers?

3. What is the "hidden curriculum" of Anyon's title? How is this curriculum taught, and what social, cultural, or political purposes does it serve?

EXPLORING CONNECTIONS

4. Which of the four types of schools that Anyon describes do you think Michael Moore attended, given the experiences he offers from his own education in "Idiot Nation" (p. 128)? Why? Do you think his attitude toward the state of schooling in America would be different if he had attended a different kind of school?

5. How might Anyon explain the boredom, absurdity, and childishness that John Taylor Gatto (p. 148) associates with compulsory public education? To what extent do Anyon and Gatto seem to agree about the relationship between school and social class?

---

[11]*physical and symbolic capital:* Elsewhere Anyon defines *capital* as "property that is used to produce profit, interest, or rent"; she defines *symbolic capital* as the knowledge and skills that "may yield social and cultural power." [Eds.]

6. Draw a Groening-like (see pp. 147 and 156) cartoon or comic strip about a classroom situation in a working-class, middle-class, professional, or elite school (but do not identify the type of school explicitly). Pool all the cartoons from the class. In small groups, sort the comics according to the type of school they represent.

7. Analyze the teaching styles that Mike Rose encounters at Our Lady of Mercy (p. 157). Which of Anyon's categories would they fit best? Do Rose's experiences at his high school tend to confirm or complicate Anyon's analysis?

Extending the Critical Context

8. Should all schools be run like professional or elite schools? What would be the advantages of making these schools models for all social classes? Do you see any possible disadvantages?

9. Choose a common elementary school task or skill that Anyon does not mention. Outline four ways it might be taught in the four types of schools.

Visual Portfolio

READING IMAGES OF EDUCATION
AND EMPOWERMENT

The Spirit of Education (1934), by Norman Rockwell.

The Graduate (1959), by Norman Rockwell.

The Problem We All Live With (1964), by Norman Rockwell.

Visual Portfolio
Reading Images of Education and Empowerment

1. What is happening in *The Spirit of Education* (p. 187)? What is Norman Rockwell saying about the situation — and about education — through the attitudes of the boy and the seated woman?

2. What meaning can you find in the elements that make up the boy's costume? What significance is there in the book, the torch, the laurel crown, the toga and sandals? What are these symbols supposed to suggest about education? If you were to costume someone to represent education today, how would you do it?

3. In *The Graduate* (p. 188), why has Rockwell chosen to place his subject in front of a newspaper? To what extent are the headlines of the paper relevant? What is Rockwell suggesting through the young man's posture and attitude?

4. Plan an updated version of the portrait on page 188, featuring a twenty-first-century graduate and a more contemporary background.

5. What is the setting of *The Problem We All Live With* (p. 189)? What event does it commemorate? How do you interpret the painting's title?

6. What does Rockwell suggest about the relationship of education, society, power, and violence through the visual details included in this painting? What significance do you see, for example, in the absence of the men's faces, the position of their hands and arms, the rhythm of their strides, the smallness of the girl, her attitude, the materials she carries, and so forth?

7. Working in groups, write an imaginary dialogue among the three college students in the photograph on page 190. What do you think they'd have to say about the class they're in, the subject, or their professor? What do you think their professor might have to say to them? How common are scenes like this in your college? What could be done to change them?

8. What's your reaction to the image of the texting elementary-school student on page 191? What do you think her teacher's reaction might be? Working in groups, discuss how cell phones, laptops, and the Internet are reshaping students' and teachers' experience of the classroom — and of each other. Do you think access to information technology should be limited in class? At all levels of education? Why or why not?

9. What does the sign on page 192 suggest about the real priorities of the North Georgia Falcons? How might John Taylor Gatto (p. 148) and Michael Moore (p. 128) assess the sign and interpret what it says about contemporary American secondary education? Make a similar sign stating the priorities of the high school you attended. Share these in class and discuss what they reveal.

The Achievement of Desire

RICHARD RODRIGUEZ

Hunger of Memory, *the autobiography of Richard Rodriguez and the source of the following selection, set off a storm of controversy in the Chicano community when it appeared in 1981. Some hailed it as an uncompromising portrayal of the difficulties of growing up between two cultures; others condemned it because it seemed to blame Mexican Americans for the difficulties they encountered assimilating into mainstream American society. Rodriguez was born in 1944 into an immigrant family outside San Francisco. Though he was unable to speak English when he entered school, his educational career can only be described as brilliant: undergraduate work at Stanford University, graduate study at Berkeley and Columbia, a Fulbright fellowship to study English literature in London, a subsequent grant from the National Endowment for the Humanities. In this selection, Rodriguez analyzes the motives that led him to abandon his study of Renaissance literature and return to live with his parents. He is currently an associate editor with the* Pacific News Service *in San Francisco, an essayist for the* PBS NewsHour, *and a contributing editor for* Harper's *magazine and for the* Opinion *section of the* Los Angeles Times. *His other books include* Mexico's Children *(1991),* Days of Obligation: An Argument with My Mexican Father *(1993), which was nominated for the Pulitzer Prize in nonfiction, and* Brown: The Last Discovery of America *(2002).*

I stand in the ghetto classroom — "the guest speaker" — attempting to lecture on the mystery of the sounds of our words to rows of diffident students. "Don't you hear it? Listen! The music of our words. '*Sumer is i-cumen in.*[1] . . .' And songs on the car radio. We need Aretha Franklin's voice to fill plain words with music — her life." In the face of their empty stares, I try to create an enthusiasm. But the girls in the back row turn to watch some boy passing outside. There are flutters of smiles, waves. And someone's mouth elongates heavy, silent words through the barrier of glass. Silent words — the lips straining to shape each voiceless syllable: "*Meet meee late errr.*" By the door, the instructor smiles at me, apparently hoping that I will be able to spark some enthusiasm in the class. But only one student seems to be listening. A girl, maybe fourteen. In this gray room her eyes shine with ambition. She keeps nodding and nodding at all that I say; she even takes notes. And each time I ask a question, she jerks up and down in her desk like a marionette, while her hand waves over the bowed heads of her classmates. It is myself (as a boy) I see as she faces me now (a man in my thirties).

[1]*Sumer is i-cumen in:* Opening line of a Middle English poem ("Summer has come").

The boy who first entered a classroom barely able to speak English, twenty years later concluded his studies in the stately quiet of the reading room in the British Museum. Thus with one sentence I can summarize my academic career. It will be harder to summarize what sort of life connects the boy to the man.

With every award, each graduation from one level of education to the next, people I'd meet would congratulate me. Their refrain always the same: "Your parents must be very proud." Sometimes then they'd ask me how I managed it — my "success." (How?) After a while, I had several quick answers to give in reply. I'd admit, for one thing, that I went to an excellent grammar school. (My earliest teachers, the nuns, made my success their ambition.) And my brother and both my sisters were very good students. (They often brought home the shiny school trophies I came to want.) And my mother and father always encouraged me. (At every graduation they were behind the stunning flash of the camera when I turned to look at the crowd.)

As important as these factors were, however, they account inadequately for my academic advance. Nor do they suggest what an odd success I managed. For although I was a very good student, I was also a very bad student. I was a "scholarship boy," a certain kind of scholarship boy. Always successful, I was always unconfident. Exhilarated by my progress. Sad. I became the prized student — anxious and eager to learn. Too eager, too anxious — an imitative and unoriginal pupil. My brother and two sisters enjoyed the advantages I did, and they grew to be as successful as I, but none of them ever seemed so anxious about their schooling. A second-grade student, I was the one who came home and corrected the "simple" grammatical mistakes of our parents. ("Two negatives make a positive.") Proudly I announced — to my family's startled silence — that a teacher had said I was losing all trace of a Spanish accent. I was oddly annoyed when I was unable to get parental help with a homework assignment. The night my father tried to help me with an arithmetic exercise, he kept reading the instructions, each time more deliberately, until I pried the textbook out of his hands, saying, "I'll try to figure it out some more by myself."

When I reached the third grade, I outgrew such behavior. I became   5
more tactful, careful to keep separate the two very different worlds of my day. But then, with ever-increasing intensity, I devoted myself to my studies. I became bookish, puzzling to all my family. Ambition set me apart. When my brother saw me struggling home with stacks of library books, he would laugh, shouting: "Hey, Four Eyes!" My father opened a closet one day and was startled to find me inside, reading a novel. My mother would find me reading when I was supposed to be asleep or helping around the house or playing outside. In a voice angry or worried or just curious, she'd ask: "What do you see in your books?" It became the family's joke. When I was called and wouldn't reply, someone would say I must be hiding under my bed with a book.

(How did I manage my success?)

What I am about to say to you has taken me more than twenty years to admit: A *primary reason for my success in the classroom was that I couldn't forget that schooling was changing me and separating me from the life I enjoyed before becoming a student.* That simple realization! For years I never spoke to anyone about it. Never mentioned a thing to my family or my teachers or classmates. From a very early age, I understood enough, just enough about my classroom experiences to keep what I knew repressed, hidden beneath layers of embarrassment. Not until my last months as a graduate student, nearly thirty years old, was it possible for me to think much about the reasons for my academic success. Only then. At the end of my schooling, I needed to determine how far I had moved from my past. The adult finally confronted, and now must publicly say, what the child shuddered from knowing and could never admit to himself or to those many faces that smiled at his every success. ("Your parents must be very proud. . . .")

At the end, in the British Museum (too distracted to finish my dissertation) for weeks I read, speed-read, books by modern educational theorists, only to find infrequent and slight mention of students like me. (Much more is written about the more typical case, the lower-class student who barely is helped by his schooling.) Then one day, leafing through Richard Hoggart's *The Uses of Literacy,* I found, in his description of the scholarship boy, myself. For the first time I realized that there were other students like me, and so I was able to frame the meaning of my academic success, its consequent price — the loss.

Hoggart's description is distinguished, at least initially, by deep understanding. What he grasps very well is that the scholarship boy must move between environments, his home and the classroom, which are at cultural extremes, opposed. With his family, the boy has the intense pleasure of intimacy, the family's consolation in feeling public alienation. Lavish emotions texture home life. *Then,* at school, the instruction bids him to trust lonely reason primarily. Immediate needs set the pace of his parents' lives. From his mother and father the boy learns to trust spontaneity and nonrational ways of knowing. *Then,* at school, there is mental calm. Teachers emphasize the value of a reflectiveness that opens a space between thinking and immediate action.

Years of schooling must pass before the boy will be able to sketch the   10 cultural differences in his day as abstractly as this. But he senses those differences early. Perhaps as early as the night he brings home an assignment from school and finds the house too noisy for study.

> He has to be more and more alone, if he is going to "get on." He will have, probably unconsciously, to oppose the ethos[2] of the hearth, the intense gregariousness of the working-class family group. Since everything centres upon the living-room, there is unlikely to be a room of

[2]*ethos:* The fundamental spirit or character of a thing.

his own; the bedrooms are cold and inhospitable, and to warm them or the front room, if there is one, would not only be expensive, but would require an imaginative leap — out of the tradition — which most families are not capable of making. There is a corner of the living-room table. On the other side Mother is ironing, the wireless is on, someone is singing a snatch of song or Father says intermittently whatever comes into his head. The boy has to cut himself off mentally, so as to do his homework, as well as he can.[3]

The next day, the lesson is as apparent at school. There are even rows of desks. Discussion is ordered. The boy must rehearse his thoughts and raise his hand before speaking out in a loud voice to an audience of classmates. And there is time enough, and silence, to think about ideas (big ideas) never considered at home by his parents.

Not for the working-class child alone is adjustment to the classroom difficult. Good schooling requires that any student alter early childhood habits. But the working-class child is usually least prepared for the change. And, unlike many middle-class children, he goes home and sees in his parents a way of life not only different but starkly opposed to that of the classroom. (He enters the house and hears his parents talking in ways his teachers discourage.)

Without extraordinary determination and the great assistance of others — at home and at school — there is little chance for success. Typically most working-class children are barely changed by the classroom. The exception succeeds. The relative few become scholarship students. Of these, Richard Hoggart estimates, most manage a fairly graceful transition. Somehow they learn to live in the two very different worlds of their day. There are some others, however, those Hoggart pejoratively terms "scholarship boys," for whom success comes with special anxiety. Scholarship boy: good student, troubled son. The child is "moderately endowed," intellectually mediocre, Hoggart supposes — though it may be more pertinent to note the special qualities of temperament in the child. High-strung child. Brooding. Sensitive. Haunted by the knowledge that one *chooses* to become a student. (Education is not an inevitable or natural step in growing up.) Here is a child who cannot forget that his academic success distances him from a life he loved, even from his own memory of himself.

Initially, he wavers, balances allegiance. ("The boy is himself [until he reaches, say, the upper forms[4]] very much of *both* the worlds of home and school. He is enormously obedient to the dictates of the world of school, but emotionally still strongly wants to continue as part of the family circle.") Gradually, necessarily, the balance is lost. The boy needs to spend more and more time studying, each night enclosing himself in the silence permitted

---

[3]All quotations are from Richard Hoggart, *The Uses of Literacy* (London: Chatto and Windus, 1957), Chapter 10. [Rodriguez's note]

[4]*upper forms:* Upper grades or classes in British secondary schools.

and required by intense concentration. He takes his first step toward academic success, away from his family.

From the very first days, through the years following, it will be with his   15
parents — the figures of lost authority, the persons toward whom he feels deepest love — that the change will be most powerfully measured. A separation will unravel between them. Advancing in his studies, the boy notices that his mother and father have not changed as much as he. Rather, when he sees them, they often remind him of the person he once was and the life he earlier shared with them. He realizes what some Romantics[5] also know when they praise the working class for the capacity for human closeness, qualities of passion and spontaneity, that the rest of us experience in like measure only in the earliest part of our youth. For the Romantic, this doesn't make working-class life childish. Working-class life challenges precisely because it is an *adult* way of life.

The scholarship boy reaches a different conclusion. He cannot afford to admire his parents. (How could he and still pursue such a contrary life?) He permits himself embarrassment at their lack of education. And to evade nostalgia for the life he has lost, he concentrates on the benefits education will bestow upon him. He becomes especially ambitious. Without the support of old certainties and consolations, almost mechanically, he assumes the procedures and doctrines of the classroom. The kind of allegiance the young student might have given his mother and father only days earlier, he transfers to the teacher, the new figure of authority. "[The scholarship boy] tends to make a father-figure of his form-master,"[6] Hoggart observes.

But Hoggart's calm prose only makes me recall the urgency with which I came to idolize my grammar school teachers. I began by imitating their accents, using their diction, trusting their every direction. The very first facts they dispensed, I grasped with awe. Any book they told me to read, I read — then waited for them to tell me which books I enjoyed. Their every casual opinion I came to adopt and to trumpet when I returned home. I stayed after school "to help" — to get my teacher's undivided attention. It was the nun's encouragement that mattered most to me. (She understood exactly what — my parents never seemed to appraise so well — all my achievements entailed.) Memory gently caressed each word of praise bestowed in the classroom so that compliments teachers paid me years ago come quickly to mind even today.

The enthusiasm I felt in second-grade classes I flaunted before both my parents. The docile, obedient student came home a shrill and precocious son who insisted on correcting and teaching his parents with the remark: "My teacher told us. . . ."

---

[5]*Romantics:* Adherents of the principles of romanticism — a literary and philosophical movement that emphasized the imagination, freedom, nature, the return to a simple life, and the ordinary individual.

[6]*form-master:* A teacher in a British secondary school.

I intended to hurt my mother and father. I was still angry at them for having encouraged me toward classroom English. But gradually this anger was exhausted, replaced by guilt as school grew more and more attractive to me. I grew increasingly successful, a talkative student. My hand was raised in the classroom; I yearned to answer any question. At home, life was less noisy than it had been. (I spoke to classmates and teachers more often each day than to family members.) Quiet at home, I sat with my papers for hours each night. I never forgot that schooling had irretrievably changed my family's life. That knowledge, however, did not weaken ambition. Instead, it strengthened resolve. Those times I remembered the loss of my past with regret, I quickly reminded myself of all the things my teachers could give me. (They could make me an educated man.) I tightened my grip on pencil and books. I evaded nostalgia. Tried hard to forget. But one does not forget by trying to forget. One only remembers. I remembered too well that education had changed my family's life. I would not have become a scholarship boy had I not so often remembered.

Once she was sure that her children knew English, my mother would   20
tell us, "You should keep up your Spanish." Voices playfully groaned in response. "*¡Pochos!*"[7] my mother would tease. I listened silently.

After a while, I grew more calm at home. I developed tact. A fourth-grade student, I was no longer the show-off in front of my parents. I became a conventionally dutiful son, politely affectionate, cheerful enough, even — for reasons beyond choosing — my father's favorite. And much about my family life was easy then, comfortable, happy in the rhythm of our living together: hearing my father getting ready for work; eating the breakfast my mother had made me; looking up from a novel to hear my brother or one of my sisters playing with friends in the backyard; in winter, coming upon the house all lighted up after dark.

But withheld from my mother and father was any mention of what most mattered to me: the extraordinary experience of first-learning. Late afternoon: in the midst of preparing dinner, my mother would come up behind me while I was trying to read. Her head just over mine, her breath warmly scented with food. "What are you reading?" Or, "Tell me about your new courses." I would barely respond, "Just the usual things, nothing special." (A half smile, then silence. Her head moving back in the silence. Silence! Instead of the flood of intimate sounds that had once flowed smoothly between us, there was this silence.) After dinner, I would rush to a bedroom with papers and books. As often as possible, I resisted parental pleas to "save lights" by coming to the kitchen to work. I kept so much, so often, to myself. Sad. Enthusiastic. Troubled by the excitement of coming upon new ideas. Eager. Fascinated by the promising texture of a brand-new book. I

---

[7]*Pocho:* A derogatory Spanish word for a Mexican American who has adopted the attitudes, values, and lifestyle of Anglo culture.

hoarded the pleasures of learning. Alone for hours. Enthralled. Nervous. I rarely looked away from my books — or back on my memories. Nights when relatives visited and the front rooms were warmed by Spanish sounds, I slipped quietly out of the house.

It mattered that education was changing me. It never ceased to matter. My brother and sisters would giggle at our mother's mispronounced words. They'd correct her gently. My mother laughed girlishly one night, trying not to pronounce *sheep* as *ship*. From a distance I listened sullenly. From that distance, pretending not to notice on another occasion, I saw my father looking at the title pages of my library books. That was the scene on my mind when I walked home with a fourth-grade companion and heard him say that his parents read to him every night. (A strange-sounding book — *Winnie the Pooh.*) Immediately, I wanted to know, "What is it like?" My companion, however, thought I wanted to know about the plot of the book. Another day, my mother surprised me by asking for a "nice" book to read. "Something not too hard you think I might like." Carefully I chose one, Willa Cather's[8] *My Ántonia.* But when, several weeks later, I happened to see it next to her bed unread except for the first few pages, I was furious and suddenly wanted to cry. I grabbed up the book and took it back to my room and placed it in its place, alphabetically on my shelf.

"Your parents must be very proud of you." People began to say that to me about the time I was in sixth grade. To answer affirmatively, I'd smile. Shyly I'd smile, never betraying my sense of the irony: I was not proud of my mother and father. I was embarrassed by their lack of education. It was not that I ever thought they were stupid, though stupidly I took for granted their enormous native intelligence. Simply, what mattered to me was that they were not like my teachers.

But, "Why didn't you tell us about the award?" my mother demanded,   25
her frown weakened by pride. At the grammar school ceremony several weeks after, her eyes were brighter than the trophy I'd won. Pushing back the hair from my forehead, she whispered that I had "shown" the *gringos*.[9] A few minutes later, I heard my father speak to my teacher and felt ashamed of his labored, accented words. Then guilty for the shame. I felt such contrary feelings. (There is no simple roadmap through the heart of the scholarship boy.) My teacher was so soft-spoken and her words were edged sharp and clean. I admired her until it seemed to me that she spoke too carefully. Sensing that she was condescending to them, I became nervous. Resentful. Protective. I tried to move my parents away. "You both must be very proud of Richard," the nun said. They responded quickly. (They were proud.) "We are proud of all our children." Then this afterthought: "They sure didn't get their brains from us." They all laughed. I smiled.

---

[8]*Willa Cather:* American novelist (1876–1947).
[9]*gringos:* Anglos.

In fourth grade I embarked upon a grandiose reading program. "Give me the names of important books," I would say to startled teachers. They soon found out that I had in mind "adult books." I ignored their suggestion of anything I suspected was written for children. (Not until I was in college, as a result, did I read *Huckleberry Finn* or *Alice's Adventures in Wonderland.*) Instead, I read *The Scarlet Letter* and Franklin's *Autobiography.* And whatever I read I read for extra credit. Each time I finished a book, I reported the achievement to a teacher and basked in the praise my effort earned. Despite my best efforts, however, there seemed to be more and more books I needed to read. At the library I would literally tremble as I came upon whole shelves of books I hadn't read. So I read and I read and I read: *Great Expectations;* all the short stories of Kipling; *The Babe Ruth Story;* the entire first volume of the *Encyclopaedia Britannica* (A–ANSTEY); the *Iliad; Moby Dick; Gone with the Wind; The Good Earth; Ramona; Forever Amber; The Lives of the Saints; Crime and Punishment; The Pearl. . . .* Librarians who initially frowned when I checked out the maximum ten books at a time started saving books they thought I might like. Teachers would say to the rest of the class, "I only wish the rest of you took reading as seriously as Richard obviously does."

But at home I would hear my mother wondering, "What do you see in your books?" (Was reading a hobby like her knitting? Was so much reading even healthy for a boy? Was it the sign of "brains"? Or was it just a convenient excuse for not helping around the house on Saturday mornings?) Always, "What do you see . . . ?"

What *did* I see in my books? I had the idea that they were crucial for my academic success, though I couldn't have said exactly how or why. In the sixth grade I simply concluded that what gave a book its value was some major idea or theme it contained. If that core essence could be mined and memorized, I would become learned like my teachers. I decided to record in a notebook the themes of the books that I read. After reading *Robinson Crusoe,* I wrote that its theme was "the value of learning to live by oneself." When I completed *Wuthering Heights,* I noted the danger of "letting emotions get out of control." Rereading these brief moralistic appraisals usually left me disheartened. I couldn't believe that they were really the source of reading's value. But for many more years, they constituted the only means I had of describing to myself the educational value of books.

I entered high school having read hundreds of books. My habit of reading made me a confident speaker and writer of English. Reading also enabled me to sense something of the shape, the major concerns, of Western thought. (I was able to say something about Dante[10] and Descartes[11]

---

[10]*Dante:* Dante Alighieri, Italian poet (1265–1321); author of *The Divine Comedy.*

[11]*Descartes:* René Descartes, French philosopher and mathematician (1596–1650).

and Engels[12] and James Baldwin[13] in my high school term papers.) In these various ways, books brought me academic success as I hoped that they would. But I was not a good reader. Merely bookish, I lacked a point of view when I read. Rather, I read in order to acquire a point of view. I vacuumed books for epigrams, scraps of information, ideas, themes — anything to fill the hollow within me and make me feel educated. When one of my teachers suggested to his drowsy tenth-grade English class that a person could not have a "complicated idea" until he had read at least two thousand books, I heard the remark without detecting either its irony or its very complicated truth. I merely determined to compile a list of all the books I had ever read. Harsh with myself, I included only once a title I might have read several times. (How, after all, could one read a book more than once?) And I included only those books over a hundred pages in length. (Could anything shorter be a book?)

There was yet another high school list I compiled. One day I came   30
across a newspaper article about the retirement of an English professor at a nearby state college. The article was accompanied by a list of the "hundred most important books of Western Civilization." "More than anything else in my life," the professor told the reporter with finality, "these books have made me all that I am." That was the kind of remark I couldn't ignore. I clipped out the list and kept it for the several months it took me to read all of the titles. Most books, of course, I barely understood. While reading Plato's *Republic*, for instance, I needed to keep looking at the book jacket comments to remind myself what the text was about. Nevertheless, with the special patience and superstition of a scholarship boy, I looked at every word of the text. And by the time I reached the last word, relieved, I convinced myself that I had read *The Republic*. In a ceremony of great pride, I solemnly crossed Plato off my list.

. . . The scholarship boy does not straddle, cannot reconcile, the two great opposing cultures of his life. His success is unromantic and plain. He sits in the classroom and offers those sitting beside him no calming reassurance about their own lives. He sits in the seminar room — a man with brown skin, the son of working-class Mexican immigrant parents. (Addressing the professor at the head of the table, his voice catches with nervousness.) There is no trace of his parents' accent in his speech. Instead he approximates the accents of teachers and classmates. Coming from *him* those sounds seem suddenly odd. Odd too is the effect produced when *he* uses academic jargon — bubbles at the tip of his tongue: "*Topos* . . . negative capability . . . vegetation imagery in Shakespearean comedy."[14] He lifts an

---

[12]*Engels:* Friedrich Engels, German socialist (1820–1895); coauthor with Karl Marx of *The Communist Manifesto* in 1848.

[13]*James Baldwin:* American novelist and essayist (1924–1987).

[14]*topos . . . negative capability . . .:* Technical terms associated with the study of literary criticism.

opinion from Coleridge, takes something else from Frye or Empson or Leavis.[15] He even repeats exactly his professor's earlier comment. All his ideas are clearly borrowed. He seems to have no thought of his own. He chatters while his listeners smile — their look one of disdain.

When he is older and thus when so little of the person he was survives, the scholarship boy makes only too apparent his profound lack of *self-confidence*. This is the conventional assessment that even Richard Hoggart repeats:

> [The scholarship boy] tends to over-stress the importance of examinations, of the piling-up of knowledge and of received opinions. He discovers a technique of apparent learning, of the acquiring of facts rather than of the handling and use of facts. He learns how to receive a purely literate education, one using only a small part of the personality and challenging only a limited area of his being. He begins to see life as a ladder, as a permanent examination with some praise and some further exhortation at each stage. He becomes an expert imbiber and doler-out; his competence will vary, but will rarely be accompanied by genuine enthusiasms. He rarely feels the reality of knowledge, of other men's thoughts and imaginings, on his own pulses. . . . He has something of the blinkered pony about him. . . .

But this is criticism more accurate than fair. The scholarship boy is a very bad student. He is the great mimic; a collector of thoughts, not a thinker; the very last person in class who ever feels obliged to have an opinion of his own. In large part, however, the reason he is such a bad student is because he realizes more often and more acutely than most other students — than Hoggart himself — that education requires radical self-reformation. As a very young boy, regarding his parents, as he struggles with an early homework assignment, he knows this too well. That is why he lacks self-assurance. He does not forget that the classroom is responsible for remaking him. He relies on his teacher, depends on all that he hears in the classroom and reads in his books. He becomes in every obvious way the worst student, a dummy mouthing the opinions of others. But he would not be so bad — nor would he become so successful, a *scholarship* boy — if he did not accurately perceive that the best synonym for primary "education" is "imitation."

Like me, Hoggart's imagined scholarship boy spends most of his years in the classroom afraid to long for his past. Only at the very end of his schooling does the boy-man become nostalgic. In this sudden change of heart, Richard Hoggart notes:

> He longs for the membership he lost, "he pines for some Nameless Eden where he never was." The nostalgia is the stronger and the more ambiguous because he is really "in quest of his own absconded self yet

---

[15]*Coleridge . . . Frye . . . Empson . . . Leavis:* Important literary critics.

scared to find it." He both wants to go back and yet thinks he has gone beyond his class, feels himself weighted with knowledge of his own and their situation, which hereafter forbids him the simpler pleasures of his father and mother. . . .

According to Hoggart, the scholarship boy grows nostalgic because he   35
remains the uncertain scholar, bright enough to have moved from his past, yet unable to feel easy, a part of a community of academics.

This analysis, however, only partially suggests what happened to me in my last years as a graduate student. When I traveled to London to write a dissertation on English Renaissance literature, I was finally confident of membership in a "community of scholars." But the pleasure that confidence gave me faded rapidly. After only two or three months in the reading room of the British Museum, it became clear that I had joined a lonely community. Around me each day were dour faces eclipsed by large piles of books. There were the regulars, like the old couple who arrived every morning, each holding a loop of the shopping bag which contained all their notes. And there was the historian who chattered madly to herself. ("Oh dear! Oh! Now, what's this? What? Oh, my!") There were also the faces of young men and women worn by long study. And everywhere eyes turned away the moment our glance accidentally met. Some persons I sat beside day after day, yet we passed silently at the end of the day, strangers. Still, we were united by a common respect for the written word and for scholarship. We did form a union, though one in which we remained distant from one another.

More profound and unsettling was the bond I recognized with those writers whose books I consulted. Whenever I opened a text that hadn't been used for years, I realized that my special interests and skills united me to a mere handful of academics. We formed an exclusive — eccentric! — society, separated from others who would never care or be able to share our concerns. (The pages I turned were stiff like layers of dead skin.) I began to wonder: Who, beside my dissertation director and a few faculty members, would ever read what I wrote? and: Was my dissertation much more than an act of social withdrawal? These questions went unanswered in the silence of the Museum reading room. They remained to trouble me after I'd leave the library each afternoon and feel myself shy — unsteady, speaking simple sentences at the grocer's or the butcher's on my way back to my bed-sitter.[16]

Meanwhile my file cards accumulated. A professional, I knew exactly how to search a book for pertinent information. I could quickly assess and summarize the usability of the many books I consulted. But whenever I started to write, I knew too much (and not enough) to be able to write anything but sentences that were overly cautious, timid, strained brittle under the heavy weight of footnotes and qualifications. I seemed unable to dare a passionate statement. I felt drawn by professionalism to the edge of sterility, capable of no more than pedantic, lifeless, unassailable prose.

[16]*bed-sitter:* A one-room apartment.

Then nostalgia began.

After years spent unwilling to admit its attractions, I gestured nostalgi-   40
cally toward the past. I yearned for that time when I had not been so alone. I
became impatient with books. I wanted experience more immediate. I feared
the library's silence. I silently scorned the gray, timid faces around me. I grew
to hate the growing pages of my dissertation on genre[17] and Renaissance literature. (In my mind I heard relatives laughing as they tried to make sense of its
title.) I wanted something — I couldn't say exactly what. I told myself that I
wanted a more passionate life. And a life less thoughtful. And above all, I
wanted to be less alone. One day I heard some Spanish academics whispering
back and forth to each other, and their sounds seemed ghostly voices recalling
my life. Yearning became preoccupation then. Boyhood memories beckoned,
flooded my mind. (Laughing intimate voices. Bounding up the front steps of
the porch. A sudden embrace inside the door.)

For weeks after, I turned to books by educational experts. I needed to
learn how far I had moved from my past — to determine how fast I would
be able to recover something of it once again. But I found little. Only a
chapter in a book by Richard Hoggart . . . I left the reading room and the
circle of faces.

I came home. After the year in England, I spent three summer months
living with my mother and father, relieved by how easy it was to be home. It
no longer seemed very important to me that we had little to say. I felt easy
sitting and eating and walking with them. I watched them, nevertheless,
looking for evidence of those elastic, sturdy strands that bind generations in
a web of inheritance. I thought as I watched my mother one night: of course
a friend had been right when she told me that I gestured and laughed just
like my mother. Another time I saw for myself: my father's eyes were much
like my own, constantly watchful.

But after the early relief, this return, came suspicion, nagging until I
realized that I had not neatly sidestepped the impact of schooling. My
desire to do so was precisely the measure of how much I remained an academic. *Negatively* (for that is how this idea first occurred to me): my need
to think so much and so abstractly about my parents and our relationship
was in itself an indication of my long education. My father and mother did
not pass their time thinking about the cultural meanings of their experience.
It was I who described their daily lives with airy ideas. And yet, *positively:*
the ability to consider experience so abstractly allowed me to shape into
desire what would otherwise have remained indefinite, meaningless longing
in the British Museum. If, because of my schooling, I had grown culturally
separated from my parents, my education finally had given me ways of
speaking and caring about that fact.

My best teachers in college and graduate school, years before, had tried
to prepare me for this conclusion, I think, when they discussed texts of

[17]*genre:* A class or category of artistic work; e.g., the genre of poetry.

aristocratic pastoral literature. Faithfully, I wrote down all that they said. I memorized it: "The praise of the unlettered by the highly educated is one of the primary themes of 'elitist' literature." But, "the importance of the praise given the unsolitary, richly passionate and spontaneous life is that it simultaneously reflects the value of a reflective life." I heard it all. But there was no way for any of it to mean very much to me. I was a scholarship boy at the time, busily laddering my way up the rungs of education. To pass an examination, I copied down exactly what my teachers told me. It would require many more years of schooling (an inevitable miseducation) in which I came to trust the silence of reading and the habit of abstracting from immediate experience — moving away from a life of closeness and immediacy I remembered with my parents, growing older — before I turned unafraid to desire the past, and thereby achieved what had eluded me for so long — the end of education.

ENGAGING THE TEXT

1. How does education affect Rodriguez's relationship to his family, his past, and his culture? Do you agree with him that education requires "radical self-reformation" (para. 33)?

2. What is a "scholarship boy"? Why does Rodriguez consider himself a bad student despite his academic success?

3. What happens to Rodriguez in London? Why does he ultimately abandon his studies there?

4. What drives Rodriguez to succeed? What does education represent to him? To his father and mother?

5. What is Rodriguez's final assessment of what he has gained and lost through his education? Do you agree with his analysis?

EXPLORING CONNECTIONS

6. Compare Rodriguez's attitude toward education and success with that of Mike Rose (p. 157) in "'I Just Wanna Be Average.'"

7. To what extent do Rodriguez's experiences as a "scholarship boy" confirm or complicate Jean Anyon's analysis (p. 169) of the relationship between social class, education, and success?

8. Read "Stephen Cruz" (p. 366) and compare his attitudes toward education and success with those of Rodriguez.

EXTENDING THE CRITICAL CONTEXT

9. What are your personal motives for academic success? How do they compare with those of Rodriguez?

10. Today many college students find that they're following in the footsteps of family members — not breaking ground as Rodriguez did. What special difficulties do such second- or third-generation college students face?

Para Teresa[1]

INÉS HERNÁNDEZ-ÁVILA

This poem explores and attempts to resolve an old conflict between its speaker and her schoolmate, two Chicanas at "Alamo which-had-to-be-its-name" Elementary School who have radically different ideas about what education means and does. Inés Hernández-Ávila (b. 1947) is director of the Chicana/Latina Research Center at the University of California, Davis. This poem appeared in her collection Con Razón, Corazón *(1987).*

A tí-Teresa
Te dedico las palabras estás
que explotan de mi corazón[2]

That day during lunch hour
at Alamo which-had-to-be-its-name   5
Elementary
my dear raza
That day in the bathroom
Door guarded
Myself cornered   10
I was accused by you, Teresa
Tú y las demás de tus amigas
Pachucas todas
Eran Uds. cinco.[3]

Me gritaban que porque me creía tan grande[4]   15
What was I trying to do, you growled
Show you up?
Make the teachers like me, pet me,
Tell me what a credit to my people I was?
I was playing right into their hands, you challenged   20
And you would have none of it.
I was to stop.

I was to be like you
I was to play your game of deadly defiance
Arrogance, refusal to submit.   25

---

[1] *Para Teresa:* For Teresa. [All notes are Hernández-Ávila's.]
[2] *A . . . corazón:* To you, Teresa, I dedicate these words that explode from my heart.
[3] *Tú . . . cinco:* You and the rest of your friends, all Pachucas, there were five of you.
[4] *Me . . . grande:* You were screaming at me, asking me why I thought I was so hot.

The game in which the winner takes nothing
Asks for nothing
Never lets his weaknesses show.

But I didn't understand.
My fear salted with confusion   30
Charged me to explain to you
I did nothing *for the teachers.*
I studied for my parents and for my grandparents
Who cut out honor roll lists
Whenever their nietos'[5] names appeared   35
For my shy mother who mastered her terror
to demand her place in mother's clubs
For my carpenter-father who helped me patiently with my math.
For my abuelos que me regalaron lápices en la Navidad[6]
And for myself.   40

Porque reconocí en aquel entonces
una verdad tremenda
que me hizo a mi un rebelde
Aunque tú no te habías dadocuenta[7]
We were not inferior   45
You and I, y las demás de tus amigas
Y los demás de nuestra gente[8]
I knew it the way I knew I was alive
We were good, honorable, brave
Genuine, loyal, strong   50
And smart.
Mine was a deadly game of defiance, also.
My contest was to prove
beyond any doubt
that we were not only equal but superior to them.   55
That was why I studied.
If I could do it, we all could.

You let me go then.
Your friends unblocked the way
I who-did-not-know-how-to-fight   60
was not made to engage with you-who-grew-up-fighting
Tu y yo,[9] Teresa

---

[5]*nietos':* Grandchildren's.
[6]*abuelos . . . Navidad:* Grandparents who gave me gifts of pencils at Christmas.
[7]*Porque . . . dadocuenta:* Because I recognized a great truth then that made me a rebel,
even though you didn't realize it.
[8]*Y . . . gente:* And the rest of your friends / And the rest of our people.
[9]*Tu y yo:* You and I.

We went in different directions
Pero fuimos juntas.[10]

In sixth grade we did not understand   65
Uds. with the teased, dyed-black-but-reddening hair,
Full petticoats, red lipsticks
and sweaters with the sleeves
pushed up
Y yo conformándome con lo que deseaba mi mamá[11]   70
Certainly never allowed to dye, to tease, to paint myself
I did not accept your way of anger,
Your judgements
You did not accept mine.

But now in 1975, when I am twenty-eight   75
Teresa
I remember you.
Y sabes —
Te comprendo,
Es más, te respeto.   80
Y si me permites,
Te nombro — "hermana."[12]

ENGAGING THE TEXT

1. The speaker says that she didn't understand Teresa at the time of the incident she describes. What didn't she understand, and why? How have her views of Teresa and of herself changed since then? What seems to have brought about this change?

2. What attitudes toward school and the majority culture do Teresa and the speaker represent? What about the speaker's family? In what way are both girls playing a game of "deadly defiance"? What arguments can you make for each form of rebellion?

3. Why do you think Hernández-Ávila wrote this poem in both Spanish and English? What does doing so say about the speaker's life? About her change of attitude toward Teresa?

EXPLORING CONNECTIONS

4. Compare the speaker's attitude toward school and family with those of Richard Rodriguez (p. 194). What motivates each of them? What tensions do they feel?

---

[10]*Pero fuimos juntas:* But we were together.

[11]*Y . . . mamá:* And I conforming to my mother's wishes.

[12]*Y sabes . . . "hermana":* And do you know what, I understand you. Even more, I respect you. And, if you permit me, I name you my sister.

5. Write a dialogue between the speaker of this poem, who wants to excel, and Ken Harvey, the boy whom Mike Rose said just wanted to be average (p. 157). Explore the uncertainties, pressures, and desires that these students felt. In what ways are these two apparently contrasting students actually similar?

Extending the Critical Context

6. Was there a person or group you disliked, feared, or fought with in elementary school? Has your understanding of your adversary or of your own motives changed since then? If so, what brought about this change?

Learning to Read
Malcolm X

Born Malcolm Little on May 19, 1925, Malcolm X was one of the most articulate and powerful leaders of black America during the 1960s. A street hustler convicted of robbery in 1946, he spent seven years in prison, where he educated himself and became a disciple of Elijah Muhammad, founder of the Nation of Islam. In the days of the civil rights movement, Malcolm X emerged as the leading spokesman for black separatism, a philosophy that urged black Americans to cut political, social, and economic ties with the white community. After a pilgrimage to Mecca, the capital of the Muslim world, in 1964, he became an orthodox Muslim, adopted the Muslim name El Hajj Malik El-Shabazz, and distanced himself from the teachings of the black Muslims. He was assassinated in 1965. In the following excerpt from his autobiography (1965), coauthored with Alex Haley and published the year of his death, Malcolm X describes his self-education.

It was because of my letters that I happened to stumble upon starting to acquire some kind of a homemade education.

I became increasingly frustrated at not being able to express what I wanted to convey in letters that I wrote, especially those to Mr. Elijah Muhammad.[1] In the street, I had been the most articulate hustler out

---

[1]*Elijah Muhammad:* American clergyman (1897–1975); leader of the Nation of Islam, 1935–1975.

there — I had commanded attention when I said something. But now, trying to write simple English, I not only wasn't articulate, I wasn't even functional. How would I sound writing in slang, the way I would *say* it, something such as, "Look, daddy, let me pull your coat about a cat, Elijah Muhammad — "

Many who today hear me somewhere in person, or on television, or those who read something I've said, will think I went to school far beyond the eighth grade. This impression is due entirely to my prison studies.

It had really begun back in the Charlestown Prison, when Bimbi[2] first made me feel envy of his stock of knowledge. Bimbi had always taken charge of any conversations he was in, and I had tried to emulate him. But every book I picked up had few sentences which didn't contain anywhere from one to nearly all of the words that might as well have been in Chinese. When I just skipped those words, of course, I really ended up with little idea of what the book said. So I had come to the Norfolk Prison Colony still going through only book-reading motions. Pretty soon, I would have quit even these motions, unless I had received the motivation that I did.

I saw that the best thing I could do was get hold of a dictionary — to study, to learn some words. I was lucky enough to reason also that I should try to improve my penmanship. It was sad. I couldn't even write in a straight line. It was both ideas together that moved me to request a dictionary along with some tablets and pencils from the Norfolk Prison Colony school.   5

I spent two days just riffling uncertainly through the dictionary's pages. I'd never realized so many words existed! I didn't know *which* words I needed to learn. Finally, just to start some kind of action, I began copying.

In my slow, painstaking, ragged handwriting, I copied into my tablet everything printed on that first page, down to the punctuation marks.

I believe it took me a day. Then, aloud, I read back, to myself, everything I'd written on the tablet. Over and over, aloud, to myself, I read my own handwriting.

I woke up the next morning, thinking about those words — immensely proud to realize that not only had I written so much at one time, but I'd written words that I never knew were in the world. Moreover, with a little effort, I also could remember what many of these words meant. I reviewed the words whose meanings I didn't remember. Funny thing, from the dictionary first page right now, that "aardvark" springs to my mind. The dictionary had a picture of it, a long-tailed, long-eared, burrowing African mammal, which lives off termites caught by sticking out its tongue as an anteater does for ants.

I was so fascinated that I went on — I copied the dictionary's next page.   10 And the same experience came when I studied that. With every succeeding page, I also learned of people and places and events from history. Actually the dictionary is like a miniature encyclopedia. Finally the dictionary's A

---

[2]*Bimbi:* A fellow inmate whose encyclopedic learning and verbal facility greatly impressed Malcolm X.

section had filled a whole tablet — and I went on into the B's. That was the way I started copying what eventually became the entire dictionary. It went a lot faster after so much practice helped me to pick up handwriting speed. Between what I wrote in my tablet, and writing letters, during the rest of my time in prison I would guess I wrote a million words.

I suppose it was inevitable that as my word-base broadened, I could for the first time pick up a book and read and now begin to understand what the book was saying. Anyone who has read a great deal can imagine the new world that opened. Let me tell you something: from then until I left that prison, in every free moment I had, if I was not reading in the library, I was reading on my bunk. You couldn't have gotten me out of books with a wedge. Between Mr. Muhammad's teachings, my correspondence, my visitors, . . . and my reading of books, months passed without my even thinking about being imprisoned. In fact, up to then, I never had been so truly free in my life.

The Norfolk Prison Colony's library was in the school building. A variety of classes was taught there by instructors who came from such places as Harvard and Boston universities. The weekly debates between inmate teams were also held in the school building. You would be astonished to know how worked up convict debaters and audiences would get over subjects like "Should Babies Be Fed Milk?"

Available on the prison library's shelves were books on just about every general subject. Much of the big private collection that Parkhurst[3] had willed to the prison was still in crates and boxes in the back of the library — thousands of old books. Some of them looked ancient: covers faded, old-time parchment-looking binding. Parkhurst . . . seemed to have been principally interested in history and religion. He had the money and the special interest to have a lot of books that you wouldn't have in a general circulation. Any college library would have been lucky to get that collection.

As you can imagine, especially in a prison where there was heavy emphasis on rehabilitation, an inmate was smiled upon if he demonstrated an unusually intense interest in books. There was a sizable number of well-read inmates, especially the popular debaters. Some were said by many to be practically walking encyclopedias. They were almost celebrities. No university would ask any student to devour literature as I did when this new world opened to me, of being able to read and *understand*.

I read more in my room than in the library itself. An inmate who was   15
known to read a lot could check out more than the permitted maximum number of books. I preferred reading in the total isolation of my own room.

When I had progressed to really serious reading, every night at about ten P.M. I would be outraged with the "lights out." It always seemed to catch me right in the middle of something engrossing.

---

[3]*Parkhurst:* Charles Henry Parkhurst (1842–1933); American clergyman, reformer, and president of the Society for the Prevention of Crime.

Fortunately, right outside my door was a corridor light that cast a glow into my room. The glow was enough to read by, once my eyes adjusted to it. So when "lights out" came, I would sit on the floor where I could continue reading in that glow.

At one-hour intervals at night guards paced past every room. Each time I heard the approaching footsteps, I jumped into bed and feigned sleep. And as soon as the guard passed, I got back out of bed onto the floor area of that light-glow, where I would read for another fifty-eight minutes until the guard approached again. That went on until three or four every morning. Three or four hours of sleep a night was enough for me. Often in the years in the streets I had slept less than that.

The teachings of Mr. Muhammad stressed how history had been "whitened" — when white men had written history books, the black man simply had been left out. Mr. Muhammad couldn't have said anything that would have struck me much harder. I had never forgotten how when my class, me and all of those whites, had studied seventh-grade United States history back in Mason, the history of the Negro had been covered in one paragraph, and the teacher had gotten a big laugh with his joke, "Negroes' feet are so big that when they walk, they leave a hole in the ground."

This is one reason why Mr. Muhammad's teachings spread so swiftly all over the United States, among *all* Negroes, whether or not they became followers of Mr. Muhammad. The teachings ring true — to every Negro. You can hardly show me a black adult in America — or a white one, for that matter — who knows from the history books anything like the truth about the black man's role. In my own case, once I heard of the "glorious history of the black man," I took special pains to hunt in the library for books that would inform me on details about black history.   20

I can remember accurately the very first set of books that really impressed me. I have since bought that set of books and I have it at home for my children to read as they grow up. It's called *Wonders of the World.* It's full of pictures of archeological finds, statues that depict, usually, non-European people.

I found books like Will Durant's[4] *Story of Civilization.* I read H. G. Wells'[5] *Outline of History. Souls of Black Folk* by W. E. B. Du Bois[6] gave me a glimpse into the black people's history before they came to this

[4]*Will Durant:* American author and historian (1885–1981). Durant, with his wife Ariel (1898–1981), won the Pulitzer Prize for literature for volume ten of their eleven-volume *The Story of Civilization,* published from 1935 to 1975.

[5]*H. G. Wells:* English novelist and historian (1866–1946).

[6]*W. E. B. Du Bois:* William Edward Burghardt Du Bois, distinguished black scholar, author, and activist (1868–1963). Du Bois was the first director of the NAACP and was an important figure in the Harlem Renaissance; his best-known book is *The Souls of Black Folk.*

country. Carter G. Woodson's[7] *Negro History* opened my eyes about black empires before the black slave was brought to the United States, and the early Negro struggles for freedom.

J. A. Rogers'[8] three volumes of *Sex and Race* told about race-mixing before Christ's time; and Aesop being a black man who told fables; about Egypt's Pharaohs; about the great Coptic Christian Empire;[9] about Ethiopia, the earth's oldest continuous black civilization, as China is the oldest continuous civilization.

Mr. Muhammad's teaching about how the white man had been created led me to *Findings in Genetics,* by Gregor Mendel.[10] (The dictionary's G section was where I had learned what "genetics" meant.) I really studied this book by the Austrian monk. Reading it over and over, especially certain sections, helped me to understand that if you started with a black man, a white man could be produced; but starting with a white man, you never could produce a black man — because the white chromosome is recessive. And since no one disputes that there was but one Original Man, the conclusion is clear.

During the last year or so, in the *New York Times,* Arnold Toynbee[11]   25 used the word "bleached" in describing the white man. His words were: "White (i.e., bleached) human beings of North European origin...." Toynbee also referred to the European geographic area as only a peninsula of Asia. He said there was no such thing as Europe. And if you look at the globe, you will see for yourself that America is only an extension of Asia. (But at the same time Toynbee is among those who have helped to bleach history. He has written that Africa was the only continent that produced no history. He won't write that again. Every day now, the truth is coming to light.)

I never will forget how shocked I was when I began reading about slavery's total horror. It made such an impact upon me that it later became one of my favorite subjects when I became a minister of Mr. Muhammad's. The world's most monstrous crime, the sin and the blood on the white man's hands, are almost impossible to believe. Books like the one by Frederick Olmsted[12] opened my eyes to the horrors suffered when the slave was landed in the United States. The European woman, Fanny Kemble,[13] who had married a Southern white slaveowner, described how human beings

---

[7]*Carter G. Woodson:* Distinguished African American historian (1875–1950); considered the father of black history.

[8]*J. A. Rogers:* African American historian and journalist (1883–1965).

[9]*Coptic Christian Empire:* The domain of the Coptic Church, a native Egyptian Christian church that retains elements of its African origins.

[10]*Gregor Mendel:* Austrian monk, botanist, and pioneer in genetic research (1822–1884).

[11]*Arnold Toynbee:* English historian (1889–1975).

[12]*Frederick Olmsted:* Frederick Law Olmsted (1822–1903), American landscape architect, city planner, and opponent of slavery.

[13]*Fanny Kemble:* Frances Anne Kemble, English actress and author (1809–1893); best known for her autobiographical *Journal of a Residence on a Georgia Plantation,* published in 1863 to win support in Britain for the abolitionist cause.

were degraded. Of course I read *Uncle Tom's Cabin*.[14] In fact, I believe that's the only novel I have ever read since I started serious reading.

Parkhurst's collection also contained some bound pamphlets of the Abolitionist[15] Anti-Slavery Society of New England. I read descriptions of atrocities, saw those illustrations of black slave women tied up and flogged with whips; of black mothers watching their babies being dragged off, never to be seen by their mothers again; of dogs after slaves, and of the fugitive slave catchers, evil white men with whips and clubs and chains and guns. I read about the slave preacher Nat Turner, who put the fear of God into the white slavemaster. Nat Turner wasn't going around preaching pie-in-the-sky and "non-violent" freedom for the black man. There in Virginia one night in 1831, Nat and seven other slaves started out at his master's home and through the night they went from one plantation "big house" to the next, killing, until by the next morning 57 white people were dead and Nat had about 70 slaves following him. White people, terrified for their lives, fled from their homes, locked themselves up in public buildings, hid in the woods, and some even left the state. A small army of soldiers took two months to catch and hang Nat Turner. Somewhere I have read where Nat Turner's example is said to have inspired John Brown[16] to invade Virginia and attack Harpers Ferry nearly thirty years later, with thirteen white men and five Negroes.

I read Herodotus,[17] "the father of History," or, rather, I read about him. And I read the histories of various nations, which opened my eyes gradually, then wider and wider, to how the whole world's white men had indeed acted like devils, pillaging and raping and bleeding and draining the whole world's non-white people. I remember, for instance, books such as Will Durant's *The Story of Oriental Civilization*, and Mahatma Gandhi's[18] accounts of the struggle to drive the British out of India.

Book after book showed me how the white man had brought upon the world's black, brown, red, and yellow peoples every variety of the suffering of exploitation. I saw how since the sixteenth century, the so-called "Christian trader" white man began to ply the seas in his lust for Asian and African empires, and plunder, and power. I read, I saw, how the white man never has gone among the non-white peoples bearing the Cross in the true manner and spirit of Christ's teachings — meek, humble, and Christlike.

I perceived, as I read, how the collective white man had been actually   30
nothing but a piratical opportunist who used Faustian machinations[19] to

---

[14]*Uncle Tom's Cabin:* Harriet Beecher Stowe's 1852 antislavery novel.

[15]*Abolitionist:* Advocating the prohibition of slavery.

[16]*John Brown:* American abolitionist (1800–1859); leader of an attack on Harpers Ferry, West Virginia, in 1859.

[17]*Herodotus:* Early Greek historian (484?–425? B.C.E.).

[18]*Mahatma Gandhi:* Hindu religious leader, social reformer, and advocate of nonviolence (1869–1948).

[19]*Faustian machinations:* Evil plots or schemes. Faust was a legendary character who sold his soul to the devil for knowledge and power.

make his own Christianity his initial wedge in criminal conquests. First, always "religiously," he branded "heathen" and "pagan" labels upon ancient non-white cultures and civilizations. The stage thus set, he then turned upon his non-white victims his weapons of war.

I read how, entering India — half a *billion* deeply religious brown people — the British white man, by 1759, through promises, trickery, and manipulations, controlled much of India through Great Britain's East India Company. The parasitical British administration kept tentacling out to half of the sub-continent. In 1857, some of the desperate people of India finally mutinied — and, excepting the African slave trade, nowhere has history recorded any more unnecessary bestial and ruthless human carnage than the British suppression of the non-white Indian people.

Over 115 million African blacks — close to the 1930s population of the United States — were murdered or enslaved during the slave trade. And I read how when the slave market was glutted, the cannibalistic white powers of Europe next carved up, as their colonies, the richest areas of the black continent. And Europe's chancelleries for the next century played a chess game of naked exploitation and power from Cape Horn to Cairo.

Ten guards and the warden couldn't have torn me out of those books. Not even Elijah Muhammad could have been more eloquent than those books were in providing indisputable proof that the collective white man had acted like a devil in virtually every contact he had with the world's collective non-white man. I listen today to the radio, and watch television, and read the headlines about the collective white man's fear and tension concerning China. When the white man professes ignorance about why the Chinese hate him so, my mind can't help flashing back to what I read, there in prison, about how the blood forebears of this same white man raped China at a time when China was trusting and helpless. Those original white "Christian traders" sent into China millions of pounds of opium. By 1839, so many of the Chinese were addicts that China's desperate government destroyed twenty thousand chests of opium. The first Opium War[20] was promptly declared by the white man. Imagine! Declaring *war* upon someone who objects to being narcotized! The Chinese were severely beaten, with Chinese-invented gunpowder.

The Treaty of Nanking made China pay the British white man for the destroyed opium; forced open China's major ports to British trade; forced China to abandon Hong Kong; fixed China's import tariffs so low that cheap British articles soon flooded in, maiming China's industrial development.

After a second Opium War, the Tientsin Treaties legalized the ravaging opium trade, legalized a British-French-American control of China's customs. China tried delaying that Treaty's ratification; Peking was looted and burned.

35

---

[20]*Opium War:* 1839–1842 war between Britain and China that ended with China's cession of Hong Kong to British rule.

"Kill the foreign white devils!" was the 1901 Chinese war cry in the Boxer Rebellion.[21] Losing again, this time the Chinese were driven from Peking's choicest areas. The vicious, arrogant white man put up the famous signs, "Chinese and dogs not allowed."

Red China after World War II closed its doors to the Western white world. Massive Chinese agricultural, scientific, and industrial efforts are described in a book that *Life* magazine recently published. Some observers inside Red China have reported that the world never has known such a hate-white campaign as is now going on in this non-white country where, present birth-rates continuing, in fifty more years Chinese will be half the earth's population. And it seems that some Chinese chickens will soon come home to roost, with China's recent successful nuclear tests.

Let us face reality. We can see in the United Nations a new world order being shaped, along color lines — an alliance among the non-white nations. America's U.N. Ambassador Adlai Stevenson[22] complained not long ago that in the United Nations "a skin game"[23] was being played. He was right. He was facing reality. A "skin game" *is* being played. But Ambassador Stevenson sounded like Jesse James accusing the marshal of carrying a gun. Because who in the world's history ever has played a worse "skin game" than the white man?

Mr. Muhammad, to whom I was writing daily, had no idea of what a new world had opened up to me through my efforts to document his teachings in books.

When I discovered philosophy, I tried to touch all the landmarks of philosophical development. Gradually, I read most of the old philosophers, Occidental and Oriental. The Oriental philosophers were the ones I came to prefer; finally, my impression was that most Occidental philosophy had largely been borrowed from the Oriental thinkers. Socrates, for instance, traveled in Egypt. Some sources even say that Socrates was initiated into some of the Egyptian mysteries. Obviously Socrates got some of his wisdom among the East's wise men. 40

I have often reflected upon the new vistas that reading opened to me. I knew right there in prison that reading had changed forever the course of my life. As I see it today, the ability to read awoke inside me some long dormant craving to be mentally alive. I certainly wasn't seeking any degree, the way a college confers a status symbol upon its students. My homemade education gave me, with every additional book that I read, a little bit more sensitivity to the deafness, dumbness, and blindness that was afflicting the black race in America. Not long ago, an English writer telephoned me from London, asking questions. One was, "What's your alma mater?" I told him,

---

[21]*Boxer Rebellion:* The 1898–1900 uprising by members of a secret Chinese society who opposed foreign influence in Chinese affairs.

[22]*Adlai Stevenson:* American politician (1900–1965); Democratic candidate for the presidency in 1952 and 1956.

[23]*skin game:* A dishonest or fraudulent scheme, business operation, or trick, with the added reference in this instance to skin color.

"Books." You will never catch me with a free fifteen minutes in which I'm not studying something I feel might be able to help the black man.

Yesterday I spoke in London, and both ways on the plane across the Atlantic I was studying a document about how the United Nations proposes to insure the human rights of the oppressed minorities of the world. The American black man is the world's most shameful case of minority oppression. What makes the black man think of himself as only an internal United States issue is just a catch-phrase, two words, "civil rights." How is the black man going to get "civil rights" before first he wins his *human* rights? If the American black man will start thinking about his *human* rights, and then start thinking of himself as part of one of the world's great peoples, he will see he has a case for the United Nations.

I can't think of a better case! Four hundred years of black blood and sweat invested here in America, and the white man still has the black man begging for what every immigrant fresh off the ship can take for granted the minute he walks down the gangplank.

But I'm digressing. I told the Englishman that my alma mater was books, a good library. Every time I catch a plane, I have with me a book that I want to read — and that's a lot of books these days. If I weren't out here every day battling the white man, I could spend the rest of my life reading, just satisfying my curiosity — because you can hardly mention anything I'm not curious about. I don't think anybody ever got more out of going to prison than I did. In fact, prison enabled me to study far more intensively than I would have if my life had gone differently and I had attended some college. I imagine that one of the biggest troubles with colleges is there are too many distractions, too much panty-raiding, fraternities, and boola-boola and all of that. Where else but in a prison could I have attacked my ignorance by being able to study intensely sometimes as much as fifteen hours a day?

ENGAGING THE TEXT

1. What motivated Malcolm X to educate himself?
2. What kind of knowledge did Malcolm X gain by learning to read? How did this knowledge free or empower him?
3. Would it be possible for public schools to empower students in the way that Malcolm X's self-education empowered him? If so, how? If not, why not?
4. Some readers are offended by the strength of Malcolm X's accusations and by his grouping of all members of a given race into "collectives." Given the history of racial injustice he recounts here, do you feel he is justified in taking such a position?

EXPLORING CONNECTIONS

5. Compare and contrast Malcolm X's views on the meaning and purpose of education — or on the value and nature of reading — with those of Richard Rodriguez (p. 194). How can you account for the differences in their attitudes?

THE BOONDOCKS   **by AARON MCGRUDER**

6. Imagine that John Taylor Gatto (p. 148), Mike Rose (p. 157), Richard Rodriguez (p. 194), and Malcolm X have been appointed to redesign American education. Working in groups, role-play a meeting in which the committee attempts to reach consensus on its recommendations. Report to the class the results of the committee's deliberations and discuss them.

7. What does the *Boondocks* cartoon above suggest about the possibility of teaching and learning "revolutionary" ideas within the setting of a public school system?

EXTENDING THE CRITICAL CONTEXT

8. Survey some typical elementary or secondary school textbooks to test the currency of Malcolm X's charge that the educational establishment presents a "whitened" view of America. What view of America is presently being projected in public school history and social science texts?

9. Go to the library and read one page of a dictionary chosen at random. Study the meanings of any unfamiliar words and follow up on the information on your page by consulting encyclopedias, books, or articles. Let yourself be guided by chance and by your interests. After you've tried this experiment, discuss in class the benefits and drawbacks of an unsystematic self-education like Malcolm X's.

Still Separate, Still Unequal

JONATHAN KOZOL

In Brown v. Board of Education *(1954), the U.S. Supreme Court overturned its ruling in* Plessy v. Ferguson *(1896), which had sanctioned "separate but equal" facilities for blacks and whites throughout the South for more than half a century. The Court's decision in* Brown *ended the deliberate segregation of U.S. schools and promised to usher in a new era of equality in American education. But according to longtime educational critic Jonathan Kozol, American schools today may be more segregated than at any time since 1954. And the "educational apartheid" that Kozol sees in U.S. schools isn't just about color. Kozol associates the "resegregation" of public education with a deterioration of classroom conditions and teaching practices that threatens an entire generation of Americans.*

After graduating from Harvard with a degree in literature and studying as a Rhodes Scholar at Oxford University, Kozol (b. 1936) took his first job teaching in an inner-city elementary school near Boston. His account of that experience, Death at an Early Age: The Destruction of the Hearts and Minds of Negro Children in the Boston Public Schools *(1967) won national acclaim and established him as one of the country's foremost educational activists and social reformers. Since then, his work with poor children and their families has resulted in a dozen books, including* Free Schools *(1972),* Illiterate America *(1980),* On Being a Teacher *(1981),* Rachael and Her Children: Homeless Families in America *(1988),* Savage Inequalities *(1991), and* The Shame of the Nation: The Restoration of Apartheid Schooling in America *(2005), the source of this selection. His most recent book is* Letters to a Young Teacher *(2007).*

Many Americans who live far from our major cities and who have no firsthand knowledge of the realities to be found in urban public schools seem to have the rather vague and general impression that the great extremes of racial isolation that were matters of grave national significance some thirty-five or forty years ago have gradually but steadily diminished in more recent years. The truth, unhappily, is that the trend, for well over a decade now, has been precisely the reverse. Schools that were already deeply segregated twenty-five or thirty years ago are no less segregated now, while thousands of other schools around the country that had been integrated either voluntarily or by the force of law have since been rapidly resegregating.

In Chicago, by the academic year 2002–2003, 87 percent of public-school enrollment was black or Hispanic; less than 10 percent of children in the schools were white. In Washington, D.C., 94 percent of children were black or Hispanic; less than 5 percent were white. In St. Louis, 82 percent of the student population were black or Hispanic; in Philadelphia and Cleveland, 79 percent; in Los Angeles, 84 percent, in Detroit, 96 percent; in Baltimore, 89 percent. In New York City, nearly three quarters of the students were black or Hispanic.

Even these statistics, as stark as they are, cannot begin to convey how deeply isolated children in the poorest and most segregated sections of these cities have become. In the typically colossal high schools of the Bronx, for instance, more than 90 percent of students (in most cases, more than

95 percent) are black or Hispanic. At John F. Kennedy High School in 2003, 93 percent of the enrollment of more than 4,000 students were black and Hispanic; only 3.5 percent of students at the school were white. At Harry S. Truman High School, black and Hispanic students represented 96 percent of the enrollment of 2,700 students; 2 percent were white. At Adlai Stevenson High School, which enrolls 3,400 students, blacks and Hispanics made up 97 percent of the student population; a mere eight-tenths of one percent were white.

A teacher at P.S. 65 in the South Bronx once pointed out to me one of the two white children I had ever seen there. His presence in her class was something of a wonderment to the teacher and to the other pupils. I asked how many white kids she had taught in the South Bronx in her career. "I've been at this school for eighteen years," she said. "This is the first white student I have ever taught."

One of the most disheartening experiences for those who grew up in the years when Martin Luther King Jr. and Thurgood Marshall[1] were alive is to visit public schools today that bear their names, or names of other honored leaders of the integration struggles that produced the temporary progress that took place in the three decades after *Brown v. Board of Education*,[2] and to find out how many of these schools are bastions of contemporary segregation. It is even more disheartening when schools like these are not in deeply segregated inner-city neighborhoods but in racially mixed areas where the integration of a public school would seem to be most natural, and where, indeed, it takes a conscious effort on the part of parents or school officials in these districts to avoid the integration option that is often right at their front door.

In a Seattle neighborhood that I visited in 2002, for instance, where approximately half the families were Caucasian, 95 percent of students at the Thurgood Marshall Elementary School were black, Hispanic, Native American, or of Asian origin. An African American teacher at the school told me — not with bitterness but wistfully — of seeing clusters of white parents and their children each morning on the corner of a street close to the school, waiting for a bus that took the children to a predominantly white school.

"At Thurgood Marshall," according to a big wall poster in the school's lobby, "the dream is alive." But school-assignment practices and federal court decisions that have countermanded long-established policies that previously fostered integration in Seattle's schools make the realization of the dream identified with Justice Marshall all but unattainable today. In San Diego there is a school that bears the name of Rosa Parks in which 86 percent of students are black and Hispanic and only some 2 percent are white. In Los Angeles there is a school that bears the name of Dr. King that is

[1]*Thurgood Marshall:* First African American justice on the Supreme Court (1908–1993).

[2]*Brown v. Board of Education:* 1954 Supreme Court case outlawing public school segregation. The court ruled, "Separate educational facilities are inherently unequal."

99 percent black and Hispanic, and another in Milwaukee in which black and Hispanic children also make up 99 percent of the enrollment. There is a high school in Cleveland that is named for Dr. King in which black students make up 97 percent of the student body, and the graduation rate is only 35 percent. In Philadelphia, 98 percent of children at a high school named for Dr. King are black. At a middle school named for Dr. King in Boston, black and Hispanic children make up 98 percent of the enrollment. . . .

There is a well-known high school named for Martin Luther King Jr. in New York City too. This school, which I've visited repeatedly in recent years, is located in an upper-middle-class white neighborhood, where it was built in the belief — or hope — that it would draw large numbers of white students by permitting them to walk to school, while only their black and Hispanic classmates would be asked to ride the bus or come by train. When the school was opened in 1975, less than a block from Lincoln Center in Manhattan, "it was seen," according to the *New York Times,* "as a promising effort to integrate white, black and Hispanic students in a thriving neighborhood that held one of the city's cultural gems." Even from the start, however, parents in the neighborhood showed great reluctance to permit their children to enroll at Martin Luther King, and, despite "its prime location and its name, which itself creates the highest of expectations," notes the *Times,* the school before long came to be a destination for black and Hispanic students who could not obtain admission into more successful schools. It stands today as one of the nation's most visible and problematic symbols of an expectation rapidly receding and a legacy substantially betrayed.

Perhaps most damaging to any serious effort to address racial segregation openly is the refusal of most of the major arbiters of culture in our northern cities to confront or even clearly name an obvious reality they would have castigated with a passionate determination in another section of the nation fifty years before — and which, moreover, they still castigate today in retrospective writings that assign it to a comfortably distant and allegedly concluded era of the past. There is, indeed, a seemingly agreed-upon convention in much of the media today not even to use an accurate descriptor like "racial segregation" in a narrative description of a segregated school. Linguistic sweeteners, semantic somersaults, and surrogate vocabularies are repeatedly employed. Schools in which as few as 3 or 4 percent of students may be white or Southeast Asian or of Middle Eastern origin, for instance — and where *every other child* in the building is black or Hispanic — are referred to as "diverse." Visitors to schools like these discover quickly the eviscerated meaning of the word, which is no longer a proper adjective but a euphemism for a plainer word that has apparently become unspeakable.

School systems themselves repeatedly employ this euphemism in   10 describing the composition of their student populations. In a school I visited in the fall of 2004 in Kansas City, Missouri, for example, a document distributed to visitors reports that the school's curriculum "addresses the needs of children from diverse backgrounds." But as I went from class to class, I did not encounter any children who were white or Asian — or Hispanic, for that matter — and when I was later provided with precise statistics for the demographics of the school, I learned that 99.6 percent of students there were African American. In a similar document, the school board of another district, this one in New York State, referred to "the diversity" of its student population and "the rich variations of ethnic backgrounds." But when I looked at the racial numbers that the district had reported to the state, I learned that there were 2,800 black and Hispanic children in the system, 1 Asian child, and 3 whites. Words, in these cases, cease to have real meaning; or, rather, they mean the opposite of what they say.

High school students whom I talk with in deeply segregated neighborhoods and public schools seem far less circumspect than their elders and far more open in their willingness to confront these issues. "It's more like being hidden," said a fifteen-year-old girl named Isabel[3] I met some years ago in Harlem, in attempting to explain to me the ways in which she and her classmates understood the racial segregation of their neighborhoods and schools. "It's as if you have been put in a garage where, if they don't have room for something but aren't sure if they should throw it out, they put it there where they don't need to think of it again."

I asked her if she thought America truly did not "have room" for her or other children of her race. "Think of it this way," said a sixteen-year-old girl sitting beside her. "If people in New York woke up one day and learned that we were gone, that we had simply died or left for somewhere else, how would they feel?"

"How do you think they'd feel?" I asked.

"I think they'd be relieved," this very solemn girl replied.

Many educators make the argument today that given the demographics   15
of large cities like New York and their suburban areas, our only realistic goal should be the nurturing of strong, empowered, and well-funded schools in segregated neighborhoods. Black school officials in these situations have sometimes conveyed to me a bitter and clear-sighted recognition that they're being asked, essentially, to mediate and render functional an uncontested separation between children of their race and children of white people living sometimes in a distant section of their town and sometimes in almost their own immediate communities. Implicit in this mediation is a willingness to set aside the promises of *Brown* and — though never stating this or even thinking of it clearly in these terms — to settle for the promise made more than a century ago in *Plessy v. Ferguson,* the 1896 Supreme Court ruling in which

---

[3]The names of children mentioned in this article have been changed to protect their privacy. [Kozol's note]

"separate but equal" was accepted as a tolerable rationale for the perpetuation of a dual system in American society.

Equality itself — equality alone — is now, it seems, the article of faith to which most of the principals of inner-city public schools subscribe. And some who are perhaps most realistic do not even dare to ask for, or expect, complete equality, which seems beyond the realm of probability for many years to come, but look instead for only a sufficiency of means — "adequacy" is the legal term most often used today — by which to win those practical and finite victories that appear to be within their reach. Higher standards, higher expectations, are repeatedly demanded of these urban principals, and of the teachers and students in their schools, but far lower standards — certainly in ethical respects — appear to be expected of the dominant society that isolates these children in unequal institutions.

"Dear Mr. Kozol," wrote the eight-year-old, "we do not have the things you have. You have Clean things. We do not have. You have a clean bathroom. We do not have that. You have Parks and we do not have Parks. You have all the thing and we do not have all the thing. Can you help us?"

The letter, from a child named Alliyah, came in a fat envelope of twenty-seven letters from a class of third-grade children in the Bronx. Other letters that the students in Alliyah's classroom sent me registered some of the same complaints. "We don't have no gardens," "no Music or Art," and "no fun places to play," one child said. "Is there a way to fix this Problem?" Another noted a concern one hears from many children in such overcrowded schools: "We have a gym but it is for lining up. I think it is not fair." Yet another of Alliyah's classmates asked me, with a sweet misspelling, if I knew the way to make her school into a "good" school — "like the other kings have" — and ended with the hope that I would do my best to make it possible for "all the kings" to have good schools.

The letter that affected me the most, however, had been written by a child named Elizabeth. "It is not fair that other kids have a garden and new things. But we don't have that," said Elizabeth. "I wish that this school was the most beautiful school in the whole why world."

"The whole why world" stayed in my thoughts for days. When I later 20 met Elizabeth, I brought her letter with me, thinking I might see whether, in reading it aloud, she'd change the "why" to "wide" or leave it as it was. My visit to her class, however, proved to be so pleasant, and the children seemed so eager to bombard me with their questions about where I lived, and why I lived there rather than in New York, and who I lived with, and how many dogs I had, and other interesting questions of that sort, that I decided not to interrupt the nice reception they had given me with questions about usages and spelling. I left "the whole why world" to float around unedited and unrevised in my mind. The letter itself soon found a resting place on the wall above my desk.

In the years before I met Elizabeth, I had visited many other schools in the South Bronx and in one northern district of the Bronx as well. I had made repeated visits to a high school where a stream of water flowed down one of the main stairwells on a rainy afternoon and where green fungus molds were growing in the office where the students went for counseling. A large blue barrel was positioned to collect rainwater coming through the ceiling. In one makeshift elementary school housed in a former skating rink next to a funeral establishment in yet another nearly all-black-and-Hispanic section of the Bronx, class size rose to thirty-four and more; four kindergarten classes and a sixth-grade class were packed into a single room that had no windows. The air was stifling in many rooms, and the children had no place for recess because there was no outdoor playground and no indoor gym.

In another elementary school, which had been built to hold 1,000 children but was packed to bursting with some 1,500, the principal poured out his feelings to me in a room in which a plastic garbage bag had been attached somehow to cover part of the collapsing ceiling. "This," he told me, pointing to the garbage bag, then gesturing around him at the other indications of decay and disrepair one sees in ghetto schools much like it elsewhere, "would not happen to white children."

Libraries, once one of the glories of the New York City school system, were either nonexistent or, at best, vestigial in large numbers of the elementary schools. Art and music programs had also for the most part disappeared. "When I began to teach in 1969," the principal of an elementary school in the South Bronx reported to me, "every school had a full-time licensed art and music teacher and librarian." During the subsequent decades, he recalled, "I saw all of that destroyed."

School physicians also were removed from elementary schools during these years. In 1970, when substantial numbers of white children still attended New York City's public schools, 400 doctors had been present to address the health needs of the children. By 1993 the number of doctors had been cut to 23, most of them part-time — a cutback that affected most severely children in the city's poorest neighborhoods, where medical facilities were most deficient and health problems faced by children most extreme. Teachers told me of asthmatic children who came into class with chronic wheezing and who at any moment of the day might undergo more serious attacks, but in the schools I visited there were no doctors to attend to them.

In explaining these steep declines in services, political leaders in New York tended to point to shifting economic factors, like a serious budget crisis in the middle 1970s, rather than to the changing racial demographics of the student population. But the fact of economic ups and downs from year to year, or from one decade to the next, could not convincingly explain the permanent shortchanging of the city's students, which took place   25 routinely in good economic times and bad. The bad times were seized upon politically to justify the cuts, and the money was never restored once the crisis years were past.

"If you close your eyes to the changing racial composition of the schools and look only at budget actions and political events," says Noreen Connell, the director of the nonprofit Educational Priorities Panel in New York, "you're missing the assumptions that are underlying these decisions." When minority parents ask for something better for their kids, she says, "the assumption is that these are parents who can be discounted. These are kids who just don't count — children we don't value."

This, then, is the accusation that Alliyah and her classmates send our way: "You have . . . We do not have." Are they right or are they wrong? Is this a case of naive and simplistic juvenile exaggeration? What does a third-grader know about these big-time questions of fairness and justice? Physical appearances apart, how in any case do you begin to measure something so diffuse and vast and seemingly abstract as having more, or having less, or not having at all?

Around the time I met Alliyah in the school year 1997–1998, New York's Board of Education spent about $8,000 yearly on the education of a third-grade child in a New York City public school. If you could have scooped Alliyah up out of the neighborhood where she was born and plunked her down in a fairly typical white suburb of New York, she would have received a public education worth about $12,000 a year. If you were to lift her up once more and set her down in one of the wealthiest white suburbs of New York, she would have received as much as $18,000 worth of public education every year and would likely have had a third-grade teacher paid approximately $30,000 more than her teacher in the Bronx was paid.

The dollars on both sides of the equation have increased since then, but the discrepancies between them have remained. The present per-pupil spending level in the New York City schools is $11,700, which may be compared with a per-pupil spending level in excess of $22,000 in the well-to-do suburban district of Manhasset, Long Island. The present New York City level is, indeed, almost exactly what Manhasset spent per pupil eighteen years ago, in 1987, when that sum of money bought a great deal more in services and salaries than it can buy today. In dollars adjusted for inflation, New York City has not yet caught up to where its wealthiest suburbs were a quarter-century ago. . . .

As racial isolation deepens and the inequalities of education finance 30 remain unabated and take on new and more innovative forms, the principals of many inner-city schools are making choices that few principals in public schools that serve white children in the mainstream of the nation ever need to contemplate. Many have been dedicating vast amounts of time and effort to create an architecture of adaptive strategies that promise incremental gains within the limits inequality allows.

New vocabularies of stentorian determination, new systems of incentive, and new modes of castigation, which are termed "rewards and sanctions," have emerged. Curriculum materials that are alleged to be aligned with governmentally established goals and standards and particularly suited to what are regarded as "the special needs and learning styles" of low-income urban children have been introduced. Relentless emphasis on raising test scores, rigid policies of nonpromotion and nongraduation, a new empiricism and the imposition of unusually detailed lists of named and numbered "outcomes" for each isolated parcel of instruction, an oftentimes fanatical insistence upon uniformity of teachers in their management of time, an openly conceded emulation of the rigorous approaches of the military and a frequent use of terminology that comes out of the world of industry and commerce — these are just a few of the familiar aspects of these new adaptive strategies.

Although generically described as "school reform," most of these practices and policies are targeted primarily at poor children of color; and although most educators speak of these agendas in broad language that sounds applicable to all, it is understood that they are valued chiefly as responses to perceived catastrophe in deeply segregated and unequal schools.

"If you do what I tell you to do, how I tell you to do it, when I tell you to do it, you'll get it right," said a determined South Bronx principal observed by a reporter for the *New York Times.* She was laying out a memorizing rule for math to an assembly of her students. "If you don't, you'll get it wrong." This is the voice, this is the tone, this is the rhythm and didactic certitude one hears today in inner-city schools that have embraced a pedagogy of direct command and absolute control. "Taking their inspiration from the ideas of B. F. Skinner[4] . . ." says the *Times,* proponents of scripted rote-and-drill curricula articulate their aim as the establishment of "faultless communication" between "the teacher, who is the stimulus," and "the students, who respond."

The introduction of Skinnerian approaches (which are commonly employed in penal institutions and drug-rehabilitation programs), as a way of altering the attitudes and learning styles of black and Hispanic children, is provocative, and it has stirred some outcries from respected scholars. To actually go into a school where you know some of the children very, very well and see the way that these approaches can affect their daily lives and thinking processes is even more provocative.

On a chilly November day four years ago in the South Bronx, I entered 35
P.S. 65, a school I had been visiting since 1993. There had been major changes since I'd been there last. Silent lunches had been instituted in the

---

[4]*B. F. Skinner:* American psychologist (1904–1990) known for his theories on stimulus and response.

cafeteria, and on days when children misbehaved, silent recess had been introduced as well. On those days the students were obliged to sit in rows and maintain perfect silence on the floor of a small indoor room instead of going out to play. The words SUCCESS FOR ALL, the brand name of a scripted curriculum — better known by its acronym, SFA — were prominently posted at the top of the main stairway and, as I would later find, in almost every room. Also frequently displayed within the halls and classrooms were a number of administrative memos that were worded with unusual didactic absoluteness. "Authentic Writing," read a document called "Principles of Learning" that was posted in the corridor close to the principal's office, "is driven by curriculum and instruction." I didn't know what this expression meant. Like many other undefined and arbitrary phrases posted in the school, it seemed to be a dictum that invited no interrogation.

I entered the fourth grade of a teacher I will call Mr. Endicott, a man in his mid-thirties who had arrived here without training as a teacher, one of about a dozen teachers in the building who were sent into this school after a single summer of short-order preparation. Now in his second year, he had developed a considerable sense of confidence and held the class under a tight control.

As I found a place to sit in a far corner of the room, the teacher and his young assistant, who was in her first year as a teacher, were beginning a math lesson about building airport runways, a lesson that provided children with an opportunity for measuring perimeters. On the wall behind the teacher, in large letters, was written: "Portfolio Protocols: 1. You are responsible for the selection of [your] work that enters your portfolio. 2. As your skills become more sophisticated this year, you will want to revise, amend, supplement, and possibly replace items in your portfolio to reflect your intellectual growth." On the left side of the room: "Performance Standards Mathematics Curriculum: M-5 Problem Solving and Reasoning. M-6 Mathematical Skills and Tools . . ."

My attention was distracted by some whispering among the children sitting to the right of me. The teacher's response to this distraction was immediate: his arm shot out and up in a diagonal in front of him, his hand straight up, his fingers flat. The young co-teacher did this, too. When they saw their teachers do this, all the children in the classroom did it, too.

"Zero noise," the teacher said, but this instruction proved to be unneeded. The strange salute the class and teachers gave each other, which turned out to be one of a number of such silent signals teachers in the school were trained to use, and children to obey, had done the job of silencing the class.

"Active listening!" said Mr. Endicott. "Heads up! Tractor beams!" which meant, "Every eye on me." 40

On the front wall of the classroom, in handwritten words that must have taken Mr. Endicott long hours to transcribe, was a list of terms that could be used to praise or criticize a student's work in mathematics. At Level Four, the highest of four levels of success, a child's "problem-solving strategies" could be described, according to this list, as "systematic, complete, efficient, and possibly elegant," while the student's capability to draw conclusions from the work she had completed could be termed "insightful" or "comprehensive." At Level Two, the child's capability to draw conclusions was to be described as "logically unsound"; at Level One, "not present." Approximately 50 separate categories of proficiency, or lack of such, were detailed in this wall-sized tabulation.

A well-educated man, Mr. Endicott later spoke to me about the form of classroom management that he was using as an adaptation from a model of industrial efficiency. "It's a kind of 'Taylorism'[5] in the classroom," he explained, referring to a set of theories about the management of factory employees introduced by Frederick Taylor in the early 1900s. "Primitive utilitarianism" is another term he used when we met some months later to discuss these management techniques with other teachers from the school. His reservations were, however, not apparent in the classroom. Within the terms of what he had been asked to do, he had, indeed, become a master of control. It is one of the few classrooms I had visited up to that time in which almost nothing even hinting at spontaneous emotion in the children or the teacher surfaced while I was there.

The teacher gave the "zero noise" salute again when someone whispered to another child at his table. "In two minutes you will have a chance to talk and share this with your partner." Communication between children in the class was not prohibited but was afforded time slots and, remarkably enough, was formalized in an expression that I found included in a memo that was posted on the wall beside the door. "An opportunity . . . to engage in Accountable Talk."

Even the teacher's words of praise were framed in terms consistent with the lists that had been posted on the wall. "That's a Level Four suggestion," said the teacher when a child made an observation other teachers might have praised as simply "pretty good" or "interesting" or "mature."

There was, it seemed, a formal name for every cognitive event within this school: "Authentic Writing," "Active Listening," "Accountable Talk." The ardor to assign all items of instruction or behavior a specific name was unsettling me. The adjectives had the odd effect of hyping every item of endeavor. "Authentic Writing" was, it seemed, a more important act than what the children in a writing class in any ordinary school might try to do. "Accountable Talk" was something more self-conscious and significant than merely useful conversation.

Since that day at P.S. 65, I have visited nine other schools in six different cities where the same Skinnerian curriculum is used. The signs on the walls, the silent signals, the curious salute, the same insistent naming

45

---

[5]*Taylorism:* Approach to management named after American engineer and business school professor Frederick Taylor. His *Principles of Scientific Management* (1911) sought to increase efficiency and productivity.

of all cognitive particulars, became familiar as I went from one school to the next.

"Meaningful Sentences," began one of the many listings of proficiencies expected of the children in the fourth grade of an inner-city elementary school in Hartford (90 percent black, 10 percent Hispanic) that I visited a short time later. "Noteworthy Questions," "Active Listening," and other designations like these had been posted elsewhere in the room. Here, too, the teacher gave the kids her outstretched arm, with hand held up, to reestablish order when they grew a little noisy, but I noticed that she tried to soften the effect of this by opening her fingers and bending her elbow slightly so it did not look quite as forbidding as the gesture Mr. Endicott had used. A warm and interesting woman, she later told me she disliked the regimen intensely.

Over her desk, I read a "Mission Statement," which established the priorities and values for the school. Among the missions of the school, according to the printed statement, which was posted also in some other classrooms of the school, was "to develop productive citizens" who have the skills that will be needed "for successful global competition," a message that was reinforced by other posters in the room. Over the heads of a group of children at their desks, a sign anointed them BEST WORKERS OF 2002.

Another signal now was given by the teacher, this one not for silence but in order to achieve some other form of class behavior, which I could not quite identify. The students gave exactly the same signal in response. Whatever the function of this signal, it was done as I had seen it done in the South Bronx and would see it done in other schools in months to come. Suddenly, with a seeming surge of restlessness and irritation — with herself, as it appeared, and with her own effective use of all the tricks that she had learned — she turned to me and said, "I can do this with my dog." . . .

In some inner-city districts, even the most pleasant and old-fashioned   50
class activities of elementary schools have now been overtaken by these ordering requirements. A student teacher in California, for example, wanted to bring a pumpkin to her class on Halloween but knew it had no ascertainable connection to the California standards. She therefore had developed what she called "The Multi-Modal Pumpkin Unit" to teach science (seeds), arithmetic (the size and shape of pumpkins, I believe — this detail wasn't clear), and certain items she adapted out of language arts, in order to position "pumpkins" in a frame of state proficiencies. Even with her multi-modal pumpkin, as her faculty adviser told me, she was still afraid she would be criticized because she knew the pumpkin would not really help her children to achieve expected goals on state exams.

Why, I asked a group of educators at a seminar in Sacramento, was a teacher being placed in a position where she'd need to do preposterous curricular gymnastics to enjoy a bit of seasonal amusement with her kids on Halloween? How much injury to state-determined "purpose" would it do to let the children of poor people have a pumpkin party once a year for no other reason than because it's something fun that other children get to do on autumn days in public schools across most of America?

"Forcing an absurdity on teachers does teach something," said an African-American professor. "It teaches acquiescence. It breaks down the will to thumb your nose at pointless protocols — to call absurdity 'absurd.'" Writing out the standards with the proper numbers on the chalkboard has a similar effect, he said; and doing this is "terribly important" to the principals in many of these schools. "You *have* to post the standards, and the way you know the children know the standards is by asking them to *state* the standards. And they *do* it — and you want to be quite certain that they do it if you want to keep on working at that school."

In speaking of the drill-based program in effect at P.S. 65, Mr. Endicott told me he tended to be sympathetic to the school administrators, more so at least than the other teachers I had talked with seemed to be. He said he believed his principal had little choice about the implementation of this program, which had been mandated for all elementary schools in New York City that had had rock-bottom academic records over a long period of time. "This puts me into a dilemma," he went on, "because I love the kids at P.S. 65." And even while, he said, "I know that my teaching SFA is a charade . . . if I don't do it I won't be permitted to teach these children."

Mr. Endicott, like all but two of the new recruits at P.S. 65 — there were about fifteen in all — was a white person, as were the principal and most of the administrators at the school. As a result, most of these neophyte instructors had had little or no prior contact with the children of an inner-city neighborhood; but, like the others I met, and despite the distancing between the children and their teachers that resulted from the scripted method of instruction, he had developed close attachments to his students and did not want to abandon them. At the same time, the class- and race-specific implementation of this program obviously troubled him. "There's an expression now," he said. "'The rich get richer, and the poor get SFA.'" He said he was still trying to figure out his "professional ethics" on the problem that this posed for him.

White children made up "only about one percent" of students in the New York City schools in which this scripted teaching system was imposed,[6] according to the *New York Times*, which also said that "the prepackaged lessons" were intended "to ensure that all teachers — even novices or the most inept" — would be able to teach reading. As seemingly pragmatic and hardheaded as such arguments may be, they are desperation strategies that come out of the acceptance of inequity. If we did not have a deeply

55

---

[6]SFA has since been discontinued in the New York City public schools, though it is still being used in 1,300 U.S. schools, serving as many as 650,000 children. Similar scripted systems are used in schools (overwhelmingly minority in population) serving several million children. [Kozol's note]

segregated system in which more experienced instructors teach the children of the privileged and the least experienced are sent to teach the children of minorities, these practices would not be needed and could not be so convincingly defended. They are confections of apartheid,[7] and no matter by what arguments of urgency or practicality they have been justified, they cannot fail to further deepen the divisions of society.

There is no misery index for the children of apartheid education. There ought to be; we measure almost everything else that happens to them in their schools. Do kids who go to schools like these enjoy the days they spend in them? Is school, for most of them, a happy place to be? You do not find the answers to these questions in reports about achievement levels, scientific methods of accountability, or structural revisions in the modes of governance. Documents like these don't speak of happiness. You have to go back to the schools themselves to find an answer to these questions. You have to sit down in the little chairs in first and second grade, or on the reading rug with kindergarten kids, and listen to the things they actually say to one another and the dialogue between them and their teachers. You have to go down to the basement with the children when it's time for lunch and to the playground with them, if they have a playground, when it's time for recess, if they still have recess at their school. You have to walk into the children's bathrooms in these buildings. You have to do what children do and breathe the air the children breathe. I don't think that there is any other way to find out what the lives that children lead in school are really like.

High school students, when I first meet them, are often more reluctant than the younger children to open up and express their personal concerns; but hesitation on the part of students did not prove to be a problem when I visited a tenth-grade class at Fremont High School in Los Angeles. The students were told that I was a writer, and they took no time in getting down to matters that were on their minds.

"Can we talk about the bathrooms?" asked a soft-spoken student named Mireya.

In almost any classroom there are certain students who, by the force of their directness or the unusual sophistication of their way of speaking, tend to capture your attention from the start. Mireya later spoke insightfully about some of the serious academic problems that were common in the school, but her observations on the physical and personal embarrassments she and her schoolmates had to undergo cut to the heart of questions of essential dignity that kids in squalid schools like this one have to deal with all over the nation.

Fremont High School, as court papers filed in a lawsuit against the state of California document, has fifteen fewer bathrooms than the law requires. 60

---

[7]*Apartheid:* Literally "apartness," the policy of racial segregation and discrimination in South Africa, restricting the rights of nonwhites, which ended in 1990.

Of the limited number of bathrooms that are working in the school, "only one or two . . . are open and unlocked for girls to use." Long lines of girls are "waiting to use the bathrooms," which are generally "unclean" and "lack basic supplies," including toilet paper. Some of the classrooms, as court papers also document, "do not have air conditioning," so that students, who attend school on a three-track schedule that runs year-round, "become red-faced and unable to concentrate" during "the extreme heat of summer." The school's maintenance records report that rats were found in eleven classrooms. Rat droppings were found "in the bins and drawers" of the high school's kitchen, and school records note that "hamburger buns" were being "eaten off [the] bread-delivery rack."

No matter how many tawdry details like these I've read in legal briefs or depositions through the years, I'm always shocked again to learn how often these unsanitary physical conditions are permitted to continue in the schools that serve our poorest students — even after they have been vividly described in the media. But hearing of these conditions in Mireya's words was even more unsettling, in part because this student seemed so fragile and because the need even to speak of these indignities in front of me and all the other students was an additional indignity.

"The problem is this," she carefully explained. "You're not allowed to use the bathroom during lunch, which is a thirty-minute period. The only time that you're allowed to use it is between your classes." But "this is a huge building," she went on. "It has long corridors. If you have one class at one end of the building and your next class happens to be way down at the other end, you don't have time to use the bathroom and still get to class before it starts. So you go to your class and then you ask permission from your teacher to go to the bathroom and the teacher tells you, 'No. You had your chance between the periods . . .'

"I feel embarrassed when I have to stand there and explain it to a teacher."

"This is the question," said a wiry-looking boy named Edward, leaning forward in his chair. "Students are not animals, but even animals need to relieve themselves sometimes. We're here for eight hours. What do they think we're supposed to do?"

"It humiliates you," said Mireya, who went on to make the interesting   65
statement that "the school provides solutions that don't actually work," and this idea was taken up by several other students in describing course requirements within the school. A tall black student, for example, told me that she hoped to be a social worker or a doctor but was programmed into "Sewing Class" this year. She also had to take another course, called "Life Skills," which she told me was a very basic course — "a retarded class," to use her words — that "teaches things like the six continents," which she said she'd learned in elementary school.

When I asked her why she had to take these courses, she replied that she'd been told they were required, which as I later learned was not exactly so.

What was required was that high school students take two courses in an area of study called "The Technical Arts," and which the Los Angeles Board of Education terms "Applied Technology." At schools that served the middle class or upper-middle class, this requirement was likely to be met by courses that had academic substance and, perhaps, some relevance to college preparation. At Beverly Hills High School, for example, the technical-arts requirement could be fulfilled by taking subjects like residential architecture, the designing of commercial structures, broadcast journalism, advanced computer graphics, a sophisticated course in furniture design, carving and sculpture, or an honors course in engineering research and design. At Fremont High, in contrast, this requirement was far more often met by courses that were basically vocational and also obviously keyed to low-paying levels of employment.

Mireya, for example, who had plans to go to college, told me that she had to take a sewing class last year and now was told she'd been assigned to take a class in hairdressing as well. When I asked her teacher why Mireya could not skip these subjects and enroll in classes that would help her to pursue her college aspirations, she replied, "It isn't a question of what students want. It's what the school may have available. If all the other elective classes that a student wants to take are full, she has to take one of these classes if she wants to graduate."

A very small girl named Obie, who had big blue-tinted glasses tilted up across her hair, interrupted then to tell me with a kind of wild gusto that she'd taken hairdressing *twice*! When I expressed surprise that this was possible, she said there were two levels of hairdressing offered here at Fremont High. "One is in hairstyling," she said. "The other is in braiding."

Mireya stared hard at this student for a moment and then suddenly began to cry. "I don't *want* to take hairdressing. I did not need sewing either. I knew how to sew. My mother is a seamstress in a factory. I'm trying to go to college. I don't need to sew to go to college. My mother sews. I hoped for something else."

"What would you rather take?" I asked. 70

"I wanted to take an AP class," she answered.

Mireya's sudden tears elicited a strong reaction from one of the boys who had been silent up till now: a thin, dark-eyed student named Fortino, who had long hair down to his shoulders. He suddenly turned directly to Mireya and spoke into the silence that followed her last words.

"Listen to me," he said. "The owners of the sewing factories need laborers. Correct?"

"I guess they do," Mireya said.

"It's not going to be their own kids. Right?" 75

"Why not?" another student said.

"So they can grow beyond themselves," Mireya answered quietly. "But we remain the same."

"You're ghetto," said Fortino, "so we send you to the factory." He sat low in his desk chair, leaning on one elbow, his voice and dark eyes loaded with a cynical intelligence. "You're ghetto — so you sew!"

"There are higher positions than these," said a student named Samantha. "You're ghetto," said Fortino unrelentingly, "So sew!"   80

Admittedly, the economic needs of a society are bound to be reflected to some rational degree within the policies and purposes of public schools. But, even so, there must be *something* more to life as it is lived by six-year-olds or ten-year-olds, or by teenagers, for that matter, than concerns about "successful global competition." Childhood is not merely basic training for utilitarian adulthood. It should have some claims upon our mercy, not for its future value to the economic interests of competitive societies but for its present value as a perishable piece of life itself.

Very few people who are not involved with inner-city schools have any real idea of the extremes to which the mercantile distortion of the purposes and character of education have been taken or how unabashedly proponents of these practices are willing to defend them. The head of a Chicago school, for instance, who was criticized by some for emphasizing rote instruction that, his critics said, was turning children into "robots," found no reason to dispute the charge. "Did you ever stop to think that these robots will never burglarize your home?" he asked, and "will never snatch your pocketbooks. . . . These robots are going to be producing taxes."

Corporate leaders, when they speak of education, sometimes pay lip-service to the notion of "good critical and analytic skills," but it is reasonable

"The Feds have authorized me to leave your child behind."

to ask whether they have in mind the critical analysis of *their* priorities. In principle, perhaps some do; but, if so, this is not a principle that seems to have been honored widely in the schools I have been visiting. In all the various business-driven inner-city classrooms I have observed in the past five years, plastered as they are with corporation brand names and managerial vocabularies, I have yet to see the two words "labor unions." Is this an oversight? How is that possible? Teachers and principals themselves, who are almost always members of a union, seem to be so beaten down that they rarely even question this omission.

It is not at all unusual these days to come into an urban school in which the principal prefers to call himself or herself "building CEO" or "building manager." In some of the same schools teachers are described as "classroom managers."[8] I have never been in a suburban district in which principals were asked to view themselves or teachers in this way. These terminologies remind us of how wide the distance has become between two very separate worlds of education. . . .

ENGAGING THE TEXT

1. Compare notes in class on your own elementary and secondary school experiences. How do the schools you attended compare with the public schools Kozol describes, both in terms of physical condition and teaching approach?

2. What evidence have you seen of reluctance on the part of politicians, educators, and the media to talk about the segregated state of America's public schools? Would you agree that the current state of public education in the United States amounts to "resegregation" and is, in fact, evidence of "apartheid" in American society?

---

[8]A school I visited three years ago in Columbus, Ohio, was littered with "Help Wanted" signs. Starting in kindergarten, children in the school were being asked to think about the jobs that they might choose when they grew up. In one classroom there was a poster that displayed the names of several retail stores: J. C. Penney, Wal-Mart, Kmart, Sears, and a few others. "It's like working in a store," a classroom aide explained. "The children are learning to pretend they're cashiers." At another school in the same district, children were encouraged to apply for jobs in their classrooms. Among the job positions open to the children in this school, there was an "Absence Manager" and a "Behavior Chart Manager," a "Form Collector Manager," a "Paper Passer Outer Manager," a "Paper Collecting Manager," a "Paper Returning Manager," an "Exit Ticket Manager," even a "Learning Manager," a "Reading Corner Manager," and a "Score Keeper Manager." I asked the principal if there was a special reason why those two words "management" and "manager" kept popping up throughout the school. "We want every child to be working as a manager while he or she is in this school," the principal explained. "We want to make them understand that, in this country, companies will give you opportunities to work, to prove yourself, no matter what you've done." I wasn't sure what she meant by "no matter what you've done," and asked her if she could explain it. "Even if you have a felony arrest," she said, "we want you to understand that you can be a manager someday." [Kozol's note]

3. Who is to blame for the current resegregation of American public schools, according to Kozol? Whom — or what — would you blame? To what extent would you agree that the state of inner-city schools represents a "moral failure" in America? Why might it be so important to Kozol to see this issue in moral — and not simply in political or social — terms?

EXPLORING CONNECTIONS

4. Compare Mike Rose's account of his own school experience during the 1950s and 1960s (p. 157) with the contemporary urban classrooms described by Kozol in this selection. How might Rose assess the teaching methods that dominate the school reforms Kozol describes? Do you think a Jack MacFarland would succeed in today's inner-city schools? Why or why not?

5. Compare what Kozol, Michael Moore (p. 128), and John Taylor Gatto (p. 148) have to say about the impact of corporate America on U.S. schools. To what extent does your own prior educational experience suggest that corporate influence is undermining American education?

6. How well do the schools that Kozol describes fit any of the four categories of schools presented by Jean Anyon (p. 169)? To what extent do you think it would be possible to adapt the approaches and methods used in Anyon's professional or elite schools more broadly?

EXTENDING THE CRITICAL CONTEXT

7. Working in groups, sample news and magazine stories published in the last year to determine if Kozol is correct when he says that the media are reluctant to discuss the "segregation" of American public education. How many of the articles you identify address the idea of segregation? Of the inequalities of public education?

8. Learn more about the "No Child Left Behind Act" and other aspects of the accountability reform movement in education. What kinds of accountability reforms have been implemented in your area? What evidence do you find that these measures have worked? To what extent would you agree that accountability reforms have turned children into robots and reduced teaching to mechanical drill?

9. Over the past few years, a number of states have begun requiring high school students to take standardized "exit exams" to guarantee that they meet minimum academic standards before graduation. Research this educational reform to find out more about its impact on students, and then debate its merits in class. Would you support recent proposals that would require a similar nationwide test for college students before they receive their degrees? Why or why not?

In the Basement of the Ivory Tower
"Professor X"

Fair warning! The essay you are about to read may trouble you, infuriate you, or confirm some of your worst suspicions about the policies and standards of American higher education. Remediation — the need to do preparatory work in math and English — has been an issue in higher education since the late 1950s, when American colleges and universities first opened their doors to a larger, more economically and ethnically diverse student population. Today, particularly in public two-year colleges, as many as eight out of ten students may need serious work in "basic skills" before enrolling in regular college courses. And even in many major universities, faculty sometimes complain about students being "underprepared." But does this mean that these students shouldn't be given a crack at college? A part-time English composition instructor, "Professor X" makes the case that many of the students admitted to college today simply aren't ready to cope with the challenges of real college work. This selection originally appeared in The Atlantic *(2008).*

I work part-time in the evenings as an adjunct instructor[1] of English. I teach two courses, Introduction to College Writing (English 101) and Introduction to College Literature (English 102), at a small private college and at a community college. The campuses are physically lovely — quiet havens of ornate stonework and columns, Gothic Revival archways, sweeping quads, and tidy Victorian scalloping. Students chat or examine their cell phones or study languidly under spreading trees. Balls click faintly against bats on the athletic fields. Inside the arts and humanities building, my students and I discuss Shakespeare, *Dubliners*,[2] poetic rhythms, and Edward Said.[3] We might seem, at first glance, to be enacting some sort of college idyll.[4] We could be at Harvard. But this is not Harvard, and our classes are no idyll. Beneath the surface of this serene and scholarly mise-en-scène[5] roil waters of frustration and bad feeling, for these colleges teem with students who are in over their heads.

I work at colleges of last resort. For many of my students, college was not a goal they spent years preparing for, but a place they landed in. Those I

---

[1]*adjunct instructor:* A part-time instructor.

[2]*Dubliners:* 1914 collection of short stories by Irish author James Joyce (1882–1941), one of the most intellectually challenging writers of the twentieth century.

[3]*Edward Said:* Edward Wadie Said (1935–2003), Palestinian American literary scholar.

[4]*idyll:* A happy, carefree time or experience, and also an indirect reference to a type of ancient Greek or Roman poem that idealized simple country life.

[5]*mise-en-scène:* The physical arrangement of props and actors on a stage or in a film.

teach don't come up in the debates about adolescent overachievers and cut-throat college admissions. Mine are the students whose applications show indifferent grades and have blank spaces where the extracurricular activities would go. They chose their college based not on the *U.S. News & World Report* rankings[6] but on MapQuest; in their ideal academic geometry, college is located at a convenient spot between work and home. I can relate, for it was exactly this line of thinking that dictated where I sent my teaching résumé.

Some of their high-school transcripts are newly minted, others decades old. Many of my students have returned to college after some manner of life interregnum:[7] a year or two of post-high-school dissolution, or a large swath of simple middle-class existence, twenty years of the demands of home and family. They work during the day and come to class in the evenings. I teach young men who must amass a certain number of credits before they can become police officers or state troopers, lower-echelon health-care workers who need credits to qualify for raises, and municipal employees who require college-level certification to advance at work.

My students take English 101 and English 102 not because they want to but because they must. Both colleges I teach at require that all students, no matter what their majors or career objectives, pass these two courses. For many of my students, this is difficult. Some of the young guys, the police-officers-to-be, have wonderfully open faces across which play their every passing emotion, and when we start reading "Araby"[8] or "Barn Burning,"[9] their boredom quickly becomes apparent. They fidget; they prop their heads on their arms; they yawn and sometimes appear to grimace in pain, as though they had been tasered. Their eyes implore: *How could you do this to me?*

The goal of English 101 is to instruct students in the sort of expository   5
writing that theoretically will be required across the curriculum. My students must venture the compare-and-contrast paper, the argument paper, the process-analysis paper (which explains how some action is performed — as a lab report might), and the dreaded research paper, complete with parenthetical citations and a listing of works cited, all in Modern Language Association[10] format. In 102, we read short stories, poetry, and *Hamlet*, and we take several stabs at the only writing more dreaded than the research paper: the absolutely despised Writing About Literature.

---

[6]*U. S. News & World Report* rankings: *U. S. News & World Report* magazine publishes a controversial annual ranking of the top 100 colleges and universities in the United States.

[7]*interregnum:* The period between the reign of two monarchs; here, a period between two phases of life.

[8]*"Araby":* A short story from Joyce's *Dubliners*, commonly taught in college English classes.

[9]*"Barn Burning":* A short story by Nobel Prize–winning American writer William Faulkner (1897–1962) and also a common assignment in college English classes.

[10]*Modern Language Association:* The principal professional association in the United States for scholars of languages and literature.

Class time passes in a flash — for me, anyway, if not always for my students. I love trying to convey to a class my passion for literature, or the immense satisfaction a writer can feel when he or she nails a point. When I am at my best, and the students are in an attentive mood — generally, early in the semester — the room crackles with positive energy. Even the cops-to-be feel driven to succeed in the class, to read and love the great books, to explore potent themes, to write well.

The bursting of our collective bubble comes quickly. A few weeks into the semester, the students must start actually writing papers, and I must start grading them. Despite my enthusiasm, despite their thoughtful nods of agreement and what I have interpreted as moments of clarity, it turns out that in many cases it has all come to naught.

Remarkably few of my students can do well in these classes. Students routinely fail; some fail multiple times, and some will never pass, because they cannot write a coherent sentence.

In each of my courses, we discuss thesis statements and topic sentences, the need for precision in vocabulary, why economy of language is desirable, what constitutes a compelling subject. I explain, I give examples, I cheerlead, I cajole, but each evening, when the class is over and I come down from my teaching high, I inevitably lose faith in the task, as I'm sure my students do. I envision the lot of us driving home, solitary scholars in our cars, growing sadder by the mile.

Our textbook boils effective writing down to a series of steps. It devotes   10
pages and pages to the composition of a compare-and-contrast essay, with lots of examples and tips and checklists. "Develop a plan of organization and stick to it," the text chirrups not so helpfully. Of course any student who can, does, and does so automatically, without the textbook's directive. For others, this seems an impossible task. Over the course of fifteen weeks, some of my best writers improve a little. Sometimes my worst writers improve too, though they rarely, if ever, approach base-level competence.

How I envy professors in other disciplines! How appealing seems the straightforwardness of their task! *These are the properties of a cell membrane, kid. Memorize 'em, and be ready to spit 'em back at me.* The biology teacher also enjoys the psychic ease of grading multiple-choice tests. Answers are right or wrong. The grades cannot be questioned. Quantifying the value of a piece of writing, however, is intensely subjective, and English teachers are burdened with discretion. (My students seem to believe that my discretion is limitless. Some of them come to me at the conclusion of a course and matter-of-factly ask that I change a failing grade because they need to graduate this semester or because they worked really hard in the class or because they need to pass in order to receive tuition reimbursement from their employer.)

I wonder, sometimes, at the conclusion of a course, when I fail nine out of fifteen students, whether the college will send me a note either (1) informing me of a serious bottleneck in the march toward commencement and demanding that I pass more students, or (2) commending me on my fiscal ingenuity — my high failure rate forces students to pay for classes two or three times over.

What actually happens is that nothing happens. I feel no pressure from the colleges in either direction. My department chairpersons, on those rare occasions when I see them, are friendly, even warm. They don't mention all those students who have failed my courses, and I don't bring them up. There seems, as is often the case in colleges, to be a huge gulf between academia and reality. No one is thinking about the larger implications, let alone the morality, of admitting so many students to classes they cannot possibly pass. The colleges and the students and I are bobbing up and down in a great wave of societal forces — social optimism on a large scale, the sense of college as both a universal right and a need, financial necessity on the part of the colleges and the students alike, the desire to maintain high academic standards while admitting marginal students — that have coalesced into a mini-tsunami of difficulty. No one has drawn up the flowchart and seen that, although more-widespread college admission is a bonanza for the colleges and nice for the students and makes the entire United States of America feel rather pleased with itself, there is one point of irreconcilable conflict in the system, and that is the moment when the adjunct instructor, who by the nature of his job teaches the worst students, must ink the F on that first writing assignment.

Recently, I gave a student a failing grade on her research paper. She was a woman in her forties; I will call her Ms. L. She looked at her paper, and my comments, and the grade. "I can't believe it," she said softly. "I was so proud of myself for having written a college paper."

From the beginning of our association vis-à-vis the research paper, I knew that there would be trouble with Ms. L.   15

When I give out this assignment, I usually bring the class to the college library for a lesson on Internet-based research. I ask them about their computer skills, and some say they have none, fessing up to being computer illiterate and saying, timorously, how hopeless they are at that sort of thing. It often turns out, though, that many of them have at least sent and received e-mail and Googled their neighbors, and it doesn't take me long to demonstrate how to search journal articles in such databases as Academic Search Premier[11] and JSTOR.[12]

Ms. L., it was clear to me, had never been on the Internet. She quite possibly had never sat in front of a computer. The concept of a link was news to her. She didn't know that if something was blue and underlined, you could click on it. She was preserved in the amber of 1990, struggling with the basic syntax of the World Wide Web. She peered intently at the screen and chewed a fingernail. She was flummoxed.

[11]*Academic Search Premiere:* An online database of scholarly and academic journals.
[12]JSTOR: An online database of scholarly and academic journals.

I had responsibilities to the rest of my students, so only when the class ended could I sit with her and work on some of the basics. It didn't go well. She wasn't absorbing anything. The wall had gone up, the wall known to every teacher at every level: the wall of defeat and hopelessness and humiliation, the wall that is an impenetrable barrier to learning. She wasn't hearing a word I said.

"You might want to get some extra help," I told her. "You can schedule a private session with the librarian."

"I'll get it," she said. "I just need a little time."   20

"You have some computer-skills deficits," I told her. "You should address them as soon as you can." I don't have cause to use much educational jargon, but *deficits* has often come in handy. It conveys the seriousness of the situation, the student's jaw-dropping lack of ability, without being judgmental. I tried to jostle her along. "You should schedule that appointment right now. The librarian is at the desk."

"I realize I have a lot of work to do," she said.

Our dialogue had turned oblique, as though we now inhabited a Pinter[13] play.

The research-paper assignment is meant to teach the fundamental mechanics of the thing: how to find sources, summarize or quote them, and cite them, all the while not plagiarizing. Students must develop a strong thesis, not just write what is called a "passive report," the sort of thing one knocks out in fifth grade on Thomas Edison.[14] This time around, the students were to elucidate the positions of scholars on two sides of a historical controversy. Why did Truman remove MacArthur?[15] Did the United States covertly support the construction of the Berlin Wall?[16] What really happened in the Gulf of Tonkin?[17] Their job in the paper, as I explained it, was to take my arm and introduce me as a stranger to scholars A, B, and C, who stood on one side of the issue, and to scholars D, E, and F, who were firmly on the other — as though they were hosting a party.

A future state trooper snorted. "That's some dull party," he said.   25

---

[13]*Pinter:* Harold Pinter (1930–2008), English playwright and 2005 Nobel Prize winner famed for writing plays with mysterious conflicts, menacing characters, and repeated breakdowns in communication.

[14]*Thomas Edison:* Thomas Alva Edison (1847–1931), American inventor and businessman known for creating the phonograph and the first practical electric lightbulb.

[15]*Why did Truman . . . :* In 1951, the 33rd president of the United States, Harry S. Truman (1884–1972), removed General Douglas MacArthur (1880–1964) from his command overseeing the postwar reconstruction of Japan due to a disagreement over Truman's Korean War policy.

[16]*Berlin Wall:* A physical barrier erected in 1961 in the city of Berlin by the communist regime of the German Democratic Republic (East Germany) to separate its population from that of West Germany.

[17]*Gulf of Tonkin:* Refers to two disputed attacks by communist gun boats against U.S. warships in the Gulf of Tonkin in 1964 that resulted in the escalation of American involvement in the Vietnam War.

At our next meeting after class in the library, Ms. L. asked me whether she could do her paper on abortion. What exactly, I asked, was the historical controversy? Well, she replied, whether it should be allowed. She was stuck, I realized, in the well-worn groove of assignments she had done in high school. I told her that I thought the abortion question was more of an ethical dilemma than a historical controversy.

"I'll have to figure it all out," she said.

She switched her topic a half-dozen times; perhaps it would be fairer to say that she never really came up with one. I wondered whether I should just give her one, then decided against it. Devising a topic was part of the assignment.

"What about gun control?" she asked.

I sighed. You could write, I told her, about a particular piece of firearms-related legislation. Historians might disagree, I said, about certain aspects of the bill's drafting. Remember, though, the paper must be grounded in history. It could not be a discussion of the pros and cons of gun control.

"All right," she said softly.

Needless to say, the paper she turned in was a discussion of the pros and cons of gun control. At least, I think that was the subject. There was no real thesis. The paper often lapsed into incoherence. Sentences broke off in the middle of a line and resumed on the next one, with the first word inappropriately capitalized. There was some wavering between single- and double-spacing. She did quote articles, but cited only databases — where were the journals themselves? The paper was also too short: a bad job, and such small portions.

"I can't believe it," she said when she received her F. "I was so proud of myself for having written a college paper."

She most certainly hadn't written a college paper, and she was a long way from doing so. Yet there she was in college, paying lots of tuition for the privilege of pursuing a degree, which she very likely needed to advance at work. Her deficits don't make her a bad person or even unintelligent or unusual. Many people cannot write a research paper, and few have to do so in their workaday life. But let's be frank: she wasn't working at anything resembling a college level.

I gave Ms. L. the F and slept poorly that night. Some of the failing grades I issue gnaw at me more than others. In my ears rang her plaintive words, so emblematic of the tough spot in which we both now found ourselves. Ms. L. had done everything that American culture asked of her. She had gone back to school to better herself, and she expected to be rewarded for it, not slapped down. She had failed not, as some students do, by being absent too often or by blowing off assignments. She simply was not qualified for college. *What exactly*, I wondered, *was I grading?* I thought briefly of passing Ms. L., of slipping her the old gentlewoman's C-minus.[18] But I

[18]*a gentlewoman's C-minus:* A play on the term "gentleman's C," referring to the practice of giving minimally passing grades to undeserving students at Ivy League colleges to appease their wealthy or powerful families.

couldn't do it. It wouldn't be fair to the other students. By passing Ms. L., I would be eroding the standards of the school for which I worked. Besides, I nurse a healthy ration of paranoia. What if she were a plant from the *New York Times* doing a story on the declining standards of the nation's colleges? In my mind's eye, the front page of a newspaper spun madly, as in old movies, coming to rest to reveal a damning headline:

THIS IS A *C*?
Illiterate Mess Garners "Average" Grade
Adjunct Says Student "Needed" to Pass, "Tried Hard"

No, I would adhere to academic standards, and keep myself off the front page.

We think of college professors as being profoundly indifferent to the grades they hand out. My own professors were fairly haughty and aloof, showing little concern for the petty worries, grades in particular, of their students. There was an enormous distance between students and professors. The full-time, tenured professors at the colleges where I teach may likewise feel comfortably separated from those whom they instruct. Their students, the ones who attend class during daylight hours, tend to be younger than mine. Many of them are in school on their parents' dime. Professors can fail these young people with emotional impunity because many such failures are the students' own fault: too much time spent texting, too little time with the textbooks.

But my students and I are of a piece. I could not be aloof, even if I wanted to be. Our presence together in these evening classes is evidence that we all have screwed up. I'm working a second job; they're trying desperately to get to a place where they don't have to. All any of us wants is a free evening. Many of my students are in the vicinity of my own age. Whatever our chronological ages, we are all adults, by which I mean thoroughly saddled with children and mortgages and sputtering careers. We all show up for class exhausted from working our full-time jobs. We carry knapsacks and briefcases overspilling with the contents of our hectic lives. We smell of the food we have eaten that day, and of the food we carry with us for the evening. We reek of coffee and tuna oil. The rooms in which we study have been used all day, and are filthy. Candy wrappers litter the aisles. We pile our trash daintily atop filled garbage cans.

During breaks, my students scatter to various corners and niches of the building, whip out their cell phones, and try to maintain a home life. Burdened with their own assignments, they gamely try to stay on top of their children's. *Which problems do you have to do? . . . That's not too many. Finish that and then do the spelling . . . No, you can't watch* Grey's Anatomy.

Adult education, nontraditional education, education for returning students — whatever you want to call it — is a substantial profit center for many colleges. Like factory owners, school administrators are delighted with this idea of mounting a second shift of learning in their classrooms, in the evenings, when the full-time students are busy with such regular extra-curricular pursuits of higher education as reading Facebook and playing beer pong. If colleges could find a way to mount a third, graveyard shift,[19] as Henry Ford's Willow Run[20] did at the height of the Second World War, I believe that they would.

There is a sense that the American workforce needs to be more profes-   40 sional at every level. Many jobs that never before required college now call for at least some post-secondary course work. School custodians, those who run the boilers and spread synthetic sawdust on vomit, may not need col-lege — but the people who supervise them, who decide which brand of syn-thetic sawdust to procure, probably do. There is a sense that our bank tellers should be college educated, and so should our medical-billing techs, and our child-welfare officers, and our sheriffs and federal marshals. We want the police officer who stops the car with the broken taillight to have a nodding acquaintance with great literature. And when all is said and done, my personal economic interest in booming college enrollments aside, I don't think that's such a boneheaded idea. Reading literature at the college level is a route to spacious thinking, to an acquaintance with certain pro-found ideas, that is of value to anyone. Will having read *Invisible Man*[21] make a police officer less likely to indulge in racial profiling? Will a familiar-ity with Steinbeck[22] make him more sympathetic to the plight of the poor, so that he might understand the lives of those who simply *cannot* get their taillights fixed? Will it benefit the correctional officer to have read *The Autobiography of Malcolm X*?[23] The health-care worker *Arrowsmith*?[24] Should the child-welfare officer read Plath's "Daddy"?[25] Such one-to-one correspondences probably don't hold. But although I may be biased, being an English instructor and all, I can't shake the sense that reading literature is informative and broadening and ultimately good for you. If I should fall ill, I suppose I would rather the hospital billing staff had read *The Pickwick Papers*,[26] particularly the parts set in debtors' prison.

[19]*graveyard shift:* A late work shift typically running from midnight until 8 A.M.

[20]*Henry Ford's Willow Run:* One of the largest manufacturing plants ever built, Willow Run was created by the Ford Motor Company near Ypsilanti, Michigan, in 1941 to produce B-24 warplanes.

[21]*Invisible Man:* Novel by American author Ralph Ellison (1913–1994) depicting the racism African Americans faced prior to the civil rights era.

[22]*Steinbeck:* John Ernst Steinbeck (1902–1968), Nobel Prize–winning American writer renowned for his sympathetic portrayal of the working poor in novels like *The Grapes of Wrath* (1939).

[23]*The Autobiography of Malcolm X:* See page 210.

[24]*Arrowsmith:* 1925 novel by American author Sinclair Lewis (1885–1951) focusing on the career of an idealistic American doctor and medical researcher.

[25]*Plath's "Daddy":* A poem by American poet and author Sylvia Plath (1932–1963) deal-ing with her difficult relationship with her father.

[26]*The Pickwick Papers: The Posthumous Papers of the Pickwick Club* (1837) was the first novel published by famed English author Charles Dickens (1812–1870).

America, ever-idealistic, seems wary of the vocational-education track. We are not comfortable limiting anyone's options. Telling someone that college is not for him seems harsh and classist and British, as though we were sentencing him to a life in the coal mines. I sympathize with this stance; I subscribe to the American ideal. Unfortunately, it is with me and my red pen that that ideal crashes and burns.

Sending everyone under the sun to college is a noble initiative. Academia is all for it, naturally. Industry is all for it; some companies even help with tuition costs. Government is all for it; the truly needy have lots of opportunities for financial aid. The media applauds it — try to imagine someone speaking out against the idea. To oppose such a scheme of inclusion would be positively churlish. But one piece of the puzzle hasn't been figured into the equation, to use the sort of phrase I encounter in the papers submitted by my English 101 students. The zeitgeist[27] of academic possibility is a great inverted pyramid, and its rather sharp point is poking, uncomfortably, a spot just about midway between my shoulder blades.

For I, who teach these low-level, must-pass, no-multiple-choice-test classes, am the one who ultimately delivers the news to those unfit for college: that they lack the most-basic skills and have no sense of the volume of work required; that they are in some cases barely literate; that they are so bereft of schemata,[28] so dispossessed of contexts in which to place newly acquired knowledge, that every bit of information simply raises more questions. They are not ready for high school, some of them, much less for college.

I am the man who has to lower the hammer.

We may look mild-mannered, we adjunct instructors, but we are academic button men. I roam the halls of academe like a modern Coriolanus[29] bearing sword and grade book, "a thing of blood, whose every motion / Was timed with dying cries."[30]   45

I knew that Ms. L.'s paper would fail. I knew it that first night in the library. But I couldn't tell her that she wasn't ready for an introductory English class. I wouldn't be saving her from the humiliation of defeat by a class she simply couldn't handle. I'd be a sexist, ageist, intellectual snob.

In her own mind, Ms. L. had triumphed over adversity. In her own mind, she was a feel-good segment on Oprah. Everyone wants to triumph. But not everyone can — in fact, most can't. If they could, it wouldn't be any

---

[27]*zeitgeist:* German term meaning "the spirit of the age."

[28]*schemata:* A term used in psychology to denote mental structures that organize knowledge and provide intellectual frameworks that facilitate future learning.

[29]*Coriolanus:* The tragedy *Coriolanus* (1623) by William Shakespeare (1564–1616) tells the story of a brilliant Roman general who opposes democratic rule and is assassinated.

[30]*"a thing of blood, whose every motion …":* Description of Coriolanus's violence on the battlefield (*Coriolanus,* act 2, scene 2, 104–09).

kind of a triumph at all. Never would I want to cheapen the accomplishments of those who really have conquered college, who were able to get past their deficits and earn a diploma, maybe even climbing onto the college honor roll. That is truly something.

One of the things I try to do on the first night of English 102 is relate the literary techniques we will study to novels that the students have already read. I try to find books familiar to everyone. This has so far proven impossible. My students don't read much, as a rule, and though I think of them monolithically, they don't really share a culture. *To Kill a Mockingbird?*[31] Nope. (And I thought everyone had read that!) *Animal Farm?*[32] No. If they have read it, they don't remember it. *The Outsiders?*[33] *The Chocolate War?*[34] No and no. *Charlotte's Web?*[35] You'd think so, but no. So then I expand the exercise to general works of narrative art, meaning movies, but that doesn't work much better. Oddly, there are no movies that they all have seen — well, except for one. They've all seen *The Wizard of Oz*. Some have caught it multiple times. So we work with the old warhorse of a *quest narrative*.[36] The farmhands' early conversation illustrates *foreshadowing*.[37] The witch melts at the *climax*. *Theme?* Hands fly up. Everybody knows that one — perhaps all too well. Dorothy learns that she can do anything she puts her mind to and that all the tools she needs to succeed are already within her. I skip the *denouement:*[38] the intellectually ambitious scarecrow proudly mangles the Pythagorean theorem[39] and is awarded a questionable diploma in a dreamland far removed from reality. That's art holding up a mirror all too closely to our own poignant scholarly endeavors.[40]

---

[31]*To Kill a Mockingbird:* 1960 novel by American author Harper Lee (b. 1926) that is commonly assigned in U.S. high schools.

[32]*Animal Farm:* 1945 novel by English author and social critic George Orwell (born Eric Arthur Blair, 1903–1950).

[33]*The Outsiders:* Popular 1967 coming-of-age teen novel by American author S. E. Hinton (b. 1950).

[34]*The Chocolate War:* Young adult novel published in 1974 by American author Robert Cormier (1925–2000).

[35]*Charlotte's Web:* Award-winning 1952 children's novel by American author E. B. White (1899–1985).

[36]*quest narrative:* A common story form in which a hero must undertake a journey and endure challenges or tests to reach a goal, obtain a prize, or attain knowledge.

[37]*foreshadowing:* A literary technique that involves offering clues that allow readers to predict future events in the story.

[38]*denouement:* A literary term that refers to the events that occur after the climax of a story.

[39]*Pythagorean theorem:* The Greek mathematician Pythagoras (572 B.C.E.–490 B.C.E.) theorized that the sum of the squares of the two legs of a right triangle is equal to the square of its hypotenuse.

[40]*That's art holding . . . endeavors:* In Shakespeare's *Tragedy of Hamlet, Prince of Denmark* (1600–1601), Hamlet explains that the purpose of theater is to "hold a mirror up to nature," or to reflect reality.

ENGAGING THE TEXT

1. What do we learn about Professor X's students? How does he portray them? How does he seem to view them and their problems?

2. How does Professor X view his role as an English teacher? Does he think that writing can actually be taught? How does he view the role played by teachers in other disciplines? Would you agree that he is a "sexist, ageist, intellectual snob"?

3. Why does Professor X reject the topics that Ms. L. chooses for her research paper? Is he right to do so? What experience have you had writing research papers? Has it been as "dull" as Professor X's students seem to find it? Why or why not?

4. To what extent do you agree with Professor X's belief that some students are simply not "qualified for college"? Would you agree that allowing students like Ms. L. (para. 14) to enter college raises moral or ethical questions? Would it be better if all students had to meet the same standards to enter college, regardless of type or purpose of institution?

5. At one point in his dealings with Ms. L, Professor X notes that a "wall of hopelessness and humiliation, an impenetrable barrier to learning" arose between them. In your own earlier education, have you ever experienced a moment when you felt a "wall of hopelessness" go up between you and an instructor — or seen this happen to someone else? How do you think such "walls" should be dealt with?

EXPLORING CONNECTIONS

6. How might John Taylor Gatto (p. 148) view Professor X and his assessment of what's wrong with higher education? How might Gatto explain the failure of a student like Ms. L.?

7. Write an imaginary dialogue between Michael Moore (p. 128) and Professor X about why the United States has become an "idiot nation." How would each of these authors likely explain the failure of America's schools?

8. How does Professor X compare as an instructor with Mike Rose's Mr. MacFarland (p. 165)? What distinguishes these two teachers in terms of their attitudes towards their students, the subjects they teach, and the way they seem to view the role of education in society?

9. How might Jonathan Kozol (p. 219) explain the unreadiness of Professor X's students? To what extent would you consider the segregation of college students by different levels of remediation or readiness — or by their access to different types of college institutions (Ivy League, state, community college, etc.) — as a kind of "educational apartheid"?

EXTENDING THE CRITICAL CONTEXT

10. Watch the 2008 French film *The Class* and compare the attitudes of its teacher protagonist with those of Professor X. How do they differ in terms

of their relationships with their students and their views of education? How common, in your opinion, are teachers like the protagonist in this film?

11. Professor X complains about the lack of information technology skills among students like Ms. L. Survey the IT skills of your classmates. Try to quantify, for example, how many hours per day they spend online, how many different Web sites they access on a regular basis, and how frequently they use the Web to search for information or for social networking. Then give the same survey to your college instructors. What do the results of your surveys suggest?

12. Toward the end of this essay, Professor X talks about trying to connect with his students by exploring the works of literature they have read. To what extent does your class share a common literary culture? What books have you read in common? What movies have most of you seen? What conclusions, if any, can you draw from this list about your intelligence or your readiness for college?

FURTHER CONNECTIONS

1. In the United States, the notion of schooling as the road to success has always been balanced by a pervasive distrust of education. This phenomenon, known as "American anti-intellectualism" grew out of the first settlers' suspicion of anything that reminded them of the "corrupting" influences of European sophistication. American anti-intellectualism often shows up most vividly in pop-cultural portrayals of school, students, and educators. Working in groups, survey recent treatments of school on television, in films, and on Internet blogs and Web sites. How is schooling treated in the mass media and by popular bloggers on the left and the right? Overall, how powerful does anti-intellectualism seem to be in American culture today?

2. Over the past few years, educational critics across the political spectrum have voiced concern about declining success rates for males in America's schools and colleges. During the last decade, for example, the number of women in America's colleges and universities has steadily increased until, today, women outnumber men in almost every academic field outside the so-called hard sciences. Research this issue to learn more about how males are faring in America's schools. Do you think, as some critics claim, that school in America has become a "feminized" institution that is particularly hostile to boys? What other reasons might explain declines in male educational achievement over the past two decades?

3. In his recent book on the impact of globalization, *The World Is Flat: A Brief History of the 21st Century* (2005), journalist and social commentator Thomas Friedman argues that America's schools are failing to equip students with the essential math, science, and language skills they'll need to compete in a global world economy. Compare notes with your classmates about how well you feel your own school experiences have prepared you for competition in the global marketplace. How much math and science did you study in high school? How would you rate your own ability in math and science? How much did you learn about other cultures and languages? In general, do you feel that America's schools today are preparing most students to compete successfully in a globalizing world?

4. Working in groups, research the educational systems in other countries to see how they compare with secondary education in the United States. For example, how is secondary school education handled in countries like England, France, Germany, Denmark, Japan, China, Cuba, and Russia? What role do testing and the rote memorization of facts play in the educational system

you selected to study? To what extent does this system emphasize creativity, personal expression, and critical thinking? Overall, how effective is this nation's educational system in terms of
preparing students for a productive and successful life? What, if
anything, might we as a nation learn from this approach to secondary education?

5. Educational researchers estimate that 25 percent to 60 percent
of the ninth graders in America's urban public schools will drop
out before graduation. Do additional research on the "dropout
crisis" to learn more about the scope and causes of this problem.
Why are so many Americans opting out of school today? Which
groups are most in danger of leaving school before graduation?
What can be done to encourage young Americans to stay in
school?

6. Under the principle of affirmative action, American colleges and
universities were permitted to consider the racial background of
applicants in admissions decisionmaking. As a result, the percentage of minority students in America's colleges and universities increased steadily from 1965 until the late 1990s when
several states reversed or seriously weakened earlier affirmative
action admissions policies. Since then, the diversity of many college campuses across the country has declined significantly. Research the history of the college systems in your state. How has
the decline of affirmative action affected college enrollments?
What are the arguments for and against the consideration of race
as an element of college admissions?

3

Money and Success

The Myth of Individual Opportunity

Affluence, photo by Steven Weinrebe.

FAST FACTS

1. Roughly 10% of white Americans, 21% of Latinos, and 25% of blacks are below the official poverty line.

2. The average American household was projected to save about $400 in 2008; at the same time, its mortgages, credit card debt, and other debt amounted to nearly $118,000 per household.

3. The average college student graduates with about $20,000 of education debt.

4. Full-time female workers in the U.S. earn 78 cents for every dollar earned by their male counterparts; this 22% gap is smaller than it has ever been before.

5. Americans' net worth declined by $1.33 trillion in the first three months of 2009.

Sources: (1) U.S. Census Bureau; (2) *New York Times*, July 20, 2008; (3) *New York Times*, July 20, 2008; (4) U.S. Census Bureau; (5) U.S. Federal Reserve.

AMERICANS CHERISH THE NOTION that the United States is a land of unequaled opportunity, where hard work and smart choices yield big rewards, where no one is stuck on the lower rungs of the economic ladder. Yet statistically speaking, upward mobility is no easier here than in England and France, and it is harder here than in Canada and some Scandinavian countries. Moreover, it is extraordinarily difficult to escape poverty if you've "chosen" the wrong parents: 95 percent of children born to poor parents will themselves be poor all their lives. Even for more fortunate Americans, the recession that battered world economies in 2008 made maintaining the comfortable lifestyle of the middle class seem increasingly dependent not on hard work but on global economic forces like the price of crude oil and the migration of American jobs overseas.

Despite the profound effects of money, or the lack thereof, on our daily lives, most Americans dislike talking about social class. For example, both our rich and our poor shun those terms. When we do talk about money and success, most of us favor a "meritocracy," a fair competition for success that's not rigged according to race, gender, or family history. A wealth of data relating success to education, ethnicity, gender, and inheritance, however, suggests that our reality falls short of our ideals; no individual is guaranteed success or doomed to failure, but the odds are stacked against women, people of color, and those born into poverty.

Our current cultural myths about success have deep roots and a long history. Indeed, the dream of individual opportunity has been at home in

America since Europeans discovered a "new world" in the Western hemi-sphere. Early immigrants like J. Hector St. John de Crèvecoeur extolled the freedom and opportunity to be found in this new land. His glowing descriptions of a classless society where anyone could attain success through honesty and hard work fired the imaginations of many European readers: in *Letters from an American Farmer* (1782) he wrote, "We are all animated with the spirit of an industry which is unfettered and unre-strained, because each person works for himself. . . . We have no princes, for whom we toil, starve, and bleed: we are the most perfect society now existing in the world." The promise of a land where "the rewards of [a man's] industry follow with equal steps the progress of his labor" drew poor immigrants from Europe and fueled national expansion into the western territories.

Our national mythology abounds with illustrations of the American suc-cess story. There's Benjamin Franklin, the very model of the self-educated, self-made man, who rose from modest origins to become a renowned scien-tist, philosopher, and statesman. In the nineteenth century, Horatio Alger, a writer of pulp fiction for young boys — fiction that you will get to sample below — became America's best-selling author with rags-to-riches tales like *Struggling Upward* (1886) and *Bound to Rise* (1873). The notion of success haunts us: we spend millions every year reading about the rich and famous, learning how to "make a fortune in real estate with no money down," and "dressing for success." The myth of success has even invaded our personal relationships: today it's as important to be "successful" in marriage or parenthood as it is to come out on top in business.

But dreams easily turn into nightmares. Every American who hopes to "make it" also knows the fear of failure, because the myth of success inevitably implies comparison between the haves and the have-nots, the achievers and the drones, the stars and the anonymous crowd. Under pres-sure of the myth, we become engrossed in status symbols: we try to live in the "right" neighborhoods, wear the "right" clothes, eat the "right" foods. These emblems of distinction assure us and others that we are different, that we stand out from the crowd. It is one of the great paradoxes of our culture that we believe passionately in the fundamental equality of all yet strive as hard as we can to separate ourselves from our fellow citizens. This separation is particularly true of our wealthiest citizens, who have increas-ingly isolated themselves from everyone else with gated communities, exclusive schools, and private jets.

Steeped in a Puritan theology that vigorously preached the individual's responsibility to the larger community, colonial America balanced the drive for individual gain with concern for the common good. To Franklin, the way to wealth lay in practicing the virtues of honesty, hard work, and thrift: "Without industry and frugality nothing will do, and with them every thing. He that gets all he can honestly, and saves all he gets . . . will certainly become RICH" ("Advice to a Young Tradesman," 1748). And Alger's heroes were as concerned with moral rectitude as they were with financial gain: a benefactor advises Ragged Dick, "If you'll try to be somebody, and grow up into a respectable member of society, you will. You may not become rich, — it isn't everybody that becomes rich, you know, — but you can obtain a good position and be respected." But in the twentieth century the mood of the myth changed.

In the 1970s, Robert Ringer's enormously popular *Looking Out for Number One* urged readers to "forget foundationless traditions, forget the 'moral' standards others may have tried to cram down your throat . . . and, most important, think of yourself — Number One. . . . You and you alone will be responsible for your success or failure." The myth of success may have been responsible for making the United States what it is today, but it also seems to be pulling us apart. Can we exist as a living community if our greatest value can be summed up by the slogan "Me first"?

The chapter opens with a pair of strongly contrasting narratives about young people learning about money and opportunity. The first, an excerpt from Horatio Alger's classic rags-to-riches novel *Ragged Dick,* unambiguously promotes the myth of individual success. The second, Toni Cade Bambara's "The Lesson," dramatizes economic inequality through the eyes of a group of Harlem kids who travel uptown to see how the rich live and spend. Next, in "Horatio Alger," Harlon L. Dalton examines the cultural meanings of such storytelling and finds the myth Alger popularized not just misleading but "socially destructive." Robert Frank's "Living It: Tim Blixseth" serves as the chapter's conservative selection — not because of Frank's politics, but because Blixseth seems to prove that the rags-to-riches myth remains viable. Born into a family that needed welfare, he became a billionaire. (Astonishingly, the empire he built has recently begun to unravel amid bankruptcies, defaults on loans, and multiple lawsuits.)

The next pair of readings, Barbara Ehrenreich's "Serving in Florida" and Gregory Mantsios's "Class in America — 2006," offer a wealth of hard facts about social class, from two very different perspectives. Ehrenreich investigates the daily grind of working-class life by recounting her personal experience of struggling to make ends meet on waitressing wages. Mantsios, taking a broad sociological view and citing numerous compelling statistics, offers a stark portrayal of a social and economic system that serves the powerful and wealthy.

The chapter next turns to visual and pop-culture riffs on money and success. The Visual Portfolio, "Reading Images of Individual Opportunity," explores dreams of success, the cost of failure, and the relationship of opportunity to race, gender, and education. The chapter's media selection — Diana Kendall's "Framing Class, Vicarious Living, and Conspicuous Consumption" — studies how TV tends to distort our view of economic inequalities, for example by treating poverty as individual misfortune rather than systematic oppression.

The chapter concludes with four diverse perspectives on the realities of class in America. In a selection from their book *The Missing Class*, Katherine S. Newman and Victor Tan Chen describe the predicament of workers like Valerie Rushing, a single mom who cleans commuter railroad cars for a living and hovers at the brink of poverty. In "Tent City, USA," journalist Maria L. La Ganga offers a glimpse of people thrown into true poverty, at least temporarily, by the recession of 2008–2009. Next, in an excerpt from *America's New Working Class*, political scientist Kathleen R. Arnold makes the provocative argument that government programs usually thought to aid poor Americans are in fact systems designed to punish, control, and monitor them. The chapter concludes with "Stephen Cruz," an oral history by Studs Terkel about a man who has moved beyond pursuing money to a way of life he finds more rewarding.

Sources

Baida, Peter. *Poor Richard's Legacy: American Business Values from Benjamin Franklin to Donald Trump.* New York: William Morrow, 1990. Print.

Correspondents of the New York Times. *Class Matters.* New York: Times Books / Henry Holt and Company, 2005. Print.

McNamee, Stephen J. and Robert K. Miller Jr. *The Meritocracy Myth.* New York: Rowman & Littlefield, 2004. Print.

St. John de Crèvecoeur, J. Hector. *Letters from an American Farmer.* New York: Dolphin Books, 1961. First published in London, 1782. Print.

BEFORE READING

- Working alone or in groups, make a list of people who best represent your idea of success. (You may want to consider public and political figures, leaders in government, entertainment, sports, education, or other fields.) List the specific qualities or accomplishments that make these people successful. Compare notes with your classmates, then freewrite about the meaning of success: What does it mean to you? To the class as a whole? Keep your list and your definition. As you work through this chapter, reread and reflect on what you've written, comparing your ideas with those of the authors included here.

- Write a journal entry that captures the thoughts of the man pictured in the photo at the beginning of this chapter (p. 253). What feelings or attitudes can you read in his expression, his dress, and his body language? How do you think he got where he is today? How easy or difficult is it to "read" social class in the dress, speech, possessions, and behavior of people you see at school, work, or other environments?

From *Ragged Dick*

HORATIO ALGER

The choice of Horatio Alger to exemplify the myth of individual oppor-
tunity is almost automatic. Alger's rags-to-riches stories have become syn-
onymous with the notion that anyone can succeed — even to generations of
Americans who have never read one of the books that were best-sellers a
century ago. The excerpt below is typical of Alger's work in that it focuses on
a young man's progress from a poor background toward "fame and for-
tune." Alger (1832–1899) published over a hundred such stories; most
observers agree that their popularity depended less on their literary accom-
plishments than on the promises they made about opportunity in America
and the rewards of hard work.

Dick now began to look about for a position in a store or counting-
room. Until he should obtain one he determined to devote half the day to
blacking boots, not being willing to break in upon his small capital. He
found that he could earn enough in half a day to pay all his necessary
expenses, including the entire rent of the room. Fosdick desired to pay his
half; but Dick steadily refused, insisting upon paying so much as compensation for his friend's services as instructor.

It should be added that Dick's peculiar way of speaking and use of
slang terms had been somewhat modified by his education and his intimacy
with Henry Fosdick. Still he continued to indulge in them to some extent,
especially when he felt like joking, and it was natural to Dick to joke, as my
readers have probably found out by this time. Still his manners were considerably improved, so that he was more likely to obtain a situation than when
first introduced to our notice.

Just now, however, business was very dull, and merchants, instead of
hiring new assistants, were disposed to part with those already in their
employ. After making several ineffectual applications, Dick began to think
he should be obliged to stick to his profession until the next season. But
about this time something occurred which considerably improved his
chances of preferment.

This is the way it happened.

As Dick, with a balance of more than a hundred dollars in the savings   5
bank, might fairly consider himself a young man of property, he thought
himself justified in occasionally taking a half holiday from business, and
going on an excursion. On Wednesday afternoon Henry Fosdick was sent by
his employer on an errand to that part of Brooklyn near Greenwood Ceme-
tery. Dick hastily dressed himself in his best, and determined to accompany him.

The two boys walked down to the South Ferry, and, paying their two cents each, entered the ferry-boat. They remained at the stern, and stood by the railing, watching the great city, with its crowded wharves, receding from view. Beside them was a gentleman with two children, — a girl of eight and a little boy of six. The children were talking gayly to their father. While he was pointing out some object of interest to the little girl, the boy managed to creep, unobserved, beneath the chain that extends across the boat, for the protection of passengers, and, stepping incautiously to the edge of the boat, fell over into the foaming water.

At the child's scream, the father looked up, and, with a cry of horror, sprang to the edge of the boat. He would have plunged in, but, being unable to swim, would only have endangered his own life, without being able to save his child.

"My child!" he exclaimed in anguish, — "who will save my child? A thousand — ten thousand dollars to any one who will save him!"

There chanced to be but few passengers on board at the time, and nearly all these were either in the cabins or standing forward. Among the few who saw the child fall was our hero.

Now Dick was an expert swimmer. It was an accomplishment which he 10 had possessed for years, and he no sooner saw the boy fall than he resolved to rescue him. His determination was formed before he heard the liberal offer made by the boy's father. Indeed, I must do Dick the justice to say that, in the excitement of the moment, he did not hear it at all, nor would it have stimulated the alacrity with which he sprang to the rescue of the little boy.

Little Johnny had already risen once, and gone under for the second time, when our hero plunged in. He was obliged to strike out for the boy, and this took time. He reached him none too soon. Just as he was sinking for the third and last time, he caught him by the jacket. Dick was stout and strong, but Johnny clung to him so tightly, that it was with great difficulty he was able to sustain himself.

"Put your arms round my neck," said Dick.

The little boy mechanically obeyed, and clung with a grasp strengthened by his terror. In this position Dick could bear his weight better. But the ferry-boat was receding fast. It was quite impossible to reach it. The father, his face pale with terror and anguish, and his hands clasped in suspense, saw the brave boy's struggles, and prayed with agonizing fervor that he might be successful. But it is probable, for they were now midway of the river, that both Dick and the little boy whom he had bravely undertaken to rescue would have been drowned, had not a row-boat been fortunately near. The two men who were in it witnessed the accident, and hastened to the rescue of our hero.

"Keep up a little longer," they shouted, bending to their oars, "and we will save you."

Dick heard the shout, and it put fresh strength into him. He battled 15 manfully with the treacherous sea, his eyes fixed longingly upon the approaching boat.

"Hold on tight, little boy," he said. "There's a boat coming."

The little boy did not see the boat. His eyes were closed to shut out the fearful water, but he clung the closer to his young preserver. Six long, steady strokes, and the boat dashed along side. Strong hands seized Dick and his youthful burden, and drew them into the boat, both dripping with water.

"God be thanked!" exclaimed the father, as from the steamer he saw the child's rescue. "That brave boy shall be rewarded, if I sacrifice my whole fortune to compass it."

"You've had a pretty narrow escape, young chap," said one of the boat-men to Dick. "It was a pretty tough job you undertook."

"Yes," said Dick. "That's what I thought when I was in the water. If it hadn't been for you, I don't know what would have 'come of us."   20

"Anyhow you're a plucky boy, or you wouldn't have dared to jump into the water after this little chap. It was a risky thing to do."

"I'm used to the water," said Dick, modestly. "I didn't stop to think of the danger, but I wasn't going to see that little fellow drown without tryin' to save him."

The boat at once headed for the ferry wharf on the Brooklyn side. The captain of the ferry-boat, seeing the rescue, did not think it necessary to stop his boat, but kept on his way. The whole occurrence took place in less time than I have occupied in telling it.

The father was waiting on the wharf to receive his little boy, with what feeling of gratitude and joy can be easily understood. With a burst of happy tears he clasped him to his arms. Dick was about to withdraw modestly, but the gentleman perceived the movement, and, putting down the child, came forward, and, clasping his hand, said with emotion, "My brave boy, I owe you a debt I can never repay. But for your timely service I should now be plunged into an anguish which I cannot think of without a shudder."

Our hero was ready enough to speak on most occasions, but always felt awkward when he was praised.   25

"It wasn't any trouble," he said, modestly. "I can swim like a top."

"But not many boys would have risked their lives for a stranger," said the gentleman. "But," he added with a sudden thought, as his glance rested on Dick's dripping garments, "both you and my little boy will take cold in wet clothes. Fortunately I have a friend living close at hand, at whose house you will have an opportunity of taking off your clothes, and having them dried."

Dick protested that he never took cold; but Fosdick, who had now joined them, and who, it is needless to say, had been greatly alarmed at Dick's danger, joined in urging compliance with the gentleman's proposal, and in the end our hero had to yield. His new friend secured a hack, the driver of which agreed for extra recompense to receive the dripping boys into his carriage, and they were whirled rapidly to a pleasant house in a side street, where matters were quickly explained, and both boys were put to bed.

"I aint used to goin' to bed quite so early," thought Dick. "This is the queerest excursion I ever took."

Like most active boys Dick did not enjoy the prospect of spending half   30
a day in bed; but his confinement did not last as long as he anticipated.

In about an hour the door of his chamber was opened, and a servant appeared, bringing a new and handsome suit of clothes throughout.

"You are to put on these," said the servant to Dick; "but you needn't get up till you feel like it."

"Whose clothes are they?" asked Dick.

"They are yours."

"Mine! Where did they come from?"   35

"Mr. Rockwell sent out and bought them for you. They are the same size as your wet ones."

"Is he here now?"

"No. He bought another suit for the little boy, and has gone back to New York. Here's a note he asked me to give you."

Dick opened the paper, and read as follows, —

"Please accept this outfit of clothes as the first instalment of a debt   40
which I can never repay. I have asked to have your wet suit dried, when you can reclaim it. Will you oblige me by calling to-morrow at my counting room, No. — , Pearl Street.

> "Your friend,
> "JAMES ROCKWELL."

When Dick was dressed in his new suit, he surveyed his figure with pardonable complacency. It was the best he had ever worn, and fitted him as well as if it had been made expressly for him.

"He's done the handsome thing," said Dick to himself; "but there wasn't no 'casion for his givin' me these clothes. My lucky stars are shinin' pretty bright now. Jumpin' into the water pays better than shinin' boots; but I don't think I'd like to try it more'n once a week."

About eleven o'clock the next morning Dick repaired to Mr. Rockwell's counting-room on Pearl Street. He found himself in front of a large and handsome warehouse. The counting-room was on the lower floor. Our hero entered, and found Mr. Rockwell sitting at a desk. No sooner did that gentleman see him than he arose, and, advancing, shook Dick by the hand in the most friendly manner.

"My young friend," he said, "you have done me so great a service that I wish to be of some service to you in return. Tell me about yourself, and what plans or wishes you have formed for the future."

Dick frankly related his past history, and told Mr. Rockwell of his   45
desire to get into a store or counting-room, and of the failure of all his applications thus far. The merchant listened attentively to Dick's statement, and,

when he had finished, placed a sheet of paper before him, and, handing him a pen, said, "Will you write your name on this piece of paper?"

Dick wrote, in a free, bold hand, the name Richard Hunter. He had very much improved his penmanship, as has already been mentioned, and now had no cause to be ashamed of it.

Mr. Rockwell surveyed it approvingly.

"How would you like to enter my counting-room as clerk, Richard?" he asked.

Dick was about to say "Bully," when he recollected himself, and answered, "Very much."

"I suppose you know something of arithmetic, do you not?"   50

"Yes, sir."

"Then you may consider yourself engaged at a salary of ten dollars a week. You may come next Monday morning."

"Ten dollars!" repeated Dick, thinking he must have misunderstood.

"Yes; will that be sufficient?"

"It's more than I can earn," said Dick, honestly.   55

"Perhaps it is at first," said Mr. Rockwell, smiling; "but I am willing to pay you that. I will besides advance you as fast as your progress will justify it."

Dick was so elated that he hardly restrained himself from some demonstration which would have astonished the merchant; but he exercised self-control, and only said, "I'll try to serve you so faithfully, sir, that you won't repent having taken me into your service."

"And I think you will succeed," said Mr. Rockwell, encouragingly. "I will not detain you any longer, for I have some important business to attend to. I shall expect to see you on Monday morning."

Dick left the counting-room, hardly knowing whether he stood on his head or his heels, so overjoyed was he at the sudden change in his fortunes. Ten dollars a week was to him a fortune, and three times as much as he had expected to obtain at first. Indeed he would have been glad, only the day before, to get a place at three dollars a week. He reflected that with the stock of clothes which he had now on hand, he could save up at least half of it, and even then live better than he had been accustomed to do; so that his little fund in the savings bank, instead of being diminished, would be steadily increasing. Then he was to be advanced if he deserved it. It was indeed a bright prospect for a boy who, only a year before, could neither read nor write, and depended for a night's lodging upon the chance hospitality of an alley-way or old wagon. Dick's great ambition to "grow up 'spectable" seemed likely to be accomplished after all.

"I wish Fosdick was as well off as I am," he thought generously. But he   60
determined to help his less fortunate friend, and assist him up the ladder as he advanced himself.

When Dick entered his room on Mott Street, he discovered that some one else had been there before him, and two articles of wearing apparel had disappeared.

"By gracious!" he exclaimed; "somebody's stole my Washington coat and Napoleon pants. Maybe it's an agent of Barnum's, who expects to make a fortun' by exhibitin' the valooable wardrobe of a gentleman of fashion."

Dick did not shed many tears over his loss, as, in his present circumstances, he never expected to have any further use for the well-worn garments. It may be stated that he afterwards saw them adorning the figure of Micky Maguire; but whether that estimable young man stole them himself, he never ascertained. As to the loss, Dick was rather pleased that it had occurred. It seemed to cut him off from the old vagabond life which he hoped never to resume. Henceforward he meant to press onward, and rise as high as possible.

Although it was yet only noon, Dick did not go out again with his brush. He felt that it was time to retire from business. He would leave his share of the public patronage to other boys less fortunate than himself. That evening Dick and Fosdick had a long conversation. Fosdick rejoiced heartily in his friend's success, and on his side had the pleasant news to communicate that his pay had been advanced to six dollars a week.

"I think we can afford to leave Mott Street now," he continued. "This   65
house isn't as neat as it might be, and I should like to live in a nicer quarter of the city."

"All right," said Dick. "We'll hunt up a new room tomorrow. I shall have plenty of time, having retired from business. I'll try to get my reg'lar customers to take Johnny Nolan in my place. That boy hasn't any enterprise. He needs somebody to look out for him."

"You might give him your box and brush, too, Dick."

"No," said Dick; "I'll give him some new ones, but mine I want to keep, to remind me of the hard times I've had, when I was an ignorant boot-black, and never expected to be anything better."

"When, in short, you were 'Ragged Dick.' You must drop that name, and think of yourself now as" —

"Richard Hunter, Esq.," said our hero, smiling.   70

"A young gentleman on the way to fame and fortune," added Fosdick.

ENGAGING THE TEXT

1. List the values, characteristics, and actions that help Ragged Dick succeed. How valuable do you consider these today? How important is virtue compared to good luck — in the story and in your own experience?

2. Skim the Alger selection to find as many mentions of money as you can. How frequent are they? What seem to be Alger's ideas about money, wealth, salaries, and other financial issues?

3. By the time we reach the end of this story, quite a few things have changed from the time Dick "was an ignorant boot-black, and never expected to be anything better" (para. 68). Working in small groups, list as many changes as you can. What seems to be Alger's attitude toward them?

4. Why is Alger careful to note that Dick does not hear Mr. Rockwell's offer of $10,000 to whoever would save Little Johnny? Is Dick being short-changed by getting a job and clothes but not a $10,000 reward?

EXPLORING CONNECTIONS

5. Look ahead to "Horatio Alger" by Harlon L. Dalton later in this chapter (p. 272). Does Dalton's analysis of the Alger myth change your understanding of this excerpt? Explain. What elements in this story might Dalton cite to support his claims?
6. Read "Looking for Work" by Gary Soto (p. 26). Compare and contrast Alger's ideas about work, money, and aspiration to those found in Soto's narrative.

EXTENDING THE CRITICAL CONTEXT

7. Dick considers himself a "young man of property" when he has $100 in the bank. Talk to classmates and see if you can reach any consensus about what it would take today to be a "young man or woman of property." Similarly, see if you can agree on what a good starting salary would be for a recent college graduate, or on what levels of wealth and income define the poor, the middle class, and the upper class in the United States today. Write a note summarizing your conclusions and keep it for reference as you read the rest of this chapter.
8. If you did the first "Before Reading" assignment on page 257, compare and contrast the qualities that made the people on your list successful with the qualities Alger gives to Ragged Dick.

The Lesson

TONI CADE BAMBARA

"The Lesson" looks at wealth through the eyes of a poor black girl whose education includes a field trip to one of the world's premier toy stores. The story speaks to serious social issues with a comic, energetic, and utterly engaging voice. Toni Cade Bambara (1939–1995) grew up in the Harlem and Bedford-Stuyvesant areas of New York City. Trained at Queens College and City College of New York in dance, drama, and literature, she is best known for her collections of stories, Gorilla, My Love *(1972) and* The Seabirds Are Still Alive and Other Stories *(1977), and for her novels,* If Blessing Comes *(1987) and* The Salt Eaters *(1980), winner of the American Book Award. Her*

novel Those Bones Are Not My Child, *edited by Toni Morrison, was pub-lished posthumously in 1999. "The Lesson" is taken from* Gorilla, My Love.

Back in the days when everyone was old and stupid or young and fool-ish and me and Sugar were the only ones just right, this lady moved on our block with nappy hair and proper speech and no makeup. And quite natu-rally we laughed at her, laughed the way we did at the junk man who went about his business like he was some big-time president and his sorry-ass horse his secretary. And we kinda hated her too, hated the way we did the winos who cluttered up our parks and pissed on our handball walls and stank up our hallways and stairs so you couldn't halfway play hide-and-seek without a goddamn gas mask. Miss Moore was her name. The only woman on the block with no first name. And she was black as hell, cept for her feet, which were fish-white and spooky. And she was always planning these boring-ass things for us to do, us being my cousin, mostly, who lived on the block cause we all moved North the same time and to the same apartment then spread out gradual to breathe. And our parents would yank our heads into some kinda shape and crisp up our clothes so we'd be presentable for travel with Miss Moore, who always looked like she was going to church, though she never did. Which is just one of the things the grownups talked about when they talked behind her back like a dog. But when she came call-ing with some sachet[1] she'd sewed up or some gingerbread she'd made or some book, why then they'd all be too embarrassed to turn her down and we'd get handed out all spruced up. She'd been to college and said it only right that she should take responsibility for the young ones' education, and she not even related by marriage or blood. So they'd go for it. Specially Aunt Gretchen. She was the main gofer in the family. You got some ole dumb shit foolishness you want somebody to go for, you send for Aunt Gretchen. She been screwed into the go-along for so long, it's a blood-deep natural thing with her. Which is how she got saddled with me and Sugar and Junior in the first place while our mothers were in a la-de-da apartment up the block having a good ole time.

So this one day Miss Moore rounds us all up at the mailbox and it's puredee hot and she's knockin herself out about arithmetic. And school suppose to let up in summer I heard, but she don't never let up. And the starch in my pinafore scratching the shit outta me and I'm really hating this nappy-head bitch and her goddamn college degree. I'd much rather go to the pool or to the show where it's cool. So me and Sugar leaning on the mailbox being surly, which is a Miss Moore word. And Flyboy checking out what everybody brought for lunch. And Fat Butt already wasting his

---

[1]*sachet:* A small bag filled with a sweet-smelling substance. Sachets are often placed in drawers to scent clothes.

peanut-butter-and-jelly sandwich like the pig he is. And Junebug punchin on Q.T.'s arm for potato chips. And Rosie Giraffe shifting from one hip to the other waiting for somebody to step on her foot or ask her if she from Georgia so she can kick ass, preferably Mercedes'. And Miss Moore asking us do we know what money is, like we a bunch of retards. I mean real money, she say, like it's only poker chips or monopoly papers we lay on the grocer. So right away I'm tired of this and say so. And would much rather snatch Sugar and go to the Sunset and terrorize the West Indian kids and take their hair ribbons and their money too. And Miss Moore files that remark away for next week's lesson on brotherhood, I can tell. And finally I say we oughta get to the subway cause it's cooler and besides we might meet some cute boys. Sugar done swiped her mama's lipstick, so we ready.

So we heading down the street and she's boring us silly about what things cost and what our parents make and how much goes for rent and how money ain't divided up right in this country. And then she gets to the part about we all poor and live in the slums, which I don't feature. And I'm ready to speak on that, but she steps out in the street and hails two cabs just like that. Then she hustles half the crew in with her and hands me a five-dollar bill and tells me to calculate 10 percent tip for the driver. And we're off. Me and Sugar and Junebug and Flyboy hangin out the window and hollering to everybody, putting lipstick on each other cause Flyboy a faggot anyway, and making farts with our sweaty armpits. But I'm mostly trying to figure how to spend this money. But they all fascinated with the meter ticking and Junebug starts laying bets as to how much it'll read when Flyboy can't hold his breath no more. Then Sugar lays bets as to how much it'll be when we get there. So I'm stuck. Don't nobody want to go for my plan, which is to jump out at the next light and run off to the first bar-b-que we can find. Then the driver tells us to get the hell out cause we are there already. And the meter reads eighty-five cents. And I'm stalling to figure out the tip and Sugar say give him a dime. And I decide he don't need it bad as I do, so later for him. But then he tries to take off with Junebug foot still in the door so we talk about his mama something ferocious. Then we check out that we on Fifth Avenue[2] and everybody dressed up in stockings. One lady in a fur coat, hot as it is. White folks crazy.

"This is the place," Miss Moore say, presenting it to us in the voice she uses at the museum. "Let's look in the windows before we go in."

"Can we steal?" Sugar asks very serious like she's getting the ground rules square away before she plays. "I beg your pardon," say Miss Moore, and we fall out. So she leads us around the windows of the toy store and me and Sugar screamin, "This is mine, that's mine, I gotta have that, that was made for me, I was born for that," till Big Butt drowns us out.

"Hey, I'm goin to buy that there."

5

[2] *Fifth Avenue:* The street in New York most famous for its expensive stores.

"That there? You don't even know what it is, stupid."

"I do so," he say punchin on Rosie Giraffe. "It's a microscope."

"Whatcha gonna do with a microscope, fool?"

"Look at things." 10

"Like what, Ronald?" ask Miss Moore. And Big Butt ain't got the first notion. So here go Miss Moore gabbing about the thousands of bacteria in a drop of water and the somethinorother in a speck of blood and the million and one living things in the air around us is invisible to the naked eye. And what she say that for? Junebug go to town on that "naked" and we rolling. Then Miss Moore ask what it cost. So we all jam into the window smudgin it up and the price tag say $300. So then she ask how long'd take for Big Butt and Junebug to save up their allowances. "Too long," I say. "Yeh," adds Sugar, "outgrown it by that time." And Miss Moore say no, you never outgrow learning instruments. "Why, even medical students and interns and," blah, blah, blah. And we ready to choke Big Butt for bringing it up in the first damn place.

"This here costs four hundred eighty dollars," say Rosie Giraffe. So we pile up all over her to see what she pointin out. My eyes tell me it's a chunk of glass cracked with something heavy, and different-color inks dripped into the splits, then the whole thing put into a oven or something. But for $480 it don't make sense.

"That's a paperweight made of semi-precious stones fused together under tremendous pressure," she explains slowly, with her hands doing the mining and all the factory work.

"So what's a paperweight?" asks Rosie Giraffe.

"To weigh paper with, dumbbell," say Flyboy, the wise man from the 15 East.

"Not exactly," say Miss Moore, which is what she say when you warm or way off too. "It's to weigh paper down so it won't scatter and make your desk untidy." So right away me and Sugar curtsy to each other and then to Mercedes who is more the tidy type.

"We don't keep paper on top of the desk in my class," say Junebug, figuring Miss Moore crazy or lyin one.

"At home, then," she say. "Don't you have a calendar and a pencil case and a blotter and a letter-opener on your desk at home where you do your homework?" And she know damn well what our homes look like cause she nosys around in them every chance she gets.

"I don't even have a desk," say Junebug. "Do we?"

"No. And I don't get no homework neither," say Big Butt. 20

"And I don't even have a home," say Flyboy like he do at school to keep the white folks off his back and sorry for him. Send this poor kid to camp posters, is his speciality.

"I do," say Mercedes. "I have a box of stationery on my desk and a picture of my cat. My godmother bought the stationery and the desk. There's a big rose on each sheet and the envelopes smell like roses."

"Who want to know about your smelly-ass stationery," say Rosie Giraffe fore I can get my two cents in.

"It's important to have a work area all your own so that . . ."

"Will you look at this sailboat, please," say Flyboy, cuttin her off and pointin to the thing like it was his. So once again we tumble all over each other to gaze at this magnificent thing in the toy store which is just big enough to maybe sail two kittens across the pond if you strap them to the posts tight. We all start reciting the price tag like we in assembly. "Hand-crafted sailboat of fiberglass at one thousand one hundred ninety-five dollars."

"Unbelievable," I hear myself say and am really stunned. I read it again for myself just in case the group recitation put me in a trance. Same thing. For some reason this pisses me off. We look at Miss Moore and she lookin at us, waiting for I dunno what.

"Who'd pay all that when you can buy a sailboat set for a quarter at Pop's, a tube of glue for a dime, and a ball of string for eight cents? It must have a motor and a whole lot else besides," I say. "My sailboat cost me about fifty cents."

"But will it take water?" say Mercedes with her smart ass.

"Took mine to Alley Pond Park once," say Flyboy. "String broke. Lost it. Pity."

"Sailed mine in Central Park and it keeled over and sank. Had to ask my father for another dollar."

"And you got the strap," laugh Big Butt. "The jerk didn't even have a string on it. My old man wailed on his behind."

Little Q.T. was staring hard at the sailboat and you could see he wanted it bad. But he too little and somebody'd just take it from him. So what the hell. "This boat for kids, Miss Moore?"

"Parents silly to buy something like that just to get all broke up," say Rosie Giraffe.

"That much money it should last forever," I figure.

"My father'd buy it for me if I wanted it."

"Your father, my ass," say Rosie Giraffe getting a chance to finally push Mercedes.

"Must be rich people shop here," say Q.T.

"You are a very bright boy," say Flyboy. "What was your first clue?" And he rap him on the head with the back of his knuckles, since Q.T. the only one he could get away with. Though Q.T. liable to come up behind you years later and get his licks in when you half expect it.

"What I want to know is," I says to Miss Moore though I never talk to her, I wouldn't give the bitch that satisfaction, "is how much a real boat costs? I figure a thousand'd get you a yacht any day."

"Why don't you check that out," she says, "and report back to the group?" Which really pains my ass. If you gonna mess up a perfectly good swim day least you could do is have some answers. "Let's go in," she say like

she got something up her sleeve. Only she don't lead the way. So me and
Sugar turn the corner to where the entrance is, but when we get there I
kinda hang back. Not that I'm scared, what's there to be afraid of, just a toy
store. But I feel funny, shame. But what I got to be shamed about? Got as
much right to go in as anybody. But somehow I can't seem to get hold on
the door, so I step away for Sugar to lead. But she hangs back too. And I
look at her and she looks at me and this is ridiculous. I mean, damn, I have
never ever been shy about doing nothing or going nowhere. But then Mercedes steps up and then Rosie Giraffe and Big Butt crowd in behind and
shove, and next thing we all stuffed into the doorway with only Mercedes
squeezing past us, smoothing out her jumper and walking right down the
aisle. Then the rest of us tumble in like a glued-together jigsaw done all
wrong. And people lookin at us. And it's like the time me and Sugar crashed
into the Catholic church on a dare. But once we got in there and everything
so hushed and holy and the candles and the bowin and the handkerchiefs on
all the drooping heads, I just couldn't go through with the plan. Which was
for me to run up to the altar and do a tap dance while Sugar played the nose
flute and messed around in the holy water. And Sugar kept givin me the
elbow. Then later teased me so bad I tied her up in the shower and turned
it on and locked her in. And she'd be there till this day if Aunt Gretchen
hadn't finally figured I was lying about the boarder takin a shower.

Same thing in the store. We all walkin on tiptoe and hardly touchin the
games and puzzles and things. And I watched Miss Moore who is steady
watchin us like she waitin for a sign. Like Mama Drewery watches the sky
and sniffs the air and takes note of just how much slant is in the bird formation. Then me and Sugar bump smack into each other, so busy gazing at the
toys, 'specially the sailboat. But we don't laugh and go into our fat-lady
bump-stomach routine. We just stare at that price tag. Then Sugar run a
finger over the whole boat. And I'm jealous and want to hit her. Maybe not
her, but I sure want to punch somebody in the mouth.

"Watcha bring us here for, Miss Moore?"

"You sound angry, Sylvia. Are you mad about something?" Give me one
of them grins like she tellin a grown-up joke that never turns out to be
funny. And she's lookin very closely at me like maybe she plannin to do my
portrait from memory. I'm mad, but I won't give her that satisfaction. So I
slouch around the store bein very bored and say, "Let's go."

Me and Sugar at the back of the train watchin' the tracks whizzin by
large then small then gettin gobbled up in the dark. I'm thinkin about this
tricky toy I saw in the store. A clown that somersaults on a bar then does
chin-ups just cause you yank lightly at his leg. Cost $35. I could see me askin
my mother for a $35 birthday clown. "You wanna who that costs what?" she'd
say, cockin her head to the side to get a better view of the hole in my head.
Thirty-five dollars could buy new bunk beds for Junior and Gretchen's boy.
Thirty-five dollars and the whole household could go visit Granddaddy
Nelson in the country. Thirty-five dollars would pay for the rent and the

piano bill too. Who are these people that spend that much for performing clowns and $1,000 for toy sailboats? What kinda work they do and how they live and how come we ain't in on it? Where we are is who we are, Miss Moore always pointin out. But it don't necessarily have to be that way, she always adds then waits for somebody to say that poor people have to wake up and demand their share of the pie and don't none of us know what kind of pie she talkin about in the first damn place. But she ain't so smart cause I still got her four dollars from the taxi and she sure ain't gettin it. Messin up my day with this shit. Sugar nudges me in my pocket and winks.

Miss Moore lines us up in front of the mailbox where we started from,   45
seem like years ago, and I got a headache for thinkin so hard. And we lean all over each other so we can hold up under the draggy-ass lecture she always finishes us off with at the end before we thank her for borin us to tears. But she just looks at us like she readin tea leaves. Finally she say, "Well, what did you think of F.A.O. Schwarz?"[3]

Rosie Giraffe mumbles, "White folks crazy."

"I'd like to go in there again when I get my birthday money," says Mercedes, and we shove her out the pack so she has to lean on the mailbox by herself.

"I'd like a shower. Tiring day," say Flyboy.

Then Sugar surprises me by saying, "You know, Miss Moore, I don't think all of us here put together eat in a year what that sailboat costs." And Miss Moore lights up like somebody goosed her. "And?" she say, urging Sugar on. Only I'm standin on her foot so she don't continue.

"Imagine for a minute what kind of society it is in which some people   50
can spend on a toy what it would cost to feed a family of six or seven. What do you think?"

"I think," say Sugar pushing me off her feet like she never done before, cause I whip her ass in a minute, "that this is not much of a democracy if you ask me. Equal chance to pursue happiness means an equal crack at the dough, don't it?" Miss Moore is besides herself and I am disgusted with Sugar's treachery. So I stand on her foot one more time to see if she'll shove me. She shuts up, and Miss Moore looks at me, sorrowfully I'm thinkin. And somethin weird is going on, I can feel it in my chest.

"Anybody else learn anything today?" lookin dead at me. I walk away and Sugar has to run to catch up and don't even seem to notice when I shrug her arm off my shoulder.

"Well, we got four dollars anyway," she says.

"Uh hunh."

"We could go to Hascombs and get half a chocolate layer and then go to   55
the Sunset and still have plenty money for potato chips and ice-cream sodas."

"Uh hunh."

---

[3]*F.A.O. Schwarz:* The name and the toy store are real. The store, in fact, has become a tourist attraction.

"Race you to Hascombs," she say.

We start down the block and she gets ahead which is O.K. by me cause I'm goin to the West End and then over to the Drive to think this day through. She can run if she want to and even run faster. But ain't nobody gonna beat me at nuthin.

Engaging the Text

1. What is the lesson Miss Moore is trying to teach in this story? How well is it received by Mercedes, Sugar, and the narrator, Sylvia? Why does the narrator react differently from Sugar, and what is the meaning of her last line in the story, "But ain't nobody gonna beat me at nuthin"?

2. Why did Bambara write the story from Sylvia's point of view? How would the story change if told from Miss Moore's perspective? From Sugar's? How would it change if the story were set today as opposed to three decades ago?

3. The story mentions several expensive items: a fur coat, a microscope, a paperweight, a sailboat, and a toy clown. Why do you think the author chose each of these details? If the story were set in the present instead of circa 1970, what items might serve the same purposes?

4. In paragraph 44 Sylvia says, "Where we are is who we are, Miss Moore always pointin out. But it don't necessarily have to be that way." What does Miss Moore mean by this? Do you agree? What does Miss Moore expect the children to do to change the situation?

Exploring Connections

5. Both Sylvia and Ragged Dick (p. 258) can be seen as trying to find their place in the world of money and social status. Compare their situations and their attitudes about class and upward mobility. How do Bambara's ideas about money and opportunity differ from Alger's?

6. "The Lesson" describes education outside of the schoolroom. How might John Taylor Gatto (p. 148) or Jean Anyon (p. 169) assess the effectiveness of Miss Moore's teaching? Do you think Miss Moore's lessons directly challenge the children's classroom learning? Explain.

7. Compare Sylvia and Sugar's relationship here with that of Teresa and the speaker of the poem in "Para Teresa" (p. 207). Which girls stand the better chance of achieving success? Why?

Extending the Critical Context

8. For the next class meeting, browse the Internet or magazines, newspapers, and catalogs to find the most overpriced, unnecessary item you can. Spend a few minutes swapping examples, then discuss the information you've gathered: Are there any lessons to be learned here about wealth, success, and status?

9. The opening lines of "The Lesson" suggest that Sylvia is now a mature woman looking back on her youth. Working in groups, write a brief biography explaining what has happened to Sylvia since the day of "The Lesson." What has she done? Who has she become? Read your profiles aloud to the class and explain your vision of Sylvia's development.

Horatio Alger

Harlon L. Dalton

The first selection in this chapter dramatizes the American Dream coming true in an uncomplicated if rather contrived way: the ambitious young "Ragged Dick" determines to improve himself, works hard, seizes his opportunity, and quickly makes his way to "fame and fortune." This piece by Harlon L. Dalton (b. 1947) questions that myth, calling it not only false, but worse — "socially destructive." Using Alger as his prime example, Dalton systematically explains how the rags-to-riches myth can conceal important social realities like race and class. A professor at Yale Law School, Harlon L. Dalton specializes in the relationship of law to theology, psychology, and race theory. He has served on the board of directors for the American Civil Liberties Union and was a member of the National Commission on AIDS. "Horatio Alger" is taken from his book Racial Healing: Confronting the Fear Between Blacks and Whites *(1995).*

Ah, Horatio Alger, whose name more than any other is associated with the classic American hero. A writer of mediocre fiction, Alger had a formula for commercial success that was simple and straightforward: his lead characters, young boys born into poverty, invariably managed to transcend their station in life by dint of hard work, persistence, initiative, and daring.[1] Nice story line. There is just one problem — it is a myth. Not just in the sense that it is fictional, but more fundamentally because the lesson Alger conveys is a false one. To be sure, many myths are perfectly benign, and more than a few are salutary, but on balance Alger's myth is socially destructive.

The Horatio Alger myth conveys three basic messages: (1) each of us is judged solely on her or his own merits; (2) we each have a fair opportunity

---

[1] Edwin P. Hoyt, *Horatio's Boys: The Life and Works of Horatio Alger, Jr.* (Radnor, Penn.: Chilton Book Company, 1974). [All notes are Dalton's.]

to develop those merits; and (3) ultimately, merit will out. Each of them is, to be charitable, problematic. The first message is a variant on the rugged individualism ethos. . . . In this form, it suggests that success in life has nothing to do with pedigree, race, class background, gender, national origin, sexual orientation — in short, with anything beyond our individual control. Those variables may exist, but they play no appreciable role in how our actions are appraised.

This simply flies in the face of reality. There are doubtless circumstances — the hiring of a letter carrier in a large metropolitan post office, for example — where none of this may matter, but that is the exception rather than the rule. Black folk certainly know what it is like to be favored, disfavored, scrutinized, and ignored all on the basis of our race. Sometimes we are judged on a different scale altogether. Stephen Carter has written movingly about what he calls "the best black syndrome," the tendency of White folk to judge successful Black people only in relation to each other rather than against all comers. Thus, when Carter earned the second-highest score in his high school on the National Merit Scholarship qualifying test, he was readily recognized as "the best Black" around, but somehow not seen as one of the best students, period.[2]

Although I would like to think that things are much different now, I know better. Not long ago a student sought my advice regarding how to deal with the fact that a liberal colleague of mine (and of Stephen Carter's) had written a judicial clerkship recommendation for her in which he described her as the best Black student to have ever taken his class. Apparently the letter caused a mild stir among current law clerks in several courthouses, one of whom saw fit to inform the student. "What was the professor [whom she declined to name] thinking of?" she wondered aloud. "What does his comment mean? What is a judge supposed to make of it? 'If for some reason you think you have to hire one of them, then she's the way to go'? I could understand if he said I was one of the top ten students or even the top thousand, but what does the 'best Black' mean?"

Black folk also know what it is like to be underestimated because of the   5
color of their skin. For example, those of us who communicate in standard English are often praised unduly for how well we speak. This is, I might add, an experience all too familiar to Asian-Americans, including those born and bred in the U.S.A. And we know what it is like to be feared, pitied, admired, and scorned on account of our race, before we even have a chance to say boo! We, in turn, view White people through the prism of our own race-based expectations. I honestly am surprised every time I see a White man who can play basketball above the rim, just as Puerto Ricans and Cubans tend to be surprised to discover "Americans" who salsa truly well.

---

[2]Stephen L. Carter, *Reflections of an Affirmative Action Baby* (New York: Basic Books, 1991), 47–49.

All of which is to say that the notion that every individual is judged solely on personal merit, without regard for sociological wrapping, is mythical at best.

The second message conveyed by Horatio Alger is that we all have a shot at reaching our true potential. To be fair, neither Alger nor the myth he underwrote suggests that we start out equal. Nor does the myth necessarily require that we be given an equal opportunity to succeed. Rather, Alger's point is that each of us has the power to create our own opportunities. That turns out to be a difficult proposition to completely disprove, for no matter what evidence is offered up to show that a particular group of people have not fared well, it can always be argued that they did not try hard enough, or that they spent too much time wallowing in their predicament and not enough figuring out how to rise above it. Besides, there are always up-by-the-bootstraps examples to point to, like Colin Powell, whose name has so frequently been linked with that of Horatio Alger's that he must think they are related.[3] Nevertheless, it is by now generally agreed that there is a large category of Americans — some have called it the underclass — for whom upward mobility is practically impossible without massive changes in the structure of the economy and in the allocation of public resources.

As for the notion that merit will out, it assumes not only a commitment to merit-based decision making but also the existence of standards for measuring merit that do not unfairly favor one individual over another. Such standards, of course, must come from somewhere. They must be decided upon by somebody. And that somebody is rarely without a point of view. Ask a devotee of West Coast basketball what skills you should look for in recruiting talent and near the top of his list will be the ability to "get out on the break," to "be creative in the open court," and "to finish the play." On the other hand, ask someone who prefers East Coast basketball and her list will rank highly the ability "to d-up [play defense]," "to board [rebound]," and "to maintain focus and intensity."

Or, to take another example, what makes a great Supreme Court justice? Brains to spare? Common sense? Proper judicial temperament? Political savvy? Extensive lawyering experience? A well-developed ability to abstract? Vision? Well-honed rhetorical skills? A reverence for our rich legal heritage? The capacity to adapt to changing times? Even if one is tempted to say "all of the above," how should these (or any other set of characteristics) be ranked? Measured? Evaluated?

[3]Sandy Grady, "Will He or Won't He?: Win or Lose, Presidential Pursuit by Colin Powell Would Do America a Necessary Service," *Kansas City Star,* 24 April 1995; Thomas B. Edsall, "For Powell, Timing Could be Crucial: As Gulf War Hero Hints at 1996 Bid, Associates Look into Details," *Washington Post,* 6 April 1995; J. F. O. McAllister, "The Candidate of Dreams," *Time,* 13 March 1995; Deroy Murdock, "Colin Powell: Many Things to Many People," *Washington Times,* 16 January 1995; Doug Fischer, "U.S. Politics: War Hero Well-Placed to Become First Black President," *Ottawa Citizen,* 8 October 1994; "General Nice Guy: Profile Colin Powell," *Sunday Telegraph,* 25 September 1994; Otto Kreisher, "As a Civilian, Powell's Options Are Enviable," *San Diego Union-Tribune,* 26 September 1993.

THE BOONDOCKS   by **AARON MCGRUDER**

The answers depend in part on whom you ask. Practicing lawyers, for example, are probably likely to rank extensive lawyering experience more highly than, say, brains. They are also likely to pay close attention to judicial temperament, which for them means whether the prospective justice would be inclined to treat them with respect during a court appearance. Sitting judges are also likely to rank judicial temperament highly, meaning whether the prospective justice would be a good colleague. In choosing among the other characteristics, they might each favor the ones that they happen to possess in abundance. Politicians might well see more merit in political savvy than would, say, academics, who could be expected to favor brains, the ability to abstract, and perhaps rhetorical skills.

All of these relevant actors might be honestly trying to come up with appropriate standards for measuring merit, but they would arrive at markedly different results. And any given result would screen out people who would succeed under another, equally plausible set of standards. Thus, if there is a genuine commitment to merit-based decision making it is possible that merit will out, but only for those who have the right kind of merit.

Which brings us to the prior question: is merit all we care about in deciding who gets what share of life's goodies? Clearly not. Does anyone, for example, honestly believe that any Supreme Court justice in recent memory was nominated solely on the basis of merit (however defined)? Any President? Any member of Congress? Does anyone believe that America's health-care resources are distributed solely on merit? That tax breaks are distributed solely on merit? That baseball club owners are selected solely on merit?

As I suggested earlier, the mere fact that a myth is based on false premises or conveys a false image of the world does not necessarily make it undesirable. Indeed, I place great stock in the idea that some illusions are, or at least can be, positive. As social psychologist Shelley Taylor has observed, "[normal] people who are confronted with the normal rebuffs of everyday life seem to construe their experience [so] as to develop and maintain an exaggeratedly positive view of their own attributes, an unrealistic optimism about the future, and a distorted faith in their ability to control what goes on

10

around them."[4] Taylor's research suggests that, up to a point, such self-aggrandizement actually improves one's chances of worldly success.[5]

This may well explain the deep appeal of the Horatio Alger myth. True or not, it can help to pull people in the direction they want to go. After all, in order to succeed in life, especially when the odds are stacked against you, it is often necessary to first convince yourself that there is a reason to get up in the morning. So what is my beef? Where is the harm?

In a nutshell, my objection to the Alger myth is that it serves to maintain the racial pecking order. It does so by mentally bypassing the role of race in American society. And it does so by fostering beliefs that themselves serve to trivialize, if not erase, the social meaning of race. The Alger myth encourages people to blink at the many barriers to racial equality (historical, structural, and institutional) that litter the social landscape. Yes, slavery was built on the notion that Africans were property and not persons; yes, even after that "peculiar institution" collapsed, it continued to shape the life prospects of those who previously were enslaved; yes, the enforced illiteracy and cultural disruption of slavery, together with the collapse of Reconstruction, virtually assured that the vast majority of "freedmen" and "freedwomen" would not be successfully integrated into society; yes, Jim Crow laws, segregation, and a separate and unequal social reality severely undermined the prospects for Black achievement; yes, these and other features of our national life created a racial caste system that persists to this day; yes, the short-lived civil rights era of the 1950s and 1960s was undone by a broad and sustained White backlash; yes, the majority of Black people in America are mired in poverty; yes, economic mobility is not what it used to be, given the decline in our manufacturing and industrial base; yes, the siting of the illicit drug industry in our inner cities has had pernicious effects on Black and Latino neighborhoods; yes, yes, yes, BUT (drumroll) "all it takes to make it in America is initiative, hard work, persistence, and pluck." After all, just look at Colin Powell!

There is a fundamental tension between the promise of opportunity enshrined in the Alger myth and the realities of a racial caste system. The main point of such a system is to promote and maintain inequality. The main point of the Alger myth is to proclaim that everyone can rise above her station in life. Despite this tension, it is possible for the myth to coexist with social reality. To quote Shelley Taylor once again:

> [T]he normal human mind is oriented toward mental health and . . . at every turn it construes events in a manner that promotes benign fictions about the self, the world, and the future. The mind is, with some significant exceptions, intrinsically adaptive, oriented toward

15

---

[4]Shelley E. Taylor, *Positive Illusions: Creative Self-Deception and the Healthy Mind* (New York: Basic Books, 1989), xi.

[5]Ibid., xi, 7, 228–46.

overcoming rather than succumbing to the adverse events of life.... At one level, it constructs beneficent interpretations of threatening events that raise self-esteem and promote motivation; yet at another level, it recognizes the threat or challenge that is posed by these events.[6]

Not surprisingly, then, there are lots of Black folk who subscribe to the Alger myth and at the same time understand it to be deeply false. They live with the dissonance between myth and reality because both are helpful and healthful in dealing with "the adverse events of life." Many Whites, however, have a strong interest in resolving the dissonance in favor of the myth. Far from needing to be on guard against racial "threat[s] or challenge[s]," they would just as soon put the ugliness of racism out of mind. For them, the Horatio Alger myth provides them the opportunity to do just that.[7]

Quite apart from the general way in which the myth works to submerge the social realities of race, each of the messages it projects is also incompatible with the idea of race-based advantage or disadvantage. If, as the myth suggests, we are judged solely on our individual merits, then caste has little practical meaning. If we all can acquire the tools needed to reach our full potential, then how important can the disadvantage of race be? If merit will eventually carry the day, then shouldn't we be directing our energies toward encouraging Black initiative and follow-through rather than worrying about questions of power and privilege?

By interring the myth of Horatio Alger, or at least forcing it to coexist with social reality, we can accomplish two important goals. First, we can give the lie to the idea that Black people can simply lift themselves up by their own bootstraps. With that pesky idea out of the way, it is easier to see why White folk need to take joint ownership of the nation's race problem. Second, the realization that hard work and individual merit, while certainly critical, are not guarantors of success should lead at least some White people to reflect on whether their own achievements have been helped along by their preferred social position.

Finally, quite apart from race, it is in our national interest to give the Horatio Alger myth a rest, for it broadcasts a fourth message no less false than the first three — that we live in a land of unlimited potential. Although that belief may have served us well in the past, we live today in an era of diminished possibilities. We need to make a series of hard choices, followed by yet more hard choices regarding how to live with the promise of less. Confronting that reality is made that much harder by a mythology that assures us we can have it all.

[6]Ibid., xi.

[7]Robert T. Carter, et al., "White Racial Identity Development and Work Values," *Journal of Vocational Behavior, Special Issue: Racial Identity and Vocational Behavior* 44, no. 2 (April 1994): 185–97.

ENGAGING THE TEXT

1. The first message communicated by the Alger myth, according to Dalton, is that "each of us is judged solely on her or his own merits" (para. 2). What does this message mean to Dalton, and why does he object to it? How does he make his case against it, and what kind of evidence does he provide? Explain why you agree or disagree with his claim that this first message "simply flies in the face of reality" (para. 3).

2. Dalton says it is "generally agreed," but do *you* agree that "there is a large category of Americans . . . for whom upward mobility is practically impossible" (para. 6)? Why or why not?

3. How persuasive do you find Dalton's claims that American society is far from operating as a strictly merit-based system?

4. Why does Dalton believe that the Alger myth is destructive? Do you think the power of the American Dream to inspire or motivate people is outweighed by the negative effects Dalton cites, or vice versa? Write a journal entry explaining your position.

EXPLORING CONNECTIONS

5. Test Dalton's claims against the actual excerpt from Horatio Alger's *Ragged Dick* (p. 258). For example, does the novel seem to match the formula Dalton summarizes in his first paragraph? Similarly, can you find in the novel any examples of the three messages Dalton identifies in his second paragraph? On balance, does the excerpt from Alger seem to promote ideas that you consider socially destructive? Why or why not?

6. How do you think Dalton would assess the chances for success of Sylvia and her friends in "The Lesson" (p. 264)? Explain why you think he would praise or critique Miss Moore's attempts to educate the children about social class and money.

7. What ideas and attitudes about success are expressed in the cartoon by Aaron McGruder on page 275? How do they compare with those of Ragged Dick (p. 258) and the children in "The Lesson" (p. 264)? How might Harlon Dalton explain the humor of the cartoon?

EXTENDING THE CRITICAL CONTEXT

8. Pick several contemporary cultural icons such as Barack Obama, Oprah Winfrey, Tiger Woods, Jet Li, Sammy Sosa, Will Smith, Sonia Sotomayor, Jackie Chan, and Beyoncé Knowles. Conduct a minipoll about what their success means to race relations in the United States. Do the responses you get support Dalton's contention that such figures encourage people "to blink at the many barriers to racial equality" (para. 14)?

9. Dalton argues that the Alger myth should be buried, or, to use his word, "interred." Supposing for the moment that you agree, how could that be accomplished? How is a cultural myth challenged, revised, or robbed of its mythic power?

Living It: Tim Blixseth

ROBERT FRANK

Have you ever woken up and needed a moment to remember if you were on your yacht, or in Tahiti, or simply at home in your 30,000 square-foot mansion? Tim Blixseth has. As described in this profile, Blixseth's extraordinary economic success seems a contemporary example of the American Dream writ large: he grew up as a "welfare kid" in a small town and became a billionaire. His immense wealth qualified him as a resident of "Richistan," defined by author Robert Frank as "a new country located in the heart of America, populated entirely by millionaires, most of whom acquired their wealth during the new Gilded Age of the past twenty years." Today, however, the Blixseth empire faces possible ruin: the ski resort he founded sought bankruptcy protection in 2008; his wife, citing debts of more than $500 million, has declared personal bankruptcy; assets around the world are being sold; and lawsuits are flying. Robert Frank is a senior writer for the Wall Street Journal; *his daily blog,* The Wealth Report, *can be found at www.wsj.com. The portrait of Tim Blixseth is taken from Frank's best-selling book* Richistan: A Journey through the American Wealth Boom and the Lives of the New Rich *(2007).*

Just before dawn, Tim Blixseth is standing on the deck of his 157-foot yacht in his bathrobe.

"Where the hell am I?" he asks, rubbing his eyes, somewhere off the coast of Mexico. "I've been waking up in a different place every day this week. I feel like a vagabond."

"Vagabond" is a relative term when you're traveling with Tim Blixseth. On Sunday morning, he woke up in his 3,000-square-foot cabin at the Yellowstone Club, a private golf-and-ski club that Blixseth founded in the Montana Rockies. The next day he woke up at a luxury lodge on a 3,200-acre fishing ranch near Cody, Wyoming.

Monday night, it was back home, "home" also being a relative term. Blixseth and his wife, Edra, live on a 240-acre spread near Palm Springs, California, that makes most five-star resorts look puny by comparison. The estate, called Porcupine Creek, has a 30,000-square-foot mansion, twelve guest cottages — each the size of a single-family home — a full-service spa, two swimming pools, an amphitheater, and an underground ballroom. For their backyard, the Blixseths built a private, nineteen-hole golf course (with clubhouse) that golf experts rank as one of the best in the country. The estate grounds are carpeted with emerald-green grass, fountains, burbling streams, waterfalls, and more than a million exotic flowers — all the more remarkable for being in the middle of the desert.

On Tuesday morning, Tim and Edra boarded their Gulfstream 550 and   5
flew to Manzaneo, Mexico, just south of Puerto Vallarta. There, they jumped
on their yacht and motored to Tamarindo — a secluded jungle resort that
Tim recently purchased. Two days later, it was off to Tahiti to another
Blixseth resort playground.

"Not a bad life," he says, sipping chardonnay on his yacht during sunset.
"I wish my dad could only see me now."

On its face, Tim Blixseth's life looks like one long, luxurious vacation.
And in some ways, it is. After making millions in the timber business,
Blixseth retired at the age of forty and tried living the Good Life. But when
his plans for a family retreat in Montana caught on with friends, he launched
a second career building high-end resorts. Now he's a billionaire, with his
Yellowstone Club and Yellowstone Club World becoming two of the most
popular playgrounds for the superrich.

And that's just a side business. Blixseth buys and sells land, and owns
more than 500,000 acres of property in the United States and Mexico. He
day-trades stocks, funds start-up companies, runs his own charitable foundation, develops real estate, operates his own music label, and writes pop songs.

Blixseth is so busy that he tends to forget that he officially "retired"
more than fifteen years ago.

"As you can tell," Tim says, racing around his golf course one afternoon   10
in his high-speed cart, "I have trouble sitting still."

The New Leisure Class

Tim Blixseth is a leading member of the new overachieving overclass.
Like Ed Bazinet[1] and many of today's Richistanis, Blixseth has all the trappings of the life of leisure — multiple vacation homes, planes, boats, and
cars. And he's got enough money to last generations. Yet Tim has little time
to enjoy it.

He's always building a new home, launching new companies, and sketch-
ing out new business plans on his dinner napkins. He's a serial entrepreneur
and project addict, always looking for the next big problem to solve and
industry to reinvent. He bounds up stairs two at a time, fidgets in his chair,
and rarely sleeps in the same house (or boat or jet) two nights in a row. He
fires off e-mails at 3 A.M. and keeps his drivers and pilots in a constant state
of panic as they try to keep up with his daily movements. (You can always
hear Tim approaching because of the urgent beeps and shouts from his
staffers' radios.)

Blixseth and his kind are reinventing the leisure class. The idle rich are
being replaced by the workaholic wealthy. They don't have the time or
patience to putter around the croquet court or sip away the hours in the

---

[1]*Ed Bazinet:* American businessman profiled in *Richistan* who made his fortune designing and importing miniature ceramic villages.

polo box like Old Money. In an economy driven more than ever by competition and innovation, the people who succeed tend to be those who thrive on risk, reinvention, and brutal hours. Richistanis are younger than the rich of the past, and far more likely to be working or running their own businesses. They climbed their way up from the middle class and continue to define themselves by their eighteen-hour days and outsized productivity.

For Richistanis, work has become their play, and play has become their work. Yachts and jets are now loaded with communications gear to allow the rich to keep working even if they're floating in the Mediterranean or soaring above the Atlantic. The new crowd in Palm Beach . . . spends as much time on their laptops as they do on the golf course. When I asked a hedge-fund manager in Greenwich whether he'd joined a local yacht or country club, he replied, "And do what? Sit around in white pants and a blue blazer and complain about the government? Not for me."

Blixseth typifies this new ideal of working leisure. *Forbes* magazine   15 recently ranked Blixseth as one of the 400 richest Americans, putting his net worth at about $1.2 billion. Yet he looks nothing like a billionaire, at least in the traditional sense. His daily uniform consists of a pair of cargo shorts, Hawaiian shirts, sandals, and a baseball cap. He has a perpetual tan, scruffy goatee, buzz-cut brown hair, and wiry physique, making him look more like a surf-shop manager than a timber tycoon. He carries three things in his pocket — a wad of cash, a pen, and a $3 plastic calculator. When Tim has important meetings with bankers or CEO types, he'll sometimes wear a button-down shirt and long pants. Suits are out. "I only wear them a few times a year. And that's if I have weddings or funerals."

Tim looks so downscale that he's frequently kicked out of high-end stores and car dealerships. One day, dressed in muddy work boots and jeans, he took his son, Beau, to a men's boutique near Palm Springs to buy a graduation suit. The salesman headed them off at the door and said, "I think you'd be better off at the mall."

"You should have seen the look on that guy's face when we drove away in the Rolls," he says.

Tim loves pranks. One day when I accompanied him to Mexico, he conspired with Mexican immigration to have me briefly detained for "smuggling." (He had the officials laughing for hours.) He and Edra throw epic parties; for Tim's fiftieth birthday, they turned their golf course into a living timeline, installing a 50s diner on their driving range, complete with classic cars. They set up similar stations for the 60s, 70s, 80s, and 90s and finished with a "time tunnel" that ushered guests to a spaceship that released a giant birthday cake. Former president Gerald Ford sent birthday wishes via video. For Edra's fiftieth, Tim hired an entire cast of Munchkins from a *Wizard of Oz* production and had Paul Anka[2] sing a personalized version of "My Way."

---

[2]*Paul Anka:* Songwriter and pop singer Anka (b. 1941) wrote the lyrics to "My Way," a song popularized by Frank Sinatra whose refrain, "I did it my way," is the perfect theme for a self-made man.

For one of their wedding anniversaries, Tim set up dinner for two by their pool. On the table, he placed a crystal bowl filled with fifty raw carrots. When Edra asked why they were there, Tim said, "Count them," and underneath she found a fifty-carat diamond necklace.

Still, Tim likes to portray himself as a kind of Everyman's Billionaire — just a poor preacher's son who made good in the timber trade. He grew up in Roseburg, Oregon, a small logging town 185 miles south of Portland. His father couldn't support the family because of a heart condition so they lived off welfare. Tim also helped out by working the night shift at a local sawmill.

"I was born with a rusty spoon in my mouth," he says. (He still has an aversion to Spam, which his family got for free and ate regularly.)

Growing up poor, Tim developed something of a chip on his shoulder. In junior high school, students waited in two lines in the cafeteria: the "paying" line or the "free-lunch" line for welfare kids. Tim had to wait in the free line and was constantly badgered by other kids.

"They'd point at me and yell 'welfare kid, welfare kid!,'" he says. "Boy, that really got me seething."

Tim got his first lesson in success from his high school shop teacher.

"The guy's name was Wally Eichler. Everyone called him Rough Cut Wally, because he was one of these real tough, no-nonsense guys. On the first day of class, Rough Cut Wally said to us, 'I don't give a damn if you learn a single thing in this class. But just remember that you can do anything you want in this country if you want to. You can succeed or fail, but it's up to you. You're entirely responsible.'" Blixseth took the advice to heart and made a perfectly crafted tin box that he still keeps in his dressing room to remind him of Wally.

Despite being a preacher's son, Blixseth placed little faith in religion. His parents joined a Christian cult led by a man who claimed that the group's 167 members would be the only people admitted to heaven.

"It seemed ridiculous to me that only these 167 people would get into heaven," Tim says. "Why only those 167 people?"

At the age of fifteen, Blixseth decided to go into business. He was combing the classified ads in the local paper one day and noticed an ad for three donkeys that were being sold for $25 each. He took his savings, bought the donkeys, and brought them home. The next day, he put an ad in the paper offering "three pack mules" for $75 each. They sold instantly.

"I wasn't selling 'donkeys.' I was selling 'pack mules,'" he says. "That's how I learned about marketing."

Soon after, he saw an ad in the paper for a 360-acre piece of timber property for $90,000. Tim barely had $1,000 to his name. Yet he bought the property with $1,000 down and a promise to pay the rest within a week.

"The realtor said to me, 'Kid, I'm going to take your money to teach you a lesson. If you don't pay me the rest of the $90,000 within a week, I'm going to keep your $1,000.'"

Yet Tim found a timber company to buy the property a week later for $140,000, giving him an instant profit of $50,000.

"My dad assumed I must have done something illegal since it was so much money," he said. "He was going to turn me in to the police until I explained the whole thing."

Blixseth launched a career as a timberland trader. He combed through land records in remote towns in the Pacific Northwest, bought overlooked properties, and flipped them to logging companies or larger landowners. Later, he branched out into logging and milling. By the time he was thirty, he was earning $1 million a month. He met Edra, a successful hotelier, married, bought a large home, and started raising their four kids (all from previous marriages).

Then, in the early 1980s, it all came crashing down. Timber prices   35
plunged by more than 80 percent. Blixseth was highly leveraged and was forced to declare bankruptcy. He lost his business, sold the house, and struggled for months to pay the light bills.

"It was the best thing that ever happened to me," he says. "I learned to never again have any debt. Debt is the thing that kills you."

To this day, Blixseth doesn't have a single mortgage on his homes. The bankruptcy, and his poor childhood, are also the main reasons Tim likes buying land — and always with cash. "No one can take it away from me. It's permanent."

After bankruptcy, Blixseth went back to land trading and eventually built up enough cash to team up with a partner to form Crown-Pacific, a timber and paper company. He sold his stake in 1990 for more than $20 million and retired at age 40.

"I thought $20 million was all I could ever need for the rest of my life," he says.

He bought a Citation jet and a home in Sun River, Oregon. He kicked   40
back and returned to his first love — singing and songwriting. In the 1970s, Blixseth had become a minor pop sensation with a song called "I Hope to Find Your Rainbow" while another one of his tunes, "Coyote Ugly," became a cult college hit.

After a few months, Tim realized he wasn't cut out for retirement. He needed projects, deals, and problems to solve.

"He was miserable," Edra recalls. "So were we."

In 1991, Tim bought 164,000 acres of land in Montana from another timber company and orchestrated a complex swap with the federal government. In exchange for 37,000 acres of environmentally sensitive land (it was a breeding area for elk and grizzly bears), the government granted Tim's company about 13,500 acres of more accessible and more commercially attractive land on the northwest corner of Yellowstone National Park, near Big Sky resort. Because of its size and importance, the deal required special approval from Congress. (Tim is a generous donor to Republican and Democratic politicians.)

Initially, Tim and Edra planned to use the property for a private family ranch. But one day, they were having a picnic on the property and Tim looked up at a nearby mountain slope and said, "Why don't we put a ski lift there?"

"We thought it would be a nice little retreat for our family and friends,"   45
Tim says.

So many friends wanted to join them that they decided to turn it into a
private ski-and-golf community. Thus, the Yellowstone Club was born. The
club has nearly 300 members, each of whom pays $250,000 to join along
with millions of dollars to build or buy a house on the site. Bill Gates is a
member, along with News Corp. president Peter Chernin, Comcast president Steve Burke, and former U.S. vice president Dan Quayle. As the club's
Web site says, "Sometimes you have to pay to play."

When Tim started Yellowstone, resort owners and vacation experts said
he was crazy. People would never pay that much to join a club, especially
since they could already ski and golf on their own in Aspen and other
upscale locales. One friend asked if he also believed in the "tooth fairy."
Hence, Tim's named his new $20 million yacht "Tooth Fairy."

Being rich themselves, Tim and Edra know exactly what other wealthy
people want. Security at the Yellowstone Club is tight and is led by a former
Secret Service agent to President Ford. Members can ski more than sixty
trails without having to wait in lift lines or dodge the hoi polloi. On the golf
course, tee times are unheard-of. Legions of club staff are always on hand to
prewarm the members' ski boots, stock their homes with groceries and
flowers and, in one case, hand-slice special meat for their dogs.

Indeed, the big draw of the Yellowstone Club is the comfort of knowing
that everyone around you is wealthy.

"People can relax and be themselves," Edra says. "They can let their   50
kids run around without worrying about them."

By 2005, however, Tim was getting restless again. He needed a new
project. One day, a Yellowstone member asked him about destination clubs,
in which members pay six-figure annual dues to stay at upscale vacation
homes. Tim and Edra liked the idea so much they decided to create their
own, but on a much grander scale.

Using hundreds of millions of dollars of their own money, they went on
a global shopping spree to find the most exotic and private escapes in the
world. "They had to be places that even the wealthy can't find or afford on
their own," as Tim puts it. "They had to have the wow factor. Or more like
the double wow factor."

They bought a plot of land near St. Andrews, Scotland — the legendary
home of golf — where they're building a golf course ringed by luxury cottages. They bought a thirteenth-century castle outside Paris, restored with
an indoor swimming pool, full-service spa, and chef's kitchen. They scooped
up a plush lodge and trout-fishing lake near Cody, Wyoming, along with
property in the California desert to build a spa. They purchased three beach
retreats — Tamarindo in Mexico, a private island in Turks and Caicos, and a
resort in Tahiti.

To make it easier for guests to get around, Tim threw in two yachts and
a fleet of private jets. And he hired an army of staffers, from wine experts
and chefs to butlers and concierges.

"You might start off taking the jet to St. Andrews for some golf," Tim   55
says. "Then you fly to the French castle for a few days, then do some yacht-
ing around the Mediterranean for a few days before heading back to the
U.S. It's exactly what I would want in a vacation."

Not that he's ever vacationed at his resorts. When I asked Tim and
Edra if they can remember their last nonworking holiday, they pause.

"I think 1999, so seven years ago," Tim says.

"No," Edra says. "We worked during that one."

The Conflicted Elite

For all his wealth, Tim Blixseth hates being labeled "rich." Rich people,
he says, are stuffy, pretentious, and out of touch. Richistanis like to think of
themselves as ordinary people, albeit with extraordinary fortunes. They go
out of their way to appear normal. Richistanis wear polo shirts, casual slacks,
and open-collar dress shirts, forsaking the old uniform of monogrammed
shirts and suits. As one Palm Beacher told me: "Suits are for the people who
work for me." Richistanis describe themselves as "down to earth," even as
they take off in their private Gulfstreams. As the billionaire vulture investor
David Tepper told the *Wall Street Journal* recently, "I'm just a middle-class
dad trapped in a rich man's body."

Blixseth is equally disparaging of the "rich."   60

"I don't like most rich people," he says. "They can be arrogant."

Wealth, he adds, can bring out the worst — or best — in people, making them a more exaggerated version of themselves.

"Money is like a truth serum. It brings out people's true nature. So
if someone's already a jerk, they become more of a jerk after they're
rich."

When I remind him that he's a billionaire, he says: "When people say
that, I think they're talking about someone else. Billion is a number that
seems so far on the horizon it doesn't even sound real to me."

The confusion is common among today's Richistanis. They strive to   65
maintain their middle-class identities. These aren't the yuppie, bourgeois
bohemians that David Brooks brilliantly described in *Bobos in Paradise*;
Richistanis are much wealthier and more extravagant. Blixseth and other
Richistanis have dual personalities, with middle-class values and upper-class
lifestyles.

Every morning (or at least on those mornings when he's home),
Blixseth wakes up early, gets in his Nissan Armada, and drives to the local
Starbucks. He orders his usual café mocha, finds a chair, and sits down to
read the paper. With a private kitchen staff of ten cooks — including an
award-winning German chef — Tim could easily find coffee at home. Yet he
prefers to be around regular people.

"It keeps me sane," he says on a recent morning, sandwiched at
a Starbucks table between a screaming baby and a group of octogenar-
ian retirees.

Tim's split personality is reflected even more clearly in his choice of cars. I ask him one afternoon how many cars he owns. He starts counting, runs out of fingers and says, "I really don't know."

He once walked into a Bentley dealership and bought a $250,000 convertible on impulse. When I notice two gleaming Rolls-Royce Phantoms — one painted in two-tone black and silver and the other blue — parked at the back of his house, I ask him why he needs two. (They each retail for more than $320,000.)

"The two-tone one, that's my restaurant car. You get a better parking space [from the valets]."

At the same time, he recently phased out his family's fleet of Range Rovers for Nissan Armadas. They were, Tim boasts, half the price.

"A great deal," he says. "I paid half as much for a car that's just as good or better than the Range Rovers. Why should I pay more?"

He then offers to show me his favorite car. Bypassing the two Rolls, he walks over to a tiny, 1,600-pound Smart Car, which retails for $20,000 and gets sixty miles per gallon.

"I love it. Sixty miles per gallon, isn't that great?"

At the same time, Blixseth's lifestyle is expanding so quickly he sometimes loses track. One night over dinner, I ask Tim and Edra how many house staff they employ at Porcupine Creek.

"With the maids, security guys, spa staff, kitchen and everything," Tim says, "probably about sixty or seventy."

Edra interrupts. "It's more than that."

"More?" Tim asks.

"It's 105," she says.

"If it's 105 we have a problem," Tim says.

"I just counted yesterday. It's 105."

"Then we have a problem," Tim says, smiling as if it's really not a problem.

Porcupine Creek is one of the most lavish estates in the country. The wooden gates open up onto a Disneyesque fantasy, with flowers, waterfalls, golf greens, and private roads lit with French streetlamps that once lined the Champs Élysées.

A soaring fountain, modeled after Las Vegas's Bellagio, rises in front of the main house, a two-story Mediterranean palace. Inside is a menagerie of eighteenth-century European antiques, oversized fish tanks, mosaics, crystal chandeliers, Asian sculptures, art deco bars, carved-wood ceilings, and giant birdcages.

The Blixseths' bed came from the archbishop of Milan's quarters and has a carved Jesus on one side (Tim's) and a Mary on the other (Edra's). Their walk-in refrigerator is bigger than most New York apartments.

Their house even has its own logo, which adorns the towels in every bathroom and the shirts on every staffer. The Blixseths' dogs are equally jet set: Their shih tzus were named Learjet and G2. (They're planning an upgrade to a G550.)

At the same time, Tim and Edra give away millions each year to philanthropy. And Tim's giving style is unique, to say the least. When he reads about someone in the paper who's suffering or in need, he shows up with gifts and cash. The element of surprise is key, making him a kind of guerrilla philanthropist. In 2004, he read about a jobless, paraplegic man in California who was robbed of everything in his home. Blixseth pulled up the next morning with a truck full of new appliances, computers, and electronic equipment. When he saw Tim standing at the front door, the man thought he was being robbed a second time.

"He peeked out the door and said 'Please go away. I don't have anything left.'" Tim recalls. "Eventually, after we started unloading the refrigerator and air conditioners, he let us in."

Tim also became a big force behind the Habitat for Humanity campaign for Katrina victims. He donated $2 million to the effort and got dozens of his wealthy friends and members to contribute as well. He also wrote a song, called "Heart of America," which was later recorded to help raise Katrina funds.

Around Palm Springs, Tim is known for handing out $20 bills to valets, 90 busboys, and Starbucks baristas. One day when we were in Mexico, he handed a $100 tip to the driver, who stared at Tim like he was crazy. When I asked him if he worried that the money would be wasted, Tim responded: "I hope he *does* waste it. If that driver takes that money and buys a cold beer, and sits on his porch and drinks that beer, and it's the only moment of real pleasure he has all day, then I've done a good thing. That's worth it to me."

One day, in the summer of 2006, I called Tim and asked how he was doing. "Great," he said. "I think I just made another billion dollars." A large real-estate developer wanted to build on a 4,200-acre piece of land that Tim owned in Southern California, proposing a deal that could eventually net Tim $1 billion.

"It's true what they say — the first billion is the hardest. The second one was pretty easy."

So is losing a billion. At the end of 2006, Tim and Edra decided to divorce. They split their assets in half, through an amicable settlement, and Tim figures he's still worth about $1 billion after the split.

Yet in today's Richistan, divorce isn't the only way to lose a fortune. The increasingly volatile financial markets, while creating huge opportunies, have also created new risks for the wealthy.

Annual Expense Statement Number One°

$50 MILLION NET WORTH	
Mortgages, two homes	$400,000
Insurance	$ 70,000
Utilities	$ 24,000
Real estate taxes	$200,000
House staff and personal assistants	$500,000
Gardening/pools maintenance	$140,000
Charities	$500,000
Restaurant/bars	$ 60,000
Cars	$300,000
Schools	none
Personal beauty/salon/spa	$ 27,000
Clothing	$ 30,000
Air charters	$350,000
Club memberships	$225,000
Political contributions	$ 61,000

°This and the following two tables show the annual expense reports of three "Richistani" families.

Annual Expense Statement Number Two

$80 MILLION NET WORTH	
Mortgage	$ 64,000
Real estate taxes	$ 32,000
Insurance	$ 31,000
Utilities	$ 31,000
House staff and personal assistants	$315,000
Gardening/pools maintenance	$146,000
Home furnishing and appliances	$ 93,000
Household supplies	$ 43,500
Charity, political contributions	$ 11,000
Cars	$ 8,500
Schools	$ 34,000
Travel	$500,000

Annual Expense Statement Number Three

$1.2 BILLION NET WORTH	
Mortgages	none
Real estate taxes (per year)	$ 900,000
Insurance	$ 500,000
Utilities	$ 700,000
House staff and personal assistants	$ 2,200,000
Annual maintenance of real estate (ex. staff listed above)	$ 900,000
Charity, philanthropic events	$ 3,000,000
Restaurant/bars	$ 250,000
Cars	$ 1,000,000
Children's schools	none
Personal beauty/salon/spa (includes $80,000 for massage)	$ 200,000
Clothing	$ 300,000
Air charters/private jet	$ 3,000,000
Club memberships	$ 500,000
Political contributions	$ 100,000
Yacht(s)(purchased new boat last year) ($1,500,000 for salaries alone)	$20,000,000
Entertaining (at house)	$ 2,000,000

Engaging the Text

1. Why did Tim Blixseth succeed? What were his defining business strategies, and what seem to be his key personal characteristics? How much of his formula for success do you think can be emulated?

2. Work with classmates to list or underline all the numbers in "Living It" — dollars, acres, and gas mileage, for example. What is the point of including so much numerical detail?

3. Identify several details in "Living It" that reveal Blixseth's "ordinary" side — his Nissan Armada, for example. Why do you think the author includes such details? How do you interpret this side of Blixseth?

4. Based on this short segment from Robert Frank's *Richistan*, what are the key features of a "Richistani," and how do such people differ from "Old Money" (para. 13)? Discuss how many distinct classes exist in the United States and what they should be called.

5. What is Frank's tone in writing about Blixseth — admiring, critical, neutral, bemused? Point to specific features of "Living It" to support your observations. Then discuss with classmates your own view of Blixseth and your reactions to the descriptions of his wealth and lifestyle. Would you want to live like Blixseth? Like his wife Edra?

Exploring Connections

6. Compare Blixseth to "Ragged Dick" (p. 258), taking into account their aspirations, the keys to their success, their level of achievement, and their connection to the society around them.

7. Look ahead to the portrait of Harold S. Browning in Gregory Mantsios's "Class in America—2006" (p. 304). Do Blixseth and Browning belong to the same social class, or is Blixseth in another world?

8. What do donkeys, trees, and land mean to Blixseth? How about cars, planes, and boats? Look ahead to the excerpt from the graphic novel *As the World Burns* on page 715; write or draw a brief conversation between Blixseth and any of the characters or animals created by Derrick Jensen and Stephanie McMillan.

Extending the Critical Context

9. The man in the photo *Affluence* (p. 253) is not Blixseth, but Blixseth clearly has the credentials to represent affluence. How might Blixseth prefer to be pictured for such a portrait? How would you picture him? Using specific details from the text, create a drawing or collage of "Tim Blixseth, Richistani."

10. F. Scott Fitzgerald famously observed that "there are no second acts in American life," but Tim Blixseth's life seems to have had several acts: he has repeatedly made and lost huge fortunes, and in the aftermath of a divorce described as "amicable," his ex-wife Edra held an ostentatious party featuring Blixseth piñatas for guests to smash. Research Blixseth's and Edra's current circumstances, beginning with this article from the *New York Times*: "Checkmate at the Yellowstone Club—Bankruptcies Jolt a Ski Haven for the Superrich" (Amy Wallace, June 14, 2009, Sunday Business section, pp. 1, 6–7).

Serving in Florida

Barbara Ehrenreich

If you're considering dropping out of college and settling into a comfy minimum-wage job (or two), please read this excerpt first. As a journalist preparing to write about working-class life, Barbara Ehrenreich decided to take a series of unglamorous jobs—waitressing, housecleaning, retail sales—and to live on the meager wages these jobs paid. In this narrative, Ehrenreich describes trying to make ends meet by adding a second waitressing job (at "Jerry's") to her eight-hour shift at "The Hearthside," having dis-

covered that $2.43 an hour plus tips doesn't add up as fast as her rent and other bills. The full account of Ehrenreich's "plunge into poverty" may be found in the New York Times best-seller Nickel and Dimed: On (Not) Getting By in America (2001). Ehrenreich (b. 1941) has published articles in many of America's leading magazines and newspapers and has authored more than a dozen books. Recent works include Bait and Switch: The (Futile) Pursuit of the American Dream (2005), Dancing in the Streets: A History of Collective Joy (2007), and This Land Is Their Land: Reports from a Divided Nation (2008).

Picture a fat person's hell, and I don't mean a place with no food. Instead there is everything you might eat if eating had no bodily consequences — the cheese fries, the chicken-fried steaks, the fudge-laden desserts — only here every bite must be paid for, one way or another, in human discomfort. The kitchen is a cavern, a stomach leading to the lower intestine that is the garbage and dishwashing area, from which issue bizarre smells combining the edible and the offal: creamy carrion, pizza barf, and that unique and enigmatic Jerry's[1] scent, citrus fart. The floor is slick with spills, forcing us to walk through the kitchen with tiny steps, like Susan McDougal in leg irons.[2] Sinks everywhere are clogged with scraps of lettuce, decomposing lemon wedges, water-logged toast crusts. Put your hand down on any counter and you risk being stuck to it by the film of ancient syrup spills, and this is unfortunate because hands are utensils here, used for scooping up lettuce onto the salad plates, lifting out pie slices, and even moving hash browns from one plate to another. The regulation poster in the single unisex rest room admonishes us to wash our hands thoroughly, and even offers instructions for doing so, but there is always some vital substance missing — soap, paper towels, toilet paper — and I never found all three at once. You learn to stuff your pockets with napkins before going in there, and too bad about the customers, who must eat, although they don't realize it, almost literally out of our hands.

The break room summarizes the whole situation: there is none, because there are no breaks at Jerry's. For six to eight hours in a row, you never sit except to pee. Actually, there are three folding chairs at a table immediately adjacent to the bathroom, but hardly anyone ever sits in this, the very rectum of the gastroarchitectural system. Rather, the function of the peri-toilet area is to house the ashtrays in which servers and dishwashers leave their cigarettes burning at all times, like votive candles, so they don't have to

---

[1]*Jerry's:* Not the real name of the restaurant where Ehrenreich worked; the restaurant was part of a "well-known national chain."

[2]*Susan McDougal in leg irons:* McDougal refused to testify against President Bill Clinton and Hillary Clinton before the Whitewater grand jury in 1996; she spent almost twenty-two months in various prisons and eventually received a presidential pardon in 2001.

waste time lighting up again when they dash back here for a puff. Almost everyone smokes as if their pulmonary well-being depended on it — the multinational mélange of cooks; the dishwashers, who are all Czechs here; the servers, who are American natives — creating an atmosphere in which oxygen is only an occasional pollutant. My first morning at Jerry's, when the hypoglycemic shakes set in, I complain to one of my fellow servers that I don't understand how she can go so long without food. "Well, I don't understand how *you* can go so long without a cigarette," she responds in a tone of reproach. Because work is what you do for others; smoking is what you do for yourself. I don't know why the antismoking crusaders have never grasped the element of defiant self-nurturance that makes the habit so endearing to its victims — as if, in the American workplace, the only thing people have to call their own is the tumors they are nourishing and the spare moments they devote to feeding them.

Now, the Industrial Revolution is not an easy transition, especially, in my experience, when you have to zip through it in just a couple of days. I have gone from craft work straight into the factory, from the air-conditioned morgue of the Hearthside[3] directly into the flames. Customers arrive in human waves, sometimes disgorged fifty at a time from their tour buses, puckish and whiny. Instead of two "girls" on the floor at once, there can be as many as six of us running around in our brilliant pink-and-orange Hawaiian shirts. Conversations, either with customers or with fellow employees, seldom last more than twenty seconds at a time. On my first day, in fact, I am hurt by my sister servers' coldness. My mentor for the day is a supremely competent, emotionally uninflected twenty-three-year-old, and the others, who gossip a little among themselves about the real reason someone is out sick today and the size of the bail bond someone else has had to pay, ignore me completely. On my second day, I find out why. "Well, it's good to see *you* again," one of them says in greeting. "Hardly anyone comes back after the first day." I feel powerfully vindicated — a survivor — but it would take a long time, probably months, before I could hope to be accepted into this sorority.

I start out with the beautiful, heroic idea of handling the two jobs at once, and for two days I almost do it: working the breakfast/lunch shift at Jerry's from 8:00 till 2:00, arriving at the Hearthside a few minutes late, at 2:10, and attempting to hold out until 10:00. In the few minutes I have between jobs, I pick up a spicy chicken sandwich at the Wendy's drive-through window, gobble it down in the car, and change from khaki slacks to black, from Hawaiian to rust-colored polo. There is a problem, though. When, during the 3:00–4:00 o'clock dead time, I finally sit down to wrap silver, my flesh seems to bond to the seat. I try to refuel with a purloined cup of clam chowder, as I've seen Gail and Joan do dozens of times, but Stu[4]

---

[3]*Hearthside:* The other restaurant where Ehrenreich worked.

[4]*Gail, Joan, Stu:* Waitress, hostess, and assistant manager at the Hearthside restaurant. Phillip, mentioned in the subsequent paragraph, is the top manager.

catches me and hisses "No *eating!*" although there's not a customer around to be offended by the sight of food making contact with a server's lips. So I tell Gail I'm going to quit, and she hugs me and says she might just follow me to Jerry's herself.

But the chances of this are minuscule. She has left the flophouse 5 and her annoying roommate and is back to living in her truck. But, guess what, she reports to me excitedly later that evening, Phillip has given her permission to park overnight in the hotel parking lot, as long as she keeps out of sight, and the parking lot should be totally safe since it's patrolled by a hotel security guard! With the Hearthside offering benefits like that, how could anyone think of leaving? This must be Phillip's theory, anyway. He accepts my resignation with a shrug, his main concern being that I return my two polo shirts and aprons.

Gail would have triumphed at Jerry's, I'm sure, but for me it's a crash course in exhaustion management. Years ago, the kindly fry cook who trained me to waitress at a Los Angeles truck stop used to say: Never make an unnecessary trip; if you don't have to walk fast, walk slow; if you don't have to walk, stand. But at Jerry's the effort of distinguishing necessary from unnecessary and urgent from whenever would itself be too much of an energy drain. The only thing to do is to treat each shift as a one-time-only emergency: you've got fifty starving people out there, lying scattered on the battlefield, so get out there and feed them! Forget that you will have to do this again tomorrow, forget that you will have to be alert enough to dodge the drunks on the drive home tonight — just burn, burn, burn! Ideally, at some point you enter what servers call a "rhythm" and psychologists term a "flow state," where signals pass from the sense organs directly to the muscles, bypassing the cerebral cortex, and a Zen-like emptiness sets in. I'm on a 2:00–10:00 P.M. shift now, and a male server from the morning shift tells me about the time he "pulled a triple" — three shifts in a row, all the way around the clock — and then got off and had a drink and met this girl, and maybe he shouldn't tell me this, but they had sex right then and there and it was like *beautiful.*

But there's another capacity of the neuromuscular system, which is pain. I start tossing back drugstore-brand ibuprofens as if they were vitamin C, four before each shift, because an old mouse-related repetitive-stress injury in my upper back has come back to full-spasm strength, thanks to the tray carrying. In my ordinary life, this level of disability might justify a day of ice packs and stretching. Here I comfort myself with the Aleve commercial where the cute blue-collar guy asks: If you quit after working four hours, what would your boss say? And the not-so-cute blue-collar guy, who's lugging a metal beam on his back, answers: He'd fire me, that's what. But fortunately, the commercial tells us, we workers can exert the same kind of authority over our painkillers that our bosses exert over us. If Tylenol doesn't want to work for more than four hours, you just fire its ass and switch to Aleve.

True, I take occasional breaks from this life, going home now and then to catch up on e-mail and for conjugal visits (though I am careful to "pay" for everything I eat here, at $5 for a dinner, which I put in a jar), seeing *The Truman Show*[5] with friends and letting them buy my ticket. And I still have those what-am-I-doing-here moments at work, when I get so homesick for the printed word that I obsessively reread the six-page menu. But as the days go by, my old life is beginning to look exceedingly strange. The e-mails and phone messages addressed to my former self come from a distant race of people with exotic concerns and far too much time on their hands. The neighborly market I used to cruise for produce now looks forbiddingly like a Manhattan yuppie emporium. And when I sit down one morning in my real home to pay bills from my past life, I am dazzled by the two- and three-figure sums owed to outfits like Club Body Tech and Amazon.com.

Management at Jerry's is generally calmer and more "professional" than at the Hearthside, with two exceptions. One is Joy, a plump, blowsy woman in her early thirties who once kindly devoted several minutes of her time to instructing me in the correct one-handed method of tray carrying but whose moods change disconcertingly from shift to shift and even within one. The other is B.J., aka B.J. the Bitch, whose contribution is to stand by the kitchen counter and yell, "Nita, your order's up, move it!" or "Barbara, didn't you see you've got another table out there? Come *on*, girl!" Among other things, she is hated for having replaced the whipped cream squirt cans with big plastic whipped-cream-filled baggies that have to be squeezed with both hands — because, reportedly, she saw or thought she saw employees trying to inhale the propellant gas from the squirt cans, in the hope that it might be nitrous oxide. On my third night, she pulls me aside abruptly and brings her face so close that it looks like she's planning to butt me with her forehead. But instead of saying "You're fired," she says, "You're doing fine." The only trouble is I'm spending time chatting with customers: "That's how they're getting you." Furthermore I am letting them "run me," which means harassment by sequential demands: you bring the catsup and they decide they want extra Thousand Island; you bring that and they announce they now need a side of fries, and so on into distraction. Finally she tells me not to take her wrong. She tries to say things in a nice way, but "you get into a mode, you know, because everything has to move so fast."[6]

I mumble thanks for the advice, feeling like I've just been stripped naked 10 by the crazed enforcer of some ancient sumptuary law:[7] No chatting for *you*, girl. No fancy service ethic allowed for the serfs. Chatting with customers is for the good-looking young college-educated servers in the downtown carpaccio and ceviche joints, the kids who can make $70–$100 a night. What had I

---

[5]*The Truman Show*: 1998 film (directed by Peter Weir and starring Jim Carrey) about a man who discovers his whole life is actually a TV show.

[6]In *Workers in a Lean World: Unions in the International Economy* (Verso, 1997), Kim Moody cites studies finding an increase in stress-related workplace injuries and illness between the mid-1980s and the early 1990s. He argues that rising stress levels reflect a new system of "management by stress" in which workers in a variety of industries are being squeezed to extract maximum productivity, to the detriment of their health. [Ehrenreich's note.]

[7]*sumptuary laws*: Laws which regulate personal behavior on moral or religious grounds.

been thinking? My job is to move orders from tables to kitchen and then trays from kitchen to tables. Customers are in fact the major obstacle to the smooth transformation of information into food and food into money — they are, in short, the enemy. And the painful thing is that I'm beginning to see it this way myself. There are the traditional asshole types — frat boys who down multiple Buds and then make a fuss because the steaks are so emaciated and the fries so sparse — as well as the variously impaired — due to age, diabetes, or literacy issues — who require patient nutritional counseling. The worst, for some reason, are the Visible Christians — like the ten-person table, all jolly and sanctified after Sunday night service, who run me mercilessly and then leave me $1 on a $92 bill. Or the guy with the crucifixion T-shirt (SOMEONE TO LOOK UP TO) who complains that his baked potato is too hard and his iced tea too icy (I cheerfully fix both) and leaves no tip at all. As a general rule, people wearing crosses or WWJD? ("What Would Jesus Do?") buttons look at us disapprovingly no matter what we do, as if they were confusing waitressing with Mary Magdalene's original profession.

I make friends, over time, with the other "girls" who work my shift: Nita, the tattooed twenty-something who taunts us by going around saying brightly, "Have we started making money yet?" Ellen, whose teenage son cooks on the graveyard shift and who once managed a restaurant in Massachusetts but won't try out for management here because she prefers being a "common worker" and not "ordering people around." Easygoing fiftyish Lucy, with the raucous laugh, who limps toward the end of the shift because of something that has gone wrong with her leg, the exact nature of which cannot be determined without health insurance. We talk about the usual girl things — men, children, and the sinister allure of Jerry's chocolate peanut-butter cream pie — though no one, I notice, ever brings up anything potentially expensive, like shopping or movies. As at the Hearthside, the only recreation ever referred to is partying, which requires little more than some beer, a joint, and a few close friends. Still, no one is homeless, or cops to it anyway, thanks usually to a working husband or boyfriend. All in all, we form a reliable mutual-support group: if one of us is feeling sick or overwhelmed, another one will "bev" a table or even carry trays for her. If one of us is off sneaking a cigarette or a pee, the others will do their best to conceal her absence from the enforcers of corporate rationality.[8]

---

[8]Until April 1998, there was no federally mandated right to bathroom breaks. According to Marc Linder and Ingrid Nygaard, authors of *Void Where Prohibited: Rest Breaks and the Right to Urinate on Company Time* (Cornell University Press, 1997), "The right to rest and void at work is not high on the list of social or political causes supported by professional or executive employees, who enjoy personal workplace liberties that millions of factory workers can only dream about.... While we were dismayed to discover that workers lacked an acknowledged right to void at work, [the workers] were amazed by outsiders' naïve belief that their employers would permit them to perform this basic bodily function when necessary.... A factory worker, not allowed a break for six-hour stretches, voided into pads worn inside her uniform; and a kindergarten teacher in a school without aides had to take all twenty children with her to the bathroom and line them up outside the stall door while she voided." [Ehrenreich's note]

But my saving human connection — my oxytocin receptor, as it were — is George, the nineteen-year-old Czech dishwasher who has been in this country exactly one week. We get talking when he asks me, tortuously, how much cigarettes cost at Jerry's. I do my best to explain that they cost over a dollar more here than at a regular store and suggest that he just take one from the half-filled packs that are always lying around on the break table. But that would be unthinkable. Except for the one tiny earring signaling his allegiance to some vaguely alternative point of view, George is a perfect straight arrow — crew-cut, hardworking, and hungry for eye contact. "Czech Republic," I ask, "or Slovakia?" and he seems delighted that I know the difference. "Vaclav Havel," I try, "Velvet Revolution, Frank Zappa?" "Yes, yes, 1989," he says, and I realize that for him this is already history.

My project is to teach George English. "How are you today, George?" I say at the start of each shift. "I am good, and how are you today, Barbara?" I learn that he is not paid by Jerry's but by the "agent" who shipped him over — $5 an hour, with the agent getting the dollar or so difference between that and what Jerry's pays dishwashers. I learn also that he shares an apartment with a crowd of other Czech "dishers," as he calls them, and that he cannot sleep until one of them goes off for his shift, leaving a vacant bed. We are having one of our ESL sessions late one afternoon when B.J. catches us at it and orders "Joseph" to take up the rubber mats on the floor near the dishwashing sinks and mop underneath. "I thought your name was George," I say loud enough for B.J. to hear as she strides off back to the counter. Is she embarrassed? Maybe a little, because she greets me back at the counter with "George, Joseph — there are so many of them!" I say nothing, neither nodding nor smiling, and for this I am punished later, when I think I am ready to go and she announces that I need to roll fifty more sets of silverware, and isn't it time I mixed up a fresh four-gallon batch of blue-cheese dressing? May you grow old in this place, B.J., is the curse I beam out at her when I am finally permitted to leave. May the syrup spills glue your feet to the floor.

I make the decision to move closer to Key West. First, because of the drive. Second and third, also because of the drive: gas is eating up $4–$5 a day, and although Jerry's is as high-volume as you can get, the tips average only 10 percent, and not just for a newbie like me. Between the base pay of $2.15 an hour and the obligation to share tips with the busboys and dishwashers, we're averaging only about $7.50 an hour. Then there is the $30 I had to spend on the regulation tan slacks worn by Jerry's servers — a setback it could take weeks to absorb. (I had combed the town's two downscale department stores hoping for something cheaper but decided in the end that these marked-down Dockers, originally $49, were more likely to survive a daily washing.) Of my fellow servers, everyone who lacks a working husband or boyfriend seems to have a second job: Nita does something at a computer eight hours a day; another welds. Without the forty-five-minute commute, I can picture myself working two jobs and still having the time to shower between them.

So I take the $500 deposit I have coming from my landlord, the $400 I   15
have earned toward the next month's rent, plus the $200 reserved for emergencies, and use the $1,100 to pay the rent and deposit on trailer number 46 in the Overseas Trailer Park, a mile from the cluster of budget hotels that constitute Key West's version of an industrial park. Number 46 is about eight feet in width and shaped like a barbell inside, with a narrow region — because of the sink and the stove — separating the bedroom from what might optimistically be called the "living" area, with its two-person table and half-sized couch. The bathroom is so small my knees rub against the shower stall when I sit on the toilet, and you can't just leap out of the bed, you have to climb down to the foot of it in order to find a patch of floor space to stand on. Outside, I am within a few yards of a liquor store, a bar that advertises "free beer tomorrow," a convenience store, and a Burger King — but no supermarket or, alas, Laundromat. By reputation, the Overseas park is a nest of crime and crack, and I am hoping at least for some vibrant multicultural street life. But desolation rules night and day, except for a thin stream of pedestrians heading for their jobs at the Sheraton or the 7-Eleven. There are not exactly people here but what amounts to canned labor, being preserved between shifts from the heat.

In line with my reduced living conditions, a new form of ugliness arises at Jerry's. First we are confronted — via an announcement on the computers through which we input orders — with the new rule that the hotel bar, the Driftwood, is henceforth off-limits to restaurant employees. The culprit, I learn through the grapevine, is the ultraefficient twenty-three-year-old who trained me — another trailer home dweller and a mother of three. Something had set her off one morning, so she slipped out for a nip and returned to the floor impaired. The restriction mostly hurts Ellen, whose habit it is to free her hair from its rubber band and drop by the Driftwood for a couple of Zins[9] before heading home at the end of her shift, but all of us feel the chill. Then the next day, when I go for straws, I find the dry-storage room locked. It's never been locked before; we go in and out of it all day — for napkins, jelly containers, Styrofoam cups for takeout. Vic, the portly assistant manager who opens it for me, explains that he caught one of the dishwashers attempting to steal something and, unfortunately, the miscreant will be with us until a replacement can be found — hence the locked door. I neglect to ask what he had been trying to steal but Vic tells me who he is — the kid with the buzz cut and the earring, you know, he's back there right now.

I wish I could say I rushed back and confronted George to get his side of the story. I wish I could say I stood up to Vic and insisted that George be given a translator and allowed to defend himself or announced that I'd find a lawyer who'd handle the case pro bono.[10] At the very least I should have testified as to the kid's honesty. The mystery to me is that there's not much worth stealing in the dry-storage room, at least not in any fenceable quantity: "Is Gyorgi here, and am having 200 — maybe 250 — catsup packets. What do you say?" My guess is that he had taken — if he had taken anything at all — some Saltines or a can of cherry pie mix and that the motive for taking it was hunger.

So why didn't I intervene? Certainly not because I was held back by the kind of moral paralysis that can mask as journalistic objectivity. On the contrary, something new — something loathsome and servile — had infected me, along with the kitchen odors that I could still sniff on my bra when I finally undressed at night. In real life I am moderately brave, but plenty of brave people shed their courage in POW camps, and maybe something similar goes on in the infinitely more congenial milieu of the low-wage American workplace. Maybe, in a month or two more at Jerry's, I might have regained my crusading spirit. Then again, in a month or two I might have turned into a different person altogether — say, the kind of person who would have turned George in.

But this is not something I was slated to find out. When my month-long plunge into poverty was almost over, I finally landed my dream job — housekeeping. I did this by walking into the personnel office of the only place I figured I might have some credibility, the hotel attached to Jerry's, and confiding urgently that I had to have a second job if I was to pay my rent and, no, it couldn't be front-desk clerk. "All *right*," the personnel lady fairly spits, "so it's *housekeeping*," and marches me back to meet Millie, the housekeeping manager, a tiny, frenetic Hispanic woman who greets me as

[9]*Zins:* Glasses of zinfandel wine.
[10]*pro bono:* Free of charge.

"babe" and hands me a pamphlet emphasizing the need for a positive attitude. The pay is $6.10 an hour and the hours are nine in the morning till "whenever," which I am hoping can be defined as a little before two. I don't have to ask about health insurance once I meet Carlotta, the middle-aged African American woman who will be training me. Carlie, as she tells me to call her, is missing all of her top front teeth.

On that first day of housekeeping and last day — although I don't yet   20
know it's the last — of my life as a low-wage worker in Key West, Carlie is in a foul mood. We have been given nineteen rooms to clean, most of them "checkouts," as opposed to "stay-overs," and requiring the whole enchilada of bed stripping, vacuuming, and bathroom scrubbing. When one of the rooms that had been listed as a stay-over turns out to be a checkout, she calls Millie to complain, but of course to no avail. "So make up the motherfucker," she orders me, and I do the beds while she sloshes around the bathroom. For four hours without a break I strip and remake beds, taking about four and a half minutes per queen-sized bed, which I could get down to three if there were any reason to. We try to avoid vacuuming by picking up the larger specks by hand, but often there is nothing to do but drag the monstrous vacuum cleaner — it weighs about thirty pounds — off our cart and try to wrestle it around the floor. Sometimes Carlie hands me the squirt bottle of "Bam" (an acronym for something that begins, ominously, with "butyric" — the rest of it has been worn off the label) and lets me do the bathrooms. No service ethic challenges me here to new heights of performance. I just concentrate on removing the pubic hairs from the bathtubs, or at least the dark ones that I can see.

I had looked forward to the breaking-and-entering aspect of cleaning the stay-overs, the chance to examine the secret physical existence of strangers. But the contents of the rooms are always banal and surprisingly neat — zipped-up shaving kits, shoes lined up against the wall (there are no closets), flyers for snorkeling trips, maybe an empty wine bottle or two. It is the TV that keeps us going, from Jerry to Sally to *Hawaii Five-O* and then on to the soaps. If there's something especially arresting, like "Won't Take No for an Answer" on Jerry, we sit down on the edge of a bed and giggle for a moment, as if this were a pajama party instead of a terminally dead-end job. The soaps are the best, and Carlie turns the volume up full blast so she won't miss anything from the bathroom or while the vacuum is on. In Room 503, Marcia confronts Jeff about Lauren. In 505, Lauren taunts poor cheated-on Marcia. In 511, Helen offers Amanda $10,000 to stop seeing Eric, prompting Carlie to emerge from the bathroom to study Amanda's troubled face. "You take it, girl," she advises. "I would for sure."

The tourists' rooms that we clean and, beyond them, the far more expensively appointed interiors in the soaps begin after a while to merge. We have entered a better world — a world of comfort where every day is a day off, waiting to be filled with sexual intrigue. We are only gate-crashers in this fantasy, however, forced to pay for our presence with backaches and perpetual thirst.

The mirrors, and there are far too many of them in hotel rooms, contain the kind of person you would normally find pushing a shopping cart down a city street — bedraggled, dressed in a damp hotel polo shirt two sizes too large, and with sweat dribbling down her chin like drool. I am enormously relieved when Carlie announces a half-hour meal break, but my appetite fades when I see that the bag of hot dog rolls she has been carrying around on our cart is not trash salvaged from a checkout but what she has brought for her lunch.

Between the TV and the fact that I'm in no position, as a first dayer, to launch new topics of conversation, I don't learn much about Carlie except that she hurts, and in more than one way. She moves slowly about her work, muttering something about joint pain, and this is probably going to doom her, since the young immigrant housekeepers — Polish and Salvadoran — like to polish off their rooms by two in the afternoon, while she drags the work out till six. It doesn't make any sense to hurry, she observes, when you're being paid by the hour. Already, management has brought in a woman to do what sounds like time-motion studies and there's talk about switching to paying by the room.[11] She broods, too, about all the little evidences of disrespect that come her way, and not only from management. "They don't care about us," she tells me of the hotel guests; in fact, they don't notice us at all unless something gets stolen from a room — "then they're all over you." We're eating our lunch side by side in the break room when a white guy in a maintenance uniform walks by and Carlie calls out, "Hey you," in a friendly way, "what's your name?"

"Peter Pan," he says, his back already to us.

"That wasn't funny," Carlie says, turning to me. "That was no kind of answer. Why did he have to be funny like that?" I venture that he has an attitude, and she nods as if that were an acute diagnosis. "Yeah, he got a attitude all right."   25

"Maybe he's a having a bad day," I elaborate, not because I feel any obligation to defend the white race but because her face is so twisted with hurt.

When I request permission to leave at about 3:30, another housekeeper warns me that no one has so far succeeded in combining housekeeping with serving at Jerry's: "Some kid did it once for five days, and you're no kid." With that helpful information in mind, I rush back to number 46, down four Advils (the name brand this time), shower, stooping to fit into the stall, and attempt to compose myself for the oncoming shift. So much for what Marx termed the "reproduction of labor power," meaning the things a worker has to do just so she'll be ready to labor again. The only unforeseen obstacle to the smooth transition from job to job is that my tan Jerry's slacks, which had

---

[11]A few weeks after I left, I heard ads on the radio for housekeeping jobs at this hotel at the amazing rate of "up to $9 an hour." When I inquired, I found out that the hotel had indeed started paying by the room, and I suspect that Carlie, if she lasted, was still making the equivalent of $6 an hour or quite a bit less. [Ehrenreich's note]

looked reasonably clean by 40-watt bulb last night when I hand washed my Hawaiian shirt, prove by daylight to be mottled with catsup and ranch-dressing stains. I spend most of my hour-long break between jobs attempting to remove the edible portions of the slacks with a sponge and then drying them over the hood of my car in the sun.

I can do this two-job thing, is my theory, if I can drink enough caffeine and avoid getting distracted by George's ever more obvious suffering.[12] The first few days after the alleged theft, he seemed not to understand the trouble he was in, and our chirpy little conversations had continued. But the last couple of shifts he's been listless and unshaven, and tonight he looks like the ghost we all know him to be, with dark half-moons hanging from his eyes. At one point, when I am briefly immobilized by the task of filling little paper cups with sour cream for baked potatoes, he comes over and looks as if he'd like to explore the limits of our shared vocabulary, but I am called to the floor for a table. I resolve to give him all my tips that night, and to hell with the experiment in low-wage money management. At eight, Ellen and I grab a snack together standing at the mephitic end of the kitchen counter, but I can only manage two or three mozzarella sticks, and lunch had been a mere handful of McNuggets. I am not tired at all, I assure myself, though it may be that there is simply no more "I" left to do the tiredness monitoring. What I would see if I were more alert to the situation is that the forces of destruction are already massing against me. There is only one cook on duty, a young man named Jesus ("Hay-Sue," that is), and he is new to the job. And there is Joy, who shows up to take over in the middle of the shift dressed in high heels and a long, clingy white dress and fuming as if she'd just been stood up in some cocktail bar.

Then it comes, the perfect storm. Four of my tables fill up at once. Four tables is nothing for me now, but only so long as they are obligingly staggered. As I bev table 27, tables 25, 28, and 24 are watching enviously. As I bev 25, 24 glowers because their bevs haven't even been ordered. Twenty-eight is four yuppyish types, meaning everything on the side and agonizing instructions as to the chicken Caesars. Twenty-five is a middle-aged black couple who complain, with some justice, that the iced tea isn't fresh and the tabletop is sticky. But table 24 is the meteorological event of the century: ten British tourists who seem to have made the decision to absorb the American experience entirely by mouth. Here everyone has at least two drinks — iced tea *and* milk shake, Michelob *and* water (with lemon slice in the water, please) — and a huge, promiscuous orgy of breakfast specials, mozz sticks, chicken strips, quesadillas, burgers with cheese

---

[12]In 1996 the number of persons holding two or more jobs averaged 7.8 million, or 6.2 percent of the workforce. It was about the same rate for men and for women (6.1 versus 6.2). About two-thirds of multiple jobholders work one job full-time and the other part-time. Only a heroic minority — 4 percent of men and 2 percent of women — work two full-time jobs simultaneously (John F. Stinson Jr., "New Data on Multiple Jobholding Available from the CPS," *Monthly Labor Review,* March 1997). [Ehrenreich's note]

and without, sides of hash browns with cheddar, with onions, with gravy, seasoned fries, plain fries, banana splits. Poor Jesus! Poor me! Because when I arrive with their first tray of food — after three prior trips just to refill bevs — Princess Di refuses to eat her chicken strips with her pancake and sausage special since, as she now reveals, the strips were meant to be an appetizer. Maybe the others would have accepted their meals, but Di, who is deep into her third Michelob, insists that everything else go back while they work on their starters. Meanwhile, the yuppies are waving me down for more decaf and the black couple looks ready to summon the NAACP.

Much of what happens next is lost in the fog of war. Jesus starts going 30
under. The little printer in front of him is spewing out orders faster than he can rip them off, much less produce the meals. A menacing restlessness rises from the tables, all of which are full. Even the invincible Ellen is ashen from stress. I take table 24 their reheated main courses, which they immediately reject as either too cold or fossilized by the microwave. When I return to the kitchen with their trays (three trays in three trips) Joy confronts me with arms akimbo: "What *is* this?" She means the food — the plates of rejected pancakes, hash browns in assorted flavors, toasts, burgers, sausages, eggs. "Uh, scrambled with cheddar," I try, "and that's — " "*No,*" she screams in my face, "is it a traditional, a super-scramble, an eye-opener?" I pretend to study my check for a clue, but entropy has been up to its tricks, not only on the plates but in my head, and I have to admit that the original order is beyond reconstruction. "You don't know an eye-opener from a traditional?" she demands in outrage. All I know, in fact, is that my legs have lost interest in the current venture and have announced their intention to fold. I am saved by a yuppie (mercifully not one of mine) who chooses this moment to charge into the kitchen to bellow that his food is twenty-five minutes late. Joy screams at him to get the hell out of her kitchen, *please,* and then turns on Jesus in a fury, hurling an empty tray across the room for emphasis.

I leave. I don't walk out, I just leave. I don't finish my side work or pick up my credit card tips, if any, at the cash register or, of course, ask Joy's permission to go. And the surprising thing is that you *can* walk out without permission, that the door opens, that the thick tropical night air parts to let me pass, that my car is still parked where I left it. There is no vindication in this exit, no fuck-you surge of relief, just an overwhelming dank sense of failure pressing down on me and the entire parking lot. I had gone into this venture in the spirit of science, to test a mathematical proposition, but somewhere along the line, in the tunnel vision imposed by long shifts and relentless concentration, it became a test of myself, and clearly I have failed. Not only had I flamed out as a housekeeper/server, I had forgotten to give George my tips, and, for reasons perhaps best known to hardworking, generous people like Gail and Ellen, this hurts. I don't cry, but I am in a position to realize, for the first time in many years, that the tear ducts are still there and still capable of doing their job.

When I moved out of the trailer park, I gave the key to number 46 to Gail and arranged for my deposit to be transferred to her. She told me that

Joan was still living in her van and that Stu had been fired from the Hearth-side. According to the most up-to-date rumors, the drug he ordered from the restaurant was crack and he was caught dipping into the cash register to pay for it. I never found out what happened to George.

ENGAGING THE TEXT

1. What's the point of Ehrenreich's experiment? What do you think she was hoping to learn by stepping down the economic ladder, and what can you learn as her reader? Explain why you find her approach more or less effec-tive than one that provides economic data and analysis.

2. Throughout this selection Ehrenreich seeks not merely to narrate facts but to elicit emotional and other responses from her readers. For one or more of the passages listed below, explain what response you think Ehrenreich is after and what *specific* methods she uses to evoke it:

    the opening description of Jerry's (paras. 1–2)

    the description of customers (para. 10)

    George's story (paras. 12–13, 16–18)

    the description of trailer number 46 (para. 15)

    the footnotes throughout the narrative

3. Ehrenreich ordinarily lives much more comfortably than she did as a waitress, and of course she had an escape hatch from her experiment — she would not serve food or clean rooms forever and could have gone back to her usual life if necessary at any time. Explain the effect her status as a "tourist" in working-class culture has on you as a reader.

4. Write a journal entry about your worst job. How did your experience of being "nickeled and dimed" compare with Ehrenreich's? What was the worst aspect of this work experience for you?

EXPLORING CONNECTIONS

5. What, if anything, do you think Gail, Ellen, and George could do to sub-stantially improve their material and economic well-being? What are the greatest barriers they face? What advice might Horatio Alger (p. 258) give them, and how do you think it would be received?

6. Using Gail, Ellen, or George as a rough model for your central character, write a detailed plot summary for a novel that would be the anti–*Ragged Dick*, a story in which someone pursues the American Dream and fails. How plausible is your story line compared to the one Horatio Alger created for Ragged Dick (p. 258)?

EXTENDING THE CRITICAL CONTEXT

7. Ehrenreich made $6.10 per hour as a housekeeper. Working in groups, sketch out a monthly budget based on this salary for (a) an individual, (b) a

single parent with a preteen child, and (c) a family of four in which one adult is ill or has been laid off. Be sure to include money for basics like rent, utilities, food, clothing, transportation, and medical care.

8. Check local want ads and shop windows to identify some of the least promising job prospects in your community. Talk to potential employers and learn as much as you can about such issues as wages, working conditions, hours, drug screening, and healthcare, retirement, or other benefits.

9. Order a meal at whichever restaurant in your community is most like "Jerry's." Study the working conditions in the restaurant, paying special attention to the kinds of problems Ehrenreich faced on her shifts. Write up an informal journal entry from the imagined point of view of a server at the restaurant.

Class in America — 2006

GREGORY MANTSIOS

Which of these gifts might a high school graduate in your family receive — a corsage, a savings bond, or a BMW? The answer indicates your social class, a key factor in American lives that many of us conspire to ignore. The selection below, however, makes it hard to deny class distinctions and their nearly universal influence on our lives. The essay juxtaposes myths and realities: Mantsios (b. 1950) outlines four widely held beliefs about class in the United States and then systematically refutes them with statistical evidence. Even if your eyes are already open to the existence of classes in the United States, some of the numbers the author cites are likely to surprise you. Mantsios is director of the Joseph S. Murphy Institute for Worker Education and Labor Studies at Queens College of the City University of New York; he is editor of A New Labor Movement for the New Century *(1998). The essay reprinted below appeared in* Race, Class, and Gender in the United States: An Integrated Study, *edited by Paula S. Rothenberg (2007).*

People in the United States don't like to talk about class. Or so it would seem. We don't speak about class privileges, or class oppression, or the class nature of society. These terms are not part of our everyday vocabulary, and in most circles they are associated with the language of the rhetorical fringe. Unlike people in most other parts of the world, we shrink from using words

The author wished to thank Mark Major for his assistance in updating this article. From Gregory Mantsios, *Class in America: Myths and Realities.* Copyright © Gregory Mantsios, 2006. Reprinted by permission of the author.

Troubletown

BY LLOYD DANGLE

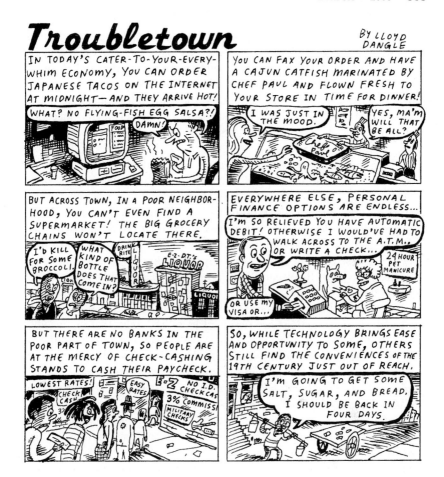

that classify along economic lines or that point to class distinctions: phrases like "working class," "upper class," and "ruling class" are rarely uttered by Americans.

For the most part, avoidance of class-laden vocabulary crosses class boundaries. There are few among the poor who speak of themselves as lower class; instead, they refer to their race, ethnic group, or geographic location. Workers are more likely to identify with their employer, industry, or occupational group than with other workers, or with the working class.[1]

Neither are those at the other end of the economic spectrum likely to use the word "class." In her study of thirty-eight wealthy and socially prominent women, Susan Ostrander asked participants if they considered themselves members of the upper class. One participant responded, "I hate to use the word 'class.' We are responsible, fortunate people, old families, the people who have something."

Another said, "I hate [the term] upper class. It is so non-upper class to use it. I just call it 'all of us,' those who are wellborn."[2]

It is not that Americans, rich or poor, aren't keenly aware of class dif-   5
ferences — those quoted above obviously are; it is that class is not in the
domain of public discourse. Class is not discussed or debated in public
because class identity has been stripped from popular culture. The institutions that shape mass culture and define the parameters of public debate
have avoided class issues. In politics, in primary and secondary education,
and in the mass media, formulating issues in terms of class is unacceptable,
perhaps even un-American.

There are, however, two notable exceptions to this phenomenon. First,
it is acceptable in the United States to talk about "the middle class." Inter-
estingly enough, such references appear to be acceptable precisely because
they mute class differences. References to the middle class by politicians,
for example, are designed to encompass and attract the broadest possible
constituency. Not only do references to the middle class gloss over differences, but these references also avoid any suggestion of conflict or injustice.

This leads us to the second exception to the class-avoidance phenomenon. We are, on occasion, presented with glimpses of the upper class and
the lower class (the language used is "the wealthy" and "the poor"). In the
media, these presentations are designed to satisfy some real or imagined
voyeuristic need of "the ordinary person." As curiosities, the ground-level
view of street life and the inside look at the rich and the famous serve as
unique models, one to avoid and one to aspire to. In either case, the two
models are presented without causal relation to each other: one is not rich
because the other is poor.

Similarly, when social commentators or liberal politicians draw attention to the plight of the poor, they do so in a manner that obscures the class
structure and denies any sense of exploitation. Wealth and poverty are
viewed as one of several natural and inevitable states of being: differences
are only differences. One may even say differences are the American way, a
reflection of American social diversity.

We are left with one of two possibilities: either talking about class and
recognizing class distinctions are not relevant to U.S. society, or we mistak-
enly hold a set of beliefs that obscure the reality of class differences and
their impact on people's lives.

Let us look at four common, albeit contradictory, beliefs about the   10
United States.

Myth 1: The United States is fundamentally a classless society. Class
distinctions are largely irrelevant today, and whatever differences do exist in
economic standing, they are — for the most part — insignificant. Rich or
poor, we are all equal in the eyes of the law, and such basic needs as health
care and education are provided to all regardless of economic standing.

Myth 2: We are, essentially, a middle-class nation. Despite some variations in economic status, most Americans have achieved relative affluence
in what is widely recognized as a consumer society.

Myth 3: We are all getting richer. The American public as a whole is
steadily moving up the economic ladder, and each generation propels itself

to greater economic well-being. Despite some fluctuations, the U.S. position in the global economy has brought previously unknown prosperity to most, if not all, Americans.

Myth 4: Everyone has an equal chance to succeed. Success in the United States requires no more than hard work, sacrifice, and perseverance: "In America, anyone can become a millionaire; it's just a matter of being in the right place at the right time."

In trying to assess the legitimacy of these beliefs, we want to ask several 15 important questions. Are there significant class differences among Americans? If these differences do exist, are they getting bigger or smaller, and do these differences have a significant impact on the way we live? Finally, does everyone in the United States really have an equal opportunity to succeed?

The Economic Spectrum

Let's begin by looking at difference. An examination of available data reveals that variations in economic well-being are, in fact, immense. Consider the following:

- The wealthiest 1 percent of the American population holds 34 percent of the total national wealth. That is, they own over one-third of all the consumer durables (such as houses, cars, and stereos) and financial assets (such as stocks, bonds, property, and savings accounts). The richest 20 percent of Americans hold nearly 85 percent of the total household wealth in the country.[3]
- Approximately 183,000 Americans, or approximately three-quarters of 1 percent of the adult population, earn more than $1 million **annually**.[4] There are nearly 400 billionaires in the U.S. today, more than three dozen of them worth more than $10 billion each. It would take the average American (earning $35,672 and spending absolutely nothing at all) a total of 28,033 years (or approximately 400 lifetimes) to earn just $1 billion.

Affluence and prosperity are clearly alive and well in certain segments of the U.S. population. However, this abundance is in contrast to the poverty and despair that is also prevalent in the United States. At the other end of the spectrum:

- Approximately 13 percent of the American population — that is, nearly one of every eight people in this country — live below the official poverty line (calculated in 2004 at $9,645 for an individual and $19,307 for a family of four).[5] An estimated 3.5 million people — of whom nearly 1.4 million are children — experience homelessness in any given year.[6]
- Approximately one out of every five children (4.4 million) in the United States under the age of six lives in poverty.[7]

The contrast between rich and poor is sharp, and with nearly one-third of the American population living at one extreme or the other, it is difficult to argue that we live in a classless society. Big-payoff reality shows, celebrity salaries, and multi-million dollar lotteries notwithstanding, evidence suggests that the level of inequality in the United States is getting higher. Census data show the gap between the rich and the poor to be the widest since the government began collecting information in 1947[8] and that this gap is continuing to grow. In 2004 alone, the average real income of 99 percent of the U.S. population grew by little more than 1 percent, while the . . . richest 1 percent saw their [real] income rise by 12 percent in the same year.[9]

Nor is such a gap between rich and poor representative of the rest of the industrialized world. In fact, the United States has by far the most unequal distribution of household income.[10] The income gap between rich and poor in the United States (measured as the percentage of total income held by the wealthiest 20 percent of the population versus the poorest 20 percent) is approximately 12 to 1, one of the highest ratios in the industrialized world. The ratio in Japan and Germany, by contrast, is 4 to 1.[11]

Reality 1: There are enormous differences in the economic standing of   20
American citizens. A sizable proportion of the U.S. population occupies opposite ends of the economic spectrum. In the middle range of the economic spectrum:

- Sixty percent of the American population holds less than 6 percent of the nation's wealth.[12]
- While the real income of the top 1 percent of U.S. families skyrocketed by more than 180 percent between 1979 and 2000, the income of the middle fifth of the population grew only slightly (12.4 percent over that same 21-year period) and its share of income (15 percent of the total compared to 48 percent of the total for the wealthiest fifth) actually declined during this period.[13]
- Regressive changes in governmental tax policies and the weakening of labor unions over the last quarter century have led to a significant rise in the level of inequality between the rich and the middle class. Between 1979 and 2000, the gap in household income between the top fifth and middle fifth of the population rose by 31 percent.[14] During the economic boom of the 1990s, the top fifth of the nation's population saw their share of net worth increase (from 59 to 63 percent) while four out of five Americans saw their share of net worth decline.[15] One prominent economist described economic growth in the United States as a "spectator sport for the majority of American families."[16] Economic decline, on the other hand, is much more "inclusive," with layoffs impacting hardest on middle- and lower-income families — those with fewer resources to fall back on.

The level of inequality is sometimes difficult to comprehend fully by looking at dollar figures and percentages. To help his students visualize the distribution of income, the well-known economist Paul Samuelson asked them to picture an income pyramid made of children's blocks, with each layer of blocks representing $1,000. If we were to construct Samuelson's pyramid today, the peak of the pyramid would be much higher than the Eiffel Tower, yet almost all of us would be within six feet of the ground.[17] In other words, the distribution of income is heavily skewed; a small minority of families take the lion's share of national income, and the remaining income is distributed among the vast majority of middle-income and low-income families. Keep in mind that Samuelson's pyramid represents the distribution of income, not wealth. The distribution of wealth is skewed even further.

Reality 2: The middle class in the United States holds a very small share of the nation's wealth and that share is declining steadily. The gap between rich and poor and between rich and the middle class is larger than it has ever been.

American Life-Styles

At last count, nearly 37 million Americans across the nation lived in unrelenting poverty.[18] Yet, as political scientist Michael Harrington once commented, "America has the best dressed poverty the world has ever known."[19] Clothing disguises much of the poverty in the United States, and this may explain, in part, its middle-class image. With increased mass marketing of "designer" clothing and with shifts in the nation's economy from blue-collar (and often better-paying) manufacturing jobs to white-collar and pink-collar jobs in the service sector, it is becoming increasingly difficult to distinguish class differences based on appearance.[20] The dress-down environment prevalent in the high-tech industry (what one author refers to as the "no-collars movement") has reduced superficial distinctions even further.[21]

Beneath the surface, there is another reality. Let's look at some "typical" and not-so-typical life-styles.

American Profile

Name:	Harold S. Browning
Father:	manufacturer, industrialist
Mother:	prominent social figure in the community
Principal child-rearer:	governess
Primary education:	an exclusive private school on Manhattan's Upper East Side *Note:* a small, well-respected primary school where teachers and administrators have a reputation for nurturing student creativity and for providing the finest educational preparation *Ambition:* "to become President"
Supplemental tutoring:	tutors in French and mathematics
Summer camp:	sleep-away camp in northern Connecticut

	Note: camp provides instruction in the creative arts, athletics, and the natural sciences
Secondary education:	a prestigious preparatory school in Westchester County *Note:* classmates included the sons of ambassadors, doctors, attorneys, television personalities, and well-known business leaders *Supplemental education:* private SAT tutor *After-school activities:* private riding lessons *Ambition:* "to take over my father's business" *High-school graduation gift:* BMW
Family activities:	theater, recitals, museums, summer vacations in Europe, occasional winter trips to the Caribbean *Note:* as members of and donors to the local art museum, the Brownings and their children attend private receptions and exhibit openings at the invitation of the museum director
Higher education:	an Ivy League liberal arts college in Massachusetts *Major:* economics and political science *After-class activities:* debating club, college newspaper, swim team *Ambition:* "to become a leader in business"
First full-time job (age 23):	assistant manager of operations, Browning Tool and Die, Inc. (family enterprise)
Subsequent employment:	*3 years* — executive assistant to the president, Browning Tool and Die *Responsibilities included:* purchasing (materials and equipment), personnel, and distribution networks *4 years* — advertising manager, Lackheed Manufacturing (home appliances) *3 years* — director of marketing and sales, Comerex, Inc. (business machines)
Present employment (age 38):	executive vice president, SmithBond and Co. (digital instruments) *Typical daily activities:* review financial reports and computer printouts, dictate memoranda, lunch with clients, initiate conference calls, meet with assistants, plan business trips, meet with associates *Transportation to and from work:* chauffeured company limousine *Annual salary:* $324,000 *Ambition:* "to become chief executive officer of the firm, or one like it, within the next five to ten years"

Present residence:	eighteenth-floor condominium on Manhattan's Upper West Side, eleven rooms, including five spacious bedrooms and terrace overlooking river
	Interior: professionally decorated and accented with elegant furnishings, valuable antiques, and expensive artwork
	Note: building management provides doorman and elevator attendant; family employs au pair for children and maid for other domestic chores
Second residence:	farm in northwestern Connecticut, used for weekend retreats and for horse breeding (investment/hobby)
	Note: to maintain the farm and cater to the family when they are there, the Brownings employ a part-time maid, groundskeeper, and horse breeder

Harold Browning was born into a world of nurses, maids, and gov- 25
ernesses. His world today is one of airplanes and limousines, five-star
restaurants, and luxurious living accommodations. The life and life-style of
Harold Browning is in sharp contrast to that of Bob Farrell.

American Profile

Name:	Bob Farrell
Father:	machinist
Mother:	retail clerk
Principal child-rearer:	mother and sitter
Primary education:	a medium-size public school in Queens, New York, characterized by large class size, outmoded physical facilities, and an educational philosophy emphasizing basic skills and student discipline
	Ambition: "to become President"
Supplemental tutoring:	none
Summer camp:	YMCA day camp
	Note: emphasis on team sports, arts and crafts
Secondary education:	large regional high school in Queens
	Note: classmates included the sons and daughters of carpenters, postal clerks, teachers, nurses, shopkeepers, mechanics, bus drivers, police officers, salespersons
	Supplemental education: SAT prep course offered by national chain

	After-school activities: basketball and handball in school park
	Ambition: "to make it through college"
	High-school graduation gift: $500 savings bond
Family activities:	family gatherings around television set, softball, an occasional trip to the movie theater, summer Sundays at the public beach
Higher education:	a two-year community college with a technical orientation
	Major: electrical technology
	After-school activities: employed as a part-time bagger in local supermarket
	Ambition: "to become an electrical engineer"
First full-time job (age 19):	service-station attendant
	Note: continued to take college classes in the evening
Subsequent employment:	mail clerk at large insurance firm, manager trainee, large retail chain
Present employment (age 38):	assistant sales manager, building supply firm
	Typical daily activities: demonstrate products, write up product orders, handle customer complaints, check inventory
	Transportation to and from work: city subway
	Annual salary: $45,261
	Ambition: "to open up my own business"
	Additional income: $6,100 in commissions from evening and weekend work as salesman in local men's clothing store
President residence:	the Farrells own their own home in a working-class neighborhood in Queens, New York

Bob Farrell and Harold Browning live very differently: the life-style of one is privileged; that of the other is not so privileged. The differences are class differences, and these differences have a profound impact on the way they live. They are differences between playing a game of handball in the park and taking riding lessons at a private stable; watching a movie on television and going to the theater; and taking the subway to work and being driven in a limousine. More important, the difference in class determines where they live, who their friends are, how well they are educated, what they do for a living, and what they come to expect from life.

Yet, as dissimilar as their life-styles are, Harold Browning and Bob Farrell have some things in common; they live in the same city, they work long hours, and they are highly motivated. More important, they are both white males.

Let's look at someone else who works long and hard and is highly motivated. This person, however, is black and female.

American Profile

Name:	Cheryl Mitchell
Father:	janitor
Mother:	waitress
Principal child-rearer:	grandmother
Primary education:	large public school in Ocean Hill-Brownsville, Brooklyn, New York
Note: rote teaching of basic skills and emphasis on conveying the importance of good attendance, good manners, and good work habits; school patrolled by security guards
Ambition: "to be a teacher"
Supplemental tutoring:	none
Summer camp:	none
Secondary education:	large public school in Ocean Hill-Brownsville
Note: classmates included sons and daughters of hairdressers, groundskeepers, painters, dressmakers, dishwashers, domestics
Supplemental education: none
After-school activities: domestic chores, part-time employment as babysitter and housekeeper
Ambition: "to be a social worker"
High-school graduation gift: corsage
Family activities:	church-sponsored socials
Higher education:	one semester of local community college
Note: dropped out of school for financial reasons
First full-time job (age 17):	counter clerk, local bakery
Subsequent employment:	file clerk with temporary-service agency, supermarket checker
Present employment (age 38):	nurse's aide at a municipal hospital
Typical daily activities: make up hospital beds, clean out bedpans, weigh patients and assist them to the bathroom, take temperature readings, pass out and collect food trays, feed patients who need help, bathe patients, and change dressings
Annual salary: $15,820
Ambition: "to get out of the ghetto"
Present residence:	three-room apartment in the South Bronx, needs painting, has poor ventilation, is in a high-crime area
Note: Cheryl Mitchell lives with her four-year-old son and her elderly mother

When we look at the lives of Cheryl Mitchell, Bob Farrell, and Harold Browning, we see life-styles that are very different. We are not looking, however, at economic extremes. Cheryl Mitchell's income as a nurse's aide puts her above the government's official poverty line.[22] Below her on the income pyramid are 33 million poverty-stricken Americans. Far from being poor, Bob Farrell has an annual income as an assistant sales manager that puts him well above the median income level — that is, more than 50 percent of the U.S. population earns less money than Bob Farrell.[23] And while Harold Browning's income puts him in a high-income bracket, he stands only a fraction of the way up Samuelson's income pyramid. Well above him are the 183,000 individuals whose annual salary exceeds $1 million. Yet Harold Browning spends more money on his horses than Cheryl Mitchell earns in a year.

Reality 3:   Even ignoring the extreme poles of the economic spectrum, we find enormous class differences in the life-styles among the haves, the have-nots, and the have-littles.   30

Class affects more than life-style and material well-being. It has a significant impact on our physical and mental well-being as well.

Researchers have found an inverse relationship between social class and health. Lower-class standing is correlated to higher rates of infant mortality, eye and ear disease, arthritis, physical disability, diabetes, nutritional deficiency, respiratory disease, mental illness, and heart disease.[24] In all areas of health, poor people do not share the same life chances as those in the social class above them. Furthermore, lower-class standing is correlated with a lower quality of treatment for illness and disease. The results of poor health and poor treatment are borne out in the life expectancy rates within each class. Researchers have found that the higher your class standing, the higher your life expectancy. Conversely, they have also found that within each age group, the lower one's class standing, the higher the death rate; in some age groups, the figures are as much as two and three times as high.[25]

Reality 4:   From cradle to grave, class standing has a significant impact on our chances for survival.

The lower one's class standing, the more difficult it is to secure appropriate housing, the more time is spent on the routine tasks of everyday life, the greater is the percentage of income that goes to pay for food and other basic necessities, and the greater is the likelihood of crime victimization.[26] Class can accurately predict chances for both survival and success.

Class and Educational Attainment

School performance (grades and test scores) and educational attainment (level of schooling completed) also correlate strongly with economic class. Furthermore, despite some efforts to make testing fairer and schooling more accessible, current data suggest that the level of inequity is staying the same or getting worse.   35

In his study for the Carnegie Council on Children twenty-five years ago, Richard De Lone examined the test scores of over half a million students who took the College Board exams (SATs). His findings were consistent with earlier studies that showed a relationship between class and scores on standardized tests; his conclusion: "the higher the student's social status, the higher the probability that he or she will get higher grades."[27] Fifteen years after the release of the Carnegie report, College Board surveys reveal data that are no different: test scores still correlate strongly with family income.

Average Combined Scores by Income (400 to 1600 scale)[28]

FAMILY INCOME	MEDIAN SCORE
More than $100,000	1119
$80,000 to $100,000	1063
$70,000 to $80,000	1039
$60,000 to $70,000	1026
$50,000 to $60,000	1014
$40,000 to $50,000	996
$30,000 to $40,000	967
$20,000 to $30,000	937
$10,000 to $20,000	906
less than $10,000	884

These figures are based on the test results of 987,584 SAT takers in 2005.

A little more than twenty years ago, researcher William Sewell showed a positive correlation between class and overall educational achievement. In comparing the top quartile (25 percent) of his sample to the bottom quartile, he found that students from upper-class families were twice as likely to obtain training beyond high school and four times as likely to attain a postgraduate degree. Sewell concluded: "Socioeconomic background . . . operates independently of academic ability at every stage in the process of educational attainment."[29]

Today, the pattern persists. There are, however, two significant changes. On the one hand, the odds of getting into college have improved for the bottom quartile of the population, although they still remain relatively low compared to the top. On the other hand, the chances of completing a college degree have deteriorated markedly for the bottom quartile. Researchers estimate the chances of completing a four-year college degree (by age 24) to be nineteen times as great for the top 25 percent of the population as it is for the bottom 25 percent.[30]

Reality 5: Class standing has a significant impact on chances for educational achievement.

Class standing, and consequently life chances, are largely determined at 40
birth. Although examples of individuals who have gone from rags to riches
abound in the mass media, statistics on class mobility show these leaps to be
extremely rare. In fact, dramatic advances in class standing are relatively
infrequent. One study showed that fewer than one in five men surpass the
economic status of their fathers.[31] For those whose annual income is in six
figures, economic success is due in large part to the wealth and privileges
bestowed on them at birth. Over 66 percent of the consumer units with
incomes of $100,000 or more have inherited assets. Of these units, over 86
percent reported that inheritances constituted a substantial portion of their
total assets.[32]

Economist Harold Wachtel likens inheritance to a series of Monopoly
games in which the winner of the first game refuses to relinquish his or her cash
and commercial property for the second game. "After all," argues the winner,
"I accumulated my wealth and income by my own wits." With such an arrangement, it is not difficult to predict the outcome of subsequent games.[33]

Reality 6: All Americans do not have an equal opportunity to succeed. Inheritance laws ensure a greater likelihood of success for the offspring of the wealthy.

Spheres of Power and Oppression

When we look at society and try to determine what it is that keeps most
people down — what holds them back from realizing their potential as
healthy, creative, productive individuals — we find institutional forces that
are largely beyond individual control. Class domination is one of these
forces. People do not choose to be poor or working class; instead, they are
limited and confined by the opportunities afforded or denied them by a
social and economic system. The class structure in the United States is a
function of its economic system: capitalism, a system that is based on private rather than public ownership and control of commercial enterprises.
Under capitalism, these enterprises are governed by the need to produce a
profit for the owners, rather than to fulfill societal needs. Class divisions
arise from the differences between those who own and control corporate
enterprise and those who do not.

Racial and gender domination are other forces that hold people down.
Although there are significant differences in the way capitalism, racism, and
sexism affect our lives, there are also a multitude of parallels. And although
class, race, and gender act independently of each other, they are at the
same time very much interrelated.

On the one hand, issues of race and gender cut across class lines. 45
Women experience the effects of sexism whether they are well-paid professionals or poorly paid clerks. As women, they are not only subjected to cat-
calls and stereotyping, but face discrimination and are denied opportunities

and privileges that men have. Similarly, a wealthy black man faces racial oppression, is subjected to racial slurs, and is denied opportunities because of his color. Regardless of their class standing, women and members of minority races are constantly dealing with institutional forces that are holding them down precisely because of their gender, the color of their skin, or both.

On the other hand, the experiences of women and minorities are differentiated along class lines. Although they are in subordinate positions vis-à-vis white men, the particular issues that confront women and people of color may be quite different depending on their position in the class structure.

Power is incremental, and class privileges can accrue to individual women and to individual members of a racial minority. While power is incremental, oppression is cumulative, and those who are poor, black, and female are often subject to all of the forces of class, race, and gender discrimination simultaneously. This cumulative situation is what is meant by the double and triple jeopardy of women and minorities.

Furthermore, oppression in one sphere is related to the likelihood of oppression in another. If you are black and female, for example, you are much more likely to be poor or working class than you would be as a white male. Census figures show that the incidence of poverty varies greatly by race and gender.

Chances of Being Poor in America[34]

WHITE MALE/ FEMALE	WHITE FEMALE HEAD°	HISPANIC MALE/ FEMALE	HISPANIC FEMALE HEAD°	BLACK MALE/ FEMALE	BLACK FEMALE HEAD°
1 in 10	1 in 5	1 in 5	1 in 3	1 in 4	1 in 3

°Persons in families with female householder, no husband present.

In other words, being female and being nonwhite are attributes in our society that increase the chances of poverty and of lower-class standing.

Reality 7: Racism and sexism significantly compound the effects of class in society.

None of this makes for a very pretty picture of our country. Despite what we like to think about ourselves as a nation, the truth is that opportunity for success and life itself are highly circumscribed by our race, our gender, and the class we are born into. As individuals, we feel hurt and anger when someone is treating us unfairly; yet as a society we tolerate unconscionable injustice. A more just society will require a radical redistribution of wealth and power. We can start by reversing the current trends that further polarize us as a people and adapt policies and practices that narrow the gaps in income, wealth, and privilege.

Notes

1. See Jay MacLead, *Ain't No Makin' It: Aspirations and Attainment in a Lower-Income Neighborhood* (Boulder, CO: Westview Press, 1995); Benjamin DeMott, *The Imperial Middle* (New York: Morrow, 1990); Ira Katznelson, *City Trenches: Urban Politics and Patterning of Class in the United States* (New York: Pantheon Books, 1981); Charles W. Tucker, "A Comparative Analysis of Subjective Social Class: 1945–1963," *Social Forces*, no. 46, June 1968, pp. 508–514; Robert Nisbet, "The Decline and Fall of Social Class," *Pacific Sociological Review*, vol. 2, Spring 1959, pp. 11–17; and Oscar Glantz, "Class Consciousness and Political Solidarity," *American Sociological Review*, vol. 23, August 1958, pp. 375–382. [All notes are Mantsios's.]

2. Susan Ostander, "Upper-Class Women: Class Consciousness as Conduct and Meaning," in G. William Domhoff, *Power Structure Research* (Beverly Hills, CA: Sage Publications, 1980), pp. 78–79. Also see Stephen Birmingham, *America's Secret Aristocracy* (Boston: Little Brown, 1987).

3. Lawrence Mishel, Jared Bernstein, and Sylvia Allegretto, *The State of Working America: 2004–2005* (Ithaca: ILR Press, Cornell University Press, 2005), p. 282.

4. The number of individuals filing tax returns showing a gross adjusted income of $1 million or more in 2003 was 182,932 (Tax Stats at a Glance, Internal Revenue Service, U.S. Treasury Department, available at http://www.irs.gov/taxstats/article/0,,id=102886,00.html).

5. Carmen DeNavas-Walt, Bernadette D. Proctor, and Cheryl Hill Lee, U.S. Census Bureau, Current Population Reports, P60-229, *Income, Poverty, and Health Insurance in the United States: 2004* (Washington, DC: U.S. Government Printing Office, 2005), pp. 9, 45.

6. National Coalition for the Homeless "How many people experience homelessness?" NCH Fact Sheet #2 (June 2006), citing a 2004 National Law Center on Homelessness and Poverty study. Available at http://www.nationalhomeless.org/publications/facts/How_Many.pdf.

7. Mishel et al., op. cit., pp. 318–319.

8. Lawrence Mishel, Jared Bernstein, and Heather Boushey, *The State of Working America: 2002–2003* (Ithaca: ILR Press, Cornell University Press, 2003), p. 53.

9. Paul Krugman, "Left Behind Economics" *New York Times*, July 14, 2006.

10. Based on a comparison of 19 industrialized states: Mishel et al., *2004–2005*, pp. 399–401.

11. Mishel et al., ibid, p. 64.

12. Derived from Mishel et al., *2002–2003*, p. 281.

13. Mishel et al., *2004–2005*, ibid, pp. 62–63.

14. Mishel et al. *2002–2003*, ibid, p. 70.

15. Mishel et al., ibid, p. 280.

16. Alan Blinder, quoted by Paul Krugman, in "Disparity and Despair," *U.S. News and World Report*, March 23, 1992, p. 54.

17. Paul Samuelson, *Economics*, 10th ed. (New York: McGraw-Hill, 1976), p. 84.

18. DeNavas-Walt et al., op. cit., p. 9.

19. Michael Harrington, *The Other America* (New York: Macmillan, 1962), pp. 12–13.

20. Stuart Ewen and Elizabeth Ewen, *Channels of Desire: Mass Images and the Shaping of American Consciousness* (New York: McGraw-Hill, 1982).

21. Andrew Ross, *No-Collar: The Humane Work Place and Its Hidden Costs* (New York: Basic Books, 2002).

22. Based on a poverty threshold for a three-person household in 2004 of $15,205. DeNavas et al., op. cit., p. 45.

23. The median income in 2004 was $40,798 for men, $31,223 for women, and $44,389 for households. DeNavas-Walt et al., op. cit., pp. 3–5.

24. E. Pamuk, D. Makuc, K. Heck, C. Reuben, and K. Lochner, *Socioeconomic Status and Health Chartbook, Health, United States, 1998* (Hyattsville, MD: National Center for Health Statistics, 1998), pp. 145–159; Vincente Navarro "Class, Race, and Health Care in the

United States," in Bersh Berberoglu, *Critical Perspectives in Sociology*, 2nd ed. (Dubuque, IA: Kendall/Hunt, 1993), pp. 148–156; Melvin Krasner, *Poverty and Health in New York City* (New York: United Hospital Fund of New York, 1989). See also U.S. Dept. of Health and Human Services, *Health Status of Minorities and Low Income Groups*, 1985; and Dan Hughes, Kay Johnson, Sara Rosenbaum, Elizabeth Butler, and Janet Simons, *The Health of America's Children* (The Children's Defense Fund, 1988).

25. E. Pamuk et al., op. cit.; Kenneth Neubeck and Davita Glassberg, *Sociology; A Critical Approach* (New York: McGraw-Hill, 1996), pp. 436–438; Aaron Antonovsky, "Social Class, Life Expectancy, and Overall Mortality," in *The Impact of Social Class* (New York: Thomas Crowell, 1972), pp. 467–491. See also Harriet Duleep, "Measuring the Effect of Income on Adult Mortality Using Longitudinal Administrative Record Data," *Journal of Human Resources*, vol. 21, no. 2, Spring 1986. See also Paul Farmer, *Pathologies of Power: Health, Human Rights, and the New War on the Poor* (Berkeley: University of California Press, 2005).

26. E. Pamuk et al., op. cit., fig. 20; Dennis W. Roncek, "Dangerous Places: Crime and Residential Environment," *Social Forces*, vol. 60, no. 1, September 1981, pp. 74–96.

27. Richard De Lone, *Small Futures* (New York: Harcourt Brace Jovanovich, 1978), pp. 14–19.

28. Derived from "2005 College-Bound Seniors, Total Group Profile," *College Board*, p. 7, available at http://www.collegeboard.com/prod_downloads/about/news_info/cbsenior/yr2005/2005-college-bound-seniors.pdf.

29. William H. Sewell, "Inequality of Opportunity for Higher Education," *American Sociological Review*, vol. 36, no. 5, 1971, pp. 793–809.

30. The Mortenson Report on Public Policy Analysis of Opportunity for Postsecondary Education, "Postsecondary Education Opportunity" (Iowa City, IA: September 1993, no. 16).

31. De Lone, op. cit., pp. 14–19.

32. Howard Tuchman, *Economics of the Rich* (New York: Random House, 1973), p. 15. For more information on inheritance, see Sam Bowles and Herbert Gintis, "The Inheritance of Inequality," *The Journal of Economic Perspectives*, vol. 16, no. 3 (summer, 2002) pp. 2–30 and Tom Hertz, *Understanding Mobility in America*, Center for American Progress, http://www.americanprogress.org/site/pp.asp?c=biJRJ8OVF&b=1579981.

33. Howard Wachtel, *Labor and the Economy* (Orlando, FL: Academic Press, 1984), pp. 161–162.

34. Derived from DeNavas et al., op. cit, pp. 46–51.

ENGAGING THE TEXT

1. Re-examine the four myths Mantsios identifies (paras. 10–14). What does Mantsios say is wrong about each myth, and what evidence does he provide to critique each? How persuasive do you find his evidence and reasoning?

2. Does the essay make a case that the wealthy are exploiting the poor? Does it simply assume this? Are there other possible interpretations of the data Mantsios provides? Explain your position, taking into account the information in "Class in America — 2006."

3. Work out a rough budget for a family of three with an annual income of $18,310, the "poverty threshold" for 2009. Be sure to include costs for food, clothing, housing, transportation, healthcare, and other unavoidable expenses. Do you think this is a reasonable "poverty line," or is it too high or too low?

4. Imagine that you are Harold S. Browning, Bob Farrell, or Cheryl Mitchell. Write an entry for this person's journal after a tough day on the job. Compare and contrast your entry with those written by other students.

5. In this essay, Mantsios does not address solutions to the problems he cites. What changes do you imagine Mantsios would like to see? What changes, if any, would you recommend?

EXPLORING CONNECTIONS

6. Working in small groups, discuss which class each of the following would belong to and how this class affiliation would shape the life chances of each:

> Mike Rose (p. 157)
>
> Richard Rodriguez (p. 194)
>
> Sylvia in "The Lesson" (p. 264)
>
> George in "Serving in Florida" (p. 290)
>
> Stephen Cruz (p. 366)
>
> Gary Soto in "Looking for Work" (p. 26)
>
> The narrator of "An Indian Story" (p. 52)

7. Although Mantsios does not focus on the Horatio Alger myth as does Harlon Dalton (p. 272), both authors concern themselves with seeing beyond myths of success to underlying realities. Compare the ways these two writers challenge the American mythology of success. Do the two readings complement one another, or do you see fundamental disagreements between the two authors? Whose approach do you find more persuasive, insightful, or informative, and why?

8. How might Tim Blixseth (p. 279) respond to Mantsios's analysis of class in America? How can a belief in individual opportunity be maintained in the face of Mantsios's statistics on social class and life chances?

EXTENDING THE CRITICAL CONTEXT

9. Mantsios points out, "Inheritance laws ensure a greater likelihood of success for the offspring of the wealthy" (para. 42). Explain why you think this is or is not a serious problem. Keeping in mind the difference between wealth and income, discuss how society might attempt to remedy this problem and what policies you would endorse.

10. Skim through a few recent issues of a financial magazine like *Forbes* or *Money*. Who is the audience for these publications? What kind of advice is offered, what kinds of products and services are advertised, and what levels of income and investment are discussed?

11. Study the employment listings at an online source such as Monster.com. Roughly what percentage of the openings would you consider upper class, middle class, and lower class? On what basis do you make your distinctions? What do the available jobs suggest about the current levels of affluence in your area?

Visual Portfolio

Reading Images of Individual Opportunity

Visual Portfolio
READING IMAGES OF INDIVIDUAL OPPORTUNITY

1. When do you think the photo of the father giving cash to his family (p. 321) was taken, and what ideas about money, social class, family, and gender was it meant to convey at that time? Explain why you think it was or was not meant to be humorous. What meanings does the image convey to you today? Compare this photograph with Norman Rockwell's *Freedom from Fear* (p. 24) in terms of cultural messages and visual composition or structure.

2. What's happening in the photograph of the bank meeting (p. 322)? Discuss such elements of the photo as the setting, the bankers' clothes, their facial expressions, and the framed portraits on the wall. What does this image tell you about money and success? Compare the women in this photo to the other females in this portfolio — the mother and daughter getting their allowance and the hungry woman who needs work. Considered as a group, what do these images say about women and money in American culture?

3. In the photograph of a man repairing novelty items during vocational training (p. 323), what else is going on? What is the man thinking? What is his relationship to his work, to the toys, and to his coworkers? What do you make of the slogan on his T-shirt, "Freedom by any means necessary"?

4. How does the urban scene with the TV (p. 324) fit into a portfolio of images about money and success? What ideas and emotions does it trigger in you? Explain the prominence of the broken TV: Why is a portion of the image framed by a TV rather than by one of countless alternatives (picture frame, doorway, window, etc.)?

5. Try to reason out the setting (time and place) of the couple with the "Hungry — Need Work" sign (p. 325). Then interpret such visual details as the cardboard sign, the couple's clothing and hair styles, and their facial expressions.

6. Do you think the hand with jewelry (p. 326) belongs to a man or a woman? Does the image give you any clues about the person's age, ethnicity, and social class or about whether the person lives in an urban or a rural environment? In trying to make such judgments, do you find it easy or difficult to distinguish between reasonable guesses and simple stereotyping?

7. What has happened to the house with boarded-up windows (p. 327)? What do you imagine has happened to its owners? Who do you think wrote the graffiti, and what might it mean?

8. The photograph on page 328 shows a "tent city" in Sacramento, California (see also the reading "Tent City, USA" by Maria L. La Ganga, p. 357). What is your primary response to the image, and what elements in the photograph do you think provoke this response? List all the kinds of structures and objects you can find in the image; then explain how a photograph of material things can comment on people's lives.

Framing Class, Vicarious Living, and Conspicuous Consumption

DIANA KENDALL

Diana Kendall, a professor of sociology at Baylor University, has performed an extensive study of how newspapers and TV have portrayed social class in the last half-century. She concludes that the media shape public opinions about the upper, middle, working, and poverty classes by "framing" their stories and their programming in a relatively small number of patterned, predictable, and misleading ways. For example, "the media glorify the upper classes, even when they are accused of wrongdoing." In this excerpt from her award-winning book Framing Class: Media Representations of Wealth and Poverty in America *(2005), Kendall analyzes how several common media frames communicate cultural messages about social class. Her most recent book is* Members Only: Elite Clubs and the Process of Exclusion *(2008).*

"The Simple Life 2" — the second season of the reality show, on which the celebutante Paris Hilton and her Best Friend Forever, the professional pop-star-daughter Nicole Richie, are set on a cross-country road trip — *once again takes the heaviest of topics and makes them as weightless as a social X-ray.*[1]

This statement by television critic Choire Sicha, in her review of FOX TV's reality-based entertainment show *The Simple Life,* sums up a recurring theme of *Framing Class:* The media typically take "the heaviest of topics," such as class and social inequality, and trivialize it. Rather than providing a meaningful analysis of inequality and showing realistic portrayals of life in various social classes, the media either play class differences for laughs or sweep the issue of class under the rug so that important distinctions are rendered invisible. By ignoring class or trivializing it, the media involve themselves in a social construction of reality that rewards the affluent and penalizes the working class and the poor. In real life, Paris Hilton and Nicole Richie are among the richest young women in the world; however, in the world of *The Simple Life,* they can routinely show up somewhere in the city or the country, pretend they are needy, and rely on the kindness of strangers who have few economic resources.

The Simple Life is only one example of many that demonstrate how class is minimized or played for laughs by the media. [Below] I have provided many examples of how class is framed in the media and what messages those framing devices might convey to audiences. In this chapter,

---

[1]Choire Sicha, "They'll Always Have Paris," *New York Times,* June 13, 2004, AR31 [emphasis added]. [All notes are Kendall's unless otherwise indicated.]

© The New Yorker Collection 2008 Roz Chast from cartoon.bank.com. All Rights Reserved.

I will look at the sociological implications of how framing contributes to our understanding of class and how it leads to vicarious living and excessive consumerism by many people. I will also discuss reasons why prospects for change in how journalists and television writers portray the various classes are limited. First, we look at two questions: How do media audiences understand and act upon popular culture images or frames? Is class understood differently today because of these frames?

Media Framing and the Performance of Class in Everyday Life

In a mass-mediated culture such as ours, the media do not simply mirror society; rather, they help to shape it and to create cultural perceptions.[2] The blurring between what is real and what is not real encourages people to emulate the upper classes and shun the working class and the poor. Television shows, magazines, and newspapers sell the idea that the only way to get ahead is to identify with the rich and powerful and to live vicariously through them. From sitcoms to reality shows, the media encourage ordinary

[2]Tim Delaney and Allene Wilcox, "Sports and the Role of the Media," in *Values, Society and Evolution*, ed. Harry Birx and Tim Delaney, 199–215 (Auburn, N.Y.: Legend, 2002).

people to believe that they may rise to fame and fortune; they too can be
the next American Idol. Constantly bombarded by stories about the
lifestyles of the rich and famous, viewers feel a sense of intimacy with elites,
with whom they have little or no contact in their daily lives.[3] According to
the social critic bell hooks, we overidentify with the wealthy, because the
media socialize us to believe that people in the upper classes are better than
we are. The media also suggest that we need have no allegiance to people in
our own class or to those who are less fortunate.[4]

Vicarious living — watching how other individuals live rather than
experiencing life for ourselves — through media representations of wealth
and success is reflected in many people's reading and viewing habits and in
their patterns of consumption. According to hooks, television promotes
hedonistic consumerism:

> Largely through marketing and advertising, television promoted the
> myth of the classless society, offering on one hand images of an
> American dream fulfilled wherein any and everyone can become rich
> and on the other suggesting that the lived experience of this lack of
> class hierarchy was expressed by our *equal right to purchase anything
> we could afford.*[5]

As hooks suggests, equality does not exist in contemporary society, but   5
media audiences are encouraged to view themselves as having an "equal
right" to purchase items that somehow will make them equal to people
above them in the social class hierarchy. However, the catch is that we must
actually be able to afford these purchases. Manufacturers and the media
have dealt with this problem by offering relatively cheap products marketed
by wealthy celebrities. Paris Hilton, an heir to the Hilton Hotel fortune, has
made millions of dollars by marketing products that give her fans a small
"slice" of the good life she enjoys. Middle- and working-class people can
purchase jewelry from the Paris Hilton Collection — sterling silver and
Swarovski crystal jewelry ranging in price from fifteen to a hundred
dollars — and have something that is "like Paris wears." For less than
twenty dollars per item, admirers can purchase the Paris Hilton Wall Calendar; a "Paris the Heiress" Paper Doll Book; Hilton's autobiography, *Confessions of an Heiress;* and even her dog's story, *The Tinkerbell Hilton Diaries:
My Life Tailing Paris Hilton.* But Hilton is only one of thousands of celebrities who make money by encouraging unnecessary consumerism among
people who are inspired by media portrayals of the luxurious and supposedly happy lives of rich celebrities. The title of Hilton's television show,
The Simple Life, appropriates the image of simple people, such as the work-

---

[3]bell hooks [Gloria Watkins], *Where We Stand: Class Matters* (New York: Routledge,
2000), 73.
[4]hooks, *Where We Stand,* 77.
[5]hooks, *Where We Stand,* 71 [emphasis added].

ing class and poor, who might live happy, meaningful lives, and transfers this image to women whose lives are anything but simple as they flaunt designer clothing and spend collectively millions of dollars on entertainment, travel, and luxuries that can be afforded only by the very wealthy.[6]

How the media frame stories about class *does* make a difference in what we think about other people and how we spend our money. Media frames constitute a mental shortcut (schema) that helps us formulate our thoughts.

The Upper Classes: Affluence and Consumerism for All

Although some media frames show the rich and famous in a negative manner, they still glorify the material possessions and lifestyles of the upper classes. Research has found that people who extensively watch television have exaggerated views of how wealthy most Americans are and what material possessions they own. Studies have also found that extensive television viewing leads to higher rates of spending and to lower savings, presumably because television stimulates consumer desires.[7]

For many years, most media framing of stories about the upper classes has been positive, ranging from *consensus framing* that depicts members of the upper class as being like everyone else, to *admiration framing* that portrays them as generous, caring individuals. The frame most closely associated with rampant consumerism is *emulation framing*, which suggests that people in all classes should reward themselves with a few of the perks of the wealthy, such as buying a piece of Paris's line of jewelry. The writers of television shows such as ABC's *Life of Luxury*, E!'s *It's Good to Be . . .* [a wealthy celebrity, such as Nicole Kidman], and VH1's *The Fabulous Life* rely heavily on admiration and price-tag framing, by which the worth of a person is measured by what he or she owns and how many assistants constantly cater to that person's whims. On programs like FOX's *The O.C.* and *North Shore* and NBC's *Las Vegas*, the people with the most expensive limousines, yachts, and jet aircraft are declared the winners in life. Reality shows like *American Idol*, *The Billionaire*, *For Love or Money*, and *The Apprentice* suggest that anyone can move up the class ladder and live like the rich if he or she displays the best looks, greatest talent, or sharpest entrepreneurial skills. It is no wonder that the economist Juliet B. Schor finds that the overriding goal of children age ten to thirteen is to get rich. In response to the statement "I want to make a lot of money when I grow up," 63 percent of the children in Schor's study agreed, whereas only 7 percent disagreed.[8]

Many adults who hope to live the good life simply plunge farther into debt. Many reports show that middle- and working-class American consumers are incurring massive consumer debts as they purchase larger

---

[6]hooks, *Where We Stand*, 72.

[7]Juliet B. Schor, *Born to Buy: The Commercialized Child and the New Consumer Culture* (New York: Scribner, 2004).

[8]Schor, *Born to Buy*.

houses, more expensive vehicles, and many other items that are beyond their means. According to one analyst, media portrayals of excessive consumer spending and a bombardment of advertisements by credit-card companies encourage people to load up on debt.[9] With the average U.S. household now spending 13 percent of its after-tax income to *service* debts (not pay off the principal!), people with average incomes who continue to aspire to lives of luxury like those of the upper classes instead may find themselves spending their way into the "poor house" with members of the poverty class.

The Poor and Homeless: "Not Me!" — Negative Role Models in the Media

The sharpest contrasts in media portrayals are between depictions of people in the upper classes and depictions of people at the bottom of the class structure. At best, the poor and homeless are portrayed as deserving of our sympathy on holidays or when disaster strikes. In these situations, those in the bottom classes are depicted as being temporarily down on their luck or as working hard to get out of their current situation but in need of public assistance. At worst, however, the poor are blamed for their own problems; stereotypes of the homeless as bums, alcoholics, and drug addicts, caught in a hopeless downward spiral because of their *individual* pathological behavior, are omnipresent in the media.

For the most part, people at the bottom of the class structure remain out of sight and out of mind for most media audiences. *Thematic framing* depicts the poor and homeless as "faceless" statistics in reports on poverty. *Episodic framing* highlights some problems of the poor but typically does not link their personal situations [and] concerns to such larger societal problems as limited educational opportunities, high rates of unemployment, and jobs that pay depressingly low wages.

The poor do not fare well on television entertainment shows, where writers typically represent them with one-dimensional, bedraggled characters standing on a street corner holding cardboard signs that read "Need money for food." When television writers tackle the issue of homelessness, they often portray the lead characters (who usually are white and relatively affluent) as helpful people, while the poor and homeless are depicted as deviants who might harm themselves or others. Hospital and crime dramas like *E.R.*, *C.S.I.*, and *Law & Order* frequently portray the poor and homeless as "crazy," inebriated in public, or incompetent to provide key information to officials. Television reality shows like *Cops* go so far as to advertise that they provide "footage of debris from the bottom tiers of the urban social order."[10] Statements such as this say a lot about the extent to which

10

---

[9]Joseph Nocera, *A Piece of the Action: How the Middle Class Joined the Money Class* (New York: Simon and Schuster, 1994).

[10]Karen De Coster and Brad Edmonds, "TV Nation: The Killing of American Brain Cells," Lewrockwell.com, 2004, www.lewrockwell.com/decoster/decoster78.html (accessed July 7, 2004).

television producers, directors, and writers view (or would have us view) the lower classes.

From a sociological perspective, framing of stories about the poor and homeless stands in stark contrast to framing of stories about those in the upper classes, and it suggests that we should distance ourselves from "those people." We are encouraged to view the poor and homeless as the *Other*, the outsider; in the media we find little commonality between our lives and the experiences of people at the bottom of the class hierarchy. As a result, it is easy for us to buy into the dominant ideological construction that views poverty as a problem of individuals, not of the society as a whole, and we may feel justified in our rejection of such people.[11]

The Working Class: Historical Relics and Jokes

The working class and the working poor do not fare much better than the poor and homeless in media representations. The working class is described as "labor," and people in this class are usually nothing more than faces in a crowd on television shows. The media portray people who *produce* goods and services as much less interesting than those who *excessively consume* them, and this problem can only grow worse as more of the workers who produce the products are thousands of miles away from us, in nations like China, very remote from the typical American consumer.[12]

Contemporary media coverage carries little information about the working class or its problems. Low wages, lack of benefits, and hazardous working conditions are considered boring and uninteresting topics, except on the public broadcasting networks or an occasional television "news show" such as *60 Minutes* or *20/20*, when some major case of worker abuse has recently been revealed. The most popular portrayal of the working class is *caricature framing*, which depicts people in negative ways, such as being dumb, white trash, buffoons, bigots, or slobs. Many television shows featuring working-class characters play on the idea that the clothing, manners, and speech patterns of the working class are not as good as those of the middle or upper classes. For example, working-class characters (such as Roseanne, the animated Homer Simpson, and *The King of Queens'* Doug) may compare themselves to the middle and upper classes by saying that they are not as "fancy as the rich people." Situation comedy writers have

15

---

[11]Judith Butler ("Performative Acts and Gender Constitution: An Essay in Phenomenology and Feminist Theory," in *Performing Feminisms: Feminist Critical Theory and Theatre*, ed. Sue-Ellen Case [Baltimore: Johns Hopkins University Press, 1990], 270) has described gender identity as performative, noting that social reality is not a given but is continually created as an illusion "through language, gesture, and all manner of symbolic social sign." In this sense, class might also be seen as performative, in that people act out their perceived class location not only in terms of their own class-related identity but in regard to how they treat other people, based on their perceived class position.

[12]See Thomas Ginsberg, "Union Hopes to Win Over Starbucks Shop Workers," *Austin American-Statesman*, July 2, 2004, D6.

perpetuated working-class stereotypes, and now a number of reality shows, such as *The Swan* and *Extreme Makeover,* try to take "ordinary" working-class people and "improve" them through cosmetic surgery, new clothing, and different hairstyles.

Like their upper-class celebrity counterparts, so-called working-class comedians like Jeff Foxworthy have ridiculed the blue-collar lifestyle. They also have marketed products that make fun of the working class. Foxworthy's website, for example, includes figurines ("little statues for *inside* the house"), redneck cookbooks, Games Rednecks Play, and calendars that make fun of the working class generally. Although some people see these items as humorous ("where's yore sense of humor?"), the real message is that people in the lower classes lack good taste, socially acceptable manners, and above all, middle-class values. If you purchase "redneck" merchandise, you too can make fun of the working class and clearly distance yourself from it.

Middle-Class Framing and Kiddy-Consumerism

Media framing of stories about the middle class tells us that this economic group is the value center and backbone of the nation. *Middle-class values framing* focuses on the values of this class and suggests that they hold the nation together. Early television writers were aware that their shows needed to appeal to middle-class audiences, who were the targeted consumers for the advertisers' products, and middle-class values of honesty, integrity, and hard work were integral ingredients of early sitcoms. However, some contemporary television writers spoof the middle class and poke fun at values supposedly associated with people in this category. The writers of FOX's *Malcolm in the Middle* and *Arrested Development,* for example, focus on the dysfunctions in a fictional middle-class family, including conflicts between husband and wife, between parents and children, and between members of the family and outsiders.

Why do these shows make fun of the middle class? Because corporations that pay for the advertisements want to capture the attention of males between ages eighteen and thirty-nine, and individuals in this category are believed to enjoy laughing at the uptight customs of conventional middle-class families. In other shows, as well, advertisers realize the influence that their programs have on families. That is why they are happy to spend billions of dollars on product placements (such as a Diet Coke can sitting on a person's desk) in the shows and on ads during commercial breaks. In recent research, Schor examined why very young children buy into the consumerism culture and concluded that extensive media exposure to products was a key reason. According to Schor, "More children [in the United States] than anywhere else believe that their clothes and brands describe who they are and define their social status. American kids display more brand affinity than their counterparts anywhere else in the world; indeed, experts describe them as increasingly 'bonded to brands.' "[13]

Part of this bonding occurs through constant television watching and Internet use, as a steady stream of ads targets children and young people. Schor concludes that we face a greater problem than just excessive consumerism. A child's well-being is undermined by the consumer culture: "High consumer involvement is a significant cause of depression, anxiety, low self-esteem, and psychosomatic complaints."[14] Although no similar studies have been conducted to determine the effects of the media's emphasis on wealth and excessive consumerism among adults, it is likely that today's children will take these values with them into adulthood if our society does not first reach the breaking point with respect to consumer debt.

The issue of class in the United States is portrayed in the media not   20
through a realistic assessment of wealth, poverty, or inequality but instead through its patterns of rampant consumerism. The general message remains, one article stated, "We pledge allegiance to the mall."[15]

Media Framing and Our Distorted View of Inequality

Class clearly permeates media culture and influences our thinking on social inequality. How the media frame stories involving class constitutes a *socially constructed reality* that is not necessarily an accurate reflection of the United States. Because of their pervasive nature, the media have the symbolic capacity to define the world for other people. In turn, readers and viewers gain information from the media that they use to construct a picture of class and inequality — a picture that becomes, at least to them, a realistic representation of where they stand in the class structure, what they should (or should not) aspire to achieve, and whether and why they should view other people as superior, equal, or inferior to themselves.

Because of the media's power to socially construct reality, we must make an effort to find out about the objective nature of class and evaluate social inequality on our own terms. Although postmodern thinkers believe that it is impossible to distinguish between real life and the fictionalized version of reality that is presented by the media, some sociologists argue that we can learn the difference between media images of reality and the actual facts pertaining to wealth, poverty, and inequality. The more we become aware that we are not receiving "raw" information or "just" entertainment from the media, the more we are capable of rationally thinking about how we are represented in media portrayals and what we are being encouraged

---

[13]Schor, *Born to Buy*, 13.

[14]Schor, *Born to Buy*, 167.

[15]Louis Uchitelle, "We Pledge Allegiance to the Mall," *New York Times,* December 6, 2004, C12.

to do (engage in hedonistic consumerism, for example) by these depictions. The print and electronic media have become extremely adept at framing issues of class in a certain manner, but we still have the ability to develop alternative frames that better explain who we are and what our nation is truly like in regard to class divisions.

The Realities of Class

What are the realities of inequality? The truth is that the rich are getting richer and that the gulf between the rich and the poor continues to widen in the United States. Since the 1990s, the poor have been more likely to stay poor, and the affluent have been more likely to stay affluent. How do we know this? Between 1991 and 2001, the income of the top one-fifth of U.S. families increased by 31 percent; during the same period, the income of the bottom one-fifth of families increased by only 10 percent.[16] The chasm is even wider across racial and ethnic categories; African Americans and Latinos/Latinas are overrepresented among those in the bottom income levels. Over one-half of African American and Latino/Latina households fall within the lowest income categories.

Wealth inequality is even more pronounced. The super-rich (the top 0.5 percent of U.S. households) own 35 percent of the nation's wealth, with net assets averaging almost nine million dollars. The very rich (the next 0.5 percent of households) own about 7 percent of the nation's wealth, with net assets ranging from $1.4 million to $2.5 million. The rich (9 percent of households) own 30 percent of the wealth, with net assets of a little over four hundred thousand dollars. Meanwhile, everybody else (the bottom 90 percent of households) owns only 28 percent of the nation's wealth. Like income, wealth disparities are greatest across racial and ethnic categories. According to the Census Bureau, the net worth of the average white household in 2000 was more than ten times that of the average African American household and more than eight times that of the average Latino/Latina household. Moreover, in 2002, almost thirty-five million people lived below the official government poverty level of $18,556 for a family of four, an increase of more than one million people in poverty since 2001.[17]

The Realities of Hedonistic Consumerism

Consumerism is a normal part of life; we purchase the things that we   25
need to live. However, hedonistic consumerism goes beyond all necessary and meaningful boundaries. As the word *hedonism* suggests, some people

[16]Carmen DeNavas-Walt and Robert W. Cleveland, "Income in the United States: 2002," *U.S. Census Bureau: Current Population Reports,* P60–221 (Washington, D.C.: U.S. Government Printing Office, 2003).
[17]Bernadette D. Proctor and Joseph Dalaker, "Poverty in the United States: 2002," *U.S. Census Bureau: Current Population Reports,* P60–222 (Washington, D.C.: U.S. Government Printing Office, 2003).

are so caught up in consumerism that this becomes the main reason for their existence, the primary thing that brings them happiness. Such people engage in the self-indulgent pursuit of happiness through what they buy. An example of this extreme was recently reported in the media. When Antoinette Millard was sued by American Express for an allegedly past-due account, she filed a counterclaim against American Express for having provided her with a big-spender's credit card that allowed her to run up bills of nearly a million dollars in luxury stores in New York.[18] Using the "victim defense," Millard claimed that, based on her income, the company should not have solicited her to sign up for the card. Although this appears to be a far-fetched defense (especially in light of some of the facts),[19] it may be characteristic of the lopsided thinking of many people who spend much more money than they can hope to earn. Recent studies have shown that the average American household is carrying more than eight thousand dollars in credit-card debt and that (statistically speaking) every fifteen seconds a person in the United States goes bankrupt.[20] Although fixed costs (such as housing, food, and gasoline) have gone up for most families over the past thirty years, these debt-and-bankruptcy statistics in fact result from more people buying items that are beyond their means and cannot properly use anyway. Our consumer expectations for ourselves and our children have risen as the media have continued to attractively portray the "good life" and to bombard us with ads for something else that we *must* have.

Are we Americans actually interested in learning about class and inequality? Do we want to know where we really stand in the U.S. class structure? Although some people may prefer to operate in a climate of denial, media critics believe that more people are finally awakening to biases in the media, particularly when they see vast inconsistencies between media portrayals of class and their everyday lives. According to the sociologists Robert Perrucci and Earl Wysong, "It is apparent that increasing experiences with and knowledge about class-based inequalities among the nonprivileged is fostering a growing awareness of and concerns about the nature and extent of superclass interests, motives, and power in the economic and

---

[18]Antoinette Millard, also known as Lisa Walker, allegedly was so caught up in hedonistic consumerism that she created a series of false identities (ranging from being a Saudi princess to being a lawyer, a model, and a wealthy divorcee) and engaged in illegal behavior (such as trying to steal $250,000 from an insurance company by reporting that certain jewelry had been stolen, when she actually had sold it). See Vanessa Grigoriadis, "Her Royal Lie-ness: The So-Called Saudi Princess Was Only One of the Many Identities Lisa Walker Tried On Like Jewelry," *New York Metro*, www.newyorkmetro.com/nymetro/news/people/columns/intelligencer/n_10418 (accessed December 18, 2004); Samuel Maull, "Antoinette Millard Countersues American Express for $2 Million for Allowing Her to Charge $951,000," credit suit.org/credit.php/blog/comments/antoinette_millard_countersues_american_express_for_2_million_for_allowing (accessed December 18, 2004).

[19]Steve Lohr, "Maybe It's Not All Your Fault," *New York Times*, December 5, 2004, WR1.

[20]Lohr, "Maybe It's Not All Your Fault."

political arenas."[21] Some individuals are becoming aware of the effect that media biases can have on what they read, see, and hear. A recent Pew Research Center poll, for example, reflects that people in the working class do not unquestioningly accept media information and commentary that preponderantly support the status quo.[22]

Similarly, Perrucci and Wysong note that television can have a paradoxical effect on viewers: It can serve both as a pacifier and as a source of heightened class consciousness. Programs that focus on how much money the very wealthy have may be a source of entertainment for nonelites, but they may also produce antagonism among people who work hard and earn comparatively little, when they see people being paid so much for doing so little work (e.g., the actress who earns seventeen million dollars per film or the sports star who signs a hundred-million-dollar multiyear contract). Even more egregious are individuals who do not work at all but are born into the "right family" and inherit billions of dollars.

Although affluent audiences might prefer that the media industry work to "reinforce and disguise privileged-class interests,"[23] there is a good chance that the United States will become more class conscious and that people will demand more accurate assessments of the problems we face if more middle- and working-class families see their lifestyles continue to deteriorate in the twenty-first century.

Is Change Likely? Media Realities Support the Status Quo

Will journalists and entertainment writers become more cognizant of class-related issues in news and in television shows? Will they more accurately portray those issues in the future? It is possible that the media will become more aware of class as an important subject to address, but several trends do not bode well for more accurate stories and portrayals of class. Among these are the issues of media ownership and control.

Media Ownership and Senior Management

Media ownership has become increasingly concentrated in recent decades. Massive mergers and acquisitions involving the three major television networks (ABC, CBS, and NBC) have created three media "behemoths" — Viacom, Disney, and General Electric — and the news and entertainment divisions of these networks now constitute only small elements of much larger, more highly diversified corporate structures. Today, these media giants control most of that industry, and a television network is viewed as "just another contributor to the bottom line."[24] As the media

30

[21]Robert Perrucci and Earl Wysong, *The New Class Society*, 2nd ed. (Lanham, Md.: Rowman & Littlefield, 2003), 199.

[22]Perrucci and Wysong, *The New Class Society*.

[23]Perrucci and Wysong, *The New Class Society*, 284.

[24]Committee of Concerned Journalists, "The State of the News Media 2004," www.journalism.org (accessed June 17, 2004).

scholar Shirley Biagi states, "The central force driving the media business in America is the desire to make money. American media are businesses, vast businesses. The products of these businesses are information and entertainment. . . . But American media are, above all, profit-centered."[25]

Concentration of media ownership through chains, broadcast networks, cross-media ownership, conglomerates, and vertical integration (when one company controls several related aspects of the same business) are major limitations to change in how class is represented in the news and entertainment industry. Social analysts like Greg Mantsios[26] are pessimistic about the prospects for change, because of the upper-class-based loyalties of media corporate elites:

> It is no wonder Americans cannot think straight about class. The mass media is neither objective, balanced, independent, nor neutral. Those who own and direct the mass media are themselves part of the upper class, and neither they nor the ruling class in general have to conspire to manipulate public opinion. Their interest is in preserving the status quo, and their view of society as fair and equitable comes naturally to them. But their ideology dominates our society and justifies what is in reality a perverse social order — one that perpetuates unprecedented elite privilege and power on the one hand and widespread deprivation on the other.[27]

According to Mantsios, wealthy media shareholders, corporate executives, and political leaders have a vested interest in obscuring class relations not only because these elites are primarily concerned about profits but because — being among the "haves" themselves — they do not see any reason to stir up class-related animosities. Why should they call attention to the real causes of poverty and inequality and risk the possibility of causing friction among the classes?

Media executives do not particularly care if the general public criticizes the *content* of popular culture as long as audiences do not begin to question the superstructure of media ownership and the benefits these corporations derive from corporate-friendly public policies. According to the sociologist Karen Sternheimer,

> Media conglomerates have a lot to gain by keeping us focused on the popular culture "problem," lest we decide to close some of the corporate tax loopholes to fund more social programs. . . . In short, the news media promote media phobia because it doesn't threaten the bottom line. Calling for social programs to reduce inequality and poverty would.[28]

[25]Shirley Biagi, *Media Impact: An Introduction to Mass Media* (Belmont, Calif.: Wadsworth, 2003), 21.

[26] *Mantsios:* See "Class in America — 2006" (p. 304). [Editors' note]

[27]Gregory Mantsios, "Media Magic: Making Class Invisible," in *Privilege: A Reader*, ed. Michael S. Kimmel and Abby L. Ferber, 99–109 (Boulder, Colo.: Westview, 2003), 108.

[28]Karen Sternheimer, *It's Not the Media: The Truth about Pop Culture's Influence on Children* (Boulder, Colo.: Westview, 2003), 211.

Although the corporate culture of the media industry may be set by shareholders and individuals in the top corporate ranks, day-to-day decisions often rest in the hands of the editor-in-chief (or a person in a similar role) at a newspaper or a television executive at a local station. Typically, the goals of these individuals reflect the profit-driven missions of their parent companies and the continual need to generate the right audiences (often young males between eighteen and thirty-five years of age) for advertisers. Television commentator Jeff Greenfield acknowledges this reality: "The most common misconception most people have about television concerns its product. To the viewer, the product is the programming. To the television executive, the product is the audience."[29] The profits of television networks and stations come from selling advertising, not from producing programs that are accurate reflections of social life.

Recent trends in the media industry — including concentration of ownership, a focus on increasing profits, and a move toward less regulation of the media by the federal government — do not offer reassurance that media representations of class (along with race, gender, age, and sexual orientation) will be of much concern to corporate shareholders or executives at the top media giants — unless, of course, this issue becomes related to the bottom line or there is public demand for change, neither of which seems likely. However, it does appear that there is a possibility for change among some journalists and entertainment writers.

Journalists: Constraints and Opportunities

Some analysts divide journalists into the "big time" players — reporters and journalists who are rich, having earned media salaries in the millions and by writing best-selling books (e.g., ABC's Peter Jennings) — and the "everyday" players, who are primarily known in their local or regional media markets.[30] Elite journalists in the first category typically are employed by major television networks (ABC, CBS, and NBC), popular cable news channels (such as CNN and FOX News), or major national newspapers such as the *Wall Street Journal, New York Times,* or *USA Today.* These journalists may be influential in national media agenda-setting, whereas the everyday media players, beat reporters, journalists, and middle- to upper-level managers at local newspapers or television stations at best can influence local markets.

[29]Quoted in Biagi, *Media Impact,* 170.
[30]One study identified the "typical journalist" as "a white Protestant male who has a bachelor's degree from a public college, is married, 36 years old, earns about $31,000 a year, has worked in journalism for about 12 years, does not belong to a journalism association, and works for a medium-sized (42 journalists), group-owned daily newspaper" (Weaver and Wilhoit 1996). Of course, many journalists today are white women, people of color, non-Protestants, and individuals who are between the ages of 45 and 54 (Committee of Concerned Journalists, "The State of the News Media 2004").

Some of these individuals — at either level — are deeply concerned about the state of journalism in this country, as one recent Pew Research Center for the People and the Press study of 547 national and local reporters, editors, and executives found.[31] One of the major concerns among these journalists was that the economic behavior of their companies was eroding the quality of journalism in the United States. By way of example, some journalists believe that business pressures in the media industry are making the news "thinner and shallower."[32] Journalists are also concerned that the news media pay "too little attention . . . to complex issues."[33] However, a disturbing finding in the Pew study was that some journalists believe that news content is becoming more shallow because that is what the public *wants*. This cynical view may become a self-fulfilling prophecy that leads journalists to produce a shallower product, based on the mistaken belief that the public cannot handle anything else.[34]

Despite all this, some opportunities do exist in the local and national news for *civic journalism* — "a belief that journalism has an obligation to public life — an obligation that goes beyond just telling the news or unloading lots of facts."[35] Civic journalism is rooted in the assumption that journalism has the ability either to empower a community or to help disable it. Based on a civic journalism perspective, a news reporter gathering information for a story has an opportunity to introduce other voices beyond those of the typical mainstream spokesperson called upon to discuss a specific issue such as the loss of jobs in a community or the growing problem of homelessness. Just as more journalists have become aware of the importance of fair and accurate representations of people based on race, gender, age, disability, and sexual orientation, it may be possible to improve media representations of class. Rather than pitting the middle class against the working class and the poor, for example, the media might frame stories in such a way as to increase people's awareness of their shared concerns in a nation where the upper class typically is portrayed as more important and more deserving than the average citizen.

The process of civic journalism encourages journalists to rethink their use of frames. Choosing a specific frame for a story is "the most powerful decision a journalist will make."[36] As journalists become more aware that the media are more than neutral storytelling devices, perhaps more of

---

[31]Pew Center for Civic Journalism, "Finding Third Places: Other Voices, Different Stories," 2004, www.pewcenter.org/doingcj/videos/thirdplaces.html (accessed July 6, 2004).

[32]Bill Kovach, Tom Rosenstiel, and Amy Mitchell, "A Crisis of Confidence: A Commentary on the Findings," Pew Research Center for the People and the Press, 2004, www.stateofthenewsmedia.org/prc.pdf (accessed July 6, 2004), 27.

[33]Kovach, Rosenstiel, and Mitchell, "A Crisis of Confidence," 29.

[34]Kovach, Rosenstiel, and Mitchell, "A Crisis of Confidence."

[35]Pew Center for Civic Journalism, "Finding Third Places."

[36]Steve Smith, "Developing New Reflexes in Framing Stories," Pew Center for Civic Journalism, 1997, www.pewcenter.org/doingcj/civiccat/displayCivcat.php?id=97 (accessed July 3, 2004).

them will develop alternative frames that look deeply into a community of interest (which might include the class-based realities of neighborhoods) to see "how the community interacts with, interrelates to, and potentially solves a pressing community problem." By asking "What is the essence of this story?" rather than "What is the conflict value of this story?" journalists might be less intent, for example, on pitting the indigenous U.S. working class against more recent immigrants or confronting unionized workers with their nonunionized counterparts. Stories that stress conflict have winners and losers, victors and villains; they suggest that people must compete, rather than cooperate, across class lines.[37] An exploration of other types of framing devices might produce better results in showing how social mobility does or does not work in the U.S. stratification system — highlighting, for example, what an individual's real chances are for moving up the class ladder (as is promised in much of the jargon about the rich and famous).

Advocates of civic journalism suggest that two practices might help journalists do a better job of framing in the public interest: *public listening* and *civic mapping*. Public listening refers to "the ability of journalists to listen with open minds and open ears; to understand what people are really saying."[38] Journalists engaged in public listening would be less interested in getting "superficial quotes or sound bites" and instead would move more deeply into the conversations that are actually taking place. Journalists would use open-ended questions in their interviews, by which they could look more deeply into people's hopes, fears, and values, rather than asking closed-ended questions to which the only allowable response choices are "yes/no" or "agree/disagree" — answers that in effect quickly (and superficially) gauge an individual's opinion on a topic. When journalists use civic mapping, they seek out underlying community concerns through discussions with people. They attempt to look beneath the surface of current public discourse on an issue. Mapping helps journalists learn about the ideas, attitudes, and opinions that really exist among diverse groups of people, not just "public opinion" or politicians' views of what is happening.

By seeking out *third places* where they can find "other voices" and hear "different stories," journalists may learn more about people from diverse backgrounds and find out what they are actually thinking and experiencing.[39] A "third place" is a location where people gather and often end up talking about things that are important to them. According to the sociologist Ray Oldenburg, the third place is "a great variety of public places that host the regular, voluntary, informal, and happily anticipated gatherings of individuals beyond the realms of home and work."[40] If the first place is the

---

[37]Richard Harwood, "Framing a Story: What's It Really About?" Pew Center for Civic Journalism, 2004, www.pewcenter.org/doingcj/videos/framing.html (accessed July 3, 2004).

[38]Smith, "Developing New Reflexes in Framing Stories."

[39]Pew Center for Civic Journalism, "Finding Third Places."

[40]Ray Oldenburg, *The Great Good Place: Cafés, Coffee Shops, Bookstores, Bars, Hair Salons and Other Hangouts at the Heart of a Community* (New York: Marlowe, 1999), 16.

home, and the second place is the work setting, then the third place includes such locations as churches, community centers, cafes, coffee shops, bookstores, bars, and other places where people informally gather. As journalists join in the conversation, they can learn what everyday people are thinking about a social issue such as tax cuts for the wealthy. They can also find out what concerns people have and what they think contributes to such problems as neighborhood deterioration.

In addition to listening to other voices and seeking out different stories in third places, journalists might look more systematically at how changes in public policies — such as in tax laws, welfare initiatives, or policies that affect publicly funded child care or public housing — might affect people in various class locations. What are the political and business pressures behind key policy decisions like these? How do policies affect the middle class? The working class? Others? For example, what part does class play in perceptions about local law enforcement agencies? How are police officers viewed in small, affluent incorporated cities that have their own police departments, as compared to low-income neighborhoods of the bigger cities? While wealthy residents in the smaller cities may view police officers as "employees" who do their bidding (such as prohibiting the "wrong kind of people" from entering their city limits at night), in some low-income sectors of larger cities the police may be viewed as "oppressors" or as "racists" who contribute to, rather than reduce, problems of lawlessness and crime in the community. Journalists who practice civic journalism might look beyond typical framing devices to tell a more compelling story about how the intersections of race *and* class produce a unique chemistry between citizens and law enforcement officials. In this way, journalists would not be using taken-for-granted framing devices that have previously been employed to "explain" what is happening in these communities.

Given current constraints on the media, including the fact that much of the new investment in journalism today is being spent on disseminating the news rather than on collecting it,[41] there is room for only cautious optimism that some journalists will break out of the standard reflexive mode to explore the microscopic realities of class at the level where people live, and at the macroscopic level of society, where corporate and governmental elites make important decisions that affect everyone else.

Some media analysts believe that greater awareness of class-related realities in the media would strengthen the democratic process in the United States. According to Mantsios, "A mass media that did not have its own class interests in preserving the status quo would acknowledge that inordinate wealth and power undermine democracy and that a 'free market' economy can ravage a people and their communities."[42] It remains to be seen, however, whether organizations like the Project for Excellence in Journalism and the Committee of Concerned Journalists will be successful in their efforts to

[41]Committee of Concerned Journalists, "The State of the News Media 2004."

[42]Mantsios, "Media Magic," 108.

encourage journalists to move beyond the standard reflexive mode so that they will use new frames that more accurately reflect class-based realities.

Like journalists, many television entertainment writers could look for better ways to frame stories. However, these writers are also beleaguered by changes in the media environment, including new threats to their economic security from reality shows that typically do not employ in-house or freelance writers like continuing series do. As a result, it has become increasingly difficult for entertainment writers to stay gainfully employed, let alone bring new ideas into television entertainment.[43]

We cannot assume that most journalists and television writers are in a   45 position to change media portrayals of class and inequality; however, in the final analysis, the responsibility rests with each of us to evaluate the media and to treat it as only one, limited, source of information and entertainment in our lives. For the sake of our children and grandchildren, we must balance the perspectives we gain from the media with our own lived experiences and use a wider sociological lens to look at what is going on around us in everyday life. Some analysts believe that the media amuse and lull audiences rather than stimulating them to think, but we must not become complacent, thinking that everything is all right as our society and world become increasingly divided between the "haves" and the "have nots."[44] If the media industry persists in retaining the same old frames for class, it will behoove each of us as readers and viewers to break out of those frames and more thoroughly explore these issues on our own.

Bibliography

Biagi, Shirley. *Media Impact: An Introduction to Mass Media,* Belmont, Calif.: Wadsworth, 2003.

Butler, Judith. "Performative Acts and Gender Constitution: An Essay in Phenomenology and Feminist Theory." In *Performing Feminisms: Feminist Critical Theory and Theatre.* Edited by Sue-Ellen Case. Baltimore: Johns Hopkins University Press, 1990.

Committee of Concerned Journalists. "The State of the News Media 2004." www.journalism.org (accessed June 17, 2004).

De Coster, Karen, and Brad Edmonds. Lewrockwell.com, 2003. "TV Nation: The Killing of American Brain Cells." www.lewrockwell.com/decoster/decoster78.html (accessed July 7, 2004).

Delaney, Tim, and Allene Wilcox. "Sports and the Role of the Media." In *Values, Society and Evolution,* edited by Harry Birx and Tim Delaney, 199–215. Auburn, N.Y. Legend, 2002.

DeNavas-Walt, Carmen, and Robert W. Cleveland. "Income in the United States: 2002." *U.S. Census Bureau: Current Population Reports,* P60–221. Washington, D.C.: U.S. Government Printing Office, 2003.

---

[43]"So You Wanna Be a Sitcom Writer?" soyouwanna.com, 2004, www.soyouwanna.com/site/syws/sitcom/sitcom.html (accessed July 7, 2004).

[44]Sternheimer, *It's Not the Media.*

Ginsberg, Thomas. "Union Hopes to Win Over Starbucks Shop Workers." *Austin American-Statesman,* July 2, 2004, D6.

Grigoriadis, Vanessa. "Her Royal Lie-ness: The So-Called Saudi Princess Was Only One of the Many Identities Lisa Walker Tried On Like Jewelry." *New York Metro.* www.newyorkmetro.com/nymetro/news/people/columns/intelligencer/n_10418 (accessed December 18, 2004).

Harwood, Richard. "Framing a Story: What's It Really About?" Pew Center for Civic Journalism, 2004. www.pewcenter.org/doingcj/videos/framing.html (accessed July 3, 2004).

hooks, bell [Gloria Watkins]. *Where We Stand: Class Matters.* New York: Routledge, 2000.

Kovach, Bill, Tom Rosenstiel, and Amy Mitchell. "A Crisis of Confidence: A Commentary on the Findings." Pew Research Center for the People and the Press, 2004. www.stateofthenewsmedia.org/prc.pdf (accessed July 6, 2004).

Mantsios, Gregory. "Media Magic: Making Class Invisible." In *Privilege: A Reader,* edited by Michael S. Kimmel and Abby L. Ferber, 99–109. Boulder, Colo.: Westview, 2003.

Maull, Samuel. "Antoinette Millard Countersues American Express for $2 Million for Allowing Her to Charge $951,000." creditsuit.org/credit.php/blog/comments/antoinette_millard_countersues_american_express_for_2_million_for_allowing (accessed December 18, 2004).

Nocera, Joseph. *A Piece of the Action: How the Middle Class Joined the Money Class.* New York: Simon and Schuster, 1994.

Oldenburg, Ray. *The Great Good Place: Cafés, Coffee Shops, Bookstores, Bars Hair Salons and Other Hangouts at the Heart of a Community.* New York: Marlowe, 1999.

Perrucci, Robert, and Earl Wysong. *The New Class Society.* 2nd edition. Lanham, Md.: Rowman & Littlefield, 2003.

Pew Center for Civic Journalism. 2004, "Finding Third Places: Other Voices, Different Stories." www.pewcenter.org/doingcj/videos/thirdplaces.html (accessed July 6, 2004).

Proctor, Bernadette D., and Joseph Dalaker. "Poverty in the United States: 2002." *U.S. Census Bureau: Current Population Reports,* P60–22. Washington, D.C.: U.S. Government Printing Office, 2003.

Schor, Juliet B. *Born to Buy: The Commercialized Child and the New Consumer Culture.* New York: Scribner, 2004.

Sicha, Choire. "They'll Always Have Paris." *New York Times,* June 13, 2004, AR31, AR41.

Smith, Steve. "Developing New Reflexes in Framing Stories." Pew Center for Civic Journalism, 1997. www.pewcenter.org/doingcj/civiccat/displayCivcat.php?id=97 (accessed July 3, 2004).

"So You Wanna Be a Sitcom Writer?" soyouwanna.com, 2004. www.soyouwanna.com/site/syws/sitcom/sitcom.html (accessed July 7, 2004).

Sternheimer, Karen. *It's Not the Media: The Truth about Pop Culture's Influence on Children.* Boulder, Colo.: Westview, 2003.

Uchitelle, Louis. "We Pledge Allegiance to the Mall." *New York Times,* December 6, 2004, C12.

Weaver, David H., and G. Cleveland Wilhoit. *The American Journalist in the 1990s.* Mahwah, N.J.: Lawrence Erlbaum, 1996.

ENGAGING THE TEXT

1. Debate Kendall's assertion that "the media do not simply mirror society; rather, they help to shape it and to create cultural perceptions" (para. 3). Do you agree with Kendall's claim that the media distort our perceptions of social inequality? Do you think that watching TV inclines Americans to run up credit card debt?

2. Review Kendall's explanation of why middle- and working-class people sometimes buy items beyond their means, particularly items associated with wealthy celebrities. Do you agree that this behavior is best understood as "vicarious living" and "unnecessary consumerism"? In small groups, brainstorm lists of purchases you think exemplify hedonistic or unnecessary consumerism. How does hedonistic consumerism appear in a college setting?

3. Kendall says the media use "thematic framing" and "episodic framing" in portraying poor Americans. Define these terms in your own words and discuss whether the media typically portray the poor as "deviant" or "Other."

4. According to Kendall, how do media representations of the working class and the middle class differ? Do you see evidence of this difference in the shows she mentions or in others you are familiar with?

5. What does Kendall mean by "civic journalism" (para. 37)? Why is she pessimistic about the future of civic journalism in national news organizations? Do you see any evidence of such journalism in your local news outlets?

EXPLORING CONNECTIONS

6. Imagine what "Looking for Work" (p. 26) or "The Lesson" (p. 264) might look like if it were turned into a TV episode. Keeping Kendall's observations in mind, how do you think TV might frame these stories about social class?

7. Re-examine the images in the Visual Portfolio (p. 321). Discuss how they "frame" issues of social class and how each image supports or challenges conventional media frames.

EXTENDING THE CRITICAL CONTEXT

8. Review Kendall's definitions of consensus framing, admiration framing, emulation framing, and price-tag framing. Then watch one of the TV shows she mentions in paragraph 8 or a similar current show and look for evidence of these framing devices. Discuss with classmates how prominent these frames seem to be in contemporary TV programs.

From *The Missing Class*

Katherine S. Newman and Victor Tan Chen

On the rare occasions that most Americans talk about social class, we tend to speak of just a few categories — usually the wealthy, the middle class, the working class, and perhaps the impoverished. Of the several readings in this chapter that complicate such simple schemes, this one is the most focused and specific: Newman and Chen explain that there is a huge "Missing Class," numbering more than 50 million, who are not homeless or destitute but who hover perilously on the brink of poverty. In this selection from the opening chapter of their book The Missing Class *(2007), the authors describe three members of the Missing Class and argue that the nation should be paying much more attention to the immense group they represent. Katherine S. Newman is professor of Sociology and Public Affairs at Princeton University and director of the Princeton Institute for International and Regional Studies; her numerous books address such topics as the working poor, downward mobility, and the social roots of school violence. Victor Tan Chen has published in* Newsday, The Chronicle of Higher Education, The Miami Herald, *and other venues; he is the founding editor of* INTHEFRAY Magazine, *a progressive online publication.*

Valerie Rushing starts her shift at midnight. A train pulls into the station, and she hops on it, mop in hand. The thirty-three-year-old mother of one is an employee for the Long Island Rail Road, the busiest commuter railroad in North America, which every morning carries an army of groggy suburbanites to their Manhattan offices, and every night shuttles them back home. When their day ends, hers begins. Most nights she'll mop twenty cars. Tonight it's twice that because she's working a double shift — midnight to 8 A.M., and 8 A.M. to 4 P.M.

Toilet duty, of course, is the worst. Long Islanders are a more slovenly sort than the city's notorious subway riders, Valerie grouses. "You figure that they would have some consideration for the next person that is going to use the bathroom, but they don't. They'll throw their whatevers there in the garbage, in the toilet. . . . And they are the most alcoholic people that I know." Every night, an eclectic assortment of paper-sheathed beer cans and bottles awaits her.

But don't feel sorry for Valerie Rushing. With a union card in her pocket, she makes $13.68 an hour, plus full benefits.[1] Her earlier life at the

---

[1] In 2006 dollars, Valerie's hourly wage of $13.68 (in 1999) would be $16.55. [All notes are Newman and Chen's unless otherwise indicated.]

THIS MODERN WORLD

by TOM TOMORROW

minimum wage — as a child-care worker, shoe-store employee, and fast-food cashier — is a distant memory.

Two years with the Long Island Rail Road have broadened Valerie's outlook. Before, she hardly ventured into the other boroughs; now she feels comfortable traversing the city and doesn't think twice about heading out to Manhattan to shop. Yes, it's janitorial work, but Valerie doesn't complain. "If it's sweeping, it's sweeping," she says. The point is, it pays the bills.

And Valerie has a lot of bills. She has sole responsibility for her daughter and has custody of her niece's six-year-old son because his own grandmother, Valerie's crack-addled sister, can't be bothered. Valerie sets aside part of every paycheck for the children's clothes, toys, and excursions. She puts aside another part to pay for her $700-a-month Brooklyn apartment, and she stashes away what she can toward that suburban house she hopes to buy someday soon.[2]

Valerie is not poor, but she is not middle class. Instead, she occupies an obscure place between rungs of the nation's social ladder — somewhere

5

[2] This sketch is a composite of details from 1999–2000 and 2002.

between working hard and succeeding, between dreaming big and living in the shadow of her ambitions. People like Valerie don't make the headlines. They aren't invited to focus groups. Blue-ribbon commissions on poverty do not include them. They are a forgotten labor force — too prosperous to be the "working poor," too insecure to be "middle income."

They are America's Missing Class.

They are people like Tomás Linares. A year shy of fifty, he is still clocking in seven days a week at two jobs in centers for people with developmental disabilities, where Tomás spends his days patiently demonstrating to his charges how to brush their teeth, reprimanding them for stealing and scratching, and occasionally wrestling an unruly resident to the floor. For his efforts, he makes a little less than $20,000 a year.

Tomás is not poor, but a look at his rundown Brooklyn apartment might suggest otherwise. He lives in an urban borderland sandwiched between two extremes: the concentrated poverty of rampant drug dealing, sporadic gang violence, and shuttered factories that Tomás has known since his youth and the collateral prosperity that middle-class newcomers and mounting real estate prices bring to Brooklyn these days. Divorced and lacking a college education, Tomás has few prospects for rising much higher in life and no illusion that he'll ever leave his seedy corner.

Gloria Hall is part of the Missing Class as well, but perhaps for not 10 much longer. An employee of the city's health department, she stopped working after falling seriously ill. She has insurance, but her policy won't cover the specialized treatment recommended for her rare form of cancer. So Gloria is a frequent visitor to the local teaching hospital, a drab health-care assembly line where patients like her are nonchalantly wheeled from room to room, waiting interminably for their release. For Gloria, living in near poverty means walking a tightrope over this frayed safety net, unsure of what each new step in her treatment will bring.

It also means worrying about what her deteriorating health will mean for her two adolescent sons, who suffer from the affliction of a deadbeat dad. What will happen to them if she dies? Who will care for them when she's not there? She knows that the odds are stacked against children like hers, those who are unlucky enough to be born black and male and statistically at risk — as crime victims and perpetrators, developmentally disabled and dropouts. Her two boys are unluckier still: they live in a household that is not poor but near poor. "I know some parents that are in worse situations than I am, financially," Gloria says. "And they get everything. Every year their kids go away to summer camp.

"You either got to be on the bottom, or you've got to be on the top."

Thirty-seven million Americans live below the poverty line. We know a lot about them because journalists, politicians, think tanks, and social scientists track their lives in great detail. Every time the poverty rate goes up or down, political parties take credit or blame for this important bell-wether.

Yet there is a much larger population of Americans that virtually no one pays attention to: the near poor. Fifty-four million Americans — including 21 percent of the nation's children — live in this nether region above the poverty line but well below a secure station.[3] This "Missing Class" is composed of households earning roughly between $20,000 and $40,000 for a family of four.[4]

The hard-won wages of Missing Class families place them beyond the   15
reach of most policies that speak to the conditions of life among the poor. Yet they are decidedly *not* middle-class Americans. In decades past we might have called them working class, but even that label fails to satisfy, now that many Missing Class workers toil in traditionally white-collar domains like health clinics and schools, even as their incomes, households, and neighborhoods lack the solidity of an earlier generation's blue-collar, union-sheltered way of life. Missing Class families earn less money, have few savings to cushion themselves, and send their kids to schools that are underfunded and crowded. The near poor live in inner-ring suburbs and city centers where many of the social problems that plague the truly poor constrain their lives as well. Crime, drugs, and delinquency are less of a problem in near-poor neighborhoods than they are in blighted ghettos, but they are down the block, within earshot, and close enough to threaten their kids.

[3] Near-poor families come in many shapes and sizes. Twenty-nine percent of the nation's children who live with single mothers are near poor. A slightly smaller portion of children who live with single fathers are near poor as well. Households with more earners in them—and more adults to share the tasks of raising the kids—are greatly advantaged, but there are still a significant number of near poor among the nation's married families; 19 percent of children who live with both parents are in the Missing Class. Younger parents are at greater risk for joining the near poor than older parents, who have more job experience. Education is a powerful force that shapes the options for employment and therefore for family income. Thirty-two percent of children growing up in homes where parents have not graduated from high school are near poor, while only 16 percent of those whose parents have had at least some college are in the Missing Class. Hsien-Hen Lu and Heather Koball, *The Changing Demographics of Low-Income Families and Their Children* (New York: National Center for Children in Poverty, Columbia University, Mailman School of Public Health, Research Brief No. 2, 2003).

[4] This is 100–200 percent of the official poverty line. The poverty line is adjusted for family size, and so are the income lines that demarcate the near poor. Therefore, a family of two would be among the near poor in 2006 if it had an annual income of $13,200–26,400, and a family of three would need $16,600–33,200 to be ranked in the Missing Class. Actual expenses vary a great deal by locality, of course; a household income of $36,000 would sustain a decent standard of living in rural Arkansas but would not go very far in San Francisco. (The poverty line as described here is taken from the Health and Human Services Department's 2006 poverty guidelines, which can be found at http://aspe.hhs.gov/poverty/06poverty.shtml. The poverty thresholds released by the Census Bureau are more precise; for instance, the 2005 federal poverty line for a family of four was $19,971. See www.census.gov/hhes/www/poverty/threshld/thresho5.html.)

Sending Missing Class teens to college, the single most important fault line in determining their long-range prospects, is difficult for the near poor. Many are unaware of the financial aid that might await their children. Parents who have never navigated the shoals of college admission are poorly prepared to offer advice, and the schools that might take over this stewardship are overwhelmed with the task of getting kids to graduate in the first place. Near-poor kids are the ones who work many hours while still in high school, who hardly ever see their guidance counselor, and who struggle to complete homework assignments that no one nearby can help them with.

Yet, because their earnings place them above the poverty line, the Missing Class is rarely on the national radar screen. We just don't think about them. This needs to change. The fate of Missing Class families is a test for this country of what it can offer to those citizens — immigrants and native-born alike — who have pulled themselves off the floor that poverty represents. If they can move up, they clear the way for those coming behind them. If they can at least stay where they are, their example will matter to others. But if their children fail to advance — if they fall back into the hole that the parents labored so hard to escape from — we will have defaulted on the promise of this wealthy nation. We will have seen a temporary respite in a single generation from the problems of poverty, only to see it emerge again in the children of the Missing Class. The danger is real — and growing with every new crack in our increasingly open and vulnerable economy.

Ironically, some of their problems stem from what most would agree is an entirely positive aspect of Missing Class life. Near-poor parents are firmly attached to the world of work. While many arrived in the Missing Class as graduates from the ranks of the welfare dependent, they are now lodged in jobs as transit workers, day-care providers, hospital attendants, teachers' aides, and clerical assistants. They pay their taxes and struggle to keep afloat on wages that are better than the minimum — if not by a huge margin. Yet even as these men and women dutifully turn the wheels of the national economy, their devotion to work takes a toll on their family life, especially on their children, who spend long hours in substandard day care or raise themselves in their teen years.

Of necessity, Missing Class families live fairly close to the margins. They have a hard time saving to buffer themselves from downturns in the economy because a large portion of their income disappears into the pockets of landlords and cash registers of grocery stores every month. As long as the adults — and many of the teens — stay on the job, they can manage. But the slightest push can send them hurtling down the income ladder again. In fact, even in the prosperous years of 1996–2002, about 16 percent of the nation's near-poor families lost a tenth or more of their income. It is important to recognize that the majority actually went in the other direction: they gained income in excess of 30 percent. These upwardly mobile families are headed out of the Missing Class for something much better. Nonetheless, the group that slides is not insignificant, and its ranks have probably grown, now that the economy has cooled.[5]

Missing Class Americans live in safer communities than the truly poor. Indeed, many look out upon their neighborhoods in amazement because they are barely recognizable from the destitute and crime-ridden days of yore. As gentrification has taken root in overheated real estate markets, once-affordable enclaves are now almost beyond the reach of the Missing Class. The arrival of affluent new neighbors brings with it more attention from city officials and the police, more investment in the aesthetics of the community, and something closer to a rainbow of complexions on the streets. For the African Americans, Dominicans, and Puerto Ricans who used to "own" these neighborhoods, this is mainly a blessing. Still, some wonder whether they still belong — whether they are still welcome on their own turf.

Sixty-eight percent of Americans are now the proud owners of their own homes. The near poor must struggle to join their ranks. Many of them missed out on the great run-up in housing prices that created so much wealth in the 1990s and the first five years of this decade. Trapped in a renter's limbo, the Missing Class cannot feather its nest for retirement or borrow against houses to pay for children's college educations. What's more, the children won't enjoy anything approaching the inheritance — in property, cash, or other assets — that their middle-class counterparts will surely reap. These wealth differences are crucial: savings are the safety net that catches you when you falter, but Missing Class families have no such

20

---

[5]The table below summarizes the percentage change in family income divided by its poverty line in the base period (1996–98) and the average in 2000–2002. The data come from the Panel Study of Income Dynamics (PSID), a nationally representative longitudinal study of nearly eight thousand U.S. families and individuals who have been followed since 1968. The sample drawn for this table includes all PSID families with an average family income in 1996 and 1998 that is *above* the poverty line but below *twice* the poverty line and hence meets our definition of the near poor (or the Missing Class). The poverty line is adjusted for family size. These data were analyzed by Professor Peter Gottschalk, Department of Economics, Boston College (personal communication).

Percentage change	Frequency	Percentage	Cumulative
More than 30% decline	250	8.81	8.81
20–30% decline	118	4.16	12.97
10–20% decline	103	3.63	16.6
0–10% decline	159	5.6	22.21
0–10% rise	165	5.82	28.02
10–20% rise	159	5.6	33.63
20–30% rise	138	4.86	38.49
More than 30% rise	1,745	61.51	100
Total	2,837	100	100

bulwark.[6] As a result, they experience an odd fusion of optimism and insecurity: the former from their upward mobility, the latter from the nagging concern that it could all disappear if just one thing goes wrong. One uninsured child sick enough to pull a parent off the job; one marriage spiraling into divorce; one layoff that shuts off the money spigot.

Like most American consumers, the Missing Class is impatient for just rewards: No one wants to sit on a couch with holes in it, but for the near poor, a new couch is beyond their means. The answer, too often, is debt. Missing Class families are generally uneducated in the ways of credit, and credit card companies are all too happy to indulge them. They deluge the mailboxes of Missing Class families with offers; they avert their eyes as Missing Class households rack up outrageous bills. (In 2005 Congress passed bankruptcy laws that prevent consumers from shielding their assets from creditors, making this kind of debt even more lethal.)[7] What's more, Missing Class families live in neighborhoods that are chronically underserved by financial institutions and scrupulously avoided by grocery chains and other major retail outlets. Denied even the most basic infrastructure for savings or loans at reasonable rates and forced to pay a premium on virtually everything they buy, these harried workers turn to check-cashing stores that exact a cut before handing over their wages. They purchase their food, household goods, and furniture at corner bodegas and other small shops with high margins.

At the same time that the pull of rising wages and the push of welfare reform have drawn millions of low-income parents deeper into the labor market, new policies governing the lives of their children have emerged that clash with the demands of the adult work world. The No Child Left Behind Act has thrust the burly arm of the state into third-grade classrooms, where kids used to the demands of finger paints and Autoharps[8] are now sweating high-stakes tests every year. Eight-year-olds wake up with stomachaches because they are afraid of being held back in school if they cannot pass these exams. Missing Class kids do not fret needlessly; the failure rates on statewide tests are high in their neighborhoods.

ENGAGING THE TEXT

1. What are the characteristics of a Missing Class individual or family? What various strategies do the authors use to define and describe this class? Do

---

[6]Melvin Oliver and Thomas Shapiro, *Black Wealth / White Wealth: A New Perspective on Racial Inequality*, 2nd ed. (New York: Routledge, 2006), and Dalton Conley, *Being Black, Living in the Red: Race, Wealth, and Social Policy in America* (Berkeley: University of California Press, 1999).

[7]Elizabeth Warren, "Show Me the Money," *New York Times*, October 24, 2005.

[8]*Autoharps:* Stringed musical instruments used most often in folk music; their design makes them relatively easy to play. [Editors' note]

you find the term useful, and do you agree with the authors that this group deserves more national attention?

2. Newman and Chen point out the vulnerability of individuals in the Missing Class to economic downturns. Discuss how Valerie Rushing, Tomás Linares, or Gloria Hall may have fared in the recession that began in 2008. Which of them was most at risk, which least, and why?

3. Analyze this reading as a problem-solution essay: what problem(s) do Newman and Chen outline in this reading, and what solutions do they offer? Based on these opening pages of their book, what call to action would you expect *The Missing Class* to make?

4. If you consider yourself in an economic class higher than the Missing Class, what put you there, and what keeps you there? How sturdy is the safety net that keeps you from poverty or near-poverty?

EXPLORING CONNECTIONS

5. Would you place the people and characters listed below in the Missing Class, above it, or below it? Use specific information from the readings to support your answers.

> The narrator of Gary Soto's "Looking for Work" (p. 26)
>
> The Bronx schoolchildren Jonathan Kozol describes in paragraphs 17–24 of "Still Separate, Still Unequal" (p. 219)
>
> Horatio Alger's "Ragged Dick" (p. 258)
>
> Sylvia, the narrator of "The Lesson" by Toni Cade Bambara (p. 264)
>
> Boyd Zimmerman, the "middle-class" resident of the Tent City described by Maria L. La Ganga (p. 357)
>
> The undocumented migrant encountered by Rubén Martínez in "The Crossing" (p. 473)

6. Compare Tim Blixseth's attitude toward credit in "Living It: Tim Blixseth" (p. 279) to the behaviors and predicaments Newman and Chen describe in para. 22. Do you think Blixseth would agree with the authors that Missing Class families are preyed upon by financial institutions? Do you think the authors' characterization of credit card companies, banks, and retailers is too harsh, about right, or perhaps too soft?

EXTENDING THE CRITICAL CONTEXT

7. Do some research to find out which employees in your area or on your campus are unionized and which are not; consider jobs in such areas as teaching, food and hospitality industries, manufacturing, agriculture, construction, and public safety (police, fire fighters, EMTs). Then research one or more specific unions and the claims it makes about having helped or protected workers over the past few years. To what extent do you think unions have benefited local workers, especially in the toughest or lowest-paying occupations?

8. The Missing Class will, by definition, appear rarely in the media. Brainstorm with classmates to think of films or TV programming (news, reality TV, soaps, etc.) that might offer a glimpse of Missing Class life. Are 50 million Americans truly invisible in our mainstream media?

Tent City, USA

Maria L. La Ganga

The recession that began in 2008 is often measured numerically—number of jobs lost, home foreclosures, or businesses gone bankrupt. Beyond the numbers, of course, are our lived experiences, and for some Americans that means struggling to fulfill the basic human needs of food, clothing, and shelter. In "Tent City, USA," journalist Maria La Ganga covers the story of some two hundred Californians, many of them newly unemployed, who sought shelter in a tent city near downtown Sacramento. La Ganga is a staff writer for the Los Angeles Times.

The capital's tent city sprawls messily on a grassed-over landfill beneath power lines, home to some two hundred men and women with nowhere else to go. It has been here for more than a year, but in the last three weeks it has transformed into a vivid symbol of a financial crisis otherwise invisible to most Americans.

The Depression had Hoovervilles. The energy crisis had snaking gas lines. The state's droughts have empty reservoirs and brown lawns. But today's deep recession is largely about disappearing wealth—painful, yes, but difficult to see. Then this tattered encampment along the American River began showing up on Oprah Winfrey, Al Jazeera,[1] and other news outlets around the world. On Thursday, city officials announced that they will shut it down within a month. "We're finding other places to go," said Steven Maviglio, a spokesman for Sacramento's mayor. The camp is "not safe. It's not humane. But we're not going in with a bulldozer."

The ragtag community captured the collective imagination through a powerful combination of geography, celebrity, and journalistic convenience. "This is the state capital of the seventh-largest economy in the world, with a

[1]*Al Jazeera:* International TV news network specializing in coverage of the Arab world and Middle East.

"Honey, we're homeless."

movie-star governor, Arnold Schwarzenegger, and an NBA pro-athlete for a new mayor, Kevin Johnson," said Barbara O'Connor, director of the Institute for the Study of Politics and Media at Cal State Sacramento. And the camp "is a wonderful visual for TV journalists."

On a recent chilly morning in the tent city, it is not yet sunrise. A Fox News van is parked nearby. A flashlight illuminates the inside of a dome tent. Traffic whines along the adjacent freeway. Cats criss-cross the encampment, eyes glowing. As the sky slowly lightens, shadowy figures emerge and head for the bushes along the riverbank. There are no portable toilets. The dumpster is a new arrival, a donation that followed the flood of news reports.

Jim Gibson heads to a neighboring tent, where two of his friends — an unemployed car salesman married to a onetime truck driver — are brewing coffee on a propane stove. Gibson looks like anybody's sunburned suburban dad, all jeans, polar fleece, and sleepy eyes, his neatly trimmed hair covered by a ball cap. Seven months ago, the fifty-year-old contractor had a job and an apartment in Sacramento. Today, he struggles to stay clean and fed. A former owner of the American dream, he is living the American nightmare. In 2004, Gibson was a semi-retired San Jose homeowner, who got bored and wanted to go back to work. Five years, two houses, and four layoffs later, the widower and grandfather says he is "trying to survive and look for work. The only work I've found is holding an advertising sign on a street corner."

Survival is the biggest time-filler here. Tents must be shored up against wind and rain. The schedule for meals, clothing giveaways, and shower times at local agencies must be strictly followed. CeCe Walker, forty-eight, is just back from coffee, breakfast, and a shower at Maryhouse, a daytime shelter for women. She has lugged a bag of ice for half a mile and cleans out a cooler with "Hobo Fridge" written on the side in thick black marker. "I've never camped in my life," she says, sorting through supplies damp from yesterday's melted ice. "This will make you old. I don't see how people want to live out here forever. God!" The tent city sprawls along the river in small clusters of ersatz neighborhoods. Walker and her neighbor, Charly Hine, thirty-eight, have pitched their tents at the distant edge to stay away from noise and trouble. Gibson's tent is in a separate, small, neat grouping. One neighbor displays an American flag and a goose with the word "welcome" on its breast. It is a favorite subject, its owner says, of news photographers. Another has a mailbox and a gate.

The largest and most raucous neighborhood is composed of about seventy tents closest to the street. Near noon, Tammie and Keith Day are drinking beer around a cold fire pit, worrying about how she'll get her diabetes medication and fretting about whether officials will shutter the tent city. "We're homeless and being evicted?" Tammie fumes. "Now I've heard everything." Keith has rheumatoid arthritis. Tammie says they both battle mental illness and alcoholism. Soon, they are in a screaming fight, hurling epithets and bricks at each other. The bricks, at least, miss their marks.

One downside to all the media attention, Tammie says before the brawl, is that her family no longer pays for her prescription. They have seen the news. Her brother is "disgusted." And her mother "doesn't even talk to me now." But an upside rolls up the dusty path about 3:30: a white Toyota pickup from the Florin Worship Center, with volunteers distributing dinner — pasta, potatoes and eggs scrambled together, beans. A maroon Ford Expedition is next, with free tents. A Roseville handyman arrives with firewood.

On this day, Sister Libby Fernandez, executive director of the homeless support group Loaves & Fishes, and attorney Cathleen Williams have convened a meeting of the tent city's leadership council. They sit on a dusty footpath under a tree and talk about the future. Fernandez says she has to return a call back at the office. "Maria Shriver[2] wants to know what the hell is going on," she says. "I'll tell her we need Porta-Potties." Last week, the city announced that it could clear out the tent city in fourteen days but backed off after the mayor called an emergency summit meeting among city officials, homeless advocates, and leaders in the homeless population. But after summit meeting No. 2 on Thursday, he announced various new measures, among them finding more shelter beds for the tent city's residents

---

[2]*Maria Shriver:* Journalist, author, and First Lady of California — that is, wife of Governor Arnold Schwarzenegger.

and studying the feasibility of a permanent encampment. But not where it is now. By April 30, he said, this one must close. "The fact that we have all this attention, people have asked me if I think it's a negative and a stain for the city," Johnson said, in a recent interview. "Now that we have a spotlight shining . . . it allows us to fix it."

Fernandez figures that about four-fifths of the tent city's residents have been homeless for more than a year. Many of them are people like Preston Anderson, fifty-seven, who would be happy if he never slept under a roof again. He has his dogs. He feeds stale croissants to wild birds and supports himself by scavenging cans. "Nobody bothers me," he said. "I'm free." The rest — a growing number — are recession victims, such as Boyd Zimmerman and his fiancee, Christina Hopper.

It is 4 P.M. The wind picks up and the shadows lengthen. Zimmerman is trying to help neighbors Jeffrey and Louise Staal pitch a big new tent. They are defeated by the gusts. Zimmerman and Hopper have lived in the tent city for the last seven months. In Phoenix, he had a job driving contract laborers from one work site to another. They owned a double-wide trailer. Then work dried up. They sold their home "for almost nothing" and headed to Sacramento, where Zimmerman grew up. He's one of the lucky ones. He got a paying job at Loaves & Fishes and is saving to rent an apartment. "I have a AAA card," he says ruefully as the sun sinks. "I'm middle-class. . . . I have to get the heck out of here. It's not a good life."

ENGAGING THE TEXT

1. La Ganga presents brief glimpses of numerous tent city residents — Jim Gibson, CeCe Walker, Charly Hine, Tammie and Keith Day, Preston Anderson, Boyd Zimmerman, Christina Hopper, and Jeffrey and Louise Staal. Review what La Ganga says about each of these individuals and explain what each profile contributes to her larger story. What composite picture of the residents emerges?

2. Aside from the actual residents of the tent city, who are all the other people in the story? What challenges does the tent city present to each of these, and how are they responding?

3. Discuss Boyd Zimmerman's comment that "I'm middle-class" (para. 11).

4. How closely does this story adhere to the usual journalistic goal of maintaining an objective tone? To what extent does the story imply a need for action or suggest a best course of action?

EXPLORING CONNECTIONS

5. In "Framing Class, Vicarious Living, and Conspicuous Consumption" (p. 330), Diana Kendall examines how media "frame" social class. Review Kendall's ideas and apply them to this story: how does La Ganga frame the story, and how would you expect Oprah Winfrey, Fox News, and Al Jazeera (all mentioned by La Ganga) to frame it?

6. The photograph on page 328 of this chapter's Visual Portfolio was taken at the tent city in Sacramento, California, in 2009. How does reading "Tent City, USA" change or enrich your understanding of the photo, and how does the photo inform your reading of La Ganga's story?

EXTENDING THE CRITICAL CONTEXT

7. La Ganga notes that by March 2009 Sacramento officials had decided to shut down the tent city within a month. Research what happened to the encampment after La Ganga's story and report to the class.

8. As La Ganga points out, the Sacramento tent city drew international attention; it was much photographed and filmed. Browse the Internet for film clips or photos from the encampment; share the most interesting of these with classmates and discuss what you learned from them.

From *America's New Working Class*

KATHLEEN R. ARNOLD

Most Americans would probably agree that the purpose of federal welfare programs is to provide economic assistance such as food stamps to people who need it, who can't quite make ends meet. Such a view regards welfare as an essentially humanitarian endeavor. In the reading below, political theorist Kathleen R. Arnold proposes a rather more sinister alternative — that the real purpose of welfare programs is to maintain a supply of cheap labor while disciplining and closely monitoring welfare recipients. Arnold teaches political science at the University of Texas, San Antonio. She is author of Homelessness, Citizenship, and Identity: The Uncanniness of Late Modernity *(2004) and* America's New Working Class: Race, Gender, and Ethnicity in a Biopolitical Age *(2007), from which this selection is excerpted.*

[Welfare and "workfare"][1] should be viewed in the same terms as parole — the recipient is not merely a client, an individual whose transaction with a bureaucracy has a beginning and end. Rather, like parole, welfare entails strict adherence to rules (including the monitoring of one's sexual activities and limits to the number of children one can have), close

---

[1]*welfare, workfare:* Welfare programs provide economic support to persons in need; workfare programs require aid recipients to work to receive social assistance. [Eds.]

scrutiny of what are normally considered private details, and harsh penalties for noncompliance. For parolees, the threat is a return to prison; for non-compliant welfare or workfare recipients, the threats involve one's very existence: homelessness, malnourishment, and a deeper descent into poverty.[2] As Sheldon Wolin states: "The state is, therefore, allowed to deal arbitrarily with all welfare recipients, not by lynching them but by redefining the conditions and categories of their existence."[3] . . .

Clearly, the word "reform" is disingenuous when applied to the welfare changes of 1996; instead of improving the situation of the poor, reform "is punishment of individuals or restriction of their rights in order to improve their characters or behaviors, as in 'reform school.' This type of welfare reform has a long tradition" in both the United States and the United Kingdom.[4] As many authors have demonstrated, the notion that poverty or joblessness is a result of personal failings is particularly American, even as some European countries have shared the values of the Protestant work ethic to a lesser extent. This explains why our policies are far more punitive and individually oriented than in other liberal capitalist countries (although England comes close).[5]

As Sheila D. Collins and Gertrude Schaffner Goldberg discuss, the history of welfare or poor relief in the United States has had the following undemocratic characteristics:[6] outdoor relief is limited or denied (this is still true — many cities ban individual food donations and regulate outdoor bread lines);[7] work is provided under coercive conditions (workfare today is not voluntary, wages are below minimum wage, benefits are not provided, and workfare wages can be garnished to pay back welfare); there is an assumption that paupers are irresponsible and individually flawed (this assumption is still evident in the ascetic prescriptions of TANF[8] and nearly all other welfare programs); the notion that the provision of aid is a causal factor in the demand for it (this is evident today in talks about welfare dependency and cheating); authorities have required relatives who are often also poor to aid their poor relations (this is still true, particularly with entrance to a homeless shelter — the individual must prove that he or she has exhausted the list of relatives with whom to stay before entering the

---

[2] On "penal welfarism," or the connection between the welfare state and criminal justice, see Garland, *Culture of Control*. [Notes are Arnold's unless otherwise indicated.]

[3] Wolin, "Democracy and the Welfare State," 159.

[4] Sheila D. Collins and Gertrude Schaffner Goldberg, *Washington's New Poor Law* (New York: Apex Press, Council on International and Public Affairs, 2001), 6.

[5] See Wilson, *When Work Disappears*.

[6] Collins and Goldberg, *Washington's New Poor Law*, 9. The characteristics listed in this paragraph are Collins and Goldberg's; the parenthetical comments are mine.

[7] For example, San Francisco has arrested individuals for feeding the homeless. In many other cities, outdoor bread lines have been hotly contested.

[8] *TANF:* Temporary Assistance for Needy Families, the formal name for the U.S. welfare program. [Eds.]

shelter);[9] aid is not viewed as an entitlement in the United States (and never has been, and furthermore, this is truer today than it was in the early part of the twentieth century); welfare relief varies from state to state (and always has); despite Supreme Court rulings that strike down residency requirements as limiting freedom of travel, local authorities deny or limit assistance to newcomers (and always have), be they citizens or immigrants;[10] and, finally, welfare has "denied recipients political and civil rights in return for a meager dole"[11] (this is still true de facto if not de jure). These broad characteristics of welfare throughout U.S. history highlight not only the punitive character of the welfare system[12] but also the coercive nature of workfare. The crucial assumptions behind workfare programs are two: participants must be forced to work; and they have no motivation to do so and thus must be guided, shaped, and disciplined. This is why they are denied choices that ordinary workers would ideally have, such as what hours to work, what they will be paid, and where their wages will go.

It needs to be emphasized that workfare is dependent *not* on job creation but rather on a flexible labor market:

> Contemporary workfare policies rarely involve job creation on any significant scale, along the lines of the old-fashioned public-works programs; they are more concerned with deterring welfare claims and necessitating the acceptance of low-paid, unstable jobs in the context of increasingly "flexible" labor markets. Stripped down to its labor-regulatory essence, workfare is not about creating jobs for people that don't have them; it is about creating workers for jobs that nobody wants. In a Foucauldian[13] sense, it is seeking to make "docile bodies" for the new economy: flexible, self-reliant, and self-disciplining.[14]

Welfare and workfare indicate bare survival — recipients are not meant to rise even to lower-middle-class status. As Piven and Cloward note:

> In New York City, some 45,000 people, mainly women, sweep the streets and clean the subways and the parks. They do the work once done by unionized municipal employees. But instead of a paycheck and

---

[9]As a housing advocate in Boston's shelter system, I was required to go through a list of relatives and friends with whom shelter residents could stay. Among other problems this causes, staying with a relative or friend can endanger the terms of that person's lease.

[10]See Sanford F. Schram, "Introduction," in *Welfare Reform: A Race to the Bottom?* ed. Schram and Samuel H. Beer (Washington, D.C.: Woodrow Wilson Center Press, n.d.). Recent changes in TANF requirements (2006) may allow American-born recipients to move from state to state without cessation of welfare; however, it is unclear whether this will be implemented efficiently.

[11]Collins and Goldberg, *Washington's New Poor Law*, 9.

[12]See, for example, Garland, *Culture of Control*.

[13]*Foucauldian:* Resembling the ideas of French philosopher Michel Foucault (1926–1984); Foucault's *Discipline and Punish: The Birth of the Prison* (1975) theorized about Western systems of punishment and control. [Eds.]

[14]Jamie Peck, *Workfare States* (New York: Guilford Press, 2001), 6.

a living wage, they get a welfare check that leaves them far below the poverty level, and they have none of the benefits and protections of unionized workers. Perhaps just as bad, they have become public spectacles of abject and degraded labor — of slave labor, many of them say.[15]

The word slavery is an exaggeration but it is not incidental: workers in Marx's analysis were also "free" to sell their labor and participate in a "free" market; but their limited choices, de facto political disenfranchisement, lack of collective bargaining or representation (i.e., unions), and inhuman work conditions indicated a profound asymmetry of political power. These dynamics, which are present today just as in Marx's time, challenge any claims about "freedom." Today, workfare and welfare programs have taken away many of the rights (not necessarily in the legal sense but broadly conceived) that ordinary citizens enjoy, including the rights to privacy and individual moral choice as well as the right to determine work conditions.

Furthermore, if the new working class (low-tier workers) is viewed as   5
part of the inner city, as composed of both formal citizens and migrants, it must be recognized that this same group is not only subject to welfare and workfare surveillance and control, but also to the War on Drugs, racial profiling, the War on Terror, immigration controls, and the resurgence of racial prejudice and sexism. . . . This set of power dynamics indicates a far more complex and intricate system of controls — one that in effect suspends the law through bureaucratic mechanisms in a systematic fashion (systematic meaning that the impact is long-lasting and that this population is treated consistently as a biological threat to national security).[16] Unlike the conditions at Guantánamo Bay (not to idealize conditions there), the ideational system that creates ethnic, racial, and gender antagonisms obscures these power dynamics and often inverts them, positing these groups as the true usurpers or exploiters (of "us": the welfare system, taxpayers' dollars, our moral sensibility, and so on).

All of these policies disproportionately affect low-tier workers and the very poor.[17] . . . Similar to workfare policies and low-wage strategies, the U.S. guest-worker program combines these two elements: "flexible" work conditions; and heavy surveillance and political control, accompanied by the political powerlessness of workers. One of the more prominent sectors of the guest-worker program is agriculture; the United States has the most physically intensive agricultural system in the West, while at the same time, agricultural jobs have been rated by various authorities as the most and second most dangerous jobs in America.[18] Because many of these workers are

---

[15]Richard Cloward and Frances Fox Piven in Peck, *Workfare States*, ix.

[16]See Arnold, *Homelessness, Citizenship, and Identity*, Chapter 4.

[17]See, for example, David L. Marcus, "Three Times and Out," *Boston Globe*, October 14, 1998, A1; Nancy Gertner and Daniel Kanstroom, "The Recent Spotlight on the INS Failed to Reveal Its Dark Side," *Boston Globe*, May 21, 2000, E1, E3.

[18]Other jobs rated among the most dangerous are mining and meatpacking work.

on agricultural visas, they are monitored by the BCIS[19] as well as by local police forces, employers, and citizens' watch groups. Guest workers are tied to one employer, must be on site twenty-four hours a day, seven days a week, are provided housing that lacks both refrigeration and sewage, often live in tents or other makeshift housing, and have no access to doctors, electricity, or outside help. As of this writing, guest workers cannot strike, change employers, or bargain for wages.[20] If they are fired from their positions, they have less than a week to leave the country and no legal recourse. Meanwhile, illegal immigrants in the meatpacking industry often work in factories that are freezing, isolated, and subject to deregulated (read "unsafe") working conditions. Often they are tracked by BCIS and citizens' watch groups and are deported or allowed to stay according to arbitrary criteria. Additionally, conditions in the Border Industrial Program, a transnational factory area established through a partnership between the United States and Mexico, are both "free" — that is, deregulated — and dangerous and exploitative for workers. Just as international companies in this program (*maquilas*) have enjoyed relaxed environmental and labor standards, female *maquiladora* workers have been subject to brutal conditions. Hundreds of these women have been rape-murdered or kidnapped. The murder investigations of these "women of Juárez" have been sluggish, but their border crossing is certainly policed. The lack of heat in these factories, the speeding up of conveyor belts so that injuries are commonplace, and the vulnerability of these workers to both the market and the police form the parameters of these workers' daily existence.[21] In all of these cases, workers are exploited and seemingly abandoned by the state; yet at the same time they are subject to much greater surveillance and control.

ENGAGING THE TEXT

1. Arnold writes in a formal style well suited to an intellectually sophisticated audience. Try writing a 100- to 200-word summary of her argument that would be accessible to high school readers.

2. Does Arnold persuade you that welfare and workfare are unreasonably invasive, punitive programs? What specific details does she cite to support her point of view? What level of supervision, if any, do you think would be appropriate for recipients of federal aid?

[19]*BCIS:* Bureau of Citizenship and Immigration Services, a component of the Homeland Security Agency. [Eds.]

[20]Legislation has been proposed to modify guest workers' conditions, but this is at the very beginning stages; moreover, the proposed legislation still does not go far enough to protect these workers from abuse, starvation, poor medical care, and exposure to the elements.

[21]See Human Rights Watch, "Human Rights Watch Welcomes U.S. Government Meat and Poultry Study," http://hrw.org/English/docs/2005/02/03/usdomio117_txt.htm; "Abusive Child Labor Found in U.S. Agriculture," http//hrw.org/English/docs/2000/06/20/usdom580_txt .thm; NCRLC, "U.S. Agricultural Workers," http: //www.ncrlc.com/Agricultural Workers.html.

3. Arnold and the writers she quotes point to ways in which welfare and work-fare resemble parole, lynching, reform schools, and slave labor. Discuss the rhetorical effect of such references, considering both their emotional impact and their logical validity.

4. Arnold's point of view is obviously not conservative. How would you characterize it — liberal, progressive, reformist, radical, revolutionary, or something else? Explain.

Exploring Connections

5. Compare the women who clean New York City streets, parks, and subways (para. 4) to Valerie Rushing, who does similar work (see *The Missing Class* by Katherine S. Newman and Victor Tan Chen, p. 349). Which labor pool would you prefer your town or city to employ to clean its parks — inexpensive workfare recipients or unionized workers like Valerie Rushing? Why?

6. Review Diana Kendall's "Framing Class, Vicarious Living, and Conspicuous Consumption" (p. 330). How would you expect media to "frame" welfare recipients? Can you think of any specific examples of media representations of welfare recipients, or are these people invisible in the media?

Extending the Critical Context

7. Research welfare/workfare in your city or county. Report to the class on the types and amount of aid, the number of recipients, and demographic data such as age, gender, and race/ethnicity of recipients.

Stephen Cruz

Studs Terkel

The speaker of the following oral history is Stephen Cruz, a man who at first glance seems to be living the American Dream of success and upward mobility. He is never content, however, and he comes to question his own values and the meaning of success in the world of corporate America. For decades, Studs Terkel (1912–2008) was the best-known practitioner of oral history in the United States. Over the course of a long career he compiled several books by interviewing widely varying people — ordinary people for the most part — about important subjects like work, race, faith, and the Great Depression. The edited versions of these interviews are often surprisingly powerful crystallizations of American social history: Terkel's subjects give voice to the frustrations and hopes of whole generations of Americans. Terkel won a Pulitzer Prize in 1985 for "The Good War": An Oral History of World War II. *His last oral history book,* Will the Circle Be Unbroken: Reflections on Death, Rebirth, and Hunger for a Faith, *appeared in 2001. This selection first appeared in his* American Dreams: Lost and Found *(1980).*

He is thirty-nine.

"*The family came in stages from Mexico. Your grandparents usually came first, did a little work, found little roots, put together a few bucks, and brought the family in, one at a time. Those were the days when controls at the border didn't exist as they do now.*"

You just tried very hard to be whatever it is the system wanted of you. I was a good student and, as small as I was, a pretty good athlete. I was well liked, I thought. We were fairly affluent, but we lived down where all the trashy whites were. It was the only housing we could get. As kids, we never understood why. We did everything right. We didn't have those Mexican accents, we were never on welfare. Dad wouldn't be on welfare to save his soul. He woulda died first. He worked during the Depression. He carries that pride with him, even today.

Of the five children, I'm the only one who really got into the business world. We learned quickly that you have to look for opportunities and add things up very quickly. I was in liberal arts, but as soon as Sputnik[1] went up, well, golly, hell, we knew where the bucks were. I went right over to the registrar's office and signed up for engineering. I got my degree in '62. If you had a master's in business as well, they were just paying all kinds of bucks. So that's what I did. Sure enough, the market was super. I had fourteen job offers. I could have had a hundred if I wanted to look around.

I never once associated these offers with my being a minority. I was   5
aware of the Civil Rights Act of 1964, but I was still self-confident enough to feel they wanted me because of my abilities. Looking back, the reason I got more offers than the other guys was because of the government edict. And I thought it was because I was so goddamned brilliant. (Laughs.) In 1962, I didn't get as many offers as those who were less qualified. You have a tendency to blame the job market. You just don't want to face the issue of discrimination.

I went to work with Procter & Gamble. After about two years, they told me I was one of the best supervisors they ever had and they were gonna promote me. Okay, I went into personnel. Again, I thought it was because I was such a brilliant guy. Now I started getting wise to the ways of the American Dream. My office was glass-enclosed, while all the other offices were enclosed so you couldn't see into them. I was the visible man.

[1]*Sputnik:* Satellite launched by the Soviet Union in 1957; this launch signaled the beginning of the "space race" between the United States and the USSR.

They made sure I interviewed most of the people that came in. I just didn't really think there was anything wrong until we got a new plant manager, a southerner. I received instructions from him on how I should interview blacks. Just check and see if they smell, okay? That was the beginning of my training program. I started asking: Why weren't we hiring more minorities? I realized I was the only one in a management position.

I guess as a Mexican I was more acceptable because I wasn't really black. I was a good compromise. I was visibly good. I hired a black secretary, which was *verboten*. When I came back from my vacation, she was gone. My boss fired her while I was away. I asked why and never got a good reason.

Until then, I never questioned the American Dream. I was convinced if you worked hard, you could make it. I never considered myself different. That was the trouble. We had been discriminated against a lot, but I never associated it with society. I considered it an individual matter. Bad people, my mother used to say. In '68 I began to question.

I was doing fine. My very first year out of college, I was making twelve   10
thousand dollars. I left Procter & Gamble because I really saw no opportunity. They were content to leave me visible, but my thoughts were not really solicited. I may have overreacted a bit, with the plant manager's attitude, but I felt there's no way a Mexican could get ahead here.

I went to work for Blue Cross. It's 1969. The Great Society[2] is in full swing. Those who never thought of being minorities before are being turned on. Consciousness raising is going on. Black programs are popping up in universities. Cultural identity and all that. But what about the one issue in this country: economics? There were very few management jobs for minorities, especially blacks.

The stereotypes popped up again. If you're Oriental, you're real good in mathematics. If you're Mexican, you're a happy guy to have around, pleasant but emotional. Mexicans are either sleeping or laughing all the time. Life is just one big happy kind of event. *Mañana*. Good to have as part of the management team, as long as you weren't allowed to make decisions.

I was thinking there were two possibilities why minorities were not making it in business. One was deep, ingrained racism. But there was still the possibility that they were simply a bunch of bad managers who just couldn't cut it. You see, until now I believed everything I was taught about the dream: the American businessman is omnipotent and fair. If we could show these turkeys there's money to be made in hiring minorities, these businessmen — good managers, good decision makers — would respond. I naively thought American businessmen gave a damn about society, that given a choice they would do the right thing. I had that faith.

I was hungry for learning about decision-making criteria. I was still too far away from top management to see exactly how they were working. I

[2]*The Great Society:* President Lyndon B. Johnson's term for the American society he hoped to establish through social reforms, including an antipoverty program.

needed to learn more. Hey, just learn more and you'll make it. That part of the dream hadn't left me yet. I was still clinging to the notion of work your ass off, learn more than anybody else, and you'll get in that sphere.

During my fifth year at Blue Cross, I discovered another flaw in the American Dream. Minorities are as bad to other minorities as whites are to minorities. The strongest weapon the white manager had is the old divide and conquer routine. My mistake was thinking we were all at the same level of consciousness. 15

I had attempted to bring together some blacks with the other minorities. There weren't too many of them anyway. The Orientals never really got involved. The blacks misunderstood what I was presenting, perhaps I said it badly. They were on the cultural kick: a manager should be crucified for saying "Negro" instead of "black." I said as long as the Negro or the black gets the job, it doesn't mean a damn what he's called. We got into a huge hassle. Management, of course, merely smiled. The whole struggle fell flat on its face. It crumpled from divisiveness. So I learned another lesson. People have their own agenda. It doesn't matter what group you're with, there is a tendency to put the other guy down regardless.

The American Dream began to look so damn complicated, I began to think: Hell, if I wanted, I could just back away and reap the harvest myself. By this time, I'm up to twenty-five thousand dollars a year. It's beginning to look good, and a lot of people are beginning to look good. And they're saying: "Hey, the American Dream, you got it. Why don't you lay off?" I wasn't falling in line.

My bosses were telling me I had all the "ingredients" for top management. All that was required was to "get to know our business." This term comes up all the time. If I could just warn all minorities and women whenever you hear "get to know our business," they're really saying "fall in line." Stay within that fence, and glory can be yours. I left Blue Cross disillusioned. They offered me a director's job at thirty thousand dollars before I quit.

All I had to do was behave myself. I had the "ingredients" of being a good Chicano, the equivalent of the good nigger. I was smart. I could articulate well. People didn't know by my speech patterns that I was of Mexican heritage. Some tell me I don't look Mexican, that I have a certain amount of Italian, Lebanese, or who knows. (Laughs.)

One could easily say: "Hey, what's your bitch? The American Dream has treated you beautifully. So just knock it off and quit this crap you're spreading around." It was a real problem. Every time I turned around, America seemed to be treating me very well. 20

Hell, I even thought of dropping out, the hell with it. Maybe get a job in a factory. But what happened? Offers kept coming in. I just said to myself: God, isn't this silly? You might as well take the bucks and continue looking for the answer. So I did that. But each time I took the money, the conflict in me got more intense, not less.

Wow, I'm up to thirty-five thousand a year. This is a savings and loan business. I have faith in the executive director. He was the kind of guy I was looking for in top management: understanding, humane, also looking for the formula. Until he was up for consideration as executive v.p. of the entire organization. All of a sudden everything changed. It wasn't until I saw this guy flip-flop that I realized how powerful vested interests are. Suddenly he's saying: "Don't rock the boat. Keep a low profile. Get in line." Another disappointment.

Subsequently, I went to work for a consulting firm. I said to myself: Okay, I've got to get close to the executive mind. I need to know how they work. Wow, a consulting firm.

Consulting firms are saving a lot of American businessmen. They're doing it in ways that defy the whole notion of capitalism. They're not allowing these businesses to fail. Lockheed was successful in getting U.S. funding guarantees because of the efforts of consulting firms working on their behalf, helping them look better. In this kind of work, you don't find minorities. You've got to be a proven success in business before you get there.

The American Dream, I see now, is governed not by education, opportunity, and hard work, but by power and fear. The higher up in the organization you go, the more you have to lose. The dream is *not losing*. This is the notion pervading America today: don't lose.

When I left the consulting business, I was making fifty thousand dollars a year. My last performance appraisal was: you can go a long way in this business, you can be a partner, but you gotta know our business. It came up again. At this point, I was incapable of being disillusioned any more. How easy it is to be swallowed up by the same set of values that governs the top guy. I was becoming that way. I was becoming concerned about losing that fifty grand or so a year. So I asked other minorities who had it made. I'd go up and ask 'em: "Look, do you owe anything to others?" The answer was: "We owe nothing to anybody." They drew from the civil rights movement but felt no debt. They've quickly forgotten how it happened. It's like I was when I first got out of college. Hey, it's really me, I'm great. I'm great. I'm as angry with these guys as I am with the top guys.

Right now, it's confused. I've had fifteen years in the business world as "a success." Many Anglos would be envious of my progress. Fifty thousand dollars a year puts you in the one or two top percent of all Americans. Plus my wife making another thirty thousand. We had lots of money. When I gave it up, my cohorts looked at me not just as strange, but as something of a traitor. "You're screwing it up for all of us. You're part of our union, we're the elite, we should govern. What the hell are you doing?" So now I'm looked at suspiciously by my peer group as well.

I'm teaching at the University of Wisconsin at Platteville. It's nice. My colleagues tell me what's on their minds. I got a farm next-door to Platteville. With farm prices being what they are (laughs), it's a losing proposition. But with university work and what money we've saved, we're gonna be all right.

25

The American Dream is getting more elusive. The dream is being governed by a few people's notion of what the dream is. Sometimes I feel it's a small group of financiers that gets together once a year and decides all the world's issues.

It's getting so big. The small-business venture is not there any more. 30 Business has become too big to influence. It can't be changed internally. A counterpower is needed.

ENGAGING THE TEXT

1. As Cruz moves up the economic ladder, he experiences growing conflict that keeps him from being content and proud of his accomplishments. To what do you attribute his discontent? Is his "solution" one that you would recommend?

2. Cruz says that the real force in America is the dream of "not losing" (para. 25). What does he mean by this? Do you agree?

3. What, according to Stephen Cruz, is wrong with the American Dream? Write an essay in which you first define and then either defend or critique his position.

4. Imagine a continuation of Stephen Cruz's life in which he gives up his teaching job and returns to the business world. What might his career have been like over the last thirty years? How would you expect Cruz to react to the business environment today?

EXPLORING CONNECTIONS

5. Compare Stephen Cruz to "Ragged Dick" (p. 258) and to Tim Blixseth (p. 279) in terms of the American Dream and individual success. What goals, beliefs, or values do they share, and what distinguishes Cruz from the others?

6. Compare Stephen Cruz to Richard Rodriguez (p. 194), Gary Soto (p. 26), and Mike Rose (p. 157) in terms of their attitudes toward education and success.

EXTENDING THE CRITICAL CONTEXT

7. According to Cruz, in 1969 few management positions were open to members of minority groups. Working in small groups, use the library or Internet to find current statistics on minorities in business (for example, the number of large minority-owned companies; the number of minority chief executives among major corporations; the distribution of minorities among top management, middle management, supervisory, and clerical positions). Compare notes with classmates and discuss.

FURTHER CONNECTIONS

1. How would you expect your county to compare with other counties in your state in terms of wealth? How would you expect your state to compare with other states? Research state and county data from the U.S. Census Bureau Web site (www.census.gov) and present or write up your findings. To what extent do you think you have had advantages or disadvantages because of where you were born or grew up?

2. The Merriam Webster Online Dictionary defines "wage slave" as "a person dependent on wages or a salary for a livelihood." Are you a wage slave now, and do you expect to be one in the future? Discuss the connotations of this term, and explain why you think the term is or is not a useful one in contemporary America. What are the alternatives to wage slavery?

3. Sketch out a rough plan of what you might try to accomplish in the five years after you receive your college diploma. How much do your career or educational plans reflect a desire to earn a high salary or to be considered "successful" in some other way? Do you see significant barriers or challenges in attaining these tentative goals? To extend this exercise, talk to a career counselor about your plans, or interview someone working in the field you are considering pursuing.

4. This chapter of *Rereading America* has been criticized by conservatives for undermining the work ethic of American college students. Rush Limbaugh, for example, claimed that the chapter "presents America as a stacked deck," thus "robbing people of the ability to see the enormous opportunities directly in front of them." Do you agree? Write a journal entry or essay in which you explain how these readings have influenced your attitudes toward work and success.

4

Created Equal

The Myth of the Melting Pot

Antiracism March, photo by Eli Reed.

FAST FACTS

1. As of 2008 there were a reported 926 active hate groups within the U.S., a 54% increase from 2000 when there were a recorded 602 such groups. The 2008 meltdown of the U.S. financial system and election of the first black American president are thought to be key contributing factors.

2. A white male born in 2003 has an average life expectancy of 75.3 years; a black male born in the same year has an average life expectancy of 69 years; the average lifespan for white and black women is 80.5 and 76.1 years, respectively.

3. In 2002, nearly three-quarters (74.5%) of white households and less than half of black (47.3%) and Latino (48.2%) households owned their own homes.

4. Nationally, 86% of whites live in neighborhoods where minorities make up less than 1% of the population.

5. Between 1980 and 2003, the number of interracial marriages in the United States more than tripled, to approximately 2.1 million.

6. As of the year 2005, more than 12% of Americans are foreign-born and over 19% speak a language other than English at home.

Sources: (1) Southern Poverty Law Center (www.splcenter.org); (2) U.S. Department of Health and Human Services/CDC, *National Vital Statistics Reports* 54.14 (April 19, 2006); (3) U.S. Census Bureau, *Housing Vacancies and Home Ownership, 2002*; (4) PBS (www.pbs.org), "Race — The Power of an Illusion" — Background Readings; (5) Vincent N. Parrillo, *Diversity in America*, 2nd ed. (Thousand Oaks, CA: Pine Forge Press, 2005), p. 186; (6) U.S. Census Bureau, *2005 American Community Survey*.

THE MYTH OF THE MELTING POT predates the drafting of the U.S. Constitution. In 1782, a year before the Peace of Paris formally ended the Revolutionary War, J. Hector St. John de Crèvecoeur envisioned the young American republic as a crucible that would forge its disparate immigrant population into a vigorous new society with a grand future:

> What, then, is the American, this new man? He is neither an European, or the descendant of an European.... He is an American, who leaving behind him all his ancient prejudices and manners, receives new ones from the new mode of life he has embraced, the new government he obeys, and the new rank he holds.... Here individuals of all nations are melted into a new race of men, whose labours and posterity will one day cause great changes in the world.

Crèvecoeur's metaphor has remained a powerful ideal for many generations of American scholars, politicians, artists, and ordinary citizens. Ralph Waldo Emerson, writing in his journal in 1845, celebrated the national vitality produced by the mingling of immigrant cultures: "In this continent — asylum of all nations, — the energy of . . . all the European tribes, — of the Africans, and of the Polynesians — will construct a new race, a new religion, a new state, a new literature." An English Jewish writer named Israel Zangwill, himself an immigrant, popularized the myth in his 1908 drama, *The Melting Pot.* In the play, the hero rhapsodizes, "Yes East and West, and North and South, the palm and the pine, the pole and the equator, the crescent and the cross — how the great Alchemist melts and fuses them with his purging flame! Here shall they all unite to build the Republic of Man and the Kingdom of God." The myth was perhaps most vividly dramatized, though, in a pageant staged by Henry Ford in the early 1920s. Decked out in the costumes of their native lands, Ford's immigrant workers sang traditional songs from their homelands as they danced their way into an enormous replica of a cast-iron pot. They then emerged from the other side wearing identical "American" business suits, waving minia-ture American flags, and singing "The Star-Spangled Banner."

The drama of becoming an American has deep roots: immigrants take on a new identity — and a new set of cultural myths — because they want to become members of the community, equal members with all the rights, responsibilities, and opportunities of their fellow citizens. The force of the melting pot myth lies in this implied promise that all Americans are indeed "created equal." However, the myth's promises of openness, harmony, unity, and equality were deceptive from the beginning. Crèvecoeur's exclusive con-cern with the mingling of *European* peoples (he lists the "English, Scotch, Irish, French, Dutch, Germans, and Swedes") utterly ignored the presence of some three-quarters of a million Africans and African Americans who then lived in this country, as well as the tribal peoples who had lived on the land for thousands of years before European contact. Crèvecoeur's vision of a country embracing "all nations" clearly applied only to northern European nations. Benjamin Franklin, in a 1751 essay, was more blunt: since Africa, Asia, and most of America were inhabited by dark-skinned people, he argued, the American colonies should consciously try to increase the white population and keep out the rest: "Why increase the Sons of Africa, by Plant-ing them in America, where we have so fair an opportunity, by excluding Blacks and Tawneys, of increasing the lovely White . . . ?" If later writers like Emerson and Zangwill saw a more inclusive cultural mix as a source of hope and renewal for the United States, others throughout this country's history have, even more than Franklin, feared that mix as a threat.

The fear of difference underlies another, equally powerful American myth — the myth of racial supremacy. This is the negative counterpart of the melting pot ideal: instead of the equal and harmonious blending of cultures, it proposes a racial and ethnic hierarchy based on the "natural superiority" of Anglo-Americans. Under the sway of this myth, differences become signs of inferiority, and "inferiors" are treated as childlike or even subhuman. This myth has given rise to some of the most shameful passages in our national life: slavery, segregation, and lynching; the near extermination of tribal peoples and cultures; the denial of citizenship and constitutional rights to African Americans, American Indians, Chinese and Japanese immigrants; the brutal exploitation of Mexican and Asian laborers. The catalog of injustices is long and painful. The melting pot ideal itself has often masked the myth of racial and ethnic superiority. "Inferiors" are expected to "melt" into conformity with Anglo-American behavior and values. Henry Ford's pageant conveys the message that ethnic identity is best left behind — exchanged for something "better," more uniform, less threatening.

This chapter explores the interaction between these two related cultural myths: the myth of unity and the myth of difference and hierarchy. It examines how the categories of race and ethnicity are defined and how they operate to divide us. These issues become crucial as the population of the United States grows increasingly diverse. The selections here challenge you to reconsider the fate of the melting pot myth as we enter the era of multi-ethnic, multicultural America. Can we learn to accept and honor our differences?

The first half of the chapter focuses on the origins and lingering consequences of racism. It opens with a selection by Thomas Jefferson that unambiguously expresses the myth of racial superiority. Pondering the future of freed slaves, Jefferson concludes that because blacks "are inferior to whites in the endowments both of body and mind," they should be prevented from intermarrying and "staining the blood" of the superior race. Surveying the most common psychological and sociological theories of prejudice, Vincent N. Parrillo provides a series of frameworks for understanding the roots of racial conflict. Studs Terkel's oral history "C. P. Ellis" at once reminds us of the persistence of racist beliefs and offers hope for change: this remarkable first-person account of Ellis's transformation from Klansman to union activist examines racism from the inside and shows how one man conquered his own bigotry. James McBride's "The Boy in the Mirror" offers another personal narrative, this time from the perspective of a child trying to make sense of his mixed racial identity. Next, an essay by Cheryl I. Harris and Devon W. Carbado examines how assumptions about race ultimately distorted media coverage of Hurricane Katrina. A Visual Portfolio gives individual faces to abstractions like race and discrimination; the images challenge us to ponder the centrality of race in American culture and to rethink ways we "read" identity.

The second half of the chapter addresses the emerging myth of the "new melting pot." First, George M. Fredrickson presents an overview of ethnic relations in American history, showing how concepts of ethnic hierarchy, assimilation, pluralism, and separatism have shaped group identities and interactions over time. Patrick J. Buchanan, in "Deconstructing America," takes a more aggressive stance, sounding the alarm about the hazards of immigration and diversity. Rubén Martínez probes the personal, cultural, and political significance of the U.S.–Mexican border in "The Crossing," which focuses on his encounter with a seriously ill undocumented immigrant in the Sonoran desert of New Mexico. In his pointedly funny short story "Assimilation," Sherman Alexie introduces us to an American Indian woman who begins to question the meaning of her marriage to a white man. Hua Hsu challenges us to think about the implications of the country's changing demographic makeup in "The End of White America?" Finally, in her poem "Child of the Americas," Aurora Levins Morales affirms both the value of her multicultural roots and the enduring power of the melting pot myth.

Sources

Franklin, John Hope. *Race and History: Selected Essays, 1938–1988*. Baton Rouge: Louisiana State University Press, 1989. 321–31. Print.

Gordon, Milton M. *Assimilation in American Life: The Role of Race, Religion, and National Origins*. New York: Oxford University Press, 1964. Print.

Njeri, Itabari. "Beyond the Melting Pot." *Los Angeles Times* 13 Jan. 1991: E1+. Print.

Pitt, Leonard. *We Americans*. 3rd ed. Vol. 2. Dubuque: Kendall/Hunt, 1987. Print.

Takaki, Ronald. "Reflections on Racial Patterns in America." In *From Different Shores: Perspectives on Race and Ethnicity in America*. Ed. Ronald Takaki. New York: Oxford University Press, 1987. 26–37. Print.

BEFORE READING

- Survey images in the popular media (newspapers, magazines, TV shows, movies, and pop music) for evidence of the myth of the melting pot. Do you find any figures in popular culture who seem to endorse the idea of a "new melting pot" in the United States? How closely do these images reflect your understanding of your own and other ethnic and racial groups? Explore these questions in a journal entry, then discuss in class.

- Alternatively, you might investigate the metaphors that are being used to describe racial and ethnic group relations or interactions between members of different groups on your campus and in your community. Consult local news sources and campus publications, and keep your ears open for conversations that touch on these issues. Do some freewriting about what you discover and compare notes with classmates.

- The frontispiece photo on page 373 was taken at an antiracism march. Why do you think that these people and this particular moment of the march caught the photographer's eye? What do the positions and expressions of the four main figures suggest about their feelings and

concerns and about the cause they are marching for? Jot down your
impressions and note the visual details that support your "reading" of
the picture. Then compare your responses in small groups: How much
consistency or variation do you find in your interpretations?

From *Notes on the State of Virginia*

THOMAS JEFFERSON

Thomas Jefferson is probably best known as the author of the Declaration of Independence. As third president of the United States (1801–1809), Thomas Jefferson (1743–1826) promoted westward expansion in the form of the Louisiana Purchase and the Lewis and Clark Expedition. In addition to his political career he was a scientist, architect, city planner (Washington, D.C.), and founder of the University of Virginia. This passage from his Notes on the State of Virginia *(1785) reveals a very different and, for many readers, shocking side of Jefferson's character — that of a slave owner and defender of white supremacy. Here he proposes that the new state of Virginia gradually phase out slavery rather than abolish it outright. He also recommends that all newly emancipated slaves be sent out of the state to form separate colonies, in part to prevent racial conflict and in part to prevent intermarriage with whites. Jefferson was not the first and was far from the last politician to advocate solving the nation's racial problems by removing African Americans from its boundaries. In 1862, the Great Emancipator himself, Abraham Lincoln, called a delegation of black leaders to the White House to enlist their support in establishing a colony for African Americans in Central America. Congress had appropriated money for this project, but it was abandoned after the governments of Honduras, Nicaragua, and Costa Rica protested the plan.*

Many of the laws which were in force during the monarchy being relative merely to that form of government, or inculcating principles inconsistent with republicanism, the first assembly which met after the establishment of the commonwealth appointed a committee to revise the whole code, to reduce it into proper form and volume, and report it to the assembly. This work has been executed by three gentlemen,[1] and reported.... The following are the most remarkable alterations proposed:

---

[1]*executed by three gentlemen:* Jefferson was one of the three men who wrote this set of proposed revisions to the legal code of Virginia.

To change the rules of descent, so as that the lands of any person dying intestate shall be divisible equally among all his children, or other representatives, in equal degree.

To make slaves distributable among the next of kin, as other movables. . . .

To emancipate all slaves born after the passing [of] the act. The bill reported by the revisers does not itself contain this proposition; but an amendment containing it was prepared, to be offered to the legislature whenever the bill should be taken up, and farther directing, that they should continue with their parents to a certain age, then to be brought up, at the public expense, to tillage, arts, or sciences, according to their geniuses, till the females should be eighteen, and the males twenty-one years of age, when they should be colonized to such place as the circumstances of the time should render most proper, sending them out with arms, implements of household and of the handicraft arts, seeds, pairs of the useful domestic animals, &c., to declare them a free and independent people, and extend to them our alliance and protection, till they have acquired strength; and to send vessels at the same time to other parts of the world for an equal number of white inhabitants; to induce them to migrate hither, proper encouragements were to be proposed. It will probably be asked, Why not retain and incorporate the blacks into the State, and thus save the expense of supplying by importation of white settlers, the vacancies they will leave? Deep-rooted prejudices entertained by the whites; ten thousand recollections, by the blacks, of the injuries they have sustained; new provocations; the real distinctions which nature has made; and many other circumstances, will divide us into parties, and produce convulsions, which will probably never end but in the extermination of the one or the other race. To these objections, which are political, may be added others, which are physical and moral. The first difference which strikes us is that of color. Whether the black of the negro resides in the reticular membrane between the skin and scarf-skin, or in the scarf-skin itself; whether it proceeds from the color of the blood, the color of the bile, or from that of some other secretion, the difference is fixed in nature, and is as real as if its seat and cause were better known to us. And is this difference of no importance? Is it not the foundation of a greater or less share of beauty in the two races? Are not the fine mixtures of red and white, the expressions of every passion by greater or less suffusions of color in the one, preferable to that eternal monotony, which reigns in the countenances, that immovable veil of black which covers the emotions of the other race? Add to these, flowing hair, a more elegant symmetry of form, their own judgment in favor of the whites, declared by their preference of them, as uniformly as is the preference of the Oranootan[2] for the black woman over those of his own species. The circumstance of superior beauty, is thought worthy of attention in the propagation of our horses, dogs, and other domestic animals; why not in that of man? Besides those of color, figure, and hair, there are other physical distinctions proving a difference of race. They have less hair on the face and body. They secrete less by the kidneys, and more by the glands of the skin, which gives them a very strong and disagreeable odor. This greater degree of transpiration, renders them more tolerant of heat, and less so of cold than the whites. Perhaps, too, a difference of structure in the pulmonary apparatus, which a late ingenious experimentalist has discovered to be the principal regulator of animal heat, may have disabled them from extricating, in the act of inspiration, so much of that fluid from the outer air, or obliged them in expiration, to part with more of it. They seem to require less sleep. A black after hard labor through the day, will be induced by the slightest amusements to sit up till midnight, or later, though knowing he must be out with the first dawn of the morning. They are at least as brave, and more adventuresome. But this may perhaps proceed from a want of forethought, which prevents their seeing a danger till it be present. When present, they do not go through it with more coolness or steadiness than the whites. They are more ardent after their female; but love seems with them to be more an eager desire, than a tender delicate mixture of sentiment and sensation. Their griefs are transient. Those numberless afflictions, which render it doubtful whether heaven has given life to us in mercy or in wrath, are less felt, and sooner forgotten with them. In general, their existence appears to participate more of sensation than reflection. To this must be ascribed their disposition to sleep when abstracted from their diversions, and

---

[2]*Oranootan:* Orangutan.

unemployed in labor. An animal whose body is at rest, and who does not reflect, must be disposed to sleep of course. Comparing them by their faculties of memory, reason, and imagination, it appears to me that in memory they are equal to the whites; in reason much inferior, as I think one could scarcely be found capable of tracing and comprehending the investigations of Euclid; and that in imagination they are dull, tasteless, and anomalous. It would be unfair to follow them to Africa for this investigation. We will consider them here, on the same stage with the whites, and where the facts are not apochryphal on which a judgment is to be formed. It will be right to make great allowances for the difference of condition, of education, of conversation, of the sphere in which they move. Many millions of them have been brought to, and born in America. Most of them, indeed, have been confined to tillage, to their own homes, and their own society; yet many have been so situated, that they might have availed themselves of the conversation of their masters; many have been brought up to the handicraft arts, and from that circumstance have always been associated with the whites. Some have been liberally educated, and all have lived in countries where the arts and sciences are cultivated to a considerable degree, and all have had before their eyes samples of the best works from abroad. The Indians, with no advantages of this kind, will often carve figures on their pipes not destitute of design and merit. They will crayon out an animal, a plant, or a country, so as to prove the existence of a germ in their minds which only wants cultivation. They astonish you with strokes of the most sublime oratory; such as prove their reason and sentiment strong, their imagination glowing and elevated. But never yet could I find that a black had uttered a thought above the level of plain narration; never saw even an elementary trait of painting or sculpture. In music they are more generally gifted than the whites with accurate ears for tune and time, and they have been found capable of imagining a small catch.[3] Whether they will be equal to the composition of a more extensive run of melody, or of complicated harmony, is yet to be proved. Misery is often the parent of the most affecting touches in poetry. Among the blacks is misery enough, God knows, but no poetry. Love is the peculiar œstrum of the poet. Their love is ardent, but it kindles the senses only, not the imagination. Religion, indeed, has produced a Phyllis Whately [*sic*];[4] but it could not produce a poet. The compositions published under her name are below the dignity of criticism. The heroes of the Dunciad[5] are to her, as Hercules to

---

[3]The instrument proper to them is the Banjar, which they brought hither from Africa, and which is the original of the guitar, its chords being precisely the four lower chords of the guitar. [Jefferson's note]

[4]*Phyllis Whately:* Phillis Wheatley (175?–1784) was born in Africa but transported to the United States and sold as a slave when she was a young child. Her *Poems on Various Subjects, Religious and Moral* (1773) was the first book of poetry to be published by an African American.

[5]*the heroes of the Dunciad:* In the mock epic poem *The Dunciad* (1728), English satirist Alexander Pope (1688–1744) lampoons his literary rivals as fools and dunces.

the author of that poem. Ignatius Sancho[6] has approached nearer to merit in composition; yet his letters do more honor to the heart than the head. They breathe the purest effusions of friendship and general philanthropy, and show how great a degree of the latter may be compounded with strong religious zeal. He is often happy in the turn of his compliments, and his style is easy and familiar, except when he affects a Shandean[7] fabrication of words. But his imagination is wild and extravagant, escapes incessantly from every restraint of reason and taste, and, in the course of its vagaries, leaves a tract of thought as incoherent and eccentric, as is the course of a meteor through the sky. His subjects should often have led him to a process of sober reasoning; yet we find him always substituting sentiment for demonstration. Upon the whole, though we admit him to the first place among those of his own color who have presented themselves to the public judgment, yet when we compare him with the writers of the race among whom he lived and particularly with the epistolary class in which he has taken his own stand, we are compelled to enroll him at the bottom of the column. This criticism supposes the letters published under his name to be genuine, and to have received amendment from no other hand; points which would not be of easy investigation. The improvement of the blacks in body and mind, in the first instance of their mixture with the whites, has been observed by every one, and proves that their inferiority is not the effect merely of their condition of life. . . .

The opinion that they are inferior in the faculties of reason and imagination, must be hazarded with great diffidence. To justify a general conclusion, requires many observations, even where the subject may be submitted to the anatomical knife, to optical glasses, to analysis by fire or by solvents. How much more then where it is a faculty, not a substance, we are examining; where it eludes the research of all the senses; where the conditions of its existence are various and variously combined; where the effects of those which are present or absent bid defiance to calculation; let me add too, as a circumstance of great tenderness, where our conclusion would degrade a whole race of men from the rank in the scale of beings which their Creator may perhaps have given them. To our reproach it must be said, that though for a century and a half we have had under our eyes the races of black and of red men, they have never yet been viewed by us as subjects of natural history. I advance it, therefore, as a suspicion only, that the blacks, whether originally a distinct race, or made distinct by time and circumstances, are inferior to the whites in the endowments both of body and mind. It is not against experience to suppose that different species of the same genus, or

5

---

[6]*Ignatius Sancho:* Born on a slave ship, Ignatius Sancho (1729–1780) became a servant in the homes of several English aristocrats, where he educated himself and became acquainted with some of the leading writers and artists of the period. He later became a grocer in London and devoted himself to writing. His letters were collected and published in 1782.

[7]*Shandean:* In the style of Laurence Sterne's comic novel, *The Life and Opinions of Tristram Shandy* (1758–1766). Sancho admired Sterne's writing and corresponded regularly with him.

varieties of the same species, may possess different qualifications. Will not a lover of natural history then, one who views the gradations in all the races of animals with the eye of philosophy, excuse an effort to keep those in the department of man as distinct as nature has formed them? This unfortunate difference of color, and perhaps of faculty, is a powerful obstacle to the emancipation of these people. Many of their advocates, while they wish to vindicate the liberty of human nature, are anxious also to preserve its dignity and beauty. Some of these, embarrassed by the question, "What further is to be done with them?" join themselves in opposition with those who are actuated by sordid avarice only. Among the Romans emancipation required but one effort. The slave, when made free, might mix with, without staining the blood of his master. But with us a second is necessary, unknown to history. When freed, he is to be removed beyond the reach of mixture.

Engaging the Text

1. Jefferson proposes colonizing — that is, sending away — all newly emancipated slaves and declaring them "a free and independent people" (para. 4). In what ways would their freedom and independence continue to be limited, according to this proposal?

2. Jefferson predicts that racial conflict in the United States "will probably never end but in the extermination of the one or the other race" (para. 4). Which of the divisive issues he mentions, if any, are still sources of conflict today? Given the history of race relations from Jefferson's time to our own, do you think his pessimism was justified? Why or why not?

3. Jefferson presents what seems on the surface to be a systematic and logical catalog of the differences he sees between blacks and whites; he then attempts to demonstrate the "natural" superiority of whites based on these differences. Working in pairs or small groups, look carefully at his observations and the conclusions he draws from them. What flaws do you find in his analysis?

Exploring Connections

4. What does the cartoonist on page 379 mean when he observes that Jefferson's words from the Declaration of Independence were "ratified" by President Obama's election on November 4, 2008? What is he suggesting about the history of equality in the United States prior to that date? Explain why you agree or disagree with the cartoonist's view of the significance of Obama's presidency.

5. Consider the picture of Jefferson's descendants on page 73. Write a journal entry or essay comparing the image of Jefferson you received in American history classes to the impression you get from the photo and from the passage above. How do you account for the differences?

6. Working in groups, write scripts for an imaginary meeting between Jefferson and Malcolm X (p. 210) and present them to the class. After each group has acted out its scenario, compare the different versions of the meeting.

What does each script assume about the motives and character of the two men?

EXTENDING THE CRITICAL CONTEXT

7. Read the Declaration of Independence and compare Jefferson's most famous document to the lesser-known passage reprinted here. How do the purposes of the two texts differ? What ideas and principles, if any, do they have in common, and where do they conflict? (The text of the Declaration is reprinted as an appendix in most unabridged dictionaries and is available online at http://lcweb2.loc.gov/const/declar.html.)

8. Write a letter to Jefferson responding to this selection and explaining your point of view. What would you tell him about how and why attitudes have changed between his time and ours?

9. Influenced by the heroic image of Jefferson as a champion of freedom and democracy, civic leaders have named libraries, schools, and other public institutions after him for the last two hundred years. Debate whether or not it is appropriate to honor Jefferson in this way given the opinions expressed in this passage.

Causes of Prejudice

VINCENT N. PARRILLO

What motivates the creation of racial categories? In the following selection, Vincent Parrillo reviews several theories that seek to explain the motives for prejudiced behavior — from socialization theory to economic competition. As Parrillo indicates, prejudice cannot be linked to any single cause: a whole network of forces and frustrations underlies this complex set of feelings and behaviors. Parrillo (b. 1938) chairs the Department of Sociology at William Paterson College in New Jersey. His books include Rethinking Today's Minorities *(1991),* Diversity in America *(2008, 3rd ed.), and* Understanding Race and Ethnic Relations *(2008, 3rd ed.). He has also written and produced two award-winning documentaries for PBS television. This excerpt originally appeared in* Strangers to These Shores *(2008, 9th ed.).*

Prejudicial attitudes may be either positive or negative. Sociologists primarily study the latter, however, because only negative attitudes can lead to turbulent social relations between dominant and minority groups. Numerous writers, therefore, have defined *prejudice* as an attitudinal "system of negative beliefs, feelings, and action-orientations regarding a certain group or groups of people."[1] The status of the strangers is an important factor in the development of a negative attitude. Prejudicial attitudes exist among members of both dominant and minority groups. Thus, in the relations between dominant and minority groups, the antipathy felt by one group for another is quite often reciprocated.

Psychological perspectives on prejudice — whether behaviorist, cognitive, or psychoanalytic — focus on the subjective states of mind of individuals. In these perspectives, a person's prejudicial attitudes may result from imitation or conditioning (behaviorist), perceived similarity–dissimilarity of beliefs (cognitive), or specific personality characteristics (psychoanalytic). In contrast, sociological perspectives focus on the objective conditions of society as the social forces behind prejudicial attitudes and behind racial and ethnic relations. Individuals do not live in a vacuum; social reality affects their states of mind.

Both perspectives are necessary to understand prejudice. As psychologist Gordon Allport argued,[2] besides needing a close study of habits, perceptions, motivation, and personality, we need an analysis of social settings, situational forces, demographic and ecological variables, and legal and economic trends.[3] Psychological and sociological perspectives complement each other in providing a fuller explanation of intergroup relations.

The Psychology of Prejudice

The psychological approach to prejudice is to examine individual behavior. We can understand more about prejudice among individuals by focusing on four areas of study: levels of prejudice, self-justification, personality, and frustration.

Levels of Prejudice.   Bernard Kramer suggested that prejudice exists   5
on three levels: cognitive, emotional, and action orientation.[4] The **cognitive level of prejudice** encompasses a person's beliefs and perceptions of a group as threatening or nonthreatening, inferior or equal (e.g., in terms of intellect, status, or biological composition), seclusive or intrusive, impulse gratifying, acquisitive, or possessing other positive or negative characteristics. Mr. X's cognitive beliefs are that Jews are intrusive and acquisitive. Other illustrations of cognitive beliefs are that the Irish are heavy drinkers

---

[1]Reported by Daniel Wilner, Rosabelle Price Walkley, and Stuart W. Cook, "Residential Proximity and Intergroup Relations in Public Housing Projects," *Journal of Social Issues* 8(1) (1952): 45. See also James W. Vander Zanden, *American Minority Relations*, 3rd ed. (New York: Ronald Press, 1972), p. 21. [All notes are Parrillo's.]

[2]Gordon W. Allport, *The Nature of Prejudice* (Reading, MA: Addison-Wesley, 1954), pp. 13–14.

[3]Gordon W. Allport, "Prejudice: Is It Societal or Personal?" *Journal of Social Issues* 18 (1962): 129–30.

[4]Bernard M. Kramer, "Dimensions of Prejudice," *Journal of Psychology* 27 (April 1949): 389–451.

and fighters, African Americans are rhythmic and lazy, and the Poles are thick-headed and unintelligent.

Generalizations shape both ethnocentric and prejudicial attitudes, but there is a difference. *Ethnocentrism* is a generalized rejection of all out-groups on the basis of an ingroup focus, whereas *prejudice* is a rejection of certain people solely on the basis of their membership in a particular outgroup.

In many societies, members of the majority group may believe that a particular low-status minority group is dirty, immoral, violent, or law break-ing. In the United States, the Irish, Italians, African Americans, Mexicans, Chinese, Puerto Ricans, and others have at one time or another been labeled with most, if not all, of these adjectives. In most European countries and in the United States, the group lowest on the socioeconomic ladder has often been depicted in caricature as also lowest on the evolutionary lad-der. The Irish and African Americans in the United States and the peasants and various ethnic groups in Europe have all been depicted in the past as apelike:

> The Victorian images of the Irish as "white Negro" and simian Celt, or a combination of the two, derived much of its force and inspiration from physiognomical beliefs . . . [but] every country in Europe had its equivalent of "white Negroes" and simianized men, whether or not they happened to be stereotypes of criminals, assassins, political radi-cals, revolutionaries, Slavs, gypsies, Jews or peasants.[5]

The **emotional level of prejudice** encompasses the feelings that a minority group arouses in an individual. Although these feelings may be based on stereotypes from the cognitive level, they represent a more intense stage of personal involvement. The emotional attitudes may be negative or positive, such as fear / envy, distrust / trust, disgust / admiration, or con-tempt / empathy. These feelings, based on beliefs about the group, may be triggered by social interaction or by the possibility of interaction. For ex-ample, whites might react with fear or anger to the integration of their schools or neighborhoods, or Protestants might be jealous of the lifestyle of a highly successful Catholic business executive.

An **action-orientation level of prejudice** is the positive or negative predisposition to engage in discriminatory behavior. A person who harbors strong feelings about members of a certain racial or ethnic group may have a tendency to act for or against them — being aggressive or nonaggressive, offering assistance or withholding it. Such an individual would also be likely to want to exclude or include members of that group both in close, personal social relations and in peripheral social relations. For example, some people would want to exclude members of the disliked group from doing business

---

[5]L. Perry Curtis Jr., *Apes and Angels: The Irishman in Victorian Caricature* (Washington, DC: Smithsonian Press, 1971).

with them or living in their neighborhood. Another manifestation of the action-orientation level of prejudice is the desire to change or maintain the status differential or inequality between the two groups, whether the area is economic, political, educational, social, or a combination. Note that an action orientation is a predisposition to act, not the action itself.

Self-Justification.   **Self-justification** involves denigrating a person or   10 group to justify maltreatment of them. In this situation, self-justification leads to prejudice and discrimination against members of another group.

Some philosophers argue that we are not so much rational creatures as we are rationalizing creatures. We require reassurance that the things we do and the lives we live are proper, that good reasons for our actions exist. If we can convince ourselves that another group is inferior, immoral, or dangerous, we may feel justified in discriminating against its members, enslaving them, or even killing them.

History is filled with examples of people who thought their maltreatment of others was just and necessary: As defenders of the "true faith," the Crusaders killed "Christ-killers" (Jews) and "infidels" (Muslims). Participants in the Spanish Inquisition imprisoned, tortured, and executed "heretics," "the disciples of the Devil." Similarly, the Puritans burned witches, whose refusal to confess "proved they were evil"; pioneers exploited or killed Native Americans who were "heathen savages"; and whites mistreated, enslaved, or killed African Americans, who were "an inferior species." According to U.S. Army officers, the civilians in the Vietnamese village of My Lai were "probably" aiding the Viet Cong; so in 1968, U.S. soldiers fighting in the Vietnam War felt justified in slaughtering over 300 unarmed people there, including women, children, and the elderly. In recent years suicide bombers and terrorists have killed innocent civilians, also justifying their actions through their religious fanaticism.

Some sociologists believe that self-justification works the other way around. That is, instead of self-justification serving as a basis for subjugating others, the subjugation occurs first and the self-justification follows, resulting in prejudice and continued discrimination.[6] The evolution of racism as a concept after the establishment of the African slave trade would seem to support this idea. Philip Mason offers an insight into this view:

> A specialized society is likely to defeat a simpler society and provide a lower tier still of enslaved and conquered peoples. The rulers and organizers sought security for themselves and their children; to perpetuate the power, the esteem, and the comfort they had achieved, it was necessary not only that the artisans and labourers should work contentedly but that the rulers should sleep without bad dreams. No one can say with certainty how the myths originated, but it is surely

---

[6]See Marvin B. Scott and Stanford M. Lyman, "Accounts," *American Sociological Review* 33 (February 1968): 40–62.

by **DARRIN BELL**

Candorville © Darrin Bell. © 2006 The Washington Post. All rights reserved. Reprinted with permission.

relevant that when one of the founders of Western thought set himself to frame an ideal state that would embody social justice, he — like the earliest city dwellers — not only devised a society stratified in tiers but believed it would be necessary to persuade the traders and work-people that, by divine decree, they were made from brass and iron, while the warriors were made of silver and the rulers of gold.[7]

Another example of self-justification serving as a source of prejudice is the dominant group's assumption of an attitude of superiority over other groups. In this respect, establishing a prestige hierarchy — ranking the status of various ethnic groups — results in differential association. To enhance or maintain self-esteem, a person may avoid social contact with groups deemed inferior and associate only with those identified as being of high status. Through such behavior, self-justification may come to intensify the social distance between groups. . . . *Social distance* refers to the degree to

[7]Philip Mason, *Patterns of Dominance* (New York: Oxford University Press, 1970), p. 7. See also Philip Mason, *Race Relations* (New York: Oxford University Press, 1970), pp. 17–29.

which ingroup members do not engage in social or primary relationships with members of various outgroups.

Personality. In 1950, in *The Authoritarian Personality*, T. W. Adorno and his colleagues reported a correlation between individuals' early childhood experiences of harsh parental discipline and their development of an **authoritarian personality** as adults.[8] If parents assume an excessively domineering posture in their relations with a child, exercising stern measures and threatening to withdraw love if the child does not respond with weakness and submission, the child tends to be insecure and to nurture much latent hostility against the parents. When such children become adults, they may demonstrate **displaced aggression,** directing their hostility against a powerless group to compensate for their feelings of insecurity and fear. Highly prejudiced individuals tend to come from families that emphasize obedience.

The authors identified authoritarianism by the use of a measuring instrument called an F scale (the *F* stands for potential fascism). Other tests included the A-S (anti-Semitism) and E (ethnocentrism) scales, the latter measuring attitudes toward various minorities. One of their major findings was that people who scored high on authoritarianism also consistently showed a high degree of prejudice against all minority groups. These highly prejudiced people were characterized by rigidity of viewpoint, dislike for ambiguity, strict obedience to leaders, and intolerance of weakness in themselves and others.

No sooner did *The Authoritarian Personality* appear than controversy began. H. H. Hyman and P. B. Sheatsley challenged the methodology and analysis.[9] Solomon Asch questioned the assumptions that the F scale responses represented a belief system and that structural variables (e.g., ideologies, stratification, and mobility) do not play a role in shaping personality.[10] E. A. Shils argued that the authors were interested only in measuring authoritarianism of the political right while ignoring such tendencies in those at the other end of the political spectrum.[11] Other investigators sought alternative explanations for the authoritarian personality. D. Stewart and T. Hoult extended the framework beyond family childhood experiences to include other social factors.[12] H. C. Kelman and Janet Barclay pointed out

15

---

[8]T. W. Adorno, Else Frankel-Brunswik, Daniel J. Levinson, and R. Nevitt Sanford, *The Authoritarian Personality* (New York: Harper & Row, 1950).

[9]H. H. Hyman and P. B. Sheatsley, "The Authoritarian Personality: A Methodological Critique," in R. Christie and M. Jahoda (eds.), *Studies in the Scope and Method of "The Authoritarian Personality"* (Glencoe, IL: Free Press, 1954).

[10]Solomon E. Asch, *Social Psychology* (Englewood Cliffs, NJ: Prentice Hall, 1952), p. 545.

[11]E. A. Shils, "Authoritarianism: Right and Left," in *Studies in the Scope and Method of "The Authoritarian Personality."*

[12]D. Stewart and T. Hoult, "A Social-Psychological Theory of 'The Authoritarian Personality,'" *American Journal of Sociology* 65 (1959): 274.

that substantial evidence exists showing that lower intelligence and less education also correlate with high authoritarianism scores on the F scale.[13]

Despite the critical attacks, the underlying conceptions of *The Authoritarian Personality* were important, and research into personality as a factor in prejudice has continued. Subsequent investigators refined and modified the original study. Correcting scores for response bias, they conducted cross-cultural studies. Respondents in Germany and Near Eastern countries, where more authoritarian social structures exist, scored higher on authoritarianism and social distance between groups. In Japan, Germany, and the United States, authoritarianism and social distance were moderately related. Other studies suggested that an inverse relationship exists between social class and F scale scores: the higher the social class, the lower the authoritarianism.[14]

Although studies of authoritarian personality have helped us understand some aspects of prejudice, they have not provided a causal explanation. Most of the findings in this area show a correlation, but the findings do not prove, for example, that harsh discipline of children causes them to become prejudiced adults. Perhaps the strict parents were themselves prejudiced, and the child learned those attitudes from them — or, as George Simpson and J. Milton Yinger say,

> One must be careful not to assume too quickly that a certain tendency — rigidity of mind, for example — that is correlated with prejudice necessarily causes that prejudice. . . . The sequence may be the other way around. . . . It is more likely that both are related to more basic factors.[15]

For some people, prejudice may indeed be rooted in subconscious   20
childhood tensions, but we simply do not know whether these tensions directly cause a high degree of prejudice in the adult or whether other powerful social forces are the determinants. Whatever the explanation, authoritarianism is a significant phenomenon worthy of continued investigation. Recent research, however, has stressed social and situational factors, rather than personality, as primary causes of prejudice and discrimination.[16]

Yet another dimension of the personality component is the role of self-esteem. Galinsky and Ku found that those with high self-esteem evaluated an outgroup more positively than those with low self-esteem.[17]

---

[13]H. C. Kelman and Janet Barclay, "The F Scale as a Measure of Breadth of Perspective," *Journal of Abnormal and Social Psychology* 67 (1963): 608–15.

[14]For an excellent summary of authoritarian studies and literature, see John P. Kirscht and Ronald C. Dillehay, *Dimensions of Authoritarianism: A Review of Research and Theory* (Lexington, KY: University of Kentucky Press, 1967).

[15]George E. Simpson and J. Milton Yinger, *Racial and Cultural Minorities: An Analysis of Prejudice and Discrimination* (New York: Harper & Row, 1953), p. 91.

[16]See, for example, Thomas F. Pettigrew, "Intergroup Contact Theory," *Annual Review of Psychology* 49 (1998): 65–85.

[17]See Adam D. Galinsky and Gillian Ku, "The Effects of Perspective-Taking on Prejudice: The Moderating Role of Self-Evaluation," *Personality and Social Psychology Bulletin* 30 (May 2004): 594–604.

Major, Kaiser, and McCoy reported that individuals' awareness of potential discrimination against themselves provided self-esteem protection,
in contrast to the lower self-esteem experienced by those less aware of
such external factors affecting themselves.[18] It would thus appear that
the level of one's self-esteem affects attitudes both about oneself and
others.

Frustration.   Frustration is the result of relative deprivation in which
expectations remain unsatisfied. **Relative deprivation** is a lack of resources,
or rewards, in one's standard of living in comparison with those of others in
the society. A number of investigators have suggested that frustrations tend
to increase aggression toward others.[19] Frustrated people may easily strike
out against the perceived cause of their frustration. However, this reaction
may not be possible because the true source of the frustration is often too
nebulous to be identified or too powerful to act against. In such instances,
the result may be displaced aggression; in this situation, the frustrated individual or group usually redirects anger against a more visible, vulnerable,
and socially sanctioned target that is unable to strike back. Minorities meet
these criteria and are thus frequently the recipients of displaced aggression
by the dominant group.

Blaming others for something that is not their fault is known as **scapegoating.** The term comes from the ancient Hebrew custom of using a goat
during the Day of Atonement as a symbol of the sins of the people. In an
annual ceremony, a priest placed his hands on the head of a goat and listed
the people's sins in a symbolic transference of guilt; he then chased the goat
out of the community, thereby freeing the people of sin.[20] Since those
times, the powerful group has usually punished the scapegoat group rather
than allowing it to escape.

There have been many instances throughout world history of minority
groups serving as scapegoats, including the Christians in ancient Rome, the
Huguenots in France, the Jews in Europe and Russia, and the Puritans and
Quakers in England. Gordon Allport suggests that certain characteristics
are necessary for a group to become a suitable scapegoat. The group must
be (1) highly visible in physical appearance or observable customs and actions;
(2) not strong enough to strike back; (3) situated within easy access of the
dominant group and, ideally, concentrated in one area; (4) a past target of
hostility for whom latent hostility still exists; and (5) the symbol of an
unpopular concept.[21]

---

[18]Brenda Major, Cheryl R. Kaiser, and Shannon K. McCoy, "It's Not My Fault: When
and Why Attributions to Prejudice Protect Self-Esteem," *Personality and Social Psychology
Bulletin* 29 (June 2003): 772–81.

[19]See Russell G. Geen, *Human Aggression*, 2nd ed. (Berkshire, England: Open University Press, 2001).

[20]Leviticus 16:5–22.

[21]Gordon W. Allport, *The Nature of Prejudice* (Cambridge, MA: Addison-Wesley, 1954),
pp. 13–14.

Some groups fit this typology better than others, but minority racial   25
and ethnic groups have been a perennial choice. Irish, Italians, Catholics,
Jews, Quakers, Mormons, Chinese, Japanese, blacks, Puerto Ricans, Mexicans, and Koreans have all been treated, at one time or another, as the
scapegoat in the United States. Especially in times of economic hardship,
societies tend to blame some group for the general conditions, which often
leads to aggressive action against the group as an expression of frustration.
For example, a study by Carl Hovland and Robert Sears found that, between 1882 and 1930, a definite correlation existed in the South between a
decline in the price of cotton and an increase in the number of lynchings of
blacks.[22]

For over twenty years, Leonard Berkowitz and his associates studied
and experimented with aggressive behavior. They concluded that, confronted with equally frustrating situations, highly prejudiced individuals are
more likely to seek scapegoats than are nonprejudiced individuals. Another
intervening variable is that personal frustrations (marital failure, injury, or
mental illness) make people more likely to seek scapegoats than do shared
frustrations (dangers of flood or hurricane).[23]

Some experiments have shown that aggression does not increase if the
frustration is understandable.[24] Other experiments have found that people
become aggressive only if the aggression directly relieves their frustration.[25]
Still other studies have shown that anger is a more likely result if the person
responsible for the frustrating situation could have acted otherwise.[26]
Clearly the results are mixed, depending on the variables within a given
social situation.

Frustration–aggression theory, although helpful, is not completely sat-
isfactory. It ignores the role of culture and the reality of actual social conflict and fails to show any causal relationship. Most of the responses measured in these studies were of people already biased. Why did one group
rather than another become the object of the aggression? Moreover, frustration does not necessarily precede aggression, and aggression does not necessarily flow from frustration.

[22]Carl I. Hovland and Robert R. Sears, "Minor Studies of Aggression: Correlation of
Lynchings with Economic Indices," *Journal of Psychology* 9 (Winter 1940): 301–10.

[23]See Leonard Berkowitz, "Whatever Happened to the Frustration-Aggression Hypothesis?" *American Behavioral Scientist* 21 (1978): 691–708; L. Berkowitz, *Aggression: A Social
Psychological Analysis* (New York: McGraw-Hill, 1962).

[24]D. Zillman, *Hostility and Aggression* (Hillsdale, NJ: Erlbaum, 1979); R. A. Baron,
Human Aggression (New York: Plenum Press, 1977); N. Pastore, "The Role of Arbitrariness in
the Frustration-Aggression Hypothesis," *Journal of Abnormal and Social Psychology* 47 (1952):
728–31.

[25]A. H. Buss, "Instrumentality of Aggression, Feedback, and Frustration as Determinants
of Physical Aggression," *Journal of Personality and Social Psychology* 3 (1966): 153–62.

[26]J. R. Averill, "Studies on Anger and Aggression: Implications for Theories of Emotion,"
American Psychologist 38 (1983): 1145–60.

The Sociology of Prejudice

The sociological approach to prejudice is not to examine individual behavior, as psychologists do, but rather to examine behavior within a group setting. Sociologist Talcott Parsons provided one bridge between psychology and sociology by introducing social forces as a variable in frustration–aggression theory. He suggested that both the family and the occupational structure may produce anxieties and insecurities that create frustration.[27] According to this view, the growing-up process (gaining parental affection and approval, identifying with and imitating sexual role models, and competing with others in adulthood) sometimes involves severe emotional strain. The result is an adult personality with a large reservoir of repressed aggression that becomes *free-floating* — susceptible to redirection against convenient scapegoats. Similarly, the occupational system is a source of frustration: Its emphasis on competitiveness and individual achievement, its function of conferring status, its requirement that people inhibit their natural impulses at work, and its ties to the state of the economy are among the factors that generate emotional anxieties. Parsons pessimistically concluded that minorities fulfill a functional "need" as targets for displaced aggression and therefore will remain targets.[28]

Perhaps most influential in staking out the sociological position on prejudice was Herbert Blumer, who suggested that prejudice always involves the "sense of group position" in society. Agreeing with Kramer's delineation of three levels of prejudice, Blumer argued that prejudice can include beliefs, feelings, and a predisposition to action, thus motivating behavior that derives from the social hierarchy.[29] By emphasizing historically established group positions and relationships, Blumer shifted the focus away from attitudes and personality compositions of individuals. As a social phenomenon, prejudice rises or falls according to issues that alter one group's position vis-à-vis that of another group.

Socialization.   In the **socialization process,** individuals acquire the values, attitudes, beliefs, and perceptions of their culture or subculture, including religion, nationality, and social class. Generally, the child conforms to the parents' expectations in acquiring an understanding of the world and its people. Being impressionable and knowing of no alternative conceptions of the world, the child usually accepts these concepts without

30

---

[27]Talcott Parsons, "Certain Primary Sources and Patterns of Aggression in the Social Structure of the Western World," in *Essays in Sociological Theory* (New York: Free Press, 1964), pp. 298–322.

[28]For an excellent review of Parsonian theory in this area, see Stanford M. Lyman, *The Black American in Sociological Thought: A Failure of Perspective* (New York: Putnam, 1972), pp. 145–69.

[29]Herbert Blumer, "Race Prejudice as a Sense of Group Position," *Pacific Sociological Review* 1 (1958): 3–7.

questioning. We thus learn the prejudices of our parents and others, which then become part of our values and beliefs. Even when based on false stereotypes, prejudices shape our perceptions of various peoples and influence our attitudes and actions toward particular groups. For example, if we develop negative attitudes about Jews because we are taught that they are shrewd, acquisitive, and clannish — all-too-familiar stereotypes — as adults we may refrain from business or social relationships with them. We may not even realize the reason for such avoidance, so subtle has been the prejudice instilled within us.

People may learn certain prejudices because of their pervasiveness. The cultural screen that we develop and through which we view the surrounding world is not always accurate, but it does permit transmission of shared values and attitudes, which are reinforced by others. Prejudice, like cultural values, is taught and learned through the socialization process. The prevailing prejudicial attitudes and actions may be deeply embedded in custom or law (e.g., the **Jim Crow laws** of the 1890s and early twentieth century establishing segregated public facilities throughout the South, which subsequent generations accepted as proper and maintained in their own adult lives).

Although socialization explains how prejudicial attitudes may be transmitted from one generation to the next, it does not explain their origin or why they intensify or diminish over the years. These aspects of prejudice must be explained in another way.

Economic Competition. People tend to be more hostile toward others when they feel that their security is threatened; thus, many social scientists conclude that economic competition and conflict breed prejudice. Certainly, considerable evidence shows that negative stereotyping, prejudice, and discrimination increase markedly whenever competition for available jobs increases.

An excellent illustration relates to the Chinese sojourners in the nineteenth-century United States. Prior to the 1870s, the transcontinental railroad was being built, and the Chinese filled many of the jobs made available by this project in the sparsely populated West. Although they were expelled from the region's gold mines and schools and could obtain no redress of grievances in the courts, they managed to convey to some whites the image of being clean, hard-working, law-abiding people. The completion of the railroad, the flood of former Civil War soldiers into the job market, and the economic depression of 1873 worsened their situation. The Chinese became more frequent victims of open discrimination and hostility. Their positive stereotype among some whites was widely displaced by a negative one: They were now "conniving," "crafty," "criminal," "the yellow menace." Only after they retreated into Chinatowns and entered specialty occupations that minimized their competition with whites did the intense hostility abate.

35

One pioneer in the scientific study of prejudice, John Dollard, demonstrated how prejudice against the Germans, which had been virtually nonexistent in a small U.S. industrial town, arose when times got bad:

> Local Whites largely drawn from the surrounding farms manifested considerable direct aggression toward the newcomers. Scornful and derogatory opinions were expressed about the Germans, and the native Whites had a satisfying sense of superiority toward them. . . . The chief element in the permission to be aggressive against the Germans was rivalry for jobs and status in the local woodenware plants. The native Whites felt definitely crowded for their jobs by the entering German groups and in case of bad times had a chance to blame the Germans who by their presence provided more competitors for the scarcer jobs. There seemed to be no traditional pattern of prejudice against Germans unless the skeletal suspicion of all out-groupers (always present) be invoked in this place.[30]

Both experimental studies and historical analyses have added credence to the economic-competition theory. Muzafer Sherif directed several experiments showing how intergroup competition at a boys' camp led to conflict and escalating hostility.[31] Donald Young pointed out that, throughout U.S. history, in times of high unemployment and thus intense job competition, nativist movements against minorities have flourished.[32] This pattern has held true regionally — against Asians on the West Coast, Italians in Louisiana, and French Canadians in New England — and nationally, with the antiforeign movements always peaking during periods of depression. So it was with the Native American Party in the 1830s, the Know-Nothing Party in the 1850s, the American Protective Association in the 1890s, and the Ku Klux Klan after World War I. Since the passage of civil rights laws on employment in the twentieth century, researchers have consistently detected the strongest antiblack prejudice among working-class and middle-class whites who feel threatened by blacks entering their socioeconomic group in noticeable numbers.[33] It seems that any group applying the pressure of job competition most directly on another group becomes a target of its prejudice.

---

[30]John Dollard, "Hostility and Fear in Social Life," *Social Forces* 17 (1938): 15–26.

[31]Muzafer Sherif, O. J. Harvey, B. Jack White, William Hood, and Carolyn Sherif, *Intergroup Conflict and Cooperation: The Robbers Cave Experiment* (Norman: University of Oklahoma Institute of Intergroup Relations, 1961). See also M. Sherif, "Experiments in Group Conflict," *Scientific American* 195 (1956): 54–58.

[32]Donald Young, *Research Memorandum on Minority Peoples in the Depression* (New York: Social Science Research Council, 1937), pp. 133–41.

[33]Andrew Greeley and Paul Sheatsley, "The Acceptance of Desegregation Continues to Advance," *Scientific American* 210 (1971): 13–19; T. F. Pettigrew, "Three Issues in Ethnicity: Boundaries, Deprivations, and Perceptions," in M. Yinger and S. J. Cutler (eds.), *Major Social Issues: A Multidisciplinary View* (New York: Free Press, 1978); R. D. Vanneman and T. F. Pettigrew, "Race and Relative Deprivation in the United States," *Race* 13 (1972): 461–86.

Once again, a theory that offers some excellent insights into prejudice — in particular, that adverse economic conditions correlate with increased hostility toward minorities — also has some serious shortcomings. Not all groups that have been objects of hostility (e.g., Quakers and Mormons) have been economic competitors. Moreover, why is hostility against some groups greater than against others? Why do the negative feelings in some communities run against groups whose numbers are so small that they cannot possibly pose an economic threat? Evidently, values besides economic ones cause people to be antagonistic to a group perceived as an actual or potential threat.

Social Norms. Some sociologists have suggested that a relationship exists between prejudice and a person's tendency to conform to societal expectations.[34] **Social norms** — the norms of one's culture — form the generally shared rules defining what is and is not proper behavior in one's culture. By learning and automatically accepting the prevailing prejudices, an individual is simply conforming to those norms.

This theory holds that a direct relationship exists between degree of conformity and degree of prejudice. If so, people's prejudices should decrease or increase significantly when they move into areas where the prejudicial norm is different. Evidence supports this view. Thomas Pettigrew found that southerners in the 1950s became less prejudiced against blacks when they interacted with them in the army, where the social norms were less prejudicial.[35] In another study, Jeanne Watson found that people moving into an anti-Semitic neighborhood in New York City became more anti-Semitic.[36]

John Dollard's study, *Caste and Class in a Southern Town* (1937/1957), provides an in-depth look at the emotional adjustment of whites and blacks to rigid social norms.[37] In his study of the processes, functions, and maintenance of accommodation, Dollard detailed the "carrot-and-stick" method social groups employed. Intimidation — sometimes even severe reprisals for going against social norms — ensured compliance. However, reprisals usually were unnecessary. The advantages whites and blacks gained in psychological, economic, or behavioral terms served to perpetuate the caste order. These gains in personal security and stability set in motion a vicious circle. They encouraged a way of life that reinforced the rationale of the social system in this community.

Two 1994 studies provided further evidence of the powerful influence of social norms. Joachim Krueger and Russell W. Clement found that con-

40

---

[34]See Harry H. L. Kitano, "Passive Discrimination in the Normal Person," *Journal of Social Psychology* 70 (1966): 23–31.

[35]Thomas Pettigrew, "Regional Differences in Anti-Negro Prejudice," *Journal of Abnormal and Social Psychology* 59 (1959): 28–36.

[36]Jeanne Watson, "Some Social and Psychological Situations Related to Change in Attitude," *Human Relations* 3 (1950): 15–56.

[37]John Dollard, *Caste and Class in a Southern Town*, 3rd ed. (Garden City, NY: Doubleday Anchor Books, 1957).

sensus bias persisted despite the availability of statistical data and knowledge about such bias.[38] Michael R. Leippe and Donna Eisenstadt showed
that induced compliance can change socially significant attitudes and that
the change generalizes to broader beliefs.[39]

Although the social-norms theory explains prevailing attitudes, it does
not explain either their origins or the reasons new prejudices develop when
other groups move into an area. In addition, the theory does not explain
why prejudicial attitudes against a particular group rise and fall cyclically
over the years.

Although many social scientists have attempted to identify the causes of
prejudice, no single factor provides an adequate explanation. Prejudice is a
complex phenomenon, and it is most likely the product of more than one
causal agent. Sociologists today tend either to emphasize multiple-cause
explanations or to stress social forces encountered in specific and similar situations — forces such as economic conditions, stratification, and hostility
toward an outgroup.

ENGAGING THE TEXT

1. Review Parrillo's discussion of the cognitive, emotional, and action-oriented
   levels of prejudice. Do you think it's possible for an individual to hold prejudiced beliefs that do *not* affect her feelings and actions? Why or why not?

2. How can prejudice arise from self-justification? Offer some examples of
   how a group can assume an attitude of superiority in order to justify ill-
   treatment of others.

3. How, according to Parrillo, might personal factors like authoritarian attitudes, low self-esteem, or frustration promote the growth of prejudice?

4. What is the "socialization process," according to Parrillo? In what different
   ways can socialization instill prejudice?

5. What is the relationship between economic competition and prejudice? Do
   you think prejudice would continue to exist if everyone had a good job with
   a comfortable income?

EXPLORING CONNECTIONS

6. Which of the theories Parrillo outlines, if any, might help to explain the
   attitudes toward blacks expressed by Thomas Jefferson (p. 378)? Which
   apply most clearly to the life story of C. P. Ellis (p. 398)?

7. Which of the causes of prejudice that Parrillo describes are reflected in the
   comments about immigrants in Darrin Bell's cartoon (p. 388)? What is Bell

[38]Joachim Krueger and Russell W. Clement, "The Truly False Consensus Effect: An
Ineradicable and Egocentric Bias in Social Perception," *Journal of Personality and Social Psychology* 67 (1994): 596–610.

[39]Michael R. Leippe and Donna Eisenstadt, "Generalization of Dissonance Reduction:
Decreasing Prejudice through Induced Compliance," *Journal of Personality and Social Psychology* 67 (1994): 395–414.

saying about the nature of anti-immigrant attitudes in U.S. history? What does he suggest about immigrants themselves?

EXTENDING THE CRITICAL CONTEXT

8. List the various groups that you belong to (racial, economic, cultural, social, familial, and so forth) and arrange them in a status hierarchy. Which groups were you born into? Which groups did you join voluntarily? Which have had the greatest impact on your socialization? Which groups isolate you the most from contact with outsiders?

9. Working in small groups, research recent news stories for examples of incidents involving racism or prejudice. Which of the theories described by Parrillo seem most useful for analyzing the motives underlying these events?

C. P. Ellis

STUDS TERKEL

The following oral history brings us uncomfortably close to unambiguous, deadly prejudice: C. P. Ellis is a former Ku Klux Klan member who claims to have overcome his racist (and sexist) attitudes; he speaks here as a union leader who feels an alliance to other workers, including blacks and women. For decades, Studs Terkel (1912–2008) was the best-known practitioner of oral history in the United States. He compiled several books by interviewing dozens of widely varying people — ordinary people for the most part — about important subjects like work, social class, race, the Great Depression, and aging. The edited versions of these interviews are often surprisingly powerful crystallizations of American social history: Terkel's subjects give voice to the frustrations and hopes of whole generations of Americans. Terkel won a Pulitzer Prize in 1985 for "The Good War": An Oral History of World War II, and in 1997 he received a National Humanities Medal from President Bill Clinton. "C. P. Ellis" first appeared in American Dreams: Lost and Found (1980).

We're in his office in Durham, North Carolina. He is the business manager of the International Union of Operating Engineers. On the wall is a plaque: "Certificate of Service, in recognition to C. P. Ellis, for your faithful service to the city in having served as a member of the Durham Human Relations Council. February 1977."

Number of hate groups active in the U.S., by state.
Southern Poverty Law Center Intelligence Report, 2008.

At one time, he had been president (exalted cyclops) of the Durham chapter of the Ku Klux Klan. . . .
He is fifty-two years old.

My father worked in a textile mill in Durham. He died at forty-eight years old. It was probably from cotton dust. Back then, we never heard of brown lung. I was about seventeen years old and had a mother and sister depending on somebody to make a livin'. It was just barely enough insurance to cover his burial. I had to quit school and go to work. I was about eighth grade when I quit.

My father worked hard but never had enough money to buy decent clothes. When I went to school, I never seemed to have adequate clothes to wear. I always left school late afternoon with a sense of inferiority. The other kids had nice clothes, and I just had what Daddy could buy. I still got some of those inferiority feelin's now that I have to overcome once in a while.

I loved my father. He would go with me to ball games. We'd go fishin' together. I was really ashamed of the way he'd dress. He would take this money and give it to me instead of putting it on himself. I always had the feeling about somebody looking at him and makin' fun of him and makin' fun of me. I think it had to do somethin' with my life.

My father and I were very close, but we didn't talk about too many intimate things. He did have a drinking problem. During the week, he would work every day, but weekends he was ready to get plastered. I can understand when a guy looks at his paycheck and looks at his bills, and he's worked hard all the week, and his bills are larger than his paycheck. He'd

5

done the best he could the entire week, and there seemed to be no hope. It's an illness thing. Finally you just say: "The heck with it. I'll just get drunk and forget it."

My father was out of work during the depression, and I remember going with him to the finance company uptown, and he was turned down. That's something that's always stuck.

My father never seemed to be happy. It was a constant struggle with him just like it was for me. It's very seldom I'd see him laugh. He was just tryin' to figure out what he could do from one day to the next.

After several years pumping gas at a service station, I got married. We had to have children. Four. One child was born blind and retarded, which was a real additional expense to us. He's never spoken a word. He doesn't know me when I go to see him. But I see him, I hug his neck. I talk to him, tell him I love him. I don't know whether he knows me or not, but I know he's well taken care of. All my life, I had work, never a day without work, worked all the overtime I could get and still could not survive financially. I began to say there's somethin' wrong with this country. I worked my butt off and just never seemed to break even. 10

I had some real great ideas about this great nation. (Laughs.) They say to abide by the law, go to church, do right and live for the Lord, and everything'll work out. But it didn't work out. It just kept gettin' worse and worse.

I was workin' a bread route. The highest I made one week was seventy-five dollars. The rent on our house was about twelve dollars a week. I will never forget: outside of this house was a 265-gallon oil drum, and I never did get enough money to fill up that oil drum. What I would do every night, I would run up to the store and buy five gallons of oil and climb up the ladder and pour it in that 265-gallon drum. I could hear that five gallons when it hits the bottom of that oil drum, splatters, and it sounds like it's nothin' in there. But it would keep the house warm for the night. Next day you'd have to do the same thing.

I left the bread route with fifty dollars in my pocket. I went to the bank and borrowed four thousand dollars to buy the service station. I worked seven days a week, open and close, and finally had a heart attack. Just about two months before the last payments of that loan. My wife had done the best she could to keep it runnin'. Tryin' to come out of that hole, I just couldn't do it.

I really began to get bitter. I didn't know who to blame. I tried to find somebody. I began to blame it on black people. I had to hate somebody. Hatin' America is hard to do because you can't see it to hate it. You gotta have somethin' to look at to hate. (Laughs.) The natural person for me to hate would be black people, because my father before me was a member of the Klan. As far as he was concerned, it was the savior of the white people. It was the only organization in the world that would take care of the white people. So I began to admire the Klan.

I got active in the Klan while I was at the service station. Every Monday night, a group of men would come by and buy a Coca-Cola, go back to the car, take a few drinks, and come back and stand around talkin'. I couldn't 15 help but wonder: Why are these dudes comin' out every Monday? They said they were with the Klan and have meetings close-by. Would I be interested? Boy, that was an opportunity I really looked forward to! To be part of somethin'. I joined the Klan, went from member to chaplain, from chaplain to vice-president, from vice-president to president. The title is exalted cyclops.

The first night I went with the fellas, they knocked on the door and gave the signal. They sent some robed Klansmen to talk to me and give me some instructions. I was led into a large meeting room, and this was the time of my life! It was thrilling. Here's a guy who's worked all his life and struggled all his life to be something, and here's the moment to be something. I will never forget it. Four robed Klansmen led me into the hall. The lights were dim, and the only thing you could see was an illuminated cross. I knelt before the cross. I had to make certain vows and promises. We promised to uphold the purity of the white race, fight communism, and protect white womanhood.

After I had taken my oath, there was loud applause goin' throughout the building, musta been at least four hundred people. For this one little ol' person. It was a thrilling moment for C. P. Ellis.

It disturbs me when people who do not really know what it's all about are so very critical of individual Klansmen. The majority of 'em are low-income whites, people who really don't have a part in something. They have been shut out as well as the blacks. Some are not very well educated either. Just like myself. We had a lot of support from doctors and lawyers and police officers.

Maybe they've had bitter experiences in this life and they had to hate somebody. So the natural person to hate would be the black person. He's beginnin' to come up, he's beginnin' to learn to read and start votin' and run for political office. Here are white people who are supposed to be superior to them, and we're shut out.

I can understand why people join extreme right-wing or left-wing groups. They're in the same boat I was. Shut out. Deep down inside, we want to be part of this great society. Nobody listens, so we join these groups. 20

At one time, I was state organizer of the National Rights party. I organized a youth group for the Klan. I felt we were getting old and our generation's gonna die. So I contacted certain kids in schools. They were havin' racial problems. On the first night, we had a hundred high school students. When they came in the door, we had "Dixie" playin'. These kids were just thrilled to death. I begin to hold weekly meetin's with 'em, teachin' the principles of the Klan. At that time, I believed Martin Luther King had Communist connections. I began to teach that Andy Young[1] was affiliated with the Communist party.

---

[1]*Andy Young:* Andrew Jackson Young Jr. (b. 1932), prominent black leader and politician. Young was a friend and adviser of Martin Luther King Jr., and served as President Jimmy Carter's ambassador to the United Nations. In the 1980s, he was twice elected mayor of Atlanta.

I had a call one night from one of our kids. He was about twelve. He said: "I just been robbed downtown by two niggers." I'd had a couple of drinks and that really teed me off. I go downtown and couldn't find the kid. I got worried. I saw two young black people. I had the .32 revolver with me. I said: "Nigger, you seen a little young white boy up here? I just got a call from him and was told that some niggers robbed him of fifteen cents." I pulled my pistol out and put it right at his head. I said: "I've always wanted to kill a nigger and I think I'll make you the first one." I nearly scared the kid to death, and he struck off.

This was the time when the civil rights movement was really beginnin' to peak. The blacks were beginnin' to demonstrate and picket downtown stores. I never will forget some black lady I hated with a purple passion. Ann Atwater. Every time I'd go downtown, she'd be leadin' a boycott. How I hated — pardon the expression, I don't use it much now — how I just hated the black nigger. (Laughs.) Big, fat, heavy woman. She'd pull about eight demonstrations, and first thing you know they had two, three blacks at the checkout counter. Her and I have had some pretty close confrontations.

I felt very big, yeah. (Laughs.) We're more or less a secret organization. We didn't want anybody to know who we were, and I began to do some thinkin'. What am I hidin' for? I've never been convicted of anything in my life. I don't have any court record. What am I, C. P. Ellis, as a citizen and a member of the United Klansmen of America? Why can't I go to the city council meeting and say: "This is the way we feel about the matter? We don't want you to purchase mobile units to set in our schoolyards. We don't want niggers in our schools."

We began to come out in the open. We would go to the meetings, and the blacks would be there and we'd be there. It was a confrontation every time. I didn't hold back anything. We began to make some inroads with the city councilmen and county commissioners. They began to call us friend. Call us at night on the telephone: "C. P., glad you came to that meeting last night." They didn't want integration either, but they did it secretively, in order to get elected. They couldn't stand up openly and say it, but they were glad somebody was sayin' it. We visited some of the city leaders in their home and talked to 'em privately. It wasn't long before councilmen would call me up: "The blacks are comin' up tonight and makin' outrageous demands. How about some of you people showin' up and have a little balance?" I'd get on the telephone. "The niggers is comin' to the council meeting tonight. Persons in the city's called me and asked us to be there." 25

We'd load up our cars and we'd fill up half the council chambers, and the blacks the other half. During these times, I carried weapons to the meetings, outside my belt. We'd go there armed. We would wind up just hollerin' and fussin' at each other. What happened? As a result of our fightin' one another, the city council still had their way. They didn't want to give up control to the blacks nor the Klan. They were usin' us.

I began to realize this later down the road. One day I was walkin' downtown and a certain city council member saw me comin'. I expected him to shake my hand because he was talkin' to me at night on the telephone. I had been in his home and visited with him. He crossed the street. Oh shit, I began to think, somethin's wrong here. Most of 'em are merchants or maybe an attorney, an insurance agent, people like that. As long as they kept low-income whites and low-income blacks fightin', they're gonna maintain control.

I began to get that feeling after I was ignored in public. I thought: Bullshit, you're not gonna use me any more. That's when I began to do some real serious thinkin'.

The same thing is happening in this country today. People are being used by those in control, those who have all the wealth. I'm not espousing communism. We got the greatest system of government in the world. But those who have it simply don't want those who don't have it to have any part of it. Black and white. When it comes to money, the green, the other colors make no difference. (Laughs.)

I spent a lot of sleepless nights. I still didn't like blacks. I didn't want to associate with 'em. Blacks, Jews, or Catholics. My father said: "Don't have anything to do with 'em." I didn't until I met a black person and talked with him, eyeball to eyeball, and met a Jewish person and talked to him, eyeball to eyeball. I found out they're people just like me. They cried, they cussed, they prayed, they had desires. Just like myself. Thank God, I got to the point where I can look past labels. But at that time, my mind was closed.

I remember one Monday night Klan meeting. I said something was wrong. Our city fathers were using us. And I didn't like to be used. The reactions of the others was not too pleasant: "Let's just keep fightin' them niggers."

I'd go home at night and I'd have to wrestle with myself. I'd look at a black person walkin' down the street, and the guy'd have ragged shoes or his clothes would be worn. That began to do somethin' to me inside. I went through this for about six months. I felt I just had to get out of the Klan. But I wouldn't get out.

Then something happened. The state AFL–CIO[2] received a grant from the Department of HEW,[3] a $78,000 grant: how to solve racial problems in the school system. I got a telephone call from the president of the state AFL–CIO. "We'd like to get some people together from all walks of life." I said: "All walks of life? Who you talkin' about?" He said: "Blacks, whites, liberals, conservatives, Klansmen, NAACP[4] people."

30

[2]*AFL–CIO:* American Federation of Labor and Congress of Industrial Organizations — a huge federation of independent labor unions in the United States, Canada, Mexico, Panama, and elsewhere.

[3]*HEW:* Health, Education, and Welfare — at the time, a department of the federal government.

[4]*NAACP:* National Association for the Advancement of Colored People.

I said: "No way am I comin' with all those niggers. I'm not gonna be associated with those type of people." A White Citizens Council guy said: "Let's go up there and see what's goin' on. It's tax money bein' spent." I walk in the door, and there was a large number of blacks and white liberals. I knew most of 'em by face 'cause I seen 'em demonstratin' around town. Ann Atwater was there. (Laughs.) I just forced myself to go in and sit down.

The meeting was moderated by a great big black guy who was bushy-headed. (Laughs.) That turned me off. He acted very nice. He said: "I want you all to feel free to say anything you want to say." Some of the blacks stand up and say it's white racism. I took all I could take. I asked for the floor and cut loose. I said: "No, sir, it's black racism. If we didn't have niggers in the schools, we wouldn't have the problems we got today."   35

I will never forget. Howard Clements, a black guy, stood up. He said: "I'm certainly glad C. P. Ellis come because he's the most honest man here tonight." I said: "What's that nigger tryin' to do?" (Laughs.) At the end of that meeting, some blacks tried to come up shake my hand, but I wouldn't do it. I walked off.

Second night, same group was there. I felt a little more easy because I got some things off my chest. The third night, after they elected all the committees, they want to elect a chairman. Howard Clements stood up and said: "I suggest we elect two co-chairpersons." Joe Beckton, executive director of the Human Relations Commission, just as black as he can be, he nominated me. There was a reaction from some blacks. Nooo. And, of all things, they nominated Ann Atwater, that big old fat black gal that I had just hated with a purple passion, as co-chairman. I thought to myself: Hey, ain't no way I can work with that gal. Finally, I agreed to accept it, 'cause at this point, I was tired of fightin', either for survival or against black people or against Jews or against Catholics.

A Klansman and a militant black woman, co-chairmen of the school committee. It was impossible. How could I work with her? But after about two or three days, it was in our hands. We had to make it a success. This give me another sense of belongin', a sense of pride. This helped this inferiority feelin' I had. A man who has stood up publicly and said he despised black people, all of a sudden he was willin' to work with 'em. Here's a chance for a low-income white man to be somethin'. In spite of all my hatred for blacks and Jews and liberals, I accepted the job. Her and I began to reluctantly work together. (Laughs.) She had as many problems workin' with me as I had workin' with her.

One night, I called her: "Ann, you and I should have a lot of differences and we got 'em now. But there's somethin' laid out here before us, and if it's gonna be a success, you and I are gonna have to make it one. Can we lay aside some of these feelin's?" She said: "I'm willing if you are." I said: "Let's do it."

My old friends would call me at night: "C. P., what the hell is wrong with you? You're sellin' out the white race." This begin to make me have guilt feelin's. Am I doin' right? Am I doin' wrong? Here I am all of a sudden   40 makin' an about-face and tryin' to deal with my feelin's, my heart. My mind was beginnin' to open up. I was beginnin' to see what was right and what was wrong. I don't want the kids to fight forever.

We were gonna go ten nights. By this time, I had went to work at Duke University, in maintenance. Makin' very little money. Terry Sanford give me this ten days off with pay. He was president of Duke at the time. He knew I was a Klansman and realized the importance of blacks and whites getting along.

I said: "If we're gonna make this thing a success, I've got to get to my kind of people." The low-income whites. We walked the streets of Durham, and we knocked on doors and invited people. Ann was goin' into the black community. They just wasn't respondin' to us when we made these house calls. Some of 'em were cussin' us out. "You're sellin' us out, Ellis, get out of my door. I don't want to talk to you." Ann was gettin' the same response from blacks. "What are you doin' messin' with that Klansman?"

One day, Ann and I went back to the school and we sat down. We began to talk and just reflect. Ann said: "My daughter came home cryin' every day. She said her teacher was makin' fun of me in front of the other kids." I said: "Boy, the same thing happened to my kid. White liberal teacher was makin' fun of Tim Ellis's father, the Klansman. In front of other peoples. He came home cryin'." At this point — (he pauses, swallows hard, stifles a sob) — I begin to see, here we are, two people from the far ends of the fence, havin' identical problems, except hers bein' black and me bein' white. From that moment on, I tell ya, that gal and I worked together good. I begin to love the girl, really. (He weeps.)

The amazing thing about it, her and I, up to that point, had cussed each other, bawled each other, we hated each other. Up to that point, we didn't know each other. We didn't know we had things in common.

We worked at it, with the people who came to these meetings. They 45 talked about racism, sex education, about teachers not bein' qualified. After seven, eight nights of real intense discussion, these people, who'd never talked to each other before, all of a sudden came up with resolutions. It was really somethin', you had to be there to get the tone and feelin' of it.

At that point, I didn't like integration, but the law says you do this and I've got to do what the law says, okay? We said: "Let's take these resolutions to the school board." The most disheartening thing I've ever faced was the school system refused to implement any one of these resolutions. These were recommendations from the people who pay taxes and pay their salaries. (Laughs.)

I thought they were good answers. Some of 'em I didn't agree with, but I been in this thing from the beginning, and whatever comes of it, I'm gonna support it. Okay, since the school board refused, I decided I'd just run for the school board.

I spent eighty-five dollars on the campaign. The guy runnin' against me spent several thousand. I really had nobody on my side. The Klan turned against me. The low-income whites turned against me. The liberals didn't particularly like me. The blacks were suspicious of me. The blacks wanted to support me, but they couldn't muster up enough to support a Klansman on the school board. (Laughs.) But I made up my mind that what I was doin' was right, and I was gonna do it regardless what anybody said.

It bothered me when people would call and worry my wife. She's always supported me in anything I wanted to do. She was changing, and my boys were too. I got some of my youth corps kids involved. They still followed me.

I was invited to the Democratic women's social hour as a candidate.   50 Didn't have but one suit to my name. Had it six, seven, eight years. I had it cleaned, put on the best shirt I had and a tie. Here were all these high-class wealthy candidates shakin' hands. I walked up to the mayor and stuck out my hand. He give me that handshake with that rag type of hand. He said: "C. P., I'm glad to see you." But I could tell by his handshake he was lyin' to me. This was botherin' me. I know I'm a low-income person. I know I'm not wealthy. I know they were sayin': "What's this little ol' dude runnin' for school board?" Yet they had to smile and make like they're glad to see me. I begin to spot some black people in that room. I automatically went to 'em and that was a firm handshake. They said: "I'm glad to see you, C. P." I knew they meant it — you can tell about a handshake.

Every place I appeared, I said I will listen to the voice of the people. I will not make a major decision until I first contacted all the organizations in the city. I got 4,640 votes. The guy beat me by two thousand. Not bad for eighty-five bucks and no constituency.

The whole world was openin' up, and I was learnin' new truths that I had never learned before. I was beginnin' to look at a black person, shake hands with him, and see him as a human bein'. I hadn't got rid of all this stuff, I've still got a little bit of it. But somethin' was happenin' to me.

It was almost like bein' born again. It was a new life. I didn't have these sleepless nights I used to have when I was active in the Klan and slippin' around at night. I could sleep at night and feel good about it. I'd rather live now than at any other time in history. It's a challenge.

Back at Duke, doin' maintenance, I'd pick up my tools, fix the commode, unstop the drains. But this got in my blood. Things weren't right in this country, and what we done in Durham needs to be told. I was so miserable at Duke, I could hardly stand it. I'd go to work every morning just hatin' to go.

My whole life had changed. I got an eighth-grade education, and I   55 wanted to complete high school. Went to high school in the afternoons on a program called PEP — Past Employment Progress. I was about the only white in class, and the oldest. I begin to read about biology. I'd take my books home at night, 'cause I was determined to get through. Sure enough, I graduated. I got the diploma at home.

I come to work one mornin' and some guy says: "We need a union." At this time I wasn't pro-union. My daddy was anti-labor, too. We're not gettin' paid much, we're havin' to work seven days in a row. We're all starvin' to death. The next day, I meet the international representative of the Operating Engineers. He give me authorization cards. "Get these cards out and we'll have an election." There was eighty-eight for the union and seventeen no's. I was elected chief steward for the union.

Shortly after, a union man come down from Charlotte and says we need a full-time rep. We've got only two hundred people at the two plants here. It's just barely enough money comin' in to pay your salary. You'll have to get out and organize more people. I didn't know nothin' about organizin' unions, but I knew how to organize people, stir people up. (Laughs.) That's how I got to be business agent for the union.

When I began to organize, I began to see far deeper. I began to see people again bein' used. Blacks against whites. I say this without any hesitancy: management is vicious. There's two things they want to keep: all the money and all the say-so. They don't want these poor workin' folks to have none of that. I begin to see management fightin' me with everything they had. Hire anti-union law firms, badmouth unions. The people were makin' a dollar ninety-five an hour, barely able to get through weekends. I worked as a business rep for five years and was seein' all this.

Last year, I ran for business manager of the union. He's elected by the workers. The guy that ran against me was black, and our membership is seventy-five percent black. I thought: Claiborne, there's no way you can beat that black guy. People know your background. Even though you've made tremendous strides, those black people are not gonna vote for you. You know how much I beat him? Four to one. (Laughs.)

The company used my past against me. They put out letters with a picture of a robe and a cap: would you vote for a Klansman? They wouldn't deal with the issues. I immediately called for a mass meeting. I met with the ladies at an electric component plant. I said: "Okay, this is Claiborne Ellis. This is where I come from. I want you to know right now, you black ladies here, I was at one time a member of the Klan. I want you to know, because they'll tell you about it."

I invited some of my old black friends. I said: "Brother Joe, Brother Howard, be honest now and tell these people how you feel about me." They done it. (Laughs.) Howard Clements kidded me a little bit. He said: "I don't know what I'm doin' here, supportin' an ex-Klansman." (Laughs.) He said: "I know what C. P. Ellis come from. I knew him when he was. I knew him as he grew, and growed with him. I'm tellin' you now: follow, follow this Klansman." (He pauses, swallows hard.) "Any questions?" "No," the black ladies said. "Let's get on with the meeting, we need Ellis." (He laughs and weeps.) Boy, black people sayin' that about me. I won one thirty-four to forty-one. Four to one.

It makes you feel good to go into a plant and butt heads with professional union busters. You see black people and white people join hands to defeat the racist issues they use against people. They're tryin' the same things with the Klan. It's still happenin' today. Can you imagine a guy who's got an adult high school diploma runnin' into professional college graduates who are union busters? I gotta compete with 'em. I work seven days a week, nights and on Saturday and Sunday. The salary's not that great, and if I didn't care, I'd quit. But I care and I can't quit. I got a taste of it. (Laughs.)

I tell people there's a tremendous possibility in this country to stop wars, the battles, the struggles, the fights between people. People say: "That's an impossible dream. You sound like Martin Luther King." An ex-Klansman who sounds like Martin Luther King. (Laughs.) I don't think it's an impossible dream. It's happened in my life. It's happened in other people's lives in America.

I don't know what's ahead of me. I have no desire to be a big union official. I want to be right out here in the field with the workers. I want to walk through their factory and shake hands with that man whose hands are dirty. I'm gonna do all that one little ol' man can do. I'm fifty-two years old, and I ain't got many years left, but I want to make the best of 'em.

When the news came over the radio that Martin Luther King was assassi-   65
nated, I got on the telephone and begin to call other Klansmen. We just had a real party at the service station. Really rejoicin' 'cause that son of a bitch was dead. Our troubles are over with. They say the older you get, the harder it is for you to change. That's not necessarily true. Since I changed, I've set down and listened to tapes of Martin Luther King. I listen to it and tears come to my eyes 'cause I know what he's sayin' now. I know what's happenin'.

POSTSCRIPT:
The phone rings. A conversation.
"This was a black guy who's director of Operation Breakthrough in Durham. I had called his office. I'm interested in employin' some young black person who's interested in learnin' the labor movement. I want somebody who's never had an opportunity, just like myself. Just so he can read and write, that's all."

Engaging the Text

1. How does Ellis battle the racism he finds in himself? What gives him the motivation and strength to change? What specific changes does he undergo, and how successful is he in abandoning racist attitudes?

2. Would Ellis say that economic class is more important than race in determining job placement and occupational mobility? Find specific passages that reveal Ellis's beliefs about the connections between economic class, race, and success in American society. What do you believe?

3. How well does Ellis seem to understand himself, his feelings, his motives? Give evidence for your assertions.

4. What is Terkel's role in this selection? Is he unconsciously helping to rationalize or justify the actions of the Ku Klux Klan?

5. Does Ellis's story offer a credible way of overcoming misunderstanding and hatred between races? Do you think such a "solution" would be workable on a large scale? Why or why not?

EXPLORING CONNECTIONS

6. To what extent does Ellis's experience illustrate the theories of prejudice described by Vincent N. Parrillo in the previous selection (p. 384)? Which of these theories best account for Ellis's racism and for his eventual transformation?

7. Review the account of Malcolm X's self-education (p. 210). How does the dramatic self-transformation he experiences compare with C. P. Ellis's rebirth? What relationships can you find between the circumstances that led to their initial attitudes, the conditions or events that fostered their transformations, and the effects that these transformations had on their characters?

EXTENDING THE CRITICAL CONTEXT

8. Visit the Southern Poverty Law Center Web site to learn which hate groups are active in your state. As an individual or class project, do further research on these groups. How do they operate and whom do they target? What efforts by law enforcement, government, civil rights organizations, or community groups are being made to combat their influence? Which of these seem most likely to be effective, and why? What further steps, if any, do you think should be taken?

9. Interview a friend, family member, or fellow student in another class to create your own oral history on the subject of racial attitudes. Ask your subject to describe a time when he or she was forced to re-evaluate his or her thoughts or feelings about someone from a different racial or ethnic group. Try to include as many relevant details as possible in your retelling of the story. Share and edit these oral histories in small groups, and then assemble them into a class anthology.

The Boy in the Mirror

JAMES McBRIDE

James McBride's mother was the daughter of an Orthodox Jewish rabbi who disowned her when she married James's father, an African American Christian minister. His 1996 memoir, The Color of Water: A Black Man's Tribute to His White Mother, *recounts his life growing up — along with his eleven siblings — in a Brooklyn housing project. The chapter reprinted here details his struggle to come to terms with his mixed heritage. McBride (b. 1957) is a writer, composer, and jazz saxophonist, whose personal Web site notes that he is "the worst dancer in the history of African Americans, bar none. . . . He dances with one finger in the air like a white guy." In other respects he is very accomplished, having published two novels — one of which,* Miracle at St. Anna *(2003), has been made into a movie of the same name directed by Spike Lee. He has won several awards for his music and has written for a variety of major magazines and newspapers, including* Rolling Stone, Essence, *the* Washington Post, *and the* New York Times. *Presently he teaches at New York University as a Distinguished Writer-in-Residence.*

Back in the 1960s, when she had money, which was hardly ever, Mommy would take us down to Delancey Street[1] on Manhattan's Lower East Side to shop for school clothes. "You have to go where the deals are," she said. "They won't come to you."

"Where are the deals?" we asked.

"The Jews have the deals."

I thought Jews were something that was in the Bible. I'd heard about them in Sunday school, through Jesus and such. I told Ma I didn't know they were still around.

"Oh, they're around," she said. She had a funny look in her face.   5

The Hasidic[2] Jewish merchants in their black yarmulkes would stare in shock as Mommy walked in, trailed by five or six of us. When they recovered enough to make money, she would drive them to the wall, haggling them to death, lapsing into Yiddish when the going got tough. "I know what's happening here! I know what's happening!" she snapped when the merchants lapsed into Yiddish[3] amongst themselves during negotiations over a pair of shoes. She angrily whipped off some gibberish and the merchants gawked even more. We were awed.

The first time it happened, we asked, "Ma, how'd you learn to talk like that?"

"Mind your own business," she said. "Never ask questions or your mind will end up like a rock. Some of these Jews can't stand you."

Looking back, I realize that I never felt any kinetic relationship to Jews. We were insulated from their world and any other world but our own. Yet there was a part of me that recognized Jews as slightly different from other white folks, partly through information gleaned from Mommy, who consciously and unconsciously sought many things Jewish, and partly through

[1]*Delancey Street on Manhattan's Lower East Side:* A NYC thoroughfare in a predominantly Jewish neighborhood famous for its concentration of low-cost and discount shops.

[2]*Hasidic:* A sect of the Orthodox Jewish religion easily recognized by the men's traditional black clothing and "peyes," or side curls.

[3]*Yiddish:* A dialect of German spoken by Eastern European Jews.

my elder siblings. My sister Rosetta's college education at the all-black Howard University was completely paid for — tuition, books, even school clothes — by the Joseph L. Fisher Foundation, which was run out of the Stephen Wise Free Synagogue of Manhattan. In addition, my oldest brother, Dennis, guru of wisdom and source of much of our worldly news in the 1960s, came home from college with respect for Jewish friends he'd met. "They support the civil rights movement," he reported. Mommy was for anything involving the improvement of our education and condition, and while she would be quick to point out that "some Jews can't stand you," she also, in her crazy contradictory way, communicated the sense to us that if we were lucky enough to come across the right Jew in our travels — a teacher, a cop, a merchant — he would be kinder than other white folks. She never spoke about Jewish people as white. She spoke about them as Jews, which made them somehow different. It was a feeling every single one of us took into adulthood, that Jews were different from white people somehow. Later as an adult when I heard folks talk of the love/hate relationship between blacks and Jews I understood it to the bone not because of any outside sociological study, but because of my own experience with Jewish teachers and classmates — some who were truly kind, genuine, and sensitive, others who could not hide their distaste for my black face — people I'd met during my own contacts with the Jewish world, which Mommy tacitly arranged by forcing every one of us to go to predominantly Jewish public schools.

It was in her sense of education, more than any other, that Mommy 10 conveyed her Jewishness to us. She admired the way Jewish parents raised their children to be scholastic standouts, insulating them from a potentially harmful and dangerous public school system by clustering together within certain communities, to attend certain schools, to be taught by certain teachers who enforced discipline and encouraged learning, and she followed their lead. During the school year she gave us careful instructions to bring home every single paper that the teachers handed out at school, especially in January, and failure to follow these instructions resulted in severe beatings. When we dutifully arrived with the papers, she would pore over them carefully, searching — "Okay . . . okay . . . here it is!" — grabbing the little form and filling it out. Every year the mighty bureaucratic dinosaur known as the New York City Public School System would belch forth a tiny diamond: they slipped a little notice to parents giving them the opportunity to have their kids bused to different school districts if they wanted; but there was a limited time to enroll, a short window of opportunity that lasted only a few days. Mommy stood poised over that option like a hawk. She invariably chose predominantly Jewish public schools: P.S. 138 in Rosedale, J.H.S. 231 in Springfield Gardens, Benjamin Cardozo,[4] Francis Lewis,[5]

---

[4]*Benjamin Cardozo:* Progressive high school located in Queens, New York, named after the eminent Jewish Supreme Court justice (1870–1938).

[5]*Francis Lewis:* The largest public high school in Queens, New York, named after a signer of the Declaration of Independence and early governor of New York (1713–1803).

Forest Hills, Music and Art. Every morning we hit the door at six-thirty, fanning out across the city like soldiers, armed with books, T squares, musical instruments, an "S" bus pass that allowed you to ride the bus and subway for a nickel, and a free-school-lunch coupon in our pocket. Even the tiniest of us knew the subway and local city bus schedules and routes by heart. *The number 3 bus lets you off at the corner, but the 3A turns, so you have to get off . . .* By age twelve, I was traveling an hour and a half one way to junior high school by myself, taking two buses each direction every day. My homeroom teacher, Miss Allison, a young white woman with glasses who generally ignored me, would shrug as I walked in ten minutes late, apologizing about a delayed bus. The white kids stared at me in the cafeteria as I gobbled down the horrible school lunch. Who cared. It was all I had to eat.

In this pre-busing era, my siblings and I were unlike most other kids in our neighborhood, traveling miles and miles to largely white, Jewish communities to attend school while our friends walked to the neighborhood school. We grew accustomed to being the only black, or "Negro," in school and were standout students, neat and well-mannered, despite the racist attitudes of many of our teachers, who were happy to knock our 95 test scores down to 85's and 80's over the most trivial mistakes. Being the token Negro was something I was never entirely comfortable with. I was the only black kid in my fifth-grade class at P.S. 138 in the then all-white enclave of Rosedale, Queens, and one afternoon as the teacher dutifully read aloud from our history book's one page on "Negro history," someone in the back of the class whispered, "James is a nigger!" followed by a ripple of tittering and giggling across the room. The teacher shushed him and glared, but the damage had been done. I felt the blood rush to my face and sank low in my chair, seething inside, yet I did nothing. I imagined what my siblings would have done. They would have gone wild. They would have found that punk and bum-rushed him. They never would've allowed anyone to call them a nigger. But I was not them. I was shy and passive and quiet, and only later did the anger come bursting out of me, roaring out of me with such blast-furnace force that I would wonder who that person was and where it all came from.

Music arrived in my life around that time, and books. I would disappear inside whole worlds comprised of *Gulliver's Travels*,[6] *Shane*,[7] and books by Beverly Cleary.[8] I took piano and clarinet lessons in school, often squirreling myself away in some corner with my clarinet to practice, wandering

---

[6]*Gulliver's Travels:* Published in 1726 by the Irish writer Jonathan Swift, *Gulliver's Travels* follows protagonist Lemuel Gulliver on his adventures around the globe.

[7]*Shane:* This classic Western, published in 1949 by Jack Schaefer, depicts a lost gunfighter's effect on the lives of a rancher's family in Wyoming.

[8]*Beverly Cleary:* American children's author (b. 1916) whose books — including *Henry Huggins* and *Ramona* — feature spunky, freckled, white protagonists.

away in Tchaikovsky[9] or John Philip Sousa,[10] trying to improvise like jazz saxophonist James Moody, only to blink back to reality an hour or two later. To further escape from painful reality, I created an imaginary world for myself. I believed my true self was a boy who lived in the mirror. I'd lock myself in the bathroom and spend long hours playing with him. He looked just like me. I'd stare at him. Kiss him. Make faces at him and order him around. Unlike my siblings, he had no opinions. He would listen to me. "If I'm here and you're me, how can *you* be there at the same time?" I'd ask. He'd shrug and smile. I'd shout at him, abuse him verbally. "Give me an answer!" I'd snarl. I would turn to leave, but when I wheeled around he was always there, waiting for me. I had an ache inside, a longing, but I didn't know where it came from or why I had it. The boy in the mirror, he didn't seem to have an ache. He was free. He was never hungry, he had his own bed probably, and his mother wasn't white. I hated him. "Go away!" I'd shout. "Hurry up! Get on out!" but he'd never leave. My siblings would hold their ears to the bathroom door and laugh as I talked to myself. "What a doofus you are," my brother Richie snickered.

Even though my siblings called me "Big Head" because I had a big head and a skinny body, to the outer world I was probably on the "most likely to succeed" list. I was a smart kid. I read a lot. I played music well. I went to church. I had what black folks called "good" hair, because it was curly as opposed to nappy. I was light-skinned or brown-skinned, and girls thought I was cute despite my shyness. Yet I myself had no idea who I was. I loved my mother yet looked nothing like her. Neither did I look like the role models in my life — my stepfather, my godparents, other relatives — all of whom were black. And *they* looked nothing like the other heroes I saw, the guys in the movies, white men like Steve McQueen and Paul Newman who beat the bad guys and in the end got the pretty girl — who, incidentally, was always white.

One afternoon I came home from school and cornered Mommy while she was cooking dinner. "Ma, what's a tragic mulatto?"[11] I asked.

Anger flashed across her face like lightning and her nose, which tends to redden and swell in anger, blew up like a balloon. "Where'd you hear that?" she asked.   15

"I read it in a book."

"For God's sake, you're no tragic mul — What book is this?"

"Just a book I read."

"Don't read that book anymore." She sucked her teeth. "Tragic mulatto. What a stupid thing to call somebody! Somebody called you that?"

[9]*Tchaikovsky:* Russian composer (1840–1893) of famous works such as *The Nutcracker Suite*, *Swan Lake*, and the *1812 Overture*.

[10]*John Philip Sousa:* American composer of military and patriotic tunes (1854–1932); known as "The March King."

[11]*tragic mulatto:* An unflattering and negatively charged stereotype of a person of mixed race who wanders through life confused, angry, and unsure of his/her identity.

"No." 20

"Don't ever ever use that term."

"Am I black or white?"

"You're a human being," she snapped. "Educate yourself or you'll be a nobody!"

"Will I be a black nobody or just a nobody?"

"If you're a nobody," she said dryly, "it doesn't matter what color you 25 are."

"That doesn't make sense," I said.

She sighed and sat down. "I bet you never heard the joke about the teacher and the beans," she said. I shook my head. "The teacher says to the class, 'Tell us about different kinds of beans.'

"The first little boy says, 'There's pinto beans.'

"'Correct,' says the teacher.

"Another boy raises his hand. 'There's lima beans.' 30

"'Very good,' says the teacher.

"Then a little girl in the back raises her hand and says, 'We're all *human* beans!'"

She laughed. "That's what you are, a *human* bean! And a *fartbuster* to boot!" She got up and went back to cooking, while I wandered away, bewildered.

Perplexed to the point of bursting, I took the question to my elder siblings. Although each had drawn from the same bowl of crazy logic Mommy served up, none seemed to share my own confusion. "Are we black or white?" I asked my brother David one day.

"*I'm* black," said David, sporting his freshly grown Afro the size of Mil- 35 waukee. "But *you* may be a Negro. You better check with Billy upstairs."

I approached Billy, but before I could open my mouth, he asked, "Want to see something?"

"Sure," I said.

He led me through our house, past Mommy, who was absorbed in changing diapers, past a pile of upended chairs, books, music stands, and musical instruments that constituted the living room, up the stairs into the boys' bedroom, and over to a closet which was filled, literally, from floor to ceiling, with junk. He stuck his head inside, pointed to the back, and said, "Look at this." When I stuck my head in, he shoved me in from behind and slammed the door, holding it shut. "Hey, man! It's dark in here!" I shouted, banging at the door and trying to keep the fear out of my voice. Suddenly, in the darkness, I felt hands grabbing me and heard a monster roar. My panic zoomed into high-level terror and I frantically pounded on the door with all my might, screaming in a high-pitched, fervent squawk, "BILLLLYYYYYYYY!" He released the door and I tore out of the closet, my brother David tumbling out behind me. My two brothers fell to the floor laughing, while I ran around the house crying for Ma, zooming from room to room, my circuits blown.

The question of race was like the power of the moon in my house. It's what made the river flow, the ocean swell, and the tide rise, but it was a silent power, intractable, indomitable, indisputable, and thus completely ignorable. Mommy kept us at a frantic living pace that left no time for the problem. We thrived on thought, books, music, and art, which she fed to us instead of food. At every opportunity she loaded five or six of us onto the subway, paying one fare and pushing the rest of us through the turnstiles while the token-booth clerks frowned and subway riders stared, parading us to every free event New York City offered: festivals, zoos, parades, block parties, libraries, concerts. We walked for hours through the city, long meandering walks that took in whole neighborhoods which we would pass through without buying a thing or speaking to anyone. Twice a year she marched us to the Guggenheim dental clinic in Manhattan for free care, where foreign dental students wearing tunics and armed with drills, picks, and no novocaine, manned a row of dental chairs and reduced each of us to a screaming mass of tears while the others waited in line, watching, horrified. They pulled teeth like maniacs, barking at us in whatever their native tongues were while they yanked our heads back and forth like rag dolls'. They once pulled my brother Billy's tooth and then sent him out to Ma in the waiting room, whereupon she looked into the mouth full of gauze and blood and discovered they had yanked the wrong tooth. She marched back in and went wild. In summer she was the Pied Piper, leading the whole pack of us to public swimming pools, stripping down to her one-piece bathing suit and plunging into the water like a walrus, the rest of us following her like seals, splashing and gurgling in terror behind her as Mommy flailed along, seemingly barely able to swim herself until one of us coughed and sputtered, at which time she whipped through the water and grabbed the offending child, pulling him out and slapping him on the back, laughing. We did not consider ourselves poor or deprived, or depressed, for the rules of the outside world seemed meaningless to us as children. But as we grew up and fanned out into the world as teenagers and college students, we brought the outside world home with us, and the world that Mommy had so painstakingly created began to fall apart.

The sixties roared through my house like a tidal wave. My sister Helen's   40
decision to drop out of school and run off at age fifteen, though she returned home five years later with a nursing degree and a baby girl, was the first sign of impending doom. Now the others began to act out, and the sense of justice and desire for equal rights that Mommy and my father had imparted to us began to backfire. Kind, gentle, Sunday school children who had been taught to say proudly, "I am a Negro," and recite the deeds of Jackie Robinson[12] and Paul Robeson[13] now turned to Malcolm X and

---

[12]*Jackie Robinson:* First black American (1919–1972) to play in Major League Baseball; also a prominent civil rights activist.
[13]*Paul Robeson:* African American stage and film actor, singer, and civil rights activist (1898–1976).

H. Rap Brown[14] and Martin Luther King for inspiration. Mommy was the wrong color for black pride and black power, which nearly rent my house in two.

One by one, my elder siblings broke with her rules, coming home bearing fruits of their own confusion, which we jokingly called their "revolution." An elder brother disappeared to Europe. Another sister had an affair at college and came home with a love child, fairly big news in 1967. My brother Richie got married at eighteen over Mommy's objections, divorced, then entered college, and was home on summer break when he got stopped by two cops while walking down the street with a friend. A group of boys who were walking about ten yards in front of Richie and his friend had ditched what appeared to be a bag of heroin as the cop car approached. The cops grouped the boys together, lined them up against a fence, and demanded to know which of them had jettisoned the bag, which later turned out to be filled with quinine, not heroin. All denied it, so the cops searched them all and found ninety dollars of Richie's college-bank-loan money in his pocket. When the policeman asked him where he got the money from, Richie told him it was his college money and he'd forgotten he'd had it. If you knew Richie, you'd nod and say, "Uh-huh," because it was perfectly in character for him to forget he was carrying around ninety precious dollars, which was a huge sum in those days. We used to call him "the Mad Scientist" when he was little. His science experiments would nearly blow up the house because whatever he created, he'd leave it bubbling and boiling while he went to search for food, forgetting it completely. He could remember the toughest calculus formulas and had nearly perfect pitch as a musician, but he literally could not remember to put his pants on. He would play John Coltrane[15]–type solos on his sax for hours and be dressed in a winter jacket and gym shorts the whole time. He was that kind of kid, absent-minded, and very smart, and later in life he became a chemist. But to the cops, he was just another black perpetrator with a story, and he was arrested and jailed.

Mommy paced the house all night when she got the news. She showed up early at Richie's arraignment the next day and took a seat right behind the defense table. When they brought him out in handcuffs and she saw him cuffed and dirty after being in the holding pen all night, she could not contain her grief and began muttering like a crazy woman, wringing her hands. Through her reverie of mumbo jumbo she heard the court-appointed lawyer lean over to Richie and offer two words of legal advice: "Plead guilty." She jumped up and screamed. "Wait!" She charged past the court officers, shouting to the judge that it was a mistake, that none of her kids had ever been in trouble with the law before, that her son was a college

---

[14]*H. Rap Brown:* Hubert Gerold Brown (b. 1943), radical 1960s civil rights activist who was later sentenced to life in prison for murdering a police officer.

[15]*John Coltrane:* Jazz saxophonist and composer (1926–1967).

student, and so forth. The white judge, who had noticed Mommy sitting in the largely black courtroom, released Richie to her custody and the charges were later dropped.

But that experience made Mommy bear down on the younger ones like me even more. She was, in retrospect, quite brilliant when it came to manipulating us. She depended heavily on the "king/queen system" which she established in our house long before I was born: the eldest sibling was the king or queen and you could not defy him or her, because you were a slave. When the eldest left for college, the next ascended to the throne. The king/queen system gave us a sense of order, rank, and self. It gave the older ones the sense that they were in charge, when in actuality it was Mommy who ruled the world. It also harked back to her own traditional Orthodox upbringing where the home was run by one dominating figure with strict rules and regulations. Despite the orchestrated chaos of our home, we always ate meals at a certain time, always did homework at a certain time, and always went to bed at a certain time. Mommy also aligned herself with any relative or friend who had any interest in any of her children and would send us off to stay with whatever relative promised to straighten us out, and many did. The extended black family was Mommy's hole card, and she played it as often as the times demanded because her family was not available to her. As I grew older, it occurred to me at some point that we had some relatives we had never seen. "How come we don't have any aunts and uncles on your side?" I asked her one day.

"I had a brother who died and my sister . . . I don't know where she is," she said.

"Why not?"   45

"We got separated."

"How's that?"

"I'm removed from my family."

"Removed?"

"Removed. Dead."   50

"Who's dead?"

"I'm dead. They're dead too by now probably. What's the difference? They didn't want me to marry on the black side."

"But if you're black already, how can they be mad at you?"

Boom. I had her. But she ignored it, "Don't ask me any more questions."

My stepfather, a potential source of information about her background,   55 was not helpful. "Oh, your mama, you mind her," he grunted when I asked him. He loved her. He seemed to have no problem with her being white, which I found odd, since she was clearly so different from him. Whereas he was largely easygoing and open-minded about most worldly matters, she was suspicious, strict, and inaccessible. Whenever she stepped out of the house with us, she went into a sort of mental zone where her attention span went no farther than the five kids trailing her and the tightly balled fist in which she held her small bit of money, which she always counted to the last penny. She had absolutely no interest in a world that seemed incredibly agitated by our presence. The stares and remarks, the glances and cackles that we heard as we walked about the world went right over her head, but not over mine. By age ten, I was coming into my own feelings about myself and my own impending manhood, and going out with Mommy, which had been a privilege and an honor at age five, had become a dreaded event. I had reached a point where I was ashamed of her and didn't want the world to see my white mother. When I went out with my friends, I'd avoid telling her where we were playing because I didn't want her coming to the park to fetch me. I grew secretive, cautious, passive, angry, and fearful, always afraid that the baddest cat on the block would call her a "honky," in which case I'd have to respond and get my ass kicked. "Come and let's walk to the store," she said one afternoon.

"I can go by myself," I said. The intent was to hide my white mom and go it alone.

"Okay," she said. She didn't seem bothered by my newfound independence. Relieved, I set off to a neighborhood grocery store. The store owner was a gruff white man who, like many of the whites in St. Albans, was on his way out as we blacks began to move in. He did not seem to like black children and he certainly took no particular liking to or interest in me. When I got home, Mommy placed the quart of milk he sold me on the table, opened it up, and the smell of sour milk filled the room. She closed the carton and handed it to me. "Take it back and get my money back."

"Do I have to?"

"Take it back." It was an order. I was a Little Kid in my house, not a Big Kid who could voice opinions and sway the master. I had to take orders.

I dragged myself back to the store, dreading the showdown I knew was coming. The owner glared at me when I walked in. "I have to return this," I said.   60

"Not here," he said. "The milk is opened. I'm not taking it back."

I returned home. Ten minutes later Mommy marched into the store, doing her "madwalk," the bowlegged strut that meant thunder and lightning was coming — body pitched forward, jaw jutted out, hands balled into tight fists, nose red, stomping like Cab Calloway[16] with the Billy Eckstein[17] band blowing full blast behind him. I followed her sheepishly, my plan to go it alone and hide my white mother now completely awash, backfired in the worst way.

She angrily placed the milk on the counter. The merchant looked at her, then at me. Then back at her. Then at me again. The surprise written on his face changed to anger and disgust, and it took me completely by surprise. I thought the man would see Ma, think they had something in common, then give her the dough and we'd be off. "That milk is sold," he said.

"Smell it," Ma said. "It's spoiled."

---

[16]*Cab Calloway:* Noted bandleader and jazz singer (1907–1994).
[17]*Billy Eckstein:* Big-band singer (1914–1993) during the swing era of the 1940s.

"I don't smell milk. I sell milk."

Right away they were at each other, I mean really going at it. A crowd of black kids gathered, watching my white mother arguing with this white man. I wanted to sink into the floor and disappear. "It's okay, Ma . . ." I said. She ignored me. In matters of money, of which she had so little, I knew it was useless. She was going full blast — " . . . fool . . . think you are . . . idiot!" — her words flying together like gibberish, while the neighborhood kids howled, woofing like dogs and enjoying the show.

After a while it was clear the man was not going to return her money, so she grabbed my hand and was heading toward the door, when he made another remark, something that I missed, something he murmured beneath his breath so softly that I couldn't hear, but it made the crowd murmur "Ooohhhh." Ma stiffened. Still holding the milk in her right hand, she turned around and flung it at him like a football. He ducked and the milk missed him, smashing into the cigarette cabinet behind him and sending milk and cigarettes splattering everywhere.

I could not understand such anger. I could not understand why she didn't just give up the milk. Why cause a fuss? I thought. My own embarrassment overrode all other feelings. As I walked home, holding Mommy's hand while she fumed, I thought it would be easier if we were just one color, black or white. I didn't want to be white. My siblings had already instilled the notion of black pride in me. I would have preferred that Mommy were black. Now, as a grown man, I feel privileged to have come from two worlds. My view of the world is not merely that of a black man but that of a black man with something of a Jewish soul. I don't consider myself Jewish, but when I look at Holocaust photographs of Jewish women whose children have been wrenched from them by Nazi soldiers, the women look like my own mother and I think to myself, *There but for the grace of God goes my own mother — and by extension, myself.* When I see two little Jewish old ladies giggling over coffee at a Manhattan diner, it makes me smile, because I hear my own mother's laughter beneath theirs. Conversely, when I hear black "leaders" talking about "Jewish slave owners" I feel angry and disgusted, knowing that they're inflaming people with lies and twisted history, as if all seven of the Jewish slave owners in the antebellum South, or however few there were, are responsible for the problems of African Americans now. Those leaders are no better than their Jewish counterparts who spin statistics in marvelous ways to make African Americans look like savages, criminals, drags on society, and "animals" (a word quite popular when used to describe blacks these days). I don't belong to any of those groups. I belong to the world of one God, one people. But as a kid, I preferred the black side, and often wished that Mommy had sent me to black schools like my friends. Instead I was stuck at that white school, P.S. 138, with white classmates who were convinced I could dance like James Brown.[18] They

---

[18]*James Brown:* Iconic singer, dancer, songwriter, and bandleader known for his electrifying performance style (1933–2006).

constantly badgered me to do the "James Brown" for them, a squiggling of the feet made famous by the "Godfather of Soul" himself, who back in the sixties was bigger than life. I tried to explain to them that I couldn't dance. I have always been one of the worst dancers that God has ever put upon this earth. My sisters would spend hours at home trying out new dances to Archie Bell and the Drells, Martha Reeves, King Curtis, Curtis Mayfield, Aretha Franklin, and the Spinners.[19] "Come on and dance!" they'd shout, boogying across the room. Even Ma would join in, sashaying across the floor, but when I joined in I looked so odd and stupid they fell to the floor laughing. "Give it up," they said. "You can't dance."

The white kids in school did not believe me, and after weeks of encouragement I found myself standing in front of the classroom on talent day, wearing my brother's good shoes and hitching up my pants, soul singer–style like one of the Temptations,[20] as someone dropped the needle on a James Brown record. I slid around the way I'd seen him do, shouting "Owww — shabba-na!" They were delighted. Even the teacher was amused. They really believed I could dance! I had them fooled. They screamed for more and I obliged, squiggling my feet and slip-sliding across the wooden floor, jumping into the air and landing in a near split by the blackboard, shouting "Eeeee-yowwww!" They went wild, but even as I sat down with their applause ringing in my ears, with laughter on my face, happy to feel accepted, to be part of them, knowing I had pleased them, I saw the derision on their faces, the clever smiles, laughing at the oddity of it, and I felt the same ache I felt when I gazed at the boy in the mirror. I remembered him, and how free he was, and I hated him even more.

Engaging the Text

1. Why did McBride identify more strongly with his African American heritage during his childhood, even though he was raised primarily by his white mother? How does his attitude toward his Jewish heritage change as he gets older?

2. In what ways does McBride's mother deal with the racist attitudes and discrimination her family encounters? How does McBride himself respond to his experiences with prejudice and stereotypes? How and why does "Mommy's" attitude toward race differ from her son's?

3. How do the social movements of the 1960s affect McBride's feelings about his mixed heritage? What is his brother David implying when he teases, "*I'm* black . . . but *you* may be a Negro" (para. 35)? How important are such labels, in your opinion?

---

[19]*Archie Bell and the Drells . . . the Spinners:* Singers and musicians responsible for many of the top soul, R & B, and Motown hits of the 1960s.

[20]*the Temptations:* One of the most successful and longest performing vocal groups of the Motown music era.

4. What does the boy in the mirror represent to McBride? What do you think motivates him to create this alter ego? Why do his James Brown dance and his classmates' reaction to it remind him so painfully of the mirror image?

5. Does Mommy strike you as a good mother? Why or why not?

EXPLORING CONNECTIONS

6. Naomi Gerstel and Natalia Sarkisian (p. 61) observe that "family strategies and behaviors often emerge in response to the challenges of living in economic deprivation or constant economic insecurity" (para. 18). To what extent does McBride's family reflect the class-based family patterns discussed in Gerstel and Sarkisian's article? What aspects of the family's life are not dictated by economic necessity?

7. Write an essay examining the role of books in the lives of McBride and one or more of the following authors: Richard Rodriguez (p. 194), Malcolm X (p. 210), and Judith Ortiz Cofer (p. 537). How do books influence each writer's sense of self and his or her relationship to other people?

EXTENDING THE CRITICAL CONTEXT

8. If your own family is "mixed" in terms of race, ethnicity, culture, or religion, have you experienced conflicts between the different aspects of your

"*You look like this sketch of someone who's thinking about committing a crime.*"

family heritage? Write a journal entry or essay describing those tensions and analyzing your responses to them.

Loot or Find: Fact or Frame?

Cheryl I. Harris
and Devon W. Carbado

In 2005, Hurricane Katrina slammed into the Gulf Coast, killing more than 1,800 people and destroying thousands of homes and businesses. Hardest hit was New Orleans, where the hurricane damage was compounded by massive flooding caused by the failure of the city's levee system. Although residents were ordered to evacuate before the storm hit, many — overwhelmingly black and poor — lacked the resources to escape, and were trapped for days in attics, on roofs, on freeway overpasses, and in overcrowded emergency shelters. In this article, Cheryl I. Harris and Devon W. Carbado (b. 1965) analyze the media coverage of this disaster and the public response to the stories that emerged from the crisis in New Orleans. Both Harris and Carbado teach at UCLA's School of Law; they have written widely on constitutional issues, civil rights, gender, and critical race theory. Harris, who has also worked in the area of international human rights, served for several years as cochair for the National Conference of Black Lawyers and in 2005 received the Distinguished Professor Award for Civil Rights Education from the ACLU Foundation of Southern California. Carbado has edited or coedited several books, including Time on Two Crosses: The Collected Writings of Bayard Rustin *(2003) and* Race Law Stories *(2008); he has won multiple awards for distinguished teaching.*

Evidence of Things Seen

What do [the images on page 423] represent? What facts do they convey? We could say that image A depicts a man who, in the aftermath of Katrina, is wading through high waters with food supplies and a big black plastic bag. We might say that image B depicts a man and woman, both wearing backpacks. They, too, are wading through high waters in the aftermath of Katrina, and the woman appears to be carrying food supplies.

A

B

This is not how these images were presented in the press. The captions that appeared with the two photos, both of which ran on Yahoo! news, were quite different. The caption for image A read: "A young man walks through chest-deep flood water after looting a grocery store in New Orleans." The caption for image B read: "Two residents wade through chest-deep waters after finding bread and soda from a local grocery store after Hurricane Katrina came through the area." The caption for image A, then, tells us that a crime has been committed; the caption for image B tells that a fierce, poignant struggle for survival is under way — the subjects have just found food. Image A depicts a young black man; image B shows a white man and woman.

The images and their respective captions almost immediately stirred up significant controversy. People complained that the captions accompanying the images were racially suggestive: black people "loot" and white people "find." *Boston Globe* correspondent Christina Pazzanese wondered, "I am curious how one photographer knew the food was looted by one but not the other. Were interviews conducted as they swam by?"[1]

Not everyone agreed, however, that the images and captions reflected a racial problem. As one commentator put it:

> It's difficult to draw any substantiated conclusions from these photos' captions. Although they were both carried by many news outlets, they were taken by two different photographers and came from two different services, the Associated Press (AP) and the Getty Images via Agence France-Presse (AFP). Services make different stylistic standards for how they caption photographs, or the dissimilar wordings may have been due to nothing more than the preferences of different photographers and editors, or the difference might be the coincidental result of a desire to avoid repetitive wording (similar photographs from the same news services variously describe the depicted actions as "looting," "raiding," "taking," "finding" and "making off"). The viewer also isn't privy to the contexts in which the photographs were taken — it's possible that in one case the photographer actually saw his subject exiting an unattended grocery store with an armful of goods, while in the other case the photographer came upon his subjects with supplies in hand and could only make assumptions about how they obtained them.[2]

For the most part, this controversy focused on a question of fact. Did the black person really loot the goods he was carrying? Did the white man and white woman really find the food they were carrying? Indeed, the director of media relations at the Associated Press suggested that, as to image A, "he [the photographer] saw the person go into the shop and take the goods. . . . that's why he wrote 'looting' in the article."[3] In other words, the fact of the matter was that the black man in image A was a looter.

The photographer of image B, Chris Graythen, maintained,

> I wrote the caption about the two people who "found" the items. I believed in my opinion, that they did simply find them, and not "looted" them in the definition of the word. The people were swimming in chest deep water, and there were other people in the water, both white and black. I looked for the best picture. There were a million items floating in the water — we were right near a grocery store that had 5+ feet of water in it. It had no doors. The water was moving, and the stuff was floating away. These people were not ducking into a store and busting down windows to get electronics. They picked up bread and Cokes that were floating in the water. They would have floated away anyhow.[4]

To some extent, the credibility of Graythen's explanation is beside the point here. That is, the loot-or-find problem of image A and image B cannot fully be addressed with reference to the individual intent of those who either took the picture or produced the accompanying interpretive text. Indeed, it is entirely plausible that had the photos appeared without any captions, they would have been read the same way.[5] This is because while neither "loot" nor "find" is written on either image, in the context of public disorder, the race of the subjects inscribes those meanings.

The "Color-Blind" Frame

Drawing on facts about both Hurricane Katrina and the public's response to it, this [essay] queries whether efforts to change the racial status quo and eliminate inequality should or can rely solely on facts or empiricism. There is a growing sense within the civil rights community that more empirical research is needed to persuade mainstream Americans that racism remains a problem in American society and that the elimination of racial disadvantage is not a do-it-yourself project. The idea seems to be that if only more Americans knew certain "facts" (for example, about the existence of implicit bias) they would be more inclined to support civil rights initiatives (for example, affirmative action). We agree that more empirical research is needed. Facts are important — indeed crucial — since so much of public opinion is grounded in misinformation. We simply do not think that there is a linear progression between raw empiricism and more enlightened public opinion about race and racism. Put another way, we do not believe that facts speak for themselves.

It is precisely the recognition that facts don't speak for themselves that helps to explain why scholars across academic fields and politicians across the political spectrum continue to pay significant attention to the social and cognitive processes that shape how we interpret facts. Of the variety of theories — in sociology, political science, law, anthropology, psychology, and economics — that attempt to explain these processes, most share the idea that we interpret events through frames — interpretational structures that, consciously and unconsciously, shape what we see and how we see it. In the words of one scholar, framing refers to "understanding a story you already know and saying, 'Oh yeah, that one.'"[6] As we process and make sense of an event, we take account of and simultaneously ignore facts that do not fit the frame, and sometimes we supply ones that are missing. Thus, it is sometimes said that "frames trump facts."[7]

The most relevant and dominant frame is color blindness, or the belief that race is *not* a factor in how we make sense of the world. Color blindness is a kind of metaframe that comprises three interwoven racial scripts: (1) because of *Brown v. Board of Education*[8] and the civil rights reforms it inaugurated, racism is by and large a thing of the past; (2) when racism does rear its ugly head, it is the product of misguided and irrational behavior on the part of self-declared racial bigots, who are few and far between; and (3) racial consciousness — whether in the form of affirmative action or Jim Crow[9]–like racism — should be treated with suspicion, if not rejected outright. The gradual ascendancy and eventual racial dominance of color blindness frames the facts of racial inequality (manifested, for example, in disparities in wealth and

10

educational outcomes between blacks and whites) as a function of something other than racism. Because scientists have largely repudiated the notion of biological inferiority, color blindness frames the problem of racial disadvantage in terms of conduct. The problem is not genes but culture, not blood but behavior: were black people to engage in normatively appropriate cultural practices — work hard, attend school, avoid drugs, resist crime — they would transcend their current social status and become part of the truly advantaged. On this view, black disadvantage is both expected and deserved — a kind of natural disaster not produced by racism.

At least initially, Katrina challenged the supremacy of color blindness. The tidal wave of suffering that washed over New Orleans seemed incontrovertible evidence of the salience of race in contemporary U.S. society.[10] The simple fact that the faces of those left to fend for themselves or die were overwhelmingly black raised questions about the explanatory power of color blindness under which race is deemed irrelevant.[11] Racial suffering was everywhere. And black people were dying — prime time live. One had to close one's eyes, or willfully blind oneself, not to see this racial disaster. Everyone, it seemed, except government officials, was riveted. And there was little disagreement that Katrina exposed shameful fissures in America's social fabric; that the precipitating event was an act of God, not the cultural pathology of the victims; and that the government's response, at least in the initial phases, was woefully inadequate. Seasoned mainstream journalists wept and railed, while ordinary Americans flooded relief organizations with money.

The tragedy of Katrina created a rupture in the racial-progress narrative that had all but erased the suffering of poor black people from the political landscape. In contrast to the pre-Katrina picture, black people were perceived to be innocent victims. Black people were perceived to have a legitimate claim on the nation-state. Black people were perceived to be deserving of government help. Katrina — or the *facts* the public observed about its effects — disrupted our tendency to *frame* black disadvantage in terms of cultural deficiency. But how did that happen? And doesn't this disruption undermine our central point about facts and frames?

Not at all. Frames are not static. Epic events like Katrina push up against and can temporarily displace them. All those people. All that suffering. This can't be America. How could we let this happen? That question — how could we let this happen? — reflected a genuine humanitarian concern for fellow human beings. Moreover, the compelling facts about Katrina raised a number of questions about racial inequality previously suppressed under color blindness. Indeed, as the humanitarian crisis peaked with the retreating floodwaters, a debate over the role of race in the disaster quickly emerged. The unrelenting spectacle of black suffering bodies demanded an explanation. Why were those New Orleans residents who remained trapped during Katrina largely black and poor? Was it, as hip-hop artist Kanye West argued, a case of presidential indifference to, or dislike of, poor black people?[12] Or was it, as Ward Connerly[13] asserted, the predictable consequence of a natural disaster that befell a city that just happened to be predominantly black? Was it, as Linda Chavez[14] claimed, the result of a culture of dependency combined with local bureaucratic incompetence? Was race a factor in determining who survived and who did not?[15] Or did class provide a better explanation?[16] Finally, could we ever fully understand Katrina without meaningfully engaging the legacy of slavery?[17] These and other, similar questions were pushed into the foreground by the force of Katrina's devastation.

But the frame of color blindness did not disappear. It manifested itself in the racial divide that emerged with respect to how people answered the foregoing questions. While there is some intraracial diversity of opinion among public figures about the role of race and racism in explaining what happened, there remains a striking racial difference in how the disaster is viewed. According to public opinion polls, whites largely reject the notion that race explains the governmental disregard, while blacks assert that the fact that the victims were black and poor was a significant part of the story.[18] This difference over the difference that race makes reflects competing racial frames. Thus, while the facts of what happened in Katrina's aftermath unsettled the familiar color-blind racial script that poor black people were the authors of their own plight, those facts did not ultimately displace core ideas embedded in the color-blind frame: race is irrelevant and racism largely does not exist. Most whites were able to see black people as victims, but they were unwilling to link their victim status to race or racism. A more acceptable story was that black people in New Orleans suffered only because of bureaucratic inefficiencies in the wake of a natural disaster. Race simply could not be a factor. Katrina then only partially destabilized the frame of color blindness. To the extent that our starting point for thinking about race is that it does not matter, other racial frames or scripts more easily fit within the overarching frame. These frames can both explicitly invoke race and, even more powerfully, implicitly play the race card. After the initial uncertainty, what emerged in the wake of Katrina was the frame of "law and order" — a racial script that permeated the debate over the iconic photographs with which we began our essay, and over the post-Katrina relief efforts. The media were both author and reader of events in ways that both challenged and underwrote this racial frame.

A Picture Is Worth a Thousand Words

Recall Chris Graythen's response to the racial controversy concerning the images with which we began this chapter. With regard to image B, Graythen asserted that he "looked for the best picture." More specifically, Graythen searched for an image that would best narrate a particular factual story: that people were wading through water to find food. According

15

to Graythen, both whites and blacks were finding food in the chest-high water. Unlike pre-Katrina New Orleans, this space was racially integrated. Graythen searched this racially integrated body of water for a picture that would most successfully convey the idea of people finding food (as distinct from people "ducking into a store and busting down windows to get electronics"). Graythen's "best picture" — his "Oh yeah, that one" — emerged when he saw the two white people photographed in image B. Their images best fit the caption that Graythen already had in mind, people wading through water to find food. Because people are more likely to associate blacks with looting ("ducking into a store and busting down windows to get electronics") than with finding food, Graythen's selection makes sense. Indeed, one can infer from Graythen's decision to photograph white people that it was easier to frame white people as despondent people finding food than it was to frame black people in that way. To put the point slightly differently, there would be some dissonance between the image of black people in those high waters and a caption describing people finding food. This dissonance is not about facts — whether in fact the black people were finding food; the dissonance is about frames — the racial association between black people and looting, particularly on the heels of a natural disaster or social upheaval.

Two caveats before moving on. First, nothing above is intended to suggest that Graythen's decision to photograph the two white people was racially conscious — that is, intentionally motivated by race. Frames operate both consciously and unconsciously; his selection of whites to photograph (and his "natural selection" against blacks) converged with existing racial frames about criminality and perpetrators, on the one hand, and law-abidingness and victims, on the other. The two photos were perfect mirror images of each other. But only image B could convey a story of survival against adversity; image A was inconsistent with that script. The presence of a black man with a big plastic bag in the context of a natural disaster is already inscribed with meaning. In that sense, the black man in image A did not require a caption to be framed; nor did the white man and woman in image B. The stereotype of black criminality was activated by image A and the many images like it, which showed the central problem in New Orleans not to be the lack of humanitarian aid, but the lack of law and order.

The second caveat: our analysis should not be read as an argument against empiricism or a claim that facts are irrelevant. We simply mean to say that racial frames shape our perceptions of the facts. This does not mean that we are overdetermined by frames or that we are unable to escape their interpretative strictures. Rather, the point is that dependence on "just the facts" will seldom be enough to dislodge racial frames.[19] Partly this is because racial frames are installed not as the result of empiricism, but in spite of it. Consider color blindness. It is the dominant racial frame for understanding race not because of facts but because of a well-financed political project to entrench and naturalize a color-blind understanding of American race relations.[20] Accordingly, something more than facts is required to undo the racial work color blindness continues to perform; and something more than facts is required to dislodge the normativity of color blindness itself.

From Rescue to Occupation: Seeing the Invisible

> I'd rather have them here dead than alive. And at least they're not robbing you and you [don't] have to worry about feeding them.[21]
> —A resident of St. Gabriel when asked for her reactions to the decision to designate the town as a collective morgue

To the extent that our discussion of the problem of racial frames has largely examined representational issues, one might reasonably ask: What are the material consequences of this problem? And how, if at all, did it injure black New Orleanians in the wake of Hurricane Katrina? The answer relates to two interconnected frames: the frame of law and order and the frame of black criminality. Working together, these frames rendered black New Orleanians dangerous, unprotectable, and unrescuable.

In the immediate aftermath of Katrina, the media pointedly criticized the slow pace at which the federal government was responding to the disaster. But the critical stance was short-lived and quickly gave way to a focus on the breakdown of law and order, a frame that activated a familiar stereotype about black criminality. While initially blacks were seen as victims of Hurricane Katrina and a failed governmental response, this victim status proved to be highly unstable. Implicit in the frame that "this can't be America" is the notion that the neglect in the wake of Katrina was a violation of the duty of care owed to all citizens of the nation. This social contract includes blacks as citizens; and indeed the claim by blacks, "We are American"—a statement vigorously asserted by those contained in the convention center[22]—responded to and relied upon that frame.[23]

As time progressed, the social currency of the image of blacks as citizens of the state to whom a duty of care is owed diminished. It rubbed uneasily against the more familiar racial framing of poor black people as lazy, undeserving, and inherently criminal. Concern over the looting of property gradually took precedence over the humanitarian question of when people might be rescued and taken off of the highways and rooftops. Thus, while armed white men were presumed to be defending their property, black men with guns constituted gangs of violent looters who had to be contained. Under this frame, the surrounding towns and parishes that constituted potential refuge for black New Orleans residents who had no means to evacuate before the storm became no-go areas because of concerns about black criminality.

A particularly stark example of this came during the CNN interview on September 8 between Christiane Amanpour[24] and the resident of St. Gabriel quoted above. The sentiment that dead blacks were better than live ones was enforced not only by local authorities who, like the Gretna police, turned people away at gunpoint, but by the National Guard and other local authorities who purportedly denied the Red Cross permission to enter the city shortly after the storm because of concerns about the safety of the rescuers.[25]

These fears were grounded in what ultimately proved to be grossly exaggerated or completely unsubstantiated media accounts of violence and attacks particularly in the Superdome and the convention center.[26] The tone of these reports were hyperbolic, evoking all of the familiar racial subtexts: FOX News, for example, issued a news report the day before the Superdome was evacuated that "there were many reports of robberies, rapes, car-jackings, rioters and murder and that violent gangs are roaming the streets at night, hidden by the cover of darkness." The *Los Angeles Times* was no less sensational, reporting that National Guard troops had to take rooftop positions to scan for snipers and armed mobs as gunfire rang out.[27] These reports were taken as authoritative by police and other law enforcement officials. Indeed, even the mayor of the city, Ray Nagin, who is black, spoke of "hundreds of armed gang members" killing and raping people inside the Superdome, such that the crowd had descended to an "almost animalistic state.[28]

We are not arguing that there was no violence. There was. But the frames of black criminality and law and order overdetermined how we interpreted both the extent and nature of that violence. For example, consider how the "facts" about rape were interpreted and discussed. Recently, advocacy groups for victims of sexual assault have begun to challenge the official count of reported rapes — four — as unrealistically low. A national database newly created by the National Sexual Violence Resource Center reports more than forty sexual assaults, while another victim's rights organization has reported more than 150 post-Katrina violent crimes, of which about one-third were sexual assaults, including those committed in the homes of host families.[29] This suggests that reports of sexual assaults were underreported. Paradoxically, at the same time that reports of rape were cited to confirm stereotypes of black criminality, the black women victims of *actual* rapes suffered an unconscionable degree of official disregard. While accounts of rape were invoked as signs of the disintegration of social order in New Orleans, some of the black women who experienced sexual violence were unable to file reports with law enforcement officials despite their efforts to do so, notwithstanding the city's ostensible mission to maintain law and order to protect victims from crime.

One of the more prominent examples of this official disregard was Charmaine Neville, a member of the family of renowned New Orleans musicians, who was raped by a roving group of men who invaded her community in the Lower Ninth Ward while she and her neighbors struggled unsuccessfully over a series of days to be evacuated and to obtain medical care.[30] Neville's searing account of what happened to her is a clear indictment of the government for its neglect: "What I want people to understand is that if we hadn't been left down there like animals that they were treating us like, all of those things would not have happened." Neville reported that her efforts to tell law enforcement officers and the National Guard of her assault were ignored. Neville's prominence and her fortuitous encounter with a member of the Catholic archdiocese in New Orleans during an interview at a local news station meant that her assault received media attention. Others did not.

Obviously, we are not excusing the conduct of the rapists or blaming that conduct on the government. Our point is simply that the overall governmental response in the aftermath of Katrina, shaped as it was by the racial frame of law and order, created conditions of possibility for rape and increased the likelihood that those rapes would be unaddressed. The sexual assaults against women — the vast majority of them black — became markers of black disorder, chaos, and the "animalistic" nature of New Orleans residents; but black women themselves could not occupy the position of victims worthy of rescue. Their injuries were only abstractions that were marshaled to make the larger point about the descent of New Orleans into a literal and figurative black hole. Black women's rape was invoked but not addressed. To borrow from Kimberle Crenshaw, their stories of rape were "voyeuristically included" in a law-and-order campaign.[31] Their specific injury — the fact that they were actually victims — was largely ignored.

The government focused its attention on violence directed against property and violence directed against the rescuers — reports of which have proven to be false or grossly embellished. While these acts of violence could fit comfortably within the frame of law and order, violence against black women's bodies could not. Images of black criminality could work concomitantly with and help to instantiate the law-and-order frame that relies on black disorder; images of black women as innocent victims could do neither. The frames of law and order and black criminality influenced both the exaggeration (overreporting) and the marginalization (underreporting) of violent crimes in ways that make clear that facts don't speak for themselves.

In another example of the law-and-order and black-criminality frames at work in New Orleans, the characterization of the Superdome and the convention center as unsafe facilitated the shift from humanitarian rescue mission to military occupation and security. In part because of the perception of the severe security threat to rescuers, no food, water, or medical care was provided to the convention center until a force of a thousand soldiers and police in full battle gear was sent in to secure the center on

25

September 2 at noon. They were able to do so in twenty minutes and encountered absolutely no resistance, though thousands of people were in the building.

Only one shooting was confirmed in the Superdome, when a soldier shot himself during a scuffle with an attacker. Though New Orleans police chief Eddie Compass reported that he and his officers had retrieved more than thirty weapons from criminals who had been shooting at the rescuers, he later modified his statement to say that this had happened to another unit, a SWAT team at the convention center. The director of the SWAT team, however, reported that his unit had heard gunshots only one time and that his team had recovered no weapons despite aggressive searches.

In retrospect, it is clear that the media both mischaracterized and exaggerated the security threat to the rescue mission. Certainly the chaos in the wake of Katrina and the breakdown of the communications network helped develop a climate in which rumors could and did flourish. Yet under similarly difficult conditions during other natural disasters and even war, reporters have adhered to basic journalistic standards. That they did not under these conditions could be explained as an isolated case of failure under extremely trying circumstances. That might very well be so. Yet, the important part of this story is not that the media failed to observe the basic rules of journalism; it is that the story they told was one people were all too ready to accept. It was a narrative that made sense within the commonly accepted racial frames of law and order and black criminality.

These frames made it difficult for us to make sense of reported   30 instances of "guys who looked like thugs, with pants hanging down around their asses," engaged in frantic efforts to get people collapsing from heat and exhaustion out of the Superdome and into a nearby makeshift medical facility. These images did not make racial sense. There was no ready-made social frame within which the image of black male rescuers could be placed. Existing outside of standard racial frames, black male rescuers present a socially unintelligible image. That we have trouble *seeing* "guys who look like thugs" as rescuers is not a problem of facts. It is a problem of frames. Indeed, the very use of the term "thug" already frames the fact of what they might be doing in a particular way.

Conclusion

Lessons from Hurricane Katrina include those about preparedness for natural disasters; coordination among local, state, and federal rescue efforts; and a nation's capacity for empathy and compassion. While it is less than clear that all of these lessons are being learned, we are at least discussing these lessons. Not so with respect to race. As a nation, we rarely talk about race and Katrina anymore. It is almost unspeakable to do so.

Yet, Katrina offers profound insights into how race operates in American society, insights into how various facts about our social life are racially interpreted through frames. As a result of racial frames, black people are both visible (as criminals) and invisible (as victims). Racial frames both capture and displace us — discursively and materially. More than shaping whether we see black people as criminal or innocent, perpetrator or victim, these frames shape whether we see black people at all. Indeed, one might reasonably ask: Where have all the black people gone, long time passing? It is not hyperbolic to say that post-Katrina black New Orleanians have become a part of an emerging social category: the disappeared. A critical lesson of Katrina is that civil rights advocacy groups need to think harder about frames, particularly when making interventions into natural disasters involving African Americans.

As Michele Landis Dauber reminds us, the template for the American social welfare system has been disaster relief, and the extent to which people are entitled to any form of government resources has always depended upon the claimants' ability to "narrat[e] their deprivation as a disaster — a sudden loss for which the claimant is not responsible."[32] In the case of Katrina, this disaster-relief conception of welfare would seem to promote an immediate national response to aid the hurricane victims. The problem for black people and for other nonwhites, however, as Dauber herself notes, is that racial minorities' claims to victim status have always been fraught "because they are highly likely to be cast as a 'disaster' for the dominant racial group.[33] Implicit in Dauber's analysis is the idea that the move to realign America's racial discourse and policy away from its current distortions must confront the complex problem of racial frames. The existence of racial frames makes it enormously difficult to incorporate "just the facts" into an argument about racism. Those facts will rarely, if ever, be able to escape completely the interpretational reach and normative appeal of racial frames about color blindness and black cultural dysfunctionality.

What is required is likely to be more in the nature of a social movement than a social survey. Facts will always play a crucial role, but just as the successes of the civil rights movement were born of organized struggle, so too must our efforts to shift racial frames ground themselves in a broader and more organic orientation than raw empiricism. People came to see the facts of de jure segregation differently not because new facts emerged about its harms but because new interpretations of those facts were made possible by social organization on the ground that pushed the courts toward a new consensus. We believe the same is true today.

Notes

This chapter draws from and builds upon Cheryl I. Harris, "White Washing Race; Scapegoating Culture," *California Law Review* (2006) (forthcoming) (book review). [All notes are Harris and Carbado's unless otherwise indicated.]

1. Cited in Aaron Kinney, "'Looting' or 'finding'?" *Salon*, September 1, 2005.
2. www.snopes.com/Katrina/photos/looters.asp.
3. Cited in Kinney, "'Looting' or 'Finding'?"

4. Ibid.

5. One study of local television news stories on crime and public opinion illustrates the strong association between criminal behavior and racial identity. Participants were shown an identical news story under three different conditions: one group witnessed a version in which the perpetrator was white; another group saw a version in which the perpetrator was black; and a third group viewed a version in which there was no picture of the perpetrator. Following the screening, the participants in the first, white-perpetrator group were less likely to recall having seen a suspect than subjects in the second, black-perpetrator group. Among those in the third group, who saw no image of the perpetrator, over 60 percent erroneously recalled seeing a perpetrator, and in 70 percent of those cases viewers identified that nonexistent image as black. See Franklin Gilliam Jr. and Shanto Iyengar, "Prime Suspects: The Influence of Local Television News on the Viewing Public," *American Journal of Political Science* 44 (2000):560.

6. Roger Schank, "Tell Me a Story," *Narrative and Intelligence* 71 (1995).

7. A more nuanced formulation suggests, "Like well-accepted theories that guide our interpretation of data, schemas incline us to interpret data consistent with our biases." See Jerry Kang, "Trojan Horses of Races," *Harvard Law Review* 118 (2005):1489,1515.

8. *Brown v. Board of Education:* The 1954 landmark Supreme Court case that outlawed segregated schools. [Eds.]

9. *Jim Crow:* System of legalized segregation that dominated the South from 1866 to the mid 1960s. Black Americans were denied access to schools, voting, and public restrooms and transportation as well as subjected to systemic racism and violence. [Eds.]

10. We do not intend to ignore the tremendous loss suffered in the Gulf region more broadly: we focus on New Orleans because of its unique position in the national imagination, as well as its pre-Katrina racial demographics. Indeed, New Orleans was not just a city that had come to be predominantly black; it was a city that was culturally marked as black. As one noted historian has stated, "The unique culture of south Louisiana derives from black Creole culture." Quoted in "Buffetted by Katrina, City's Complex Black Community Struggles to Regroup," Associated Press, October 4, 2005, www.msnbc.com.

11. Or fend for themselves and be punished for it. A particularly harrowing account of official indifference and hostility comes from the ordeal of two emergency room workers who had the misfortune of being in New Orleans for a conference when Hurricane Katrina struck. After their hotel in the French Quarter closed, they, along with several hundred others, collected money to hire buses for their evacuation, but the buses were prevented from entering the city. When the workers attempted to flee on foot, they were directed to wait on the interstate for rescue that never came. Neither the police nor the National Guard provided them with food or water. When the group managed to find food for themselves and set up a makeshift camp, they were repeatedly dispersed at gunpoint by the police. When they attempted to walk across the bridge into the neighboring city of Gretna, they were again turned back at gunpoint by Gretna police. See Larry Bradshaw and Lorrie Beth Slonsky, "Trapped in New Orleans," September 6, 2005, www.counterpunch.org/bradshaw09062005 .html.

12. On a nationally broadcast telethon to raise money for the victims of Katrina, Kanye West departed from the scripted remarks to say, "I hate the way they portray us in the media. You see a black family: it says they are looting. You see a white family; it says they have been looking for food. And you know, it has been five days, because most of the people are black, and even for me to complain about it, I would be a hypocrite, because I have tried to turn away from the TV because it is too hard to watch. So now I am calling my business manager right now to see what is the biggest amount I can give. And just imagine if I was down there and those are my people down there." Commenting on the slow pace of the government's response, he said, "George Bush doesn't care about black people." NBC immediately cut to another star on the program and censored West's remarks from the West Coast feed of the program. It also issued the following disclaimer: "Kanye West departed from the scripted com-

ments that were prepared for him, and his opinions in no way represent the views of the networks. It would be most unfortunate if the efforts of the artists who participated tonight and the generosity of millions of Americans who are helping those in need are overshadowed by one person's opinion." "Rapper Kanye West Accuses Bush of Racism; NBC Apologizes," *CBC Arts*, September 3, 2005, www.cbc.ca/story/arts/national/2005/09/03/Arts/kanye_west_katrina20050903.html.

13. *Ward Connerly:* Conservative African American political activist (b. 1939). [Eds.]

14. *Linda Chavez:* The first Latina (b. 1947) nominated to the U.S. Cabinet, now an author and conservative political commentator. [Eds.]

15. This was Howard Dean's view. In an address to the National Baptist Convention he stated, "As survivors are evacuated, order is restored, the water slowly begins to recede, and we sort through the rubble, we must also begin to come to terms with the ugly truth that skin color, age and economics played a deadly role in who survived and who did not." "Excerpts of DNC Chairman Howard Dean's Remarks to the National Baptist Convention of America, Inc.," U.S. Newswire, September 8, 2005, www.usnewswire.com.

16. While some have argued that class was a more salient factor than race in explaining who was affected, we do not think that given the country's history of de jure and de facto racial subordination, race can be so neatly disaggregated from class. Particularly in the context of New Orleans — a city that was predominantly black and predominantly poor — the fact that those left on the overpasses and in the Superdome were black had everything to do with why they were poor. The point is not to reproduce another unhelpful version of the race-versus-class debate but to avoid sublimating the racial dimension of the issues raised by Katrina. Recent survey analysis suggests that race was in fact a crucial factor in explaining who was in harm's way. See "Katrina Hurts Blacks and Poor Victims Most," CNN/*USA Today*/Gallup Poll, October 25, 2005.

17. Both the Reverend Jesse Jackson and Representative Cynthia McKinney drew a link between the events in the Gulf and slavery. In response to a question by Anderson Cooper on CNN about whether race was a determinative factor in the federal government's response to Katrina, Jackson replied, "It is at least a factor. Today I saw 5,000 African Americans on the I-10 causeway desperate, perishing, dehydrated, babies dying. It looked like Africans in the hull of a slave ship. It was so ugly and so obvious. Have we missed this catastrophe because of indifference and ineptitude or is it a combination of both? And certainly I think the issue of race as a factor will not go away from this equation." Jesse Jackson, Remarks on *360 Degrees*, CNN, September 2, 2005. In an address on the floor of the House of Representatives on September 8, 2005, Representative McKinney said, "As I saw the African Americans, mostly African-American families ripped apart, I could only think about slavery, families ripped apart, herded into what looked like concentration camps." Cynthia McKinney, "Text of Remarks Delivered on the Floor of the House on Sept. 8, 2005," reprinted in "A Few Thoughts on the State of Our Nation," September 12, 2005, www.counterpunch.org/mckinney09122005.html.

18. "Huge Racial Divide over Katrina and Its Consequences," Report of the Pew Research Center for People and the Press, September 8, 2005, 2; available at http://people-press.org/reports/display.php3?Report ID=255.

19. As Gary Blasi contends, "If we store social categories in our heads by means of prototypes or exemplars rather than statistics, then our basic cognitive mechanisms not only predispose us toward stereotypes . . ., but also limit the potentially curative effect of information that contradicts the statistical assumptions about base rates that are embedded in our stereotypes." Gary Blasi, "Advocacy Against the Stereotype," *UCLA Law Review* 49 (2002):1241, 1256–57.

20. See Lee Cokorinos, *The Assault on Diversity* (Institute for Democracy Studies, 2002), tracing the network of conservative activists and organizations that have waged a well-funded campaign over two decades to change the corpus of civil rights laws, end affirmative action, and reframe the political discourse on race and racism.

21. This should not suggest that she was without any compassion. She went on to say, "[The bodies] have to go somewhere. These are people's families. They have to — they still have to have dignity." It's precisely our point that one can have compassion and still see black people through racial frames. *Paula Zahn Now*, CNN, September 8, 2005.

22. See Michael Ignatieff, "The Broken Contract," *New York Times*, September 25, 2005 (reporting that a woman held at the convention center asserted, "We are American" during a TV interview, demonstrating both anger and astonishment that she would have to remind Americans of that fact and that the social contract had failed).

23. Note that this frame is simultaneously inclusionary and exclusionary. To the extent that it asserts black citizenship, it seeks to include black people within the nation-state. However, it excludes noncitizens, black as well as others, from the circle of care based on lack of formal American belonging. This is deeply problematic but it reveals the limited space within which blacks could assert legitimate claims on national empathy.

24. *Christiane Amanpour:* Chief International Correspondent for CNN News. [Eds.]

25. See Anna Johnson, "Jackson Lashes Out at Bush over Hurricane Response, Criticizes Media for Katrina Coverage," AP Alert, September 3, 2005 (reporting that the Red Cross asserted that it could not enter New Orleans on orders from the National Guard and local authorities). A principal reason for the delay was that government officials believed that they had to prepare a complicated military operation rather than a relief effort. See "Misinformation Seen Key in Katrina Delays," UPI Top Stories, September 30, 2005.

26. See Brian Thevenot and Gordon Russell, "Reports of Anarchy at the Superdome Overstated," *Seattle Times*, September 26, 2005 (reporting that "the vast majority of reported atrocities committed by evacuees have turned out to be false, or at least unsupported by any evidence, according to key military, law enforcement, medical and civilian officers in a position to know." See also Andrew Gumbel, "After the Storm, US Media Held to Account for Exaggerated Tales of Katrina Chaos," *Los Angeles Times*, September 28, 2005.

27. Susannah Rosenblatt and James Rainey, "Reports of Post-Katrina Mayhem May Have Been Overblown," *Los Angeles Times*, September 27, 2005.

28. Thevenot and Russell, "Reports of Anarchy."

29. See "40 Rapes Reported in Hurricane Katrina, Rita Aftermath," NewOrleans Channel.com, wsdu, http://msnbc.msn.com/id/10590305; Nancy Cook Lauer, "Rape-Reporting Procedure Missing After Hurricane" Women's eNews, www.womensenews.org/article.cfm/dyn/aid/2448.

30. See Charmaine Neville, "How We Survived the Flood," transcript of interview given to New Orleans media outlets, September 5, 2005, www.counterpunch.org/neville09072005.html.

31. Kimberle Crenshaw, "Mapping the Margins: Intersectionality, Identity Politics, and Violence Against Women of Color," *Stanford Law Review* 43 (1991): 1241, 1261.

32. Michele Landis Dauber, "Fate, Responsibility, and 'Natural' Disaster Relief: Narrating the American Welfare State," *Law and Society* 33 (1999):257, 264.

33. Ibid., 307.

ENGAGING THE TEXT

1. What is an interpretive frame? According to Harris and Carbado, what role did framing play in the controversy over the two photos of Hurricane Katrina victims wading through the water? What alternative explanations of the photos and their captions are mentioned in the article? Which explanation seems most plausible to you, and why?

2. Harris and Carbado identify several unspoken assumptions underlying the "metaframe" of color blindness. What are they, and how do they affect the way "color blind" people explain racial inequality? Do you agree that color blindness is a problem? Why or why not?

3. In what ways did Hurricane Katrina challenge existing racial frameworks? How did the public understanding of the disaster change over time, and what role did framing play in those evolving interpretations?

4. How were the interpretive frames of the government and media at odds with facts in the aftermath of Hurricane Katrina? How persuasive do you find Harris and Carbado's argument that "frames trump facts" (para. 9)?

5. Harris and Carbado contend that that it's essential to "shift racial frames" (para. 34) in order to combat racial injustice. How would you go about trying to change the frame of color blindness? Brainstorm strategies and discuss their feasibility and likelihood of success.

Exploring Connections

6. In the cartoon on page 421, what frame is suggested by the policeman's comment to the black "suspect"? What frame does the cartoonist rely on as the source of humor here?

7. Would you explain C. P. Ellis's transformation (p. 398) as a result of exposure to new facts, new frames, or both? What details in the narrative support your view?

8. Analyze the role played by framing in the following experiences detailed by James McBride (p. 409): the reactions of the Hasidic salesmen to Mommy and the children, the behavior of the police in Richie's arrest, the words and actions of the grocer with the sour milk, and the response of McBride's classmates to his James Brown dance.

Extending the Critical Context

9. Write a journal entry describing an experience that made you question a preconception you had about another race, ethnicity, or nationality. What did you believe about the group before this experience, and what happened to make you question your view? Did you change as a result? If so, how and why?

10. Read news reports, editorials, blogs, or letters to the editor that address a current incident or issue that creates controversy over race (for example, charges of racial profiling, police brutality, insensitive remarks by a public figure, or "reverse discrimination"). How are the facts of the situation framed by participants, politicians, and pundits? What evidence, if any, do you see of the color-blindness frame? What other frames do you detect? Compare notes in class and discuss your observations.

11. As a class project, develop and conduct a mini-survey on color blindness on your campus. For example, you might ask participants to agree or disagree with a series of short statements like these: "Racism is a serious problem today" or "It's better not to talk about race." Compile your results and write a paper discussing what you found and what further questions your survey raises.

12. Watch the award-winning documentary *Trouble the Water*. How does the film's depiction of Hurricane Katrina and its aftermath differ from the mainstream media accounts discussed by Harris and Carbado?

Visual Portfolio

Reading Images of the Melting Pot

Visual Portfolio
READING IMAGES OF THE MELTING POT

1. What is your emotional response to the photo of the woman wrapped in the flag blanket (p. 439)? How do you interpret the photograph's meaning? What does the woman's body language and expression suggest about her situation? Why do you think the photographer chose to focus so closely on this individual rather than including more of her surroundings?

2. Write a narrative that explains the situation pictured in the second image of the portfolio (p. 440). What is happening and what led up to this scene? Who are these people and what are their relationships? Identify specific details of setting, dress, body language, and facial expression that support your interpretation. Compare narratives and discuss the assumptions that inform the stories as well as the persuasiveness of the evidence they are based on.

3. How many different ways could you describe the ethnic or cultural identity of each of the four friends on page 441 based on the visual cues provided by the photo? What knowledge or assumptions about race, ethnicity, and culture underlie your interpretations?

4. In the fourth photo (p. 442), several residents of New Orleans wait for rescue on the roof of an apartment building following Hurricane Katrina. What practical and symbolic purposes do the flags serve for the survivors? For the photographer? Should the photographer have tried to assist these people rather than take their picture? Why or why not?

5. How might Cheryl I. Harris and Devon W. Carbado read the significance of the rooftop image and the next one (pp. 442–43), which was also taken in New Orleans following Katrina?

6. What messages do you think the photo on page 443 conveys about power, survival, and American values? Why do you think the photographer chose to focus on the figures in the foreground? How would the effect of the image change if the entire scene were clearly in focus? If the shot had been taken from a different angle — from above, for example, or from the side of the street?

7. The image on page 444 depicts a section of the fence that divides the United States from Mexico. What sense does the picture give you of the photographer's views of immigration, the fence, the border, and the relationship between the two countries? What details of the picture itself — angle, lighting, proportion, position of the figures — suggest these views?

8. How do you think the people in the "Close the Border" photo (p. 445) would explain the motives for their protest? What motives might Vincent N. Parrillo (p. 384) or George M. Fredrickson (p. 449) attribute to them? Write an imaginary conversation among the protesters and the two writers.

9. The image of Rev. Jesse Jackson (p. 446) fills a huge screen as supporters (including Jackson) wait for Barack Obama to deliver his acceptance speech on election night 2008. What history does Jackson's presence and

his reaction to the election results evoke? (If you don't know much about him, do some quick online research to learn some of the highlights of Jackson's career.) What conclusions or questions about race in the United States are suggested by the election data at the bottom of the screen?

10. The Obamas' visit to the Lincoln Memorial took place the night before inauguration day. What is the intended symbolism of this photo (p. 447)? How do you respond to it? What political and civic purposes were served by the visit, and by photographs like this one?

Models of American Ethnic Relations: A Historical Perspective

George M. Fredrickson

Are Irish Americans white? The answer is so self-evident that the question seems absurd, but as historian George Fredrickson notes, the idea of "whiteness" has in the past excluded many Europeans, including the Irish. A survey of ethnic and racial categories in American history shows how much they change with the politics and prejudices of the time. Yet citizenship, civil rights, even human status have been granted or withheld on the basis of these shifting definitions. Fredrickson examines four models of ethnic relations — hierarchy, assimilation, pluralism, and separatism — that have defined how groups perceived as different from each other should interact. Fredrickson (1934–2009) wrote extensively about race in the history of the United States and South Africa, served as president of the Organization for American Historians, and taught for many years at Stanford University. His books include The Inner Civil War *(1965),* The Black Image in the White Mind *(1972),* White Supremacy *(1981),* Black Liberation *(1995), and* Racism: A Short History *(2002).*

Throughout its history, the United States has been inhabited by a variety of interacting racial or ethnic groups. In addition to the obvious "color line" structuring relationships between dominant whites and lower-status blacks, Indians, and Asians, there have at times been important social distinctions among those of white or European ancestry. Today we think of the differences between white Anglo-Saxon Protestants and Irish, Italian, Polish, and Jewish Americans as purely cultural or religious, but in earlier times these groups were sometimes thought of as "races" or "subraces" — people possessing innate or inborn characteristics and capabilities that affected their fitness for American citizenship. Moreover, differences apparently defined as cultural have sometimes been so reified[1] as to serve as the functional equivalent of physical distinctions. Indians, for example, were viewed by most nineteenth-century missionaries and humanitarians as potentially equal and similar to whites. Their status as noncitizens was not attributed to skin color or physical appearance; it was only their obdurate adherence to "savage ways" that allegedly stood in the way of their possessing equal rights and being fully assimilated. Analogously, conservative opponents of affirmative action and other antiracist policies in the 1990s may provide a "rational" basis for prejudice and discrimination by attributing the disadvantages and alleged shortcomings of African Americans to persistent cultural "pathology" rather than to genetic deficiencies (D'Souza 1995).

It can therefore be misleading to make a sharp distinction between race and ethnicity when considering intergroup relations in American history. As I have argued extensively elsewhere, ethnicity is "racialized" whenever distinctive group characteristics, however defined or explained, are used as the basis for a status hierarchy of groups who are thought to differ in ancestry or descent (Fredrickson 1997, ch. 5).

Four basic conceptions of how ethnic or racial groups should relate to each other have been predominant in the history of American thought about group relations — ethnic hierarchy, one-way assimilation, cultural pluralism, and group separatism. This [essay] provides a broad outline of the historical career of each of these models of intergroup relations, noting some of the changes in how various groups have defined themselves or been defined by others.

Ethnic Hierarchy

Looking at the entire span of American history, we find that the most influential and durable conception of the relations among those American racial or ethnic groups viewed as significantly dissimilar has been hierarchical. A dominant group — conceiving of itself as society's charter membership — has claimed rights and privileges not to be fully shared with outsiders or "others," who have been characterized as unfit or unready for equal rights and full citizenship. The hierarchical model has its deepest roots and most enduring consequences in the conquest of Indians and the enslavement of blacks during the colonial period (Axtell 1981; Jordan 1968). But it was also applied in the nineteenth century to Asian immigrants and in a less severe and more open-ended way to European immigrants who differed in culture and religion from old-stock Americans of British origin (Higham 1968; Miller 1969). The sharpest and most consequential distinction was always between "white" and "nonwhite." The first immigration law passed by Congress in 1790 specified that only white immigrants were eligible for naturalization. This provision would create a crucial difference in

---

[1]*reified:* Treated as if real, concrete, but actually abstract.

the mid-nineteenth century between Chinese "sojourners," who could not become citizens and voters, and Irish immigrants, who could.

Nevertheless, the Irish who fled the potato famine of the 1840s by emi- 5 grating to the United States also encountered discrimination. Besides being Catholic and poor, the refugees from the Emerald Isle were Celts rather than Anglo-Saxons, and a racialized discourse,[2] drawing on British prece- dents, developed as an explanation for Irish inferiority to Americans of En- glish ancestry (Knobel 1986). The dominant group during the nineteenth and early twentieth centuries was not simply white but also Protestant and Anglo-Saxon. Nevertheless, the Irish were able to use their right to vote and the patronage they received from the Democratic Party to improve their status, an option not open to the Chinese. Hence, they gradually gained the leverage and respectability necessary to win admission to the dominant caste, a process that culminated in Al Smith's nomination for the presidency in 1928 and John F. Kennedy's election in 1960.

The mass immigration of Europeans from eastern and southern Europe in the late nineteenth and early twentieth centuries inspired new concerns about the quality of the American stock. In an age of eugenics,[3] scientific racism,[4] and social Darwinism,[5] the notion that northwestern Europeans were innately superior to those from the southern and eastern parts of the continent — to say nothing of those light-skinned people of actual or pre- sumed west Asian origin (such as Jews, Syrians, and Armenians) — gained wide currency. A determined group of nativists, encouraged by the latest racial "science," fought for restrictive immigration policies that discriminated against those who were not of "Nordic" or "Aryan" descent (Higham 1968). In the 1920s the immigration laws were changed to reflect these prejudices. Low quotas were established for white people from nations or areas outside of those that had supplied the bulk of the American population before 1890. In the minds of many, true Americans were not merely white but also north- ern European. In fact, some harbored doubts about the full claim to "white- ness" of swarthy immigrants from southern Italy.

After immigration restriction had relieved ethnic and racial anxieties, the status of the new immigrants gradually improved as a result of their political involvement, their economic and professional achievement, and a decline in the respectability of the kind of scientific racism that had ranked some European groups below others. World War II brought revulsion

[2]*racialized discourse:* Language that defines a group of people as a race and attributes distinctive "racial" characteristics to them.

[3]*eugenics:* Movement that advocated improving the human race by encouraging geneti- cally "superior" people to reproduce and promoting the sterilization of "undesirables," includ- ing minorities, poor people, and those with mental and physical disorders.

[4]*scientific racism:* Refers to various efforts to find some scientific basis for white superior- ity, the results of which were inevitably bad science.

[5]*social Darwinism:* The belief that Darwin's theory of evolution and natural selection applies to society; thus the existence of extreme wealth and poverty (whether of individuals or nations) is rationalized as a "natural" result of competition and the survival of the fittest.

against the genocidal anti-Semitism and eugenic experiments of the Nazis, dealing a coup de grâce to the de facto hierarchy that had placed Anglo-Saxons, Nordics, or Aryans at the apex of American society. All Americans of European origin were now unambiguously white and, for most purposes, ethnically equal to old-stock Americans of Anglo-Saxon, Celtic, and Germanic ancestry. Hierarchy was now based exclusively on color. Paradoxically, it might be argued, the removal of the burden of "otherness" from virtually all whites made more striking and salient than ever the otherness of people of color, especially African Americans.

The civil rights movement of the 1960s was directed primarily at the legalized racial hierarchy of the southern states. The Civil Rights Acts of 1964 and 1965 brought an end to government-enforced racial segregation and the denial of voting rights to blacks in that region. But the legacy of four centuries of white supremacy survives in the disadvantaged social and economic position of blacks and other people of color in the United States. The impoverished, socially deprived, and physically unsafe ghettos, barrios, and Indian reservations of this nation are evidence that ethnic hierarchy in a clearly racialized form persists in practice if not in law.

One-Way Assimilation

Policies aimed at the assimilation of ethnic groups have usually assumed that there is a single and stable American culture of European, and especially English, origin to which minorities are expected to conform as the price of admission to full and equal participation in the society and polity of the United States (Gordon 1964, ch. 4). Assimilationist thinking is not racist in the classic sense: it does not deem the outgroups in question to be innately or biologically inferior to the ingroup. The professed goal is equality — but on terms that presume the superiority, purity, and unchanging character of the dominant culture. Little or nothing in the cultures of the groups being invited to join the American mainstream is presumed worthy of preserving. When carried to its logical conclusion, the assimilationist project demands what its critics have described — especially in reference to the coercive efforts to "civilize" Native Americans — as "cultural genocide."

Estimates of group potential and the resulting decisions as to which   10
groups are eligible for assimilation have varied in response to changing definitions of race. If an ethnic group is definitely racialized, the door is closed because its members are thought to possess ineradicable traits (biologically or culturally determined) that make them unfit for inclusion. At times there have been serious disagreements within the dominant group about the eligibility of particular minorities for initiation into the American club.

Although one-way assimilationism was mainly a twentieth-century ideology, it was anticipated in strains of nineteenth-century thinking about Irish immigrants, Native Americans, and even blacks. Radical white abolitionists and even some black antislavery activists argued that prejudice

LA CUCARACHA   by **LALO ALCARAZ**

against African Americans was purely and simply a result of their peculiarly degraded and disadvantaged circumstances and that emancipation from slavery would make skin color irrelevant and open the way to their full equality and social acceptability (Fredrickson 1987, ch. 1). These abolitionists had little or no conception that there was a rich and distinctive black culture that could become the source of a positive group identity, and that African modes of thought and behavior had been adapted to the challenge of surviving under slavery.

If the hope of fully assimilating blacks into a color-blind society was held by only a small minority of whites, a majority probably supposed that the Irish immigrants of the 1840s and 1850s could become full-fledged Americans, if they chose to do so, simply by changing their behavior and beliefs. The doctrine of the innate inferiority of Celts to Anglo-Saxons was not even shared by all of the nativists who sought to slow down the process of Irish naturalization (Knobel 1986). A more serious problem for many of them was the fervent Catholicism of the Irish; Anglo-Protestant missionaries hoped to convert them en masse. The defenders of unrestricted Irish immigration came mostly from the ranks of the Democratic Party, which relied heavily on Irish votes. Among them were strong believers in religious toleration and a high wall of separation between church and state. They saw religious diversity as no obstacle to the full and rapid Americanization of all white-skinned immigrants.

The most sustained and serious nineteenth-century effort to assimilate people who differed both culturally and phenotypically[6] from the majority was aimed at American Indians. Frontier settlers, military men who fought Indians, and many other whites had no doubts that Indians were members of an inherently inferior race that was probably doomed to total extinction as a result of the conquest of the West. Their views were graphically expressed by General Philip Sheridan when he opined that "the only good Indian is a dead Indian." But an influential group of eastern philanthropists, humanitarian reformers, and government officials thought of the Indians as having been "noble savages" whose innate capacities were not inferior to those of whites.

[6]*phenotypically:* Physically.

Thomas Jefferson, who had a much dimmer view of black potentialities, was one of the first to voice this opinion (Koch and Peden 1944, 210–11). For these ethnocentric humanitarians, the "Indian problem" was primarily cultural rather than racial, and its solution lay in civilizing the "savages" rather than exterminating them. Late in the century, the assimilationists adopted policies designed to force Indians to conform to Euro-American cultural norms; these included breaking up communally held reservations into privately owned family farms and sending Indian children to boarding schools where they were forbidden to speak their own languages and made to dress, cut their hair, and in every possible way act and look like white people. The policy was a colossal failure; most Native Americans refused to abandon key aspects of their traditional cultures, and venal whites took advantage of the land reforms to strip Indians of much of their remaining patrimony[7] (Berkhofer 1978; Hoxie 1984; Mardock 1971).

In the early twentieth century, the one-way assimilation model was applied to the southern and eastern European immigrants who had arrived in massive numbers before the discriminatory quota system of the 1920s was implemented. While some nativists called for their exclusion on the grounds of their innate deficiencies, other champions of Anglo-American cultural homogeneity hoped to assimilate those who had already arrived through education and indoctrination. The massive "Americanization" campaigns of the period just prior to World War I produced the concept of America as a "melting pot" in which cultural differences would be obliterated. The metaphor might have suggested that a new mixture would result — and occasionally it did have this meaning — but a more prevalent interpretation was that non-Anglo-American cultural traits and inclinations would simply disappear, making the final brew identical to the original one (Gordon 1964, ch. 5).

Before the 1940s, people of color, and especially African Americans, were generally deemed ineligible for assimilation because of their innate inferiority to white ethnics, who were now thought capable of being culturally reborn as Anglo-Americans. Such factors as the war-inspired reaction against scientific racism and the gain in black political power resulting from mass migration from the South (where blacks could not vote) to the urban North (where the franchise was again open to them) led to a significant reconsideration of the social position of African Americans and threw a spotlight on the flagrant denial in the southern states of the basic constitutional rights of African Americans. The struggle for black civil rights that emerged in the 1950s and came to fruition in the early 1960s was premised on a conviction that white supremacist laws and policies violated an egalitarian "American Creed" — as Gunnar Myrdal had argued in his influential wartime study *An American Dilemma* (1944). The war against Jim Crow[8]

15

---

[7] *patrimony:* Inheritance.
[8] *Jim Crow:* Collective term for southern segregation laws.

was fought under the banner of "integration," which, in the minds of white liberals at least, generally meant one-way assimilation. Blacks, deemed by Myrdal and others as having no culture worth saving, would achieve equal status by becoming just like white Americans in every respect except pigmentation.

When it became clear that the civil rights legislation of the 1960s had failed to improve significantly the social and economic position of blacks in the urban ghettos of the North, large numbers of African Americans rejected the integrationist ideal on the grounds that it had been not only a false promise but an insult to the culture of African Americans for ignoring or devaluing their distinctive experience as a people. The new emphasis on "black power" and "black consciousness" conveyed to those whites who were listening that integration had to mean something other than one-way assimilation to white middle-class norms if it was to be a solution to the problem of racial inequality in America (Marable 1991; Van Deburg 1992).

It should be obvious by now that the one-way assimilation model has not proved to be a viable or generally acceptable way of adjusting group differences in American society. It is based on an ethnocentric ideal of cultural homogeneity that has been rejected by Indians, blacks, Asians, Mexican Americans, and even many white ethnics. It reifies and privileges one cultural strain in what is in fact a multicultural society. It should be possible to advocate the incorporation of all ethnic or racial groups into a common civic society without requiring the sacrifice of cultural distinctiveness and diversity.

Cultural Pluralism

Unlike assimilationists, cultural pluralists celebrate differences among groups rather than seek to obliterate them. They argue that cultural diversity is a healthy and normal condition that does not preclude equal rights and the mutual understandings about civic responsibilities needed to sustain a democratic nation-state. This model for American ethnic relations is a twentieth-century invention that would have been virtually inconceivable at an earlier time. The eighteenth and nineteenth centuries lacked the essential concept of the relativity of cultures. The model of cultural development during this period was evolutionary, progressive, and universalistic. People were either civilized or they were not. Mankind was seen as evolving from a state of "savagery" or "barbarism" to "civilization," and all cultures at a particular level were similar in every way that mattered. What differentiated nations and ethnic groups was their ranking on the scale of social evolution. Modern Western civilization stood at the apex of this universal historical process. Even nineteenth-century black nationalists accepted the notion that there were universal standards of civilization to which people of African descent should aspire. They differed from white supremacists in believing that blacks had the natural capability to reach the same heights as Caucasians if they were given a chance (Moses 1978).

The concept of cultural pluralism drew on the new cultural anthropology of the early twentieth century, as pioneered by Franz Boas. Boas and his disciples attempted to look at each culture they studied on its own terms and as an integrated whole. They rejected theories of social evolution that ranked cultures in relation to a universalist conception of "civilization." But relativistic cultural anthropologists were not necessarily cultural pluralists in their attitude toward group relations within American society. Since they generally believed that a given society or community functioned best with a single, integrated culture, they could favor greater autonomy for Indians on reservations but also call for the full assimilation of new immigrants or even African Americans. Boas himself was an early supporter of the National Association for the Advancement of Colored People (NAACP) and a pioneering advocate of what would later be called racial integration.

An effort to use the new concept of culture to validate ethnic diversity within the United States arose from the negative reaction of some intellectuals to the campaign to "Americanize" the new immigrants from eastern and southern Europe in the period just before and after World War I. The inventors of cultural pluralism were cosmopolitan critics of American provincialism or representatives of immigrant communities, especially Jews, who valued their cultural distinctiveness and did not want to be melted down in an Americanizing crucible. The Greenwich Village intellectual Randolph Bourne described his ideal as a "transnational America" in which various ethnic cultures would interact in a tolerant atmosphere to create an enriching variety of ideas, values, and lifestyles (Bourne 1964, ch. 8). The Jewish philosopher Horace Kallen, who coined the phrase "cultural pluralism," compared the result to a symphony, with each immigrant group represented as a section of the orchestra (Higham 1984, ch. 9; Kallen 1924). From a different perspective, W. E. B. DuBois celebrated a distinctive black culture rooted in the African and slave experiences and heralded its unacknowledged contributions to American culture in general (Lewis 1993). But the dominant version advocated by Kallen and Bourne stopped, for all practical purposes, at the color line. Its focus was on making America safe for a variety of European cultures. As a Zionist, Kallen was especially concerned with the preservation of Jewish distinctiveness and identity.

Since it was mainly the viewpoint of ethnic intellectuals who resisted the assimilationism of the melting pot, cultural pluralism was a minority persuasion in the twenties, thirties, and forties. A modified version reemerged in the 1950s in Will Herberg's (1960) conception of a "triple melting pot" of Protestants, Catholics, and Jews. The revulsion against Nazi anti-Semitism and the upward mobility of American Jews and Catholics inspired a synthesis of cultural pluralism and assimilationism that made religious persuasion the only significant source of diversity among white Americans. Herberg conceded, however, that black Protestants constituted a separate group that was not likely to be included in the Protestant melting pot. He therefore sharpened the distinction between race or color and ethnicity that was central to postwar thinking about group differences. Nevertheless, Herberg's

20

view that significant differences between, say, Irish and Italian Catholics were disappearing was challenged in the 1960s and later, especially in the "ethnic revival" of the 1970s, which proclaimed that differing national origins among Euro-Americans remained significant and a valuable source of cultural variations.

The "multiculturalism" of the 1980s operated on assumptions that were similar to those of the cultural pluralist tradition, except that the color line was breached and the focus was shifted from the cultures and contributions of diverse European ethnic groups to those of African Americans, Mexican Americans, Asian Americans, and Native Americans. Abandonment of the earlier term "multiracialism" signified a desire to escape from the legacy of biological or genetic determinism and to affirm that the differences among people who happened to differ in skin color or phenotype were the result of their varying cultural and historical experiences. Under attack was the doctrine, shared by assimilationists and most earlier proponents of cultural pluralism, that the cultural norm in the United States was inevitably European in origin and character. Parity was now sought for groups of Asian, African, and American Indian ancestry. This ideal of cultural diversity and democracy was viewed by some of its critics as an invitation to national disunity and ethnic conflict (Schlesinger 1992). But its most thoughtful proponents argued that it was simply a consistent application of American democratic values and did not preclude the interaction and cooperation of groups within a common civic society (Hollinger 1995). Nevertheless, the mutual understandings upon which national unity and cohesion could be based needed to be negotiated rather than simply imposed by a Euro-American majority.

Group Separatism

Sometimes confused with the broadened cultural pluralism described here is the advocacy of group separatism. It originates in the desire of a culturally distinctive or racialized group to withdraw as much as possible from American society and interaction with other groups. Its logical outcome, autonomy in a separate, self-governing community, might conceivably be achieved either in an ethnic confederation like Switzerland or in the dissolution of the United States into several ethnic nations. But such a general theory is a logical construction rather than a program that has been explicitly advocated. Group separatism emanates from ethnocentric concerns about the status and destiny of particular groups, and its advocates rarely if ever theorize about what is going to happen to other groups. Precedents for group separatism based on cultural differences can be found in American history in the toleration of virtually autonomous religious communities like the Amish and the Hutterites[9] and in the modicum of self-government and

---

[9]*the Amish and the Hutterites:* Religious groups that reject the values and technology of contemporary society, living in relatively isolated, self-sufficient farming communities.

immunity from general laws accorded to Indian tribes and reservations since the 1930s.

The most significant and persistent assertion of group separatism in American history has come from African Americans disillusioned with the prospects for equality within American society. In the nineteenth century, several black leaders and intellectuals called on African Americans to emigrate from the United States in order to establish an independent black republic elsewhere; Africa was the most favored destination. In the 1920s, Marcus Garvey created a mass movement based on the presumption that blacks had no future in the United States and should identify with the independence and future greatness of Africa, ultimately by emigrating there. More recently, the Nation of Islam has proposed that several American states be set aside for an autonomous black nation (Fredrickson 1995, chs. 2, 4, 7). At the height of the black power movement of the 1960s and early 1970s, a few black nationalists even called for the establishment of a noncontiguous federation of black urban ghettos — a nation of islands like Indonesia or the Philippines, but surrounded by white populations rather than the Pacific Ocean.

The current version of black separatism — "Afrocentrism"[10] — has not   25
as yet produced a plan for political separation. Its aim is a cultural and spiritual secession from American society rather than the literal establishment of a black nation. Advocates of total separation could be found among other disadvantaged groups. In the late 1960s and 1970s Mexican American militants called for the establishment of the independent Chicano nation of Aztlán[11] in the American Southwest (Gutierrez 1995, 184–85) and some Native American radicals sought the reestablishment of truly independent tribal nations.

Group separatism might be viewed as a utopian vision or rhetorical device expressing the depths of alienation felt by the most disadvantaged racial or ethnic groups in American society. The extreme unlikelihood of realizing such visions has made their promulgation more cathartic than politically efficacious. Most members of groups exposed to such separatist appeals have recognized their impracticality, and the clash between the fixed and essentialist[12] view of identity that such projects entail and the fluid and hybrid quality of group cultures in the United States has become increasingly evident to many people of color, as shown most dramatically by the recent movement among those of mixed parentage to affirm a biracial identity. Few African Americans want to celebrate the greater or lesser

---

[10]*Afrocentrism:* An academic movement intended to counter the dominant European bias of Western scholarship; Afrocentric scholars seek to show the influence of African cultures, languages, and history on human civilization.

[11]*Aztlán:* Includes those parts of the United States once governed by Mexico.

[12]*essentialist:* Refers to the idea that group characteristics are innate, or "essential," rather than cultural.

degree of white ancestry most of them possess, but many have acknowledged not only their ancestral ties to Africa but their debt to Euro-American culture (and its debt to them). Most Mexican Americans value their cultural heritage but do not have the expectation or even the desire to establish an independent Chicano nation in the Southwest. Native Americans have authentic historical and legal claims to a high degree of autonomy but generally recognize that total independence on their current land base is impossible and would worsen rather than improve their circumstances. Asian Americans are proud of their various cultures and seek to preserve some of their traditions but have shown little or no inclination to separate themselves from other Americans in the civic, professional, and economic life of the nation. Afrocentrism raises troubling issues for American educational and cultural life but hardly represents a serious threat to national unity.

Ethnic separatism, in conclusion, is a symptom of racial injustice and a call to action against it, but there is little reason to believe that it portends "the disuniting of America." It is currently a source of great anxiety to many Euro-Americans primarily because covert defenders of ethnic hierarchy or one-way assimilation have tried to confuse the broad-based ideal of democratic multiculturalism with the demands of a relatively few militant ethnocentrists for thoroughgoing self-segregation and isolation from the rest of American society.

Of the four models of American ethnic relations, the one that I believe offers the best hope for a just and cohesive society is a cultural pluralism that is fully inclusive and based on the free choices of individuals to construct or reconstruct their own ethnic identities. We are still far from achieving the degree of racial and ethnic tolerance that realization of such an ideal requires. But with the demographic shift that is transforming the overwhelmingly Euro-American population of thirty or forty years ago into one that is much more culturally and phenotypically heterogeneous, a more democratic form of intergroup relations is a likely prospect, unless there is a desperate reversion to overt ethnic hierarchicalism by the shrinking Euro-American majority. It that were to happen, national unity and cohesion would indeed be hard to maintain. If current trends continue, minorities of non-European ancestry will constitute a new majority sometime in the next century. Well before that point is reached, they will have the numbers and the provocation to make the country virtually ungovernable if a resurgent racism brings serious efforts to revive the blatantly hierarchical policies that have prevailed in the past.

References

Axtell, James. (1981). *The European and the Indian: Essays in the Ethnohistory of Colonial North America*. New York: Oxford University Press.

Berkhofer, Robert F., Jr. (1978). *The White Man's Indian: Image of the American Indian from Columbus to the Present*. New York: Alfred A. Knopf.

Bourne, Randolph S. (1964). *War and the Intellectuals: Collected Essays, 1915–1919.* New York: Harper Torch.

D'Souza, Dinesh. (1995). *The End of Racism: Principles for a Multiracial Society.* New York: Free Press.

Fredrickson, George M. (1987). *The Black Image in the White Mind: The Debate on Afro-American Character and Destiny, 1817–1914.* Middletown, Conn.: Wesleyan University Press.

———. (1995). *Black Liberation: A Comparative History of Black Ideologies in the United States and South Africa.* New York: Oxford University Press.

———. (1997). *The Comparative Imagination: On the History of Racism, Nationalism, and Social Movements.* Berkeley: University of California Press.

Gordon, Milton M. (1964). *Assimilation in American Life: The Role of Race, Religion, and National Origins.* New York: Oxford University Press.

Gutierrez, David. (1995). *Walls and Mirrors: Mexican Americans, Mexican Immigrants, and the Politics of Ethnicity.* Berkeley: University of California Press.

Herberg, Will. (1960). *Protestant-Catholic-Jew: An Essay in American Religious Sociology.* Garden City, N.Y.: Anchor Books.

Higham, John. (1968). *Strangers in the Land: Patterns of American Nativism, 1860–1925.* New York: Atheneum.

———. (1984). *Send These to Me: Jews and Other Immigrants in Urban America.* Baltimore: Johns Hopkins University Press.

Hollinger, David. (1995). *Postethnic America: Beyond Multiculturalism.* New York: Basic Books.

Hoxie, Frederick E. (1984). A *Final Promise: The Campaign to Assimilate the Indians, 1880–1920.* Lincoln: University of Nebraska Press.

Jordan, Winthrop D. (1968). *White Over Black: American Attitudes Toward the Negro, 1550–1812.* New York: University of North Carolina Press.

Kallen, Horace. (1924). *Culture and Democracy in the United States: Studies in the Group Psychology of American Peoples.* New York: Boni & Liveright.

Koch, Adrienne, and Peden, William (eds.). (1944). *The Life and Selected Writings of Thomas Jefferson.* New York: Modern Library.

Knobel, Dale T. (1986). *Paddy and the Republic: Ethnicity and Nationality in Antebellum America.* Middletown, Conn.: Wesleyan University Press.

Lewis, David Levering. (1993). *W. E. B. DuBois: Biography of a Race, 1868–1919.* New York: Henry Holt.

Marable, Manning. (1991). *Race, Reform, and Rebellion: The Second Reconstruction in Black America.* Jackson, Miss.: University of Mississippi Press.

Mardock, Robert W. (1971). *The Reformers and the American Indian.* Columbia: University of Missouri Press.

Miller, Stuart Creighton. (1969). *The Unwelcome Immigrant: The American Image of the Chinese, 1785–1882.* Berkeley: University of California Press.

Moses, Wilson Jeremiah. (1978). *The Golden Age of Black Nationalism, 1850–1925.* Hamden, Conn.: Archon Books.

Myrdal, Gunnar. (1944). *An American Dilemma.* New York: Harper and Row.

Schlesinger, Arthur M., Jr. (1992). *The Disuniting of America.* New York: Norton.

Van Deburg, William L. (1992). *New Day in Babylon: The Black Power Movement and American Culture, 1965–1975.* Chicago: University of Chicago Press.

ENGAGING THE TEXT

1. How does Fredrickson distinguish between race and ethnicity? How and under what circumstances can ethnicity become "racialized" (para. 2)?

2. What does Fredrickson mean by "the burden of 'otherness' "? Summarize the ways in which racial categories and definitions of "whiteness" have changed during the course of American history.

3. What are some of the ways that ethnic hierarchy has been eliminated? In what ways does it persist, according to Fredrickson? What evidence can you think of that would support or challenge this contention?

4. Fredrickson writes that "assimilationist thinking is not racist in the classic sense" (para. 9) — thereby implying that such thinking may be racist in some other sense. What does he mean by this? Do you agree?

5. How does Fredrickson distinguish cultural pluralism from assimilation? How did earlier forms of pluralism differ from the current concept of multiculturalism?

6. Why does Fredrickson reject the claim that an emphasis on ethnic identity threatens the unity and stability of American society? Why does a Euro-American backlash against ethnic diversity pose a greater risk in his view? Have you observed any recent examples of either divisiveness or backlash? Compare your observations with those of classmates.

EXPLORING CONNECTIONS

7. Write an essay examining the ways in which various models of ethnic relations can be seen operating in one or more of the following selections:

> Richard Rodriguez, "The Achievement of Desire" (p. 194)
> Malcolm X, "Learning to Read" (p. 210)
> Studs Terkel, "Stephen Cruz" (p. 366)
> Studs Terkel, "C. P. Ellis" (p. 398)
> James McBride, "The Boy in the Mirror" (p. 409)
> Sherman Alexie, "Assimilation" (p. 483)
> Judith Ortiz Cofer, "The Story of My Body" (p. 537)

8. What model or models of ethnic relations do you see represented in the cartoon by Lalo Alcaraz on page 453?

9. Examine the Visual Portfolio on pages 439–47. Identify the model of ethnic relations you see embodied in each image and explain your reasoning.

EXTENDING THE CRITICAL CONTEXT

10. If your campus or community is involved in a debate concerning affirmative action, immigration, bilingual education, multiculturalism, or ethnic studies, analyze several opinion pieces or position papers on the issue. What models of ethnic relations are expressed or assumed by each side of the debate?

Deconstructing America

Patrick J. Buchanan

> *One of the most influential and outspoken conservative voices in the United States, Patrick J. Buchanan (b. 1938) lives and breathes politics. He served as a senior advisor to Presidents Nixon, Ford, and Reagan, and has campaigned for the presidency himself three times — as a candidate in the Republican primaries of 1992 and 1996 and as the nominee of the Reform Party in 2000. Six of his ten books have been best-sellers. The titles speak for themselves: they include* The Great Betrayal: How American Sovereignty and Social Justice Are Being Sacrificed to the Gods of the Global Economy *(1998);* The Death of the West: How Dying Populations and Immigrant Invasions Imperil Our Country and Civilization *(2002);* Where the Right Went Wrong: How Neoconservatives Subverted the Reagan Revolution and Hijacked the Bush Presidency *(2004); and* State of Emergency: The Third World Invasion and Conquest of America *(2006). Buchanan founded* The American Conservative *magazine, writes a syndicated column on politics, and appears daily on cable TV news shows as a political analyst. The following selection is taken from his 2007 book,* Day of Reckoning: How Hubris, Ideology, and Greed Are Tearing America Apart.

> Yet at present, the United States is unwinding strand by strand, rather like the Soviet Union.
>
> — William Rees-Mogg, 1992[1]

> The histories of bilingual and bicultural societies that do not assimilate are histories of turmoil, tension and tragedy.
>
> — Seymour Martin Lipset[2]

In 2007, on the 400th anniversary of the Jamestown[3] settlement, Queen Elizabeth II arrived to commemorate the occasion. But it took some fancy footwork by Her Majesty to run the Powhatan gauntlet.[4]

---

[1] Daniel Patrick Moynihan, *Pandaemonium: Ethnicity in International Politics* (New York: Oxford University Press, 1994), p. 24. [All notes are Buchanan's unless otherwise indicated.]

[2] Stanley Monteith, "The Diabolic Plan," Reprise of Richard Lamm's Address, "A Plan to Destroy America," May 2006. RaidersNewsNetwork.com

[3] *Jamestown:* Founded in 1607, Jamestown, Virginia, was the first permanent English settlement in North America. [Eds.]

[4] *Powhatan gauntlet:* The Powhatan tribe led a confederacy of more than thirty other tribes during the period of the Jamestown settlement; the gauntlet refers to a tribal initiation ritual in which young men submitted to an extended period of severe physical and mental discipline before emerging as mature men and recognized leaders. [Eds.]

CANDORVILLE By Darrin Bell

Candorville © Darrin Bell. © 2006 The Washington Post. All rights reserved. Reprinted with permission.

For the queen had been there before, fifty years ago, for the 350th anniversary, in a less progressive era. As the Associated Press reported, "the last time the queen helped Virginia mark the anniversary of its colonial founding, it was an all-white affair in a state whose government was in open defiance of a 1954 Supreme Court order to desegregate public schools."[5]

That was the time of massive resistance to integration in Virginia. And the queen was quick to recognize and embrace the change: "Since I visited Jamestown in 1957, my country has become a much more diverse society just as the Commonwealth of Virginia and the whole United States of America have also undergone a major social change."[6]

Both nations are indeed more diverse. But the most recent reminder of diversity in Virginia, to which the queen alluded, was the massacre of thirty-two students and teachers at Virginia Tech by an immigrant madman.

And now that London is Londonistan,[7] Muslim imams preach hatred of   5
the West in mosques, and Pakistani subway bombers find support in their madrassas.[8] Race riots are common in the northern industrial cities. Crime rates have soared. In parts of London, people fear to walk. Yes, the Britain of Tony Blair and Gordon Brown[9] is more diverse than the Britain of Victoria and Lord Salisbury,[10] Lloyd George and Churchill.[11] Is it also a better,

---

[5]"Queen Elizabeth Sees Virginia Anew," May 3, 2007, Associated Press, MSNBC.com.
[6]Ibid.

[7]*Londonistan:* Ironic reference to the large immigrant Pakistani population of London. [Eds.]

[8]*madrassas:* Islamic religious schools. [Eds.]

[9]*Tony Blair and Gordon Brown:* Blair (b. 1953) served as the British prime minister, 1997–2007; he was succeeded by Brown (b. 1951). [Eds.]

[10]*Victoria and Lord Salisbury:* Queen Victoria (1819–1901) was Britain's longest-reigning monarch; Robert Cecil, Third Marquess of Salisbury (1830–1903) served as her prime minister three times. [Eds.]

[11]*Lloyd George and Churchill:* David Lloyd George (1863–1945) was Britain's prime minister during much of World War I, 1916–1922; Sir Winston Churchill served as prime minister throughout World War II, 1940–1945, and again in the early 1950s, 1951–1955. [Eds.]

lovelier, stronger, more respected nation than the Britannia that ruled the waves and a fourth of the world?

The prevailing orthodoxy demands that we parrot such platitudes. And Her Majesty was careful to conform. "Fifty years on, we are now in a position to reflect more candidly on the Jamestown legacy," said the queen, as she began to reflect less candidly on that legacy.[12]

Here, at Jamestown, "Three great civilizations came together for the first time — western European, native American and African."[13]

Well, that is certainly one way of putting it.

Even Her Majesty must have smiled inwardly as she delivered this comic rendition of history. For the Jamestown settlers were not Western Europeans but English Christians. They despised French Catholics and the great event in their lives had been the sinking of the Spanish Armada. And the first decision taken at Jamestown was to build a fort to protect them from Chief Powhatan's tribe, whom they thought might massacre them, as they suspected Indians had massacred the Roanoke[14] colony. Their leader, Capt. John Smith, would escape being clubbed to death by Powhatan, thanks only to the princess Pocahontas. Or so Smith liked to tell the tale. In 1622, the Indians succeeded in massacring a third of all the inhabitants of Jamestown.[15]

As for the Africans, they arrived in 1619 in slave ships, and were not freed for 246 years. Then they were segregated for a century.   10

Jamestown was no coming together of "three great civilizations." It was the beginning of centuries of imperial conquest by British Christians who drove the pagan Indians westward, repopulated their lands, and imposed their own faith, customs, laws, language, and institutions upon their New World. Jamestown was the beginning of America — and of the British Empire.

"With the benefit of hindsight, we can see in that event [Jamestown] the origins of a singular endeavor — the building of a great nation, founded on the eternal values of democracy and equality," said the queen.[16]

A great nation did indeed arise from Jamestown, but, intending no disrespect to Her Majesty, democracy and equality had nothing to do with it.

---

[12]Patrick J. Buchanan, "Queen's Fancy PC Footwork in Jamestown," May 7, 2007. VDARE.com

[13]Ibid.

[14]*Roanoke:* Located in what is now North Carolina, Roanoke Island was the site of the first attempts by the English to settle in North America. The first group of settlers, in 1585, encountered such hardship that they returned to England the following year; a small group of men who remained were killed by Indians. The second group of colonists, in 1587, mysteriously vanished. [Eds.]

[15]"From Jamestown's Swamp: Pocahontas Was the Least of It," editorial, *Washington Post,* May 12, 2007, p. A14.

[16]Ibid.

The House of Burgesses, formed in 1619, was restricted to white males, men of property. The American Revolution was not fought for equality, but to be rid of British rule. Four of the first five presidents — Washington, Jefferson, Madison, and Monroe — were Virginia slaveholders. Exactly two and a half centuries after Jamestown, in 1857, came Chief Justice Roger B. Taney's *Dred Scott* decision declaring that slaves were not Americans and that none of them had any of the rights of American citizens. Few Americans then, certainly not Abe Lincoln, believed in social or political equality.

Now, if, in 1957 — 350 years after Jamestown, 100 years after *Dred Scott* — the state of Virginia had a declared policy of massive resistance to racial integration, how can the queen claim that Jamestown or Virginia or America were always about "the eternal values of democracy and equality"?

History contradicts the politically correct version the queen had to   15
recite about the Jamestown settlement — and raises another question.

If Jamestown and Virginia were not about democracy, equality, and diversity for the 350 years between 1607 and 1957, who invented this myth that America was always about democracy, equality, and diversity? And what was their motive?

At Jamestown the queen performed a service to America of which she was surely unaware. By radically revising her views of fifty years ago, about what Jamestown was, the queen revealed the real revolution that occurred between the era of Eisenhower and that of George W. Bush.

It is a revolution in thought and belief about who we are as a nation. In the half century since massive resistance, Virginia has indeed become a radically changed society. No longer does Richmond proudly call herself the Capital of the Confederacy. Lee-Jackson Day is out. Martin Luther King Day is in. The Confederate flag flies nowhere. On Monument Avenue, which features the statues of Robert E. Lee, "Stonewall" Jackson, J. E. B. Stuart, and Jefferson Davis,[17] a statue of Arthur Ashe, an African American tennis player, has been added.[18] "Carry Me Back to Old Virginny" was retired by the legislature as the state song ten years before the queen's return. Within days of her arrival in 2007, the Virginia legislature apologized for slavery.

Virginia 2007 is ashamed of who she was in 1957. But how then can Virginia be proud of what Jamestown was in 1607? For the first Jamestown was not some multicultural village but the first outpost of an imperial nation determined to settle and conquer North America for English Christians, to wipe out or drive out Indians who got in its way, and to bring in Africans as slaves to do the labor English settlers would not do.

---

[17]*Robert E. Lee . . . and Jefferson Davis:* Lee (1807–1870), Jackson (1824–1863), and Stuart (1833–1864) were Confederate generals; Davis (1808–1889) served as president of the Confederate States. [Eds.]

[18]"Multimedia Tour: Monument Ave," *Discover Richmond*. discoverrichmond.com

An Inconvenient Truth

The point here is unpleasant to modernity but critical to recognize: The   20
United States, the greatest republic since Rome, and the British Empire,
the greatest empire since Rome, may be said to have arisen from that three-
cornered fort the Jamestown settlers began to build the day they arrived.
But that republic and that empire did not rise because the settlers and those
who followed believed in diversity, equality, and democracy, but because
they rejected diversity, equality, and democracy. The English, the Virgini-
ans, the Americans were all "us-or-them" people.

They believed in the superiority of their Christian faith and English
culture and civilization. And they transplanted that unique faith, culture,
and civilization to America's fertile soil. Other faiths, cultures, and civilizations — like the ones the Indians had here, or the Africans brought, or the
French had planted in Quebec, or the Spanish in Mexico — they rejected
and resisted with cannon, musket, and sword. This was *our* land, not anybody else's.

But today America and Britain have embraced ideas about the innate
equality of all cultures, civilizations, languages, and faiths, and about the
mixing of all tribes, races, and peoples, that are not only ahistorical, they are
suicidal for America and the West. For all over the world, rising faiths like
Islam, rising movements like the indigenous peoples' movement rolling out
of Latin America to Los Angeles, rising powers like China reaching for
Asian and world hegemony — ignore the kumbaya we preach, and look to
what our fathers practiced when *they* conquered the world.

What the queen said at Jamestown 2007 was that we are not the same
people we were in 1957. She is right. For we now reject as repellent and
ethnocentric the idea that the British who founded our republic and created
the British Empire were not only unique but superior to other peoples and
civilizations. And to show the world how resolutely we reject those old
ideas, we threw open our borders in the last forty years to peoples of all
creeds, cultures, countries, and civilizations, inviting them to come and convert the old America into the most multicultural, multilingual, multiethnic,
multiracial nation in history — "The First Universal Nation"[19] of Ben Wattenberg's[20] warblings. But if the Jamestown settlers had believed in equality
and diversity, and had shared their fort with the Indians, the settlers would
never have been heard from again.

No matter the lies we tell ourselves and teach our children, no great
republic or empire — not Persia, Rome, Islam, Spain, France, Britain, Russia, China, the United States — ever arose because it embraced democracy,

---

[19]*The First Universal Nation:* Title of a 1990 book by Ben Wattenberg which argued that
the United States, due to its increasing ethnic diversity, is becoming a "universal" country.
[Eds.]

[20]*Ben Wattenberg:* Conservative author (b. 1933) and host of a number of PBS television
shows dealing with current events. [Eds.]

diversity, and equality. None. The real question is not whether the values the queen celebrated at Jamestown created America — they had nothing to do with it — but whether America can survive having embraced them. . . .

The Disuniting of America

America is today less a nation than an encampment of suspicious and   25
hostile tribes quarreling viciously over the spoils of politics and power. We live on the same land, under the same set of laws, but we are no longer the one people of whom John Jay[21] wrote in *Federalist* No. 2.

> Providence has been pleased to give this one connected country to one united people — a people descended from the same ancestors, speaking the same language, professing the same religion, attached to the same principles of government, very similar in their manners and customs, and who, by their joint counsels, arms, and efforts, fighting side by side throughout a long and bloody war, have nobly established their general liberty and independence.[22]

"This country and this people seem to have been made for each other," Jay wrote, calling his countrymen "a band of brethren." Even before the Constitution had been ratified, Jay regarded Americans as "one united people," "one connected country," "brethren," of common blood.[23]

But what held this "one united people" together — a common heritage, history, faith, language, manners, customs, and culture — today pulls us apart.

Are we united by language? Children in Chicago are taught in two hundred languages. Our fastest growing media are Spanish speaking. Half the 9 million in Los Angeles County speak a language other than English in their homes. Today's vile talk on radio and television, in the movies, magazines, and books, would have been an embarrassment in a marine barracks fifty years ago.

Are we united by faith? While 99 percent Protestant in 1789, we are now Protestant, Catholic, Jewish, Mormon, Muslim, Hindu, Buddhist, Taoist, Shintoist, Santería, Sikh, New Age, voodoo, agnostic, atheist, Rastafarian. The mention of the name of Jesus by the preachers President Bush chose to give invocations at his inauguration evoked cries of "insensitive," "divisive," "exclusionary." A *New Republic* editorial lashed out at these "crushing Christological thuds" from the inaugural stand.[24]

Many of the Christian churches have split asunder over abortion,   30
female bishops, homosexual clergy, and gay marriage.

---

[21]*John Jay:* Founding father (1745–1829) and first chief justice of the United States. [Eds.]

[22]James Madison, Alexander Hamilton, John Jay, *The Federalist Papers*, with an introduction by Willmore Kendall and George W. Carey (New Rochelle, N.Y.: Arlington House), p. 38.

[23]Ibid.

[24]Jeff Jacoby, "The Role of Religion in Government: Invoking Jesus at the Inauguration," *Boston Globe*, Feb. 2, 2001, p. A15; Patrick J. Buchanan, *The Death of the West* (New York: St. Martin's Press, 2002), p. 144.

In 2007, after a court battle by the American Civil Liberties Union, the U.S. Department of Veterans Affairs agreed to add the five-point star of the Wiccan neo-pagan religion to the list of thirty-eight "emblems of belief" allowed on VA grave markers. The thirty-eight include "symbols for Christianity, Buddhism, Islam and Judaism, as well as . . . for . . . Sufism Reoriented, Eckiankar and the Japanese faith Seicho-No-Ie."[25]

Are we united by a common culture? To the contrary. We are in a raging culture war in which peaceful coexistence is a myth.

In the nineteenth century, America was torn apart by slavery and the tariff. Those issues were settled in a civil war that resulted in 600,000 dead. Today, America is divided over issues of race, ethnicity, religion, language, culture, history, morality, the very things that once defined us and united us as a people and a nation.

Protestants and Catholics, a hundred years ago, disagreed passionately over whether beer, wine, and spirits were wicked. Today, we Americans disagree over whether annihilating 45 million unborn babies in the womb since *Roe v. Wade*[26] is a mark of progress or a monstrous national evil causing us to echo Jefferson, "I tremble for my country when I reflect that God is just."

In the 1960s, to do penance for all her sins, from Jamestown on, the United States threw open its doors to peoples of all colors, continents, and creeds. And today, the America of John F. Kennedy, 89 percent white and 10 percent of African descent, an essentially biracial country united by a common culture, creed, history, and tradition, is gone. We threw it away.

Today, America is twice as populous as in 1950 — with 300 million people. Instead of 1 to 2 million Hispanics, there are 45 million, with 102 million expected by 2050, concentrated in a Southwest that 58 percent of Mexicans say belongs to them. Our population is down to 67 percent European, and falling; 14.5 percent Hispanic and rising rapidly, 13 percent black and holding, and 4.5 percent Asian and rising. By 2040, Americans of European descent will be less than half the population, when, as President Bill Clinton told an audience of cheering California students, we will all belong to minorities. White Americans are already a minority in California, New Mexico, Texas, Hawaii. Twelve to 20 million illegal aliens are in the country. We may not have believed in diversity in the old America, but we are practicing it now. But has all this diversity made us a stronger nation than we were in the time of Eisenhower and Kennedy?

In October 2006, the *Financial Times* reported the findings of Robert Putnam, author of *Bowling Alone*, on diversity in America.

---

[25]Scott Bauer, "VA Allows Wiccan Symbols on Headstones," April 23, 2007, Associated Press. Yahoo.News.

[26]*Roe v. Wade:* The 1973 Supreme Court case that legalized abortion. [Eds.]

A bleak picture of the corrosive effects of ethnic diversity has been revealed in research by Harvard University's Robert Putnam, one of the world's most influential political scientists.

His research shows that the more diverse a community is, the less likely its inhabitants are to trust anyone — from their next-door neighbour to the mayor.

The core message . . . was that, "in the presence of diversity, we hunker down," he said. "We act like turtles. The effect of diversity is worse than had been imagined. And it's not just that we don't trust people who are not like us. In diverse communities, we don't trust people who do look like us."

Prof. Putnam found trust was lowest in Los Angeles, "the most diverse human habitation in human history. . . ."[27]

The city Professor Putnam references, Los Angeles, was the scene of the Academy Award–winning film *Crash*, which portrayed a feral zone in which whites, blacks, Asians, and Hispanics clashed violently again and again, as they could not understand one another or communicate with one another.

Wrote columnist John Leo, after perusing the report, "Putnam adds a crushing footnote: his findings 'may underestimate the real effect of diversity on social withdrawal.'"[28]

With another 100 million people anticipated in the United States by 2050, most of them immigrants and their children, legal and illegal, Putnam's findings are ominous. If the greater the diversity the greater the mistrust, Balkanization beckons — for all of us.

Is diversity a strength? In the ideology of modernity, yes. But history teaches otherwise. For how can racial diversity be a strength when racial diversity was behind the bloodiest war in U.S. history and has been the most polarizing issue among us ever since?

Our most divisive Supreme Court decision, *Dred Scott*, was about race. The War Between the States was about race. Reconstruction was about race. Segregation was about race. The riots in Harlem, Watts, Newark, Detroit, then Washington, DC, and a hundred other cities after the assassination of Dr. King were about race. The riot in Los Angeles following the Simi Valley jury's acquittal of the cops who beat Rodney King was about race. Forced busing, affirmative action, quotas, profiling are about race. The O. J. trial, the Tawana Brawley and Duke rape-case hoaxes, and the Don Imus affair[29] were

---

[27]John Lloyd, "Study Paints Bleak Picture of Ethnic Diversity," Oct. 8, 2006. FT.com

[28]John Leo, "Bowling with Our Own," *City Journal*, Summer 2007, vol. 17, no. 3.

[29]*"The O. J. trial . . . the Don Imus affair:"* In 1995, O. J. Simpson was found not guilty of murder after a long and highly publicized criminal trial; in 1986, a New York grand jury found that Tawana Brawley's claim that she was raped and brutalized by white men was fabricated; in 2006, another African American woman charged that she had been raped by a group of white Duke University lacrosse players, but the charges were dropped the following year; talk-radio host Don Imus was fired in 2007 after making racist comments about female African American basketball players. In each case, opinions tended to divide along racial lines. [Eds.]

about race. When Gunnar Myrdal wrote his classic *American Dilemma*, about the crisis of our democracy, the subject was — race.

All Americans believe slavery was evil and the denial of equal justice under law was wrong. But because they were wrong, does that make what we are doing — inviting the whole world to come to America — right or wise?

Today, tens of thousands of corporate and government bureaucrats monitor laws against discrimination and laws mandating integration in housing and employment. To achieve equality, Americans are sacrificing freedom. Police are ever on the lookout for hate crimes. Hardly a month passes without some controversy or crime rooted in race being forced through cable TV and talk radio onto the national agenda. How does all this make us a more united, stronger people?

Among the educated and affluent young, resegregation is in vogue.   45
Columnist Leo writes that at UCLA, racially separate graduations have become the norm. "The core reason," he writes, "is the obvious one."

> On campus, assimilation is a hostile force, the domestic version of American imperialism. On many campuses, identity-group training begins with separate freshman orientation programs for nonwhites, who arrive earlier and are encouraged to bond before the first Caucasian freshmen arrive. Some schools have separate orientations for gays as well. Administrations tend to foster separatism by arguing that bias is everywhere, justifying double standards that favor identity groups.[30]

Leo concludes on a note of despair, "As in so many areas of national life, the preposterous is now normal."[31]

Quo Vadis,[32] America?

Again, history teaches that multiethnic states are held together either by an authoritarian regime or a dominant ethnocultural core, or they are ever at risk of disintegration in ethnic conflict.

The Soviet Union, Czechoslovakia, and Yugoslavia, artificial nations all, disintegrated when the dictatorships collapsed.

In democracies it is an ethnocultural core that holds the country together. England created a United Kingdom of English, Scots, Welsh, and Irish, with England predominant. Now that Britain is no longer great, the core nations have begun to pull apart, to seek their old independence, as the English have begun to abandon the land they grew up in.

In "Vanishing England," in August 2007, columnist Cal Thomas   50
reported a startling fact: Between June 2005 and June 2006, 200,000 British

---

[30]John Leo, "Let the Segregation Commence . . . Separatist Graduations Proliferate at UCLA," June 13, 2007, *City Journal*, Spring 2007, vol. 17, no. 2.

[31]Ibid.

[32]*Quo Vadis:* Latin phrase meaning "Where are you going?" [Eds.]

citizens (the equivalent of a million Americans) left their country for good, as more than a half million legal immigrants and unknown thousands of illegals entered. "Britons give many reasons for leaving, but their stories share one commonality," Thomas wrote; "life in Britain has become unbearable for them."[33] There is the lawlessness and the constant threat of Muslim terror, but also

> the loss of a sense of Britishness, exacerbated by the growing refusal of public schools to teach the history and culture of the nation to the next generation. What it means to be British has been watered down in a plague of political correctness that has swept the country faster than hoof-and-mouth disease. Officials says they do not wish to "offend" others.[34]

Intellectuals deceive themselves if they believe the new trinity of their faith — democracy, equality, and diversity — can replace the old idea of what it meant to be a Briton, what it meant to be an Englishman.

In the thirteen North American colonies, the ethnocultural core was British-Protestant, with a smattering of Germans whose growing numbers alarmed Ben Franklin. After the wave of Irish from 1845 to 1849, and the steady German influx, and then the great wave from Southern and Eastern Europe between 1890 and 1920, America was no longer British-Protestant, but a European-Christian nation whose institutions, language, and culture remained British. Bismarck said the most important fact of the twentieth century would be that the North Americans spoke English. Indeed, that is why we fought on Britain's side in two world wars. Despite our eighteenth- and nineteenth-century quarrels and wars, the Brits were still "the cousins."

By 1960, 88.6 percent of our nation was of European stock and 95 percent Christian. America had never been a more united nation. African Americans had been assimilated into the Christian faith and national culture if not fully into society. While Jews, perhaps 4 percent of the population, were non-Christians, their parents or grandparents had come from European Christian nations.

Since the cultural revolution of the 1960s and the Immigration Act of 1965, however, the ethnocultural core has begun to dissolve. Secularism has displaced Christianity as the faith of the elites. The nation has entered a post-Christian era. There is no longer a unifying culture. Rather, we are fighting a culture war. And the European ethnic core is shrinking. From near 90 percent in 1960, it is down to 67 percent today, and will be less than 50 percent by 2040.

Here we come to the heart of the matter.

Quo Vadis, America? Where are you going?

55

---

[33]Cal Thomas, "Vanishing England," *Washington Times*, Aug. 29, 2007, p. A17.
[34]Ibid.

If we have no common faith and are divided by morality and culture, and are separated by ethnicity and race, what holds us together? Especially in light of Putnam's report that "diversity" dilutes "social capital," erodes community, and engenders mutual mistrust.

Realizing we are divided on the things that constitute a true nation — blood and soil, tradition and faith, history and heroes — intellectuals have sought to construct, in lieu of the real nation, the nation of the heart that is passing away, an artificial nation, a nation of the mind, an ideological nation, a creedal nation, united by a belief in the new trinity: diversity, democracy, and equality. As Christianity is purged from the public schools, this civil religion is taught in its stead. The dilemma of those who conjured up this civil religion and creedal nation, liberals and neoconservatives, is that it has no roots and does not touch the heart. Americans will not send their sons to fight and die for such watery abstractions.

ENGAGING THE TEXT

1. What kind of "revolution" (para. 17) does Buchanan believe has occurred in the United States and Britain in the fifty years between Queen Elizabeth's two visits to Jamestown? What illustrations of social change does he offer? How would you characterize his attitude toward these changes?

2. Why does Buchanan object to Queen Elizabeth's reference to the Jamestown colony as a meeting of "three great civilizations" (para. 7)? In his view, what is the real significance of Jamestown?

3. How does Buchanan differentiate between earlier groups of immigrants to the United States and those who have come since the 1965 Immigration Act? What effects does he believe immigrants are having on this country? Do you agree with his assessment? Why or why not?

4. Buchanan suggests that a nation based on "democracy, diversity, and equality" (para. 24) is unlikely to thrive or even to survive. Debate the merits of the logic and evidence he presents in support of his claim.

5. According to Buchanan, laws prohibiting discrimination, hate crimes, and segregated housing and employment require "sacrificing freedom" (para. 44) in order to attain greater equality. How and for whom is freedom restricted by such laws? Explain why you think the tradeoff is or is not worthwhile.

EXPLORING CONNECTIONS

6. Which of the models of ethnic relations described by George M. Fredrickson (p. 449) does Buchanan appear to endorse, which does he reject, and why? How would you describe his ideal vision of America?

7. How might Hua Hsu (p. 497) respond to Buchanan's assertion that "Among the educated and affluent young, resegregation is in vogue" (para. 45)? Role-play a debate between the two writers, then discuss which position you find more compelling, and why.

8. Buchanan mentions the practice, on some campuses, of holding separate orientations or graduation ceremonies for different "identity groups" (para. 45). If your school offers such functions, organize a group or whole class project and interview students, family members, and faculty who have attended one of these events. Pool your interview notes: do you find any consistency or patterns of response in your interviewees' comments about the event? Write a paper based on your research assessing the purpose and value of separate functions.

9. Buchanan quotes a newspaper article reporting on research done by political scientist Robert Putnam. Look up Putnam's original article, "*E Pluribus Unum*: Diversity and Community in the Twenty-first Century" (available online). Discuss the extent to which Putnam's research supports or challenges Buchanan's contention that diversity undermines social cohesion.

The Crossing

RUBÉN MARTÍNEZ

Although the United States prides itself on being a nation of immigrants, Americans' attitudes toward immigrants can be complex and contradictory. One recent poll showed opinion evenly divided over whether immigration helps or hurts the country, and while Americans overwhelmingly oppose illegal immigration, a consistent majority believes that undocumented workers fill jobs that citizens don't want. In this essay, adapted from his book Burning Sand *(2006), Rubén Martínez explores the cultural contradictions that arise in our representations of the border and of those who cross it searching for a better life. Martínez is an award-winning journalist and associate professor of creative writing at the University of Houston. His earlier books include* The Other Side: Notes from the New L.A., Mexico City and Beyond *(1993),* Crossing Over: A Mexican Family on the Migrant Trail *(2002), and* The New Americans *(2004).*

I am, again, on the line.

I've been drawn to it my entire life, beginning with frequent childhood jaunts across it to Tijuana and back — that leap from the monochrome suburban grids of Southern California to the Technicolor swirl of urban Baja California and back. I am an American today because of that line — and my parents' will to erase it with their desire.

I return to it again and again because I am from both sides. So for me, son of a mother who emigrated from El Salvador and a Mexican American father who spent his own childhood leaping back and forth, the line is a sieve. And it is a brick wall.

It defines me even as I defy it. It is a book without a clear beginning or end, and despite the fact that we refer to it as a "line," it is not even linear; to compare it to an actual book I'd have to invoke Cortázar's[1] *Hopscotch*. This line does and does not exist. It is a historical, political, economic, and cultural fact. It is a laughable, puny, meaningless thing. It is a matter of life and death. And it is a matter of representation. It is a very productive trope[2] in both American and Mexican pop.

The cowboy crosses the line to evade the law, because he imagines there is no law in the South. The immigrant crosses the line to embrace the future because he imagines there is no past in the North. Usually rendered by the River (the Rio Grande/Río Bravo — its name changes from one shore to the other), the line appears again and again in film and literature and music from both sides.

Just a few: Cormac McCarthy and Carlos Fuentes, Marty Robbins and Los Tigres del Norte, Sam Peckinpah and Emilio "El Indio" Fernández, Charles Bowden and Gloria Anzaldúa.[3]

In the Western, the moment of the crossing (the lawless gang fleeing the lawmen, their horses' hooves muddying the muddy waters all the more) is heralded by a stirring musical figure, brassy and percussive, leaping several tonal steps with each note. Once we're safely on the other side, the melodic strings of Mexico take over. The swaggering American will have his way with a Mexican señorita. The post-colonial[4] representations of borderlands literature — produced by Mexicans and Americans alike — have yet to soften the edges of this Spring Break syndrome. The whorehouse-across-the-river is there for a spurned Jake Gyllenhaal to get off with smooth-skinned brown boys in an otherwise liberatory *Brokeback Mountain*. Americans fictional and real always fantasize remaining in that racy, lazy South, but business or vengeance or a respectable marriage (the señorita is a puta, and

5

---

[1]*Cortázar:* Julio Florencio Cortázar (1914–1986), Argentine writer known for his short stories.

[2]*trope:* Figure of speech, such as metaphor.

[3]*Cormac McCarthy . . . Gloria Anzaldúa:* Cormac McCarthy (b. 1933), American novelist known for writing about the Southwest; Carlos Fuentes (b. 1928), Mexican essayist and fiction writer; Marty Robbins (1925–1982), American country-western singer; Los Tigres del Norte, Grammy-winning musical group formed in the late 1960s; Sam Peckinpah (1925–1984), American writer, director, and producer of western films and television series; Emilio Fernández (1903–1968), Mexican actor, writer, and director; Charles Bowden (b. 1945), American nonfiction writer and editor; Gloria Anzaldúa (1942–2004), Chicana writer and editor, best known for *Borderlands/La Frontera: The New Mestiza* (1987).

[4]*post-colonial:* Refers to the time following the independence of a colony; postcolonial literature often deals with the impact and legacy of colonial rule.

you can't marry a puto[5] on either side of the border) usually call the cowboy back home.

The Mexican or Chicano production is an inverted mirror of the same. The climax of Cheech Marin's *Born in East L.A.* (and dozens of Mexican B-movies) fulfills every migrant's fantasy of a joyous rush of brown humanity breaching a hapless Border Patrol, the victory of simple desire over military technology that occurs thousands of times a day on the border and feeds the paranoid vision of a reconquista[6] (which, a handful of crackpot Chicano nationalists notwithstanding, has been largely invented by the likes of the Minutemen,[7] white dudes with real economic insecurities unfortunately marinated in traditional borderlands racism).

Every step across the line is a breach of one code or another. Some of these laws are on the books; some have never been written down; some are matters more private than public.

I've been drawn to that line my whole life. Sometimes it's a metaphor. 10
Sometimes it's not.

This time, I am close to the line on the Buenos Aires National Wildlife Refuge in southern Arizona. It is a late August afternoon, a day that will not make headlines because there are no Minuteman patrols out hunting migrants, no Samaritans out seeking to save them. Nor is there, for the moment, any Border Patrol in the immediate vicinity. The land is as its public designation intended: a unique Sonoran desert habitat bizarrely and beautifully traversed by grasslands that are home to hundreds of unique species, including the endangered pronghorn antelope; it is also an outstanding birding location. But there are no birders in the dead of summer. The birders and the Minutemen have no wish to be out in temperatures that often rise to more than 110 degrees. (Some Samaritans who belong to a group called No More Deaths are indeed in the area, but the day's final patrol is probably heading back to the church-based group's campground near the town of Arivaca, which borders the refuge.)

I park at the Arivaca Creek trailhead. The interpretive sign tells of the possibility of hearing the "snap of vermilion flycatchers snatching insects on the wing." It also tells of another species, a relative newcomer to this "riparian ribbon":

"Visitors to BANWR are advised to remain alert for illegal activity associated with the presence of undocumented aliens (UDAs). There is also increased law enforcement activity by several agencies & organizations."

The bulleted visitor guidelines advise not to let the "UDAs approach you or your vehicle," a Homeland Security variation of "do not feed the wildlife."

[5]*puta/puto:* Whore.

[6]*reconquista:* Reconquest; much of the American southwest once belonged to Mexico.

[7]*Minutemen:* Self-appointed anti-immigrant guardians of the U.S. borders, particularly in the southwest. This contemporary group has adopted the name of the well-known American military unit that fought in the Revolutionary War.

The humidity from recent monsoonal deluges is stifling, making   15
100 degrees feel much hotter — and wetter. The reed-like branches of ocotil-
los have sprouted their tiny lime-green leaves, hiding their terrifically sharp
thorns. Moss flourishes on arroyo stones. Mosquitoes zip and whine through
the thick air. The desert jungle.

I tell myself that I'll take a short stroll; it's getting late. I climb the trail
from the creek bed, which is dominated by mammoth cottonwood trees,
south toward the red dirt hills — a trail used by birders and "UDAs" alike.
I can imagine an Audubon guide leading a gaggle of khaki-clad tourists
peering through binoculars, first at a vermilion flycatcher and then at a
Mexican rushing through a mesquite thicket, *Profugus mexicanus.* On the
line everything seems to attract its opposite or, more accurately, everything
seems to attract a thing that seems to have no relation to it, not parallel uni-
verses but saw-toothed eruptions, the crumpled metal of a collision. These
pairings occur not just near the political border — I am about 11 miles from
the boundary between the United States of America and the United States
of Mexico — but throughout the West. The border is no longer a line. Its
ink has diffused, an ambiguous veil across the entire territory.

Take the microcosm of the BANWR and its immediate vicinity. The
birders and the migrants, the Samaritans and the Minutemen. Hunters and
stoners. A "dude ranch" that charges city slickers up to $2,500 a week.
Retirees of modest means. Hellfire Protestants and Catholic penitents and
New Age vortex-seekers. Living here or passing through are Americans and
Native Americans and Mexicans and Mexican Americans and Mexican Indians, all of varying shades and accents, and there are Iranians and Guatemalans
and Chinese. This kind of situation was once affectionately referred to as
the Melting Pot. But no, it is more like speaking in tongues, speaking in
Babel.[8] The tower is crumbling. Melting pot meltdown.

I climb into the red hills as the sun nears the horizon. The sky at the
zenith is a stunning true blue. Reaching a saddle, I stumble on to a huge
migrant encampment — water jugs and backpacks and soiled underwear
and tubes of toothpaste and a brand-new denim jacket finely embroidered
with the name of a car club, opened cans of refried beans, bottles of men's
cologne, Tampax, tortillas curled hard in the heat. The things they carried
and left behind because 11 miles into the 50-mile hike they'd begun to realize the weight of those things, and they'd resolved to travel lighter. If something was to go wrong and they got lost and hyperthermic, they might even
begin stripping the clothes off their backs.

It is possible, too, that they've just broken camp; it is possible that they
saw me coming and are hiding behind one of the saddle's humps. I call out:

---

[8]*Babel:* Refers to an ancient city whose inhabitants tried to build a tower to heaven, which
God destroyed. He then made the people speak different languages so that they could no
longer work together.

¡No soy migra![9] This is a line from the script of the Samaritan Patrol, who, like the activists of No More Deaths, scour the desert searching for migrants in distress. They call out so that the fearful migrants might reveal themselves to receive food and water. It is a good line in the borderlands; I can't think of a better one. The real problem is, what am I going to say if someone actually responds? Buenas tardes señoras y señores, soy periodista y quería entervistarles, si es que no les es mucha molestia[10] . . . the journalist's lame introduction. Of course, they would have no reason to stop and speak to me — just the opposite. Indeed, why would they believe that I am not migra? And what if the smugglers are hauling a load of narcotics instead of humans? What if they are carrying weapons? This is not idle paranoia — this desert is armed with Mexican and American government-issue sidearms and the assault rifles of the paramilitary brigades on both sides. It is no surprise that there is bloodshed. Assault, rape, torture, and murder are common.

In any event, I have nothing to offer the trekkers; they have not run out   20
of water yet (though by tomorrow, after 15 or 20 miles, they well might). I am suddenly ashamed, as if I've intruded on a tremendously private moment, as if I've stumbled upon a couple in erotic embrace, bodies vulnerable to the harshness of the landscape and my gaze.

The sun sets, a funnel of gold joining cerulean canopy to blood-red earth. The land is completely still. I hold my breath. I realize that I want them to appear. I want to join them on the journey. The Audubon birder needs the vermilion flycatcher; right now, the writer needs a mojado.[11]

The migrant stumbles through the desert and I after him — he's on a pilgrimage and I'm in pursuit of him. Thus I am the literary migra: I will trap the mojado within the distorting borders of representation — a problem no writer has ever resolved. But aren't I also representing the origins of my own family's journey? Don't I also return to the line because it was upon my parents and grandparents' crossing it that I became possible?

¡No soy migra! I call out again.

There is no response. I sweat profusely, soaking through my UNM[12] Lobos T-shirt. Even my jeans hang heavy with moisture. Swatting mosquitoes, I retrace my footsteps back to the car.

I drive west in the dimming light. There is no one on this road but me.   25

Suddenly, a flutter in my peripheral vision. And now a figure stumbles out of the desert green to remind me that the border is, above all else, a moral

---

[9]*¡No soy migra!:* I'm not immigration ("la migra" refers generically to any branch or agent of the U.S. immigration authority, such as the Border Patrol).

[10]*Buenas tardes . . . mucha molestia:* Good afternoon, ladies and gentlemen, I'm a journalist and would like to interview you, if it's not too much trouble.

[11]*mojado:* Wetback.

[12]*UNM:* University of New Mexico.

U.S. Immigration Policy

line. He crawls from the brush and waves to me from the south side of the road. I stop the truck and roll down my window. He is a plaintive-looking fellow in his thirties, with thick black curls, a sweaty and smudged moon of a face. He has large brown eyes ringed by reddened whites. He is wearing a black T-shirt, blue jeans, and white tennis shoes. He carries a small blue vinyl bag.

¿Qué pasó? I ask. What happened?

With the first syllables of his response I can tell that he is from El Salvador. It is an accent that splits the difference between the typically muted tones of the Latin American provinces and the urgent desire of urban speech. It is the accent of my mother and her family; it is the Spanish accent I associate most with my childhood.

He says his name is Victor and that he had hiked about 12 miles into U.S. territory and could not make it any farther. His migrant crew had traveled all night and started up again late in the afternoon — just a couple of hours ago — but he'd become extremely fatigued and his vision began to blur.

Soy diabético,[13] says Victor.   30

Immediately I grab my phone to dial 911. It chirps a complaint: there is no signal. I think: Hypoglycemia, he needs something sweet. I think this because of the hundreds of plot lines in television dramas I've watched since I was a kid. In the backseat I have enough supplies to keep a dozen

[13]*Soy diabético:* I'm diabetic.

hikers going for at least a day in the desert — power bars, fruit cups, tins of Vienna sausages, peanut butter crackers, bags of trail mix, several bottles of Gatorade and gallon-jugs of drinking water. I expect him to tear ravenously into the strawberry-flavored bar I give him, but he eats it very slowly, taking modest sips of water between bites.

I flip open the cellphone again. Still no signal.

The particulars of a problem begin to form in my mind. Although I am not a medical expert, it is apparent that Victor needs urgent attention. But there is no way to contact medical personnel. The only option is to drive Victor to the nearest town, which is Arivaca, about 10 miles away. I become aware that by doing so, both Victor and I will be risking apprehension by the Border Patrol. More than one border denizen has told me that merely giving a migrant a ride can place one in a tenuous legal situation.

U.S. Code (Title 8, Chapter 12, Subchapter II, Part VIII, Section 1324) stipulates that an American citizen breaks the law when "knowing or in reckless disregard of the fact that an alien has come to, entered, or remains in the United States in violation of law, transports, or moves or attempts to transport or move such alien within the United States by means of trans-portation or otherwise, in furtherance of such violation of law."

The ethical calculation is simple enough. The law might contradict my 35 moral impulse, but the right thing to do is obvious. I also tell myself that in the event of apprehension by the Border Patrol, the truth of the situation will suffice. I am a Samaritan, after all, not a coyote. The truth will suffice at least for me, that is: I will go free, and Victor will be deported.

I tell Victor to get in the car.

The night falls fast. Soon the only things we can see through the bug-splattered windshield are the grainy blacktop ahead and the tangle of mesquites lining the road. I keep expecting more migrants to appear in the headlights and wave us down. At any given moment on this stretch of bor-derland there may be hundreds of migrants attempting passage.

It is a winding road and I'm a conservative driver, so there's time for small talk. Victor is much more animated now. He says he is feeling better.

He is from Soyapango, a working-class suburb of San Salvador that I remember well from my time in the country during the civil war, when it had the reputation of being a rebel stronghold. Right now, Victor is 1,800 miles from Soyapango.

¿Y a qué se dedica usted? He asks what I do for a living. 40

I reply that I am a writer, and then there is silence for about a quarter of a mile.

The Border Patrol will appear any minute now, I think to myself.

His large round eyes glisten, reflecting the light from my dashboard. More questions. ¿Cómo se llama el pueblo al que vamos? ¿Qué lejos queda Phoenix? ¿Qué lejos queda Los Angeles? What's the name of the town we're heading to? How far is Phoenix? How far is Los Angeles? Phoenix: where the coyote told him he'd be dropped off at a safe house. Los Angeles:

where his sister lives. He has memorized a phone number. It begins with the area code 818. Yes, he is feeling quite fine now, Victor says, and he realizes that I can't drive him all the way to L.A. But Phoenix is only 100 miles away. That's like from San Salvador to Guatemala City.

There is still no Border Patrol in sight. This does not make any sense. There are hundreds of agents on duty in what is called the Tucson Sector, the busiest and deadliest crossing along the U.S.–Mexico line. Is it the changing of the guard? Are the agents on dinner break? Are they tracking down Osama bin Laden, disguised as a Mexican day laborer?

Now, I realize, the problem is a bit different. Victor is apparently no longer experiencing a medical emergency, although I cannot be absolutely certain of this. The law is ambiguous on the matter of Samaritan aid. I am aware of a pending federal court case against two young No More Deaths activists, Shanti Sellz and Daniel Strauss, who recently attempted to conduct a "medical evacuation" by taking two apparently ailing migrants directly to a hospital rather than handing them over to the BP. Federal prosecutors decided that the activists were transporting the migrants "in furtherance" of their illegal presence in the U.S. and indicted the pair on several felony charges. The activists and their supporters say that the ethical imperative of offering aid in the context of a medical emergency supersedes the letter of immigration law — a moral argument without juridical precedent on the border. The activists are clearly hoping to set one.

But the law is decidedly less ambiguous about what Victor is now asking me to do. If I drive him to Phoenix and put him in touch with his sister, I will clearly have provided transportation "in furtherance of" his illegal presence. He is no longer asking for medical aid.

The air-conditioning chills the sweat on the wet rag that my Lobos T-shirt has become. It seems that there are now several possibilities, several problems. It seems that there are many right and wrong things to do. The scenarios tumble through my mind.

Risk the trip to Phoenix. (Where is that BP checkpoint on I-19? Is it north or south of Arivaca Junction? I look into the sky — are there thunderheads? Checkpoints often close when it rains.) What if Victor is actually still sick and on the verge of a seizure — shouldn't I turn him over to the BP? But will the BP give him the medical care he needs? And, not least of all, what of Victor's human right to escape the living hell that is Soyapango (poverty and crime there today are taking nearly as much a toll as the civil war did)? If Victor has that essential human right to seek a better life for himself and his family, what is my moral duty when he literally stumbles into my life on the border? Am I willing to risk federal charges to fulfill an ethical responsibility that I decide trumps the laws of my country?

I slow down to a crawl as we near the outskirts of Arivaca, a town famed for a 60s-era commune and the weed-growing hippies that hung on long past the Summer of Love. It will all end here in Arivaca, I tell myself. The BP trucks will be lined up outside the one small grocery store in town, or

45

maybe up at the Grubsteak, which is presided over by a gregarious Mexican who waits on the graying hippies and handful of outsider artists who arrived years ago thinking they'd found the grail of Western living, long before chaos came to the border.

But when I pull up to the store, there is only the heat of the night and a   50
flickering street lamp gathering a swarm of moths. I notice a few local kids — white, shaved heads — standing by a pay phone. Now it occurs to me that there is a possible solution to this mess. In the rush of events, I'd forgotten that No More Deaths had a camp about four miles east of town. Because it is a faith-based organization, the camp was baptized "Ark of the Covenant." Since 2004, No More Deaths had recruited student activists — like Sellz and Strauss, the pair under federal indictment — from around the country to come to southern Arizona and walk the lethal desert trails. There would be activists there with more experience than I in these matters. They could easily consult the doctors and lawyers supporting their cause to deter- mine the right thing to do — or at least their version of the right thing.

I walk into the store. I tell Victor to stay inside the car. The clerk behind the counter is reading the newspaper, head cupped in her hands and elbows leaning on the food scale next to the cash register.

I briefly blurt out my story.

She asks me where Victor is. In the car, I say. Immediately she tells me that the BP can impound my vehicle, they can file charges. She tells me that she can call the Border Patrol for me. She seems to know exactly what the right thing to do is. The only thing to do. She places her hand on the phone.

A few seconds later I'm back in the heat of the night and I ask the first passerby, a young blond woman named Charity, for directions to the Ark of the Covenant. Do you have a map? She asks. She means a local map. No. Now she is drawing one on a page of my reporter's notebook. She draws many lines. Here there is a hill, she says; here, a llama ranch. She says a quarter of a mile, then a couple of miles, then three-quarters of a mile and left and right and across. It is a moonless night. Good luck, she says.

I climb back in the truck, I turn the ignition. I give Victor the notebook   55
with the map. In a minute we're out of town and on to the first dirt road of the route. Still no BP in sight. The map is accurate. I pass by the llama ranch, barely catching the sign in the dimness.

For several minutes I ride on impulse — no thoughts at all. But as I turn left just where Charity told me to, a thought powerful enough to take my foot off the gas seizes me.

I can't ride into the Ark of the Covenant with Victor in the truck. What I'd forgotten in my haste was the political reality of the moment: the feds had called No More Deaths' bluff and were going after them in court. I remem- bered hearing from a couple of activists that before and since the arrests of Sellz and Strauss, there had been constant BP surveillance on the encampment.

If the BP were to see me dropping off Victor at the camp now, would they, could they use this as more evidence of running a de facto smuggling operation? Perhaps this could strengthen the federal case against Sellz and Strauss. And what if there was a conviction? And what if a judge ordered the camp closed?

Now I was weighing Victor's singular rights and desire and the goals and strategy of an activist movement that had helped dozens of migrants in distress over the past two summers and that could continue to help many more. The problem was, my cellphone was dead. The problem was my desire to capture a mojado. The problem was, I didn't have enough information to know what the "right" decision was. I had placed myself on the line, and I wasn't ready for what it would ask of me.

I slow down, and the dust kicked up by the tires envelops the truck. Victor and I turn to each other.   60

Fifteen minutes later, I pull up, for the second time, to the convenience store in Arivaca. The clerk is still reading the paper. I tell her to call the Border Patrol. I tell her that Victor has diabetes and symptoms of hypoglycemia.

She picks up the phone: "We've got a diabetic UDA."

I walk out to Victor, who is standing next to my truck, staring into the black desert night. He asks me again how far it is to Tucson. I tell him that he'll die if he tries to hike.

I tell myself that Victor is probably living and working somewhere in America now. It is quite possible that he attempted to cross over again after his apprehension by the Border Patrol, and that he succeeded. This thought does and does not comfort me.

I tell myself I did the right thing. I tell myself I did the wrong thing. I tell myself that every decision on the line is like that, somewhere in between.   65

ENGAGING THE TEXT

1. What different meanings — personal, geographic, cultural, metaphoric — does Martínez associate with the border? Why does he emphasize this complexity? In what ways is he "on the line" (para. 1)?

2. How does Martínez's role as a journalist influence his decisions and actions? To what extent does his family history affect his thinking and behavior?

3. Martínez refers to trapping his subject "within the distorting borders of representation" (para. 22). How does he represent or misrepresent Victor? How might Victor represent himself differently?

4. What is the effect of Martínez's use of the derogatory word "mojado" in the passage describing his search for an undocumented immigrant to interview? Why do you think he chooses to use the term here and in paragraph 59 and not elsewhere in the essay?

5. Debate the ethical dilemma Martínez faces: Does the moral imperative to obtain medical assistance for Victor outweigh Martínez's legal obligation to turn him over to the Border Patrol? Write a journal entry explaining what you would have done in Martínez's place, and why. Share your responses in class.

Exploring Connections

6. Which of George M. Fredrickson's models of ethnic relations (p. 449) appear to be operating along the U.S.–Mexican border as Martínez describes it? Do you see evidence of more than one model coexisting?

7. How might Martínez respond to the depiction of immigrants in the preceding essay by Patrick J. Buchanan? Write an imaginary letter from Martínez to Buchanan expressing these views.

8. In "U.S. Immigration Policy" (p. 478) what is the cartoonist suggesting about American attitudes and laws regarding immigration? To what extent does Martínez share the cartoonist's view? How does his perspective differ?

Extending the Critical Context

9. Write an essay comparing Martínez's representation of the U.S.–Mexican border to another depiction that you are familiar with in music, film, or literature.

10. Work in groups to research the Minutemen and No More Deaths. What is the history and purpose of each organization? What appear to be their primary values?

11. Examine the language used by news reporters, politicians, and pro- and anti-immigrant groups in discussing immigration issues: How are documented and undocumented immigrants portrayed? What metaphors are used to describe the number of immigrants entering the United States (e.g., flood) and what are their implications?

Assimilation

Sherman Alexie

Sherman Alexie won the 1999 World Heavyweight Championship Poetry Bout by improvising, in thirty seconds, a poetic riff on the word "dumbass." The poem, according to one reporter, was both humorous and poignant. Alexie's performance captured his sense of humor, his inventiveness, and his ability to wring insight from unlikely material. True to form, this story — about a Coeur d'Alene Indian woman who decides to cheat on her white husband — is a comedy that poses serious questions about race, class, culture, deception, and love. Alexie (b. 1966) grew up on the Spokane Indian Reservation in Washington State, but attended a high school where, in his words, he was "the only Indian . . . except the school mascot." He claims not to believe in writer's block, and has the publications to prove it: four novels, Reservation Blues *(1995),* Indian Killer *(1996),* Flight *(2007), and* The

Absolutely True Diary of a Part-Time Indian *(2007); fourteen volumes of poems and short stories; many essays and reviews. He coauthored the script for the award-winning film* Smoke Signals *(1998) and both wrote and directed* The Business of Fancydancing *(2002).* "Assimilation" *comes from Alexie's short story collection* The Toughest Indian in the World *(2000).*

Regarding love, marriage, and sex, both Shakespeare and Sitting Bull knew the only truth: treaties get broken. Therefore, Mary Lynn wanted to have sex with any man other than her husband. For the first time in her life, she wanted to go to bed with an Indian man only because he was Indian. She was a Coeur d'Alene Indian married to a white man; she was a wife who wanted to have sex with an indigenous stranger. She didn't care about the stranger's job or his hobbies, or whether he was due for a Cost of Living raise, or owned ten thousand miles of model railroad track. She didn't care if he was handsome or ugly, mostly because she wasn't sure exactly what those terms meant anymore and how much relevance they truly had when it came to choosing sexual partners. Oh, she'd married a very handsome man, there was no doubt about that, and she was still attracted to her husband, to his long, graceful fingers, to his arrogance and utter lack of fear in social situations — he'd say anything to anybody — but lately, she'd been forced to concentrate too hard when making love to him. If she didn't focus completely on him, on the smallest details of his body, then she would drift away from the bed and float around the room like a bored angel. Of course, all this made her feel like a failure, especially since it seemed that her husband had yet to notice her growing disinterest. She wanted to be a good lover, wife, and partner, but she'd obviously developed some form of sexual dyslexia or had picked up a mutant, contagious, and erotic strain of Attention Deficit Disorder. She felt baffled by the complications of sex. She haunted the aisles of bookstores and desperately paged through every book in the self-help section and studied every diagram and chart in the human sensuality encyclopedias. She wanted answers. She wanted to feel it again, whatever *it* was.

A few summers ago, during Crow Fair, Mary Lynn had been standing in a Montana supermarket, in the produce aisle, when a homely white woman, her spiky blond hair still wet from a trailer-house shower, walked by in a white t-shirt and blue jeans, and though Mary Lynn was straight — having politely declined all three lesbian overtures thrown at her in her life — she'd felt a warm breeze pass through her DNA in that ugly woman's wake, and had briefly wanted to knock her to the linoleum and do beautiful things to her. Mary Lynn had never before felt such lust — in Montana, of all places, for a white woman who was functionally illiterate and underemployed! — and had not since felt that sensually about any other woman or man.

Who could explain such things, these vagaries of love? There were many people who would blame Mary Lynn's unhappiness, her dissatisfaction, on her ethnicity. God, she thought, how simple and earnest was that particular bit of psychotherapy! Yes, she was most certainly a Coeur d'Alene — she'd grown up on the rez, had been very happy during her time there, and had left without serious regrets or full-time enemies — but that wasn't the only way to define her. She wished that she could be called Coeur d'Alene as a description, rather than as an excuse, reason, prescription, placebo, prediction, or diminutive. She only wanted to be understood as eccentric and complicated!

Her most cherished eccentricity: when she was feeling her most lonely, she'd put one of the Big Mom Singers' powwow CDs on the stereo (*I'm not afraid of death, hey, ya, hey, death is my cousin, hey, ya, ha, ha*) and read from Emily Dickinson's poetry (*Because I could not stop for Death — /He kindly stopped for me —).*

Her most important complication: she was a woman in a turbulent marriage that was threatening to go bad, or had gone bad and might get worse.   5

Yes, she was a Coeur d'Alene woman, passionately and dispassionately, who wanted to cheat on her white husband because he was white. She wanted to find an anonymous lover, an Indian man who would fade away into the crowd when she was done with him, a man whose face could appear on the back of her milk carton. She didn't care if he was the kind of man who knew the punch lines to everybody's dirty jokes, or if he was the kind of man who read Zane Grey before he went to sleep, or if he was both of those men simultaneously. She simply wanted to find the darkest Indian in Seattle — the man with the greatest amount of melanin — and get naked with him in a cheap motel room. Therefore, she walked up to a flabby Lummi Indian man in a coffee shop and asked him to make love to her.

"Now," she said. "Before I change my mind."

He hesitated for a brief moment, wondering why he was the chosen one, and then took her by the hand. He decided to believe he was a handsome man.

"Don't you want to know my name?" he asked before she put her hand over his mouth.

"Don't talk to me," she said. "Don't say one word. Just take me to the   10
closest motel and fuck me."

The obscenity bothered her. It felt staged, forced, as if she were an actress in a three-in-the-morning cable-television movie. But she was acting, wasn't she? She was not an adulteress, was she?

Why exactly did she want to have sex with an Indian stranger? She told herself it was because of pessimism, existentialism, even nihilism, but those reasons — *those words* — were a function of her vocabulary and not of her motivations. If forced to admit the truth, or some version of the truth, she'd testify she was about to go to bed with an Indian stranger because she wanted to know how it would feel. After all, she'd slept with a white stranger in her life, so why not include a Native American? Why not practice a carnal form of affirmative action? By God, her infidelity was a political act! Rebellion, resistance, revolution!

In the motel room, Mary Lynn made the Indian take off his clothes first. Thirty pounds overweight, with purple scars crisscrossing his pale chest and belly, he trembled as he undressed. He wore a wedding ring on his right hand. She knew that some Europeans wore their wedding bands on the right hand — so maybe this Indian was married to a French woman — but Mary Lynn also knew that some divorced Americans wore rings on their right hands as symbols of pain, of mourning. Mary Lynn didn't care if he was married or not, or whether he shared custody of the sons and daughters, or whether he had any children at all. She was grateful that he was plain and desperate and lonely.

Mary Lynn stepped close to him, took his hand, and slid his thumb into her mouth. She sucked on it and felt ridiculous. His skin was salty and oily, the taste of a working man. She closed her eyes and thought about her husband, a professional who had his shirts laundered. In one hour, he was going to meet her at a new downtown restaurant.

She walked a slow, tight circle around the Indian. She stood behind   15
him, reached around his thick waist, and held his erect penis. He moaned and she decided that she hated him. She decided to hate all men. Hate, hate, hate, she thought, and then let her hate go.

She was lovely and intelligent, and had grown up with Indian women who were more lovely and more intelligent, but who also had far less ambition and mendacity. She'd once read in a book, perhaps by Primo Levi or Elie Wiesel, that the survivors of the Nazi death camps were the Jews who lied, cheated, murdered, stole, and subverted. You must remember, said Levi or Wiesel, that the best of us did not survive the camps. Mary Lynn felt the same way about the reservation. Before she'd turned ten, she'd attended the funerals of seventeen good women — the best of the Coeur d'Alenes — and had read about the deaths of eighteen more good women since she'd left the rez. But what about the Coeur d'Alene men — those liars, cheats, and thieves — who'd survived, even thrived? Mary Lynn wanted nothing to do with them, then or now. As a teenager, she'd dated only white boys. As an adult, she'd only dated white men. God, she hated to admit it, but white men — her teachers, coaches, bosses, and lovers — had always been more dependable than the Indian men in her life. White men had rarely disappointed her, but they'd never surprised her either. White men were neutral, she thought, just like Belgium! And when has Belgium ever been sexy? When has Belgium caused a grown woman to shake with fear and guilt? She didn't want to feel Belgian; she wanted to feel dangerous.

In the cheap motel room, Mary Lynn breathed deeply. The Indian smelled of old sweat and a shirt worn twice before washing. She ran her finger along the ugly scars on his belly and chest. She wanted to know the scars' creation story — she hoped this Indian man was a warrior with a history of knife fighting — but she feared he was only carrying the transplanted heart and lungs of another man. She pushed him onto the bed, onto the scratchy comforter. She'd once read that scientists had examined a hotel-room comforter and discovered four hundred and thirty-two different samples of sperm. God, she thought, those scientists obviously had too much time on their hands and, in the end, had failed to ask the most important questions: Who left the samples? Spouses, strangers? Were these exchanges of money, tenderness, disease? Was there love?

"This has to be quick," she said to the stranger beside her.

Jeremiah, her husband, was already angry when Mary Lynn arrived thirty minutes late at the restaurant and he nearly lost all of his self-control when they were asked to wait for the next available table. He often raged at strangers, though he was incredibly patient and kind with their four children. Mary Lynn had seen that kind of rage in other white men when their wishes and desires were ignored. At ball games, in parking lots, and especially in airports, white men demanded to receive the privileges whose very existence they denied. White men could be so predictable, thought Mary Lynn. She thought: O, Jeremiah! O, season ticket holder! O, monthly parker! O, frequent flyer! She dreamed of him out there, sitting in the airplane with eighty-seven other white men wearing their second-best suits, all of them traveling toward small rooms in the Ramadas, Radissons, and sometimes the Hyatts, where they all separately watched the same pay-per-view porno that showed everything except penetration. What's the point of porno without graphic penetration? Mary Lynn knew it only made these lonely men feel all that more lonely. And didn't they deserve better, these white salesmen and middle managers, these twenty-first-century Willy Lomans,[1] who only wanted to be better men than their fathers had been? Of course, thought Mary Lynn, these sons definitely deserved better — they were smarter and more tender and generous than all previous generations of white American men — but they'd never receive their just rewards, and thus their anger was justified and banal.

"Calm down," Mary Lynn said to her husband as he continued to rage   20
at the restaurant hostess.

Mary Lynn said those two words to him more often in their marriage than any other combination of words.

"It could be twenty, thirty minutes," said the hostess. "Maybe longer."

"We'll wait outside," said Jeremiah. He breathed deeply, remembering some mantra that his therapist had taught him.

Mary Lynn's mantra: I cheated on my husband, I cheated on my husband.

"We'll call your name," said the hostess, a white woman who was tired   25
of men no matter what their color. "When."

---

[1]*Willy Lomans:* Willy Loman, the protagonist of Arthur Miller's play *Death of a Salesman,* is an ordinary but driven man struggling to find meaning in his work and family life; he becomes a symbol of the problems and despair faced by the "little guy" in an increasingly impersonal world.

Their backs pressed against the brick wall, their feet crossed on the sidewalk, on a warm Seattle evening, Mary Lynn and Jeremiah smoked faux cigarettes filled with some foul-tasting, overwhelmingly organic herb substance. For years they had smoked unfiltered Camels, but had quit after all four of their parents had simultaneously suffered through at least one form of cancer. Mary Lynn had called them the Mormon Tabernacle Goddamn Cancer Choir, though none of them was Mormon and all of them were altos. With and without grace, they had all survived the radiation, chemotherapy, and in-hospital cable-television bingo games, with their bodies reasonably intact, only to resume their previously self-destructive habits. After so many nights spent in hospital corridors, waiting rooms, and armchairs, Mary Lynn and Jeremiah hated doctors, all doctors, even the ones on television, especially the ones on television. United in their obsessive hatred, Mary Lynn and Jeremiah resorted to taking vitamins, eating free-range chicken, and smoking cigarettes rolled together and marketed by six odoriferous white liberals in Northern California.

As they waited for a table, Mary Lynn and Jeremiah watched dozens of people arrive and get seated immediately.

"I bet they don't have reservations," he said.

"I hate these cigarettes," she said.

"Why do you keep buying them?"   30

"Because the cashier at the health-food store is cute."

"You're shallow."

"Like a mud puddle."

Mary Lynn hated going out on weeknights. She hated driving into the city. She hated waiting for a table. Standing outside the downtown restaurant, desperate to hear their names, she decided to hate Jeremiah for a few seconds. Hate, hate, hate, she thought, and then she let her hate go. She wondered if she smelled like sex, like indigenous sex, and if a white man could recognize the scent of an enemy. She'd showered, but the water pressure had been weak and the soap bar too small.

"Let's go someplace else," she said.   35

"No. Five seconds after we leave, they'll call our names."

"But we won't know they called our names."

"But I'll feel it."

"It must be difficult to be psychic and insecure."

"I knew you were going to say that."   40

Clad in leather jackets and black jeans, standing inches apart but never quite touching, both handsome to the point of distraction, smoking crappy cigarettes that appeared to be real cigarettes, they could have been the subjects of a Schultz photograph or a Runnette poem.

The title of the photograph: "Infidelity."

The title of the poem: "More Infidelity."

Jeremiah's virtue was reasonably intact, though he'd recently been involved in a flirtatious near-affair with a coworker. At the crucial moment, when the last button was about to be unbuttoned, when consummation was just a fingertip away, Jeremiah had pushed his potential lover away and said I can't, I just can't, I love my marriage. He didn't admit to love for his spouse, partner, wife. No, he confessed his love for marriage, for the blessed union, for the legal document, for the shared mortgage payments, and for their four children.

Mary Lynn wondered what would happen if she grew pregnant with   45
the Lummi's baby. Would this full-blood baby look more Indian than her half-blood sons and daughters?

"Don't they know who I am?" she asked her husband as they waited outside the downtown restaurant. She wasn't pregnant; there would be no paternity tests, no revealing of great secrets. His secret: he was still in love with a white woman from high school he hadn't seen in decades. What Mary Lynn knew: he was truly in love with the idea of a white woman from a mythical high school, with a prom queen named *If Only* or a homecoming princess named *My Life Could Have Been Different*.

"I'm sure they know who you are," he said. "That's why we're on the wait list. Otherwise, we'd be heading for McDonald's or Denny's."

"Your kinds of places."

"Dependable. The Big Mac you eat in Hong Kong or Des Moines tastes just like the Big Mac in Seattle."

"Sounds like colonialism to me."   50

"Colonialism ain't all bad."

"Put that on a bumper sticker."

This place was called Tan Tan, though it would soon be trendy enough to go by a nickname: Tan's. Maybe Tan's would become T's, and then T's would be identified only by a slight turn of the head or a certain widening of the eyes. After that, the downhill slide in reputation would be inevitable, whether or not the culinary content and quality of the restaurant remained exactly the same or improved. As it was, Tan Tan was a pan-Asian restaurant whose ownership and chefs — head, sauce, and line — were white, though most of the wait staff appeared to be one form of Asian or another.

"Don't you hate it?" Jeremiah asked. "When they have Chinese waiters in sushi joints? Or Korean dishwashers in a Thai noodle house?"

"I hadn't really thought about it," she said.   55

"No, think about it, these restaurants, these Asian restaurants, they hire Asians indiscriminately because they think white people won't be able to tell the difference."

"White people can't tell the difference."

"I can."

"Hey, Geronimo, you've been hanging around Indians too long to be white."

"Fucking an Indian doesn't make me Indian."   60

"So, that's what we're doing now? Fucking?"

"You have a problem with fucking?"

"No, not with the act itself, but I do have a problem with your sexual thesaurus."

Mary Lynn and Jeremiah had met in college, when they were still called Mary and Jerry. After sleeping together for the first time, after her first orgasm and his third, Mary had turned to Jerry and said, with absolute seriousness: If this thing is going to last, we have to stop the end rhyme. She had majored in Milton and Blake. He'd been a chemical engineer since the age of seven, with the degree being only a matter of formality, so he'd had plenty of time to wonder how an Indian from the reservation could be so smart. He still wondered how it had happened, though he'd never had the courage to ask her.

Now, a little more than two decades after graduating with a useless   65
degree, Mary Lynn worked at Microsoft for a man named Dickinson. Jeremiah didn't know his first name, though he hoped it wasn't Emery, and had never met the guy, and didn't care if he ever did. Mary Lynn's job title and responsibilities were vague, so vague that Jeremiah had never asked her to elaborate. She often worked sixty-hour weeks and he didn't want to reward that behavior by expressing an interest in what specific tasks she performed for Bill Gates.

Waiting outside Tan Tan, he and she could smell ginger, burned rice, beer.

"Are they ever going to seat us?" she asked.

"Yeah, don't they know who you are?"

"I hear this place discriminates against white people."

"Really?"   70

"Yeah, I heard once, these lawyers, bunch of white guys in Nordstrom's suits, had to wait, like, two hours for a table."

"Were those billable hours?"

"It's getting hard for a white guy to find a place to eat."

"Damn affirmative action is what it is."

Their first child had been an accident, the result of a broken condom and   75
a missed birth control pill. They named her Antonya, Toni for short. The second and third children, Robert and Michael, had been on purpose, and the fourth, Ariel, came after Mary Lynn thought she could no longer get pregnant.

Toni was fourteen, immature for her age, quite beautiful and narcissistic, with her translucent skin, her long blond hair, and eight-ball eyes. Botticelli eyes, she bragged after taking an Introduction to Art class. She never bothered to tell anybody she was Indian, mostly because nobody asked.

Jeremiah was quite sure that his daughter, his Antonya, had lost her virginity to the pimply quarterback of the junior varsity football team. He found the thought of his daughter's adolescent sexuality both curious and disturbing. Above all else, he believed that she was far too special to sleep with a cliché, let alone a junior varsity cliché.

Three months out of every year, Robert and Michael were the same age. Currently, they were both eleven. Dark-skinned, with their mother's black hair, strong jawline, and endless nose, they looked Indian, very Indian.

Robert, who had refused to be called anything other than Robert, was the smart boy, a math prodigy, while Mikey was the basketball player.

When Mary Lynn's parents called from the reservation, they always asked after the boys, always invited the boys out for the weekend, the holidays, and the summer, and always sent the boys more elaborate gifts than they sent the two girls.

When Jeremiah had pointed out this discrepancy to Mary Lynn, she   80
had readily agreed, but had made it clear that his parents also paid more attention to the boys. Jeremiah never mentioned it again, but had silently vowed to love the girls a little more than he loved the boys.

As if love were a thing that could be quantified, he thought.

He asked himself: What if I love the girls more because they look more like me, because they look more white than the boys?

Towheaded Ariel was two, and the clay of her personality was just beginning to harden, but she was certainly petulant and funny as hell, with the ability to sleep in sixteen-hour marathons that made her parents very nervous. She seemed to exist in her own world, enough so that she was periodically monitored for incipient autism. She treated her siblings as if they somehow bored her, and was the kind of kid who could stay alone in her crib for hours, amusing herself with all sorts of personal games and imaginary friends.

Mary Lynn insisted that her youngest daughter was going to be an artist, but Jeremiah didn't understand the child, and despite the fact that he was her father and forty-three years older, he felt inferior to Ariel.

He wondered if his wife was ever going to leave him because he was   85
white.

When Tan Tan's doors swung open, laughter and smoke rolled out together.

"You got another cigarette?" he asked.

"Quit calling them cigarettes. They're not cigarettes. They're more like rose bushes. Hell, they're more like the shit that rose bushes grow in."

"You think we're going to get a table?"

"By the time we get a table, this place is going to be very unpopular."   90

"Do you want to leave?"

"Do you?"

"If you do."

"We told the baby-sitter we'd be home by ten."

They both wished that Toni were responsible enough to baby-sit her   95
siblings, rather than needing to be sat along with them.

"What time is it?" she asked.

"Nine."

"Let's go home."

Last Christmas, when the kids had been splayed out all over the living room, buried to their shoulders in wrapping paper and expensive toys, Mary Lynn had studied her children's features, had recognized most of her face in her sons' faces and very little of it in her daughters', and had decided, quite facetiously, that the genetic score was tied.

We should have another kid, she'd said to Jeremiah, so we'll know if   100
this is a white family or an Indian family.

It's a family family, he'd said, without a trace of humor.

Only a white guy would say that, she'd said.

Well, he'd said, you married a white guy.

The space between them had grown very cold at that moment, in that silence, and perhaps one or both of them might have said something truly destructive, but Ariel had started crying then, for no obvious reason, relieving both parents of the responsibility of finishing that particular conversation. During the course of their relationship, Mary Lynn and Jeremiah had often discussed race as a concept, as a foreign country they occasionally visited, or as an enemy that existed outside their house, as a destructive force they could fight against as a couple, as a family. But race was also a constant presence, a houseguest and permanent tenant who crept around all the rooms in their shared lives, opening drawers, stealing utensils and small articles of clothing, changing the temperature.

Before he'd married Mary Lynn, Jeremiah had always believed there   105
was too much talk of race, that white people were all too willing to be racist and that brown people were just as willing and just as racist. As a rational scientist, he'd known that race was primarily a social construct, illusionary, but as the husband of an Indian woman and the father of Indian children, he'd since learned that race, whatever its construction, was real. Now, there were plenty of white people who wanted to eliminate the idea of race, to cast it aside as an unwanted invention, but it was far too late for that. If white people are the mad scientists who created race, thought Jeremiah, then we created race so we could enslave black people and kill Indians, and now race has become the Frankenstein monster that has grown beyond our control. Though he'd once been willfully blind, Jeremiah had learned how to recognize that monster in the faces of whites and Indians and in their eyes.

Long ago, Jeremiah and Mary Lynn had both decided to challenge those who stared by staring back, by flinging each other against walls and tongue-kissing with pornographic élan.

Long ago, they'd both decided to respond to any questions of why, how, what, who, or when by simply stating: Love is Love. They knew it was romantic bullshit, a simpleminded answer only satisfying for simpleminded people, but it was the best available defense.

Listen, Mary Lynn had once said to Jeremiah, asking somebody why they fall in love is like asking somebody why they believe in God.

You start asking questions like that, she had added, and you're either going to start a war or you're going to hear folk music.

You think too much, Jeremiah had said, rolling over and falling asleep.   110

Then, in the dark, as Jeremiah slept, Mary Lynn had masturbated while fantasizing about an Indian man with sundance scars on his chest.

After they left Tan Tan, they drove a sensible and indigenous Ford Taurus over the 520 bridge, back toward their house in Kirkland, a five-bedroom rancher only ten blocks away from the Microsoft campus. Mary Lynn walked to work. That made her feel privileged. She estimated there were twenty-two American Indians who had ever felt even a moment of privilege.

"We still have to eat," she said as she drove across the bridge. She felt strange. She wondered if she was ever going to feel normal again.

"How about Taco Bell drive-thru?" he asked.

"You devil, you're trying to get into my pants, aren't you?"   115

Impulsively, he dropped his head into her lap and pressed his lips against her black-jeaned crotch. She yelped and pushed him away. She wondered if he could smell her, if he could smell the Lummi Indian. Maybe he could, but he seemed to interpret it as something different, as something meant for him, as he pushed his head into her lap again. What was she supposed to do? She decided to laugh, so she did laugh as she pushed his face against her pubic bone. She loved the man for reasons she could not always explain. She closed her eyes, drove in that darkness, and felt dangerous.

Halfway across the bridge, Mary Lynn slammed on the brakes, not because she'd seen anything — her eyes were still closed — but because she'd felt something. The car skidded to a stop just inches from the bumper of a truck that had just missed sliding into the row of cars stopped ahead of it.

"What the hell is going on?" Jeremiah asked as he lifted his head from her lap.

"Traffic jam."

"Jesus, we'll never make it home by ten. We better call."   120

"The cell phone is in the glove."

Jeremiah dialed the home number but received only a busy signal.

"Toni must be talking to her boyfriend," she said.

"I don't like him."

"He doesn't like you."   125

"What the hell is going on? Why aren't we moving?"

"I don't know. Why don't you go check?"

Jeremiah climbed out of the car.

"I was kidding," she said as he closed the door behind him.

He walked up to the window of the truck ahead of him.   130

"You know what's going on?" Jeremiah asked the truck driver.

"Nope."

Jeremiah walked farther down the bridge. He wondered if there was a disabled car ahead, what the radio liked to call a "blocking accident." There was also the more serious "injury accident" and the deadly "accident with fatality involved." He had to drive this bridge ten times a week. The commute. White men had invented the commute, had deepened its meaning, had diversified its complications, and now spent most of the time trying to shorten it, reduce it, lessen it.

In the car, Mary Lynn wondered why Jeremiah always found it necessary to insert himself into every situation. He continually moved from the
passive to the active. The man was kinetic. She wondered if it was a white
thing. Possibly. But more likely, it was a Jeremiah thing. She remembered
Mikey's third-grade-class's school play, an edited version of *Hamlet*. Jeremiah had walked onto the stage to help his son drag the unconscious Polo-
nius, who had merely been clubbed over the head rather than stabbed to
death, from the stage. Mortally embarrassed, Mikey had cried himself to
sleep that night, positive that he was going to be an elementary-school
pariah, while Jeremiah vainly tried to explain to the rest of the family why
he had acted so impulsively.

I was just trying to be a good father, he had said.   135

Mary Lynn watched Jeremiah walk farther down the bridge. He was
just a shadow, a silhouette. She was slapped by the brief, irrational fear that
he would never return.

Husband, come back to me, she thought, and I will confess.

Impatient drivers honked their horns. Mary Lynn joined them. She
hoped Jeremiah would recognize the specific sound of their horn and return
to the car.

Listen to me, listen to me, listen to me, she thought as she pounded the
steering wheel.

Jeremiah heard their car horn, but only as one note in the symphony of   140
noise playing on the bridge. He walked through that noise, through an ever-
increasing amount of noise, until he pushed through a sudden crowd of
people and found himself witnessing a suicide.

Illuminated by headlights, the jumper was a white woman, pretty,
wearing a sundress and good shoes. Jeremiah could see that much as she
stood on the bridge railing, forty feet above the cold water.

He could hear sirens approaching from both sides of the bridge, but
they would never make it through the traffic in time to save this woman.

The jumper was screaming somebody's name.

Jeremiah stepped closer, wanting to hear the name, wanting to have
that information so that he could use it later. To what use, he didn't know,
but he knew that name had value, importance. That name, the owner of
that name, was the reason why the jumper stood on the bridge.

"Aaron," she said. The jumper screamed, "Aaron."   145

In the car, Mary Lynn could not see either Jeremiah or the jumper, but
she could see dozens of drivers leaving their cars and running ahead.

She was suddenly and impossibly sure that her husband was the reason
for this commotion, this emergency. He's dying, thought Mary Lynn, he's
dead. This is not what I wanted, she thought, this is not why I cheated on
him, this is not what was supposed to happen.

As more drivers left their cars and ran ahead, Mary Lynn dialed 911 on
the cell phone and received only a busy signal.

She opened her door and stepped out, placed one foot on the pavement, and stopped.

The jumper did not stop. She turned to look at the crowd watching her. She looked into the anonymous faces, into the maw, and then looked back down at the black water.

Then she jumped.

Jeremiah rushed forward, along with a few others, and peered over the edge of the bridge. One brave man leapt off the bridge in a vain rescue attempt. Jeremiah stopped a redheaded young man from jumping.

"No," said Jeremiah. "It's too cold. You'll die too."

Jeremiah stared down into the black water, looking for the woman who'd jumped and the man who'd jumped after her.

In the car, or rather with one foot still in the car and one foot placed on the pavement outside of the car, Mary Lynn wept. Oh, God, she loved him, sometimes because he was white and often despite his whiteness. In her fear, she found the one truth Sitting Bull never knew: there was at least one white man who could be trusted.

The black water was silent.

Jeremiah stared down into that silence.

"Jesus, Jesus," said a lovely woman next to him. "Who was she? Who was she?"

"I'm never leaving," Jeremiah said.

"What?" asked the lovely woman, quite confused.

"My wife," said Jeremiah, strangely joyous. "I'm never leaving her." Ever the scientist and mathematician, Jeremiah knew that his wife was a constant. In his relief, he found the one truth Shakespeare never knew: gravity is overrated.

Jeremiah looked up through the crossbeams above him, as he stared at the black sky, at the clouds that he could not see but knew were there, the invisible clouds that covered the stars. He shouted out his wife's name, shouted it so loud that he could not speak in the morning.

In the car, Mary Lynn pounded the steering wheel. With one foot in the car and one foot out, she honked and honked the horn. She wondered if this was how the world was supposed to end, with everybody trapped on a bridge, with the black water pushing against their foundations.

Out on the bridge, four paramedics arrived far too late. Out of breath, exhausted from running across the bridge with medical gear and stretchers, the paramedics could only join the onlookers at the railing.

A boat, a small boat, a miracle, floated through the black water. They found the man, the would-be rescuer, who had jumped into the water after the young woman, but they could not find her.

Jeremiah pushed through the crowd, as he ran away from the place where the woman had jumped. Jeremiah ran across the bridge until he could see Mary Lynn. She and he loved each other across the distance.

ENGAGING THE TEXT

1. What is the significance of the title "Assimilation" in the context of this story? How do you interpret the "truths" that Mary Lynn and Jeremiah discover at the end of the story? Do you think that Alexie is endorsing assimilation in this story? Why or why not?

2. What is the purpose and effect of the paired cultural references — to Shakespeare and Sitting Bull, the Big Mom Singers and Emily Dickinson — that Alexie includes in the story?

3. What glimpses does Alexie give us of reservation life and of Indians less privileged than Mary Lynn? What do these allusions tell us about her character and motives? What do they suggest about the nature of the "white" culture she is immersed in?

4. Mary Lynn and the narrator make a number of observations about white men — that they are dependable but "neutral . . . like Belgium," that they invented the commute, and so forth. What overall portrait of white men emerges from these comments and from the character of Jeremiah? Explain why you think that Alexie is being fair or unfair in his characterization of white men.

5. What attitudes, behavior, and cultural phenomena does Alexie make fun of, and why? What values and ideas does he appear to take seriously? Are these categories mutually exclusive? Why or why not?

EXPLORING CONNECTIONS

6. Review the passages in the story that speak specifically about race. To what extent would Alexie endorse George M. Fredrickson's (p. 449) assertion that "ethnic hierarchy in a clearly racialized form persists in practice if not in law" in the United States?

7. Rubén Martínez (p. 473), like Mary Lynn, has a complex relationship to the dominant culture. What do they enjoy or value about mainstream American life? What do they dislike or distrust? To what extent are they assimilated, and how does that affect their relationship to their home cultures?

EXTENDING THE CRITICAL CONTEXT

8. Watch a film written and directed by Native American artists (e.g., *Smoke Signals, The Fast Runner, Skins, The Business of Fancydancing*) and compare it to any recent film that portrays, but was not created by, Indians (e.g., *Pocahontas, Apocalypto, Windtalkers*). What differences, if any, do you see in the way the films depict Indian and white cultures and relationships?

The End of White America?

Hua Hsu

In this provocative essay, Hua Hsu surveys the cultural landscape of an America in which white people will become a minority group within the next few decades. Does hip-hop point the way toward a multi-ethnic, post-racial future? What do NASCAR and "white trash studies" say about the condition of the white psyche? Can we escape entrenched racial hierarchy? Hsu (b. 1977) is an assistant professor of English at Vassar College where he teaches in the American Culture Program. His work has appeared in Slate, *the* Village Voice, *the* New York Times, *and* The Atlantic, *where this article was first published (January / February 2009).*

"Civilization's going to pieces," he remarks. He is in polite company, gathered with friends around a bottle of wine in the late-afternoon sun, chatting and gossiping. "I've gotten to be a terrible pessimist about things. Have you read *The Rise of the Colored Empires* by this man Goddard?" They hadn't. "Well, it's a fine book, and everybody ought to read it. The idea is if we don't look out the white race will be — will be utterly submerged. It's all scientific stuff; it's been proved."

He is Tom Buchanan, a character in F. Scott Fitzgerald's *The Great Gatsby*, a book that nearly everyone who passes through the American education system is compelled to read at least once. Although *Gatsby* doesn't gloss as a book on racial anxiety — it's too busy exploring a different set of anxieties entirely — Buchanan was hardly alone in feeling besieged. The book by "this man Goddard" had a real-world analogue: Lothrop Stoddard's *The Rising Tide of Color Against White World-Supremacy*, published in 1920, five years before *Gatsby*. Nine decades later, Stoddard's polemic remains oddly engrossing. He refers to World War I as the "White Civil War" and laments the "cycle of ruin" that may result if the "white world" continues its infighting. The book features a series of foldout maps depicting the distribution of "color" throughout the world and warns, "Colored migration is a universal peril, menacing every part of the white world."

As briefs for racial supremacy go, *The Rising Tide of Color* is eerily serene. Its tone is scholarly and gentlemanly, its hatred rationalized and, in Buchanan's term, "scientific." And the book was hardly a fringe phenomenon. It was published by Scribner, also Fitzgerald's publisher, and Stoddard, who received a doctorate in history from Harvard, was a member of many professional academic associations. It was precisely the kind of book that a 1920s man of Buchanan's profile — wealthy, Ivy League–educated, at once pretentious and intellectually insecure — might have been expected to bring up in casual conversation.

*"Instead of just sitting around, why don't you kids
go out and co-opt some black culture?"*

As white men of comfort and privilege living in an age of limited social mobility, of course, Stoddard and the Buchanans in his audience had nothing literal to fear. Their sense of dread hovered somewhere above the concerns of everyday life. It was linked less to any immediate danger to their class's political and cultural power than to the perceived fraying of the fixed, monolithic identity of whiteness that sewed together the fortunes of the fair-skinned.

From the hysteria over Eastern European immigration to the vibrant cultural miscegenation of the Harlem Renaissance,[1] it is easy to see how this imagined worldwide white kinship might have seemed imperiled in the 1920s. There's no better example of the era's insecurities than the 1923 Supreme Court case *United States v. Bhagat Singh Thind*, in which an Indian American veteran of World War I sought to become a naturalized citizen by proving that he was Caucasian.[2] The Court considered new anthropological studies that expanded the definition of the Caucasian race

5

---

[1] *Harlem Renaissance:* Harlem in the 1920s and early 30s was the center of intense literary and cultural activity among African American writers, intellectuals, artists, and musicians; white readers embraced the work of writers like Langston Hughes and Zora Neale Hurston, and white patrons flocked to popular Harlem nightspots like the Cotton Club.

[2] *"sought . . . Caucasian":* The Naturalization Act of 1870 restricted U.S. citizenship to "white persons and persons of African descent."

to include Indians, and the justices even agreed that traces of "Aryan blood" coursed through Thind's body. But these technicalities availed him little. The Court determined that Thind was not white "in accordance with the understanding of the common man" and therefore could be excluded from the "statutory category" of whiteness. Put another way: Thind was white, in that he was Caucasian and even Aryan. But he was not *white* in the way Stoddard or Buchanan were white.

The 20s debate over the definition of whiteness — A legal category? A commonsense understanding? A worldwide civilization? — took place in a society gripped by an acute sense of racial paranoia, and it is easy to regard these episodes as evidence of how far we have come. But consider that these anxieties surfaced when whiteness was synonymous with the American mainstream, when threats to its status were largely imaginary. What happens once this is no longer the case — when the fears of Lothrop Stoddard and Tom Buchanan are realized, and white people actually become an American minority?

Whether you describe it as the dawning of a post-racial age or just the end of white America, we're approaching a profound demographic tipping point. According to an August 2008 report by the U.S. Census Bureau, those groups currently categorized as racial minorities — blacks and Hispanics, East Asians and South Asians — will account for a majority of the U.S. population by the year 2042. Among Americans under the age of eighteen, this shift is projected to take place in 2023, which means that every child born in the United States from here on out will belong to the first post-white generation.

Obviously, steadily ascending rates of interracial marriage complicate this picture, pointing toward what Michael Lind has described as the "beiging" of America. And it's possible that "beige Americans" will self-identify as "white" in sufficient numbers to push the tipping point further into the future than the Census Bureau projects. But even if they do, whiteness will be a label adopted out of convenience and even indifference, rather than aspiration and necessity. For an earlier generation of minorities and immigrants, to be recognized as a "white American," whether you were an Italian or a Pole or a Hungarian, was to enter the mainstream of American life; to be recognized as something else, as the *Thind* case suggests, was to be permanently excluded. As Bill Imada, head of the IW Group, a prominent Asian American communications and marketing company, puts it: "I think in the 1920s, 1930s, and 1940s, [for] anyone who immigrated, the aspiration was to blend in and be as American as possible so that white America wouldn't be intimidated by them. They wanted to imitate white America as much as possible: learn English, go to church, go to the same schools."

Today, the picture is far more complex. To take the most obvious example, whiteness is no longer a precondition for entry into the highest levels of public office. The son of Indian immigrants doesn't have to become "white" in order to be elected governor of Louisiana.[3] A half-Kenyan, half-Kansan politician can self-identify as black and be elected president of the United States.

As a purely demographic matter, then, the "white America" that Lothrop   10
Stoddard believed in so fervently may cease to exist in 2040, 2050, or 2060,
or later still. But where the culture is concerned, it's already all but finished.
Instead of the long-standing model of assimilation toward a common center, the culture is being remade in the image of white America's multiethnic, multicolored heirs.

For some, the disappearance of this centrifugal core heralds a future rich with promise. In 1998, President Bill Clinton, in a now-famous address to students at Portland State University, remarked:

> Today, largely because of immigration, there is no majority race in Hawaii or Houston or New York City. Within five years, there will be no majority race in our largest state, California. In a little more than fifty years, there will be no majority race in the United States. No other nation in history has gone through demographic change of this magnitude in so short a time . . . [These immigrants] are energizing our culture and broadening our vision of the world. They are renewing our most basic values and reminding us all of what it truly means to be American.

Not everyone was so enthused. Clinton's remarks caught the attention of another anxious Buchanan — Pat Buchanan, the conservative thinker. Revisiting the president's speech in his 2001 book, *The Death of the West*, Buchanan wrote: "Mr. Clinton assured us that it will be a better America when we are all minorities and realize true 'diversity.' Well, those students [at Portland State] are going to find out, for they will spend their golden years in a Third World America."

Today, the arrival of what Buchanan derided as "Third World America" is all but inevitable. What will the new mainstream of America look like, and what ideas or values might it rally around? What will it mean to be white after "whiteness" no longer defines the mainstream? Will anyone mourn the end of white America? Will anyone try to preserve it?

Another moment from *The Great Gatsby*: as Fitzgerald's narrator and Gatsby drive across the Queensboro Bridge into Manhattan, a car passes them, and Nick Carraway notices that it is a limousine "driven by a white chauffeur, in which sat three modish negroes, two bucks and a girl." The novelty of this topsy-turvy arrangement inspires Carraway to laugh aloud and think to himself, "Anything can happen now that we've slid over this bridge, anything at all . . . "

For a contemporary embodiment of the upheaval that this scene por-   15
tended, consider Sean Combs, a hip-hop mogul and one of the most famous

---

[3]*The son of . . . governor of Louisiana:* Bobby Jindal (b. 1971) was elected governor of Louisiana in 2007.

African Americans on the planet. Combs grew up during hip-hop's late-1970s rise, and he belongs to the first generation that could safely make a living working in the industry — as a plucky young promoter and record-label intern in the late 1980s and early 1990s, and as fashion designer, artist, and music executive worth hundreds of millions of dollars a brief decade later.

In the late 1990s, Combs made a fascinating gesture toward New York's high society. He announced his arrival into the circles of the rich and pow-erful not by crashing their parties, but by inviting them into his own spec-tacularly over-the-top world. Combs began to stage elaborate annual parties in the Hamptons,[4] not far from where Fitzgerald's novel takes place. These "white parties" — attendees are required to wear white — quickly became legendary for their opulence (in 2004, Combs showcased a 1776 copy of the Declaration of Independence) as well as for the cultures-colliding quality of Hamptons elites paying their respects to someone so comfortably nouveau riche. Prospective business partners angled to get close to him and praised him as a guru of the lucrative "urban" market, while grateful partygoers hailed him as a modern-day Gatsby.

"Have I read *The Great Gatsby*?" Combs said to a London newspaper in 2001. "I am the Great Gatsby."

Yet whereas Gatsby felt pressure to hide his status as an arriviste, Combs celebrated his position as an outsider-insider — someone who appropriates elements of the culture he seeks to join without attempting to assimilate outright. In a sense, Combs was imitating the old WASP establishment; in another sense, he was subtly provoking it, by over-enunciating its formality and never letting his guests forget that there was something slightly off about his presence. There's a silent power to throwing parties where the best-dressed man in the room is also the one whose public profile once con-sisted primarily of dancing in the background of Biggie Smalls videos. ("No one would ever expect a young black man to be coming to a party with the Declaration of Independence, but I got it, and it's coming with me," Combs joked at his 2004 party, as he made the rounds with the document, promis-ing not to spill champagne on it.)

In this regard, Combs is both a product and a hero of the new cultural mainstream, which prizes diversity above all else, and whose ultimate goal is some vague notion of racial transcendence, rather than subversion or assim-ilation. Although Combs's vision is far from representative — not many hip-hop stars vacation in St. Tropez with a parasol-toting manservant shading their every step — his industry lies at the heart of this new mainstream. Over the past thirty years, few changes in American culture have been as significant as the rise of hip-hop. The genre has radically reshaped the way we listen to and consume music, first by opposing the pop mainstream and then by becoming it. From its constant sampling of past styles and eras — old

---

[4]*the Hamptons:* A prestigious seaside resort area on Long Island, New York.

records, fashions, slang, anything — to its mythologization of the self-made black antihero, hip-hop is more than a musical genre: it's a philosophy, a political statement, a way of approaching and remaking culture. It's a lingua franca[5] not just among kids in America, but also among young people worldwide. And its economic impact extends beyond the music industry, to fashion, advertising, and film. (Consider the producer Russell Simmons — the ur-Combs and a music, fashion, and television mogul — or the rapper 50 Cent, who has parlayed his rags-to-riches story line into extracurricular successes that include a clothing line; book, video-game, and film deals; and a startlingly lucrative partnership with the makers of Vitamin Water.)

But hip-hop's deepest impact is symbolic. During popular music's rise   20
in the twentieth century, white artists and producers consistently "main-streamed" African American innovations. Hip-hop's ascension has been different. Eminem notwithstanding, hip-hop never suffered through anything like an Elvis Presley moment, in which a white artist made a musical form safe for white America. This is no dig at Elvis — the constrictive racial logic of the 1950s demanded the erasure of rock and roll's black roots, and if it hadn't been him, it would have been someone else. But hip-hop — the sound of the post-civil-rights, post-soul generation — found a global audience on its own terms.

Today, hip-hop's colonization of the global imagination, from fashion runways in Europe to dance competitions in Asia, is Disney-esque, This transformation has bred an unprecedented cultural confidence in its black originators. Whiteness is no longer a threat, or an ideal: it's kitsch to be appropriated, whether with gestures like Combs's "white parties" or the trickle-down epidemic of collared shirts and cuff links currently afflicting rappers. And an expansive multiculturalism is replacing the us-against-the-world bunker mentality that lent a thrilling edge to hip-hop's mid-1990s rise.

Peter Rosenberg, a self-proclaimed "nerdy Jewish kid" and radio personality on New York's Hot 97 FM — and a living example of how hip-hop has created new identities for its listeners that don't fall neatly along lines of black and white — shares another example: "I interviewed [the St. Louis rapper] Nelly this morning, and he said it's now very cool and *in* to have multicultural friends. Like you're not really considered hip or 'you've made it' if you're rolling with all the same people."

Just as Tiger Woods forever changed the country-club culture of golf, and Will Smith confounded stereotypes about the ideal Hollywood leading man, hip-hop's rise is helping redefine the American mainstream, which no longer aspires toward a single iconic image of style or class. Successful network-television shows like *Lost*, *Heroes*, and *Grey's Anatomy* feature wildly diverse casts, and an entire genre of half-hour comedy, from *The Colbert Report* to *The Office*, seems dedicated to having fun with the persona of the clueless

---

[5]*lingua franca:* Italian term meaning "common language."

white male. The youth market is following the same pattern: consider the Cheetah Girls, a multicultural, multiplatinum, multiplatform trio of teeny-boppers who recently starred in their third movie, or Dora the Explorer, the precocious bilingual seven-year-old Latina adventurer who is arguably the most successful animated character on children's television today. In a recent address to the Association of Hispanic Advertising Agencies, Brown Johnson, the Nickelodeon executive who has overseen Dora's rise, explained the importance of creating a character who does not conform to "the white, middle-class mold." When Johnson pointed out that Dora's wares were outselling Barbie's in France, the crowd hooted in delight.

Pop culture today rallies around an ethic of multicultural inclusion that seems to value every identity — except whiteness. "It's become harder for the blond-haired, blue-eyed commercial actor," remarks Rochelle Newman-Carrasco, of the Hispanic marketing firm Enlace. "You read casting notices, and they like to cast people with brown hair because they could be Hispanic. The language of casting notices is pretty shocking because it's so specific: 'Brown hair, brown eyes, could look Hispanic.' Or, as one notice put it: 'Ethnically ambiguous.'"

"I think white people feel like they're under siege right now — like it's   25 not okay to be white right now, especially if you're a white male," laughs Bill Imada, of the IW Group. Imada and Newman-Carrasco are part of a movement within advertising, marketing, and communications firms to reimagine the profile of the typical American consumer. (Tellingly, every person I spoke with from these industries knew the Census Bureau's projections by heart.)

"There's a lot of fear and a lot of resentment," Newman-Carrasco observes, describing the flak she caught after writing an article for a trade publication on the need for more-diverse hiring practices. "I got a response from a friend — he's, like, a sixty-something white male, and he's been involved with multicultural recruiting," she recalls. "And he said, 'I really feel like the hunted. It's a hard time to be a white man in America right now, because I feel like I'm being lumped in with all white males in America, and I've tried to do stuff, but it's a tough time.'"

"I always tell the white men in the room, 'We need you,'" Imada says. "We cannot talk about diversity and inclusion and engagement without you at the table. It's okay to be white!

"But people are stressed out about it. 'We used to be in control! We're losing control!'"

If they're right — if white America is indeed "losing control," and if the future will belong to people who can successfully navigate a post-racial, multicultural landscape — then it's no surprise that many white Americans are eager to divest themselves of their whiteness entirely.

For some, this renunciation can take a radical form. In 1994, a young   30 graffiti artist and activist named William "Upski" Wimsatt, the son of a university professor, published *Bomb the Suburbs*, the spiritual heir to Norman Mailer's celebratory 1957 essay, "The White Negro." Wimsatt was deeply committed to hip-hop's transformative powers, going so far as to embrace the status of the lowly "wigger," a pejorative term popularized in the early 1990s to describe white kids who steep themselves in black culture. Wimsatt viewed the wigger's immersion in two cultures as an engine for change. "If channeled in the right way," he wrote, "the wigger can go a long way toward repairing the sickness of race in America."

Wimsatt's painfully earnest attempts to put his own relationship with whiteness under the microscope coincided with the emergence of an academic discipline known as "whiteness studies." In colleges and universities across the country, scholars began examining the history of "whiteness" and unpacking its contradictions. Why, for example, had the Irish and the Italians fallen beyond the pale at different moments in our history? Were Jewish Americans *white*? And, as the historian Matthew Frye Jacobson asked, "Why is it that in the United States, a white woman can have black children but a black woman cannot have white children?"

Much like Wimsatt, the whiteness-studies academics — figures such as Jacobson, David Roediger,[6] Eric Lott,[7] and Noel Ignatiev — were attempting to come to terms with their own relationships with whiteness, in its past and present forms. In the early 1990s, Ignatiev, a former labor activist and the author of *How the Irish Became White*, set out to "abolish" the idea of the white race by starting the New Abolitionist Movement and founding a journal titled *Race Traitor*. "There is nothing positive about white identity," he wrote in 1998. "As James Baldwin said, 'As long as you think you're white, there's no hope for you.'"

Although most white Americans haven't read *Bomb the Suburbs* or *Race Traitor*, this view of whiteness as something to be interrogated, if not shrugged off completely, has migrated to less academic spheres. The perspective of the whiteness-studies academics is commonplace now, even if the language used to express it is different.

"I get it: as a straight white male, I'm the worst thing on Earth," Christian Lander says. Lander is a Canadian-born, Los Angeles–based satirist who in January 2008 started a blog called Stuff White People Like (stuffwhitepeoplelike.com), which pokes fun at the manners and mores of a specific species of young, hip, upwardly mobile whites. (He has written more than one hundred entries about whites' passion for things like bottled water, "the idea of soccer," and "being the only white person around.") At its best, Lander's site — which formed the basis for a recently published book of the same name (reviewed in the October 2008 *Atlantic*) — is a cunningly pre-

---

[6]*David Roediger:* American historian (b. 1952) who has written extensively about race in the United States.

[7]*Eric Lott:* Professor of English (b. 1959) and cultural studies who has written books on racism and minstrelsy.

cise distillation of the identity crisis plaguing well-meaning, well-off white kids in a post-white world.

"Like, I'm aware of all the horrible crimes that my demographic has   35 done in the world," Lander says. "And there's a bunch of white people who are desperate — *desperate* — to say, 'You know what? My skin's white, but I'm not one of the white people who's destroying the world.'"

For Lander, whiteness has become a vacuum. The "white identity" he limns on his blog is predicated on the quest for authenticity — usually other people's authenticity. "As a white person, you're just desperate to find something else to grab onto. You're jealous! Pretty much every white person I grew up with wished they'd grown up in, you know, an ethnic home that gave them a second language. White culture is *Family Ties* and Led Zeppelin and Guns N' Roses — like, this is white culture. This is all we have."

Lander's "white people" are products of a very specific historical moment, raised by well-meaning Baby Boomers to reject the old ideal of white American gentility and to embrace diversity and fluidity instead. ("It's strange that we are the kids of Baby Boomers, right? How the hell do you rebel against that? Like, your parents will march against the World Trade Organization next to you. They'll have bigger white dreadlocks than you. What do you do?") But his lighthearted anthropology suggests that the multicultural harmony they were raised to worship has bred a kind of self-denial.

Matt Wray, a sociologist at Temple University who is a fan of Lander's humor, has observed that many of his white students are plagued by a racial-identity crisis: "They don't care about socioeconomics; they care about culture. And to be white is to be culturally broke. The classic thing white students say when you ask them to talk about who they are is, 'I don't have a culture.' They might be privileged, they might be loaded socioeconomically, but they feel bankrupt when it comes to culture . . . They feel disadvantaged, and they feel marginalized. They don't have a culture that's cool or oppositional." Wray says that this feeling of being culturally bereft often prevents students from recognizing what it means to be a child of privilege — a strange irony that the first wave of whiteness-studies scholars, in the 1990s, failed to anticipate.

Of course, the obvious material advantages that come with being born white — lower infant-mortality rates and easier-to-acquire bank loans, for example — tend to undercut any sympathy that this sense of marginalization might generate. And in the right context, cultural-identity crises can turn well-meaning whites into instant punch lines. Consider *ego trip's The (White) Rapper Show*, a brilliant and critically acclaimed reality show that VH1 debuted in 2007. It depicted ten (mostly hapless) white rappers living together in a dilapidated house — dubbed "Tha White House" — in the South Bronx. Despite the contestants' best intentions, each one seemed like a profoundly confused caricature, whether it was the solemn graduate student committed to fighting racism or the ghetto-obsessed suburbanite who had, seemingly by accident, named himself after the abolitionist John Brown.

Similarly, Smirnoff struck marketing gold in 2006 with a viral music   40 video titled "Tea Partay," featuring a trio of strikingly bad, V-neck-sweater-clad white rappers called the Prep Unit. "Haters like to clown our Ivy League educations / But they're just jealous 'cause our families run the nation," the trio brayed, as a pair of bottle-blond women in spiffy tennis whites shimmied behind them. There was no nonironic way to enjoy the video; its entire appeal was in its self-aware lampooning of WASP culture: verdant country clubs, "old money," croquet, popped collars, and the like.

"The best defense is to be constantly pulling the rug out from underneath yourself," Wray remarks, describing the way self-aware whites contend with their complicated identity. "Beat people to the punch. You're forced as a white person into a sense of ironic detachment. Irony is what fuels a lot of white subcultures. You also see things like Burning Man,[8] when a lot of white people are going into the desert and trying to invent something that is entirely new and not a form of racial mimicry. That's its own kind of flight from whiteness. We're going through a period where whites are really trying to figure out: Who are we?"

The "flight from whiteness" of urban, college-educated, liberal whites isn't the only attempt to answer this question. You can flee *into* whiteness as well. This can mean pursuing the authenticity of an imagined past: think of the deliberately white-bread world of Mormon America, where the 50s never ended, or the anachronistic WASP entitlement flaunted in books like last year's *A Privileged Life: Celebrating Wasp Style*, a handsome coffee-table book compiled by Susanna Salk, depicting a world of seersucker blazers, whale pants, and deck shoes. (What the book celebrates is the "inability to be outdone," and the "self-confidence and security that comes with it," Salk tells me. "That's why I call it 'privilege.' It's this privilege of time, of heritage, of being in a place longer than anybody else.") But these enclaves of preserved-in-amber whiteness are likely to be less important to the American future than the construction of whiteness as a somewhat pissed-off minority culture.

This notion of a self-consciously white expression of minority empowerment will be familiar to anyone who has come across the comedian Larry the Cable Guy — he of "Farting Jingle Bells" — or witnessed the transformation of Detroit-born-and-bred Kid Rock from teenage rapper into "American Bad Ass" southern-style rocker. The 1990s may have been a decade when multiculturalism advanced dramatically — when American culture

[8]*Burning Man:* This annual event, which takes place in Nevada's Black Rock Desert throughout the week leading up to Labor Day, attracts tens of thousands of participants; the festival encourages "radical self-expression," which takes the form of amplified music; large temporary art installations; fanciful costumes and identies; and the sharing or bartering of food, handcrafted work, and frequently, drugs.

became "colorized," as the critic Jeff Chang put it — but it was also an era when a very different form of identity politics crystallized. Hip-hop may have provided the decade's soundtrack, but the highest-selling artist of the 90s was Garth Brooks. Michael Jordan and Tiger Woods may have been the faces of athletic superstardom, but it was NASCAR that emerged as professional sports' fastest-growing institution, with ratings second only to the NFL's.

As with the unexpected success of the apocalyptic Left Behind novels,[9] or the Jeff Foxworthy–organized Blue Collar Comedy Tour, the rise of country music and auto racing took place well off the American elite's radar screen. (None of Christian Lander's white people would be caught dead at a NASCAR race.) These phenomena reflected a growing sense of cultural solidarity among lower-middle-class whites — a solidarity defined by a yearning for American "authenticity," a folksy realness that rejects the global, the urban, and the effete in favor of nostalgia for "the way things used to be."

Like other forms of identity politics, white solidarity comes complete   45
with its own folk heroes, conspiracy theories (Barack Obama is a secret Muslim! The U.S. is going to merge with Canada and Mexico!), and laundry lists of injustices. The targets and scapegoats vary — from multiculturalism and affirmative action to a loss of moral values, from immigration to an economy that no longer guarantees the American worker a fair chance — and so do the political programs they inspire. (Ross Perot[10] and Pat Buchanan both tapped into this white identity politics in the 1990s; today, its tribunes run the ideological gamut, from Jim Webb to Ron Paul to Mike Huckabee to Sarah Palin.)[11] But the core grievance, in each case, has to do with cultural and socioeconomic dislocation — the sense that the system that used to guarantee the white working class some stability has gone off-kilter.

Wray is one of the founders of what has been called "white-trash studies," a field conceived as a response to the perceived elite-liberal marginalization of the white working class. He argues that the economic downturn of the 1970s was the precondition for the formation of an "oppositional" and "defiant" white-working-class sensibility — think of the rugged, anti-everything individualism of 1977's *Smokey and the Bandit*. But those anxieties took their shape from the aftershocks of the identity-based movements of the 1960s. "I think that the political space that the civil-rights movement

---

[9]*Left Behind novels:* A series of novels by evangelical writer Tim LaHaye, which depict the "last days of earth."

[10]*Ross Perot:* Wealthy businessman who founded the Reform Party and ran for president in 1992 and 1996.

[11]*Jim Webb . . . Sarah Palin:* Webb (b. 1946) is a Democratic senator from Virginia; Paul (b. 1935) is a libertarian Republican congressman from Texas; Huckabee, a former Baptist minister, served as governor of Arkansas and ran in the 2008 Republican presidential primary, as did Ron Paul; Sarah Palin (b. 1964) served briefly as governor of Alaska before being chosen as Republican John McCain's vice presidential running mate in 2008.

opens up in the mid-1950s and 60s is the transformative thing," Wray observes. "Following the black-power movement, all of the other minority groups that followed took up various forms of activism, including brown power and yellow power and red power. Of course the problem is, if you try and have a 'white power' movement, it doesn't sound good."

The result is a racial pride that dares not speak its name, and that defines itself through cultural cues instead — a suspicion of intellectual elites and city dwellers, a preference for folksiness and plainness of speech (whether real or feigned), and the association of a working-class white minority with "the real America." (In the Scots-Irish belt that runs from Arkansas up through West Virginia, the most common ethnic label offered to census takers is "American.") Arguably, this white identity politics helped swing the 2000 and 2004 elections, serving as the powerful counterpunch to urban white liberals, and the McCain-Palin campaign relied on it almost to the point of absurdity (as when a McCain surrogate dismissed Northern Virginia as somehow not part of "the real Virginia") as a bulwark against the threatening multiculturalism of Barack Obama. Their strategy failed, of course, but it's possible to imagine white identity politics growing more potent and more forthright in its racial identifications in the future, as "the real America" becomes an ever-smaller portion of, well, the real America, and as the soon-to-be white minority's sense of being besieged and disdained by a multicultural majority grows apace.

This vision of the aggrieved white man lost in a world that no longer values him was given its most vivid expression in the 1993 film *Falling Down*. Michael Douglas plays Bill Foster, a downsized defense worker with a buzz cut and a pocket protector who rampages through a Los Angeles overrun by greedy Korean shop-owners and Hispanic gangsters, railing against the eclipse of the America he used to know. (The film came out just eight years before California became the nation's first majority-minority state.) *Falling Down* ends with a soulful police officer apprehending Foster on the Santa Monica Pier, at which point the middle-class vigilante asks, almost innocently: *"I'm* the bad guy?"

But this is a nightmare vision. Of course most of America's Bill Fosters aren't the bad guys — just as civilization is not, in the words of Tom Buchanan, "going to pieces" and America is not, in the phrasing of Pat Buchanan, going "Third World." The coming white minority does not mean that the racial hierarchy of American culture will suddenly become inverted, as in 1995's *White Man's Burden*, an awful thought experiment of a film, starring John Travolta, that envisions an upside-down world in which whites are subjugated to their high-class black oppressors. There will be dislocations and resentments along the way, but the demographic shifts of the next forty years are likely to reduce the power of racial hierarchies over everyone's lives, producing a culture that's more likely than any before to treat its inhabitants as individuals, rather than members of a caste or identity group.

Consider the world of advertising and marketing, industries that set out   50
to mold our desires at a subconscious level. Advertising strategy once assumed a "general market" — "a code word for 'white people,'" jokes one ad executive — and smaller, mutually exclusive, satellite "ethnic markets." In recent years, though, advertisers have begun revising their assumptions and strategies in anticipation of profound demographic shifts. Instead of herding consumers toward a discrete center, the goal today is to create versatile images and campaigns that can be adapted to highly individualized tastes. (Think of the dancing silhouettes in Apple's iPod campaign, which emphasizes individuality and diversity without privileging — or even representing — any specific group.)

At the moment, we can call this the triumph of multiculturalism, or post-racialism. But just as *whiteness* has no inherent meaning — it is a vessel we fill with our hopes and anxieties — these terms may prove equally empty in the long run. Does being post-racial mean that we are past race completely, or merely that race is no longer essential to how we identify ourselves? Karl Carter, of Atlanta's youth-oriented GTM Inc. (Guerrilla Tactics Media), suggests that marketers and advertisers would be better off focusing on matrices like "lifestyle" or "culture" rather than race or ethnicity. "You'll have crazy in-depth studies of the white consumer or the Latino consumer," he complains. "But how do skaters feel? How do hip-hoppers feel?"

The logic of online social networking points in a similar direction. The New York University sociologist Dalton Conley has written of a "network nation," in which applications like Facebook and MySpace create "crosscutting social groups" and new, flexible identities that only vaguely overlap with racial identities. Perhaps this is where the future of identity after whiteness lies — in a dramatic departure from the racial logic that has defined American culture from the very beginning. What Conley, Carter, and others are describing isn't merely the displacement of whiteness from our cultural center; they're describing a social structure that treats race as just one of a seemingly infinite number of possible self-identifications.

The problem of the twentieth century, W. E. B. Du Bois[12] famously predicted, would be the problem of the color line. Will this continue to be the case in the twenty-first century, when a black president will govern a country whose social networks increasingly cut across every conceivable line of identification? The ruling of *United States v. Bhagat Singh Thind* no longer holds weight, but its echoes have been inescapable: we aspire to be post-racial, but we still live within the structures of privilege, injustice, and racial categorization that we inherited from an older order. We can talk about

[12]*W. E. B. Du Bois:* Scholar, author, and civil rights activist (1868–1963).

defining ourselves by lifestyle rather than skin color, but our lifestyle choices are still racially coded. We know, more or less, that race is a fiction that often does more harm than good, and yet it is something we cling to without fully understanding why — as a social and legal fact, a vague sense of belonging and place that we make solid through culture and speech.

But maybe this is merely how it used to be — maybe this is already an outdated way of looking at things. "You have a lot of young adults going into a more diverse world," Carter remarks. For the young Americans born in the 1980s and 1990s, culture is something to be taken apart and remade in their own image. "We came along in a generation that didn't have to follow that path of race," he goes on. "We saw something *different.*" This moment was not the end of white America; it was not the end of anything. It was a bridge, and we crossed it.

ENGAGING THE TEXT

1. In what ways does Hsu suggest that white America is coming to an end? Why do you think he ended his title with a question mark?

2. According to Hsu, how are white racial attitudes of the 1920s, as represented by *The Great Gatsby* and the Thind case, relevant to twenty-first-century America?

3. What evidence does Hsu offer to support his contention that hip-hop represents "the new cultural mainstream" (para. 19)? Do you find his argument persuasive? Why or why not?

4. How does Hsu interpret the following cultural phenomena: wiggers, whiteness studies, redneck humor, the popularity of NASCAR? Working in pairs or groups, choose one of these topics and develop an alternative interpretation of its significance. Present your analyses to the class and discuss. Which interpretations (including Hsu's) seem most compelling, and why?

5. Hsu quotes a teacher who observes that many white students claim not to have a culture. What constitutes a culture in general? List as many characteristics of your own culture as you can think of, then share your lists in class. How much agreement is there about the defining characteristics of your and your classmates' cultures?

6. How do marketing trends and online networking point toward a potentially "post racial" future, according to Hsu? How likely or unlikely does this seem, and why?

EXPLORING CONNECTIONS

7. How does Hsu characterize Patrick J. Buchanan's view of diversity? How might Buchanan (p. 462) respond to Hsu's analysis of "white identity politics" (para. 47)? Is awareness of ethnic or cultural identity inherently divisive, a resource to be celebrated, or something more complicated? Explain your reasoning.

8. Compare Hsu's discussion of hip-hop to Joan Morgan's (p. 601). Does one writer's view of its cultural significance more closely reflect your own? Are both authors equally right? Equally wrong? Do you find any agreement in the class as a whole about the meaning and importance of hip-hop culture?

Extending the Critical Context

9. Analyze the profiles and postings on a social networking site that you belong to, looking for evidence of the "crosscutting social groups" that Hsu mentions (para. 52). Are the groups you interact with primarily defined by ethnicity, culture, language, mutual interests, or something else? To what extent would you define your online identity as "post racial"?

10. Examine advertising on television or in magazines for images that reflect ethnic ambiguity or diversity. How common are these images in media directed toward broad audiences (e.g., national news magazines, prime time network TV) versus media that target more narrowly defined audiences (e.g., *Vibe*, *Essence*, cable TV)?

Child of the Americas

Aurora Levins Morales

This poem concentrates on the positive aspects of a multicultural heritage, as Morales celebrates her uniqueness, her diversity, and her wholeness. It's an up-to-date and sophisticated reinterpretation of the melting pot myth. As this autobiographical poem states, Aurora Levins Morales (b. 1954) was the child of a Puerto Rican mother and a Jewish father. She moved to the United States when she was thirteen and now writes, performs, and teaches in the San Francisco Bay Area. "Child of the Americas" is from the collection Getting Home Alive *(1986), which she coauthored with her mother, Rosario Morales. Her mother has written that the book "began in long, budget-breaking telephone calls stretched across the width of this country . . . the phone line strung between us like a 3,000-mile umbilical cord from navel to navel, mine to hers, hers to mine, each of us mother and daughter by turns, feeding each other the substance of our dreams." Morales has taught Jewish studies and women's studies at Berkeley and lectures on a variety of issues, including Puerto Rican history and culture, Latina feminism, and community activism. She is the author of* Remedios: Stories of Earth and Iron from the History of Puertorriqueñas *(1998) and* Medicine Stories: History, Culture, and the Politics of Integrity *(1998).*

I am a child of the Americas,
a light-skinned mestiza of the Caribbean,
a child of many diaspora,[1] born into this continent at a crossroads.

I am a U.S. Puerto Rican Jew,
a product of the ghettos of New York I have never known.   5
An immigrant and the daughter and granddaughter of immigrants.
I speak English with passion: it's the tongue of my consciousness,
a flashing knife blade of crystal, my tool, my craft.

I am Caribeña,[2] island grown. Spanish is in my flesh,
ripples from my tongue, lodges in my hips: 10
the language of garlic and mangoes,
the singing in my poetry, the flying gestures of my hands.
I am of Latinoamerica, rooted in the history of my continent:
I speak from that body.

I am not african. Africa is in me, but I cannot return.   15
I am not taína.[3] Taíno is in me, but there is no way back.
I am not european. Europe lives in me, but I have no home there.

I am new. History made me. My first language was spanglish.[4]
I was born at the crossroads
and I am whole.   20

ENGAGING THE TEXT

1. Does this poem do more to challenge or to promote the myth of the melting pot? Explain.

2. Why does the poet list elements of her background that she scarcely knows ("the ghettos of New York" and Taíno)? How can they be part of her?

3. How do you interpret the last stanza? Rephrase its messages in more complete, more explicit statements.

EXPLORING CONNECTIONS

4. Many of the writers in this book express a sense of internal fragmentation or cultural conflict. How does the speaker of this poem avoid the feeling of cultural schizophrenia? How does her response compare to those of Richard Rodriguez (p. 194), Stephen Cruz (p. 366), James McBride (p. 409),

---

[1]*diaspora:* Scattered colonies. The word originally referred to Jews scattered outside Palestine after the Babylonian exile; it is now used to refer to African and other peoples scattered around the world.
[2]*Caribeña:* Caribbean woman.
[3]*taína:* Describing the Taíno, an aboriginal people of the Greater Antilles and Bahamas.
[4]*spanglish:* Spanish and English combined.

Rubén Martínez (p. 473), and Judith Ortiz Cofer (p. 537). Which responses do you find most appealing or most realistic, and why?

EXTENDING THE CRITICAL CONTEXT

5. Write your own version of "Child of the Americas," following Morales's structure but substituting ideas and images from your own heritage. Read it to the class.

FURTHER CONNECTIONS

1. Research the history of the native peoples of your state. Learn as much as you can about a specific aspect or period of that history. What tribal groups inhabited the area before Europeans arrived? What is known about the cultures and languages of these tribes? How much and why did the native population decrease following European contact? What alliances and treaties were made between the tribes and the newcomers as non-natives began to occupy native lands? To what extent were treaties upheld or abandoned, and why? How were local native populations affected by relocation, the establishment of reservations, the creation of Indian boarding schools, the Dawes Act, or other legislation? What role has the Bureau of Indian Affairs played in protecting or failing to protect tribal interests? What issues are of greatest concern to the tribes in your area today? Write up the results of your research and present them to the class.

2. Some states and communities have responded to the rise in illegal immigration by enacting laws or ordinances that ban any language other than English, deny government services to undocumented immigrants, and penalize citizens (such as employers, landlords, and merchants) who "assist" them. Has your state or community adopted any such regulations? Research the arguments for and against such legislation and discuss your findings in class. Which arguments are the most compelling, and why?

3. Investigate a recent conflict between ethnic, racial, or cultural groups on your campus or in your community. Research the issue, and interview people on each side. What event triggered the conflict? How do the groups involved perceive the issue differently? What tension, prior conflict, or injustice has contributed to the conflict and to the perceptions of those affected by it? Has the conflict been resolved? If so, write a paper discussing why you feel that the resolution was appropriate or not. If the conflict is continuing, write a paper proposing how a fair resolution might be reached.

4. Contentious debates over issues like affirmative action often hinge on whether or not the debaters accept the idea of structural racism (also called systemic racism). Proponents argue that structural racism is largely responsible for persistent racial disparities in wealth, income, home ownership, education, health care, and life expectancy. Investigate the concept of structural racism: What is it? How does it differ from individual racism or intentional discrimination? What evidence and examples of systemic racism do proponents cite? How do opponents of the concept explain racial inequalities, and what supporting evidence do they offer? Argue a position: Is it necessary to address structural discrimination in order to achieve racial equality in the United States?

5

True Women and Real Men

Myths of Gender

Bree Scott-Hartland as Delphinia Blue, photo by Carolyn Jones. (From *Living Proof,* Abbeville Press, 1994.)

FAST FACTS

1. Women hold 50.3% of all management and professional positions. Yet, only 7.9% of *Fortune* 500 top earners and 1.4 % of *Fortune* 500 CEOs are women.

2. Every year approximately 4 million American women are victims of serious assault by their husbands or partners.

3. Gay and lesbian teenagers are about four times more likely than their heterosexual classmates to be threatened with a weapon at school and are five times more likely to skip school because they feel unsafe.

4. Among men aged 15–44, 76.3% agree or strongly agree with the statement, "It is more important for a man to spend a lot of time with his family than to be successful at his career."

5. Some 73% of college and university faculty and 74% of students describe the climate of their campus as homophobic.

6. In thirty-four states employers may legally fire employees based on their sexual orientation; in forty-four states they may fire employees based on gender identity.

Sources: (1) Catalyst (www.catalyst.org), "Women 'Take Care,' Men 'Take Charge,'" 2005; (2) The National Domestic Violence Hotline (www.ndvh.org), "Abuse in America"; (3) ACLU (www.aclu.org), "Doing the Math: What the Numbers Say About Harassment of Gay, Lesbian, Bisexual, and Transgendered Students"; (4) CDC National Center for Health Statistics, "Fertility, Contraception, and Fatherhood," May 2006; (5) Susan R. Rankin, *Campus Climate for Gay, Lesbian, Bisexual, and Transgender People: A National Perspective* (New York: The National Gay and Lesbian Task Force Policy Institute, 2003); (6) Human Rights Campaign (www.hrc.org), "GLBT Workplace Issues."

COMMON SENSE TELLS US that there are obvious differences between females and males: after all, biology, not culture, determines whether you're able to bear children. But culture and cultural myths do shape the roles men and women play in our public and private relationships: we may be born female and male, but we are made women and men. Sociologists distinguish between sex and gender — between one's biological identity and the conventional patterns of behavior we learn to associate with each sex. While biological sex remains relatively stable, the definition of "appropriate" gender behavior varies dramatically from one cultural group or historical period to the next. The variations show up markedly in the way we dress. For example, in Thailand, men who act and dress like women are not only socially accepted but encouraged to participate in popular, male-only beauty pageants; in contemporary Anglo-American culture, on the other hand, cross-dressers are usually seen as deviant or ridiculous. Male clothing in late-seventeenth- and early-eighteenth-century England would also have failed our current "masculinity" tests: in that period, elaborate laces, brocades, wigs, and even makeup signaled wealth, status, and sexual attractiveness for men and women alike.

History shows us how completely our gender derives from cultural myths about what is proper for men and women to think, enjoy, and do. And history is replete with examples of how the apparent "naturalness" of gender has been used to regulate political, economic, and personal relations between the sexes.

Many nineteenth-century scientists argued that it was "unnatural" for women to attend college; rigorous intellectual activity, they asserted, would draw vital energy away from a woman's reproductive organs and make her sterile. According to this line of reasoning, women who sought higher education threatened the natural order by jeopardizing their ability to bear children and perpetuate the species. Arguments based on nature were likewise used to justify women's exclusion from political life. In his classic 1832 treatise on American democracy, James Fenimore Cooper remarked that women's domestic role and "necessary" subordination to men made them unsuitable for participation in public affairs. Thus denying women the right to vote was perfectly consistent with the principles of American democracy:

> In those countries where the suffrage is said to be universal, exceptions exist, that arise from the necessity of things. . . . The interests of women being thought to be so identified with those of their male relatives as to become, in a great degree, inseparable, females are, almost generally, excluded from the possession of political rights. There can be no doubt that society is greatly the gainer, by thus excluding one half its members, and the half that is best adapted to give a tone to its domestic happiness, from the strife of parties, and the fierce struggles of political controversies. . . . These exceptions, however, do not very materially affect the principle of political equality. (*The American Democrat*)

Resistance to gender equality has been remarkably persistent in the United States. It took over seventy years of hard political work by both black and white women's organizations to win the right to vote. But while feminists gained the vote for women in 1920 and the legal right to equal educational and employment opportunities in the 1970s, attitudes change even more slowly than laws. Contemporary antifeminist campaigns voice some of the same anxieties as their nineteenth-century counterparts over the "loss" of femininity and domesticity.

Women continue to suffer economic inequities based on cultural assumptions about gender. What's defined as "women's work" — nurturing, feeding, caring for family and home — is devalued and pays low wages or none at all. When women enter jobs traditionally held by men, they often encounter discrimination, harassment, or "glass ceilings" that limit their advancement. But men, too, pay a high price for their culturally imposed roles. Psychological research shows higher rates of depression among people of both sexes who adhere closely to traditional roles than among those who do not. Moreover, studies of men's mental and physical health suggest that social pressure to "be a man" (that is, to be emotionally controlled, powerful, and successful) can contribute to isolation, anxiety, stress, and illness, and may be partially responsible for men's shorter life spans. As sociologist Margaret Andersen observes, "traditional gender roles limit the psychological and social possibilities for human beings."

Even our assumption that there are "naturally" only two genders is a cultural invention that fails to accommodate the diversity of human experience. Some cultures have three or more gender categories. One of the best-known third genders is the American Indian *berdache,* a role that is found in as many as seventy North and South American tribes. The berdache is a biological male who takes the social role of a woman, does women's work (or in some cases both women's and men's work), and often enjoys high status in the society; the berdache has sex with men who are not themselves berdaches and in some cultures may also marry a man. Euro-American culture, by contrast, offers no socially acceptable alternative gender roles. As a result, gay men, lesbians, bisexuals, transsexuals, cross-dressers, and other gender rebels confront pervasive and often legally sanctioned discrimination similar to that once experienced by women. Just as many Americans in the past considered it "unnatural" and socially destructive for women to vote or go to college, many now consider it "unnatural" and socially destructive for gays and lesbians to marry, or for individuals to express a gender identity that violates conventional notions of masculinity or femininity.

This chapter focuses on cultural myths of gender and the influence they wield over human development and personal identity. The first three selections examine how dominant American culture defines female and male gender roles — and how those roles may define us. In "How the Americans Understand the Equality of the Sexes," Alexis de Tocqueville describes the status of American women in the early years of the Republic. Jamaica Kincaid's "Girl," a story framed as a mother's advice to her daughter, presents a more contemporary take on what it means to be raised a woman. Aaron H. Devor's "Becoming Members of Society" examines gender as a socially constructed category and discusses the psychological processes that underlie gender role acquisition. Next, two personal narratives and a Visual Portfolio offer contemporary rereadings of conventional gender roles. Judith Ortiz Cofer's personal reflection, "The Story of My Body," traces the shifting meanings of gender and identity for a woman of color who moves among different social and cultural contexts. In "A Boy's Life," journalist Hanna Rosin tells the story of Brandon Simms, an eight-year-old boy who desperately wants to be a girl. The portfolio presents both conventional and unconventional images of women and men that provide an opportunity to think about the ways that we "read" gender visually.

The second half of the chapter opens with two essays that examine the power of the media to reflect our attitudes and shape our behavior as women and men. Jean Kilbourne's " 'Two Ways a Woman Can Get Hurt': Advertising and Violence" argues that the objectification of women in ads constitutes a form of cultural abuse. In "From Fly-Girls to Bitches and Hos," self-described "hip-hop feminist" Joan Morgan takes a different approach to analyzing the depiction of women in popular culture: she maintains that it's necessary to look behind the violent misogyny of many rap lyrics in order to understand and heal the pain of the African American men who compose and perform the songs. The chapter concludes with three essays that focus on men. Michael Kimmel's " 'Bros Before Hos': The Guy Code" lays out the "rules" of masculinity that govern and at times distort the behavior and emotions of young men. "The Descent of Men," by Dan Kindlon, considers the growing dominance of women in higher education and predicts a major shift in men's roles as women achieve greater economic power. Reihan Salam, in "The Death of Macho," offers a counterpoint to Kindlon: he envisions men rebelling rather than adapting to their loss of power, warning that "We have no precedent for a world after the death of macho. But we can expect the transition to be wrenching, uneven, and possibly very violent."

Sources

Andersen, Margaret L. *Thinking About Women: Sociological Perspectives on Gender.* 3rd ed. New York: Macmillan, 1993. Print.

Cooper, James Fenimore. *The American Democrat.* N.p.: Minerva Press, 1969. Print.

French, Marilyn. *Beyond Power: On Women, Men, and Morals.* New York: Ballantine Books, 1985. Print.

Giddings, Paula. *When and Where I Enter: The Impact of Black Women on Race and Sex in America.* New York: Bantam Books, 1984. Print.

Hubbard, Ruth. *The Politics of Women's Biology.* New Brunswick, NJ: Rutgers University Press, 1990. Print.

Lorber, Judith. *Paradoxes of Gender.* New Haven and London: Yale University Press, 1994. Print.

Weinrich, James D. and Walter L. Williams, "Strange Customs, Familiar Lives: Homosexualities in Other Cultures." *Homosexuality: Research Implications for Public Policy.* Ed. John C. Gonsiorek and James D. Weinrich. Newbury Park, CA: Sage, 1991. Print.

BEFORE READING

- Imagine for a moment that you were born female (if you're a man) or male (if you're a woman). How would your life be different? Would any of your interests and activities change? How about your relationships with other people? Write a journal entry describing your past, present, and possible future in this alternate gender identity.

- Collect and bring to class images of girls and boys, women and men taken from popular magazines and newspapers. Working in groups, make a collage of either male or female gender images; then compare and discuss your results. What do these media images tell you about what it means to be a woman or a man in this culture?

- Do a brief freewrite focusing on the performer in the frontispiece to this chapter (p. 515). How would you describe this person's gender? In what ways does this image challenge traditional ideas about maleness and femaleness?

How the Americans Understand the Equality of the Sexes

ALEXIS DE TOCQUEVILLE

In 1831, Alexis de Tocqueville (1805–1859), a French aristocrat, left Europe to study the American penal system. The young democracy that he observed in the United States left a deep impression on Tocqueville, and in 1835 he published his reflections on this new way of life in Democracy in America — *a work that has since become the point of departure for many studies of American culture. In the following passage from* Democracy in America, *Tocqueville compares the social condition of American women to that of their European counterparts. Tocqueville's concept of equality and assumptions about women can seem foreign to modern readers, so it would be a good idea to take your time as you read this short passage.*

I have shown how democracy destroys or modifies the different inequalities which originate in society; but is that all? or does it not ultimately affect that great inequality of man and woman which has seemed, up to the present day, to be eternally based in human nature? I believe that the social changes which bring nearer to the same level the father and son, the master and servant, and, in general, superiors and inferiors, will raise woman, and make her more and more the equal of man. But here, more than ever, I feel the necessity of making myself clearly understood; for there is no subject on which the coarse and lawless fancies of our age have taken a freer range.

There are people in Europe who, confounding together the different characteristics of the sexes, would make man and woman into beings not only equal, but alike. They would give to both the same functions, impose on both the same duties, and grant to both the same rights; they would mix them in all things, — their occupations, their pleasures, their business. It may readily be conceived, that, by thus attempting to make one sex equal to the other, both are degraded; and from so preposterous a medley of the works of nature, nothing could ever result but weak men and disorderly women.

It is not thus that the Americans understand that species of democratic equality which may be established between the sexes. They admit that, as nature has appointed such wide differences between the physical and moral constitution of man and woman, her manifest design was to give a distinct employment to their various faculties; and they hold that improvement does not consist in making beings so dissimilar do pretty nearly the same things, but in causing each of them to fulfil their respective tasks in the best possible manner. The Americans have applied to the sexes the great principle of political economy which governs the manufactures of our age, by carefully dividing the duties of man from those of woman, in order that the great work of society may be the better carried on.

In no country has such constant care been taken as in America to trace two clearly distinct lines of action for the two sexes, and to make them keep pace one with the other, but in two pathways which are always different. American women never manage the outward concerns of the family, or conduct a business, or take a part in political life; nor are they, on the other hand, ever compelled to perform the rough labor of the fields, or to make any of those laborious exertions which demand the exertion of physical strength. No families are so poor as to form an exception to this rule. If, on the one hand, an American woman cannot escape from the quiet circle of domestic employments, she is never forced, on the other, to go beyond it. Hence it is, that the women of America, who often exhibit a masculine strength of understanding and a manly energy, generally preserve great delicacy of personal appearance, and always retain the manners of women, although they sometimes show that they have the hearts and minds of men.

Nor have the Americans ever supposed that one consequence of democratic principles is the subversion of marital power, or the confusion of the natural authorities in families. They hold that every association must have a head in order to accomplish its object, and that the natural head of the conjugal association is man. They do not therefore deny him the right of directing his partner; and they maintain that, in the smaller association of husband and wife, as well as in the great social community, the object of democracy is to regulate and legalize the powers which are necessary, and not to subvert all power.

5

This opinion is not peculiar to one sex, and contested by the other: I never observed that the women of America consider conjugal authority as a fortunate usurpation of their rights, nor that they thought themselves degraded by submitting to it. It appeared to me, on the contrary, that they attach a sort of pride to the voluntary surrender of their own will, and make it their boast to bend themselves to the yoke, — not to shake it off. Such, at least, is the feeling expressed by the most virtuous of their sex; the others are silent; and, in the United States, it is not the practice for a guilty wife to clamor for the rights of women, whilst she is trampling on her own holiest duties.[1]

It has often been remarked, that in Europe a certain degree of contempt lurks even in the flattery which men lavish upon women: although a European frequently affects to be the slave of woman, it may be seen that he never sincerely thinks her his equal. In the United States, men seldom compliment women, but they daily show how much they esteem them. They constantly display an entire confidence in the understanding of a wife, and a profound respect for her freedom; they have decided that her mind is just as fitted as that of a man to discover the plain truth, and her heart as firm to embrace it; and they have never sought to place her virtue, any more than his, under the shelter of prejudice, ignorance, and fear.

It would seem that, in Europe, where man so easily submits to the despotic sway of women, they are nevertheless deprived of some of the greatest attributes of the human species, and considered as seductive but imperfect beings; and (what may well provoke astonishment) women ultimately look upon themselves in the same light, and almost consider it as a privilege that they are entitled to show themselves futile, feeble, and timid. The women of America claim no such privileges.

Again, it may be said that in our morals we have reserved strange immunities to man; so that there is, as it were, one virtue for his use, and another for the guidance of his partner; and that, according to the opinion of the public, the very same act may be punished alternately as a crime, or only as a fault. The Americans know not this iniquitous division of duties and rights; amongst them, the seducer is as much dishonored as his victim.

It is true that the Americans rarely lavish upon women those eager   10
attentions which are commonly paid them in Europe; but their conduct to women always implies that they suppose them to be virtuous and refined; and such is the respect entertained for the moral freedom of the sex, that in the presence of a woman the most guarded language is used, lest her ear

---

[1]Allusion to Mary Wollstonecraft (1759–1797), English radical, political theorist, and author of *Vindication of the Rights of Woman,* who argued that women should enjoy complete political, economic, and sexual freedom; Wollstonecraft scandalized the "polite" society of her day by living according to her feminist principles.

should be offended by an expression. In America, a young unmarried woman may, alone and without fear, undertake a long journey.

The legislators of the United States, who have mitigated almost all the penalties of criminal law, still make rape a capital offence, and no crime is visited with more inexorable severity by public opinion. This may be accounted for; as the Americans can conceive nothing more precious than a woman's honor, and nothing which ought so much to be respected as her independence, they hold that no punishment is too severe for the man who deprives her of them against her will. In France, where the same offence is visited with far milder penalties, it is frequently difficult to get a verdict from a jury against the prisoner. Is this a consequence of contempt of decency, or contempt of women? I cannot but believe that it is a contempt of both.

Thus, the Americans do not think that man and woman have either the duty or the right to perform the same offices, but they show an equal regard for both their respective parts; and though their lot is different, they consider both of them as beings of equal value. They do not give to the courage of woman the same form or the same direction as to that of man; but they never doubt her courage: and if they hold that man and his partner ought not always to exercise their intellect and understanding in the same manner, they at least believe the understanding of the one to be as sound as that of the other, and her intellect to be as clear. Thus, then, whilst they have allowed the social inferiority of woman to subsist, they have done all they could to raise her morally and intellectually to the level of man; and in this respect they appear to me to have excellently understood the true principle of democratic improvement.

As for myself, I do not hesitate to avow, that, although the women of the United States are confined within the narrow circle of domestic life, and their situation is, in some respects, one of extreme dependence, I have nowhere seen woman occupying a loftier position; and if I were asked, now that I am drawing to the close of this work, in which I have spoken of so many important things done by the Americans, to what the singular prosperity and growing strength of that people ought mainly to be attributed, I should reply, To the superiority of their women.

ENGAGING THE TEXT

1. What roles does Tocqueville assume are natural and appropriate for women? For men? Which of his assumptions, if any, seem contemporary? Which ones seem antiquated, and why?

2. How do American and European attitudes toward women differ, according to Tocqueville? In what ways does he suggest that American democracy is enabling women to become "more and more the equal of man" (para. 1)?

3. By the time Tocqueville wrote this selection, the first feminist manifesto, Mary Wollstonecraft's *Vindication of the Rights of Woman* (1792), had been read and discussed in Europe for over forty years. Which parts of Tocqueville's essay seem to be intended as a response to feminist arguments for women's equality?

4. Tocqueville finds some forms of equality between women and men more desirable than others. Which forms does he approve of, which does he disapprove of, and why?

EXPLORING CONNECTIONS

5. Read the selection by Aaron H. Devor (p. 527); how and why does Devor's understanding of gender roles differ from Tocqueville's assumption that the "great inequality of man and woman" appears to be "eternally based in human nature" (para. 1)?

6. Both Tocqueville and Thomas Jefferson (p. 378) attempt to justify or rationalize a particular form of inequality. What strategies does each writer use to build his case for the subjection of women or for the enslavement of blacks? Which of their arguments appear least effective to you as a modern reader, and why?

EXTENDING THE CRITICAL CONTEXT

7. Work in groups to list the specific tasks involved in maintaining a household in the 1830s (keep in mind that electricity, indoor plumbing, ready-made clothing, and prepared foods were not available). How credible is Tocqueville's claim that no American woman is "ever compelled...to make any of those laborious exertions which demand the exertion of physical strength" (para. 4)? How do you explain his failure to acknowledge the hard physical labor routinely performed by many women during this time?

Girl

JAMAICA KINCAID

Although she now lives in New England, Jamaica Kincaid (b. 1949) retains strong ties, including citizenship, to her birthplace — the island of Antigua in the West Indies. After immigrating to the United States to attend college, she ended up educating herself instead, eventually becoming a staff writer for The New Yorker, *the author of several critically acclaimed books, and an instructor at Harvard University. About the influence of parents on children she says, "The magic is they carry so much you don't know about. They know you in a way you don't know yourself." Some of that magic is exercised in the story "Girl," which was first published in* The New Yorker *and later appeared in Kincaid's award-winning collection* At the Bottom of the River *(1983). She has written and edited many volumes of nonfiction on subjects ranging from colonialism to gardening and travel. She has published four novels:* Annie John *(1985),* Lucy *(1990),* The Autobiography of My Mother *(1996), and* Mr. Potter *(2002).*

Wash the white clothes on Monday and put them on the stone heap; wash the color clothes on Tuesday and put them on the clothesline to dry; don't walk barehead in the hot sun; cook pumpkin fritters[1] in very hot sweet oil; soak your little clothes right after you take them off; when buying cotton to make yourself a nice blouse, be sure that it doesn't have gum[2] on it, because that way it won't hold up well after a wash; soak salt fish overnight before you cook it; is it true that you sing benna[3] in Sunday school?; always eat your food in such a way that it won't turn someone else's stomach; on Sundays try to walk like a lady and not like the slut you are so bent on becoming; don't sing benna in Sunday school; you mustn't speak to wharf-rat boys, not even to give directions; don't eat fruits on the street — flies will follow you; *but I don't sing benna on Sundays at all and never in Sunday school;* this is how to sew on a button; this is how to make a buttonhole for the button you have just sewed on; this is how to hem a dress when you see the hem coming down and so to prevent yourself from looking like the slut I know you are so bent on becoming; this is how you iron your father's khaki shirt so that it doesn't have a crease; this is how you iron your father's khaki pants so that they don't have a crease; this is how you grow okra[4] — far from the house, because okra tree harbors red ants; when you are growing dasheen,[5] make sure it gets plenty of water or else it makes your throat itch when you are eating it; this is how you sweep a corner; this is how you sweep a whole house; this is how you sweep a yard; this is how you smile to someone you don't like too much; this is how you smile to someone you don't like at all; this is how you smile to someone you like completely; this is how you set a table for tea; this is how you set a table for dinner; this is how you set a table for dinner with an important guest; this is how you set a table for lunch; this is how you set a table for breakfast; this is how to behave in the presence of men who don't know you very well, and this way they won't recognize immediately the

---

[1]*fritters:* Small fried cakes of batter, often containing vegetables, fruit, or other fillings.
[2]*gum:* Plant residue on cotton.
[3]*sing benna:* Sing popular music (not appropriate for Sunday school).
[4]*okra:* A shrub whose pods are used in soups, stews, and gumbo.
[5]*dasheen:* The taro plant, cultivated, like the potato, for its edible tuber.

slut I have warned you against becoming; be sure to wash every day, even if it is with your own spit; don't squat down to play marbles — you are not a boy, you know; don't pick people's flowers — you might catch something; don't throw stones at blackbirds, because it might not be a blackbird at all; this is how to make a bread pudding; this is how to make doukona;[6] this is how to make pepper pot;[7] this is how to make a good medicine for a cold; this is how to make a good medicine to throw away a child before it even becomes a child; this is how to catch a fish; this is how to throw back a fish you don't like, and that way something bad won't fall on you; this is how to bully a man; this is how a man bullies you; this is how to love a man, and if this doesn't work there are other ways, and if they don't work don't feel too bad about giving up; this is how to spit up in the air if you feel like it, and this is how to move quick so that it doesn't fall on you; this is how to make ends meet; always squeeze bread to make sure it's fresh; *but what if the baker won't let me feel the bread?; you mean to say that after all you are really going to be the kind of woman who the baker won't let near the bread?

ENGAGING THE TEXT

1. What are your best guesses as to the time and place of the story? Who is telling the story? What does this dialogue tell you about the relationship between the characters, their values and attitudes? What else can you surmise about these people (for instance, ages, occupation, social status)? On what evidence in the story do you base these conclusions?

2. Why does the story juxtapose advice on cooking and sewing, for example, with the repeated warning not to act like a slut?

3. Explain the meaning of the last line of the story: "you mean to say that after all you are really going to be the kind of woman who the baker won't let near the bread?"

4. What does the story tell us about male-female relationships? According to the speaker, what roles are women and men expected to play? What kinds of power, if any, does the speaker suggest that women may have?

EXPLORING CONNECTIONS

5. To what extent would Tocqueville approve of the behaviors and attitudes that the mother is trying to teach her daughter in this selection?

6. What does it mean to be a successful mother in "Girl"? How does this compare to being a good mother or parent in "An Indian Story" (p. 52) or "Looking for Work" (p. 26)? Of all the parents in these narratives, which do you consider most successful, which least, and why?

---

[6]*doukona:* Plaintain pudding; the plaintain fruit is similar to the banana.
[7]*pepper pot:* A spicy West Indian stew.

Extending the Critical Context

7. Write an imitation of the story. If you are a woman, record some of the advice or lessons your mother or another woman gave you; if you are a man, put down advice received from your father or from another male. Read what you have written aloud in class, alternating between male and female speakers, and discuss the results: How does parental guidance vary according to gender?

8. Write a page or two recording what the daughter might be thinking as she listens to her mother's advice; then compare notes with classmates.

Becoming Members of Society: Learning the Social Meanings of Gender

Aaron H. Devor

Gender is the most transparent of all social categories: we acquire gender roles so early in life and so thoroughly that it's hard to see them as the result of lessons taught and learned. Maleness and femaleness seem "natural," not the product of socialization. In this wide-ranging scholarly essay, Aaron H. Devor suggests that many of our notions of what it means to be female or male are socially constructed. He also touches on the various ways that different cultures define gender. A professor of sociology and Dean of Graduate Studies at the University of Victoria in British Columbia, Devor is a member of the International Academy of Sex Research and author of FTM: Female-to-Male Transsexuals in Society *(1997). Born Holly Devor in 1951, Devor announced in 2002 his decision to live as a man and to adopt the name Aaron H. Devor. This selection is taken from his groundbreaking book,* Gender Blending: Confronting the Limits of Duality *(1989).*

The Gendered Self

The task of learning to be properly gendered members of society only begins with the establishment of gender identity. Gender identities act as cognitive filtering devices guiding people to attend to and learn gender role behaviors appropriate to their statuses. Learning to behave in accordance with one's gender identity is a lifelong process. As we move through our lives, society demands different gender performances from us and rewards, tolerates, or punishes us differently for conformity to, or digression from, social norms. As children, and later adults, learn the rules of membership in society, they come to see themselves in terms they have learned from the people around them.

Children begin to settle into a gender identity between the age of eighteen months and two years.[1] By the age of two, children usually understand that they are members of a gender grouping and can correctly identify other members of their gender.[2] By age three they have a fairly firm and consistent concept of gender. Generally, it is not until children are five to seven years old that they become convinced that they are permanent members of their gender grouping.[3]

Researchers test the establishment, depth, and tenacity of gender identity through the use of language and the concepts mediated by language. The language systems used in populations studied by most researchers in this field conceptualize gender as binary and permanent. All persons are either male or female. All males are first boys and then men; all females are first girls and then women. People are believed to be unable to change genders without sex change surgery, and those who do change sex are considered to be both disturbed and exceedingly rare.

This is by no means the only way that gender is conceived in all cultures. Many aboriginal cultures have more than two gender categories and accept the idea that, under certain circumstances, gender may be changed without changes being made to biological sex characteristics. Many North and South American native peoples had a legitimate social category for persons who wished to live according to the gender role of another sex. Such people were sometimes revered, sometimes ignored, and occasionally scorned. Each culture had its own word to describe such persons, most commonly translated into English as "berdache." Similar institutions and linguistic concepts have also been recorded in early Siberian, Madagascan, and Polynesian societies, as well as in medieval Europe.[4]

---

[1]Much research has been devoted to determining when gender identity becomes solidified in the sense that a child knows itself to be unequivocally either male or female. John Money and his colleagues have proposed eighteen months of age because it is difficult or impossible to change a child's gender identity once it has been established around the age of eighteen months. Money and Ehrhardt, p. 243. [All notes are Devor's unless otherwise indicated.]

[2]Mary Driver Leinbach and Beverly I. Fagot, "Acquisition of Gender Labels: A Test for Toddlers," *Sex Roles* 15 (1986), pp. 655–66.

[3]Maccoby, pp. 225–29; Kohlberg and Ullian, p. 211.

[4]See Susan Baker, "Biological Influences on Human Sex and Gender," in *Women: Sex and Sexuality*, ed. Catherine R. Stimpson and Ethel S. Person (Chicago: University of Chicago Press, 1980), p. 186; Evelyn Blackwood, "Sexuality and Gender in Certain Native American Tribes: The Case of Cross-Gender Females," *Signs* 10 (1984), pp. 27–42; Vern L. Bullough, "Transvestites in the Middle Ages," *American Journal of Sociology* 79 (1974), 1381–89; J. Cl. DuBois, "Transsexualisme et Anthropologie Culturelle," *Gynecologie Practique* 6 (1969), pp. 431–40; Donald C. Forgey, "The Institution of Berdache among the North American Plains Indians," *Journal of Sex Research* 11 (Feb. 1975), pp. 1–15; Walter L. Williams, *The Spirit and the Flesh: Sexual Diversity in American Indian Culture* (Boston: Beacon, 1986).

Very young children learn their culture's social definitions of gender   5
and gender identity at the same time that they learn what gender behaviors
are appropriate for them. But they only gradually come to understand the
meaning of gender in the same way as the adults of their society do. Very
young children may learn the words which describe their gender and be
able to apply them to themselves appropriately, but their comprehension of
their meaning is often different from that used by adults. Five-year-olds, for
example, may be able to accurately recognize their own gender and the genders of the people around them, but they will often make such ascriptions
on the basis of role information, such as hair style, rather than physical
attributes, such as genitals, even when physical cues are clearly known to
them. One result of this level of understanding of gender is that children in
this age group often believe that people may change their gender with a
change in clothing, hair style, or activity.[5]

The characteristics most salient to young minds are the more culturally
specific qualities which grow out of gender role prescriptions. In one study,
young school age children, who were given dolls and asked to identify their
gender, overwhelmingly identified the gender of the dolls on the basis of
attributes such as hair length or clothing style, in spite of the fact that the dolls
were anatomically correct. Only 17 percent of the children identified the
dolls on the basis of their primary or secondary sex characteristics.[6] Children
five to seven years old understand gender as a function of role rather than as a
function of anatomy. Their understanding is that gender (role) is supposed to
be stable but that it is possible to alter it at will. This demonstrates that
although the standard social definition of gender is based on genitalia, this is
not the way that young children first learn to distinguish gender. The process
of learning to think about gender in an adult fashion is one prerequisite to
becoming a full member of society. Thus, as children grow older, they learn
to think of themselves and others in terms more like those used by adults.

Children's developing concepts of themselves as individuals are necessarily bound up in their need to understand the expectations of the society
of which they are a part. As they develop concepts of themselves as individuals, they do so while observing themselves as reflected in the eyes of
others. Children start to understand themselves as individuals separate from
others during the years that they first acquire gender identities and gender
roles. As they do so, they begin to understand that others see them and
respond to them as particular people. In this way they develop concepts of
themselves as individuals, as an "I" (a proactive subject) simultaneously with
self-images of themselves as individuals, as a "me" (a member of society, a
subjective object). Children learn that they are both as they see themselves
and as others see them.[7]

---

[5]Maccoby, p. 255.

[6]Ibid., p. 227.

[7]George Herbert Mead, "Self," in *The Social Psychology of George Herbert Mead*, ed.
Anselm Strauss (Chicago: Phoenix Books, 1962, 1934), pp. 212–60.

To some extent, children initially acquire the values of the society around them almost indiscriminately. To the degree that children absorb the generalized standards of society into their personal concept of what is correct behavior, they can be said to hold within themselves the attitude of the "generalized other."[8] This "generalized other" functions as a sort of monitoring or measuring device with which individuals may judge their own actions against those of their generalized conceptions of how members of society are expected to act. In this way members of society have available to them a guide, or an internalized observer, to turn the more private "I" into the object of public scrutiny, the "me." In this way, people can monitor their own behavioral impulses and censor actions which might earn them social disapproval or scorn. The tension created by the constant interplay of the personal "I" and the social "me" is the creature known as the "self."

But not all others are of equal significance in our lives, and therefore not all others are of equal impact on the development of the self. Any person is available to become part of one's "generalized other," but certain individuals, by virtue of the sheer volume of time spent in interaction with someone, or by virtue of the nature of particular interactions, become more significant in the shaping of people's values. These "significant others" become prominent in the formation of one's self-image and one's ideals and goals. As such they carry disproportionate weight in one's personal "generalized other."[9] Thus, children's individualistic impulses are shaped into a socially acceptable form both by particular individuals and by a more generalized pressure to conformity exerted by innumerable faceless members of society. Gender identity is one of the most central portions of that developing sense of self. . . .

Gender Role Behaviors and Attitudes

The clusters of social definitions used to identify persons by gender are collectively known as femininity and masculinity. Masculine characteristics are used to identify persons as males, while feminine ones are used as signifiers for femaleness. People use femininity or masculinity to claim and communicate their membership in their assigned, or chosen, sex or gender. Others recognize our sex or gender more on the basis of these characteristics than on the basis of sex characteristics, which are usually largely covered by clothing in daily life.

These two clusters of attributes are most commonly seen as mirror images of one another with masculinity usually characterized by dominance and aggression, and femininity by passivity and submission. A more even- 10

[8]G. H. Mead.
[9]Hans Gerth and C. Wright Mills, *Character and Social Structure: The Psychology of Social Institutions* (New York: Harcourt, Brace and World, 1953), p. 96.

handed description of the social qualities subsumed by femininity and masculinity might be to label masculinity as generally concerned with egoistic dominance and femininity as striving for cooperation or communion.[10] Characterizing femininity and masculinity in such a way does not portray the two clusters of characteristics as being in a hierarchical relationship to one another but rather as being two different approaches to the same question, that question being centrally concerned with the goals, means, and use of power. Such an alternative conception of gender roles captures the hierarchical and competitive masculine thirst for power, which can, but need not, lead to aggression, and the feminine quest for harmony and communal well-being, which can, but need not, result in passivity and dependence.

Many activities and modes of expression are recognized by most members of society as feminine. Any of these can be, and often are, displayed by persons of either gender. In some cases, cross gender behaviors are ignored by observers, and therefore do not compromise the integrity of a person's gender display. In other cases, they are labeled as inappropriate gender role behaviors. Although these behaviors are closely linked to sexual status in the minds and experiences of most people, research shows that dominant persons of either gender tend to use influence tactics and verbal styles usually associated with men and masculinity, while subordinate persons, of either gender, tend to use those considered to be the province of women.[11] Thus it seems likely that many aspects of masculinity and femininity are the result, rather than the cause, of status inequalities.

Popular conceptions of femininity and masculinity instead revolve around hierarchical appraisals of the "natural" roles of males and females. Members of both genders are believed to share many of the same human characteristics, although in different relative proportions; both males and females are popularly thought to be able to do many of the same things, but most activities are divided into suitable and unsuitable categories for each gender class. Persons who perform the activities considered appropriate for another gender will be expected to perform them poorly; if they succeed adequately, or even well, at their endeavors, they may be rewarded with ridicule or scorn for blurring the gender dividing line.

---

[10]Egoistic dominance is a striving for superior rewards for oneself or a competitive striving to reduce the rewards for one's competitors even if such action will not increase one's own rewards. Persons who are motivated by desires for egoistic dominance not only wish the best for themselves but also wish to diminish the advantages of others whom they may perceive as competing with them. See Maccoby, p. 217.

[11]Judith Howard, Philip Blumstein, and Pepper Schwartz, "Sex, Power, and Influence Tactics in Intimate Relationships," *Journal of Personality and Social Psychology* 51 (1986), pp. 102–09; Peter Kollock, Philip Blumstein, and Pepper Schwartz, "Sex and Power in Interaction: Conversational Privileges and Duties," *American Sociological Review* 50 (1985), pp. 34–46.

The patriarchal gender schema[12] currently in use in mainstream North American society reserves highly valued attributes for males and actively supports the high evaluation of any characteristics which might inadvertently become associated with maleness. The ideology which the schema grows out of postulates that the cultural superiority of males is a natural outgrowth of the innate predisposition of males toward aggression and dominance, which is assumed to flow inevitably from evolutionary and biological sources. Female attributes are likewise postulated to find their source in innate predispositions acquired in the evolution of the species. Feminine characteristics are thought to be intrinsic to the female facility for childbirth and breastfeeding. Hence, it is popularly believed that the social position of females is biologically mandated to be intertwined with the care of children and a "natural" dependency on men for the maintenance of mother-child units. Thus the goals of femininity and, by implication, of all biological females are presumed to revolve around heterosexuality and maternity.[13]

Femininity, according to this traditional formulation, "would result in   15
warm and continued relationships with men, a sense of maternity, interest in caring for children, and the capacity to work productively and continuously in female occupations."[14] This recipe translates into a vast number of proscriptions and prescriptions. Warm and continued relations with men and an interest in maternity require that females be heterosexually oriented. A heterosexual orientation requires women to dress, move, speak, and act in ways that men will find attractive. As patriarchy has reserved active expressions of power as a masculine attribute, femininity must be expressed through modes of dress, movement, speech, and action which communicate weakness, dependency, ineffectualness, availability for sexual or emotional service, and sensitivity to the needs of others.

Some, but not all, of these modes of interrelation also serve the demands of maternity and many female job ghettos. In many cases, though, femininity is not particularly useful in maternity or employment. Both mothers and workers often need to be strong, independent, and effectual in order to do their jobs well. Thus femininity, as a role, is best suited to satisfying a masculine vision of heterosexual attractiveness.

Body postures and demeanors which communicate subordinate status and vulnerability to trespass through a message of "no threat" make people appear to be feminine. They demonstrate subordination through a minimizing of spatial use: people appear feminine when they keep their arms closer to

---

[12]*schema:* A mental framework, scheme, or pattern that helps us make sense of experience. [Eds.]

[13]Chodorow, p. 134.

[14]Jon K. Meyer and John E. Hoopes, "The Gender Dysphoria Syndromes: A Position Statement on So-Called 'Transsexualism'," *Plastic and Reconstructive Surgery* 54 (Oct. 1974), pp. 444–51.

their bodies, their legs closer together, and their torsos and heads less vertical then do masculine-looking individuals. People also look feminine when they point their toes inward and use their hands in small or childlike gestures. Other people also tend to stand closer to people they see as feminine, often invading their personal space, while people who make frequent appeasement gestures, such as smiling, also give the appearance of femininity. Perhaps as an outgrowth of a subordinate status and the need to avoid conflict with more socially powerful people, women tend to excel over men at the ability to correctly interpret, and effectively display, nonverbal communication cues.[15]

Speech characterized by inflections, intonations, and phrases that convey nonaggression and subordinate status also make a speaker appear more feminine. Subordinate speakers who use more polite expressions and ask more questions in conversation seem more feminine. Speech characterized by sounds of higher frequencies are often interpreted by listeners as feminine, childlike, and ineffectual.[16] Feminine styles of dress likewise display subordinate status through greater restriction of the free movement of the body, greater exposure of the bare skin, and an emphasis on sexual characteristics. The more gender distinct the dress, the more this is the case.

Masculinity, like femininity, can be demonstrated through a wide variety of cues. Pleck has argued that it is commonly expressed in North American society through the attainment of some level of proficiency at some, or all, of the following four main attitudes of masculinity. Persons who display success and high status in their social group, who exhibit "a manly air of toughness, confidence, and self-reliance" and "the aura of aggression, violence, and daring," and who conscientiously avoid anything associated with femininity are seen as exuding masculinity.[17] These requirements reflect the patriarchal ideology that masculinity results from an excess of testosterone, the assumption being that androgens supply a natural impetus toward aggression, which in turn impels males toward achievement and success. This vision of masculinity also reflects the ideological stance that ideal maleness (masculinity) must remain untainted by female (feminine) pollutants.

Masculinity, then, requires of its actors that they organize themselves and their society in a hierarchical manner so as to be able to explicitly quantify the achievement of success. The achievement of high status in one's social group   20

---

[15]Erving Goffman, *Gender Advertisements* (New York: Harper Colophon Books, 1976); Judith A. Hall, *Non-Verbal Sex Differences: Communication Accuracy and Expressive Style* (Baltimore: Johns Hopkins University Press, 1984); Nancy M. Henley, *Body Politics: Power, Sex and Non-Verbal Communication* (Englewood Cliffs, New Jersey: Prentice Hall, 1979); Marianne Wex, *"Let's Take Back Our Space": "Female" and "Male" Body Language as a Result of Patriarchal Structures* (Berlin: Frauenliteraturverlag Hermine Fees, 1979).

[16]Karen L. Adams, "Sexism and the English Language: The Linguistic Implications of Being a Woman," in *Women: A Feminist Perspective*, 3rd edition, ed. Jo Freeman (Palo Alto, Calif.: Mayfield, 1984), pp. 478–91; Hall, pp. 37, 130–37.

[17]Elizabeth Hafkin Pleck, *Domestic Tyranny: The Making of Social Policy Against Family Violence from Colonial Times to the Present* (Cambridge: Oxford University Press, 1989), p. 139.

requires competitive and aggressive behavior from those who wish to obtain it. Competition which is motivated by a goal of individual achievement, or egoistic dominance, also requires of its participants a degree of emotional insensitivity to feelings of hurt and loss in defeated others, and a measure of emotional insularity to protect oneself from becoming vulnerable to manipulation by others. Such values lead those who subscribe to them to view feminine persons as "born losers" and to strive to eliminate any similarities to feminine people from their own personalities. In patriarchally organized societies, masculine values become the ideological structure of the society as a whole. Masculinity thus becomes "innately" valuable and femininity serves a contrapuntal function to delineate and magnify the hierarchical dominance of masculinity.

Body postures, speech patterns, and styles of dress which demonstrate and support the assumption of dominance and authority convey an impression of masculinity. Typical masculine body postures tend to be expansive and aggressive. People who hold their arms and hands in positions away from their bodies, and who stand, sit, or lie with their legs apart — thus maximizing the amount of space that they physically occupy — appear most physically masculine. Persons who communicate an air of authority or a readiness for aggression by standing erect and moving forcefully also tend to appear more masculine. Movements that are abrupt and stiff, communicating force and threat rather than flexibility and cooperation, make an actor look masculine. Masculinity can also be conveyed by stern or serious facial expressions that suggest minimal receptivity to the influence of others, a characteristic which is an important element in the attainment and maintenance of egoistic dominance.[18]

Speech and dress which likewise demonstrate or claim superior status are also seen as characteristically masculine behavior patterns. Masculine speech patterns display a tendency toward expansiveness similar to that found in masculine body postures. People who attempt to control the direction of conversations seem more masculine.[19] Those who tend to speak more loudly, use less polite and more assertive forms, and tend to interrupt the conversations of others more often also communicate masculinity to others. Styles of dress which emphasize the size of upper body musculature, allow freedom of movement, and encourage an illusion of physical power and a look of easy physicality all suggest masculinity. Such appearances of strength and readiness to action serve to create or enhance an aura of aggressiveness and intimidation central to an appearance of masculinity. Expansive postures and gestures combine with these qualities to insinuate that a position of secure dominance is a masculine one.

Gender role characteristics reflect the ideological contentions underlying the dominant gender schema in North American society. That schema

---

[18]Goffman, *Gender Advertisements;* Hall; Henley; Wex.
[19]Adams; Hall, pp. 37, 130–37.

"We don't believe in pressuring the children. When the time is right, they'll choose the appropriate gender."

leads us to believe that female and male behaviors are the result of socially directed hormonal instructions which specify that females will want to have children and will therefore find themselves relatively helpless and dependent on males for support and protection. The schema claims that males are innately aggressive and competitive and therefore will dominate over females. The social hegemony[20] of this ideology ensures that we are all raised to practice gender roles which will confirm this vision of the nature of the sexes. Fortunately, our training to gender roles is neither complete nor uniform. As a result, it is possible to point to multitudinous exceptions to, and variations on, these themes. Biological evidence is equivocal about the source of gender roles; psychological androgyny[21] is a widely accepted concept. It seems most likely that gender roles are the result of systematic power imbalances based on gender discrimination.[22]

---

[20]*hegemony:* System of preponderant influence, authority, or dominance. [Eds.]

[21]*androgyny:* The state of having both male and female characteristics. [Eds.]

[22]Howard, Blumstein, and Schwartz; Kollock, Blumstein, and Schwartz.

ENGAGING THE TEXT

1. Devor charges that most languages present gender as "binary and permanent" (para. 3). Has this been your own view? How does Devor challenge this idea — that is, what's the alternative to gender being binary and permanent — and how persuasive do you find his evidence?

2. How, according to Devor, do children "acquire" gender roles? What are the functions of the "generalized other" and the "significant other" in this process?

3. Explain the distinction Devor makes between the "I" and the "me" (paras. 7 and 8). Write a journal entry describing some of the differences between your own "I" and "me."

4. Using examples from Devor and from other reading or observation, list some "activities and modes of expression" (para. 12) that society considers characteristically female and characteristically male. Which are acceptable cross-gender behaviors, and which are not? Search for a "rule" that defines what types of cross-gender behaviors are tolerated.

5. Do some aspects of the traditional gender roles described by Devor seem to be changing? If so, which ones, and how?

EXPLORING CONNECTIONS

6. To what extent do Alexis de Tocqueville's views of women and men (p. 520) reflect the "patriarchal gender schema" as Devor defines it?

7. Drawing on Devor's discussion of gender role formation, analyze the difference between the "I" and the "me" of the girl in Jamaica Kincaid's story (p. 524).

8. How would Devor explain the humor of the cartoon on page 535? How do the details of the cartoon — the setting, the women's appearance, the three pictures on the coffee table — contribute to its effect?

EXTENDING THE CRITICAL CONTEXT

9. As a class, identify at least half a dozen men living today who are widely admired in American culture. To what extent do they embody the "four main attitudes of masculinity" outlined by Devor (para. 19)?

10. Write an essay or journal entry analyzing your own gender role socialization. To what extent have you been pressured to conform to conventional roles? To what extent have you resisted them? What roles have "generalized others" and "significant others" played in shaping your identity?

The Story of My Body
JUDITH ORTIZ COFER

Accepting the idea that gender roles are socially constructed might not be too difficult, but it may come as a shock to realize that even the way we see our bodies is filtered through the lens of social values and beliefs. In this personal essay, Judith Ortiz Cofer reflects on the different roles her own body has assumed in different contexts and cultures — the ways that different societies have "read" the meanings of her physical appearance. The story of her body becomes, to some extent, the story of her life, and woven into the tale are intriguing comments on gender and on cross-cultural perception. A native of Puerto Rico, Ortiz Cofer (b. 1952) is the Franklin Professor of English and Creative Writing at the University of Georgia. Her publications include three novels and many collections of poetry and prose, including Silent Dancing: A Partial Remembrance of a Puerto Rican Childhood *(1990),* An Island Like You: Stories of the Barrio *(1995),* Woman in Front of the Sun: On Becoming a Writer *(2000), and most recently,* A Love Story Beginning in Spanish: Poems *(2005). "The Story of My Body" appeared in* The Latin Deli *(1993).*

> Migration is the story of my body.
> — VICTOR HERNÁNDEZ CRUZ

Skin

I was born a white girl in Puerto Rico but became a brown girl when I came to live in the United States. My Puerto Rican relatives called me tall; at the American school, some of my rougher classmates called me Skinny Bones, and the Shrimp because I was the smallest member of my classes all through grammar school until high school, when the midget Gladys was given the honorary post of front row center for class pictures and score-keeper, bench warmer, in P.E. I reached my full stature of five feet in sixth grade.

I started out life as a pretty baby and learned to be a pretty girl from a pretty mother. Then at ten years of age I suffered one of the worst cases of chicken pox I have ever heard of. My entire body, including the inside of my ears and in between my toes, was covered with pustules which in a fit of panic at my appearance I scratched off my face, leaving permanent scars. A cruel school nurse told me I would always have them — tiny cuts that looked as if a mad cat had plunged its claws deep into my skin. I grew my hair long and hid behind it for the first years of my adolescence. This was when I learned to be invisible.

Color

In the animal world it indicates danger: the most colorful creatures are often the most poisonous. Color is also a way to attract and seduce a mate. In the human world color triggers many more complex and often deadly reactions. As a Puerto Rican girl born of "white" parents, I spent the first years of my life hearing people refer to me as *blanca,* white. My mother insisted that I protect myself from the intense island sun because I was more prone to sunburn than some of my darker, *trigueño*[1] playmates. People were always commenting within my hearing about how my black hair contrasted so nicely with my "pale" skin. I did not think of the color of my skin consciously except when I heard the adults talking about complexion. It seems to me that the subject is much more common in the conversation of mixed-race peoples than in mainstream United States society, where it is a touchy and sometimes even embarrassing topic to discuss, except in a political context. In Puerto Rico I heard many conversations about skin color. A pregnant woman could say, "I hope my baby doesn't turn out *prieto*" (slang for "dark" or "black") "like my husband's grandmother, although she was a good-looking *negra*[2] in her time." I am a combination of both, being olive-skinned — lighter than my mother yet darker than my fair-skinned father. In America, I am a person of color, obviously a Latina. On the Island I have been called everything from a *paloma blanca,*[3] after the song (by a black suitor), to *la gringa.*[4]

My first experience of color prejudice occurred in a supermarket in Paterson, New Jersey. It was Christmastime, and I was eight or nine years old. There was a display of toys in the store where I went two or three times a day to buy things for my mother, who never made lists but sent for milk, cigarettes, a can of this or that, as she remembered from hour to hour. I enjoyed being trusted with money and walking half a city block to the new, modern grocery store. It was owned by three good-looking Italian brothers. I liked the younger one with the crew-cut blond hair. The two older ones watched me and the other Puerto Rican kids as if they thought we were going to steal something. The oldest one would sometimes even try to hurry me with my purchases, although part of my pleasure in these expeditions came from looking at everything in the well-stocked aisles. I was also teaching myself to read English by sounding out the labels on packages: L&M cigarettes, Borden's

[1]*trigueño:* Brown-skinned.
[2]*negra:* Black.
[3]*paloma blanca:* White dove.
[4]*la gringa:* A white, non-Latina woman.

homogenized milk, Red Devil potted ham, Nestle's chocolate mix, Quaker oats, Bustelo coffee, Wonder bread, Colgate toothpaste, Ivory soap, and Goya (makers of products used in Puerto Rican dishes) everything — these are some of the brand names that taught me nouns. Several times this man had come up to me, wearing his blood-stained butcher's apron, and towering over me had asked in a harsh voice whether there was something he could help me find. On the way out I would glance at the younger brother who ran one of the registers and he would often smile and wink at me.

It was the mean brother who first referred to me as "colored." It was a few days before Christmas, and my parents had already told my brother and me that since we were in Los Estados[5] now, we would get our presents on December 25 instead of Los Reyes, Three Kings Day, when gifts are exchanged in Puerto Rico. We were to give them a wish list that they would take to Santa Claus, who apparently lived in the Macy's store downtown — at least that's where we had caught a glimpse of him when we went shopping. Since my parents were timid about entering the fancy store, we did not approach the huge man in the red suit. I was not interested in sitting on a stranger's lap anyway. But I did covet Susie, the talking schoolteacher doll that was displayed in the center aisle of the Italian brothers' supermarket. She talked when you pulled a string on her back. Susie had a limited repertoire of three sentences: I think she could say: "Hello, I'm Susie Schoolteacher," "Two plus two is four," and one other thing I cannot remember. The day the older brother chased me away, I was reaching to touch Susie's blond curls. I had been told many times, as most children have, not to touch anything in the store that I was not buying. But I had been looking at Susie for weeks. In my mind, she was my doll. After all, I had put her on my Christmas wish list. The moment is frozen in my mind as if there were a photograph of it on file. It was not a turning point, a disaster, or an earth-shaking revelation. It was simply the first time I considered — if naively — the meaning of skin color in human relations.

I reached to touch Susie's hair. It seems to me that I had to get on tiptoe, since the toys were stacked on a table and she sat like a princess on top of the fancy box she came in. Then I heard the booming "Hey, kid, what do you think you're doing!" spoken very loudly from the meat counter. I felt caught, although I knew I was not doing anything criminal. I remember not looking at the man, but standing there, feeling humiliated because I knew everyone in the store must have heard him yell at me. I felt him approach, and when I knew he was behind me, I turned around to face the bloody butcher's apron. His large chest was at my eye level. He blocked my way. I started to run out of the place, but even as I reached the door I heard him shout after me: "Don't come in here unless you gonna buy something. You PR kids put your dirty hands on stuff. You always look dirty. But maybe

5

---

[5]*Los Estados:* "The States" — that is, the United States.

dirty brown is your natural color." I heard him laugh and someone else too in the back. Outside in the sunlight I looked at my hands. My nails needed a little cleaning as they always did, since I liked to paint with watercolors, but I took a bath every night. I thought the man was dirtier than I was in his stained apron. He was also always sweaty — it showed in big yellow circles under his shirt-sleeves. I sat on the front steps of the apartment building where we lived and looked closely at my hands, which showed the only skin I could see, since it was bitter cold and I was wearing my quilted play coat, dungarees, and a knitted navy cap of my father's. I was not pink like my friend Charlene and her sister Kathy, who had blue eyes and light brown hair. My skin is the color of the coffee my grandmother made, which was half milk, *leche con café* rather than *café con leche*.[6] My mother is the opposite mix. She has a lot of café in her color. I could not understand how my skin looked like dirt to the supermarket man.

I went in and washed my hands thoroughly with soap and hot water, and borrowing my mother's nail file, I cleaned the crusted watercolors from underneath my nails. I was pleased with the results. My skin was the same color as before, but I knew I was clean. Clean enough to run my fingers through Susie's fine gold hair when she came home to me.

Size

My mother is barely four feet eleven inches in height, which is average for women in her family. When I grew to five feet by age twelve, she was amazed and began to use the word tall to describe me, as in "Since you are tall, this dress will look good on you." As with the color of my skin, I didn't consciously think about my height or size until other people made an issue of it. It is around the preadolescent years that in America the games children play for fun become fierce competitions where everyone is out to "prove" they are better than others. It was in the playground and sports fields that my size-related problems began. No matter how familiar the story is, every child who is the last chosen for a team knows the torment of waiting to be called up. At the Paterson, New Jersey, public schools that I attended, the volleyball or softball game was the metaphor for the battle-field of life to the inner city kids — the black kids versus the Puerto Rican kids, the whites versus the blacks versus the Puerto Rican kids; and I was 4F,[7] skinny, short, bespectacled, and apparently impervious to the blood thirst that drove many of my classmates to play ball as if their lives depended on it. Perhaps they did. I would rather be reading a book than sweating, grunting, and running the risk of pain and injury. I simply did not

---

[6]*leche con café . . . café con leche:* Milk with coffee (light brown) . . . coffee with milk (dark brown).

[7]*4F:* Draft-board classification meaning "unfit for military service;" hence, not physically fit.

see the point in competitive sports. My main form of exercise then was walking to the library, many city blocks away from my barrio.

Still, I wanted to be wanted. I wanted to be chosen for the team. Physical education was compulsory, a class where you were actually given a grade. On my mainly all A report card, the C for compassion I always received from the P.E. teachers shamed me the same as a bad grade in a real class. Invariably, my father would say: "How can you make a low grade for *playing games?*" He did not understand. Even if I had managed to make a hit (it never happened) or get the ball over that ridiculously high net, I already had a reputation as a "shrimp," a hopeless nonathlete. It was an area where the girls who didn't like me for one reason or another — mainly because I did better than they on academic subjects — could lord it over me; the playing field was the place where even the smallest girl could make me feel powerless and inferior. I instinctively understood the politics even then; how the *not* choosing me until the teacher forced one of the team captains to call my name was a coup of sorts — there, you little show-off, tomorrow you can beat us in spelling and geography, but this afternoon you are the loser. Or perhaps those were only my own bitter thoughts as I sat or stood in the sidelines while the big girls were grabbed like fish and I, the little brown tadpole, was ignored until Teacher looked over in my general direction and shouted, "Call Ortiz," or, worse, "Somebody's *got* to take her."

No wonder I read Wonder Woman comics and had Legion of Super Heroes daydreams. Although I wanted to think of myself as "intellectual," my body was demanding that I notice it. I saw the little swelling around my once-flat nipples, the fine hairs growing in secret places; but my knees were still bigger than my thighs, and I always wore long- or half-sleeve blouses to hide my bony upper arms. I wanted flesh on my bones — a thick layer of it. I saw a new product advertised on TV. Wate-On. They showed skinny men and women before and after taking the stuff, and it was a transformation like the ninety-seven-pound-weakling-turned-into-Charles-Atlas ads that I saw on the back covers of my comic books. The Wate-On was very expensive. I tried to explain my need for it in Spanish to my mother, but it didn't translate very well, even to my ears — and she said with a tone of finality, eat more of my good food and you'll get fat — anybody can get fat. Right. Except me. I was going to have to join a circus someday as Skinny Bones, the woman without flesh.

Wonder Woman was stacked. She had a cleavage framed by the spread wings of a golden eagle and a muscular body that has become fashionable with women only recently. But since I wanted a body that would serve me in P.E., hers was my ideal. The breasts were an indulgence I allowed myself. Perhaps the daydreams of bigger girls were more glamorous, since our ambitions are filtered through our needs, but I wanted first a powerful body. I daydreamed of leaping up above the gray landscape of the city to where the sky was clear and blue, and in anger and self-pity, I fantasized about scooping my enemies up by their hair from the playing fields and dumping them on a barren asteroid. I would put the P.E. teachers each on

10

their own rock in space too, where they would be the loneliest people in the universe, since I knew they had no "inner resources," no imagination, and in outer space, there would be no air for them to fill their deflated volleyballs with. In my mind all P.E. teachers have blended into one large spiky-haired woman with a whistle on a string around her neck and a volleyball under one arm. My Wonder Woman fantasies of revenge were a source of comfort to me in my early career as a shrimp.

I was saved from more years of P.E. torment by the fact that in my sophomore year of high school I transferred to a school where the midget, Gladys, was the focal point of interest for the people who must rank according to size. Because her height was considered a handicap, there was an unspoken rule about mentioning size around Gladys, but of course, there was no need to say anything. Gladys knew her place: front row center in class photographs. I gladly moved to the left or to the right of her, as far as I could without leaving the picture completely.

Looks

Many photographs were taken of me as a baby by my mother to send to my father, who was stationed overseas during the first two years of my life. With the army in Panama when I was born, he later traveled often on tours of duty with the navy. I was a healthy, pretty baby. Recently, I read that people are drawn to big-eyed round-faced creatures, like puppies, kittens, and certain other mammals and marsupials, koalas, for example, and, of course, infants. I was all eyes, since my head and body, even as I grew older, remained thin and small-boned. As a young child I got a lot of attention from my relatives and many other people we met in our barrio. My mother's beauty may have had something to do with how much attention we got from strangers in stores and on the street. I can imagine it. In the pictures I have seen of us together, she is a stunning young woman by Latino standards: long, curly black hair, and round curves in a compact frame. From her I learned how to move, smile, and talk like an attractive woman. I remember going into a bodega[8] for our groceries and being given candy by the proprietor as a reward for being *bonita*, pretty.

I can see in the photographs, and I also remember, that I was dressed in the pretty clothes, the stiff, frilly dresses, with layers of crinolines underneath, the glossy patent leather shoes, and, on special occasions, the skull-hugging little hats and the white gloves that were popular in the late fifties and early sixties. My mother was proud of my looks, although I was a bit too thin. She could dress me up like a doll and take me by the hand to visit relatives, or go to the Spanish mass at the Catholic church and show me off. How was I to know that she and the others who called me "pretty" were

[8]*bodega:* Market.

representatives of an aesthetic that would not apply when I went out into the mainstream world of school?

In my Paterson, New Jersey, public schools there were still quite a few white children, although the demographics of the city were changing rapidly. The original waves of Italian and Irish immigrants, silk-mill workers, and laborers in the cloth industries had been "assimilated." Their children were now the middle-class parents of my peers. Many of them moved their children to the Catholic schools that proliferated enough to have leagues of basketball teams. The names I recall hearing still ring in my ears: Don Bosco High versus St. Mary's High, St. Joseph's versus St. John's. Later I too would be transferred to the safer environment of a Catholic school. But I started school at Public School Number 11. I came there from Puerto Rico, thinking myself a pretty girl, and found that the hierarchy for popularity was as follows: pretty white girl, pretty Jewish girl, pretty Puerto Rican girl, pretty black girl. Drop the last two categories; teachers were too busy to have more than one favorite per class, and it was simply understood that if there was a big part in the school play, or any competition where the main qualification was "presentability" (such as escorting a school visitor to or from the principal's office), the classroom's public address speaker would be requesting the pretty and/or nice-looking white boy or girl. By the time I was in the sixth grade, I was sometimes called by the principal to represent my class because I dressed neatly (I knew this from a progress report sent to my mother, which I translated for her) and because all the "presentable" white girls had moved to the Catholic schools (I later surmised this part). But I was still not one of the popular girls with the boys. I remember one incident where I stepped out into the playground in my baggy gym shorts and one Puerto Rican boy said to the other: "What do you think?" The other one answered: "Her face is OK, but look at the toothpick legs." The next best thing to a compliment I got was when my favorite male teacher, while handing out the class pictures, commented that with my long neck and delicate features I resembled the movie star Audrey Hepburn. But the Puerto Rican boys had learned to respond to a fuller figure: long necks and a perfect little nose were not what they looked for in a girl. That is when I decided I was a "brain." I did not settle into the role easily. I was nearly devastated by what the chicken pox episode had done to my self-image. But I looked into the mirror less often after I was told that I would always have scars on my face, and I hid behind my long black hair and my books.

After the problems at the public school got to the point where even nonconfrontational little me got beaten up several times, my parents enrolled me at St. Joseph's High School. I was then a minority of one among the Italian and Irish kids. But I found several good friends there — other girls who took their studies seriously. We did our homework together and talked about the Jackies. The Jackies were two popular girls, one blonde and the other red-haired, who had women's bodies. Their curves showed even in the blue jumper uniforms with straps that we all wore. The blonde

Jackie would often let one of the straps fall off her shoulder, and although she, like all of us, wore a white blouse underneath, all the boys stared at her arm. My friends and I talked about this and practiced letting our straps fall off our shoulders. But it wasn't the same without breasts or hips.

My final two and a half years of high school were spent in Augusta, Georgia, where my parents moved our family in search of a more peaceful environment. There we became part of a little community of our army-connected relatives and friends. School was yet another matter. I was enrolled in a huge school of nearly two thousand students that had just that year been forced to integrate. There were two black girls and there was me. I did extremely well academically. As to my social life, it was, for the most part, uneventful — yet it is in my memory blighted by one incident. In my junior year, I became wildly infatuated with a pretty white boy. I'll call him Ted. Oh, he was pretty: yellow hair that fell over his forehead, a smile to die for — and he was a great dancer. I watched him at Teen Town, the youth center at the base where all the military brats gathered on Saturday nights. My father had retired from the navy, and we had all our base privileges — one other reason we moved to Augusta. Ted looked like an angel to me. I worked on him for a year before he asked me out. This meant maneuvering to be within the periphery of his vision at every possible occasion. I took the long way to my classes in school just to pass by his locker, I went to football games, which I detested, and I danced (I too was a good dancer) in front of him at Teen Town — this took some fancy footwork, since it involved subtly moving my partner toward the right spot on the dance floor. When Ted finally approached me, "A Million to One" was playing on the jukebox, and when he took me into his arms, the odds suddenly turned in my favor. He asked me to go to a school dance the following Saturday. I said yes, breathlessly. I said yes, but there were obstacles to surmount at home. My father did not allow me to date casually. I was allowed to go to major events like a prom or a concert with a boy who had been properly screened. There was such a boy in my life, a neighbor who wanted to be a Baptist missionary and was practicing his anthropological skills on my family. If I was desperate to go somewhere and needed a date, I'd resort to Gary. This is the type of religious nut that Gary was: when the school bus did not show up one day, he put his hands over his face and prayed to Christ to get us a way to get to school. Within ten minutes a mother in a station wagon, on her way to town, stopped to ask why we weren't in school. Gary informed her that the Lord had sent her just in time to find us a way to get there in time for roll call. He assumed that I was impressed. Gary was even good-looking in a bland sort of way, but he kissed me with his lips tightly pressed together. I think Gary probably ended up marrying a native woman from wherever he may have gone to preach the Gospel according to Paul. She probably believes that all white men pray to God for transportation and kiss with their mouths closed. But it was Ted's mouth, his whole beautiful self, that concerned me in those days. I knew my father would say no to our date, but I planned to run away from home if necessary. I told my mother how important this date was. I cajoled and pleaded with her from Sunday to Wednesday. She listened to my arguments and must have heard the note of desperation in my voice. She said very gently to me: "You better be ready for disappointment." I did not ask what she meant. I did not want her fears for me to taint my happiness. I asked her to tell my father about my date. Thursday at breakfast my father looked at me across the table with his eyebrows together. My mother looked at him with her mouth set in a straight line. I looked down at my bowl of cereal. Nobody said anything. Friday I tried on every dress in my closet. Ted would be picking me up at six on Saturday: dinner and then the sock hop at school. Friday night I was in my room doing my nails or something else in preparation for Saturday (I know I groomed myself nonstop all week) when the telephone rang. I ran to get it. It was Ted. His voice sounded funny when he said my name, so funny that I felt compelled to ask: "Is something wrong?" Ted blurted it all out without a preamble. His father had asked who he was going out with. Ted had told him my name. "Ortiz? That's Spanish, isn't it?" the father had asked. Ted had told him yes, then shown him my picture in the yearbook. Ted's father had shaken his head. No. Ted would not be taking me out. Ted's father had known Puerto Ricans in the army. He had lived in New York City while studying architecture and had seen how the spics lived. Like rats. Ted repeated his father's words to me as if I should understand *his* predicament when I heard why he was breaking our date. I don't remember what I said before hanging up. I do recall the darkness of my room that sleepless night and the heaviness of my blanket in which I wrapped myself like a shroud. And I remember my parents' respect for my pain and their gentleness toward me that weekend. My mother did not say "I warned you," and I was grateful for her understanding silence.

In college, I suddenly became an "exotic" woman to the men who had survived the popularity wars in high school, who were now practicing to be worldly: they had to act liberal in their politics, in their lifestyles, and in the women they went out with. I dated heavily for a while, then married young. I had discovered that I needed stability more than social life. I had brains for sure and some talent in writing. These facts were a constant in my life. My skin color, my size, and my appearance were variables — things that were judged according to my current self-image, the aesthetic values of the time, the places I was in, and the people I met. My studies, later my writing, the respect of people who saw me as an individual person they cared about, these were the criteria for my sense of self-worth that I would concentrate on in my adult life.

ENGAGING THE TEXT

1. Ortiz Cofer writes a good deal about how people perceived her and about how their perceptions changed according to time and place. Trace the stages Ortiz Cofer lived through, citing examples from the text, and discuss

in each instance how her self-image was affected by people around her. What main point(s) do you think Ortiz Cofer may be trying to make with the narrative?

2. Which of the difficulties Ortiz Cofer faces are related specifically to gender (or made more serious by gender)? Do boys face comparable problems?

3. In your opinion, did Ortiz Cofer make the right decisions throughout her story? Is there anything she or her parents could have done to avoid or resist the various mistreatments she describes?

4. What role do media images play in Ortiz Cofer's story?

5. Does everyone have a story similar to Ortiz Cofer's, or not? Other people may be overweight, wear braces, mature very early or very late, have big noses or unusual voices, and so on. What, if anything, sets Ortiz Cofer's experience apart from the usual "traumas" of childhood?

EXPLORING CONNECTIONS

6. Review Aaron H. Devor's "Becoming Members of Society" (p. 527). How do Ortiz Cofer's experiences support and/or complicate Devor's explanation of gender role socialization?

7. Compare the childhood experiences of Ortiz Cofer and Gary Soto (p. 26). To what extent do their relationships, concerns, and behavior appear to be influenced by gender? What other social forces shape their lives?

EXTENDING THE CRITICAL CONTEXT

8. In her self-analysis, Ortiz Cofer discusses the "variables" in her physical appearance — the socially determined values that influence her perception of her body. She also reflects on personal "facts" or "constants" — more durable features, like her writing and her need for stability — that contribute to her identity. Write a series of journal entries that tell the story of your own body. What "variables" have influenced your perception of your appearance? What "facts" about yourself have become "constants"?

A Boy's Life
HANNA ROSIN

In this article, Hanna Rosin introduces us to Brandon Simms, a lively eight-year-old boy who prefers Barbies to toy grenades and is happiest when he can wear girls' clothing. Rosin follows Brandon's mother, Tina, as she struggles to understand a transgender child and to do what's right for her son. The story first appeared in The Atlantic *(November 2008). Rosin writes frequently about the intersection of religion and politics; her first book,* God's Harvard: A Christian College on a Mission to Save America *was published in 2007. Her work has appeared in* The New Republic, The New Yorker, GQ, *and the* Washington Post *as well as* The Atlantic.

The local newspaper recorded that Brandon Simms was the first millennium baby born in his tiny southern town, at 12:50 A.M. He weighed eight pounds, two ounces and, as his mother, Tina, later wrote to him in his baby book, "had a darlin' little face that told me right away you were innocent." Tina saved the white knit hat with the powder-blue ribbon that hospitals routinely give to new baby boys. But after that, the milestones took an unusual turn. As a toddler, Brandon would scour the house for something to drape over his head — a towel, a doily, a moons-and-stars bandanna he'd snatch from his mother's drawer. "I figure he wanted something that felt like hair," his mother later guessed. He spoke his first full sentence at a local Italian restaurant: "I like your high heels," he told a woman in a fancy red dress. At home, he would rip off his clothes as soon as Tina put them on him, and instead try on something from her closet — a purple undershirt, lingerie, shoes. "He ruined all my heels in the sandbox," she recalls.

At the toy store, Brandon would head straight for the aisles with the Barbies or the pink and purple dollhouses. Tina wouldn't buy them, instead steering him to neutral toys: puzzles or building blocks or cool neon markers. One weekend, when Brandon was two and a half, she took him to visit her ten-year-old cousin. When Brandon took to one of the many dolls in her huge collection — a blonde Barbie in a pink sparkly dress — Tina let him bring it home. He carried it everywhere, "even slept with it, like a teddy bear."

For his third Christmas, Tina bought Brandon a first-rate army set — complete with a Kevlar hat, walkie-talkies, and a hand grenade. Both Tina and Brandon's father had served in the army, and she thought their son might identify with the toys. A photo from that day shows him wearing a towel around his head, a bandanna around his waist, and a glum expression [see p. 551]. The army set sits unopened at his feet. Tina recalls his joy, by contrast, on a day later that year. One afternoon, while Tina was on the phone, Brandon climbed out of the bathtub. When she found him, he was dancing in front of the mirror with his penis tucked between his legs. "Look, Mom, I'm a girl," he told her. "Happy as can be," she recalls.

"Brandon, God made you a boy for a special reason," she told him before they said prayers one night when he was five, the first part of a speech she'd prepared. But he cut her off: "God made a mistake," he said.

Tina had no easy explanation for where Brandon's behavior came from. Gender roles are not very fluid in their no-stoplight town, where Confederate flags line the main street. Boys ride dirt bikes through the woods starting

Brandon Simms at age 5 in a Disney princess
costume (courtesy of the family).

at age five; local county fairs feature muscle cars for boys and beauty
pageants for girls of all ages. In the army, Tina operated heavy machinery,
but she is no tomboy. When she was younger, she wore long flowing dresses
to match her long, wavy blond hair; now she wears it in a cute, Renée
Zellweger–style bob. Her husband, Bill (Brandon's stepfather), lays wood
floors and builds houses for a living. At a recent meeting with Brandon's
school principal about how to handle the boy, Bill aptly summed up the town
philosophy: "The way I was brought up, a boy's a boy and a girl's a girl."

School had always complicated Brandon's life. When teachers divided
the class into boys' and girls' teams, Brandon would stand with the girls. In
all of his kindergarten and first-grade self-portraits — "I have a pet," "I love
my cat," "I love to play outside" — the "I" was a girl, often with big red lips,
high heels, and a princess dress. Just as often, he drew himself as a mermaid
with a sparkly purple tail, or a tail cut out from black velvet. Late in second
grade, his older stepbrother, Travis, told his fourth-grade friends about
Brandon's "secret" — that he dressed up at home and wanted to be a girl.
After school, the boys cornered and bullied him. Brandon went home crying and begged Tina to let him skip the last week.

Since he was four, Tina had been taking Brandon to a succession of
therapists. The first told her he was just going through a phase; but the phase
never passed. Another suggested that Brandon's chaotic early childhood
might have contributed to his behavior. Tina had never married Brandon's

"Me and My Pets," a self-portrait drawn by
Brandon in kindergarten (courtesy of the family).

father, whom she'd met when they were both stationed in Germany. Twice,
she had briefly stayed with him, when Brandon was five months old and
then when he was three. Both times, she'd suspected his father of being too
rough with the boy and had broken off the relationship. The therapist suggested that perhaps Brandon overidentified with his mother as the protector in the family, and for a while, this theory seemed plausible to Tina. In
play therapy, the therapist tried to get Brandon to discuss his feelings about
his father. She advised Tina to try a reward system at home. Brandon could
earn up to $21 a week for doing three things: looking in the mirror and say-
ing "I'm a boy"; not dressing up; and not wearing anything on his head. It
worked for a couple of weeks, but then Brandon lost interest.

Tina recounted much of this history to me in June at her kitchen table,
where Brandon, now eight, had just laid out some lemon pound cake he'd
baked from a mix. She, Bill, Brandon, his half sister, Madison, and Travis live
in a comfortable double-wide trailer that Bill set up himself on their half acre
of woods. I'd met Tina a month earlier, and she'd agreed to let me follow
Brandon's development over what turned out to be a critical few months of
his life, on the condition that I change their names and disguise where they
live. While we were at the table talking, Brandon was conducting a kind of
nervous fashion show; over the course of several hours, he came in and out
of his room wearing eight or nine different outfits, constructed from his costume collection, his mom's shoes and scarves, and his little sister's bodysuits

and tights. Brandon is a gymnast and likes to show off splits and back bends. On the whole, he is quiet and a little somber, but every once in a while — after a great split, say — he shares a shy, crooked smile.

About a year and a half ago, Tina's mom showed her a Barbara Walters 20/20 special she'd taped. The show featured a six-year-old boy named "Jazz" who, since he was a toddler, had liked to dress as a girl. Everything about Jazz was familiar to Tina: the obsession with girls' clothes, the Barbies, wishing his penis away, even the fixation on mermaids. At the age of three, Jazz had been diagnosed with "gender-identity disorder" and was considered "transgender," Walters explained. The show mentioned a "hormone imbalance," but his parents had concluded that there was basically nothing wrong with him. He "didn't ask to be born this way," his mother explained. By kindergarten, his parents were letting him go to school with shoulder-length hair and a pink skirt on.

Tina had never heard the word *transgender*; she'd figured no other little   10
boy on Earth was like Brandon. The show prompted her to buy a computer and Google "transgender children." Eventually, she made her way to a subculture of parents who live all across the country; they write in to listservs with grammar ranging from sixth-grade-level to professorial, but all have family stories much like hers. In May, she and Bill finally met some of them at the Trans-Health Conference in Philadelphia, the larger of two annual gatherings in the U.S. that many parents attend. Four years ago, only a handful of kids had come to the conference. This year, about fifty showed up, along with their siblings — enough to require a staff dedicated to full-time children's entertainment, including Jack the Balloon Man, Sue's Sand Art, a pool-and-pizza party, and a treasure hunt.

Diagnoses of gender-identity disorder among adults have tripled in Western countries since the 1960s; for men, the estimates now range from one in 7,400 to one in 42,000 (for women, the frequency of diagnosis is lower). Since 1952, when army veteran George Jorgensen's sex-change operation hit the front page of the New York *Daily News*, national resistance has softened a bit, too. Former NASCAR driver J. T. Hayes recently talked to *Newsweek* about having had a sex-change operation. Women's colleges have had to adjust to the presence of "trans-men," and the president-elect of the Gay and Lesbian Medical Association is a trans-woman and a successful cardiologist. But nothing can do more to normalize the face of transgender America than the sight of a seven-year-old (boy or girl?) with pink cheeks and a red balloon puppy in hand saying to Brandon, as one did at the conference:

"Are you transgender?"

"What's that?" Brandon asked.

"A boy who wants to be a girl."

"Yeah. Can I see your balloon?"   15

Around the world, clinics that specialize in gender-identity disorder in children report an explosion in referrals over the past few years. Dr. Kenneth

Brandon on Christmas Day 2002, wearing
his mother's bandanna around his waist and a
towel around his head (courtesy of the family).

Zucker, who runs the most comprehensive gender-identity clinic for youth
in Toronto, has seen his waiting list quadruple in the past four years, to
about eighty kids—an increase he attributes to media coverage and the
proliferation of new sites on the Internet. Dr. Peggy Cohen-Kettenis, who
runs the main clinic in the Netherlands, has seen the average age of her
patients plummet since 2002. "We used to get calls mostly from parents
who were concerned about their children being gay," says Catherine Tuerk,
who since 1998 has run a support network for parents of children with gender-
variant behavior, out of Children's National Medical Center in Washington,
DC. "Now about 90 percent of our calls are from parents with some concern that their child may be transgender."

   In breakout sessions at the conference, transgender men and women
in their fifties and sixties described lives of heartache and rejection: years
of hiding makeup under the mattress, estranged parents, suicide attempts.
Those in their twenties and thirties conveyed a dedicated militancy: they
wore nose rings and Mohawks, ate strictly vegan, and conducted heated
debates about the definitions of *queer* and *he-she* and *drag queen*. But the
kids treated the conference like a family trip to Disneyland. They ran around

with parents chasing after them, fussing over twisted bathing-suit straps or wiping crumbs from their lips. They looked effortlessly androgynous, and years away from sex, politics, or any form of rebellion. For Tina, the sight of them suggested a future she'd never considered for Brandon: a normal life as a girl. "She could end up being a *mommy* if she wants, just like me," one adoring mother leaned over and whispered about her five-year-old (natal) son.

It took the gay-rights movement thirty years to shift from the Stonewall riots[1] to gay marriage; now its transgender wing, long considered the most subversive, is striving for suburban normalcy too. The change is fueled mostly by a community of parents who, like many parents of this generation, are open to letting even preschool children define their own needs. Faced with skeptical neighbors and school officials, parents at the conference discussed how to use the kind of quasi-therapeutic language that, these days, inspires deference: tell the school the child has a "medical condition" or a "hormonal imbalance" that can be treated later, suggested a conference speaker, Kim Pearson; using terms like *gender-identity disorder* or *birth defect* would be going too far, she advised. The point was to take the situation out of the realm of deep pathology or mental illness, while at the same time separating it from voluntary behavior, and to put it into the idiom of garden-variety "challenge." As one father told me, "Between all the kids with language problems and learning disabilities and peanut allergies, the school doesn't know who to worry about first."

A recent medical innovation holds out the promise that this might be the first generation of transsexuals who can live inconspicuously. About three years ago, physicians in the U.S. started treating transgender children with puberty blockers, drugs originally intended to halt precocious puberty. The blockers put teens in a state of suspended development. They prevent boys from growing facial and body hair and an Adam's apple, or developing a deep voice or any of the other physical characteristics that a male-to-female transsexual would later spend tens of thousands of dollars to reverse. They allow girls to grow taller, and prevent them from getting breasts or a period.

At the conference, blockers were the hot topic. One mother who'd   20 found out about them too late cried, "The guilt I feel is overwhelming." The preteens sized each other up for signs of the magic drug, the way other teens might look for hip, expensive jeans: a sixteen-year-old (natal) girl, shirtless, with no sign of breasts; a seventeen-year-old (natal) boy with a face as smooth as Brandon's. "Is there anybody out there," asked Dr. Nick Gorton, a physician and trans-man from California, addressing a room full

---

[1]*Stonewall riots:* On June 28, 1969, patrons of the Stonewall Inn, a gay bar in New York's Greenwich Village, rioted in response to a police raid; this event marked the beginning of the gay rights movement.

of older transsexuals, "who would not have taken the shot if it had been offered?" No one raised a hand.

After a day of sessions, Tina's mind was moving fast. "These kids look happier," she told me. "This is nothing we can fix. In his brain, in his *mind*, Brandon's a girl." With Bill, she started to test out the new language. "What's it they say? It's nothing wrong. It's just a medical condition, like diabetes or something. Just a variation on human behavior." She made an unlikely friend, a lesbian mom from Seattle named Jill who took Tina under her wing. Jill had a five-year-old girl living as a boy and a future already mapped out. "He'll just basically be living life," Jill explained about her (natal) daughter. "I already legally changed his name and called all the parents at the school. Then, when he's in eighth grade, we'll take him to the [endocrinologist] and get the blockers, and no one will ever know. He'll just sail right through."

"I live in a small town," Tina pleaded with Jill. "This is all just really *new*. I never even heard the word *transgender* until recently, and the shrinks just kept telling me this is fixable."

In my few months of meeting transgender children, I talked to parents from many different backgrounds, who had made very different decisions about how to handle their children. Many accepted the "new normalcy" line, and some did not. But they all had one thing in common: in such a loaded situation, with their children's future at stake, doubt about their choices did not serve them well. In Brandon's case, for example, doubt would force Tina to consider that if she began letting him dress as a girl, she would be defying the conventions of her small town, and the majority of psychiatric experts, who advise strongly against the practice. It would force her to consider that she would have to begin making serious medical decisions for Brandon in only a couple of years, and that even with the blockers, he would face a lifetime of hormone injections and possibly major surgery. At the conference, Tina struggled with these doubts. But her new friends had already moved past them.

"Yeah, it is fixable," piped up another mom, who'd been on the *20/20* special. "We call it the disorder we cured with a skirt."

In 1967, Dr. John Money launched an experiment that he thought 25 might confirm some of the more radical ideas emerging in feminist thought. Throughout the 60s, writers such as Betty Friedan[2] were challenging the notion that women should be limited to their prescribed roles as wives, housekeepers, and mothers. But other feminists pushed further, arguing that the whole notion of gender was a social construction, and easy to manipulate. In a 1955 paper, Money had written: "Sexual behavior and orientation as

---

[2]*Betty Friedan:* Author of *The Feminine Mystique,* a book that helped spur the feminist movement of the 1960s and 1970s; throughout her life, Friedan (1921–2006) continued to be a strong advocate for women's rights.

male or female does not have an innate, instinctive basis." We learn whether we are male or female "in the course of the various experiences of growing up." By the 60s, he was well-known for having established the first American clinic to perform voluntary sex-change operations, at the Johns Hopkins Hospital, in Baltimore. One day, he got a letter from the parents of infant twin boys, one of whom had suffered a botched circumcision that had burned off most of his penis.

Money saw the case as a perfect test for his theory. He encouraged the parents to have the boy, David Reimer, fully castrated and then to raise him as a girl. When the child reached puberty, Money told them, doctors could construct a vagina and give him feminizing hormones. Above all, he told them, they must not waver in their decision and must not tell the boy about the accident.

In paper after paper, Money reported on Reimer's fabulous progress, writing that "she" showed an avid interest in dolls and dollhouses, that she preferred dresses, hair ribbons, and frilly blouses. Money's description of the child in his book *Sexual Signatures* prompted one reviewer to describe her as "sailing contentedly through childhood as a genuine girl." *Time* magazine concluded that the Reimer case cast doubt on the belief that sex differences are "immutably set by the genes at conception."

The reality was quite different, as *Rolling Stone* reporter John Colapinto brilliantly documented in the 2000 best-seller *As Nature Made Him*. Reimer had never adjusted to being a girl at all. He wanted only to build forts and play with his brother's dump trucks, and insisted that he should pee standing up. He was a social disaster at school, beating up other kids and misbehaving in class. At fourteen, Reimer became so alienated and depressed that his parents finally told him the truth about his birth, at which point he felt mostly relief, he reported. He eventually underwent phalloplasty, and he married a woman. Then four years ago, at age thirty-eight, Reimer shot himself dead in a grocery-store parking lot.

Today, the notion that gender is purely a social construction seems nearly as outmoded as bra-burning or free love. Feminist theory is pivoting with the rest of the culture, and is locating the key to identity in genetics and the workings of the brain. In the new conventional wisdom, we are all prewired for many things previously thought to be in the realm of upbringing, choice, or subjective experience: happiness, religious awakening, cheating, a love of chocolate. Behaviors are fundamental unless we are chemically altered. Louann Brizendine, in her 2006 best-selling book, *The Female Brain*, claims that everything from empathy to chattiness to poor spatial reasoning is "hardwired into the brains of women." Dr. Milton Diamond, an expert on human sexuality at the University of Hawaii and long the intellectual nemesis of Money, encapsulated this view in an interview on the BBC in 1980, when it was becoming clear that Money's experiment was failing: "Maybe we really have to think . . . that we don't come to this world neutral; that we come to this world with some degree of maleness and femaleness which will transcend whatever the society wants to put into [us]."

Diamond now spends his time collecting case studies of transsexuals   30
who have a twin, to see how often both twins have transitioned to the opposite sex. To him, these cases are a "confirmation" that "the biggest sex organ is not between the legs but between the ears." For many gender biologists like Diamond, transgender children now serve the same allegorical purpose that David Reimer once did, but they support the opposite conclusion: they are seen as living proof that "gender identity is influenced by some innate or immutable factors," writes Melissa Mines, the author of *Brain Gender*.

This is the strange place in which transsexuals have found themselves. For years, they've been at the extreme edges of transgressive sexual politics. But now children like Brandon are being used to paint a more conventional picture: before they have much time to be shaped by experience, before they know their sexual orientation, even in defiance of their bodies, children can know their gender, from the firings of neurons deep within their brains. What better rebuke to the *Our Bodies, Ourselves* era of feminism than the notion that even the body is dispensable, that the hard nugget of difference lies even deeper?

In most major institutes for gender-identity disorder in children worldwide, a psychologist is the central figure. In the United States, the person intending to found "the first major academic research center," as he calls it, is Dr. Norman Spack, an endocrinologist who teaches at Harvard Medical School and is committed to a hormonal fix. Spack works out of a cramped office at Children's Hospital in Boston, where the walls are covered with diplomas and notes of gratitude scrawled in crayons or bright markers ("Thanks, Dr. Spack!!!"). Spack is bald, with a trim beard, and often wears his Harvard tie under his lab coat. He is not confrontational by nature, but he can hold his own with his critics: "To those who say I am interrupting God's work, I point to Leviticus, which says, 'Thou shalt not stand idly by the blood of your neighbor'" — an injunction, as he sees it, to prevent needless suffering.

Spack has treated young-adult transsexuals since the 1980s, and until recently he could never get past one problem: "They are never going to fail to draw attention to themselves." Over the years, he'd seen patients rejected by families, friends, and employers after a sex-change operation. Four years ago, he heard about the innovative use of hormone blockers on transgender youths in the Netherlands; to him, the drugs seemed like the missing piece of the puzzle.

The problem with blockers is that parents have to begin making medical decisions for their children when the children are quite young. From the earliest signs of puberty, doctors have about eighteen months to start the blockers for ideal results. For girls, that's usually between ages ten and twelve; for boys, between twelve and fourteen. If the patients follow through with cross-sex hormones and sex-change surgery, they will be permanently sterile, something Spack always discusses with them. "When you're talking to a twelve-year-old, that's a heavy-duty conversation," he said in a recent interview. "Does a kid that age really think about fertility? But if you don't start treatment, they will always have trouble fitting in."

When Beth was eleven, she told her mother, Susanna, that she'd "rather   35 be dead" than go to school anymore as a girl. (The names of all the children and parents used as case studies in this story are pseudonyms.) For a long time, she had refused to shower except in a bathing suit, and had skipped out of health class every Thursday, when the standard puberty videos were shown. In March 2006, when Beth, now Matt, was twelve, they went to see Spack. He told Matt that if he went down this road, he would never biologically have children.

"I'll adopt!" Matt said.

"What is most important to him is that he's comfortable in who he is," says Susanna. They left with a prescription — a "godsend," she calls it.

Now, at fifteen and on testosterone, Matt is tall, with a broad chest and hairy legs. Susanna figures he's the first trans-man in America to go shirtless without having had any chest surgery. His mother describes him as "happy" and "totally at home in his masculine body." Matt has a girlfriend; he met her at the amusement park where Susanna works. Susanna is pretty sure he's said something to the girl about his situation, but knows he hasn't talked to her parents.

Susanna imagines few limitations in Matt's future. Only a minority of trans-men get what they call "bottom" surgery, because phalloplasty is still more cosmetic than functional, and the procedure is risky. But otherwise? Married? "Oh, yeah. And his career prospects will be good because he gets very good grades. We envision a kind of family life, maybe in the suburbs, with a good job." They have "no fears" about the future, and "zero doubts" about the path they've chosen.

Blockers are entirely reversible; should a child change his or her mind   40 about becoming the other gender, a doctor can stop the drugs and normal puberty will begin. The Dutch clinic has given them to about seventy children since it started the treatment, in 2000; clinics in the United States and Canada have given them to dozens more. According to Dr. Peggy Cohen-Kettenis, the psychologist who heads the Dutch clinic, no case of a child stopping the blockers and changing course has yet been reported.

This suggests one of two things: either the screening is excellent, or once a child begins, he or she is set firmly on the path to medical intervention. "Adolescents may consider this step a guarantee of sex reassignment," wrote Cohen-Kettenis, "and it could make them therefore less rather than more inclined to engage in introspection." In the Netherlands, clinicians try to guard against this with an extensive diagnostic protocol, including testing and many sessions "to confirm that the desire for treatment is very persistent," before starting the blockers.

Spack's clinic isn't so comprehensive. A part-time psychologist, Dr. Laura Edwards-Leeper, conducts four-hour family screenings by appointment. (When I visited during the summer, she was doing only one or two a month.) But often she has to field emergency cases directly with Spack, which sometimes means skipping the screening altogether. "We get these calls from parents who are just frantic," she says. "They need to get in immediately, because their child is about to hit puberty and is having serious mental-health issues, and we really want to accommodate that. It's like they've been waiting their whole lives for this and they are just desperate, and when they finally get in to see us . . . it's like a rebirth."

Spack's own conception of the psychology involved is uncomplicated: "If a girl starts to experience breast budding and feels like cutting herself, then she's probably transgendered. If she feels immediate relief on the [puberty-blocking] drugs, that confirms the diagnosis," he told the *Boston Globe*. He thinks of the blockers not as an addendum to years of therapy but as "preventative" because they forestall the trauma that comes from social rejection. Clinically, men who become women are usually described as "male-to-female," but Spack, using the parlance of activist parents, refers to them as "affirmed females" — "because how can you be a male-to-female if really you were always a female in your brain?"

For the transgender community, *born in the wrong body* is the catchphrase that best captures this moment. It implies that the anatomy deceives where the brain tells the truth; that gender destiny is set before a baby takes its first breath. But the empirical evidence does not fit this argument so neatly. Milton Diamond says his study of identical transgender twins shows the same genetic predisposition that has been found for homosexuality: if one twin has switched to the opposite sex, there is a 50 percent chance that the other will as well. But his survey has not yet been published, and no one else has found nearly that degree of correlation. Eric Vilain, a geneticist at UCLA who specializes in sexual development and sex differences in the brain, says the studies on twins are mixed and that, on the whole, "there is no evidence of a biological influence on transsexualism yet."

In 1995, a study published in *Nature* looked at the brains of six adult male-to-female transsexuals and showed that certain regions of their brains were closer in size to those of women than of men. This study seemed to echo a famous 1991 study about gay men, published in *Science* by the neuroscientist Simon LeVay. LeVay had studied a portion of the hypothalamus that governs sexual behavior, and he discovered that in gay men, its size was much closer to women's than to straight men's; his findings helped legitimize the notion that homosexuality is hardwired. But in the transsexual study, the sample size was small, and the subjects had already received significant feminizing hormone treatments, which can affect brain structure.

Transsexualism is far less common than homosexuality, and the research is in its infancy. Scattered studies have looked at brain activity, finger size, familial recurrence, and birth order. One hypothesis involves hormonal imbalances during pregnancy. In 1988, researchers injected hormones into pregnant rhesus monkeys; the hormones seemed to masculinize the brains but not the bodies of their female babies. "Are we expecting to find some biological component [to gender identity]?" asks Vilain. "Certainly I am. But my hunch is, it's going to be mild. My hunch is that sexual orientation is probably much more hardwired than gender identity. I'm not saying [gender identity is] entirely determined by the social environment. I'm just saying that it's much more malleable."

Vilain has spent his career working with intersex patients, who are born with the anatomy of both sexes. He says his hardest job is to persuade the parents to leave the genitals ambiguous and wait until the child has grown up, and can choose his or her own course. This experience has influenced his views on parents with young transgender kids. "I'm torn here. I'm very ambivalent. I know [the parents] are saying the children are born this way. But I'm still on the fence. I consider the child my patient, not the parents, and I don't want to alleviate the anxiety of the parents by surgically fixing the child. We don't know the long-term effects of making these decisions for the child. We're playing God here, a little bit."

Even some supporters of hormone blockers worry that the availability of the drugs will encourage parents to make definitive decisions about younger and younger kids. This is one reason why doctors at the clinic in the Netherlands ask parents not to let young children live as the other gender until they are about to go on blockers. "We discourage it because the chances are very high that your child will not be a transsexual," says Cohen-Kettenis. The Dutch studies of their own patients show that among young children who have gender-identity disorder, only 20 to 25 percent still want to switch gender at adolescence; other studies show similar or even lower rates of persistence.

The most extensive study on transgender boys was published in 1987 as *The "Sissy Boy Syndrome" and the Development of Homosexuality*. For fifteen years, Dr. Richard Green followed forty-four boys who exhibited extreme feminine behaviors, and a control group of boys who did not. The boys in the feminine group all played with dolls, preferred the company of girls to boys, and avoided "rough-and-tumble play." Reports from their parents sound very much like the testimonies one reads on the listservs today. "He started . . . cross-dressing when he was about three," reported one mother. "[He stood] in front of the mirror and he took his penis and he folded it under, and he said, 'Look, Mommy, I'm a girl,'" said another.

Green expected most of the boys in the study to end up as transsexuals, but nothing like that happened. Three-fourths of the forty-four boys turned out to be gay or bisexual (Green says a few more have since contacted him and told him they too were gay). Only one became a transsexual. "We can't tell a pre-gay from a pre-transsexual at eight," says Green, who recently retired from running the adult gender-identity clinic in England. "Are you helping or hurting a kid by allowing them to live as the other gender? If everyone is caught up in facilitating the thing, then there may be a hell of a lot of pressure to remain that way, regardless of how strongly the kid still feels gender-dysphoric. Who knows? That's a study that hasn't found its investigator yet."

Out on the sidewalk in Philadelphia, Tina was going through Marlboro after Marlboro, stubbing them out half-smoked against city buildings. The conference's first day had just ended, with Tina asking another mom, "So how do you know if one of these kids stays that way or if he changes?" and the mom suggesting she could wait awhile and see.

"Wait? Wait for what?" Tina suddenly said to Bill. "He's already waited six years, and now I don't care about any of that no more." Bill looked worried, but she threw an army phrase at him: "Suck it up and drive on, soldier."

The organizers had planned a pool party for that night, and Tina had come to a decision: Brandon would wear exactly the kind of bathing suit he'd always wanted. She had spotted a Macy's a couple of blocks away. I walked with her and Bill and Brandon into the hush and glow, the headless mannequins sporting golf shorts with $80 price tags. They quietly took the escalator one floor up, to the girls' bathing-suit department. Brandon leaped off at the top and ran to the first suit that caught his eye: a teal Hannah Montana bikini studded with jewels and glitter. "Oh, I love this one," he said.

"So that's the one you want?" asked Tina.

Brandon hesitated. He was used to doing his cross-dressing somewhat furtively. Normally he would just grab the shiniest thing he saw, for fear his chance would evaporate. But as he came to understand that both Tina and Bill were on board, he slowed down a bit. He carefully looked through all the racks. Bill, calm now, was helping him. "You want a one-piece or two-piece?" Bill asked. Tina, meanwhile, was having a harder time. "I'll get used to it," she said. She had tried twice to call Brandon "she," Tina suddenly confessed, but "it just don't sound right," she said, her eyes tearing.

Brandon decided to try on an orange one-piece with polka dots, a sky-blue-and-pink two-piece, and a Hawaiian-print tankini with a brown background and pink hibiscus flowers. He went into a dressing room and stayed there a long, long time. Finally, he called in the adults. Brandon had settled on the least showy of the three: the Hawaiian print with the brown background. He had it on and was shyly looking in the mirror. He wasn't doing backflips or grinning from ear to ear; he was still and at peace, gently fingering the price tag. He mentioned that he didn't want to wear the suit again until he'd had a chance to wash his feet.

At the pool party, Brandon immediately ran into a friend he'd made earlier, the transgender boy who'd shared his balloon puppy. The pool was in a small room in the corner of a hotel basement, with low ceilings and no windows. The echoes of seventy giddy children filled the space. Siblings were there, too, so it was impossible to know who had been born a boy and who a girl. They were all just smooth limbs and wet hair and an occasional slip that sent one crying to his or her mother.

Bill sat next to me on a bench and spilled his concerns. He was worried about Tina's stepfather, who would never accept this. He was worried that Brandon's father might find out and demand custody. He was worried about Brandon's best friend, whose parents were strict evangelical Christians. He was worried about their own pastor, who had sternly advised them to take away all of Brandon's girl-toys and girl-clothes. "Maybe if we just pray hard enough," Bill had told Tina.

Brandon raced by, arm in arm with his new friend, giggling. Tina and Bill didn't know this yet, but Brandon had already started telling the other kids that his name was Bridget, after the pet mouse he'd recently buried ("My beloved Bridget. Rest With the Lord," the memorial in his room read). The comment of an older transsexual from Brooklyn who'd sat behind Tina in a session earlier that day echoed in my head. He'd had his sex-change operation when he was in his fifties, and in his wild, wispy wig, he looked like a biblical prophet, with breasts. "You think you have troubles now," he'd yelled out to Tina. "Wait until next week. Once you let the genie out of the bottle, she's not going back in!"

Dr. Kenneth Zucker has been seeing children with gender-identity 60 disorder in Toronto since the mid-70s and has published more on the subject than any other researcher. But lately he has become a pariah to the most-vocal activists in the American transgender community. In 2012, the *Diagnostic and Statistical Manual of Mental Disorders* — the bible for psychiatric professionals — will be updated. Many in the transgender community see this as their opportunity to remove gender-identity disorder from the book, much the same way homosexuality was delisted in 1973. Zucker is in charge of the committee that will make the recommendation. He seems unlikely to bless the condition as psychologically healthy, especially in young children.

I met Zucker in his office at the Centre for Addiction and Mental Health, where piles of books alternate with the Barbies and superheroes that he uses for play therapy. Zucker has a white mustache and beard, and his manner is somewhat Talmudic. He responds to every question with a methodical three-part answer, often ending by climbing a chair to pull down a research paper he's written. On one of his file cabinets, he's tacked up a flyer from a British parents' advocacy group that reads: "Gender dysphoria is increasingly understood . . . as having biological origins," and describes "small parts of the brain" as "progressing along different pathways." During the interview, he took it down to make a point: "In terms of empirical data, this is not true. It's just dogma, and I've never liked dogma. Biology is not destiny."

In his case studies and descriptions of patients, Zucker usually explains gender dysphoria in terms of what he calls "family noise": neglectful parents who caused a boy to overidentify with his domineering older sisters; a mother who expected a daughter and delayed naming her newborn son for eight weeks. Zucker's belief is that with enough therapy, such children can be made to feel comfortable in their birth sex. Zucker has compared young children who believe they are meant to live as the other sex to people who want to amputate healthy limbs, or who believe they are cats, or those with something called ethnic-identity disorder. "If a five-year-old black kid came into the clinic and said he wanted to be white, would we endorse that?" he told me. "I don't think so. What we would want to do is say, 'What's going on with this kid that's making him feel that it would be better to be white?'"

Young children, he explains, have very concrete reasoning; they may believe that if they want to wear dresses, they are girls. But he sees it as his job — and the parents' — to help them think in more flexible ways. "If a kid has massive separation anxiety and does not want to go to school, one solution would be to let them stay home. That would solve the problem at one level, but not at another. So it is with gender identity." Allowing a child to switch genders, in other words, would probably not get to the root of the psychological problem, but only offer a superficial fix.

Zucker calls his approach "developmental," which means that the most important factor is the age of the child. Younger children are more malleable, he believes, and can learn to "be comfortable in their own skin." Zucker says that in twenty-five years, not one of the patients who started seeing him by age six has switched gender. Adolescents are more fixed in their identity. If a parent brings in, say, a thirteen-year-old who has never been treated and who has severe gender dysphoria, Zucker will generally recommend hormonal treatment. But he considers that a fraught choice. "One has to think about the long-term developmental path. This kid will go through lifelong hormonal treatment to approximate the phenotype of a male and may require some kind of surgery and then will have to deal with the fact that he doesn't have a phallus; it's a tough road, with a lot of pain involved."

Zucker put me in touch with two of his success stories, a boy and a girl, 65 now both living in the suburbs of Toronto. Meeting them was like moving into a parallel world where every story began the same way as those of the American families I'd met, but then ran in the opposite direction.

When he was four, the boy, John, had tested at the top of the gender-dysphoria scale. Zucker recalls him as "one of the most anxious kids I ever saw." He had bins full of Barbies and Disney princess movies, and he dressed in homemade costumes. Once, at a hardware store, he stared up at the glittery chandeliers and wept, "I don't want to be a daddy! I want to be a mommy!"

His parents, well-educated urbanites, let John grow his hair long and play with whatever toys he preferred. But then a close friend led them to Zucker, and soon they began to see themselves as "in denial," recalls his mother, Caroline. "Once we came to see his behavior for what it was, it became painfully sad." Zucker believed John's behavior resulted from early-childhood medical trauma — he was born with tumors on his kidneys and had had invasive treatments every three months — and from his dependence during that time on his mother, who has a dominant personality.

When they reversed course, they dedicated themselves to the project with a thoroughness most parents would find exhausting and off-putting. They boxed up all of John's girl-toys and videos and replaced them with neutral ones. Whenever John cried for his girl-toys, they would ask him, "Do you think playing with those would make you feel better about being a boy?" and then would distract him with an offer to ride bikes or take a walk. They turned their house into a 1950s kitchen-sink drama, intended to inculcate respect for patriarchy, in the crudest and simplest terms: "Boys don't wear pink, they wear blue," they would tell him, or "Daddy is smarter than Mommy — ask him." If John called for Mommy in the middle of the night, Daddy went, every time.

When I visited the family, John was lazing around with his older brother, idly watching TV and playing video games, dressed in a polo shirt and Abercrombie & Fitch shorts. He said he was glad he'd been through the therapy, "because it made me feel happy," but that's about all he would say; for the most part, his mother spoke for him. Recently, John was in the basement watching the Grammys. When Caroline walked downstairs to say good night, she found him draped in a blanket, vamping. He looked up at her, mortified. She held his face and said, "You never have to be embarrassed of the things you say or do around me." Her position now is that the treatment is "not a cure; this will always be with him" — but also that he has nothing to be ashamed of. About a year ago, John carefully broke the news to his parents that he is gay. "You'd have to carefully break the news to me that you were straight," his dad told him. "He'll be a man who loves men," says his mother. "But I want him to be a happy man who loves men."

The girl's case was even more extreme in some ways. She insisted on peeing standing up and playing only with boys. When her mother bought her Barbies, she'd pop their heads off. Once, when she was six, her father, Mike, said out of the blue: "Chris, you're a girl." In response, he recalls, she "started screaming and freaking out," closing her hand into a fist and punching herself between the legs, over and over. After that, her parents took her to see Zucker. He connected Chris's behavior to the early years of her parents' marriage; her mother had gotten pregnant and Mike had been resentful of having to marry her, and verbally abusive. Chris, Zucker told them, saw her mother as weak and couldn't identify with her. For four years, they saw no progress. When Chris turned eleven and other girls in school started getting their periods, her mother found her on the bed one night, weeping. She "said she wanted to kill herself," her mother told me. "She said, 'In my head, I've always been a boy.'"

But about a month after that, everything began to change. Chris had joined a softball team and made some female friends; her mother figured she had cottoned to the idea that girls could be tough and competitive. Then one day, Chris went to her mother and said, "Mom, I need to talk to you. We need to go shopping." She bought clothes that were tighter and had her ears pierced. She let her hair grow out. Eventually she gave her boys' clothes away.

Now Chris wears her hair in a ponytail, walks like a girl, and spends hours on the phone, talking to girlfriends about boys. Her mother recently watched her through a bedroom window as she was jumping on their trampoline, looking slyly at her own reflection and tossing her hair around. At her parents' insistence, Chris has never been to a support group or a conference, never talked to another girl who wanted to be a boy. For all she knew, she was the only person in the world who felt as she once had felt.

The week before I arrived in Toronto, the Barbara Walters special about Jazz had been re-aired, and both sets of parents had seen it. "I was aghast," said John's mother. "It really affected us to see this poor little peanut, and her parents just going to the teacher and saying 'He is a "she" now.' Why would you assume a four-year-old would understand the ramifications of that?"

"We were shocked," Chris's father said. "They gave up on their kid too early. Regardless of our beliefs and our values, you look at Chris, and you look at these kids, and they have to go through a sex-change operation and they'll never look right and they'll never have a normal life. Look at Chris's chance for a happy, decent life, and look at theirs. Seeing those kids, it just broke our hearts."

Catherine Tuerk, who runs the support group for parents in Washington, DC, started out as an advocate for gay rights after her son came out, in his twenties. She has a theory about why some parents have become so comfortable with the transgender label: "Parents have told me it's almost easier to tell others, 'My kid was born in the wrong body,' rather than explaining that he might be gay, which is in the back of everyone's mind. When people think about being gay, they think about sex — and thinking about sex and kids is taboo." 75

Tuerk believes lingering homophobia is partly responsible for this, and in some cases, she may be right. When Bill saw two men kissing at the conference, he said, "That just don't sit right with me." In one of Zucker's case studies, a seventeen-year-old girl requesting cross-sex hormones tells him, "Doc, to be honest, lesbians make me sick . . . I want to be normal." In Iran, homosexuality is punishable by death, but sex-change operations are legal — a way of normalizing aberrant attractions.

Overall, though, Tuerk's explanation touches on something deeper than latent homophobia: a subconscious strain in American conceptions of childhood. You see it in the hyper-vigilance about "good touch" and "bad touch." Or in the banishing of Freud to the realm of the perverse. The culture seems invested in an almost Victorian notion of childhood innocence, leaving no room for sexual volition, even in the far future.

When Tuerk was raising her son, in the 70s, she and her husband, a psychiatrist, both fell prey to the idea that their son's gayness was somehow their fault, and that they could change it. These were the years when the child psychologist Bruno Bettelheim blamed cold, distant "refrigerator mothers" for everything from autism to schizophrenia in their children. Children, to Bettelheim, were messy, unhappy creatures, warped by the sins of their parents. Today's children are nothing like that, at least not in their parents' eyes. They are pure vessels, channeling biological impulses beyond their control — or their parents'. Their requests are innocent, unsullied by baggage or desire. Which makes it much easier to say yes to them.

Tuerk was thrilled when the pendulum swung from nurture toward nature; "I can tell you the exact spot where I was, in Chevy Chase Circle, when someone said the words to me: 'There's a guy in Baltimore, and he thinks people are born gay.'" But she now thinks the pendulum may have swung too far. For the minority who are truly transgender, "the sooner they get into the right clothes, the less they're going to suffer. But for the rest? I'm not sure if we're helping or hurting them by pushing them in this direction."

It's not impossible to imagine Brandon's life going in another direction. 80 His early life fits neatly into a Zucker case study about family noise. Tina describes Brandon as "never leaving my side" during his early years. The diagnosis writes itself: father, distant and threatening; mother, protector; child overidentifies with strong maternal figure. If Tina had lived in Toronto, if she'd had the patience for six years of Dr. Zucker's therapy, if the therapy had been free, then who knows?

Yet Zucker's approach has its own disturbing elements. It's easy to imagine that his methods — steering parents toward removing pink crayons from the box, extolling a patriarchy no one believes in — could instill in some children a sense of shame and a double life. A 2008 study of twenty-five girls who had been seen in Zucker's clinic showed positive results; twenty-two were no longer gender-dysphoric, meaning they were comfortable living as girls. But that doesn't mean they were happy. I spoke to the mother of one Zucker patient in her late twenties, who said her daughter was repulsed by the thought of a sex change but was still suffering — she'd become an alcoholic, and was cutting herself. "I'd be surprised if she outlived me," her mother said.

When I was reporting this story, I was visibly pregnant with my third child. My pregnancy brought up a certain nostalgia for the parents I met, because it reminded them of a time when life was simpler, when a stranger could ask them whether their baby was a boy or a girl and they could answer straightforwardly. Many parents shared journals with me that were filled with anguish. If they had decided to let their child live as the other gender, that meant cutting off ties with family and friends who weren't supportive, putting away baby pictures, mourning the loss of the child they thought they had. It meant sending their child out alone into a possibly hostile world. If they chose the other route, it meant denying their child the things he or she most wanted, day after day, in the uncertain hope that one day, it would all pay off. In either case, it meant choosing a course on the basis of hazy evidence, and resolving to believe in it.

About two months after the conference, I visited Brandon again. On Father's Day, Tina had made up her mind to just let it happen. She'd started calling him "Bridget" and, except for a few slipups, "she." She'd packed up all the boy-clothes and given them to a neighbor, and had taken Bridget to JC Penney for a new wardrobe. When I saw her, her ears were pierced and her hair was just beginning to tickle her earlobes. "If it doesn't move any faster, I'll have to get extensions!" Tina said.

That morning, Tina was meeting with Bridget's principal, and the principal of a nearby school, to see if she could transfer. "I want her to be known as Bridget, not Bridget-who-used-to-be-Brandon." Tina had memorized lots of lines she'd heard at the conference, and she delivered them well, if a little too fast. She told the principals that she had "pictures and medical documentation." She showed them a book called *The Transgender Child*. "I thought we could fix it," she said, "but gender's in your brain." Brandon's old principal looked a little shell-shocked. But the one from the nearby school, a young woman with a sweet face and cropped curly hair, seemed more open. "This is all new to me," she said. "It's a lot to learn."

The week before, Tina had gone to her mother's house, taking Bridget along. Bridget often helps care for her grandmother, who has lupus; the two are close. After lunch, Bridget went outside in a pair of high heels she'd found in the closet. Tina's stepfather saw the child and lost it: "Get them damned shoes off!" he yelled.

"Make me," Bridget answered.

Then the stepfather turned to Tina and said, "You're ruining his fucking life," loud enough for Bridget to hear.

Tina's talk with Karen, the mother of Bridget's best friend, Abby, hadn't gone too smoothly, either. Karen is an evangelical Christian, with an anti-gay-marriage bumper sticker on her white van. For two years, she'd picked up Brandon nearly every day after school, and brought him over to play with Abby. But that wasn't going to happen anymore. Karen told Tina she didn't want her children "exposed to that kind of thing." "God doesn't make mistakes," she added.

Bridget, meanwhile, was trying to figure it all out — what she could and couldn't do, where the limits were. She'd always been a compliant child, but now she was misbehaving. Her cross-dressing had amped up; she was trying on makeup, and demanding higher heels and sexier clothes. When I was over, she came out of the house dressed in a cellophane getup, four-inch heels, and lip gloss. "It's like I have to teach her what's appropriate for a girl her age," says Tina.

Thursdays, the family spends the afternoon at a local community center, 90
where both Bridget and her little sister, Madison, take gymnastics. She'd
normally see Abby there; the two of them are in the same class and usually
do their warm-up together, giggling and going over their day. On the car ride
over, Bridget was trying to navigate that new relationship, too.

"Abby's not my best friend anymore. She hits me. But she's really good
at drawing."

"Well, don't you go hitting nobody," Tina said. "Remember, sticks and
stones."

When they arrived at the center and opened the door, Abby was standing right there. She looked at Bridget / Brandon. And froze. She turned and
ran away. Madison, oblivious, followed her, yelling, "Wait for us!"

Bridget sat down on a bench next to Tina. Although they were miles
from home, she'd just seen a fourth-grade friend of her stepbrother's at the
pool table, and she was nervous.

"Hey, we need to work on this," said Tina. "If anybody says anything, 95
you say, 'I'm not Brandon. I'm Bridget, his cousin from California. You want
to try it?"

"No. I don't want to."

"Well, if someone keeps it up, you just say, 'You're crazy.' "

Tina had told me over the phone that Brandon was easily passing as a
girl, but that wasn't really true, not yet. With his hair still short, he looked
like a boy wearing tight pink pants and earrings. This meant that for the
moment, everywhere in this small town was a potential land mine. At the
McDonald's, the cashier eyed him suspiciously: "Is that Happy Meal for a
boy or a girl?" At the playground, a group of teenage boys with tattoos and
their pants pulled low down did a double take. By the evening, Tina was a
nervous wreck. "Gosh darn it! I left the keys in the car," she said. But she
hadn't. She was holding them in her hand.

After gymnastics, the kids wanted to stop at the Dairy Queen, but Tina
couldn't take being stared at in one more place. "Drive-thru!" she yelled.
"And I don't want to hear any more whining from you."

On the quiet, wooded road leading home, she could finally relax. It was 100
cool enough to roll down the windows and get some mountain air. After
high school, Tina had studied to be a travel agent; she had always wanted to
just "work on a cruise ship or something, just go, go, go." Now she wanted
things to be easy for Brandon, for him to disappear and pop back as Bridget,
a new kid from California, new to this town, knowing nobody. But in a small
town, it's hard to erase yourself and come back as your opposite.

Maybe one day they would move, she said. But thinking about that
made her head hurt. Instead of the future, she drifted to the past, when
things were easier.

"Remember that camping trip we took once, Brandon?" she asked, and
he did. And together, they started singing one of the old camp songs she'd
taught him.

Smokey the Bear, Smokey the Bear,
Howlin' and a-prowlin' and a-sniffin' the air.
He can find a fire before it starts to flame.
That's why they call him Smokey,
That's how he got his name.

"You remember that, Brandon?" she asked again. And for the first time all day, they seemed happy.

ENGAGING THE TEXT

1. Review the various theories about the origin of "gender identity disorder" or "gender dysphoria" discussed by the experts and advocates that Rosin cites. Why do some reject the whole idea that transgenderism is a "disorder"?

2. Evaluate the evidence summarized by Rosin that gender identity is "hard-wired" in the brain. How persuasive or unpersuasive do you find it, and why?

3. List the benefits and drawbacks of the puberty-blocking drug for young people like Brandon. What alternative treatments are available? If Brandon were your child, what would you do, and why?

4. What do you think of Tina Simms's decision to encourage Brandon to live as a girl? How would you describe Rosin's attitude toward this decision? Point to specific language and details in the story that support your conclusion.

EXPLORING CONNECTIONS

5. In what ways does Brandon's story support or challenge Aaron H. Devor's account of gender role socialization (p. 527)? How does his experience reflect Devor's distinction between "the personal 'I' and the social 'me'" (Devor, para. 7)?

6. Some readers are likely to be put off by the subject matter of Rosin's article. What rhetorical strategies does she use to engage readers' interest and to appeal for greater understanding of transgendered people?

EXTENDING THE CRITICAL CONTEXT

7. Watch a film that features a central character who is transgendered (e.g., *TransAmerica; Boys Don't Cry; Normal; Hedwig and the Angry Inch; The Crying Game; The Adventures of Priscilla, Queen of the Desert*). Does the movie depict gender identity as primarily psychological or biological? To what extent is the central character's identity portrayed as a problem for himself or herself, and to what extent is it a problem for others? Is she or he presented as a tragic, comic, heroic, or ordinary figure?

Visual Portfolio
READING IMAGES OF GENDER

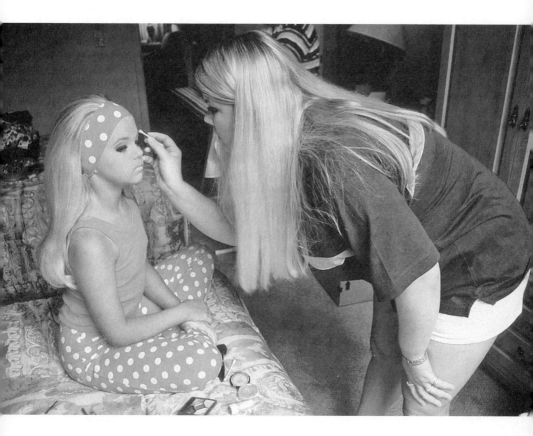

Visual Portfolio
READING IMAGES OF GENDER

1. What do you imagine is happening in the photo on page 568? Where are these boys, and who or what are they aiming at with their water guns? First, write a short narrative from the point of view of one of the boys explaining what led up to this moment and describing your thoughts and feelings. Then write an alternate account from a different point of view — perhaps that of someone who's a target of the water barrage or that of a social scientist (like Aaron H. Devor or Michael Kimmel) analyzing the significance of the scene. Share your stories and discuss the differences of interpretation they reveal.

2. The little girl getting her makeup done (p. 569) is a contestant in a beauty pageant for children. Do some online research about these pageants: How popular are they? How old are the contestants? What is the value of such pageants, according to supporters? What arguments do critics offer against them? Write a paper explaining and defending your own view.

3. Working in pairs or groups, develop an interpretation of the photo of the young woman looking in the mirror (p. 570). Take into account the framing of the photo, the setting, the young woman's outfit, her posture and expression, the direction of her gaze, and the fragmented reflection. Present these interpretations in class and evaluate the persuasiveness of each.

4. Imagine that you are one of the people in the picture of the four teens (p. 571) and freewrite about what is happening (or what has just happened). What are you thinking and feeling at this moment, and why? Compare your responses to those of classmates: Does the gender of the "character" you adopt affect your interpretation of the image? If so, how and why?

5. What does the photo of the victorious boxer (p. 572) suggest about her feelings at that moment? About her opponent's response to his loss? What other messages — about sports or gender or competition, for example — does the picture convey to you? Point to particular visual details that support your interpretations.

6. How would you describe the mood or feeling the photographer has captured in the picture of the father and child (p. 573)? How do the light, the setting, the stance, and the expression of each figure contribute to this impression?

7. Do you think that "Masculinity" would be an appropriate title for the picture of the man and child (p. 573)? Why or why not? Eli Reed, the photographer, titles the photo simply, "Mississippi, 1991"; why do you think he chose to identify it by place and time rather than by theme?

"Two Ways a Woman Can Get Hurt": Advertising and Violence

Jean Kilbourne

*Most of us like to think of ourselves as immune to the power of ads — we know that advertisers use sex to get our attention and that they make exaggerated claims about a product's ability to make us attractive, popular, and successful. Because we can see through these subtle or not-so-subtle messages, we assume that we're too smart to be swayed by them. But Jean Kilbourne argues that ads affect us in far more profound and potentially damaging ways. The way that ads portray bodies — especially women's bodies — as objects conditions us to see each other in dehumanizing ways, thus "normalizing" attitudes that can lead to sexual aggression. Kilbourne (b. 1946) has spent most of her professional life teaching and lecturing about the world of advertising. She has produced award-winning documentaries on images of women in ads (*Killing Us Softly, Slim Hopes*) *and tobacco advertising (*Pack of Lies*). She has also been a member of the National Advisory Council on Alcohol Abuse and Alcoholism and has twice served as an adviser to the surgeon general of the United States. Currently she serves on the Massachusetts Governor's Commission on Sexual and Domestic Abuse and teaches at Wellesley College. Her most recent book, coauthored by Diane E. Levin, is* So Sexy So Soon: The New Sexualized Childhood and What Parents Can Do to Protect Their Kids *(2008). The following selection is taken from her 1999 book* Can't Buy My Love: How Advertising Changes the Way We Think and Feel *(formerly titled* Deadly Persuasion*).*

Sex in advertising is more about disconnection and distance than connection and closeness. It is also more often about power than passion, about violence than violins. The main goal, as in pornography, is usually power over another, either by the physical dominance or preferred status of men or what is seen as the exploitative power of female beauty and female sexuality. Men conquer and women ensnare, always with the essential aid of a product. The woman is rewarded for her sexuality by the man's wealth, as in an ad for Cigarette boats in which the woman says, while lying in a man's embrace clearly after sex, "Does this mean I get a ride in your Cigarette?"

Sex in advertising is pornographic because it dehumanizes and objectifies people, especially women, and because it fetishizes products, imbues them with an erotic charge — which dooms us to disappointment since products never can fulfill our sexual desires or meet our emotional needs.

Two Ways A Woman Can Get Hurt.

(Heartbreaker)

(Soap and water shave)

Skintimate® Shave Gel Ultra Protection formula contains 75% moisturizers, including vitamin E, to protect your legs from nicks, cuts and razor burn. So while guys may continue to be a pain, shaving most definitely won't.

SKINTIMATE® SHAVE GEL.
LOVE YOUR LEGS

© 1997 S.C. Johnson & Son, Inc. All rights reserved. www.skintimate.com

The poses and postures of advertising are often borrowed from pornography, as are many of the themes, such as bondage, sadomasochism, and the sexual exploitation of children. When a beer ad uses the image of a man licking the high-heeled boot of a woman clad in leather, when bondage is

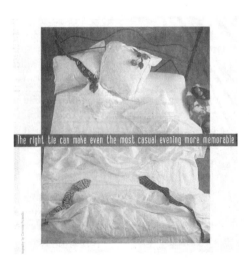

The right tie can make even the most casual evening more memorable

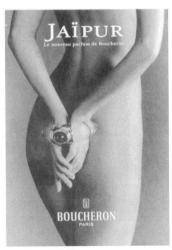

JAÏPUR
Le nouveau parfum de Boucheron

BOUCHERON
PARIS

used to sell neckties in the *New York Times,* perfume in *The New Yorker,* and watches on city buses, and when a college magazine promotes an S&M Ball, pornography can be considered mainstream.

Most of us know all this by now and I suppose some consider it kinky good fun. Pornography is more dangerously mainstream when its glorification of rape and violence shows up in mass media, in films and television shows, in comedy and music videos, and in advertising. Male violence is subtly encouraged by ads that encourage men to be forceful and dominant, and to value sexual intimacy more than emotional intimacy. "Do you want to be the one she tells her deep, dark secrets to?" asks a three-page ad for men's cologne. "Or do you want to be her deep, dark secret?" The last page advises men, "Don't be such a good boy." There are two identical women

looking adoringly at the man in the ad, but he isn't looking at either one of them. Just what is the deep, dark secret? That he's sleeping with both of them? Clearly the way to get beautiful women is to ignore them, perhaps mistreat them.

"Two ways a woman can get hurt," says an ad for shaving gel, featuring a razor and a photo of a handsome man. My first thought is that the man is a batterer or date rapist, but the ad informs us that he is merely a "heartbreaker." The gel will protect the woman so that "while guys may continue to be a pain, shaving most definitely won't." Desirable men are painful — heartbreakers at best.

Wouldn't it be wonderful if, realizing the importance of relationships in   5
all of our lives, we could seek to learn relational skills from women and to help men develop these strengths in themselves? In fact, we so often do the opposite. The popular culture usually trivializes these abilities in women, mocks men who have real intimacy with women (it is almost always married men in ads and cartoons who are jerks), and idealizes a template for relationships between men and women that is a recipe for disaster: a template that views sex as more important than anything else, that ridicules men who are not in control of their women (who are "pussy-whipped"), and that disparages fidelity and commitment (except, of course, to brand names).

Indeed the very worst kind of man for a woman to be in an intimate relationship with, often a truly dangerous man, is the one considered most sexy and desirable in the popular culture. And the men capable of real intimacy (the ones we tell our deep, dark secrets to) constantly have their very masculinity impugned. Advertising often encourages women to be attracted

sweat. Go all out. We'll keep up. New Old Spice Anti-Perspirant helps stop the sweat that causes odor. The proof? You're looking at her. For great odor protection, now you've got **proof** that performs.

to hostile and indifferent men while encouraging boys to become these men. This is especially dangerous for those of us who have suffered from "condemned isolation" in childhood: like heat-seeking missiles, we rush inevitably to mutual destruction.

Men are also encouraged to never take no for an answer. Ad after ad implies that girls and women don't really mean "no" when they say it, that women are only teasing when they resist men's advances. "NO" says an ad showing a man leaning over a woman against a wall. Is she screaming or laughing? Oh, it's an ad for deodorant and the second word, in very small print, is "sweat." Sometimes it's "all in good fun," as in the ad for Possession shirts and shorts featuring a man ripping the clothes off a woman who seems to be having a good time.

And sometimes it is more sinister. A perfume ad running in several teen magazines features a very young woman, with eyes blackened by makeup or perhaps something else, and the copy, "Apply generously to your neck so he can smell the scent as you shake your head 'no.'" In other words, he'll understand that you don't really mean it and he can respond to the scent like any other animal.

Sometimes there seems to be no question but that a man should force a woman to have sex. A chilling newspaper ad for a bar in Georgetown features a closeup of a cocktail and the headline, "If your date won't listen to reason, try a Velvet Hammer." A vodka ad pictures a wolf hiding in a flock of sheep, a hideous grin on its face. We all know what wolves do to sheep. A campaign for Bacardi Black rum features shadowy figures almost obliterated by darkness and captions such as "Some people embrace the night because

P♡SSESSION

SHIRTS AND SHORTS
1-800-229-GRVPO

the rules of the day do not apply." What it doesn't say is that people who are above the rules do enormous harm to other people, as well as to themselves.

These ads are particularly troublesome, given that between one-third   10 and three-quarters of all cases of sexual assault involve alcohol consumption by the perpetrator, the victim, or both.[1] "Make strangers your friends, and your friends a lot stranger," says one of the ads in a Cuervo campaign that uses colorful cartoon beasts and emphasizes heavy drinking. This ad is especially disturbing when we consider the role of alcohol in date rape, as is another ad in the series that says, "The night began with a bottle of Cuervo and ended with a vow of silence." Over half of all reported rapes on college campuses occur when either the victim or the assailant has been drinking.[2] Alcohol's role has different meaning for men and women, however. If a man is drunk when he commits a rape, he is considered less responsible. If a woman is drunk (or has had a drink or two or simply met the man in a bar), she is considered more responsible.

In general, females are still held responsible and hold each other responsible when sex goes wrong — when they become pregnant or are the victims of rape and sexual assault or cause a scandal. Constantly exhorted to be sexy and attractive, they discover when assaulted that that very sexiness is evidence of their guilt, their lack of "innocence." Sometimes the ads play on this by "warning" women of what might happen if they use the product.

---

[1]Wilsnack, Plaud, Wilsnack, and Klassen, 1997, 262. [All notes are Kilbourne's unless otherwise indicated.]

[2]Abbey, Ross, and McDuffie, 1991. Also Martin, 1992, 230–37.

"Wear it but beware it," says a perfume ad. Beware what exactly? Victoria's Secret tempts young women with blatantly sexual ads promising that their lingerie will make them irresistible. Yet when a young woman accused William Kennedy Smith of raping her, the fact that she wore Victoria's Secret panties was used against her as an indication of her immorality. A jury acquitted Smith, whose alleged history of violence against women was not permitted to be introduced at trial.

It is sadly not surprising that the jury was composed mostly of women. Women are especially cruel judges of other women's sexual behavior, mostly

because we are so desperate to believe we are in control of what happens to us. It is too frightening to face the fact that male violence against women is irrational and commonplace. It is reassuring to believe that we can avoid it by being good girls, avoiding dark places, staying out of bars, dressing "innocently." An ad featuring two young women talking intimately at a coffee shop says, "Carla and Rachel considered themselves open-minded and non-judgmental people. Although they did agree Brenda was a tramp." These terrible judgments from other women are an important part of what keeps all women in line.

If indifference in a man is sexy, then violence is sometimes downright erotic. Not surprisingly, this attitude too shows up in advertising. "Push my buttons," says a young woman, "I'm looking for a man who can totally floor me." Her vulnerability is underscored by the fact that she is in an elevator,

often a dangerous place for women. She is young, she is submissive (her eyes are downcast), she is in a dangerous place, and she is dressed provocatively. And she is literally asking for it.

"Wear it out and make it scream," says a jeans ad portraying a man sliding his hands under a woman's transparent blouse. This could be a seduction, but it could as easily be an attack. Although the ad that ran in the Czech version of *Elle* portraying three men attacking a woman seems unambiguous, the terrifying image is being used to sell jeans *to women.* So someone must think that women would find this image compelling or attractive. Why would we? Perhaps it is simply designed to get our attention, by shocking us and by arousing unconscious anxiety. Or perhaps the intent is more subtle and it is designed to play into the fantasies of domination and even rape that some women use in order to maintain an illusion of being in control (we are the ones having the fantasies, after all, we are the directors).

A camera ad features a woman's torso wrapped in plastic, her hands tied behind her back. A smiling woman in a lipstick ad has a padlocked chain around her neck. An ad for MTV shows a vulnerable young woman, her breasts exposed, and the simple copy "Bitch." A perfume ad features a man shadowboxing with what seems to be a woman.

Sometimes women are shown dead or in the process of being killed. "Great hair never dies," says an ad featuring a female corpse lying on a bed, her breasts exposed. An ad in the Italian version of *Vogue* shows a man aiming a gun at a nude woman wrapped in plastic, a leather briefcase covering her face. And an ad for Bitch skateboards, for God's sake, shows a cartoon version of a similar scene, this time clearly targeting young people. We

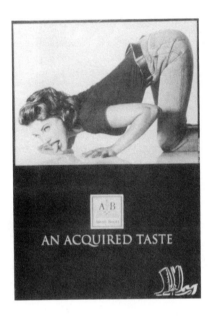

believe we are not affected by these images, but most of us experience visceral shock when we pay conscious attention to them. Could they be any less shocking to us on an unconscious level?

Most of us become numb to these images, just as we become numb to the daily litany in the news of women being raped, battered, and killed. According to former surgeon general Antonia Novello, battery is the single greatest cause of injury to women in America, more common than automobile accidents, muggings, and stranger rapes combined, and more than one-third of women slain in this country die at the hands of husbands or

boyfriends.[3] Throughout the world, the biggest problem for most women is simply surviving at home. The Global Report on Women's Human Rights concluded that "Domestic violence is a leading cause of female injury in almost every country in the world and is typically ignored by the state or only erratically punished."[4] Although usually numb to these facts on a conscious level, most women live in a state of subliminal terror, a state that, according to Mary Daly,[5] keeps us divided both from each other and from our most passionate, powerful, and creative selves.[6]

Ads don't directly cause violence, of course. But the violent images contribute to the state of terror. And objectification and disconnection create a climate in which there is widespread and increasing violence. Turning a human being into a thing, an object, is almost always the first step toward justifying violence against that person. It is very difficult, perhaps impossible, to be violent to someone we think of as an equal, someone we have empathy with, but it is very easy to abuse a thing. We see this with racism, with homophobia. The person becomes an object and violence is inevitable. This step is already taken with women. The violence, the abuse, is partly the chilling but logical result of the objectification.

An editorial in *Advertising Age* suggests that even some advertisers are concerned about this: "Clearly it's time to wipe out sexism in beer ads; for

[3]Novello, 1991. Also Blumenthal, 1995.
[4]Wright, 1995, A2.
[5]*Mary Daly:* Radical feminist scholar and author (1928–2010). [Eds.]
[6]Weil, 1999, 21.

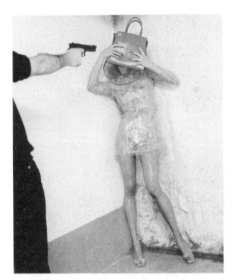

La Borsa è la Vita

the brewers and their agencies to wake up and join the rest of America in realizing that sexism, sexual harassment, and the cultural portrayal of women in advertising are inextricably linked."[7] Alas, this editorial was written in 1991 and nothing has changed.

It is this link with violence that makes the objectification of women [20] a more serious issue than the objectification of men. Our economic system constantly requires the development of new markets. Not surprisingly, men's bodies are the latest territory to be exploited. Although we are growing more used to it, in the beginning the male sex object came as a surprise. In 1994 a "gender bender" television commercial in which a bevy of women office workers gather to watch a construction worker doff his shirt to quaff a Diet Coke led to so much hoopla that you'd have thought women were mugging men on Madison Avenue.[8]

There is no question that men are used as sex objects in ads now as never before. We often see nude women with fully clothed men in ads (as in art), but the reverse was unheard of, until recently. These days some ads do feature clothed and often aggressive women with nude men. And women sometimes blatantly objectify men, as in the Metroliner ad that says, " 'She's reading Nietzsche,' Harris noted to himself as he walked towards the café car for a glass of cabernet. And as he passed her seat, Maureen looked up from her book and thought, 'Nice buns.' "

[7]Brewers can help fight sexism, 1991, 28.
[8]Kilbourne, 1994, F13.

bitch skateboards

Although these ads are often funny, it is never a good thing for human beings to be objectified. However, there is a world of difference between the objectification of men and that of women. The most important difference is that there is no danger for most men, whereas objectified women are always at risk. In the Diet Coke ad, for instance, the women are physically separated from the shirtless man. He is the one in control. His body is powerful, not passive. Imagine a true role reversal of this ad: a group of businessmen gather to leer at a beautiful woman worker on her break, who removes her shirt before drinking her Diet Coke. This scene would be frightening, not funny, as the Diet Coke ad is. And why is the Diet Coke ad funny? Because we know it doesn't describe any truth. However, the ads featuring images of male violence against women do describe a truth, a truth we are all aware of, on one level or another.

When power is unequal, when one group is oppressed and discrimi-nated against *as a group*, when there is a context of systemic and historical oppression, stereotypes and prejudice have different weight and meaning. As Anna Quindlen[9] said, writing about "reverse racism": "Hatred by the powerful, the majority, has a different weight — and often very different effects — than hatred by the powerless, the minority."[10] When men objec-tify women, they do so in a cultural context in which women are constantly objectified and in which there are consequences — from economic discrim-ination to violence — to that objectification.

For men, though, there are no such consequences. Men's bodies are not routinely judged and invaded. Men are not likely to be raped, harassed, or beaten (that is to say, men presumed to be heterosexual are not, and very few men are abused in these ways by women). How many men are fright-ened to be alone with a woman in an elevator? How many men cross the street when a group of women approaches? Jackson Katz, who writes and lectures on male violence, often begins his workshops by asking men to describe the things they do every day to protect themselves from sexual assault. The men are surprised, puzzled, sometimes amused by the ques-tion. The women understand the question easily and have no trouble at all coming up with a list of responses. We don't list our full names in the phone directory or on our mailboxes, we try not to be alone after dark, we carry our keys in our hands when we approach our cars, we always look in the back seat before we get in, we are wary of elevators and doorways and bushes, we carry pepper sprays, whistles, Mace.

Nonetheless, the rate of sexual assault in the United States is the high-est of any industrialized nation in the world.[11] According to a 1998 study by the federal government, one in five of us has been the victim of rape or attempted rape, most often before our seventeenth birthday. And more than half of us have been physically assaulted, most often by the men we live with. In fact, three of four women in the study who responded that they had been raped or assaulted as adults said the perpetrator was a current or former husband, a cohabiting partner or a date.[12] The article reporting the results of this study was buried on page twenty-three of my local news-paper, while the front page dealt with a long story about the New England Patriots football team.

A few summers ago, a Diet Pepsi commercial featured Cindy Crawford being ogled by two boys (they seemed to be about twelve years old) as she got out of her car and bought a Pepsi from a machine. The boys made very suggestive comments, which in the end turned out to be about the Pepsi's

25

---

[9]*Anna Quindlen:* Novelist and Pulitzer Prize–winning journalist who often writes about women's issues (b. 1953). [Eds.]

[10]Quindlen, 1992, E17.

[11]Blumenthal, 1995, 2.

[12]Tjaden and Thoennes, 1998.

can rather than Ms. Crawford's. There was no outcry: the boys' behavior was acceptable and ordinary enough for a soft-drink commercial.

Again, let us imagine the reverse: a sexy man gets out of a car in the countryside and two preteen girls make suggestive comments, seemingly about his body, especially his buns. We would fear for them and rightly so. But the boys already have the right to ogle, to view women's bodies as property to be looked at, commented on, touched, perhaps eventually hit and raped. The boys have also learned that men ogle primarily to impress other men (and to affirm their heterosexuality). If anyone is in potential danger in this ad, it is the woman (regardless of the age of the boys). Men are not seen

as *property* in this way by women. Indeed if a woman does whistle at a man or touches his body or even makes direct eye contact, it is still *she* who is at risk and the man who has the power.

"I always lower my eyes to see if a man is worth following," says the woman in an ad for men's pants. Although the ad is offensive to everyone, the woman is endangering only herself.

"Where women are women and men are roadkill," says an ad for motorcycle clothing featuring an angry-looking African American woman. Women are sometimes hostile and angry in ads these days, especially women of color who are often seen as angrier and more threatening than white women. But, regardless of color, we all know that women are far more likely than men to end up as roadkill — and, when it happens, they are blamed for being on the road in the first place.

Even little girls are sometimes held responsible for the violence against   30
them. In 1990 a male Canadian judge accused a three-year-old girl of being "sexually aggressive" and suspended the sentence of her molester, who was then free to return to his job of baby-sitter.[13] The deeply held belief that all women, regardless of age, are really temptresses in disguise, nymphets, sexually insatiable and seductive, conveniently transfers all blame and responsibility onto women.

[13]Two men and a baby, 1990, 10.

All women are vulnerable in a culture in which there is such wide-spread objectification of women's bodies, such glorification of disconnection, so much violence against women, and such blaming of the victim. When everything and everyone is sexualized, it is the powerless who are most at risk. Young girls, of course, are especially vulnerable. In the past twenty years or so, there have been several trends in fashion and advertising that could be seen as cultural reactions to the women's movement, as perhaps unconscious fear of female power. One has been the obsession with thinness. Another has been an increase in images of violence against women. Most disturbing has been the increasing sexualization of children, especially girls. Sometimes the little girl is made up and seductively posed. Sometimes the language is suggestive. "Very cherry," says the ad featuring a sexy little African American girl who is wearing a dress with cherries all over it. A shocking ad in a gun magazine features a smiling little girl, a toddler, in a bathing suit that is tugged up suggestively in the rear. The copy beneath the photo says, "short BUTTS from FLEMING FIREARMS."[14] Other times girls are juxtaposed with grown women, as in the ad for underpants that says "You already know the feeling."

This is not only an American phenomenon. A growing national obsession in Japan with schoolgirls dressed in uniforms is called "Loli-con," after

[14]Herbert, 1999, WK 17.

Lolita.[15] In Tokyo hundreds of "image clubs" allow Japanese men to act out their fantasies with make-believe schoolgirls. A magazine called *V-Club* featuring pictures of naked elementary-school girls competes with another called *Anatomical Illustrations of Junior High School Girls.*[16] Masao Miyamoto, a male psychiatrist, suggests that Japanese men are turning to girls because they feel threatened by the growing sophistication of older women.[17]

In recent years, this sexualization of little girls has become even more disturbing as hints of violence enter the picture. A three-page ad for Prada clothing features a girl or very young woman with a barely pubescent body, clothed in what seem to be cotton panties and perhaps a training bra, viewed through a partially opened door. She seems surprised, startled, worried, as if she's heard a strange sound or glimpsed someone watching her. I suppose this could be a woman awaiting her lover, but it could as easily be a girl being preyed upon.

The 1996 murder of six-year-old JonBenet Ramsey[18] was a gold mine for the media, combining as it did child pornography and violence. In November of 1997 *Advertising Age* reported in an article entitled "JonBenet keeps hold on magazines" that the child had been on five magazine covers in October, "Enough to capture the Cover Story lead for the month. The pre-adolescent beauty queen, found slain in her home last Christmas, garnered 6.5 points.

---

[15]*Lolita:* The title character of Vladimir Nabokov's 1955 novel, Lolita is a young girl who is sexually pursued by her stepfather. [Eds.]

[16]Schoolgirls as sex toys, 1997, 2E.

[17]Ibid.

[18]*JonBenet Ramsey:* Six-year-old beauty-pageant winner who was sexually molested and murdered in her Boulder, Colorado, home in 1996. [Eds.]

The case earned a *triple play* [italics mine] in the *National Enquirer,* and one-time appearances on *People* and *Star.*"[19] Imagine describing a six-year-old child as "pre-adolescent."

Sometimes the models in ads are children, other times they just look like children. Kate Moss was twenty when she said of herself, "I look twelve."[20] She epitomized the vacant, hollow-cheeked look known as "heroin chic" that was popular in the mid-nineties. She also often looked vulnerable, abused, and exploited. In one ad she is nude in the corner of a huge sofa, cringing as if braced for an impending sexual assault. In another she is lying nude on her stomach, pliant, available, androgynous enough to appeal to all kinds of pedophiles. In a music video she is dead and bound to a chair while Johnny Cash sings "Delia's Gone."

It is not surprising that Kate Moss models for Calvin Klein, the fashion designer who specializes in breaking taboos and thereby getting himself public outrage, media coverage, and more bang for his buck. In 1995 he brought the federal government down on himself by running a campaign that may have crossed the line into child pornography.[21] Very young models (and others who just seemed young) were featured in lascivious print ads and in television commercials designed to mimic child porn. The models were awkward, self-conscious. In one commercial, a boy stands in what seems to be a finished basement. A male voiceover tells him he has a great body and asks him to take off his shirt. The boy seems embarrassed but he complies. There was a great deal of protest, which brought the issue into

35

[19]Johnson, 1997, 42.
[20]Leo, 1994, 27.
[21]Sloan, 1996, 27.

national consciousness but which also gave Klein the publicity and free media coverage he was looking for. He pulled the ads but, at the same time, projected that his jeans sales would almost double from $115 million to $220 million that year, partly because of the free publicity but also because the controversy made his critics seem like prudes and thus positioned Klein as the daring rebel, a very appealing image to the majority of his customers.

Having learned from this, in 1999 Klein launched a very brief advertising campaign featuring very little children frolicking in their underpants, which included a controversial billboard in Times Square.[22] Although in some ways this campaign was less offensive than the earlier one and might have gone unnoticed had the ads come from a department store catalog rather than from Calvin Klein, there was the expected protest and Klein quickly withdrew the ads, again getting a windfall of media coverage. In my opinion, the real obscenity of this campaign is the whole idea of people buying designer underwear for their little ones, especially in a country in which at least one in five children doesn't have enough to eat.

Although boys are sometimes sexualized in an overt way, they are more often portrayed as sexually precocious, as in the Pepsi commercial featuring the young boys ogling Cindy Crawford or the jeans ad portraying a very little boy looking up a woman's skirt. It may seem that I am reading too much into this ad, but imagine if the genders were reversed. We would fear for a little girl who was unzipping a man's fly in an ad (and we would be shocked, I would hope). Boys are vulnerable to sexual abuse too, but cultural attitudes make it difficult to take this seriously. As a result, boys are less likely to report abuse and to get treatment.

[22]Associated Press, 1999, February 18, A7.

Many boys grow up feeling that they are unmanly if they are not always "ready for action," capable of and interested in sex with any woman who is available. Advertising doesn't cause this attitude, of course, but it contributes to it. A Levi Strauss commercial that ran in Asia features the shock of a schoolboy who discovers that the seductive young woman who has slipped a note into the jeans of an older student is his teacher. And an ad for BIC pens pictures a young boy wearing X-ray glasses while ogling the derriere of an older woman. Again, these ads would be unthinkable if the genders were reversed. It is increasingly difficult in such a toxic environment to see children, boys or girls, as *children*.

In the past few years there has been a proliferation of sexually   40
grotesque toys for boys, such as a Spider Man female action figure whose

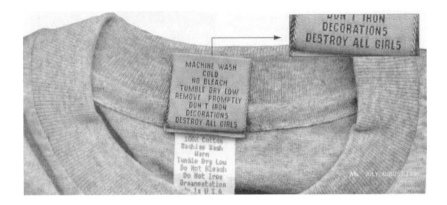

exaggerated breasts have antennae coming out of them and a female Spawn figure with carved skulls for breasts. Meantime even children have easy access to pornography in video games and on the World Wide Web, which includes explicit photographs of women having intercourse with groups of men, with dogs, donkeys, horses, and snakes; photographs of women being raped and tortured; some of these women made up to look like little girls.

It is hard for girls not to learn self-hatred in an environment in which there is such widespread and open contempt for women and girls. In 1997 a company called Senate distributed clothing with inside labels that included, in addition to the usual cleaning instructions, the line "Destroy all girls." A Senate staffer explained that he thought it was "kind of cool."[23] Given all this, it's not surprising that when boys and girls were asked in a recent study to write an essay on what it would be like to be the other gender, many boys wrote they would rather be dead. Girls had no trouble writing essays about activities, power, freedom, but boys were often stuck, could think of nothing.

It is also not surprising that, in such an environment, sexual harassment is considered normal and ordinary. According to an article in the journal *Eating Disorders:*

> In our work with young women, we have heard countless accounts of this contempt being expressed by their male peers: the girls who do not want to walk down a certain hallway in their high school because they are afraid of being publicly rated on a scale of one to ten; the girls who are subjected to barking, grunting and mooing calls and labels of "dogs, cows, or pigs" when they pass by groups of male students; those who are teased about not measuring up to buxom, bikini-clad [models]; and the girls who are grabbed, pinched, groped, and fondled as they try to make their way through the school corridors.

[23]Wire and *Times* staff reports, 1997, D1.

Harassing words do not slide harmlessly away as the taunting sounds dissipate. . . . They are slowly absorbed into the child's identity and developing sense of self, becoming an essential part of who she sees herself to be. Harassment involves the use of words as weapons to inflict pain and assert power. Harassing words are meant to instill fear, heighten bodily discomfort, and diminish the sense of self.[24]

It is probably difficult for those of us who are older to understand how devastating and cruel and pervasive this harassment is, how different from the "teasing" some of us might remember from our own childhoods (not that that didn't hurt and do damage as well). A 1993 report by the American Association of University Women found that 76 percent of female students in grades eight to eleven and 56 percent of male students said they had been sexually harassed in school.[25] One high-school junior described a year of torment at her vocational school: "The boys call me slut, bitch. They call me a ten-timer, because they say I go with ten guys at the same time. I put up with it because I have no choice. The teachers say it's because the boys think I'm pretty."[26]

High school and junior high school have always been hell for those who were different in any way (gay teens have no doubt suffered the most, although "overweight" girls are a close second), but the harassment is more extreme and more physical these days. Many young men feel they have the right to judge and touch young women and the women often feel they have no choice but to submit. One young woman recalled that "the guys at school routinely swiped their hands across girls' legs to patrol their shaving prowess and then taunt them if they were slacking off. If I were running late, I'd protect myself by faux shaving — just doing the strip between the bottom of my jeans and the top of my cotton socks."[27]

Sexual battery, as well as inappropriate sexual gesturing, touching, and   45
fondling, is increasing not only in high schools but in elementary and middle schools as well.[28] There are reports of sexual assaults by students on other students as young as eight. A fifth-grade boy in Georgia repeatedly touched the breasts and genitals of one of his fellow students while saying, "I want to get in bed with you" and "I want to feel your boobs." Authorities did nothing, although the girl complained and her grades fell. When her parents found a suicide note she had written, they took the board of education to court.[29]

[24]Larkin, Rice, and Russell, 1996, 5–26.
[25]Daley and Vigue, 1999, A12.
[26]Hart, 1998, A12.
[27]Mackler, 1998, 56.
[28]Daley and Vigue, 1999, A1, A12.
[29]Shin, 1999, 32.

A high-school senior in an affluent suburban school in the Boston area said she has been dragged by her arms so boys could look up her skirt and that boys have rested their heads on her chest while making lewd comments. Another student in the same school was pinned down on a lunch table while a boy simulated sex on top of her. Neither student reported any of the incidents, for fear of being ostracized by their peers.[30] In another school in the Boston area, a sixteen-year-old girl, who had been digitally raped by a classmate, committed suicide.[31]

According to Nan Stein, a researcher at Wellesley College:

> Schools may in fact be training grounds for the insidious cycle of domestic violence. . . . The school's hidden curriculum teaches young women to suffer abuse privately, that resistance is futile. When they witness harassment of others and fail to respond, they absorb a different kind of powerlessness — that they are incapable of standing up to injustice or acting in solidarity with their peers. Similarly, in schools boys receive permission, even training, to become batterers through the practice of sexual harassment.[32]

This pervasive harassment of and contempt for girls and women constitute a kind of abuse. We know that addictions for women are rooted in trauma, that girls who are sexually abused are far more likely to become addicted to one substance or another. I contend that all girls growing up in this culture are sexually abused — abused by the pornographic images of female sexuality that surround them from birth, abused by all the violence against women and girls, and abused by the constant harassment and threat of violence. Abuse is a continuum, of course, and I am by no means implying that cultural abuse is as terrible as literally being raped and assaulted. However, it hurts, it does damage, and it sets girls up for addictions and self-destructive behavior. Many girls turn to food, alcohol, cigarettes, and other drugs in a misguided attempt to cope.

As Marian Sandmaier said in *The Invisible Alcoholics: Women and Alcohol Abuse in America*, "In a culture that cuts off women from many of their own possibilities before they barely have had a chance to sense them, that pain belongs to all women. Outlets for coping may vary widely, and may be more or less addictive, more or less self-destructive. But at some level, all women know what it is to lack access to their own power, to live with a piece of themselves unclaimed."[33]

Today, every girl is endangered, not just those who have been physically and sexually abused. If girls from supportive homes with positive role models are at risk, imagine then how vulnerable are the girls who have been   50

---

[30]Daley and Vigue, 1999, A12.
[31]Daley and Abraham, 1999, B6.
[32]Stein, 1993, 316–17.
[33]Sandmaier, 1980, xviii.

violated. No wonder they so often go under for good — ending up in abusive marriages, in prison, on the streets. And those who do are almost always in the grip of one addiction or another. More than half of women in prison are addicts and most are there for crimes directly related to their addiction. Many who are there for murder killed men who had been battering them for years. Almost all of the women who are homeless or in prisons and mental institutions are the victims of male violence.[34]

Male violence exists within the same cultural and sociopolitical context that contributes to addiction. Both can be fully understood only within this context, way beyond individual psychology and family dynamics. It is a context of systemic violence and oppression, including racism, classism, heterosexism, weightism, and ageism, as well as sexism, all of which are traumatizing in and of themselves. Advertising is only one part of this cultural context, but it is an important part and thus is a part of what traumatizes.

Sources

Abbey, A., Ross, L., and McDuffie, D. (1991). Alcohol's role in sexual assault. In Watson, R., ed. *Addictive behaviors in women.* Totowa, NJ: Humana Press.

Associated Press (1999, February 18). Calvin Klein retreats on ad. *Boston Globe,* A7.

Blumenthal, S. J. (1995, July). *Violence against women.* Washington, DC: Department of Health and Human Services.

Brewers can help fight sexism (1991, October 28). *Advertising Age,* 28.

Daley, B., and Vigue, D. I. (1999, February 4). Sex harassment increasing amid students, officials say. *Boston Globe,* A1, A12.

Hart, J. (1998, June 8). Northampton confronts a crime, cruelty. *Boston Globe,* A1, A12.

Herbert, B. (1999, May 2). America's littlest shooters. *New York Times,* WK 17.

Johnson, J. A. (1997, November 10). JonBenet keeps hold on magazines. *Advertising Age,* 42.

Kilbourne, J. (1994, May 15). 'Gender bender' ads: Same old sexism. *New York Times,* F13.

Larkin, J., Rice, C., and Russell, V. (1996, Spring). Slipping through the cracks: Sexual harassment. *Eating Disorders: The Journal of Treatment and Prevention,* vol. 4, no. 1, 5–26.

Leo, J. (1994, June 13). Selling the woman-child. *U. S. News and World Report,* 27.

Mackler, C. (1998). Memoirs of a (sorta) ex-shaver. In Edut, O., ed. (1998). *Adios, Barbie.* Seattle, WA: Seal Press, 55–61.

Novello, A. (1991, October 18). Quoted by Associated Press, AMA to fight wife-beating. *St. Louis Post Dispatch,* 1, 15.

Quindlen, A. (1992, June 28). All of these you are. *New York Times,* E17.

Sandmaier, M. (1980). *The invisible alcoholics: Women and alcohol abuse in America.* New York: McGraw-Hill.

Schoolgirls as sex toys. *New York Times* (1997, April 16), 2E.

---

[34]Snell, 1991.

Shin, A. (1999, April/May). Testing Title IX. *Ms.*, 32.

Sloan, P. (1996, July 8). Underwear ads caught in bind over sex appeal. *Advertising Age*, 27.

Snell, T. L. (1991). *Women in prison.* Washington, DC: U.S. Department of Justice.

Stein, N. (1993). No laughing matter: Sexual harassment in K-12 schools. In Buchwald, E., Fletcher, P. R., and Roth, M. (1993). *Transforming a rape culture.* Minneapolis, MN: Milkweed Editions, 311–31.

Tjaden, R., and Thoennes, N. (1998, November). *Prevalence, incidence, and consequences of violence against women: Findings from the National Violence Against Women Survey.* Washington, DC: U.S. Department of Justice.

Two men and a baby (1990, July/August). *Ms.*, 10.

Vigue, D. J., and Abraham, Y. (1999, February 7). Harassment a daily course for students. *Boston Globe*, B1, B6.

Weil, L. (1999, March). Leaps of faith. *Women's Review of Books*, 21.

Wilsnack, S. C., Plaud, J. J., Wilsnack, R. W., and Klassen, A. D. (1997). Sexuality, gender, and alcohol use. In Wilsnack, R. W., and Wilsnack, S. C., eds. *Gender and alcohol: Individual and social perspectives.* New Brunswick, N.J.: Rutgers Center of Alcohol Studies, 262.

Wire and Times Staff Reports (1997, May 20). Orange County skate firm's 'destroy all girls' tags won't wash. *Los Angeles Times*, D1.

Wright, R. (1995, September 10). Brutality defines the lives of women around the world. *Boston Globe*, A2.

ENGAGING THE TEXT

1. What parallels does Kilbourne see between advertising and pornography? How persuasive do you find the evidence she offers? Do the photos of the ads she describes strengthen her argument? Why or why not?

2. Why is it dangerous to depict women and men as sex objects, according to Kilbourne? Why is the objectification of women *more* troubling, in her view? Do you agree?

3. How does Kilbourne explain the appeal of ads that allude to bondage, sexual aggression, and rape — particularly for female consumers? How do you respond to the ads reproduced in her essay?

4. What does Kilbourne mean when she claims that the depiction of women in advertising constitutes "cultural abuse"? How does she go about drawing connections between advertising images and social problems like sexual violence, harassment, and addiction? Which portions of her analysis do you find most and least persuasive, and why?

EXPLORING CONNECTIONS

5. Media images constitute part of the "generalized other" — the internalized sense of what is socially acceptable and unacceptable — described by Aaron H. Devor (p. 527). In addition to the violent and sexualized images

Kilbourne examines, what other images or messages about gender do you encounter regularly in the media? Which ones have been most influential in the development of your "generalized other"?

6. Drawing on the essays by Kilbourne and Joan Morgan (below), write an essay exploring the power of media to promote or curb violence.

EXTENDING THE CRITICAL CONTEXT

7. Kilbourne claims that popular culture idealizes dangerous, exploitative, or dysfunctional relationships between women and men. Working in small groups, discuss the romantic relationships depicted in movies you've seen recently. Does her critique seem applicable to those films? List the evidence you find for and against her argument and compare your results with those of other groups.

8. In her analysis of two ads (the Diet Pepsi commercial featuring Cindy Crawford and the Diet Coke ad with the shirtless construction worker), Kilbourne applies a gender reversal test in order to demonstrate the existence of a double standard. Try this test yourself on a commercial or ad that relies on sexual innuendo. Write a journal entry describing the ad and explaining the results of your test.

9. Working in pairs or small groups, survey the ads in two magazines — one designed to appeal to a predominantly female audience and one aimed at a largely male audience. What differences, if any, do you see in the kinds of images and appeals advertisers use in the two magazines? How often do you see the kinds of "pornographic" ads Kilbourne discusses? Do you find any ads depicting the "relational skills" that she suggests are rarely emphasized in popular culture?

From Fly-Girls to Bitches and Hos

JOAN MORGAN

As a music writer and fan of hip-hop, Joan Morgan loves the power of rap. As a feminist, she is troubled by the pervasive sexism of its lyrics. The misogyny of rap, she argues, is a symptom of crisis in the black community; it must be confronted and understood, not simply condemned, as a step toward healing the pain that it both expresses and inflicts. This passage comes from her collection of essays, When Chickenheads Come Home to Roost . . . My Life as a Hip-Hop Feminist (1999). *Formerly the executive editor of* Essence, *she has also written for* The Village Voice, Vibe, Ms., *and* Spin.

Feminist criticism, like many other forms of social analysis, is widely considered part of a hostile white culture. For a black feminist to chastise misogyny in rap publicly would be viewed as divisive and counterproductive. There is a widespread perception in the black community that public criticism of black men constitutes collaborating with a racist society. . . .

> — MICHELE WALLACE, "When Black Feminism
> Faces the Music, and the Music Is Rap,"
> The *New York Times*[1]

Lord knows our love jones for hip-hop is understandable. Props given to rap music's artistic merits, its irrefutable impact on pop culture, its ability to be alternately beautiful, poignant, powerful, strong, irreverent, visceral, and mesmerizing — homeboy's clearly got it like that. But in between the beats, booty shaking, and hedonistic abandon, I have to wonder if there isn't something inherently unfeminist in supporting a music that repeatedly reduces me to tits and ass and encourages pimping on the regular. While it's human to occasionally fall deep into the love thang with people or situations that simply aren't good for you, feminism alerted me long ago to the dangers of romancing a misogynist (and ridiculously fine, brilliant ones with gangsta leans are no exception). Perhaps the nonbelievers were right, maybe what I'd been mistaking for love and commitment for the last twenty years was really nothing but a self-destructive obsession that made a mockery of my feminism. . . .

I guess it all depends on how you define the f-word. My feminism places the welfare of black women and the black community on its list of priorities. It also maintains that black-on-black love is essential to the survival of both.

We have come to a point in our history, however, when black-on-black love — a love that's survived slavery, lynching, segregation, poverty, and racism — is in serious danger. The stats usher in this reality like taps before the death march: According to the U.S. Census Bureau, the number of black two-parent households has decreased from 74 percent to 48 percent since 1960. The leading cause of death among black men ages fifteen to twenty-four is homicide. The majority of them will die at the hands of other black men.[2]

Women are the unsung victims of black-on-black crime. A while back, a friend of mine, a single mother of a newborn (her "babyfather" — a brother — abdicated responsibility before their child was born) was attacked by a pit bull while walking her dog in the park. The owner (a brother) trained

---

[1]Michele Wallace, "When Black Feminism Faces the Music, and the Music Is Rap," the *New York Times*, July 29, 1990. [All notes are Morgan's.]

[2]Joan Morgan, "Real Love," *Vibe*, April 1996, p. 38.

the animal to prey on other dogs and the flesh of his fellow community members.

A few weeks later my mom called, upset, to tell me about the murder of a family friend. She was a troubled young woman with a history of substance abuse, aggravated by her son's murder two years ago. She was found beaten and burned beyond recognition. Her murderers were not "skinheads," "The Man," or "the racist white power structure." More likely than not, they were brown men whose faces resembled her own.

Clearly, we are having a very difficult time loving one another.

Any feminism that fails to acknowledge that black folks in nineties America are living and trying to love in a war zone is useless to our struggle against sexism. Though it's often portrayed as part of the problem, rap music is essential to that struggle because it takes us straight to the battlefield.

My decision to expose myself to the sexism of Dr. Dre, Ice Cube, Snoop Dogg, or the Notorious B.I.G. is really my plea to my brothers to tell me who they are. I need to know why they are so angry at me. Why is disrespecting me one of the few things that make them feel like men? What's the haps, what are you going through on the daily that's got you acting so foul?

As a black woman and a feminist I listen to the music with a willingness to see past the machismo in order to be clear about what I'm *really* dealing with. What I hear frightens me. On booming track after booming track, I hear brothers talking about spending each day high as hell on malt liquor and Chronic. Don't sleep. What passes for "40 and a blunt" good times in most of hip-hop is really alcoholism, substance abuse, and chemical dependency. When brothers can talk so cavalierly about killing each other and then reveal that they have no expectation to see their twenty-first birthday, that is straight-up depression *masquerading* as machismo.

Anyone curious about the processes and pathologies that form the psyche of the young, black, and criminal-minded needs to revisit our dearly departed Notorious B.I.G.'s first album, *Ready to Die.* Chronicling the life and times of the urban "soldier," the album is a blues-laden soul train that took us on a hustler's life journey. We boarded with the story of his birth, strategically stopped to view his dysfunctional, warring family, his first robbery, his first stint in jail, murder, drug-dealing, getting paid, partying, sexin', rap-pin', mayhem, and death. Biggie's player persona might have momentarily convinced the listener that he was livin' phat without a care in the world but other moments divulged his inner hell. The chorus of "Everyday Struggle": *I don't wanna live no more / Sometimes I see death knockin' at my front door* revealed that "Big Poppa" was also plagued with guilt, regret, and depression. The album ultimately ended with his suicide.

The seemingly impenetrable wall of sexism in rap music is really the complex mask African Americans often wear both to hide and express the pain. At the close of this millennium, hip-hop is still one of the few forums in which young black men, even surreptitiously, are allowed to express their pain.

When it comes to the struggle against sexism and our intimate relationships with black men, some of the most on-point feminist advice I've
received comes from sistas like my mother, who wouldn't dream of using
the term. During our battle to resolve our complicated relationships with
my equally wonderful and errant father, my mother presented me with the
following gem of wisdom, "One of the most important lessons you will ever
learn in life and love, is that you've got to love people for what they are —
not for who you would like them to be."

This is crystal clear to me when I'm listening to hip-hop. Yeah, sistas
are hurt when we hear brothers calling us bitches and hos. But the real
crime isn't the name-calling, it's their failure to love us — to be our brothers
in the way that we commit ourselves to being their sistas. But recognize:
Any man who doesn't truly love himself is incapable of loving us in the
healthy way we need to be loved. It's extremely telling that men who can
only see us as "bitches" and "hos" refer to themselves only as "niggas."

In the interest of our emotional health and overall sanity, black women
have got to learn to love brothers realistically, and that means differentiating between who they are and who we'd like them to be. Black men are
engaged in a war where the real enemies — racism and the white power
structure — are masters of camouflage. They've conditioned our men to
believe the enemy is brown. The effects of this have been as wicked as
they've been debilitating. Being in battle with an enemy that looks just like
you makes it hard to believe in the basics every human being needs. For too
many black men there is no trust, no community, no family. Just self.

Since hip-hop is the mirror in which so many brothers see themselves,   15
it's significant that one of the music's most prevalent mythologies is that
black boys rarely grow into men. Instead, they remain perpetually postado-
lescent or die. For all the machismo and testosterone in the music, it's
frighteningly clear that many brothers see themselves as powerless when it
comes to facing the evils of the larger society, accepting responsibility for
their lives, or the lives of their children.

So, sista friends, we gotta do what any rational, survivalist-minded person would do after finding herself in a relationship with someone whose
pain makes him abusive. We've gotta continue to give up the love but *from
a distance that's safe.* Emotional distance is a great enabler of unconditional
love and support because it allows us to recognize that the attack, the
"bitch, ho" bullshit — isn't personal but part of the illness.

And the focus of black feminists has got to change. We can't afford to
keep expending energy on banal discussions of sexism in rap when sexism is
only part of a huge set of problems. Continuing on our previous path is akin
to demanding that a fiending, broke crackhead not rob you blind because
it's *wrong* to do so.

If feminism intends to have any relevance in the lives of the majority of
black women, if it intends to move past theory and become functional it has
to rescue itself from the ivory towers of academia. Like it or not, hip-hop is

not only the dominion of the young, black, and male, it is also the world in which young black women live and survive. A functional game plan for us, one that is going to be as helpful to Shequanna on 142nd as it is to Samantha at Sarah Lawrence, has to recognize hip-hop's ability to articulate the pain our *community* is in and use that knowledge to create a redemptive, healing space.

Notice the emphasis on "community." Hip-hop isn't only instrumental in exposing black men's pain, it brings the healing sistas need right to the surface. Sad as it may be, it's time to stop ignoring the fact that rappers meet "bitches" and "hos" daily — women who reaffirm their depiction of us on vinyl. Backstage, the road, and the 'hood are populated with women who would do anything to be with a rapper sexually for an hour if not a night. It's time to stop fronting like we don't know who rapper Jeru the Damaja was talking about when he said:

> Now a queen's a queen but a stunt's a stunt
> You can tell who's who by the things they want

Sex has long been the bartering chip that women use to gain protection, material wealth, and the vicarious benefits of power. In the black community, where women are given less access to all of the above, "trickin'" becomes a means of leveling the playing field. Denying the justifiable anger of rappers — men who couldn't get the time of day from these women before a few dollars and a record deal — isn't empowering and strategic. Turning a blind eye and scampering for moral high ground diverts our attention away from the young women who are being denied access to power and are suffering for it.

It might've been more convenient to direct our sistafied rage attention to "the sexist representation of women" in those now infamous Sir Mix-A-Lot videos, to fuss over *one* sexist rapper, but wouldn't it have been more productive to address the failing self-esteem of the 150 or so half-naked young women who were willing, unpaid participants? And what about how flip we are when it comes to using the b-word to describe each other? At some point we've all been the recipients of competitive, unsisterly, "bitchiness," particularly when vying for male attention.

Since being black and a woman makes me fluent in both isms, I sometimes use racism as an illuminating analogy. Black folks have finally gotten to the point where we recognize that we sometimes engage in oppressive behaviors that white folks have little to do with. Complexion prejudices and classism are illnesses which have their *roots* in white racism but the perpetrators are certainly black.

Similarly, sistas have to confront the ways we're complicit in our own oppression. Sad to say it, but many of the ways in which men exploit our images and sexuality in hip-hop is done with our permission and cooperation. We need to be as accountable to each other as we believe "race

20

traitors" (i.e., one hundred or so brothers in blackface cooning in a skin-head's music video) should be to our community. To acknowledge this doesn't deny our victimization but it does raise the critical issue of whose responsibility it is to end our oppression. As a feminist, I believe it is too great a responsibility to leave to men.

A few years ago, on an airplane making its way to Montego Bay, I received another gem of girlfriend wisdom from a sixty-year-old self-declared nonfeminist. She was meeting her husband to celebrate her thirty-fifth wedding anniversary. After telling her I was twenty-seven and very much single, she looked at me and shook her head sadly. "I feel sorry for your generation. You don't know how to have relationships, especially the women." Curious, I asked her why she thought this was. "The women of your generation, you want to be right. The women of my generation, we didn't care about being right. We just wanted to win."

Too much of the discussion regarding sexism and the music focuses on being right. We feel we're *right* and the rappers are wrong. The rappers feel it's their *right* to describe their "reality" in any way they see fit. The store owners feel it's their *right* to sell whatever the consumer wants to buy. The consumer feels it's his *right* to be able to decide what he wants to listen to. We may be the "rightest" of the bunch but we sure as hell ain't doing the winning.

I believe hip-hop can help us win. Let's start by recognizing that its illuminating, informative narration and its incredible ability to articulate our collective pain is an invaluable tool when examining gender relations. The information we amass can help create a redemptive, healing space for brothers and sistas.

We're all winners when a space exists for brothers to honestly state and explore the roots of their pain and subsequently their misogyny, sans judg-ment. It is criminal that the only space our society provided for the late Tupac Shakur to examine the pain, confusion, drug addiction, and fear that led to his arrest and his eventual assassination was in a prison cell. How can we win if a prison cell is the only space an immensely talented but troubled young black man could dare utter these words: "Even though I'm not guilty of the charges they gave me, I'm not innocent in terms of the way I was act-ing. I'm just as guilty for not doing things. Not with this case but with my life. I had a job to do and I never showed up. I was so scared of this respon-sibility that I was running away from it."[3] We have to do better than this for our men.

And we have to do better for ourselves. We desperately need a space to lovingly address the uncomfortable issues of our failing self-esteem, the ways we sexualize and objectify ourselves, our confusion about sex and love and the unhealthy, unloving, unsisterly ways we treat each other. Commitment

25

---

[3]Kevin Powell, "The Vibe Q: Tupac Shakur, Ready to Live," *Vibe*, April 11, 1995, p. 52.

to developing these spaces gives our community the potential for remedies based on honest, clear diagnoses.

As I'm a black woman, I am aware that this doubles my workload — that I am definitely going to have to listen to a lot of shit I won't like — but without these candid discussions, there is little to no hope of exorcising the illness that hurts and sometimes kills us.

ENGAGING THE TEXT

1. What qualities of hip-hop music and rap artists does Morgan admire or appreciate? What fears does she have for rap's female fans and for the artists themselves? To what extent do you agree with Morgan's assessment of the misogyny, anger, and despair expressed by hip-hop?

2. What evidence does Morgan offer that "black folks in nineties America are living and trying to love in a war zone"? How does she explain the causes of the violence she describes? How persuasive do you find her analysis, and why?

3. How do you interpret Morgan's call for establishing "a redemptive, healing space" for confronting the pain expressed by hip-hop? What kind of "space" is she talking about, and how would you go about establishing it?

4. What audience is Morgan addressing and what persuasive strategies — of both argument and style — does she use to appeal to that audience? What do you find effective or ineffective about her approach?

5. While Morgan asserts that we need to examine the lives of rappers like Notorious B.I.G. to understand the roots of their misogyny, critics might counter that she is simply making excuses for intolerable attitudes. Write an essay explaining why you agree or disagree with Morgan's argument.

EXPLORING CONNECTIONS

6. Compare Jean Kilbourne's analysis of sexism and violence in advertising (p. 575) to Morgan's discussion of the same themes in rap. What are the causes and consequences of "pornographic" depictions of women in popular culture according to each writer? Do you think Kilbourne would concur with Morgan about how we should respond to these images? Why or why not?

7. Look ahead to "'Bros Before Hos': The Guy Code" (p. 608) and compare the features of Michael Kimmel's "Guy Code" to the images of masculinity portrayed by hip-hop artists.

8. Write an essay comparing Morgan's view of hip-hop to that of Hua Hsu (p. 497). How do you account for the differences in their perspectives?

EXTENDING THE CRITICAL CONTEXT

9. Survey the current issues of several magazines aimed at fans of rap music. What images do they present of women, men, and human relationships?

How often do they reflect the themes that Morgan discusses? What other themes and patterns do you find? To what extent, if any, have the subjects and attitudes of hip-hop artists changed since the 1990s?

10. Examine the lyrics of several female rappers and compare them to those of the male rappers Morgan mentions. What similarities and differences do you find in the subjects they address and the feelings they express? If you're not a fan of rap, you may want to consult an online hip-hop dictionary for help in decoding some of the language (www.rapdict.org).

"Bros Before Hos": The Guy Code

MICHAEL KIMMEL

According to sociologist Michael Kimmel, "guys" — young men, ages sixteen to twenty-six — represent a distinct social group. In Guyland: The Perilous World Where Boys Become Men *(2008), he investigates the values, rites, and preoccupations of these young men. This selection from the book details the code of masculinity that guys are expected to follow. Kimmel (b. 1951) has written or edited more than a dozen books on men and masculinity as well as editing the journal* Men and Masculinities; *he teaches at the State University of New York at Stony Brook. He is also a spokesperson for the National Organization for Men Against Sexism (NOMAS) and has served as an expert witness for the U.S. Department of Justice in two key sex discrimination cases against military academies which had excluded women.*

Whenever I ask young women what they think it means to be a woman, they look at me puzzled, and say, basically, "Whatever I want." "It doesn't mean anything at all to me," says Nicole, a junior at Colby College in Maine. "I can be Mia Hamm, I can be Britney Spears, I can be Madame Curie or Madonna. Nobody can tell me what it means to be a woman anymore."

For men, the question is still meaningful — and powerful. In countless workshops on college campuses and in high-school assemblies, I've asked young men what it means to be a man. I've asked guys from every state in the nation, as well as about fifteen other countries, what sorts of phrases and words come to mind when they hear someone say, "Be a man!"[1]

---

[1]*hear someone say, "Be a man!":* This workshop idea was developed by Paul Kivel of the Oakland Men's Project. I am grateful to Paul for demonstrating it to my classes. [All notes are Kimmel's.]

The responses are rather predictable. The first thing someone usually says is "Don't cry," then other similar phrases and ideas — never show your feelings, never ask for directions, never give up, never give in, be strong, be aggressive, show no fear, show no mercy, get rich, get even, get laid, win — follow easily after that.

Here's what guys say, summarized into a set of current epigrams. Think of it as a "Real Guy's Top Ten List."

1. "Boys Don't Cry"
2. "It's Better to be Mad than Sad"
3. "Don't Get Mad — Get Even"
4. "Take It Like a Man"
5. "He Who has the Most Toys When he Dies, Wins"
6. "Just Do It," or "Ride or Die"
7. "Size Matters"
8. "I Don't Stop to Ask for Directions"
9. "Nice Guys Finish Last"
10. "It's All Good"

The unifying emotional subtext of all these aphorisms involves never showing emotions or admitting to weakness. The face you must show to the world insists that everything is going just fine, that everything is under control, that there's nothing to be concerned about (a contemporary version of Alfred E. Neuman of *MAD* magazine's "What, me worry?"). Winning is crucial, especially when the victory is over other men who have less amazing or smaller toys. Kindness is not an option, nor is compassion. Those sentiments are taboo.

This is "The Guy Code," the collection of attitudes, values, and traits that together composes what it means to be a man. These are the rules that govern behavior in Guyland, the criteria that will be used to evaluate whether any particular guy measures up. The Guy Code revisits what psychologist William Pollack called "the boy code" in his bestselling book *Real Boys*[2] — just a couple of years older and with a lot more at stake. And just as Pollack and others have explored the dynamics of boyhood so well, we now need to extend the reach of that analysis to include late adolescence and young adulthood.

In 1976, social psychologist Robert Brannon summarized the four basic rules of masculinity:[3]

1. "No Sissy Stuff!" Being a man means not being a sissy, not being perceived as weak, effeminate, or gay. Masculinity is the relentless repudiation of the feminine.

---

[2]*Real Boys:* See William Pollack, *Real Boys: Rescuing Our Sons from the Myths of Boyhood* (New York: Henry Holt, 1998).

[3]*four basic rules of masculinity:* See Robert Brannon and Deborah David, "Introduction" to *The Forty-Nine Per Cent Majority* (Reading, MA: Addison-Wesley, 1976).

2. "Be a Big Wheel." This rule refers to the centrality of success and power in the definition of masculinity. Masculinity is measured more by wealth, power, and status than by any particular body part.

3. "Be a Sturdy Oak." What makes a man is that he is reliable in a crisis. And what makes him so reliable in a crisis is not that he is able to respond fully and appropriately to the situation at hand, but rather that he resembles an inanimate object. A rock, a pillar, a species of tree.

4. "Give 'em Hell." Exude an aura of daring and aggression. Live life out on the edge. Take risks. Go for it. Pay no attention to what others think.

Amazingly, these four rules have changed very little among successive generations of high-school and college-age men. James O'Neil, a developmental psychologist at the University of Connecticut, and Joseph Pleck, a social psychologist at the University of Illinois, have each been conducting studies of this normative definition of masculinity for decades. "One of the most surprising findings," O'Neil told me, "is how little these rules have changed."

Being a Man Among Men

Where do young men get these ideas? "Oh, definitely, my dad," says Mike, a twenty-year-old sophomore at Wake Forest. "He was always riding my ass, telling me I had to be tough and strong to make it in this world."

"My older brothers were always on my case," says Drew, a twenty-four-year-old University of Massachusetts grad. "They were like, always ragging on me, calling me a pussy, if I didn't want to play football or wrestle. If I just wanted to hang out and like play my Xbox, they were constantly in my face."

"It was subtle, sometimes," says Warren, a twenty-one-year-old at Towson, "and other times really out front. In school, it was the male teachers, saying stuff about how explorers or scientists were so courageous and braving the elements and all that. Then, other times, it was phys-ed class, and everyone was all over everyone else talking about 'He's so gay' and 'He's a wuss.'"

"The first thing I think of is my coach," says Don, a twenty-six-year-old former football player at Lehigh. "Any fatigue, any weakness, any sign that being hit actually hurt and he was like 'Waah! [fake crying] Widdle Donny got a boo boo. Should we kiss it guys?' He'd completely humiliate us for showing anything but complete toughness. I'm sure he thought he was building up our strength and ability to play, but it wore me out trying to pretend all the time, to suck it up and just take it."

The response was consistent: Guys hear the voices of the men in their lives — fathers, coaches, brothers, grandfathers, uncles, priests — to inform their ideas of masculinity.

This is no longer surprising to me. One of the more startling things I found when I researched the history of the idea of masculinity in America for a previous book was that men subscribe to these ideals not because they want to impress women, let alone any inner drive or desire to test themselves against some abstract standards. They do it because they want to be positively evaluated by other men. American men want to be a "man among men," an Arnold Schwarzenegger-like "man's man," not a Fabio-like "ladies' man." Masculinity is largely a "homosocial" experience: performed for, and judged by, other men.

Noted playwright David Mamet explains why women don't even enter the mix. "Women have, in men's minds, such a low place on the social ladder of this country that it's useless to define yourself in terms of a woman. What men need is men's approval." While women often become a kind of currency by which men negotiate their status with other men, women are for possessing, not for emulating.

The Gender Police

Other guys constantly watch how well we perform. Our peers are a kind of "gender police," always waiting for us to screw up so they can give us a ticket for crossing the well-drawn boundaries of manhood. As young men, we become relentless cowboys, riding the fences, checking the boundary line between masculinity and femininity, making sure that nothing slips over. The possibilities of being unmasked are everywhere. Even the most seemingly insignificant misstep can pose a threat or activate that haunting terror that we will be found out.

On the day the students in my class "Sociology of Masculinity" were scheduled to discuss homophobia, one student provided an honest and revealing anecdote. Noting that it was a beautiful day, the first day of spring after a particularly brutal Northeast winter, he decided to wear shorts to class. "I had this really nice pair of new Madras shorts," he recounted. "But then I thought to myself, these shorts have lavender and pink in them. Today's class topic is homophobia. Maybe today is not the best day to wear these shorts." Nods all around.

Our efforts to maintain a manly front cover everything we do. What we wear. How we talk. How we walk. What we eat (like the recent flap over "manwiches" — those artery-clogging massive burgers, dripping with extras). Every mannerism, every movement contains a coded gender language. What happens if you refuse or resist? What happens if you step outside the definition of masculinity? Consider the words that would be used to describe you. In workshops it generally takes less than a minute to get a list of about twenty terms that are at the tip of everyone's tongues: wimp, faggot, dork, pussy, loser, wuss, nerd, queer, homo, girl, gay, skirt, Mama's boy, pussy-whipped. This list is so effortlessly generated, so consistent, that it composes a national well from which to draw epithets and put-downs.

Ask any teenager in America what is the most common put-down in middle school or high school? The answer: "That's so gay." It's said about anything and everything — their clothes, their books, the music or TV shows they like, the sports figures they admire. "That's so gay" has become a free-floating put-down, meaning bad, dumb, stupid, wrong. It's the generic bad thing.

Listen to one of America's most observant analysts of masculinity, [20] Eminem. Asked in an MTV interview in 2001 why he constantly used "faggot" in every one of his raps to put down other guys, Eminem told the interviewer, Kurt Loder,

> The lowest degrading thing you can say to a man when you're battling him is to call him a faggot and try to take away his manhood. Call him a sissy, call him a punk. "Faggot" to me doesn't necessarily mean gay people. "Faggot" to me just means taking away your manhood.[4]

[4]*The lowest . . . your manhood:* Richard Kim, "A Bad Rap?" in *The Nation,* March 5, 2001, p. 5.

But does it mean homosexuality? Does it really suggest that you suspect the object of the epithet might actually be attracted to another guy? Think, for example, of how you would answer this question: If you see a man walking down the street, or meet him at a party, how do you "know" if he is homosexual? (Assume that he is not wearing a T-shirt with a big pink triangle on it, and that he's not already holding hands with another man.)

When I ask this question in classes or workshops, respondents invariably provide a standard list of stereotypically effeminate behaviors. He walks a certain way, talks a certain way, acts a certain way. He's well dressed, sensitive, and emotionally expressive. He has certain tastes in art and music — indeed, he has *any* taste in art and music! Men tend to focus on the physical attributes, women on the emotional. Women say they "suspect" a man might be gay if he's interested in what she's talking about, knows something about what she's talking about, or is sensitive and a good listener. One recently said, "I suspect he might be gay if he's looking at my eyes, and not down my blouse." Another said she suspects he might be gay if he shows no sexual interest in her, if he doesn't immediately come on to her.

Once I've established what makes a guy "suspect," I ask the men in the room if any of them would want to be thought of as gay. Rarely does a hand go up — despite the fact that this list of attributes is actually far preferable to the restrictive one that stands in the "Be a Man" box. So, what do straight men do to make sure that no one gets the wrong idea about them?

Everything that is perceived as gay goes into what we might call the Negative Playbook of Guyland. Avoid everything in it and you'll be all right. Just make sure that you walk, talk, and act in a different way from the gay stereotype; dress terribly; show no taste in art or music; show no emotions at all. Never listen to a thing a woman is saying, but express immediate and unquenchable sexual interest. Presto, you're a real man, back in the "Be a Man" box. Homophobia — the fear that people might *misperceive* you as gay — is the animating fear of American guys' masculinity. It's what lies underneath the crazy risk-taking behaviors practiced by boys of all ages, what drives the fear that other guys will see you as weak, unmanly, frightened. The single cardinal rule of manhood, the one from which all the other characteristics — wealth, power, status, strength, physicality — are derived is to offer constant proof that you are not gay.

Homophobia is even deeper than this. It's the fear *of* other men — that 25 other men will perceive you as a failure, as a fraud. It's a fear that others will see you as weak, unmanly, frightened. This is how John Steinbeck put it in his novel *Of Mice and Men:*

> "Funny thing," [Curley's wife] said. "If I catch any one man, and he's alone, I get along fine with him. But just let two of the guys get together

an' you won't talk. Jus' nothin' but mad." She dropped her fingers and put her hands on her hips. "You're all scared of each other, that's what. Ever'one of you's scared the rest is goin' to get something on you."[5]

In that sense, homosexuality becomes a kind of shorthand for "unmanliness" — and the homophobia that defines and animates the daily conversations of Guyland is at least as much about masculinity as it is about sexuality.

But what would happen to a young man if he were to refuse such limiting parameters on who he is and how he's permitted to act? "It's not like I want to stay in that box," says Jeff, a first-year Cornell student at my workshop. "But as soon as you step outside it, even for a second, all the other guys are like, 'What are you, dude, a fag?' It's not very safe out there on your own. I suppose as I get older, I'll get more secure, and feel like I couldn't care less what other guys say. But now, in my fraternity, on this campus, man, I'd lose everything."

The consistency of responses is as arresting as the list is disturbing: "I would lose my friends." "Get beat up." "I'd be ostracized." "Lose my self-esteem." Some say they'd take drugs or drink. Become withdrawn, sullen, a loner, depressed. "Kill myself," says one guy. "Kill them," responds another. Everyone laughs, nervously. Some say they'd get mad. And some say they'd get even. "I dunno," replied Mike, a sophomore at Portland State University. "I'd probably pull a Columbine. I'd show them that they couldn't get away with calling me that shit."

Guys know that they risk everything — their friendships, their sense of self, maybe even their lives — if they fail to conform. Since the stakes are so enormous, young men take huge chances to prove their manhood, exposing themselves to health risks, workplace hazards, and stress-related illnesses. Here's a revealing factoid. Men ages nineteen to twenty-nine are three times less likely to wear seat belts than women the same age. Before they turn nineteen though, young men are actually *more* likely to wear seat belts. It's as if they suddenly get the idea that as long as they're driving the car, they're completely in control, and therefore safe.[6] Ninety percent of all driving offenses, excluding parking violations, are committed by men, and 93 percent of road ragers are male.[7] Safety is emasculating! So they drink too much, drive too fast, and play chicken in a multitude of dangerous venues.

The comments above provide a telling riposte to all those theories of   30
biology that claim that this definition of masculinity is "hard-wired," the result of millennia of evolutionary adaptation or the behavioral response to waves of aggression-producing testosterone, and therefore inevitable. What these theories fail to account for is the way that masculinity is coerced and

[5]John Steinbeck, *Of Mice and Men* (New York: Scribner's, 1937), p. 57.

[6]*completely in control, and therefore safe:* Eric Nagourney, "Young Men with No Attachments" in *New York Times,* January 4, 2005.

[7]*and 93 percent of road ragers are male:* Mary Blume, "The Feminist Future of the Automobile" in *International Herald Tribune,* October 8, 2004, p. 11.

policed relentlessly by other guys. If it were biological, it would be as natural as breathing or blinking. In truth, the Guy Code fits as comfortably as a straightjacket.

Boys' Psychological Development: Where the Guy Code Begins

Masculinity is a constant test — always up for grabs, always needing to be proved. And the testing starts early. Recently, I was speaking with a young black mother, a social worker, who was concerned about a conversation she had had with her husband a few nights earlier. It seems that her husband had taken their son to the barber, which, she explained to me, is a central social institution in the African American community. As the barber prepared the boy's hair for treatment, using, apparently some heat and some painful burning chemicals, the boy began to cry. The barber turned to the boy's father and pronounced, "This boy is a wimp!" He went on, "This boy has been spending too much time with his mama! Man, you need to put your foot down. You have got to get this boy away from his mother!"

That evening the father came home, visibly shaken by the episode, and announced to his wife that from that moment on the boy would not be spending as much time with her, but instead would do more sports and other activities with him, "to make sure he doesn't become a sissy."

After telling me this story, the mother asked what I thought she should do. "Gee," I said, "I understand the pressures that dads feel to 'toughen up' their sons. But how old is your boy, anyway?"

"Three and a half," she said.

I tried to remind her, of course, that crying is the natural human re-   35
sponse to pain, and that her son was behaving appropriately. But her story reminded me of how early this pressure starts to affect an emotionally impervious manly stoicism.

Ever since Freud, we've believed that the key to boys' development is separation, that the boy must switch his identification from mother to father in order to "become" a man. He achieves his masculinity by repudiation, dissociation, and then identification. It is a perilous path, but a necessary one, even though there is nothing inevitable about it — and nothing biological either. Throw in an overdominant mother, or an absent father, and we start worrying that the boy will not succeed in his masculine quest.

Boys learn that their connection to mother will emasculate them, turn them into Mama's Boys. And so they learn to act *as if* they have made that leap by pushing away from their mothers. Along the way they suppress all the feelings they associate with the maternal — compassion, nurturance, vulnerability, dependency. This suppression and repudiation is the origin of the Boy Code. It's what turns those happy, energetic, playful, and emotionally expressive five-year-olds into sullen, withdrawn, and despondent nine-year-olds. In the recent spate of bestselling books about boys' development, psychologists like William Pollack, James Garbarino, Michael Thompson, Dan Kindlon, and others, argue that from an early age boys are taught to refrain from crying, to suppress their emotions, never to display vulnerability. As a result, boys feel effeminate not only if they *express* their emotions, but even if they *feel* them. In their bestseller, *Raising Cain*, Kindlon and Thompson describe a "culture of cruelty" in which peers force other boys to deny their emotional needs and disguise their feelings. It's no wonder that so many boys end up feeling emotionally isolated.

These books about boys map the inner despair that comes from such emotional numbness and fear of vulnerability. Pollack calls it the "mask of masculinity," the fake front of impervious, unemotional independence, a swaggering posture that boys believe will help them to present a stoic front. "Ruffled in a manly pose," the great Irish poet William Butler Yeats put it in his poem "Coole Park" (1929), "For all his timid heart."

The ruffling starts often by age four or five, when he enters kindergarten, and it gets a second jolt when he hits adolescence. Think of the messages boys get: Stand on your own two feet! Don't cry! Don't be a sissy! As one boy in Pollack's book summarizes it: "Shut up and take it, or you'll be sorry." When I asked my nine-year-old son, Zachary, what he thought of when I said "be a man" he said that one of his friends said something about "taking it like a man. So," he explained, "I think it means acting tougher than you actually are."

Recently a colleague told me about a problem he was having. It seems   40
his seven-year-old son, James, was being bullied by another boy on his way home from school. His wife, the boy's mother, strategized with her son about how to handle such situations in the future. She suggested he find an alternate route home, tell a teacher, or perhaps even tell the boy's parents. And she offered the standard "use your words, not your fists" conflict-reducer. "How can I get my wife to stop treating James like a baby?" my colleague asked. "How will he ever learn to stand up for himself if she turns him into a wimp?"

The Boy Code leaves boys disconnected from a wide range of emotions and prohibited from sharing those feelings with others. As they grow older, they feel disconnected from adults, as well, unable to experience the guidance towards maturity that adults can bring. When they turn to anger and violence it is because these, they believe, perhaps rightly, are the only acceptable forms of emotional expression allowed them. Just as the Boy Code shuts boys down, the Guy Code reinforces those messages, suppressing what was left of boyhood exuberance and turning it into sullen indifference.

No wonder boys are more prone to depression, suicidal behavior, and various other forms of out-of-control or out-of-touch behaviors than girls are. No wonder boys drop out of school and are diagnosed as emotionally disturbed four times more often as girls, get into fights twice as often, and are six times more likely than girls to be diagnosed with Attention Deficit and Hyperactivity Disorder (ADHD).[8]

ENGAGING THE TEXT

1. What are the "rules" associated with the Guy Code, according to Kimmel? To what extent do these rules reflect your own understanding of what it means to be a man? Discuss Kimmel's assertion that "the Guy Code fits as comfortably as a straightjacket" (para. 30).

2. Outline the psychology of the Guy Code: How do boys become men, according to Kimmel, and how does their development affect their emotional lives and relationships with others?

3. Kimmel writes that "masculinity is coerced and policed relentlessly by other guys" (para. 30). Write a journal entry detailing any encounters you've observed or experienced that involve such "gender police." What happened, and how did you react at the time? Did the incident(s) have any lasting effect on your thinking or behavior? If so, how and why?

4. Kimmel argues that homophobia plays a central role in defining and reinforcing the Guy Code. What evidence do you see that young men are or are not pressured "to offer constant proof that [they] are not gay" (para. 24)?

EXPLORING CONNECTIONS

5. What people and institutions act as the "gender police" in Brandon Simms's life (p. 546)? How do they pressure Brandon, either directly or indirectly, to conform to more conventional dress and behavior? What sources of support help him to resist these pressures?

6. In what ways does Kimmel's analysis of American masculinity help to explain the violence and misogyny described by Jean Kilbourne (p. 575) and Joan Morgan (p. 601)? What other factors contribute to these problems?

7. How does the image on page 610 reflect both the rewards and the costs of the Guy Code? How do you interpret the meaning and placement of the "Think again" message?

EXTENDING THE CRITICAL CONTEXT

8. Working in small groups, try to come up with a list of "rules" you associate with being a woman. As a class, debate whether or not a Girl Code exists, and if so, what it consists of and how it's taught and reinforced.

9. For one full day, keep track of every time you hear the word "gay" used as a pejorative term in conversation or in the media. In each case, is the

---

[8]*No wonder . . . Hyperactivity Disorder:* See, for example, Brad Knickerbocker, "Young and Male in America: It's Hard Being a Boy" in *Christian Science Monitor*, April 29, 1999.

speaker male or female? Who or what is he or she referring to? Is he joking or serious? Bring your notes to class to compare with others' observations. Do your findings bear out Kimmel's assertion that "Homophobia . . . is the animating fear of American guys' masculinity" (para. 24)?

The Descent of Men

DAN KINDLON

Dan Kindlon's research on the psychology of adolescent girls has led him to conclude that the current generation of young women is "fundamentally different" from earlier generations — more highly motivated, self-confident, and independent. His book, Alpha Girls *(2006), presents the results of his studies of these high achievers; in the following passage, he considers how the emergence of the alpha girl is likely to alter the roles of men both in the workplace and the home. Kindlon (b. 1953), a research psychologist and clinician who focuses on childhood and adolescent development, has taught child psychology at Harvard since 1985. His earlier books include* Raising Cain: Protecting the Emotional Life of Boys *(1999),* Too Much of a Good Thing: Raising Children of Character in an Indulgent Age *(2001), and* Tough Times, Strong Children: Lessons from the Past for Your Child's Future *(2003).*

> There are more girls in college now than guys — which from my point of view is great!
>
> — SAM, 18, freshman at UC Santa Cruz

When it comes to chimps, scientists have found that, as my daughters were fond of saying when they were in kindergarten, "girls rule and boys drool."

Researchers have observed that young female chimpanzees in the Gombe National Park in Tanzania are smarter than young male chimps, at least when it comes to learning how to fish for termites. Young female chimps watch carefully as their mothers select the right size stick to dip into the termite mound and quickly learn to imitate them. The young males, on the other hand, pay their mothers no mind. They are inattentive, rolling around in the dirt and generally slacking off. The young females start fishing for termites on their own at a much earlier age than the males — on average

"Ted's flamboyantly straight."

over two years earlier — and they remain more proficient fishers as adults. The study's authors conclude that given "[a] similar disparity in the ability of young males and females has been demonstrated in human children, sex-based learning differences may therefore date back at least to the last common ancestor of chimpanzees and humans."[1]

This picture of young female chimps as focused, receptive learners fits well with our portrait of academically accomplished girls. I haven't spent much time discussing their male peers and the psychological challenges and difficulties they face, but boys are obviously part of the equation when it comes to understanding the alpha girl generation and its future impact on society.

As girls move into positions of power and prominence, what will happen to boys? Will their penchant for figuratively horsing around while their female peers master important life skills mean that they are going to become increasingly irrelevant? Are our boys headed in the direction of Johnny Lechner, who, at the age of twenty-nine, is still a college undergraduate and has spent his last twelve years as a frat boy?

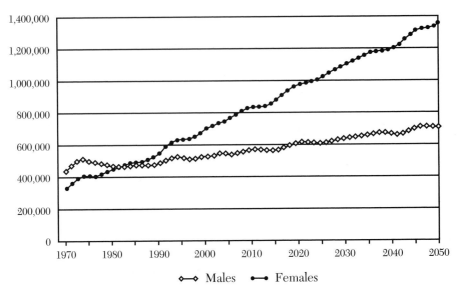

Figure 1   Number of bachelor's degrees awarded to males and females, projected to 2050.
Source data (1970–2003): U.S. Department of Education, National Center for Education Statistics.[2] Projected data (2004–2050).

Lechner has appeared on *Good Morning America* and *Letterman*. He   5
has an agent at William Morris who is trying to get him television and book deals and product endorsements. His brand image, according to the *New York Times*, where his story made front page news, will be linked to his "record of debauchery . . . a roisterous college life of beer and merrymaking." Fame, however, has come with a price. The *Times* quotes Lechner: "I'm really stressed out. All the money, the book deals, the agents. It's crazy."[3]

While not all our boys are doomed to careers as frat house party animals, it's self-evident that as girls fill more of the challenging and desirable positions in the workforce, the opportunities and positions open to men will shrink. Not all the academic and occupational gains achieved by women in recent years have come at the expense of men — but some have.

In the case of college admissions, the more spots that are given to girls, the fewer will be available for boys.* Similarly, if the board of directors at a Fortune 500 company is limited to ten members, if five are women, only

---

*Some colleges and universities are starting to admit what has been known among admissions officers for years: that they sometimes use affirmative action standards in order to increase the number of male enrollees. See Britz, J.D. "To all the girls I've rejected," *New York Times*, OP-ED, Thursday, March 23, 2006. [Kindlon's note]

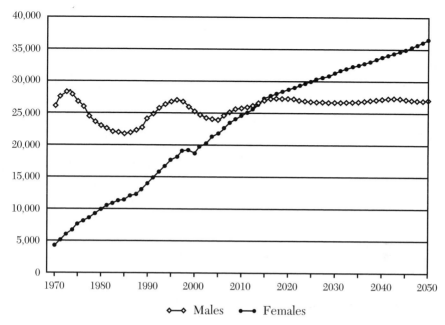

Figure 2 Number of doctorate degrees awarded to males and females, projected to 2050.
Source data (1970–2003): U.S. Department of Education, National Center for Education Statistics.[4] Projected data (2004–2050).

five can be men. There is no simple equation, however, that will tell us which sex will be better off following the kinds of gender role changes we can expect in the coming years.

As we start to look forward into the future, we see a number of significant trends. The first is the dominance of women in higher education. As we've noted, in 2005, nearly 59 percent of undergraduate degrees were granted to women. The degree gap is growing.[5] The chart [on page 620] (Figure 1) projects the changing sex-ratio in colleges into the next decade and beyond.

We see the same trend for advanced degrees. Over the next ten years, the number of degrees awarded in medicine, law, dentistry, and the theological professions is projected to increase 16 percent for men and 26 percent for women. For doctorate degrees (Ph.D.'s), the results are even more startling. As Figure 2 shows, in 2050, *fewer* men will receive Ph.D.'s than they did in 2000, while the number of doctorates awarded to women will continue to sharply rise. These degree-gap trends hold true across racial and ethnic groups. For the foreseeable future, white, black, Latina, and Asian women will all be receiving more college degrees than their male counterparts.[6]

Number of Bachelor's Degrees Awarded by Sex and Race/Ethnicity, 2004 and 2025 (projected)

	WHITE		BLACK		HISPANIC		ASIAN	
	2004	2025	2004	2025	2004	2025	2004	2025
Males	405,409	438,492	39,256	65,338	32,697	70,057	37,073	59,557
Females	533,899	692,740	76,379	158,292	49,423	113,844	44,955	107,541
Ratio F:M	1.3	1.6	1.9	2.4	1.5	1.6	1.2	1.8

Source data (2004): U.S. Department of Education, National Center for Education Statistics.[7]

What are the implications of these trends? An oddly analogous situation has occurred in China. When China instituted its One-Child Policy in 1979, male babies had long been considered the more desirable pregnancy outcome in China, a preference that only became more pronounced when couples were told by the state that they could only have one child. One upshot of the policy was that girl babies were more likely to be aborted or become victims of infanticide and medical neglect. Some parents took advantage of a loophole in the law that allowed a couple to have a second child if their first was disabled or female.

As a result, the birth ratio in China began to change. As many as 1.3 boys were born for each girl in rural areas such as Qinghai province.[8] Now that the first members of the One-Child Policy generation are well into marriageable and childbearing age, there are around 80 million men, according to one source, who can't find partners.[9]

A similar trend is emerging — although reversed — in the U.S. when we look at the mating dance open to college graduates. The degree gap between men and women is similar to the birth ratio in Qinghai.

With each passing year the ratio of college-educated women to college-educated men will grow. There will be an increasing number of college-educated women who will not be able to marry or partner with a college-educated man (see Figure 3).

In a few years, the population of the United States will have more living women college graduates than men college graduates. This preponderance of women among the "educated class" will be an event that is unprecedented in human history and promises to have far-reaching implications. Women will begin to appear in greater numbers among the applicants for prestigious, highly paid jobs. A college degree currently yields nearly one million dollars more over the course of a working life than a high school degree. A Ph.D. is estimated to return $1.5 million more, and professional degrees in medicine or law over $2.5 million more in lifetime salary than a bachelor's degree.[10] To the extent that money is power, women who obtain advanced degrees and enter the workforce will have more of it than they have in the past.

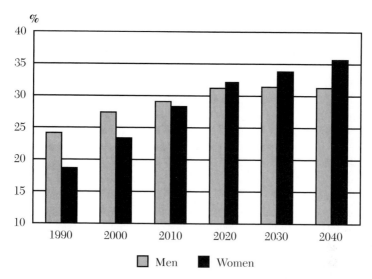

Figure 3 Percentage of U.S. population aged 25+ with a bachelor's degree or higher, projected to 2040.
Source data: U.S. Census Bureau. Current Population Survey 2003.[11]

Much of what motivated feminists in the 1960s and 1970s was a reac- 15
tion to the relative powerlessness of American housewives in the 1950s. At
the root of nearly all of the myriad meanings of power is the concept of control. If you have power, you have the ability to influence events rather than
be influenced by them. To control rather than be controlled.

Women traditionally were dependent on their husbands for financial
support; many of them had few, if any, job skills. But if the current trends in
higher education continue, men are going to have to share or relinquish
some of their power because their wives will control the proverbial purse
strings.

One consequence of women moving into highly paid jobs is that more
of the men they marry and bear children with will earn less than they do.
One out of every four women today earns more than her husband; by 2050,
it is projected that almost one in two will (see Figure 4).

Even if a married woman doesn't earn *more* than her husband, if she
earns enough to live on or has the status and job skills that come from being
better educated, she will have more control over her life. In cases of divorce
or abandonment, she won't be at the mercy of her ex-husband's goodwill or
a court's ability to enforce child support or alimony laws. Better education
and higher earnings provide a financial safety net for women today that
dependent housewives in the 1950s didn't have.

The distribution of power in a couple's relationship does not, however,
have to be a battle. Many men are happy to share power. In the future, the
following scenario will become more common. Jim Krawieki, forty-seven,

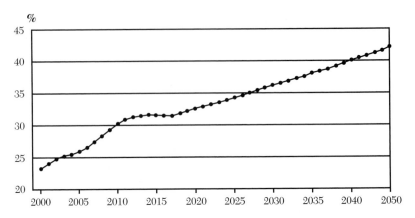

Figure 4 Percent of married couples with wives earning more than husbands, projected to 2050.
Source data (1990–2003): U.S. Department of Education, National Center for Education Statistics.

and his younger wife, Carroll, work on the Needham, Massachusetts, police force. Carroll, a sergeant, is Jim's boss, a cause for mirth among his fellow patrolmen. Despite being a political conservative, not a traditionally feminist group, Jim says, "The easiest way to deal with it is just accept it." It was Jim who originally encouraged Carroll to quit waitressing, join the force, and take the tests necessary for promotion. Jim didn't want to climb the career ladder himself because of all the "paperwork."

The couple's first child is soon due. Carroll plans to return to work after   20
her maternity leave. Her shift runs midnight to eight and Jim works days, so they'll divvy up child care.[12]

Jim and Carroll's story illustrates the degree to which gender roles are changing. Carroll is thriving in a non-traditional occupation for women, and her older, politically conservative husband, whom she outranks, not only accepts the situation, he helped create it.

Is Jim an anomaly? Will most men accept the eclipse of their traditional role as breadwinners? Or will there be a backlash against the emancipation of women fueled by wounded male pride? At least two important factors argue against backlash.

First, cultural trends suggest that men are less intent on wearing the pants in the family. In many cases, they do not feel threatened, demeaned, or emasculated by being married to a woman who is more successful than they are. Men are also more amenable to sharing household duties, particularly child care. In fact, young men hunger for more time with their kids. This is the case with Trevor, twenty-five, and his wife, Lindsay, who is pregnant with their first child. Trevor's adolescence was spent rolling around on the proverbial termite mound. Although he has a high IQ, he barely graduated from high school. "I couldn't stand school and my teachers couldn't stand me," he said. After high school, he delivered pizzas, installed carpeting, and did custodial work at a community airport. He eventually drifted back to school, taking a few classes at a community college, then tried his hand at flight school, and completed a twelve-week course in car stereo installation. When Lindsay became pregnant, Trevor had recently left a sales job that had the potential for rapid advancement. "I couldn't see myself selling boxes for the rest of my life," he said. "It wasn't going to work out for either me or the company."

Lindsay graduated from a local college and became a middle manager at a small company. Her work provides the couple with a moderate salary and decent benefits. Trevor is looking forward to doing the bulk of the child care when the baby comes. "My wife makes more than I do. I hope she always does. I'd love to stay home with the kids. Are you kidding me, it'd be a blast."

Trevor is not the only man who wants to stay home with the kids. *Business*   25
Week magazine reports that working men born between 1965 and 1979 now spend about 3.5 hours a day with their kids — the same amount as working women. Seventy percent of men said they would take a pay cut to spend more time with their family, and almost half would turn down a promotion if it meant less family time. The article states:

> The shift in attitudes among male workers is evident to veteran staffers such as Betty Purkey, who manages work-life strategies at Texas Instruments. Not only are men, who make up seventy percent of the chipmaker's employee base, clamoring for more flexibility, but they frequently crowd into the company's classes for new parents. 'They really want to spend more time with their families,' marvels Purkey, who finds a pronounced difference among younger employees.[13]

Men are better suited in many ways to be contemporary homemakers. Start with the most robust biological differences between men and women — size and strength. One of the only aspects of contemporary urban and suburban life that requires physical strength is household tasks — carrying a baby and two bags of groceries in from the car, for example. Domestic duties are one of the few remaining areas in which men's physical strength is an advantage. In addition, many men are fascinated by gadgets, tools, and machinery; these men should love hanging around the house doing minor car repairs, fixing a leaky faucet, programming the VCR, installing an electric garage door opener — all jobs for a handyman!

The large majority of boys in our survey group said that they felt that working mothers were not detrimental to their children's development, and, more important, many boys wanted to participate in child rearing. Close to 25 percent said that they expected to be a stay-at-home parent at some point in their lives. . . .

In the coming world of the alpha generation, our sons will be forced to confront some of the core psychological attributes of traditional masculinity.

Modern boys will need to go through their own "inner metamorphosis" and make similar changes in their personal psychology to those that have been made by the daughters of the feminist revolution. In particular, boys will need to strike a better balance between separation and connection, dominance and submission. As their sisters have, boys will need to incorporate elements of both their fathers and their mothers into their personalities.

As Michael Thompson and I discussed in our 1999 book *Raising Cain: Protecting the Emotional Life of Boys*,[14] the historical domination of men over women has come with a price. Boys have long been socialized not only to dominate and control others, especially women, but also to control themselves. They have been told that they have to control their "weaker" emotions. They have been pushed to be autonomous, to remain separate from others and self-sufficient. They have been taught never to ask for help.

Michael and I discussed the findings of the groundbreaking National   30
Survey of Adolescent Males (NSAM). We were struck by the fact that boys who approved of more rigid gender roles were, in the survey's word, "hypermasculine" and at greater risk for a host of problems, including school suspension, date rape, and drug and alcohol use.[15] Boys who tend towards hypermasculinity also tend be dominant in their relationships with girls. They are less likely to wear a condom during sex, for example.

In our sample, the boys with the most traditionally masculine attitudes were, similar to the NSAM findings, more likely to have had sex at an earlier age and to have more sexual partners. They were also more likely to have had sex in a non-monogamous "casual" relationship. They watch more hours of television and have more body image problems than boys with less traditionally masculine attitudes. On the flip side, they rated themselves as more dependable.

Unfortunately, boys don't have the abundance of positive media role models that girls have had in recent years. The hypermasculine male is still very much present on television. Studies by media watchdog groups find that men and boys on television rarely show signs of vulnerability, and almost three-quarters of young adult male characters use antisocial behaviors to solve problems.[16] A remarkable long-term study showed that boys who watched more violent television when they were in early elementary school were more likely as young adults to physically assault their spouses and respond to an insult with physical force. They were also three times as likely to have been convicted of a crime.[17]

In subtle and not-so-subtle ways, our culture gives boys the message that they should behave like the men they see on TV or else. In one recent television commercial, a hapless young man is crushed by a giant can of beer that falls from the sky when he displays feminine tendencies. "Men should act like men," the ad's announcer intones, giving fair warning to the boys in the audience. These are amusing commercials, but they push boys in unhealthy ways; they are part of an onslaught of media that is encouraging hypermasculinity.

When I speak to audiences about boys' psychology, I often ask parents to try to think of three male characters on television that they would like their son to emulate. Parents are surprised by how difficult this is. Male characters on prime-time television tend to be buffoons, while their female counterparts are increasingly clever and capable. . . .

When we look at the decline of men, it is easy to become alarmed. But   35 perhaps the coming generations of feminized men may be happier than men of the past. The onus of running the world, the endless problems and headaches — let alpha women have a crack at them; we'll see if they can do better! It's clear that there is much room for improvement.

Perhaps in a world run by women, men will live longer, less stress-filled lives. They will cultivate hitherto underdeveloped aspects of their masculinity; they will allow the full flowering of the tenderer, nurturing aspects of being a "good provider." They will raise the kids and keep house. Men will reassert the role as their children's primary mentor and guide that they held in agrarian America.[18] They will finally fulfill the great hope that has been the dream behind all our wealth and technology — a society where we have the leisure to enjoy one another and appreciate the simple joy of being alive. Men will be able to drop some of the burden of maleness and become more loving. The alphas will provide — fishing for termites, bringing home the bacon — while men will have more of a chance to indulge themselves in sublimely pointless play.

Notes

1. Lonsdorf, E. V.; Eberly, L. E.; and Pusey, A. E. (2004) "Sex differences in learning in chimpanzees," *Nature* 428, pp. 715–716. [All notes are Kindlon's.]

2. U.S. Department of Education, National Center for Education Statistics, Earned Degrees Conferred, 1869–70 through 1964–65; Projections of Education Statistics to 2014; Higher Education General Information Survey (HEGIS), "Degrees and Other Formal Awards Conferred" surveys, 1965–66 through 1985–86; and 1986–87 through 2002–03 Integrated Postsecondary Education Data System, "Completions Survey" (IPEDS-C:87–99), and Fall 2000 through Fall 2003.

3. Dillon, S. "For one student, a college career becomes a career." *New York Times*, Thursday, November 10, 2005, A1, A22.

4. U.S. Department of Education, National Center for Education Statistics, Higher Education General Information Survey (HEGIS), "Degrees and Other Formal Awards Conferred" surveys 1976–77 through 1984–85, and Integrated Postsecondary Education Data System (IPEDS), "Completions" surveys, 1986–87 through 1998–99, and Fall 2000 through Fall 2002 surveys. (This table was prepared August 2003.)

5. See Table 247, Digest of Educational Statistics, 2003, Washington, D.C.: U.S. Department of Education. Online source: http://nces.ed.gov/programs/digest/d04/tables/dt04_247.asp.

6. Source: U.S. Dept. of Education, NCES: Integrated Postsecondary Education Data System (IPEDS), "Completions Survey," various years; and Earned Degrees Conferred Model.

7. U.S. Department of Education, National Center for Education Statistics. (2002). The Condition of Education 2002 (NCES 2002–25), table 25-3 and previously unpublished tabulations for 2002–03 (December 2004). Data from U.S. Department of Commerce, Bureau of the Census, Current Population Survey (CPS), March Supplement, 1971–2003.

8. Hesketh, T.; Lu, L.; and Xing, Z. W. (1997) "Health in China: The one child family policy: the good, the bad, and the ugly," *British Medical Journal* 314, p. 1685. Many couples will choose to have a second child only if their first child is a girl.

9. See Hesketh, T.; Lu, L.; and Xing, Z. W. (2005) "The Effect of China's One-Child Family Policy after 25 Years," *New England Journal of Medicine* 353, pp. 1171–76. The one-child policy is not instituted in the same way across groups. For example, families in most rural areas are allowed to have a second child after an interval of 5 years. See also: Jones, S. Y: *The Descent of Men*. Boston: Houghton Mifflin (2003).

10. Source: Annual Demographic Survey, a Joint Project Between the Bureau of Labor Statistics and the Bureau of the Census, 2004.

11. U.S. Census Bureau. Current Population Survey 2003, Annual Demographic Supplements. Table F-22. Married-Couple Families with Wives' Earnings Greater Than Husbands' Earnings: 1981 to 2003.

12. Meade, L. K. "Baby makes three for partners in blue," *Boston Globe*, Thursday, January 5, 2006, W2, W3.

13. See "Hopping aboard the daddy track," *Business Week* magazine, November 8, 2004.

14. Kindlon, D. and Thompson, M. *Raising Cain: Protecting the Emotional Lives of Boys*. New York: Ballantine (1999).

15. Pleck, J. F., et al. (1993), "Masculinity ideology: Its effect of adolescent males' heterosexual relationships." *Journal of Social Issues* 49, pp. 11–29.

16. See Children Now. *Boys to Men: Entertainment Media Messages About Masculinity*. Oakland, CA: Children Now (September 1999).

17. L. Rowell Huesmann, Jessica Moise-Titus, Cheryl-Lynn Podolski, and Leonard D. Eron of the University of Michigan, "Longitudinal Relations Between Children's Exposure to TV Violence and Their Aggressive and Violent Behavior in Young Adulthood: 1977–1992." *Developmental Psychology* 39, pp. 201–21.

18. See for example: LaRossa, R. *The Modernization of Fatherhood: A Social and Political History*. Chicago: University of Chicago Press (1997).

Engaging the Text

1. How do you respond to Kindlon's repeated comparisons of boys to young chimps? What does this analogy suggest about the basis of male human behavior?

2. In the footnote on page 620, Kindlon mentions that because girls tend to outperform boys academically, some colleges now "use affirmative action standards in order to increase the number of male enrollees." Should gender be a consideration in admission decisions? Why or why not?

3. How and why are traditional gender roles changing, according to Kindlon? What potential benefits for men does he see in women's increasing levels of education and earning power?

4. Evaluate the evidence Kindlon offers to support his predictions about changing gender roles. Consider the studies he cites, the stories he tells, and the graphs he presents: What are the strengths and weaknesses of each?

Exploring Connections

5. Compare Kindlon's depiction of masculinity to Michael Kimmel's (p. 608). Which do you find more accurate, more appealing, and why?

6. Role-play or write an imaginary conversation among Dan Kindlon, Jean Kilbourne, Joan Morgan, and Michael Kimmel about how conventional gender roles affect the relationships between women and men.

7. What's the source of the humor in the cartoon on page 619? Why isn't the kind of hypermasculinity that Kindlon describes, and that Ted appears to represent, considered a "flamboyant" display?

Extending the Critical Context

8. While Kindlon praises "the abundance of positive media role models" for girls, he suggests that images of men, especially on TV, encourage an unhealthy "hypermasculinity" (para. 33). Write an essay explaining why you agree or disagree with this assessment.

The Death of Macho

Reihan Salam

Was the recent global economic collapse caused by risk-taking, macho investment bankers run amok? Reihan Salam argues that "the cult of macho" in the financial industry was largely to blame. He also contends that public backlash against this type of Wall Street "penis competition" may hasten the demise of male dominance. Presently a Fellow at the New America Foundation, Salam (b. 1979) has worked for NBC News, the New York Times, The Atlantic, *and* The New Republic. *He contributes regularly to* Slate *and the* Weekly Standard, *and edits a blog,* The American Scene; *with coauthor Ross Douthat, he wrote* Grand New Party: How Conservatives Can Win the Working Class and Save the American Dream *(2008).*

The era of male dominance is coming to an end.

Seriously.

For years, the world has been witnessing a quiet but monumental shift of power from men to women. Today, the Great Recession has turned what was an evolutionary shift into a revolutionary one. The consequence will be not only a mortal blow to the macho men's club called finance capitalism that got the world into the current economic catastrophe; it will be a collective crisis for millions and millions of working men around the globe.

The death throes of macho are easy to find if you know where to look. Consider, to start, the almost unbelievably disproportionate impact that the current crisis is having on men — so much so that the recession is now known to some economists and the more plugged-in corners of the blogosphere as the "he-cession." More than 80 percent of job losses in the United States since November have fallen on men, according to the U.S. Bureau of Labor Statistics. And the numbers are broadly similar in Europe, adding up to about 7 million more out-of-work men than before the recession just in the United States and Europe as economic sectors traditionally dominated by men (construction and heavy manufacturing) decline further and faster than those traditionally dominated by women (public-sector employment, healthcare, and education). All told, by the end of 2009, the global recession is expected to put as many as 28 million men out of work worldwide.

Things will only get worse for men as the recession adds to the pain globalization was already causing. Between 28 and 42 million more jobs in the United States are at risk for outsourcing, Princeton economist Alan Blinder estimates. Worse still, men are falling even further behind in acquiring the educational credentials necessary for success in the knowledge-based economies that will rule the post-recession world. Soon, there will be three female college graduates for every two males in the United States, and a similarly uneven outlook in the rest of the developed world.   5

Of course, macho is a state of mind, not just a question of employment status. And as men get hit harder in the he-cession, they're even less well-equipped to deal with the profound and long-term psychic costs of job loss. According to the *American Journal of Public Health*, "the financial strain of unemployment" has significantly more consequences on the mental health of men than on that of women. In other words, be prepared for a lot of unhappy guys out there — with all the negative consequences that implies.

As the crisis unfolds, it will increasingly play out in the realm of power politics. Consider the electoral responses to this global catastrophe that are starting to take shape. When Iceland's economy imploded, the country's voters did what no country has done before: Not only did they throw out the all-male elite who oversaw the making of the crisis, they named the world's first openly lesbian leader as their prime minister. It was, said Halla Tomasdottir, the female head of one of Iceland's few remaining solvent banks, a perfectly reasonable response to the "penis competition" of male-dominated investment banking. "Ninety-nine percent went to the same school, they drive the same cars, they wear the same suits and they have the same attitudes. They got us into this situation — and they had a lot of fun doing it," Tomasdottir complained to *Der Spiegel*. Soon after, tiny, debt-ridden Lithuania took a similar course, electing its first woman president: an experienced economist with a black belt in karate named Dalia Grybauskaite. On the day she won, Vilnius's leading newspaper bannered this headline: "Lithuania has decided: The country is to be saved by a woman."

Although not all countries will respond by throwing the male bums out, the backlash is real — and it is global. The great shift of power from males to females is likely to be dramatically accelerated by the economic crisis, as

more people realize that the aggressive, risk-seeking behavior that has enabled men to entrench their power — the cult of macho — has now proven destructive and unsustainable in a globalized world.

Indeed, it's now fair to say that the most enduring legacy of the Great Recession will not be the death of Wall Street. It will not be the death of finance. And it will not be the death of capitalism. These ideas and institutions will live on. What will not survive is macho. And the choice men will have to make, whether to accept or fight this new fact of history, will have seismic effects for all of humanity — women as well as men.

For several years now it has been an established fact that, as behavioral finance economists Brad Barber and Terrance Odean memorably demonstrated in 2001, of all the factors that might correlate with overconfident investment in financial markets — age, marital status, and the like — the most obvious culprit was having a Y chromosome. And now it turns out that not only did the macho men of the heavily male-dominated global finance sector create the conditions for global economic collapse, but they were aided and abetted by their mostly male counterparts in government whose policies, whether consciously or not, acted to artificially prop up macho.

One such example is the housing bubble, which has now exploded most violently in the West. That bubble actually represented an economic policy that disguised the declining prospects of blue-collar men. In the United States, the booming construction sector generated relatively high-paying jobs for the relatively less-skilled men who made up 97.5 percent of its

10

workforce — $814 a week on average. By contrast, female-dominated jobs in healthcare support pay $510 a week, while retail jobs pay about $690 weekly. The housing bubble created nearly 3 million more jobs in residential construction than would have existed otherwise, according to the U.S. Bureau of Labor Statistics. Other, mostly male-dominated, industries, such as real estate, cement production, truck transport, and architecture, saw big employment gains as well. These handsome construction wages allowed men to maintain an economic edge over women. When policymakers are asked why they didn't act to stem the housing bubble's inflation, they invariably cite the fact that the housing sector was a powerful driver of employment. Indeed, subsidizing macho had all kinds of benefits, and to puncture the housing bubble would have been political suicide.

And yet, the housing bubble is just the latest in a long string of efforts to prop up macho, the most powerful of which was the New Deal, as historian Gwendolyn Mink has argued. At the height of the Great Depression in 1933, 15 million Americans were unemployed out of a workforce that was roughly 75 percent male. This undermined the male breadwinner model of the family, and there was tremendous pressure to bring it back. The New Deal did just that by focusing on job creation for men. Insulating women from the market by keeping them in the home became a mark of status for men — a goal most fully realized in the postwar nuclear family (Rosie the Riveter[1] was a blip). In this way, according to historian Stephanie Coontz, the Great Depression and the New Deal reinforced traditional gender roles: women were promised economic security in exchange for the state's entrenchment of male economic power.

Today, this old bargain has come undone, and no state intervention will restore it. Indeed, the U.S. economic stimulus package no longer bears much resemblance to a New Deal–style public-works program. Despite early talk that the stimulus would stress shovel-ready infrastructure projects, high-speed rail lines, and other efforts that would bolster heavily male sectors of the economy, far more of the money is going — directly or indirectly — to education, healthcare, and other social services. Already in the United States, women make up nearly half of biological and medical scientists and nearly three quarters of health-industry workers. No less an authority than U.S. president Barack Obama has weighed in on the shift of power from men to women, telling the *New York Times* that, though construction and manufacturing jobs won't vanish altogether, "they will constitute a smaller percentage of the overall economy." As a result, he said, "Women are just as likely to be the primary bread earner, if not more likely, than men are today."

What this all means is that the problem of macho run amok and excessively compensated is now giving way to macho unemployed and undirected —

---

[1]*Rosie the Riveter:* Generic term referring to women who worked in aircraft assembly plants or took on other traditionally male jobs during World War II.

a different but possibly just as destructive phenomenon. Long periods of unemployment are a strong predictor of heavy drinking, especially for men ages twenty-seven to thirty-five, a study in *Social Science & Medicine* found last year. And the macho losers of globalization can forget about marrying: "Among the workers who disproportionately see their jobs moving overseas or disappearing into computer chips," says sociologist Andrew Cherlin, "we'll see fewer young adults who think they can marry." So the disciplining effects of marriage for young men will continue to fade.

Surly, lonely, and hard-drinking men, who feel as though they have been   15
rendered historically obsolete, and who long for lost identities of macho, are already common in ravaged post-industrial landscapes across the world, from America's Rust Belt to the post-Soviet wreckage of Vladimir Putin's Russia to the megalopolises of the Middle East. If this recession has any staying power, and most believe it does, the massive psychic trauma will spread like an inkblot.

How will this shift to the post-macho world unfold? That depends on the choices men make, and they only have two.

The first is adaptation: men embracing women as equal partners and assimilating to the new cultural sensibilities, institutions, and egalitarian arrangements that entails. That's not to say that all the men in the West will turn into metrosexuals while football ratings and beer sales plummet. But amid the death of macho, a new model of manhood may be emerging, especially among some educated men living in the affluent West.

Economist Betsey Stevenson has described the decline of an older kind of marriage, in which men specialized in market labor while women cared for children, in favor of "consumption" marriage, "where both people are equally contributing to production in the marketplace, but they are matching more on shared desires on how to consume and how to live their lives." These marriages tend to last longer, and they tend to involve a more even split when it comes to household duties.

Not coincidentally, the greater adaptability of educated men in family life extends to economic life, too. Economist Eric D. Gould found in 2004 that marriage tends to make men (particularly lower-wage earners) more serious about their career — more likely to study more, work more, and desire white-collar rather than blue-collar jobs. This adaptation of men may be the optimistic scenario, but it's not entirely far-fetched.

Then, however, there's the other choice: resistance. Men may decide to   20
fight the death of macho, sacrificing their own prospects in an effort to disrupt and delay a powerful historical trend. There are plenty of precedents for this. Indeed, men who have no constructive ways of venting their anger may become a source of nasty extremism; think of the KGB[2] nostalgists in Russia or the jihadi recruits in search of lost honor, to name just a couple.

---

[2]*KGB:* The notorious secret police of the former Soviet Union.

And there are still plenty of men in the West who want to "stand athwart history, yelling Stop."[3] These guys notwithstanding, however, Western developed countries are not for the most part trying to preserve the old gender imbalances of the macho order this time around.

Instead, the choice between adaptation and resistance may play out along a geopolitical divide: while North American and Western European men broadly — if not always happily — adapt to the new egalitarian order, their counterparts in the emerging giants of East and South Asia, not to mention in Russia, all places where women often still face brutal domestic oppression, may be headed for even more exaggerated gender inequality. In those societies, state power will be used not to advance the interests of women, but to keep macho on life support.

Look at Russia, where just such an effort has been unfolding for the past decade. Although there are 10.4 million more Russian women than men, this hasn't translated into political or economic power. After the Soviet collapse, the ideal of women's equality was abandoned almost entirely, and many Russians revived the cult of the full-time homemaker (with Putin's government even offering bonus payments for childbearing women). But Russian men, floored by the dislocations of the Soviet collapse and a decade of economic crisis, simply couldn't adapt. "It was common for men to fall into depression and spend their days drinking and lying on the couch smoking," Moscow writer Masha Lipman observes. Between their tremendously high rates of mortality, incarceration, and alcoholism and their low rates of education, only a small handful of Russian men were remotely able (or willing) to serve as sole breadwinners.

This left Russia's resilient women to do the work, while being forced to accept skyrocketing levels of sexual exploitation at work and massive hypocrisy at home. A higher percentage of working-age women are employed in Russia than nearly any other country, Elena Mezentseva of the Moscow Center for Gender Studies has found, but as of 2000, they were making only half the wages that Russian men earned for the same work. All the while, Putin has aided and abetted these men, turning their nostalgia for the lost macho of Soviet times into an entire ideology.

If this represents a nightmare scenario for how the death of macho could play out, another kind of threatening situation is unfolding in China. The country's $596 billion economic stimulus package bears a far stronger resemblance to a New Deal–style public-works program than anything the U.S. Democratic Party has devised. Whereas healthcare and education have attracted the bulk of U.S. stimulus dollars, more than 90 percent of the Chinese stimulus is going to construction: of low-income homes, highways, railroads, dams, sewage-treatment plants, electricity grids, airports, and much else.

---

[3]*"stand athwart history, yelling Stop"*: A phrase used by William F. Buckley Jr. to describe the mission of his conservative magazine, *The National Review*.

This frenzy of spending is designed to contain the catastrophic damage   25
caused by the loss of manufacturing jobs in China's export sector. The
Chinese Communist Party has long seen the country's 230 million migrant
workers, roughly two-thirds of whom are men, as a potential source of political unrest. Tens of millions have lost manufacturing jobs already, and so far
they've proved unwilling or unable to return to their native provinces.

Just as the housing bubble in the United States was a pro-male policy,
China's economic trajectory over the past two decades is deeply tied to its
effort to manage the threat posed by the country's massive male migrant
population. Massachusetts Institute of Technology economist Yasheng Huang
has argued that while the first decade after Deng Xiaoping's economic
reforms saw tremendous economic growth and entrepreneurship in the
Chinese hinterlands, the next two decades have seen a marked decline in
the economic prospects of rural China coupled with a concerted effort
to promote the rapid development of China's coastal cities. State-owned
enterprises and multinational corporations enjoyed generous subsidies, tax
abatements, and other insider deals, and in return, they employed millions
of migrants. The trade-off exacerbated China's internal migration, as millions of men fled rural poverty in search of short-term urban employment,
but after the Tiananmen Square uprising, Chinese elites welcomed it as a
way to stave off urban unrest.

Today, however, it's hard to see how Chinese leaders can safely unravel
this bargain. Matters are made worse by China's skewed population — there
are 119 male births for every 100 female — and the country has already seen
violent protests from its increasingly alienated young men. Of course, it's
possible that China will constructively channel this surplus of macho energy
in the direction of entrepreneurship, making the country a global source of
radical innovation, with all the military implications that entails. More likely,
if the nature of China's stimulus is any indication, Beijing will continue trying
to prop up its urban industrial economy — for if this outlet for macho
crumbles, there is good reason to believe that the Communist Party will
crumble with it.

It might be tempting to think that the death of macho is just a cyclical
correction and that the alpha males of the financial world will all be back to
work soon. Tempting, but wrong. The "penis competition" made possible
by limitless leverage, arcane financial instruments,[4] and pure unadulterated
capitalism will now be domesticated in lasting ways.

The he-cession is creating points of agreement among people not typically thought of as kindred spirits, from behavioral economists to feminist
historians. But while many blame men for the current economic mess,

---

[4]*'limitless leverage, arcane financial instruments'*: "Leverage" most often refers to debt
used to purchase an investment. One of the causes of the financial collapse of 2008 was over-
borrowing; another was that some of the investment products that had become popular were
so complicated that hardly anyone understood what they were actually investing in.

much of the talk thus far has focused on the recession's effects on women. And they are real. Women had a higher global unemployment rate before the current recession, and they still do. This leads many to agree with a UN report from earlier this year: "The economic and financial crisis puts a disproportionate burden on women, who are often concentrated in vulnerable employment and tend to have lower unemployment and social security benefits, and have unequal access to and control over economic and financial resources."

This is a valid concern, and not incompatible with the fact that billions   30
of men worldwide, not just a few discredited bankers, will increasingly lose out in the new world taking shape from the current economic wreckage. As women start to gain more of the social, economic, and political power they have long been denied, it will be nothing less than a full-scale revolution the likes of which human civilization has never experienced.

This is not to say that women and men will fight each other across armed barricades. The conflict will take a subtler form, and the main battlefield will be hearts and minds. But make no mistake: the axis of global conflict in this century will not be warring ideologies, or competing geopolitics, or clashing civilizations. It won't be race or ethnicity. It will be gender. We have no precedent for a world after the death of macho. But we can expect the transition to be wrenching, uneven, and possibly very violent.

Engaging the Text

1. What does Salam mean when he refers to "the death of macho"? Why does he believe it's dying?

2. How does Salam explain the causes of the global economic crisis? What role have macho attitudes and behavior (para. 8) played, in his opinion? In what ways is this crisis a "he-cession"? How has it affected women as well as men?

3. How has economic policy worked to sustain "the cult of macho" (para. 8) in the past? Why does Salam think that this is unlikely to continue?

4. Salam suggests that men can either adapt to or rebel against their declining power. Which does he think is more likely, and why?

Exploring Connections

5. In what ways does Salam agree with Dan Kindlon's analysis (p. 618) of the ways men may respond to the growing power of women? In what ways does he disagree? Which writer's conclusions do you find more persuasive, and why?

6. Review the selections by Reihan Salam, Dan Kindlon (p. 618), Michael Kimmel (p. 608), and Aaron H. Devor (p. 527), and work in groups to list the characteristics that they associate with American masculinity. To what extent do the men you know embody these characteristics?

EXTENDING THE CRITICAL CONTEXT

7. Do some informal research to test the idea that "the era of male dominance is coming to an end" (para. 1). Look through some business magazines for profiles of powerful executives, scan lists of the wealthiest or highest earning people in various fields, find current statistics on the percentages of male and female CEOs. Based on your findings, how immediate or distant does the death of macho appear to you?

FURTHER CONNECTIONS

1. Compare the rhetorical strategies and effectiveness of any two of the selections in this chapter. What is each writer's purpose and what audience is he or she addressing? To what extent and how does each author appeal to readers' reason and emotions? What kind of persona does each writer project? What kinds of evidence does each author rely on? How persuasive or compelling do you find each selection, and why?

2. Research the issue of domestic violence. How is it defined? How prevalent is domestic violence nationwide, in your state, and in your community? What are the risk factors for abusers and their victims? Investigate the resources in your community that offer assistance to victims of domestic abuse: hotlines, shelters, organizations, and government agencies that provide counseling or legal aid. Do these services focus on punishing abusers or "curing" them? Write a paper evaluating the effectiveness of different approaches to protecting victims from abusive partners.

3. Research the status of women in the field or profession you plan to pursue. Are women's salaries and compensation comparable to those of men with similar credentials and experience? What is the ratio of women to men in the field as a whole, in entry-level positions, and in executive or high-status positions? Interview at least one woman in this line of work: In what ways, if any, does she feel that her work experience has differed from a man's? Report your findings to the class.

4. Title IX, the law mandating equal funding for women's sports at publicly funded schools, has been praised for opening new opportunities for women athletes and criticized for siphoning money away from some popular men's sports. Research the impact of Title IX on athletics programs at your college or university: How has the picture of women's and men's sports changed since 1972, the year Title IX was enacted? Have women's and men's athletics attained equality at your school?

5. Some religious groups argue that laws and policies that prohibit harassment of or discrimination against homosexuals infringe on their religious freedom. Investigate a specific case in which a religious organization has made this claim. What arguments have been advanced on both sides of the case? What values and assumptions underlie these arguments? What rights and freedoms are at stake for each party in the dispute?

6

Ah Wilderness!

American Myths of Nature and the Environment

Kindred Spirits, by Asher B. Durand (1849).

FAST FACTS

1. During the 1830s American Indians on the Southern Plains killed an estimated 280,000 bison every year. During the height of the nineteenth-century "buffalo hunts" led by plainsmen like Buffalo Bill Cody, as many as 100,000 bison a day were destroyed. Of the 350,000 buffalo in the United States today, approximately 250,000 are being raised for human consumption.

2. At least 140 major animal and bird species have gone extinct in North America since Christopher Columbus "discovered" the New World in 1492 — including four species of whales, seventeen varieties of grizzly bears, the Eastern and Oregon buffalo, Newfoundland and Florida wolves, Eastern cougars, Badlands bighorn sheep, passenger pigeons, and probably ivory-billed woodpeckers. Of the original 2.2 billion acres of wilderness that existed in pre-Columbian America, only 90 million officially protected and 50 million unprotected acres remain today.

3. Average world temperatures have climbed 1.4 degrees Fahrenheit since 1880. Eleven of the past twelve years have rated among the warmest since 1850. Montana's Glacier National Park now has only 27 of the 150 glaciers it had in 1910. Average world temperatures could climb another 11 degrees Fahrenheit by the end of the twenty-first century, and sea levels could rise by as much as two feet.

4. Each month, Americans average 153 hours watching television and 29 hours online. During all of 2006, 12.5 million Americans spent time hunting, 30.3 million went sport fishing, and 71.1 million visited nature as "wildlife watchers" (observing, feeding, and photographing birds and animals). While the number of American hunters declined between 2001 and 2006 by 4%, the number of wildlife watchers increased by nearly 8%.

Sources: (1) "American Bison," http://en.wikipedia.org/wiki/American_Bison; (2) *Christopher Columbus and the Conquest of Paradise,* Kirkpatrick Sale, Tauris Parke Paperbacks (2006); (3) National Geographic "Global Warming Fast Facts," http://news.nationalgeographic.com/news/2004/12/1206_041206_global_warming.html; US EPA "Future Sea Level Changes," http://www.epa.gov/climatechange/science/futureslc.html; (4) *A2 / M2 Three Screen Report,* The Nielsen Company (2009); *2006 National Survey of Fishing, Hunting, and Wildlife-Associated Recreation,* U.S. Department of the Interior, http://library.fws.gov/pubs/nat_survey2006_final.pdf.

THERE'S NO DOUBT ABOUT IT: Americans love nature. Or, at least, we like to think we do. As a nation, we're wild about hiking, camping, boating, skiing, fishing, and hunting. We preserve our forests and protect wild creatures like the condor and the bald eagle. We celebrate Earth Day every April 22, we recycle, and we worry about global warming. But this wasn't always the case. American attitudes toward nature have evolved since Christopher Columbus first reported his "discovery" of a land with "trees stretching up to the stars . . . great and beautiful mountains, vast fields, groves, fertile plains . . . and [a] remarkable number of rivers contributing to the healthfulness of man . . ."

Early reports from the "New World" emphasized the fertility of the land and the limitless supply of natural resources. The logs of seventeenth-century Spanish and British explorers brim with descriptions of a world stocked with exotic animals and fragrant with the smells of grapes and ripening grain. Portraying the New World as an untouched paradise waiting to be harvested, these early sales pitches were designed to lure settlers to the Americas. They also established one of the continent's most enduring cultural myths: the belief that America's natural beauty and bounty were endless and inexhaustible.

Of course, the land that European settlers claimed was neither endless nor uninhabited. The tribal peoples who lived in the Americas for more than ten thousand years before Columbus arrived had their own complex relationship with nature. Unlike the European invaders, they didn't see nature as a pool of material resources to be exploited for profit. In Native American religions, humans, plants, animals, and land forms exist within a complex network of interdependent relationships, and all are part of a larger "spirit world." The animist idea that all creatures are locked in bonds of spiritual kinship with the earth encouraged a sense of reciprocity and restraint in Indian cultures. This is why animals, plants, rocks, rivers, clouds, stars, and sky all play important parts in Native American myths and legends. In tribal myths like those of the Crow and Hopi, Old Man Coyote and a couple of red-eyed ducks can create the world during an afternoon of casual conversation. The human race itself can be conjured to life by the song of Spider Woman and the Sun God. Because they saw all creation as deeply connected, native peoples didn't draw a sharp distinction between things natural and human, and they didn't bother with ideas like wilderness and civilization.

But the Pilgrims did. When they arrived on the *Mayflower* in 1620, the Pilgrims had no illusions about nature's bounty. Dropping anchor in midwinter, they faced a season of "cruell and fierce stormes" and felt themselves stranded in a "hideous and desolate wilderness full of wild beasts and wild men." Fleeing religious persecution in England and the Netherlands, the thirty-five original Pilgrims saw themselves and their voyage to the New World in biblical terms. Like the Israelites in the Hebrew Bible's book of Exodus, they believed that they were fleeing captivity in Europe in search of a new promised land. The Puritans saw themselves as saints, holy people who had been elected by God to restore Christian belief to its original pure state. As God's chosen, they intended to build a New Jerusalem in America, a new form of sacred civilization free of the corruption and moral decay they had left behind in Europe. According to this biblically inspired script, nature assumed the role of a fearful opponent. Just as the Israelites had been tested in the deserts of Sinai for forty years, the Pilgrims saw themselves on a "mission in the Wilderness." In their view, nature was a dangerous force aligned with the powers of darkness and full of threats and temptations. In fact, they deliberately shunned milder climates in the Virginian colonies and chose to settle in the north because they feared that rich soil and good weather would lead their people to "degenerate speedily, and to corrupt their minds and bodies too." They believed that part of their mission was to tame the "howling wilderness" and turn it into a garden, much like the fruitful and orderly paradise that God provides Adam and Eve in Genesis.

The Pilgrims were so suspicious of nature, they once put it on trial. Twenty years after landing at Plymouth, they were busily building new towns, farms, and schools to fulfill their dream of re-creating a "*New England*" out of the wasteland they inhabited. Unfortunately, as they cleared the terrain of trees and native tribes, they noted a disturbing increase in the wolf population outside their settlements. As concerns grew about what this meant, rumors began circulating about an outbreak of "bestiality cases" involving local farmers and their livestock. The result, as historian Melanie Perreault describes it, was a mass trial of animals and men gone wild: "In a bizarre scene, Puritan officials brought the suspect animals and the accused men before the courts and summarily executed both after they were found guilty." The wild was a great source of anxiety for our Pilgrim Fathers. Indeed, while they sought the challenge of wilderness, they also feared that living close to the wild would make them wild as well.

The Pilgrim fear of wilderness and "wild men" lingered in colonial culture for another two centuries. It wasn't until the post-revolutionary period that Americans began to see nature as more than a source of threat or profit. Following liberation from the British, American intellectuals grappled with the project of fashioning a unique national identity. They sought to discover something that would distinguish America from the exhausted monarchies and authoritarian cultures that dominated the Old World. To thinkers like essayist and poet Ralph Waldo Emerson, what most clearly set Americans apart from their European cousins was their close relationship with nature. Emerson, along with the other members of the American transcendentalist movement, turned the Puritan understanding of nature on its head. Instead of seeing wilderness as a threatening force aligned with dark powers, they embraced it as a reflection of the divinely inspired order of the universe. Emerson believed that direct contact with nature could help humanity "transcend" the corrupting influences of society and reconnect with the "Oversoul," the divine force uniting all creation. As Emerson expressed it, "In the woods we return to reason and faith. Standing on the bare ground, — my head bathed by the blithe air, and uplifted into infinite space . . . I am part and particle of God."

Henry David Thoreau put this revolutionary view of nature into practice. A close friend of Emerson, Thoreau left his teaching post in Concord, Massachusetts, in the spring of 1845 to conduct the most famous philosophical experiment in American history. For two years, Thoreau lived alone in the woods outside Concord near Walden Pond in a simple, one-room cabin he built from used boards, river rocks, and hand-felled trees. Trying "to suck all the marrow out of life," Thoreau moved to the woods to live as simply, as "deliberately," and as close to the land as possible, working only as much as needed to feed himself with food he grew with his own hands. For Thoreau, nature offered an antidote to the ills of civilization. As he saw it, wilderness was "the raw material of life," a "tonic" that nourishes and restores the senses and the soul. Cities, schools, churches, jobs, books — all the trappings of civilization — serve only to distract us from life's core truths and meaning. This vision of nature's purity and healing power, as expressed in *Walden*, Thoreau's 1854 account of his "Life in the Woods," still shapes our thinking about nature today.

Generations of Americans followed Thoreau into the wild. In 1860, twenty-two-year-old John Muir abandoned his strict Protestant family in Wisconsin to begin a lifelong trek across the continent that took him from Canada to the Gulf of Mexico and from there to the American West. Inspired by Emerson and Thoreau, Muir extolled the virtues of wilderness in his writings and spent fifty years fighting to protect pristine areas like California's Yosemite Valley from the impact of development. In response to these efforts, Congress passed the Yosemite Act in 1890, the first bill specifically designed to preserve a wilderness area. Two years later, Muir founded the Sierra Club, the first organization in the United States dedicated to preserving the environment. Muir's efforts on behalf of the wild inspired other Americans as well, including President Teddy Roosevelt, who became an avid hunter and outdoorsman to compensate for his frail health as a child. Roosevelt's love of "roughing it" and his dedication to the frontier virtues he saw at the heart of the American character made him a leader in the wilderness cult that swept the country at the turn of the twentieth century. As the nation became increasingly industrialized in the early 1900s, this obsession with the wild eventually led to the development of nature-oriented children's clubs that promoted outdoors encounters and crafts, including organizations like the Indian Guides and Boy Scouts.

As America moved into the twentieth century, our love affair with nature matured. Naturalists like Aldo Leopold and Rachel Carson and activists like Edward Abbey transformed America's attachment to nature into a matter of critical scientific and political concern. In his famous *Sand County Almanac*, published in 1949, Leopold argued that nature is more than the sum of all the plants, animals, and minerals that make it up. Seen from the evolutionary perspective he had adopted while working as a wildlife manager, nature became a complex network of interdependent ecosystems involving multiple communities of creatures and land forms. In Leopold's view, we humans are members of a "biotic team," and as such, we have an ethical obligation to live in harmony with the land.

Naturalist Rachel Carson carried Leopold's ecological thinking a step farther with publication of her groundbreaking book *Silent Spring* in 1962. Opening with the story of "a town in the heart of America" that is blighted by a mysterious "shadow of death," *Silent Spring* documented the toll the chemical pesticide DDT was taking on birds, animals, and children across the country. Today, Carson's pioneering work is widely credited with inspiring the creation of the Environmental Protection Agency and with kick-starting the modern environmental movement.

Not long after Carson's death, Edward Abbey began publishing a series of books on his life as a park ranger and all-around environmental roughneck, books that eventually led to a new, more aggressive form of environmental activism. Abbey's venerated 1975 novel *The Monkey Wrench Gang* traced the adventures of a group of fast-living, hard-drinking "eco-warriors" as they stormed across the American West, sabotaging bulldozers and burning billboards in the name of the environment. Widely seen as the father of "eco-anarchism," Abbey served as a role model for a new generation of radical environmental activists, from relatively nonviolent groups like Greenpeace and Earth First! to "eco-terrorist" organizations like the Earth Liberation Front, which has made headlines by firebombing tourist developments and SUV dealerships in the name of the planet.

Today, as we confront issues like climate change and global warming, the survival of nature itself may be in doubt. One hundred and fifty years into the Industrial Revolution, the scientific consensus is that greenhouse gases are raising temperatures around the world at a breathtaking rate. According to the Intergovernmental Panel on Climate Change, unless we slash greenhouse gas emissions now, average world temperatures could rise by as much as eleven degrees Fahrenheit by the end of the century, triggering a two-to-three-foot increase in sea levels around the world. If we fail to act, scientists predict that hurricanes, droughts, and famines will worsen, animal and plant species will go extinct, and millions of people will be displaced. Never before has nature itself seemed so fragile, and never in the history of America has our thinking about nature and the environment meant so much for world survival.

This chapter invites you to explore some of the most powerful American myths of nature, past and present, and to consider our options in light of the global environmental crisis we now face. The first half of the chapter features a series of readings tracing the intersection of personal and cultural encounters with nature. The chapter opens with excerpts from Henry David Thoreau's 1851 essay *Walking*. This classic account of the meaning of wilderness provides a point of departure for almost every other selection in the chapter. Next, two episodes from Annie Dillard's *An American Childhood* offer you the opportunity to consider the role that nature played in your own early experience. In "A Life of the Senses," Richard Louv probes the role that nature plays in child development and argues that we all suffer from "cultural autism" in our increasingly media-dependent world. The idea of electronically mediated nature is expanded in Charles Siebert's "The Artifice of the Natural," a thought-provoking analysis of how animals are portrayed on television. The first half of the chapter closes with "Talking to the Owls and Butterflies," a challenging alternative view of nature presented by Sioux medicine man John (Fire) Lame Deer and anthropologist Richard Erdoes.

The second half of the chapter focuses on environmental activism and the global climate change crisis. The chapter's Visual Portfolio presents a collage of historical and contemporary images illustrating the toll that industrial society has taken on the American landscape over the past two hundred years. Joy Williams follows by challenging you to consider what you've done for the environment in her scathingly personal "Save the Whales, Screw the Shrimp." Next, an excerpt from Derrick Jensen and Stephanie McMillan's graphic novel *As the World Burns* critiques some of our commonplace assumptions about how we can save the planet from global warming. In "The End of Nature," famed environmental activist Bill McKibben wonders what climate change says about our relationship with the earth and about us as a species. Graeme Wood's "Moving Heaven and Earth" rounds off this quartet of readings by examining some radical technological solutions that are being proposed for combating greenhouse gases.

The chapter concludes with two selections on environmental activism. First, U.S. Congresswoman Nydia M. Velázquez argues, in "In Search of Justice," that a healthy environment is the right of all Americans, including those who live in highly polluted urban neighborhoods. John Berlau's "Our Unhealthy Future Under Environmentalism" brings the chapter to a close by challenging us to consider if environmental activists haven't gone too far in their quest to save the earth.

Sources

Columbus, Christopher. *Letter on the First Voyage to the New World.* 1493. U of Southern Maine. Web. 02 Oct. 2009.

Emerson, Ralph Waldo. *Nature and Walking.* Boston: Beacon Press, 1994. Print.

Hawkin, Paul. *Blessed Unrest: How the Largest Social Movement in History is Restoring Grace, Justice, and Beauty to the World.* New York: Penguin Books, 2007. Print.

Leopold, Aldo. *A Sand County Almanac.* New York: Ballantine Books, 1966. Print.

Nash, Roderick Frazier. *Wilderness and the American Mind,* 4th ed. New Haven: Yale University Press, 2001. Print.

Perreault, Melanie. "American Wilderness and First Contact." *American Wilderness*. Ed. Michael Lewis. New York: Oxford University Press, 2007. Print.

Taylor, Alan. *American Colonies: The Settling of North America*. New York: Penguin Books, 2002. Print.

Thoreau, Henry David. *Walden and Other Writings*. Ed. Brooks Atkinson. Modern Library edition. New York: Random House, 2000. Print.

BEFORE READING

- Working in groups, brainstorm a list of words, ideas, and reactions that come to mind when you think about nature. What does your list suggest about how you view nature and your relationship with the natural world?

- Examine Asher B. Durand's 1849 landscape *Kindred Spirits* (p. 639), which depicts Durand's recently deceased friend, nature artist Thomas Cole, walking in the Catskill Mountains with American poet William Cullen Bryant. How is nature portrayed in this painting? Why do you think Durand chose to remember his friend by depicting him in this setting? What does this painting suggest about mid-nineteenth-century American attitudes toward nature?

- Do some quick online research to learn more about the figures mentioned in the introduction to this chapter, including Ralph Waldo Emerson, Henry David Thoreau, John Muir, Theodore Roosevelt, Aldo Leopold, Rachel Carson, and Edward Abbey. Share what you learn in class and discuss which of these American environmentalists seems most interesting to you and why.

From *Walking*

HENRY DAVID THOREAU

Born in 1817 in Concord, Massachusetts, Henry David Thoreau was a tutor, teacher, philosopher, pacifist, and self-trained naturalist. After graduating from Harvard University with a degree in English, Thoreau met Ralph Waldo Emerson, one of the nation's leading thinkers and founder of the American transcendentalist movement. In his youth, Thoreau was strongly attracted to the tenets of transcendentalism, which stressed the uniqueness of the individual spirit and the individual's duty to search for universal truth. Inspired by the transcendental ideal of harmony with nature, Thoreau left Concord in 1845 to live in a hand-built one-room cabin near Walden Pond outside Concord. He chronicled his experiences of living as simply and as close to nature as possible in Walden *(1854), which remains one of the most influential works in the history of American nature writing. Published after his death in 1862,* Walking *began as a public lecture that Thoreau delivered at the Concord Lyceum and at other venues during the 1850s. In this meditation on what it means to ramble through the woods, Thoreau offers a concise manifesto on the meaning of nature and the power of wilderness. In addition to* Walden *and* Walking, *Thoreau published a number of memorable reflections on nature and natural philosophy during his lifetime, including* A Week on the Concord and Merrimack Rivers *(1849) and* The Maine Woods *(1864).*

I wish to speak a word for Nature, for absolute freedom and wildness, as contrasted with a freedom and culture merely civil, — to regard man as an inhabitant, or a part and parcel of Nature, rather than a member of society. I wish to make an extreme statement, if so I may make an emphatic one, for there are enough champions of civilization: the minister and the school-committee and every one of you will take care of that.

I have met with but one or two persons in the course of my life who understood the art of Walking, that is, of taking walks. . . .

I think that I cannot preserve my health and spirits, unless I spend four hours a day at least, — and it is commonly more than that, — sauntering through the woods and over the hills and fields, absolutely free from all worldly engagements. You may safely say, A penny for your thoughts, or a thousand pounds. When sometimes I am reminded that the mechanics[1] and shopkeepers stay in their shops not only all the forenoon, but all the afternoon too, sitting with crossed legs, so many of them, — as if the legs were made to sit upon, and not to stand or walk upon, — I think that they deserve some credit for not having all committed suicide long ago. . . .

But the walking of which I speak has nothing in it akin to taking exercise, as it is called, as the sick take medicine at stated hours, — as the swinging of dumb-bells or chairs; but is itself the enterprise and adventure of the day. If you would get exercise, go in search of the springs of life. Think of a man's swinging dumb-bells for his health, when those springs are bubbling up in far-off pastures unsought by him!

Moreover, you must walk like a camel, which is said to be the only beast which ruminates[2] when walking. When a traveler asked Wordsworth's[3] servant   5

---

[1]*mechanics:* Skilled workers.
[2]*ruminates:* To chew the cud, as does a cow; to turn over in the mind, to reflect.
[3]*Wordsworth:* William Wordsworth (1770–1850), English poet famed for his nature poetry.

to show him her master's study, she answered, "Here is his library, but his study is out of doors." . . .

I can easily walk ten, fifteen, twenty, any number of miles, commencing at my own door, without going by any house, without crossing a road except where the fox and the mink do: first along by the river, and then the brook, and then the meadow and the woodside. There are square miles in my vicinity which have no inhabitant. From many a hill I can see civilization and the abodes of man afar. The farmers and their works are scarcely more obvious than woodchucks and their burrows. Man and his affairs, church and state and school, trade and commerce, and manufactures and agriculture, even politics, the most alarming of them all, — I am pleased to see how little space they occupy in the landscape. Politics is but a narrow field, and that still narrower highway yonder leads to it. I sometimes direct the traveler thither. If you would go to the political world, follow the great road, — follow that market-man, keep his dust in your eyes, and it will lead you straight to it; for it, too, has its place merely, and does not occupy all space. I pass from it as from a bean-field into the forest, and it is forgotten. In one half-hour I can walk off to some portion of the earth's surface where a man does not stand from one year's end to another, and there, consequently, politics are not, for they are but as the cigar-smoke of a man. . . .

When I go out of the house for a walk, uncertain as yet whither I will bend my steps, and submit myself to my instinct to decide for me, I find, strange and whimsical as it may seem, that I finally and inevitably settle southwest, toward some particular wood or meadow or deserted pasture or hill in that direction. My needle is slow to settle, — varies a few degrees, and does not always point due southwest, it is true, and it has good authority for this variation, but it always settles between west and south-southwest. The future lies that way to me, and the earth seems more unexhausted and richer on that side. The outline which would bound my walks would be, not a circle, but a parabola, or rather like one of those cometary orbits which have been thought to be non-returning curves, in this case opening westward, in which my house occupies the place of the sun. I turn round and round irresolute sometimes for a quarter of an hour, until I decide, for a thousandth time, that I will walk into the southwest or west. Eastward I go only by force; but westward I go free. Thither no business leads me. It is hard for me to believe that I shall find fair landscapes or sufficient wildness and freedom behind the eastern horizon. I am not excited by the prospect of a walk thither; but I believe that the forest which I see in the western horizon stretches uninterruptedly toward the setting sun, and there are no towns nor cities in it of enough consequence to disturb me. Let me live where I will, on this side is the city, on that the wilderness, and ever I am leaving the city more and more, and withdrawing into the wilderness. I should not lay so much stress on this fact, if I did not believe that something like this is the prevailing tendency of my countrymen. I must walk toward Oregon, and not toward Europe. And that way the nation is moving, and I may say that mankind progress from east to west. . . .

We go eastward to realize history and study the works of art and literature, retracing the steps of the race; we go westward as into the future, with a spirit of enterprise and adventure. The Atlantic is a Lethean[4] stream, in our passage over which we have had an opportunity to forget the Old World[5] and its institutions. If we do not succeed this time, there is perhaps one more chance for the race left before it arrives on the banks of the Styx;[6] and that is in the Lethe of the Pacific, which is three times as wide. . . .

Sir Francis Head, an English traveler and a Governor-General of Canada, tells us that "in both the northern and southern hemispheres of the New World, Nature has not only outlined her works on a larger scale, but has painted the whole picture with brighter and more costly colors than she used in delineating and in beautifying the Old World. . . . The heavens of America appear infinitely higher, the sky is bluer, the air is fresher, the cold is intenser, the moon looks larger, the stars are brighter, the thunder is louder, the lightning is vivider, the wind is stronger, the rain is heavier, the mountains are higher, the rivers longer, the forests bigger, the plains broader.". . .

These are encouraging testimonies. If the moon looks larger here than in Europe, probably the sun looks larger also. If the heavens of America appear infinitely higher, and the stars brighter, I trust that these facts are symbolical of the height to which the philosophy and poetry and religion of her inhabitants may one day soar. At length, perchance, the immaterial heaven will appear as much higher to the American mind, and the intimations that star it as much brighter. For I believe that climate does thus react on man, — as there is something in the mountain-air that feeds the spirit and inspires. Will not man grow to greater perfection intellectually as well as physically under these influences? Or is it unimportant how many foggy days there are in his life? I trust that we shall be more imaginative, that our thoughts will be clearer, fresher, and more ethereal as our sky, — our understanding more comprehensive and broader, like our plains, — our intellect generally on a grander scale, like our thunder and lightning, our rivers and mountains and forests, — and our hearts shall even correspond in breadth and depth and grandeur to our inland seas. Perchance there will appear to the traveler something, he knows not what, of *læta* and *glabra*,[7] of joyous

10

---

[4]*Lethean:* From Lethe, the river of forgetfulness in Greek mythology; hence, causing or related to forgetfulness.

[5]*the Old World:* Europe as opposed to the "New World" discovered by Columbus.

[6]*Styx:* River in the underworld in Greek mythology.

[7]*læta and* glabra: Quoted from Carl Linnaeus (1701–1778), known as the Father of Taxonomy (scientific classification).

and serene, in our very faces. Else to what end does the world go on, and why was America discovered?

To Americans I hardly need to say, —

"Westward the star of empire takes its way."

As a true patriot, I should be ashamed to think that Adam[8] in paradise was more favorably situated on the whole than the backwoodsman in this country. . . .

The west of which I speak is but another name for the Wild; and what I have been preparing to say is, that in Wildness is the preservation of the World. Every tree sends its fibres forth in search of the Wild. The cities import it at any price. Men plough and sail for it. From the forest and wilderness come the tonics and barks which brace mankind. Our ancestors were savages. The story of Romulus and Remus[9] being suckled by a wolf is not a meaningless fable. The founders of every state which has risen to eminence have drawn their nourishment and vigor from a similar wild source. It was because the children of the Empire[10] were not suckled by the wolf that they were conquered and displaced by the children of the northern forests who were.

I believe in the forest, and in the meadow, and in the night in which the corn grows. We require an infusion of hemlock-spruce or arbor vitæ[11] in our tea. There is a difference between eating and drinking for strength and from mere gluttony. The Hottentots[12] eagerly devour the marrow of the koodoo and other antelopes raw, as a matter of course. Some of our Northern Indians eat raw the marrow of the Arctic reindeer, as well as various other parts, including the summits of the antlers, as long as they are soft. And herein, perchance, they have stolen a march on the cooks of Paris. They get what usually goes to feed the fire. This is probably better than stall-fed beef and slaughter-house pork to make a man of. Give me a wildness whose glance no civilization can endure, — as if we lived on the marrow of koodoos devoured raw. . . .

A tanned skin is something more than respectable, and perhaps olive is a fitter color than white for a man, — a denizen of the woods. "The pale white man!" I do not wonder that the African pitied him. Darwin[13] the naturalist says, "A white man bathing by the side of a Tahitian was like a plant bleached by the gardener's art, compared with a fine, dark green one, growing vigorously in the open fields."

---

[8]*Adam:* First human created by God in the Hebrew Bible's book of Genesis.

[9]*Romulus and Remus:* Mythological founders of the city of Rome.

[10]*the Empire:* The Roman Empire (286–476).

[11]*arbor vitæ:* A type of conifer related to the cypress.

[12]*Hottentots:* Name given by white colonists to the Khoekhoe people of southern Africa.

[13]*Darwin:* Charles Darwin (1802–1882), British naturalist and writer.

Ben Jonson[14] exclaims, —

15

"How near to good is what is fair!"

So I would say, —

How near to good is what is *wild!*

Life consists with wildness. The most alive is the wildest. Not yet subdued to man, its presence refreshes him. One who pressed forward incessantly and never rested from his labors, who grew fast and made infinite demands on life, would always find himself in a new country or wilderness, and surrounded by the raw material of life. He would be climbing over the prostrate stems of primitive forest-trees. . . .

In short, all good things are wild and free. There is something in a strain of music, whether produced by an instrument or by the human voice, — take the sound of a bugle in a summer night, for instance, — which by its wildness, to speak without satire, reminds me of the cries emitted by wild beasts in their native forests. It is so much of their wildness as I can understand. Give me for my friends and neighbors wild men, not tame ones. The wildness of the savage is but a faint symbol of the awful ferity[15] with which good men and lovers meet.

I love even to see the domestic animals reassert their native rights, — any evidence that they have not wholly lost their original wild habits and vigor; as when my neighbor's cow breaks out of her pasture early in the spring and boldly swims the river, a cold, gray tide, twenty-five or thirty rods wide, swollen by the melted snow. It is the buffalo crossing the Mississippi. This exploit confers some dignity on the herd in my eyes, — already dignified. The seeds of instinct are preserved under the thick hides of cattle and horses, like seeds in the bowels of the earth, an indefinite period.

Any sportiveness in cattle is unexpected. I saw one day a herd of a dozen bullocks and cows running about and frisking in unwieldy sport, like huge rats, even like kittens. They shook their heads, raised their tails, and rushed up and down a hill, and I perceived by their horns, as well as by their activity, their relation to the deer tribe. But, alas! a sudden loud *Whoa!* would have damped their ardor at once, reduced them from venison to beef, and stiffened their sides and sinews like the locomotive. Who but the Evil One has cried, "Whoa!" to mankind? Indeed, the life of cattle, like that of many men, is but a sort of locomotiveness; they move a side at a time, and man, by his machinery, is meeting the horse and the ox half-way. Whatever part the whip has touched is thenceforth palsied. Who would ever think of a *side* of any of the supple cat tribe, as we speak of a *side* of beef?

I rejoice that horses and steers have to be broken before they can be made the slaves of men, and that men themselves have some wild oats still

---

[14]*Ben Jonson:* English playwright and poet (1572–1637).
[15]*ferity:* Wildness.

left to sow before they become submissive members of society. Undoubt-edly, all men are not equally fit subjects for civilization; and because the majority, like dogs and sheep, are tame by inherited disposition, this is no reason why the others should have their natures broken that they may be reduced to the same level. Men are in the main alike, but they were made several in order that they might be various. If a low use is to be served, one man will do nearly or quite as well as another; if a high one, individual excellence is to be regarded. Any man can stop a hole to keep the wind away,[16] but no other man could serve so rare a use as the author of this illus-tration[17] did. Confucius[18] says, "The skins of the tiger and the leopard, when they are tanned, are as the skins of the dog and the sheep tanned." But it is not the part of a true culture to tame tigers, any more than it is to make sheep ferocious; and tanning their skins for shoes is not the best use to which they can be put. . . .

I would not have every man nor every part of a man cultivated, any   20
more than I would have every acre of earth cultivated: part will be tillage,[19] but the greater part will be meadow and forest, not only serving an immedi-ate use, but preparing a mould against a distant future, by the annual decay of the vegetation which it supports.

There are other letters for the child to learn than those which Cadmus[20] invented. The Spaniards have a good term to express this wild and dusky knowledge, *Gramática parda*, tawny grammar, a kind of mother-wit derived from that same leopard to which I have referred.

We have heard of a Society for the Diffusion of Useful Knowledge. It is said that knowledge is power; and the like. Methinks there is equal need of a Society for the Diffusion of Useful Ignorance, what we will call Beautiful Knowledge, a knowledge useful in a higher sense: for what is most of our boasted so-called knowledge but a conceit that we know something, which robs us of the advantage of our actual ignorance? What we call knowledge is often our positive ignorance; ignorance our negative knowledge. By long years of patient industry and reading of the newspapers, — for what are the libraries of science but files of newspapers? — a man accumulates a myriad facts, lays them up in his memory, and then when in some spring of his life he saunters abroad into the Great Fields of thought, he, as it were, goes to grass like a horse and leaves all his harness behind in the stable. I would say to the Society for the Diffusion of Useful Knowledge, sometimes, — Go to grass. You have eaten hay long enough. The spring has come with its green

---

[16]*stop a hole to keep the wind away:* William Shakespeare (1564–1616), *Hamlet*, act 5, scene 1: "Imperious Caesar, dead and turn'd to clay, / Might stop a hole to keep the wind away."

[17]*the author of this illustration:* Refers to Shakespeare.

[18]*Confucius:* Chinese thinker and philosopher (551–479 B.C.E.).

[19]*tillage:* Plowed soil.

[20]*Cadmus:* In Greek mythology, a prince who introduced the Phoenician alphabet to Greece.

crop. The very cows are driven to their country pastures before the end of May; though I have heard of one unnatural farmer who kept his cow in the barn and fed her on hay all the year round. So, frequently, the Society for the Diffusion of Useful Knowledge treats its cattle.

A man's ignorance sometimes is not only useful, but beautiful, — while his knowledge, so called, is oftentimes worse than useless, besides being ugly. Which is the best man to deal with, — he who knows nothing about a subject, and, what is extremely rare, knows that he knows nothing, or he who really knows something about it, but thinks that he knows all?

My desire for knowledge is intermittent; but my desire to bathe my head in atmospheres unknown to my feet is perennial and constant. The highest that we can attain to is not Knowledge, but Sympathy with Intelligence. I do not know that this higher knowledge amounts to anything more definite than a novel and grand surprise on a sudden revelation of the insufficiency of all that we called Knowledge before, — a discovery that there are more things in heaven and earth[21] than are dreamed of in our philosophy. It is the lighting up of the mist by the sun. Man cannot *know* in any higher sense than this, any more than he can look serenely and with impunity in the face of the sun. . . .

There is something servile in the habit of seeking after a law which we may obey. We may study the laws of matter at and for our convenience, but a successful life knows no law. It is an unfortunate discovery certainly, that of a law which binds us where we did not know before that we were bound. Live free, child of the mist, — and with respect to knowledge we are all children of the mist. The man who takes the liberty to live is superior to all the laws, by virtue of his relation to the law-maker. "That is active duty," says the Vishnu Purana,[22] "which is not for our bondage; that is knowledge which is for our liberation: all other duty is good only unto weariness; all other knowledge is only the cleverness of an artist." . . .

We hug the earth, — how rarely we mount! Methinks we might elevate ourselves a little more. We might climb a tree, at least. I found my account in climbing a tree once. It was a tall white pine, on the top of a hill; and though I got well pitched, I was well paid for it, for I discovered new mountains in the horizon which I had never seen before, — so much more of the earth and the heavens. I might have walked about the foot of the tree for three-score years and ten, and yet I certainly should never have seen them. But, above all, I discovered around me, — it was near the end of June, — on the ends of the topmost branches only, a few minute and delicate red cone-like blossoms, the fertile flower of the white pine looking heavenward. I carried straightway to the village the topmost spire, and showed it to stranger

25

---

[21]*more things in heaven and earth: Hamlet,* act 5, scene 1.

[22]*Vishnu Purana:* One of eighteen Puranas, Hindu religious texts that tell the story of creation among other topics.

jurymen who walked the streets, — for it was court-week, — and to farmers and lumber-dealers and wood-choppers and hunters, and not one had ever seen the like before, but they wondered as at a star dropped down. Tell of ancient architects finishing their works on the tops of columns as perfectly as on the lower and more visible parts! Nature has from the first expanded the minute blossoms of the forest only toward the heavens, above men's heads and unobserved by them. We see only the flowers that are under our feet in the meadows. The pines have developed their delicate blossoms on the highest twigs of the wood every summer for ages, as well over the heads of Nature's red children as of her white ones; yet scarcely a farmer or hunter in the land has ever seen them. . . .

We had a remarkable sunset one day last November. I was walking in a meadow, the source of a small brook, when the sun at last, just before setting, after a cold gray day, reached a clear stratum in the horizon, and the softest, brightest morning sunlight fell on the dry grass and on the stems of the trees in the opposite horizon and on the leaves of the shrub-oaks on the hillside, while our shadows stretched long over the meadow eastward, as if we were the only motes in its beams.[23] It was such a light as we could not have imagined a moment before, and the air also was so warm and serene that nothing was wanting to make a paradise of that meadow. When we reflected that this was not a solitary phenomenon, never to happen again, but that it would happen forever and ever an infinite number of evenings, and cheer and reassure the latest child that walked there, it was more glorious still.

The sun sets on some retired meadow, where no house is visible, with all the glory and splendor that it lavishes on cities, and perchance as it has never set before, — where there is but a solitary marsh-hawk to have his wings gilded by it, or only a musquash[24] looks out from his cabin, and there is some little black-veined brook in the midst of the marsh, just beginning to meander, winding slowly round a decaying stump. We walked in so pure and bright a light, gilding the withered grass and leaves, so softly and serenely bright, I thought I had never bathed in such a golden flood, without a ripple or a murmur to it. The west side of every wood and rising ground gleamed like the boundary of Elysium,[25] and the sun on our backs seemed like a gentle herdsman driving us home at evening.

So we saunter toward the Holy Land,[26] till one day the sun shall shine more brightly than ever he has done, shall perchance shine into our minds

---

[23]*motes in its beams:* An allusion to Matthew 7:3 from the King James version of the Christian Bible: "And why beholdest thou the mote [speck] that is in thy brother's eye, but considerest not the beam that is in thine own eye?"

[24]*musquash:* Muskrat.

[25]*Elysium:* In Greek mythology, the final resting place for the souls of heroic warriors, often depicted as a natural paradise.

[26]*Holy Land:* In the Hebrew Bible, the area in and around Jerusalem, also known as the Land of Canaan, which God promised to the descendants of Abraham.

and hearts, and light up our whole lives with a great awakening light, as warm and serene and golden as on a bankside in autumn.

ENGAGING THE TEXT

1. Where and why does Thoreau walk? Have you ever taken walks like this? What purpose did they serve for you?

2. Why does Thoreau prefer to walk toward the West? What do East and West symbolize for him?

3. Why are wilderness and wildness important for Thoreau? To what extent would you agree that "The most alive is the wildest" (para. 15), that most people are "tame by inherited disposition" (para. 19)?

4. In the opening paragraph of *Walking*, Thoreau says that he wishes "to make an extreme statement." Which of his many claims in this essay about nature, human beings, and civilization strike you as particularly "extreme"? Why?

EXPLORING CONNECTIONS

5. What similarities can you find between the views of John Taylor Gatto (p. 148) and those of Thoreau on society, conformity, and formal education? If Thoreau were to create a school, what do you imagine it would be like?

6. Given his assessment of America as an "Idiot Nation" (p. 128), how might Michael Moore view Thoreau's assertion that "A man's ignorance sometimes is not only useful, but beautiful" (para. 23)?

7. To what extent might R. Crumb's "A Short History of America" (p. 695) be seen as a contemporary response or rebuttal to *Walking*? Do you think that today it is still possible to walk in nature the way Thoreau describes in this selection?

EXTENDING THE CRITICAL CONTEXT

8. Working in groups, survey images of nature in popular culture. To what extent is Thoreau's vision of nature as a source of freedom still with us today?

9. Conduct brief interviews with three to five fellow students or friends outside of class to learn what nature and wilderness mean to them. Share the results of your informal research in class, and discuss how contemporary views of nature and wilderness compare to Thoreau's views.

10. Visit any of the many Web sites dedicated to Thoreau and transcendentalism to learn more about the American transcendentalist movement, including:

   www.thoreau-online.org/other-essays-by-thoreau.htm
   http://thoreau.eserver.org/
   www.transcendentalists.com/

Compare your findings in class and discuss which aspects of Thoreau's views of nature and wilderness seem to reflect transcendentalist thinking most closely.

From *An American Childhood*

Annie Dillard

> *Most of us remember an early childhood experience of being alone in*
> *nature. It doesn't really matter if it was on a family camping trip, in the back-*
> *yard of an abandoned neighborhood house, or in a city park. Nature speaks*
> *directly to children, and early experiences of the natural world often form*
> *the core of some of our most powerful childhood memories. In* An American
> Childhood *(1987), Pulitzer prize–winning essayist, novelist, and poet Annie*
> *Dillard (b. 1945) tells the story of her own formative experiences in nature as*
> *she grew up during the 1950s in Pittsburgh, Pennsylvania. Dillard's childhood*
> *adventures in Frick Park and her early passion for insect collecting echo the*
> *experiences of generations of Americans who have discovered essential parts*
> *of themselves as they explored the natural world. Dillard's many publications*
> *include* Pilgrim at Tinker Creek *(1974),* Teaching a Stone to Talk *(1982),* For
> the Time Being *(1999), and* The Maytrees *(2007).*

I walked. My mother had given me the freedom of the streets as soon as
I could say our telephone number. I walked and memorized the neighborhood. I made a mental map and located myself upon it. At night in bed I
rehearsed the small world's scheme and set challenges: Find the store using
backyards only. Imagine a route from the school to my friend's house. I mastered chunks of town in one direction only; I ignored the other direction,
toward the Catholic church.

On a bicycle I traveled over the known world's edge, and the ground
held. I was seven. I had fallen in love with a red-haired fourth-grade boy
named Walter Milligan. He was tough, Catholic, from an iffy neighborhood.
Two blocks beyond our school was a field — Miss Frick's field, behind Henry
Clay Frick's mansion[1] — where boys played football. I parked my bike on the
sidelines and watched Walter Milligan play. As he ran up and down the length
of the field, following the football, I ran up and down the sidelines, following
him. After the game I rode my bike home, delirious. It was the closest we had
been, and the farthest I had traveled from home.

(My love lasted two years and occasioned a bit of talk. I knew it angered
him. We spoke only once. I caught him between classes in the school's
crowded hall and said, "I'm sorry." He looked away, apparently enraged; his
pale freckled skin flushed. He jammed his fists in his pockets, looked down,

---

[1]*Henry Clay Frick's mansion:* In 1919, industrialist Henry Clay Frick (1849–1919) be-
queathed his Point Breeze mansion and 150 acres of land to create Pittsburgh's Frick Park.

looked at me for a second, looked away, and brought out gently, "That's okay." That was the whole of it: beginning, middle, and end.)

Across the street from Walter Milligan's football field was Frick Park. Frick Park was 380 acres of woods in residential Pittsburgh. Only one trail crossed it; the gravelly walk gave way to dirt and led down a forested ravine to a damp streambed. If you followed the streambed all day you would find yourself in a distant part of town reached ordinarily by a long streetcar ride. Near Frick Park's restful entrance, old men and women from other neighborhoods were lawn bowling on the bowling green. The rest of the park was wild woods.

My father forbade me to go to Frick Park. He said bums lived there under bridges; they had been hanging around unnoticed since the Depression. My father was away all day; my mother said I could go to Frick Park if I never mentioned it. 5

I roamed Frick Park for many years. Our family moved from house to house, but we never moved so far I couldn't walk to Frick Park. I watched the men and women lawn bowling — so careful the players, so dull the game. After I got a bird book I found, in the deep woods, a downy woodpecker working a tree trunk; the woodpecker looked like a jackhammer man banging Edgerton Avenue to bits. I saw sparrows, robins, cardinals, juncos, chipmunks, squirrels, and — always disappointingly, emerging from their magnificent ruckus in the leaves — pedigreed dachshunds, which a woman across the street bred.

I never met anyone in the woods except the woman who walked her shiny dachshunds there, but I was cautious, and hoped I was braving danger. If a bum came after me I would disarm him with courtesy ("Good afternoon"). I would sneak him good food from home; we would bake potatoes together under his bridge; he would introduce me to his fellow bums; we would all feed the squirrels.

The deepest ravine, over which loomed the Forbes Avenue bridge, was called Fern Hollow. There in winter I searched for panther tracks in snow. In summer and fall I imagined the woods extending infinitely. I was the first human being to see these shadowed trees, this land; I would make my pioneer clearing here, near the water. Mine would be one of those famously steep farms: "How'd you get so beat up?" "Fell out of my cornfield." In spring I pried flat rocks from the damp streambed and captured red and black salamanders. I brought the salamanders home in a bag once and terrified my mother with them by mistake, when she was on the phone.

In the fall I walked to collect buckeyes from lawns. Buckeyes were wealth. A ripe buckeye husk splits. It reveals the shining brown sphere inside only partially, as an eyelid only partially discloses an eye's sphere. The nut so revealed looks like the calm brown eye of a buck, apparently. It was odd to imagine the settlers who named it having seen more male deer's eyes in the forest than nuts on a lawn.

Walking was my project before reading. The text I read was the town; 10
the book I made up was a map. First I had walked across one of our side yards to the blackened alley with its buried dime. Now I walked to piano lessons, four long blocks north of school and three zigzag blocks into an Irish neighborhood near Thomas Boulevard.

I pushed at my map's edges. Alone at night I added newly memorized streets and blocks to old streets and blocks, and imagined connecting them on foot. From my parents' earliest injunctions I felt that my life depended on keeping it all straight — remembering where on earth I lived, that is, in relation to where I had walked. It was dead reckoning. On darkening evenings I came home exultant, secretive, often from some exotic leafy curb a mile beyond what I had known at lunch, where I had peered up at the street sign, hugging the cold pole, and fixed the intersection in my mind. What joy, what relief, eased me as I pushed open the heavy front door! — joy and relief because, from the very trackless waste, I had located home, family, and the dinner table once again.

An infant watches her hands and feels them move. Gradually she fixes her own boundaries at the complex incurved rim of her skin. Later she touches one palm to another and tries for a game to distinguish each hand's sensation of feeling and being felt. What is a house but a bigger skin, and a neighborhood map but the world's skin ever expanding? . . .

Young children have no sense of wonder. They bewilder well, but few things surprise them. All of it is new to young children, after all, and equally gratuitous. Their parents pause at the unnecessary beauty of an ice storm coating the trees; the children look for something to throw. The children who tape colorful fall leaves to the schoolroom windows and walls are humoring the teacher. The busy teacher halts on her walk to school and stoops to pick up fine bright leaves "to show the children" — but it is she, now in her sixties, who is increasingly stunned by the leaves, their brightness all so much trash that litters the gutter.

This year at the Ellis School my sister Amy was in the fifth grade, with Mrs. McVicker. I remembered Mrs. McVicker fondly. Every year she reiterated the familiar (and, without a description of their mechanisms, the sentimental) mysteries that schoolchildren hear so often and so indifferently: that each snowflake is different, that some birds fly long distances, that acorns grow into oaks. Caterpillars turn into butterflies. The stars are large and very far away. She struck herself like a gong with these same mallets every year — a sweet old schoolteacher whom we in our time had loved and tolerated for her innocence.

Now that I was an aging veteran of thirteen or so, I was becoming case-softened myself. Imperceptibly I had shed my indifference. I was getting positively old: the hatching of wet robins in the spring moved me. I saw them from the school library window, as if on an educational film: a robin sprawled on a nest in the oak, and four miserable hatchlings appeared. They peeped. I knew this whole story; who didn't? Nevertheless I took to checking on the robins a few times a day. Their mother rammed worms and bugs down their throats; they grew feathers and began to hop up and down in the nest. Bit by bit they flew away; I saw them from the schoolyard taking test flights under the oak. Glory be, I thought during all those weeks, hallelujah, and never told a soul. . . .

Everywhere, things snagged me. The visible world turned me curious to books; the books propelled me reeling back to the world.

At school I saw a searing sight. It turned me to books; it turned me to jelly; it turned me much later, I suppose, into an early version of a runaway, a scapegrace. It was only a freshly hatched Polyphemus moth crippled because its mason jar was too small.

The mason jar sat on the teacher's desk; the big moth emerged inside it. The moth had clawed a hole in its hot cocoon and crawled out, as if agonizingly, over the course of an hour, one leg at a time; we children watched around the desk, transfixed. After it emerged, the wet, mashed thing turned around walking on the green jar's bottom, then painstakingly climbed the twig with which the jar was furnished.

There, at the twig's top, the moth shook its sodden clumps of wings. When it spread those wings — those beautiful wings — blood would fill their veins, and the birth fluids on the wings' frail sheets would harden to make them tough as sails. But the moth could not spread its wide wings at all; the jar was too small. The wings could not fill, so they hardened while they were still crumpled from the cocoon. A smaller moth could have spread its wings to their utmost in that mason jar, but the Polyphemus moth was big. Its gold furred body was almost as big as a mouse. Its brown, yellow, pink, and blue wings would have extended six inches from tip to tip, if there had been no mason jar. It would have been big as a wren.

The teacher let the deformed creature go. We all left the classroom and paraded outside behind the teacher with pomp and circumstance. She bounced the moth from its jar and set it on the school's asphalt driveway. The moth set out walking. It could only heave the golden wrinkly clumps where its wings should have been; it could only crawl down the school driveway on its six frail legs. The moth crawled down the driveway toward the rest of Shadyside, an area of fine houses, expensive apartments, and fashionable shops. It crawled down the driveway because its shriveled wings were glued shut. It crawled down the driveway toward Shadyside, one of several sections of town where people like me were expected to settle after college, renting an apartment until they married one of the boys and bought a house. I watched it go.

I knew that this particular moth, the big walking moth, could not travel more than a few more yards before a bird or a cat began to eat it, or a car ran over it. Nevertheless, it was crawling with what seemed wonderful vigor, as if, I thought at the time, it was still excited from being born. I watched it go till the bell rang and I had to go in. I have told this story before, and may yet tell it again, to lay the moth's ghost, for I still see it crawl down the broad black driveway, and I still see its golden wing clumps heave.

I had not suspected, among other things, that moths came so big. From a school library book I learned there were several such enormous American moths, all wild silk moths which spun cocoons, and all common.

Gene Stratton Porter's old *Moths of the Limberlost* caught my eye; for some years after I read it, it was my favorite book. From one of its queer painted photographs I learned what the Polyphemus moth would have looked like whole: it was an unexpected sort of beauty, brown and wild. It had pink stripes, lavender crescents, yellow ovals — all sorts of odd colors no one would think to combine. Enormous blue eye-spots stared eerily from its hind wings. Coincidentally, it was in the Polyphemus chapter that the book explained how a hatched moth must spread its wings quickly, and fill them with blood slowly, before it can fly.

Gene Stratton Porter had been a vigorous, loving kid who grew up long ago near a swampy wilderness of Indiana, and had worked up a whole memorable childhood out of insects, of all things, which I had never even noticed, and my childhood was half over.

When she was just a tot, she learned how entomologists carry living moths and butterflies without damaging them. She commonly carried a moth

20

25

or butterfly home from her forest and swamp wanderings by lightly compressing its thorax between thumb and index finger. The insect stops moving but is not hurt; when you let it go, it flies away.

One day, after years of searching, she found a yellow swallowtail. This is not the common tiger swallowtail butterfly, but *Papilio turnus:* "the largest, most beautiful butterfly I had ever seen." She held it carefully in the air, its wings high over the back of her fingers. She wanted to show the fragile, rare creature to her father and then carry it back to precisely where she found it. But she was only a child, and so she came running home with it instead of walking. She tripped, and her fingers pinched through the butterfly's thorax. She broke it to pieces. And that was that. It was like one of Father's bar jokes.

There was a terror connected with moths that attracted and repelled me. I would face down the terror. I continued reading about moths, and branched out to other insects.

I liked the weird horned beetles rumbling along everywhere, even at the country club, whose names were stag, elephant, rhinoceros. They were so big I could hear them walk; their sharp legs scraped along the poolside concrete. I liked the comical true bugs, like the red-and-blue-striped leafhoppers, whose legs looked like yellow plastic; they hopped on roses in the garden at home. At Lake Erie I watched the solitary wasps that hunted along the beach path; they buried their paralyzed caterpillar prey in holes they dug so vigorously the sand flew. I even liked the dull little two-winged insects, the diptera, because this order contained mosquitoes, about several species of which I knew something because they bore interesting diseases. I studied under the microscope our local mosquitoes in various stages — a hairy lot — dipped in a cup from Molly's wading pool.

To collect insects I equipped myself with the usual paraphernalia: glass-headed pins, a net, and a killing jar. It was insects in jars again — but unlike the hapless teacher who put the big moth's cocoon in the little mason jar, I knew, I thought, what I was doing. In the bottom of the killing jar — formerly a pickle jar — I laid a wad of cotton soaked in cleaning fluid containing carbon tetrachloride, which compound I thrilled myself by calling, offhandedly, "carbon tet." A circle of old door screen prevented the insects' tangling in the cotton. I placed each insect on the screen and quickly tightened the jar lid. Then, as if sensitively, I looked away. After a suitable interval I poured out the dead thing as carefully as I could, and pinned it and its festive, bunting-like row of fluttering labels in a cigar box. My grandfather had saved the cigar boxes, one for each order of insect; they smelled both sharp and sweet, of cedar and leaf tobacco. I pinned the insects in rows, carefully driving the pins through chitinous thoraxes just where the books indicated. Four beetles I collected were so big they had a cigar box to themselves.

Once I returned to my attic bedroom after four weeks at summer camp. There, beside the detective table, under the plaster-stain ship, was the insect collection, a stack of cigar boxes. I checked the boxes. In the big beetles' cigar box I found a rhinoceros beetle crawling on its pin. The pin entered the beetle through that triangle in the thorax between the wing-cover tops; it emerged ventrally above and between the legs. The big black beetle's six legs hung down waving in the air, well above the floor of the cigar box. It crawled and never got anywhere. It must have been pretty dehydrated; the attic was hot. Presumably the beetle's legs had been waving in the air like that in search of a footing for the past four weeks.

I hated insects; that was the fact. I never caught my stamp collection trying to crawl away.

Butterflies die with folded wings. Before they're mounted, butterflies require an elaborate chemical treatment to relax their dead muscles, a bit more every day, so you can spread their brittle wings without shattering them. After a few grueling starts at this relaxing and spreading of dead butterflies, I avoided it. When on rare occasions I killed butterflies, I stuck them away somewhere and forgot about them.

One hot evening I settled on my bed in my summer nightgown with a novel I had looked forward to reading. I lay back, opened the book, and a dead butterfly dropped headfirst on my bare neck. I jumped up, my skin crawling, and it slid down my nightgown. Somehow it stuck to my sweaty skin; when I brushed at it — whooping aloud — it fragmented, and pieces stuck to my hands and rained down on the floor. Most of the dead butterfly, which still looked as if it were demurely praying while falling apart, with folded yellow wings in shreds and a blasted black body, fell out on my foot. I brushed broken antennae and snapped legs from my neck; I wiped a glittering yellow dust of wing scales from my belly, and they stuck to my palm.

I hated insects; that I knew. Fingering insects was touching the rim of nightmare. But you have to study something. I never considered turning away from them just because I was afraid of them.

I liked their invisibility; they did not matter, so they did not exist.   35
People's nervous systems edited out the sight of insects before it reached their brains; my seeing insects let me live alongside human society in a different sensory world, just as insects themselves do. That I collected specimens at the country-club pool pleased me; I did not really mind that my friends turned bilious when I showed them my prizes. I loved the sport of catching butterflies; they took bad hops, like aerial grounders. (I did not know then that the truly athletic, life-loving entomologists study dragonflies, which are fantastically difficult to catch — fast, sharp-eyed, hard to outwit.) Cringing, I taught myself to paralyze butterflies through the net, holding them lightly at the thorax as Gene Stratton Porter had done. I brought them out of the net and let them fly away — lest they fall on me dead later.

How confidently I had overlooked all this — rocks, bugs, rain. What else was I missing?

I opened books like jars. Here between my hands, here between some book's front and back covers, whose corners poked dents in my palm, was another map to the neighborhood I had explored all my life, and fancied I knew, a map depicting hitherto invisible landmarks. After I learned to see those, I looked around for something else. I never knew where my next revelation was coming from, but I knew it was coming — some hairpin curve, some stray bit of romance or information that would turn my life around in a twinkling.

ENGAGING THE TEXT

1. What does wandering in Frick Park mean to Dillard? What does she learn there about nature and what fantasies do her excursions there awaken?
2. What does Dillard learn about nature and human beings through her encounter with the Polyphemous moth?
3. What fascinates Dillard about insects? Why does she collect them? To what extent do you think her early attitudes toward the natural world are typical of American children?

EXPLORING CONNECTIONS

4. How do Dillard's early experiences with nature confirm or complicate Henry David Thoreau's vision of nature and nature's meaning (p. 646)? Which of these authors' experiences with nature resonates more closely with your own? Why?
5. Which panel of R. Crumb's "A Short History of America" (pp. 695–98) do you think best fits the era of Dillard's childhood experiences? To what extent, if any, have childhood encounters with the natural world changed since that time?

EXTENDING THE CRITICAL CONTEXT

6. Draw your own set of childhood "neighborhood maps" — one capturing your world when you were roughly seven years old and another when you were about twelve. Compare these sketches in groups and discuss what they reveal about your own early experiences with nature. To what extent do your early experiences in nature echo those of Thoreau and Dillard?
7. Much of Dillard's early knowledge of nature comes from books. Which nature books do you recall most vividly from your own childhood? What did you learn from them? To what extent do you think children today learn about nature through direct experience or through the kinds of "mediated" experiences provided by books, films, and television programming?

A Life of the Senses

RICHARD LOUV

According to legend, long before he became the twenty-sixth president of the United States, the young Teddy Roosevelt was a sickly boy who suffered from asthma and poor general health. To build himself up, Roosevelt began a regimen of strenuous physical exercise and eventually became an avid sports enthusiast and outdoorsman. During his twenties, Roosevelt's love of nature took him back again and again to what was then the Dakota Territory. There, on the two ranches he owned throughout his life, "TR" learned to hunt buffalo and rubbed shoulders with backwoodsmen and other "rough and ready" characters. Since Roosevelt's time, the idea of nature as a source of health has been a staple of American cultural lore that's inspired movements from the Boy Scouts to Outward Bound. Today, as Richard Louv suggests in this selection, scientists are confirming the long-held American belief that children need personal experience of the natural world for healthy physical and mental development. Louv (b. 1949) is a journalist, media commentator, and author of seven works of nonfiction, including Fly-Fishing for Sharks: An American Journey *(2000) and* Last Child in the Woods: Saving Our Children from Nature Deficit Disorder *(2005), the source of this selection.*

> I go to nature to be soothed and healed,
> and to have my senses put in tune once more.
> — JOHN BURROUGHS

Children need nature for the healthy development of their senses, and, therefore, for learning and creativity. This need is revealed in two ways: by an examination of what happens to the senses of the young when they lose connection with nature, and by witnessing the sensory magic that occurs when young people — even those beyond childhood — are exposed to even the smallest direct experience of a natural setting.

The Boyz of the Woods

In just a few weeks, a group of boyz of the hood[1] become the boyz of the woods. At the Crestridge Ecological Reserve, 2,600 acres of mountainous California between the cities of El Cajon and Alpine, a dozen members of the Urban Corps, ages eighteen to twenty-five — all but one of them male, all of

---

[1]*boyz of the hood:* A reference to *Boyz in the Hood*, a 1991 film depicting Los Angeles gang life.

them Hispanic — follow two middle-aged Anglo women — park docents — through sage and patches of wild berries.

As members of the city-sponsored Urban Corps, they attend a charter school that emphasizes hands-on conservation work. They've spent the past few weeks at the nature preserve clearing trails, pulling out non-native plants, learning the art of tracking from a legendary former Border Patrol officer, and experiencing a sometimes baffling explosion of senses. The young people wear uniforms: light-green shirts, dark-green pants, military-style canvas belts. One of the docents wears a blue sunbonnet, the other a baggy T-shirt and day pack.

"Here we have the home of the dusky-footed wood rat," says Andrea Johnson, a docent who lives on a ridge overlooking this land.

She points at a mound of sticks tucked under poison oak. A wood rat's   5
nest looks something like a beaver's lodge; it contains multiple chambers, including specialized indoor latrines and areas where leaves are stored to get rid of toxins before eating. The nests can be as tall as six feet. Wood rats tend to have houseguests, Johnson explains. "Kissing bugs! Oh my, yes," she says. Kissing bugs, a.k.a. the blood-sucking assassin bug.

"This is one reason you might not want a wood-rat nest near your house. Kissing bugs are attracted to carbon dioxide, which we all exhale. Consequently, the kissing bug likes to bite people around their mouths," Johnson continues, fanning herself in the morning heat. "The bite eats away the flesh; my husband has a *big scar* on his face."

One of the Urban Corpsmen shudders so hard that his pants, fashionably belted far to the south of his hips, try to head farther south.

Leaving the wood-rat's lair, the docents lead the Urban Corps members through clusters of California fuchsia and laurel sumac into cool woods where a spring seeps into a little creek. Carlos, a husky six-footer with earrings and shaved head, leaps nimbly from rock to rock, his eyes filled with wonder. He whispers exclamations in Spanish as he crouches over a two-inch-long tarantula hawk, a wasp with orange wings, dark-blue body, and a sting considered one of the most painful of any North American insect. This wasp is no Rotarian; it will attack and paralyze a tarantula five times its size, drag it underground, plant a single egg, and seal the chamber on its way out. Later, the egg hatches into a grub that eats the spider alive. Nature is beautiful, but not always pretty.

Several of the young men spent their early childhood in rural Central America or on Mexican farms. Carlos, who now works as a brake technician, describes his grandmother's farm in Sinaloa, Mexico. "She had pigs, man. She had land. It was fine." Despite their current urban habitats, these young first- and second-generation immigrants experienced nature more directly when they were small children than have most North Americans. "In Mexico, people know how hard it is to own a piece of land up here, so they value it. They take care of it. People who live on this side of the border don't value land so much. Take it for granted. Too much cream on the taco, or something."

But right now the boyz of the woods aren't so serious. They begin to tease a nineteen-year-old with a shy grin and a hickey the size of a tarantula hawk.

"He's been sleepin' with his window open again," someone says. "Blair Witch² got him."

"Nah, man," says Carlos, laughing, "*Chupacabras* chewed him," referring to Latin America's half-bat, half-kangaroo, razor-clawed, goat-sucking mythological beast, most recently reported in Argentina. Or maybe it was just the kissing bug.

Over the weeks, Carlos has observed closely and sketches the plants and animals in notebooks. Along with the other students, he has watched a bobcat stalk game, heard the sudden percussion of disturbed rattlesnake dens, and felt a higher music. "When I come here, I can *exhale*," says Carlos. "Here, you *hear* things; in the city, you can't hear anything because you can hear everything. In the city, everything is *obvious*. Here, you get closer and you see more."

Losing Our Senses

Not that long ago, the sound track of a young person's days and nights was composed largely of the notes of nature. Most people were raised on the land, worked the land, and were often buried on the same land. The relationship was direct.

Today, the life of the senses is, literally, electrified. One obvious contributor is electronics: television and computers. But simpler, early technologies played important roles. Air-conditioning, for example: the U.S. Census Bureau reports that in 1910, only 12 percent of housing had air-conditioning. People threw open their sash windows and let in night air and the sound of wind in leaves. By the time the baby boomers came along, approximately half our homes were air-conditioned. By 1970, that figure was 72 percent, and by 2001, 78 percent.

In 1920, most farms were miles from a city of any size. Even by 1935, fewer than 12 percent of America's farms had electricity (compared to 85 percent of urban homes); not until the mid-1940s were even half of all U.S. farm homes electrified. In the 1920s, farmers gathered at feed stores or cotton gins to listen to the radio, or created their own wired networks by connecting several homes to a single radio. In 1949, only 36 percent of farms had telephone service.

Few of us are about to trade our air conditioners for fans. But one price of progress is seldom mentioned: a diminished life of the senses. Like the boyz of the hood, as human beings we need direct, natural experiences; we require fully activated senses in order to feel fully alive. Twenty-first-century Western culture accepts the view that because of omnipresent technology we are awash in data. But in this information age, vital information is missing.

²*Blair Witch: The Blair Witch Project* was a 1999 American horror film.

Nature is about smelling, hearing, tasting, seeing below the "transparent mucous-paper in which the world like a bon-bon is wrapped so carefully that we can never get at it," as D. H. Lawrence[3] put it, in a relatively obscure but extraordinary description of his own awakening to nature's sensory gift. Lawrence described his awakening in Taos, New Mexico, as an antidote to the "know-it-all state of mind," that poor substitute for wisdom and wonder:

> Superficially, the world has become small and known. Poor little globe of earth, the tourists trot round you as easily as they trot round the Bois or round Central Park. There is no mystery left, we've been there, we've seen it, we know all about it. We've done the globe and the globe is done.
>
> This is quite true, superficially. On the superficies, horizontally, we've been everywhere and done everything, we know all about it. Yet the more we know, superficially, the less we penetrate, vertically. It's all very well skimming across the surface of the ocean and saying you know all about the sea. . . .
>
> As a matter of fact, our great-grandfathers, who never went anywhere, in actuality had more experience of the world than we have, who have seen everything. When they listened to a lecture with lantern-slides,[4] they really held their breath before the unknown, as they sat in the village school-room. We, bowling along in a rickshaw in Ceylon, say to ourselves: "It's very much what you'd expect." We really know it all.
>
> We are mistaken. The know-it-all state of mind is just the result of being outside the mucous-paper wrapping of civilization. Underneath is everything we don't know and are afraid of knowing.

Some of us adults recognize the know-it-all state of mind in ourselves, sometimes at unlikely moments.

Todd Merriman, a newspaper editor and father, remembers an illuminating hike with his young son. "We were walking across a field in the mountains," he says. "I looked down and saw mountain lion tracks. They were fresh. We immediately headed back to the car, and then I saw another set of tracks. I knew they had not been there before. The lion had circled us." In that moment of dread and excitement, he became intensely aware of his surroundings. Later, he realized that he could not remember the last time he had used all of his senses so acutely. The near encounter jarred something loose.

How much of the richness of life have he and his son traded for their daily immersion in indirect, technological experience? Today, Merriman often thinks about that question — usually while he is sitting in front of a computer screen.

---

[3]*D. H. Lawrence:* David Herbert Richards Lawrence (1885–1930), English author, essayist, and literary critic.

[4]*lantern-slides:* Slides used in a "magic lantern," the nineteenth-century forerunner of the slide projector.

It doesn't take an encounter with a mountain lion for us to recognize   20
that our sensory world has shrunk. The information age is, in fact, a myth,
despite songwriter Paul Simon's[5] phrase, "These are the days of miracle and
wonder. . . . Lasers in the jungle," and all that. Our indoor life feels downsized,
as if it's lost a dimension or two. Yes, we're enamored of our gadgets — our
cell phones connected to our digital cameras connected to our laptops connected to an e-mail-spewing satellite transponder hovering somewhere over
Macon, Georgia. Of course, some of us (I include myself here) love the giz-
mology. But quality of life isn't measured only by what we gain, but also by
what we trade for it.

Instead of spending less time at the office, we work on Internet Time.
A billboard on the freeway near my home advertises an online banking service. It shows a chipper young woman in front of her computer saying, "I
expect to pay bills at 3 A.M." Electronic immersion will continue to deepen.
Researchers at the Massachusetts Institute of Technology's Media Laboratory are working to make computers invisible in the home. In New York,
architects Gisue and Mojgan Hariri promote their idea of a dream Digital
House, with walls of LCD screens.

As electronic technology surrounds us, we long for nature — even if the
nature is synthetic. Several years ago, I met Tom Wrubel, founder of the
Nature Company, the pioneering mall outlet for all things faux flora and
fauna. In the beginning, the store, which became a nationwide chain, was
aimed primarily at children. In 1973, Wrubel and his wife, Priscilla, noted a
common thread in nature-oriented retailing: the emphasis was on *getting* to
nature. "But once you got to the mountains or wherever, what do you do,
except shoot or catch things," he said. "So we emphasized books and gadgets to use in nature."

The Wrubels caught and accelerated a wave — what the Nature Company's president, Roger Bergen, called "the shift from activity-orientation in
the 1960s and 70s, to knowledge-orientation in the 80s." The Nature Company marketed nature as mood, at first to children primarily. "We go for
strong vertical stone elements, giant archways. Gives you the feeling that
you're entering Yosemite Canyon. At the entrances, we place stone creeks
with running water — but these creeks are modernistic, an architect's dream
of creekness," Tom Wrubel explained. His version of nature was both anti-
septic and whimsical. Visitors walked through the maze of products: dande-
lion blossoms preserved within crystalline domes; designer bird-feeders;
inflatable snakes and dinosaurs; bags of Nature Company natural cedar tips
from the mountains of New Mexico; "pine cones in brass cast from Actual
Cones," according to the display sign. In the air: the sounds of wind and
water, buzzing shrimp, snapping killer whales — courtesy of "The Nature
Company Presents: Nature," available on audiotape and compact disk. "Mood

---

[5]*Paul Simon:* American singer and songwriter (b. 1941).

tapes" were also available, including "Tranquility," a forty-seven-minute, musically scored video the catalog described as a "deeply calming, beautiful study in the shapes and colors of clouds, waves, unfolding blossoms and light."

Wrubel sincerely believed that his stores stimulated concern for the environment. Perhaps he was right.

Such design emphasis now permeates malls across the country. For example, Minnesota's Mall of America now has its own UnderWater World. John Beardsley, a curator who teaches at the Harvard Design School, describes this simulated natural attraction in *Earthworks and Beyond: Contemporary Art in the Landscape:* "You're in a gloomy boreal forest in the fall, descending a ramp past bubbling brooks and glass-fronted tanks stocked with freshwater fish native to the northern woodlands. At the bottom of the ramp, you step onto a moving walkway and are transported through a 300-foot-long transparent tunnel carved into a 1.2-million-gallon aquarium. All around you are the creatures of a succession of ecosystems: the Minnesota lakes, the Mississippi River, the Gulf of Mexico, and a coral reef."

There, according to the mall's promotional line, you'll "meet sharks, rays, and other exotic creatures face to face." This "piece of concocted nature," as Beardsley terms it, "is emblematic of a larger phenomenon." Beardsley calls it the growing "commodification of nature: the increasingly pervasive commercial trend that views and uses nature as a sales gimmick or marketing strategy, often through the production of replicas or simulations." This can be presented on a grand scale; more often, the commodification of nature occurs in smaller, subtler ways. As Beardsley points out, this phenomenon is new only in scale and to the degree that it permeates everyday life. "For at least five centuries — since the fifteenth-century Franciscan monk Fra Bernardino Caimi reproduced the shrines of the Holy Land at Sacro Monte in Varallo, Italy, for the benefit of pilgrims unable to travel to Jerusalem — replicas of sacred places, especially caves and holy mountains, have attracted the devout," he writes. The 1915 Panama-Pacific International Exposition in San Francisco included a small railroad, according to Beardsley, that "featured fabricated elephants, a replica of Yellowstone National Park complete with working geysers, and a mock-up Hopi village." But now, "almost everywhere we look, whether we see it or not, commodity culture is reconstructing nature. Synthetic rocks, video images of forests, Rainforest Cafés."

Mall and retail design is one way to package nature for commercial purposes, but the next stage goes a step further by using nature itself as an advertising medium. Researchers at the State University of New York at Buffalo are experimenting with a genetic technology through which they can choose the colors that appear on butterfly wings. The announcement of this in 2002 led writer Matt Richtel to conjure a brave new advertising medium: "There are countless possibilities for moving ads out of the virtual world and into the real one. Sponsorship-wise, it's time for nature to carry its weight." Advertisers already stamp their messages into the wet sands of

25

public beaches. Cash-strapped municipalities hope corporations agree to affix their company logo on parks in exchange for dollars to keep the public spaces maintained. "The sheer popularity" of simulating nature or using nature as ad space "demands that we acknowledge, even respect, their cultural importance," suggests Richtel. Culturally important, yes. But the logical extension of synthetic nature is the irrelevance of "true" nature — the certainty that it's not even worth looking at.

True, our experience of natural landscape "often occurs within an automobile looking out," as Elaine Brooks said. But now even that visual connection is optional. A friend of mine was shopping for a new luxury car to celebrate her half-century of survival in the material world. She settled on a Mercedes SUV, with a Global Positioning System: just tap in your destination and the vehicle not only provides a map on the dashboard screen, but talks you there. But she knew where to draw the line. "The salesman's jaw dropped when I said I didn't want a backseat television monitor for my daughter," she told me. "He almost refused to let me leave the dealership until he could understand why." Rear-seat and in-dash "multimedia entertainment products" as they are called, are quickly becoming the hottest add-on since rearview mirror fuzzy dice. The target market: parents who will pay a premium for a little backseat peace. Sales are brisk; the prices are falling. Some systems include wireless, infrared-connected headsets. The children can watch *Sesame Street* or play Grand Theft Auto on their PlayStation without bothering the driver.

Why do so many Americans say they want their children to watch less TV, yet continue to expand the opportunities for them to watch it? More important, why do so many people no longer consider the physical world worth watching? The highway's edges may not be postcard perfect. But for a century, children's early understanding of how cities and nature fit together was gained from the backseat: the empty farmhouse at the edge of the subdivision; the variety of architecture, here and there; the woods and fields and water beyond the seamy edges — all that was and is still available to the eye. This was the landscape that we watched as children. It was our drive-by movie.

Perhaps we'll someday tell our grandchildren stories about our version   30
of the nineteenth-century Conestoga wagon.[6]

"You did *what*?" they'll ask.

"Yes," we'll say, "it's true. We actually *looked out the car window*." In our useful boredom, we used our fingers to draw pictures on fogged glass as we watched telephone poles tick by. We saw birds on the wires and combines in the fields. We were fascinated with roadkill, and we counted cows and horses and coyotes and shaving-cream signs. We stared with a kind of reverence at the horizon, as thunderheads and dancing rain moved with us.

---

[6]*Conestoga wagon:* The type of heavy "covered wagon" used by settlers in the American West.

We held our little plastic cars against the glass and pretended that they, too, were racing toward some unknown destination. We considered the past and dreamed of the future, and watched it all go by in the blink of an eye.

> Soap
> May do
> For lads with fuzz
> But sir, you ain't
> the kid you wuz
> *Burma-Shave.*[7]

Is roadside America really so boring today? In some stretches, yes, but all the others are instructive in their beauty, even in their ugliness. Hugh A. Mulligan, in an Associated Press story about rail travel, quoted novelist John Cheever's[8] recollection of the "peaceable landscape" once seen by suburban rail commuters: "It seemed to me that fishermen and lone bathers and grade-crossing watchmen and sandlot ballplayers and owners of small sailing craft and old men playing pinochle in firehouses were the people who stitched up the big holes in the world made by people like me." Such images still exist, even in this malled America. There is a real world, beyond the glass, for children who look, for those whose parents encourage them to truly see.

The Rise of Cultural Autism

In the most nature-deprived corners of our world we can see the rise of what might be called cultural autism. The symptoms? Tunneled senses, and feelings of isolation and containment. Experience, including physical risk, is narrowing to about the size of a cathode ray tube, or flat panel if you prefer. Atrophy of the senses was occurring long before we came to be bombarded with the latest generation of computers, high-definition TV, and wireless phones. Urban children, and many suburban children, have long been isolated from the natural world because of a lack of neighborhood parks, or lack of opportunity — lack of time and money for parents who might otherwise take them out of the city. But the new technology accelerates the phenomenon. "What I see in America today is an almost religious zeal for the technological approach to every facet of life," says Daniel Yankelovich, the veteran public opinion analyst. This faith, he says, transcends mere love for new machines. "It's a value system, a way of thinking, and it can become delusional."

The late Edward Reed, an associate professor of psychology at Franklin and Marshall College, was one of the most articulate critics of the myth of   35

---

[7]*Burma-Shave:* Brand of American shaving cream famous for its early-twentieth-century advertising campaign featuring humorous rhyming verses on small, sequential highway signs.
[8]*John Cheever:* American novelist and short story writer (1912–1982).

the information age. In *The Necessity of Experience* he wrote, "There is something wrong with a society that spends so much money, as well as countless hours of human effort — to make the least dregs of processed information available to everyone everywhere and yet does little or nothing to help us explore the world for ourselves." None of our major institutions or our popular culture pay much notice to what Reed called "primary experience" — that which we can see, feel, taste, hear, or smell for ourselves. According to Reed, we are beginning "to lose the ability to experience our world directly. What we have come to mean by the term experience is impoverished; what we have of experience in daily life is impoverished as well." René Descartes[9] argued that physical reality is so ephemeral that humans can only experience their personal, internal interpretation of sensory input. Descartes' view "has become a major cultural force in our world," wrote Reed, one of a number of psychologists and philosophers who pointed to the post-modern acceleration of indirect experience. They proposed an alternative view — ecological psychology (or ecopsychology) — steeped in the ideas of John Dewey,[10] America's most influential educator. Dewey warned a century ago that worship of secondary experience in childhood came with the risk of depersonalizing human life.

North Carolina State University professor Robin Moore directs a research and design program that promotes the natural environment in the daily lives of children. He takes Reed and Dewey to heart in his contemporary examination of postmodern childhood play. Primary experience of nature is being replaced, he writes, "by the secondary, vicarious, often distorted, dual sensory (vision and sound only), one-way experience of television and other electronic media." According to Moore:

> Children live through their senses. Sensory experiences link the child's exterior world with their interior, hidden, affective world. Since the natural environment is the principal source of sensory stimulation, freedom to explore and play with the outdoor environment through the senses in their own space and time is essential for healthy development of an interior life.... This type of self-activated, autonomous interaction is what we call free play. Individual children test themselves by interacting with their environment, activating their potential and reconstructing human culture. The content of the environment is a critical factor in this process. A rich, open environment will continuously present alternative choices for creative engagement. A rigid, bland environment will limit healthy growth and development of the individual or the group.

Little is known about the impact of new technologies on children's emotional health, but we do know something about the implications for adults. In 1998, a controversial Carnegie Mellon University study found that people who spend even a few hours on the Internet each week suffer higher levels

---

[9]*René Descartes:* French philosopher and mathematician (1596–1650).
[10]*John Dewey:* American philosopher, psychologist, and educational reformer (1859–1952).

of depression and loneliness than people who use the Net infrequently. Enterprising psychologists and psychiatrists now treat Internet Addiction, or IA as they call it.

As we grow more separate from nature, we continue to separate from one another physically. The effects are more than skin deep, says Nancy Dess, senior scientist with the American Psychological Association. "None of the new communication technologies involve human touch; they all tend to place us one step removed from direct experience. Add this to control-oriented changes in the workplace and schools, where people are often forbidden, or at least discouraged, from any kind of physical contact, and we've got a problem," she says. Without touch, infant primates die; adult primates with touch deficits become more aggressive. Primate studies also show that physical touch is essential to the peace-making process. "Perversely, many of us can go through an average day and not have more than a handshake," she adds. Diminishing touch is only one by-product of the culture of technical control, but Dess believes it contributes to violence in an ever more tightly wired society.

Frank Wilson, professor of neurology at the Stanford University School of Medicine, is an expert on the co-evolution of the hominid hand and brain. In *The Hand*, he contends that one could not have evolved to its current sophistication without the other. He says, "We've been sold a bill of goods — especially parents — about how valuable computer-based experience is. We are creatures identified by what we do with our hands." Much of our learning comes from doing, from making, from feeling with our hands; and though many would like to believe otherwise, the world is not entirely available from a keyboard. As Wilson sees it, we're cutting off our hands to spite our brains. Instructors in medical schools find it increasingly difficult to teach how the heart works as a pump, he says, "because these students have so little real-world experience; they've never siphoned anything, never fixed a car, never worked on a fuel pump, may not even have hooked up a garden hose. For a whole generation of kids, direct experiences in the backyard, in the tool shed, in the fields and woods, has been replaced by indirect learning, through machines. These young people are smart, they grew up with computers, they were supposed to be superior — but now we know that something's missing."

The Infinite Reservoir

Not surprisingly, as the young grow up in a world of narrow yet over-whelming sensory input, many of them develop a wired, know-it-all state of mind. That which cannot be Googled does not count. Yet a fuller, grander, more mysterious world, one worthy of a child's awe, is available to children and the rest of us. Bill McKibben,[11] in *The Age of Missing Information*, argues that "the definition of television's global village is just the contrary — it's a place where there's as little variety as possible, where as much information   40

[11]*Bill McKibben:* American environmentalist and writer (b. 1960). (See p. 743.)

as possible is wiped away to make 'communications' easier." He describes his personal experience with a nearby mountain: "The mountain says you live in a particular place. Though it's a small area, just a square mile or two, it took me many trips to even start to learn its secrets. Here there are blue-berries, and here there are bigger blueberries . . . You pass a hundred different plants along the trail — I know maybe twenty of them. One could spend a lifetime learning a small range of mountains, and once upon a time people did."

Any natural place contains an infinite reservoir of information, and therefore the potential for inexhaustible new discoveries. As naturalist Robert Michael Pyle says, "Place is what takes me out of myself, out of the limited scope of human activity, but this is not misanthropic. A sense of place is a way of embracing humanity among all of its neighbors. It is an entry into the larger world."

During my visits with middle school, high school, and college students, a discussion of the senses would inevitably come about when we talked about nature. Sometimes I would ask directly, other times the students would raise the subject in the classroom or later, through essays. Their verbal answers were often hesitant, searching. This was apparently not a subject that many, if any, had confronted before. For some young people, nature is so abstract — the ozone layer, a faraway rain forest — that it exists beyond the senses. For others, nature is simple background, a disposable consumer item. One young man in a Potomac, Maryland, classroom described his relationship with nature as shaky, at best. "Like most I exploit what it gives and I do with it what I please," he said. He thought of nature "as a means to an end or a tool; something made to be used and admired, not something to live. Nature to me is like my house or even like my cluttered room. It has things in it which can be played with. I say play away, do what you want with it, it's your house." He made no mention of the senses, saw or understood no complexity. I admired his honesty.

Yet other young people, when prompted, did describe how experiences in nature excited their senses. For example, one boy recalled his sensory experience when camping, "the red and orange flames dancing in the darkness, the smoky fumes rising up, burning my eyes and nostrils. . . ."

The experience of irrepressible Jared Grano, a ninth-grader whose father is a middle-school principal, sends a positive message to parents who worry that they might be alienating their kids from nature by taking them on the sometimes-dreaded family vacation. He complained that, although vacations are supposed to be for getting away from it all, "Unfortunately, I had to take them all with me! My parents, younger brother, and younger sister would all be traveling with me in an oven on wheels for over a week. The Grand Canyon? I was in no hurry to see the canyon. I figured it would be there for me later." When the family arrived, Jared gazed at "the massive temples of the canyon." His first thought was, "It looks like a painting." He was impressed by the beauty and majesty of the surroundings. "But after seeing the canyon from several different vantage points, I was ready to leave. Although the canyon was magnificent, I felt that I was not part of it — and without being part of it, it seemed little more than a giant hole in the ground." But the vacation was young, and the know-it-all state of mind penetrable. After the Grand Canyon, his family drove to smaller Walnut Canyon National Monument, near Flagstaff, Arizona. Jared assumed that Walnut Canyon would be similar to the Grand Canyon, "interesting to look at, but nothing to hold my attention."

Nine hundred years ago, the Sinagua people built their homes under   45
cliff overhangs. Twenty miles long, four hundred feet deep and a quarter mile wide, the canyon is populated with soaring turkey vultures, as well as elk and javelina. Life zones overlap, mixing species that usually live apart; cacti grow beside mountain firs. Jared described details of the path they walked, how the bushes were low and straggly and looked as though they had been there for many years, and the shape of the tall green pines across the gap. "As we followed the path down into the canyon, the skies grew suddenly dark. It began raining and the rain quickly turned to sleet," Jared wrote. "We found shelter in one of the ancient Indian caves. Lightning lit up the canyon and the sound of thunder reverberated in the cave. As we stood waiting for the storm to end, my family and I talked about the Indians who once lived here. We discussed how they cooked in the caves, slept in the caves, and found shelter in the caves — just as we were doing." He looked out across the canyon through the haze of rain. "I finally felt that I was a part of nature." The context of his life shifted. He was immersed in living history, witnessing natural events beyond his control, keenly aware of it all. He was *alive.*

Surely such moments are more than pleasant memories. The young don't demand dramatic adventures or vacations in Africa. They need only a taste, a sight, a sound, a touch — or, as in Jared's case, a lightning strike — to reconnect with that receding world of the senses.

The know-it-all state of mind is, in fact, quite vulnerable. In a flash, it burns, and something essential emerges from its ashes.

ENGAGING THE TEXT

1. What forms of technology hinder direct contact with nature, according to Louv? What other aspects of modern American life diminish our direct experience of the natural world? Which, if any, of these features of modern living would you give up to improve your relationship with nature?

2. Would you agree with Louv's contention that modern technology is actually "shrinking" our sensory world? What evidence do you see that the information age is or is not creating a generation of Americans who suffer from "cultural autism" (para. 34)?

3. What's the difference for Louv between learning about nature and actually experiencing it? Would you agree that kids are better off watching the

landscape go by along a superhighway than they are watching a nature film in the back of their parents' SUV? Why or why not?

4. What does it take, in Louv's view, to break through "the know-it-all state of mind"? Have you ever had the kind of breakthrough experience he describes? If so, would you agree that it changed you in some essential way?

EXPLORING CONNECTIONS

5. To what extent might Henry David Thoreau (p. 646) agree with Louv's assessment of the impact of the "know-it-all state of mind"? What similarities can you find between Thoreau's and Louv's views of nature?

6. How might Annie Dillard's childhood memories (p. 656) be seen as challenging or supporting Louv's views on the power of nature? Do her recollections of Frick Park and her insect collection reflect Louv's understanding of "creative engagement" with nature? Does she exemplify someone free of the "know-it-all state of mind"?

7. Reread the assessments of public education offered by John Taylor Gatto (p. 148), Jean Anyon (p. 169), and Jonathan Kozol (p. 219) in Chapter Two, and discuss the role that public schools might play in the development of "cultural autism."

EXTENDING THE CRITICAL CONTEXT

8. Working in groups, create a collage of media and advertising images featuring nature and natural subjects. Share the results of your efforts in class and discuss whether they support Louv's contention that nature has become a "simple background," or "a disposable consumer item" (para. 42).

9. Survey some friends to determine the intensity of their use of electronic technology. How many hours a week, for example, do they watch TV, play video games, use computers, and communicate via their cell phones? Based on your findings, would you agree that we are in danger of losing our ability to experience the world directly?

The Artifice of the Natural

CHARLES SIEBERT

It's a hot day in the semitropics. Green grass waves beneath an azure sky as animals gather around a waterhole. Suddenly, a big cat appears on the edge of the clearing, and a dubbed-in voice, muffled to an unnecessary whisper, explains that, "Having gone for days without a kill for her cubs, the female

Sidewalk Bubblegum ©1993 Clay Butler

cheetah prepares to play her part in the never-ending struggle for survival..."
This is about as close to the wild that some of us will ever get. Many Americans
today — and certainly many urban Americans — learn about wilderness and
wild animals from television. But is nature seen through the media the same as
real nature, and is the experience of mediated nature equal to the experience
of nature in the raw? According to Charles Siebert, the author of this selection,
nature on TV offers us a unique experience — one that says more about human
tastes and obsessions than it does about the natural world. Siebert (b. 1938) is
an essayist, journalist, and the author of a number of nonfiction books on ani-
mals, including The Wauchula Woods Accord: Toward a New Understanding
of Animals (2009). *This essay originally appeared in* Harper's *magazine.*

    It's a Sunday evening, just after eight o'clock, and my TV screen is filled
with elephant seals. They crowd the beaches of a small Pacific island called
Año Nuevo. There was lighthearted Latin music as the show began, followed by a dizzying montage of the wildlife that yearly inhabits the island;
then the cameras settled on the show's subject — huge, gelatinous mammals that spend most of their life slipping seamlessly through open seas but
whose existence on land looks to be a self-contained Sisyphean nightmare:[1]

---

[1]*Sisyphean nightmare:* In Greek mythology, Sisyphus was condemned by the gods to roll a
huge rock uphill every day, only to have the rock roll back down every night; hence, any pointless task requiring extraordinary effort.

endless, exhaustive heavings of themselves back and forth across the sand. Of course, their life on land is nothing of the kind. Yet we can neither depict nor look upon beached seals without somehow articulating the ache that their limbless listing induces in us. They don't, as far as anyone knows, have a constant inner aria of grounded-seal woes playing in their brain. That is playing now in mine, as it no doubt played in the minds of those who made this film. TV nature shows are, above all else, extravagant animal opera, dramatizing, scoring, voicing in human terms the vast backdrop of inhuman action. Tonight's show is entitled *Elephant Seals: Those Magnificent Diving Machines.* "They look helpless, primitive, even absurd," the narrator, PBS's[2] George Page, intones to a shot of two beached, floppy-nosed elephant-seal bulls butting heads, "but they're precisely shaped for . . . life in the ocean. We humans, marooned in air, can only catch brief glimpses of that underwater world."

At the moment, I'm "marooned" six floors in the air in the living room of my Brooklyn, New York, apartment. At the opposite end of the sofa is my dog, Lucy. It's a clear, mild, late-autumn evening. Out my window I can see the tiered building lights of Manhattan, jet planes sliding past the highest towers, and, when I look down, directly below me, Lincoln Place, quiet for such a warm evening, none of the usual clamor coming from the stoop of the crackhouse brownstone with the chained sapling out front, every inch of its branches covered with blinking Christmas lights. Brooklyn is where I do the bulk of my nature-show viewing. The rest I do in a log cabin in the Canadian woods. It may seem a redundancy watching nature on TV while passing days — actually, months — each year, mostly alone, in the midst of what is commonly considered to be the natural world. But the two places — actual and televised nature — have little to do with each other. The woods are so wide, old, and slow as to be dismissive of me and the names I know and what I might wish and wait to see. The show, by contrast, is rapid, focused, and framed, a potent distillation of someone else's waiting designed precisely for me.

In fact, nature shows are much more like cities, both entities being elaborate human constructs: fast-paced, multistoried, and artificially lit. And both entities are, in turn, having an increasing influence on the way we view nature. Living in cities, watching our TVs, we have come to see nature not so much as that inscrutable place; that living, visitable gradualness with which, in the traditional romantic and transcendentalist conception,[3] we try to merge by abandoning our will and gauging our senses down to it; that

---

[2]*PBS's:* PBS stands for the Public Broadcasting Service.

[3]*the traditional romantic and transcendentalist conception:* In romantic philosophy, nature is typically seen as a sacred or powerful realm closely associated with the mystery of creation and opposed to the world of human activity. In American transcendentalism, a form of romanticism, nature is viewed as being allied with spiritual truth.

spiritually infused world, as Wordsworth[4] wrote, "Of eye, and ear, both what they half create, / And what perceive." Today, the natural world is for us a place of reticent and reticular wonders that command our coaxing, our active exposure and editing; a world made up of what we half create and what, even when we're there, we fully expect to see.

On the beaches of Año Nuevo now there's sexual mayhem: bulls mounting everything in sight, charging at interlopers, crushing mothers and nursing pups along the way. Suddenly, a storm hits. Waves pound the beach, dragging newborns far out to sea. "This pup," Page says as I watch a baby seal slipping under and then an adult onshore looking seaward, "drowns before his mother's eyes." Nature shows always do this, the old war- and horror-movie technique of getting you attached to the minor characters — in this instance, via countless mother / pup nuzzling and nursing scenes — so that you'll feel more deeply the pain of their loss. Now there's an overview shot of seal-strewn waves breaking softly against the shore in the storm's aftermath: "What the waves take," says our narrator, "the waves return, rolling the dead up the beach to the waiting gulls."

There's an implicit unnaturalness in our watching of nature shows: we   5
are, at once, ensconced in our day and tuned into *theirs*, that of the wild animals. There's something vaguely illicit about it to me, and, my guess is, to many among the millions of us who tune in each week. We ask ourselves questions, what I call my questions of stasis, after the poet Elizabeth Bishop's famous "Questions of Travel": "Should we," she asks from afar, "have stayed at home and thought of here? . . . Is it right to be watching strangers in a play / in this strangest of theaters?" And should we, I wonder, be making shows of them at all, and am I right to just sit here at home and think of there, and what if I and everyone else were to just suddenly pick up and go, where then would that leave them? "Oh, must we dream our dreams / and have them, too?"

Outside my window now, the night air is all soft urban thrum: the occasional bleat of a car horn; a far-off siren wobbling like a tired top along a distant side street; a light breeze moving the tops of the ailanthus in great dark waves above the neighborhood's vacant lots. Through my open windows, honeybees — dazed, listless, postsummer drones — keep drifting in and out, bristling as they bob before the TV screen, aswim now with the image of a lone seal pup in a camera-lighted sea. This is our protagonist. Separated from her mother in the storm, she's finning herself back to safety. Darkness approaches. "If she can't find a surrogate mother," our narrator explains, "she'll starve." Mournful Andean flute music sounds. The pup pulls up into a wide, slow, skyward gaze and cries. I had thought about not tuning in tonight, having

---

[4]*Wordsworth:* William Wordsworth (1770–1850), English romantic poet famed for his meditative depictions of nature.

already seen elephant seals before on past shows. In fact, insofar as this species — as I've just learned — was nearly wiped out save for a core group of a hundred seals on this island, the chances are that I've seen the very same seals or their relatives. Still, if the seals are the same, the show is different, more elaborate and engaging, which is why I tuned in. The more facts we compile about the animals' days, the more human the tales we tell of them. We've come so far from actual nature.

I remember, as a child back in the 1960s, watching a particularly riled elephant-seal bull chase Marlin Perkins up the beach in *Mutual of Omaha's Wild Kingdom*. That seemed to be about the extent of nature programming back then, close encounters with the wild: Marlin and one of his muscular, square-jawed cohorts frantically running from or wrestling with animals, bagging snakes, lassoing leopards, shooting myriad creatures with tranquilizers before releasing them again back into the wilderness. Somehow that was enough of a show then, the capture and release, perhaps because we could still believe there was someplace other and unknown — a place we could confidently call the natural world — for them to be released into. I remember as well Jacques Cousteau[5] paying a visit to Año Nuevo back in the 1970s. We had, by this time, penetrated, captured on film, a good deal of the world's wilderness, and so there was already a marked embellishment in our narrations of it as well as that hushed, somber, guilt-tinged tone that has become the hallmark of nature-show narration. Of course, Cousteau, our first existentialist naturalist, got a bit carried away, describing the very mating scene I've been told tonight is quite natural for elephant seals as if it were something out of Petronius's *Satyricon*.[6] "Zee island iz a sex and milk bank. Beasts all mating wiz each uh-there, females giving milk to any pup that passes by. What has 'appened to zee seals also 'appens with humans. In difficult times, they obey strict rules. In opulence, society degenerates." Still, Cousteau had the same lines about the seals being so ungainly on land and yet streamlined for the sea, and he too filmed a wave-swept orphan seal pup, although in this case Cousteau and his crew stepped into the scene, lifted the pup from the water, and brought it to a nursing mother's side.

In tonight's show, however, we get a whole story, a year in the life, and the makers' hands are kept out of the frame so as not to break the tension that has been the dynamic of nature-show drama since Marlin Perkins first began bringing the wild (and, not incidentally, selling life insurance) to homes across America — that tension we feel between the indifference and apparent arbitrariness of occurrences in the natural world and our own civilized stays against it. Our pup survives the storm. Now we're about to follow her on her inaugural swim with the aid of the latest underwater photography

---

[5]*Jacques Cousteau:* Jacques-Yves Cousteau (1910–1997), French marine explorer and host of a popular television series on marine life during the 1960s and 1970s.

[6]*Petronius's* Satyricon: Satirical novel by Titus Petronius Niger (d. A.D. 66), famed for its depiction of the grotesque sexual and culinary excesses of Roman society.

and the information gleaned from a "time-depth recorder," which, stuck to the back of a mature elephant seal, traced the long, deep outlines of its yearly eight-month ocean migrations. "There's so much to learn," says our narrator. "The world unfolds before the little female's eyes, and it's an amazing sight."

Deep, sonorous flute music again as the pup swirls from one lesson to the next in her "world of floating shadows": sharks, a passing whale, schools of fish; our pup "sees creature after creature feeding — and becoming food," and she is now being drawn to the surface by an eerie constellation of floating lights. She rises up through a dense, gray cloud of squid, stares a moment through a glare of unseen camera lights at the skulking shadows on the deck of a commercial fisherman's boat, and then dives again. . . .

There's a driving rainstorm tonight, the city is completely obscured   10 from view, and I'm watching a show about the rain forest. My TV screen is a brilliant canvas of bright red beads set into a field of multicolored triangles: a close-up of red mites on the back of a harlequin beetle. Now, over surreal horizons of harlequin thorax, come tiny scorpions preying upon the mites. Paper wasps, meanwhile, are spitting rainwater off of their nest and cooling their brood with wing pulsations. A poison-arrow frog is dumping its tadpoles into a droplet of water at the base of a bromeliad. Golden toads are courting in misty pools atop the one mountain in this world where they can be found. There's a sudden wide shot of a night sky with a white-gold moon that gives way now to the luminous orb of a leaf toad's eye, and then a shocking, screen-size, green triangle: the head of a katydid. I can hear its chewing, and then the soft paddings across dead leaves of an approaching tarantula. The tarantula pounces. I listen to its pincers piercing the waxen abdomen of the katydid. "We soon get through with Nature," Thoreau[7] once noted in his journals. "She excites an expectation which she cannot satisfy." Thus, the modern TV nature show: a clean and well-lighted simultaneity of the unseen; of the things you'd never see in a thousand walks in the wild.

Jungles are most remarkable for what you don't see for the longest time. How many of us would wait long enough for the lives there that retreat upon our first footfalls to start back toward us? How many of us remain who might regard such creatures? Jungles are wondrous places for precisely the reasons a nature show cannot convey. It is the mostly hidden and nonreflective enormity of their life forces, behemoth and belittling, that has most to show and tell us. To be in "nature" — by which we've come to mean the world without us — is to meet firsthand that thriving indifference and nearly insufferable gradualness that moves us to *decamp* from nature. To be alone in the jungle or in any uninterrupted wilderness, even to walk through a typical deciduous forest such as the one surrounding my cabin in Canada, is to be rapidly divested of your ego and ideas. In fact, our most inspired writing

---

[7]*Thoreau:* American writer, philosopher, and naturalist (1817–1862). See page 646.

about nature is, in essence, the evocation of this divesting, the depiction, often ecstatic, of our own thoughts' unraveling into a greater surrounding thoughtlessness.

But to sit here in front of a nature show is to have one's ego fed shamelessly via the distilled essence of that original place whose indifference and gradualness we can no longer abide. We need the time-lapsed and tightly woven tale called nature, and it is from here and not from that tale's source that we now collectively depart. We are, in a sense, a species being increasingly defined by the loss of gradualness, by the steady progress of our walk out of the woods.

Perhaps I shouldn't watch nature shows, lest I become no longer able to suffer the real place. But then I think what a shame it would be to have missed *Year of the Jackal, Sexual Encounters of the Floral Kind,* or *Tides of War,* a recent film about the Persian Gulf crisis[8] from the animals' point of view, surely the first of its kind, animals being the most available emissaries of our own outrage and outrageousness — that heron, for example, striding into a fiery expanse of oil-splattered desert as the narrator informs us that "herons were often seen in the oilfields appearing confused and miserable," when they were, of course, herons appearing in confused and miserable-looking fields. I would have missed as well *Realms of the Russian Bear,* a six-hour foray into previously unseen corners of the former Soviet Union, animals being the most easygoing ambassadors of our "new world order." (In one memorable shot a polar bear lazing among hundreds of walruses on some remote Siberian seashore gently bites one walrus after the other in search of a sick or disabled one for supper.) And while I can't say how or if seeing such things changes me, it would seem some kind of loss to miss the deep-diving films currently being shot by the wild sea lions whose backs we've strapped cameras to; or to have missed that noiseless stick spider suspended upside down above the leafy plate of its unwitting prey; or the polar bear mother emerging from her icebound winter's den with three newborns like animate snowballs beneath her; to have missed the shots — how did they get them? — from the very wing tips of a flying duck; or of those freshwater dolphins who make of themselves a fishing net and heave whole schools of fish onto the shore for supper; or of the killer whales who snatch seals from the beach and then toss them about like rubber toys in the surf. . . .

Friday night, late November, cold and clear, the city sparkling in the distance. There's no nature on this evening. (Actually, it's on somewhere in the vast TV system. There's an all-nature cable channel now, but my particular section of Brooklyn may be the last quadrant of this nation not yet wired for cable.) Lucy is, as usual, settled deep into her end of the couch, sifting for

---

[8]*the Persian Gulf crisis:* Euphemistic term for the United States' war with Iraq in response to its invasion of Kuwait in 1990.

sleep through an elaborate series of sighs. I'm thinking about the cabin in the woods, wondering if it's still there.

It was built more than 160 years ago and lists pretty badly now into a wooded hillside. Daylight leaks in everywhere through the joints and siding. Tin sheets tapped onto the old roof hold out most of the rain; and plastic sheets over the broken windows, the wind. One small combination lock on a latch holds the front door, barely, within its jamb — or it might be holding the cabin up around the door. Not that one needs a combination to get inside. At this very moment all kinds of creatures are having the run of the place, or at least the slow, sleepy refuge of its webbed nooks and thinly insulated rafters. I merely do a kind of summer time-share with them each season: the mice, moles, snakes, skinks, and spiders. The place does have pipes that bring ice-cold water through the warmest months from an underground spring, and a phone, and electricity for the little portable black-and-white TV on which Lucy and I and our assorted native stowaways can watch the narrated images of animals — the huge darkness of the night sky and surrounding woods pressing in around us.

But along with the cabin itself, it's the very essence of the time I spend there that keeps collapsing now in my mind. I'm thinking in particular of my walks in the woods, how they begin with such a deep sense of disappointment not so much in, but *from*, my surroundings. It's a disappointment rooted in the disparity between the ways in which we now represent nature to ourselves and the way it actually is; between that flitting, omniscient, nature-show overview delivering me from one available, arcane wonder to the next, and the plodding, myopic bulk of me within such a mute and long-lived presence.

At one point in Lewis Carroll's *Through the Looking-Glass*, Alice wanders tentatively into a cool, shady wood "where things have no names." Immediately upon entering, she forgets what to call the tree under which she's standing, and she entirely forgets herself. She next comes face-to-face with a fawn, which, not being recalled by Alice as such, is entirely fearless and walks farther through the woods side by side with her in a spell of peace and calm. Eventually, the two emerge back out into an open field, at which point name recognition returns and the fawn bounds off, frightened, leaving Alice "almost ready to cry with vexation at having lost her . . . fellow-traveler so suddenly." Alice's walk is, in essence, a brief pass, at once unsettling and euphoric, through a primordial world, through the world without us and the names by which we naturally put things in their place and thus proceed away from them. And it is some semblance of her experience, however remote it may be to the modern psyche, that I have when I walk in the woods, an experience exactly the opposite of watching a nature show. It is the sufferance of my own insignificance, and of the full, muted, weighty presence of things; the daring to linger in a nonspecific, unnarrated, and ongoing anonymity; a prolonged visit with that absence of us. It is a walk away from what we know toward an understanding — in both the physical and abstract senses of that word — of what surrounds us.

15

Now, however, we are increasingly incapable of suffering the silent world without us, of standing a stand of trees. We've become, in a sense, a race of armchair naturalists even as more and more of us are now visiting the places and creatures whose stories we've watched on the TV. We go as nature tourists, fully equipped and expectant of seeing those characters, as though visiting the various sets of a Universal Studios theme park.

I remember a few years ago making a trip to Nepal to write a story about a young American doctor practicing emergency wilderness medicine at an outpost high in the Himalayas. On the day of my departure I learned that I would be accompanied by twelve other doctors, who were to be led by the subject of my story through Nepalese mountains and jungle while taking courses from him in emergency medicine — that is, an extravagant adventure vacation and tax write-off for the doctors and their families. I found all the doctors waiting at the airport gate in Seattle, already decked out in the finest Banana Republic trekking gear. All except one, an ortho-pedic surgeon from southern California who, I've since decided, is the pre-figurement of humankind's next evolutionary advancement. His skin was milky white, his body a pervasive paunch bordering on shapelessness, and he wore — never departed from, in fact — a red knit polo shirt; tan slacks; brand-new, creaseless penny loafers; and a La Quinta Country Club[9] golf hat.

Yet in the course of our expedition, he outperformed everyone, always 20 arriving at the top of trails of our jungle camps hours ahead of the rest of us. We would trek and look dutifully about in hopes of spotting something in the wild, our minds mired somewhere in that disappointment between "Disney-fied" nature and the actual place, while he sped along in those loafers, noting the surroundings as though clicking off items on a checklist on the way to a more poignant encounter with a big-list item, one of the rare snow leop-ards of the region, or rhinos, or Bengal tigers. On the buses that brought us from one corner of the country to another, everyone was reading Peter Matthiessen's *Snow Leopard*. He read vampire novels. The last I remember seeing of him, we were all riding on the backs of elephants through the jungles of southwestern Nepal. He was on the lead elephant, of course, and we came into a clearing along a winding riverbank of tall grass, the white wavy wands of which we were all instructed to pause and watch a few moments in the distance for the possible movement of a rhino. I looked up and watched the La Quinta doctor instead. He raised a pair of binoculars, focused briefly on the motionless tips of grass, and then drove on, those shiny penny loafers dug firmly into his elephant as they passed back into the jungle.

It is 8:45 P.M., mid-December, light snow outside, the city subsumed in a pale orange glow. I'm watching *Great Moments with Nature's Filmmakers*, a show about the making of the shows, a guided tour of sorts through nature's studio sets and all the suddenly disengaged props of that dream:

---

[9]*La Quinta Country Club:* An exclusive private country club in La Quinta, California.

here the fur-wrapped camera-on-wheels that brought us into that pride of lions, and here the feather duster that the falcon attacked the night I saw just talons and scattered plumage. Over here is the den aquarium tank that was the wide sea in which the moray eel ate the blowfish and then spit it free; and here is the film center in England where they first perfected time-lapse and various microcosmic film techniques: room upon room with cameras clicking tight fast frames of this world's wide days of sluggish plants, fleeing insects, and shy birds. These "camera techniques," the narrator solemnly declares at show's end, "changed forever our vision of the natural world."

I pick up the phone now and dial my cabin to make sure it's still there. Of course, for all I know a strong wind has blown it over since my last visit, leaving only the lintel to which the phone's attached, so that I'm calling a snowy wooded hilltop with a few chairs, a wood stove, some scattered books on the floor, and a dark TV on a table. I dial the cold, rimless northern night. There's the cheap crackling mimicry of distance in my ear; and then, after the first ring, I begin trying to reassemble my days there, but see only a series of twitched heads and wide-eyed stares, a rooftop crow scattering like a broken fleck of night sky, and the fawn that had been rubbing its flank against an outside corner, padding off now with a near-soundless hoof-squeak through snow.

ENGAGING THE TEXT

1. Why does Siebert believe that TV nature shows amount to little more than "extravagant animal operas"? What's particularly "operatic" about the examples he offers from the PBS special on elephant seals?

2. What, according to Siebert, is the experience of real nature like, in contrast to the kind of nature we see on television? Why does he feel that there is "something vaguely illicit" about watching nature shows on television? Would you agree?

3. What is the experience of being alone in nature like for human beings, according to Siebert? What does direct contact with animals and the natural world do to or for us, in his view? Would you agree that today we tend to visit nature only as tourists (para. 18)?

4. What is the point of the three brief passages that Siebert uses to close his essay — the anecdote about the "La Quinta doctor" touring Nepal, the description of watching *Great Moments with Nature's Filmmakers*, and the story about calling his vacant cabin in Canada? What do each of these recollections suggest about television and its impact on our views of nature?

EXPLORING CONNECTIONS

5. What do you imagine a nature television show produced by Henry David Thoreau (p. 646) would be like? What would Thoreau focus on, and what would happen in it? To what extent do Siebert and Thoreau agree about how we experience nature in the wild?

6. How might you expect Richard Louv (p. 664) to assess the kind of nature television programming that Siebert describes in terms of its impact on children? In general, do you think nature shows help children develop a personal relationship with nature?

7. How do Siebert's attitudes toward animals and nature compare with those of John (Fire) Lame Deer (below)? Would Lame Deer be likely to agree with Siebert about the "Disneyfied" portrayal of nature and animal life on television or about what real nature is like? Why or why not?

EXTENDING THE CRITICAL CONTEXT

8. Working in groups, survey a number of television nature shows to test Siebert's claims about how they tend to depict animals and the natural world. Do the shows that you watch portray animals in the "operatic" way that Siebert describes? To what extent have portrayals of nature and animals on TV changed since Siebert's essay first appeared in 1993?

9. Survey portrayals of animals in popular movies — including animated films like those in the *Madagascar* and *Ice Age* series and in documentaries like *March of the Penguins, Earth,* and *Crimson Wing.* What do these films tell us about animals? To what extent do they anthropomorphize animal behavior?

Talking to the Owls and Butterflies
JOHN (FIRE) LAME DEER
AND RICHARD ERDOES

When he was just sixteen years old, John (Fire) Lame Deer spent four days and nights alone in a pit dug in a deserted hilltop on the Rosebud Reservation in South Dakota. He wasn't being punished for some adolescent transgression. He was experiencing his hanblechia *— or "vision seeking" — the first step in his preparation as a Sioux medicine man. In Sioux culture, if you want to talk to the gods, you get in touch with nature. For the traditional Sioux, nature is alive and animals are related to their human counterparts by territory, history, and blood. In this excerpt from his classic autobiography, Lame Deer castigates the "white world" for its attitude toward nature and its treatment of animals. He also offers some telling insights into Native American views of what it means to live wild.*

During his lifetime, Lame Deer (1900–1976) was a tribal leader, medicine man, storyteller, rodeo clown, and painter. Richard Erdoes (1912–2008) was nearly sixty when he met Lame Deer after being assigned by Life *maga-*

zine to paint and photograph daily existence on a Sioux reservation. The meeting convinced Erdoes to give up his career as a professional illustrator to document Indian culture. Lame Deer chose him to collaborate on the story that became Lame Deer, Seeker of Visions *(1972), the source of this selection. Erdoes went on to work with Mary Crow Dog on her autobiography,* Lakota Woman *(1990), which received the 1991 American Book Award, and, with Lame Deer's son, Archie Fire Lame Deer, on his memoir,* Gift of Power: The Life and Teachings of a Lakota Medicine Man *(1992).*

Let's sit down here, all of us, on the open prairie, where we can't see a highway or a fence. Let's have no blankets to sit on, but feel the ground with our bodies, the earth, the yielding shrubs. Let's have the grass for a mattress, experiencing its sharpness and its softness. Let us become like stones, plants, and trees. Let us be animals, think and feel like animals.

Listen to the air. You can hear it, feel it, smell it, taste it. *Woniya waken* — the holy air — which renews all by its breath. *Woniya, woniya waken* — spirit, life, breath, renewal — it means all that. *Woniya* — we sit together, don't touch, but something is there; we feel it between us, as a presence. A good way to start thinking about nature, talk about it. Rather talk to it, talk to the rivers, to the lakes, to the winds as to our relatives.

You have made it hard for us to experience nature in the good way by being part of it. Even here we are conscious that somewhere out in those hills there are missile silos and radar stations. White men always pick the few unspoiled, beautiful, awesome spots for the sites of these abominations. You have raped and violated these lands, always saying, "Gimme, gimme, gimme," and never giving anything back. You have taken 200,000 acres of our Pine Ridge[1] reservation and made them into a bombing range. This land is so beautiful and strange that now some of you want to make it into a national park. The only use you have made of this land since you took it from us was to blow it up. You have not only despoiled the earth, the rocks, the minerals, all of which you call "dead" but which are very much alive; you have even changed the animals, which are part of us, part of the Great Spirit, changed them in a horrible way, so no one can recognize them. There is power in a buffalo — spiritual, magic power — but there is no power in an Angus, in a Hereford.[2]

There is power in an antelope, but not in a goat or in a sheep, which holds still while you butcher it, which will eat your newspaper if you let it. There was great power in a wolf, even in a coyote. You have made him into

[1]*Pine Ridge:* Reservation established for the Oglala Sioux in 1978 following more than ten years of negotiation and fighting; site of the Wounded Knee massacre.

[2]*Angus, Hereford:* Breeds of cattle.

a freak — a toy poodle, a Pekingese, a lap dog. You can't do much with a cat, which is like an Indian, unchangeable. So you fix it, alter it, declaw it, even cut its vocal cords so you can experiment on it in a laboratory without being disturbed by its cries.

A partridge, a grouse, a quail, a pheasant, you have made them into   5
chickens, creatures that can't fly, that wear a kind of sunglasses so that they won't peck each other's eyes out, "birds" with a "pecking order." There are some farms where they breed chickens for breast meat. Those birds are kept in low cages, forced to be hunched over all the time, which makes the breast muscles very big. Soothing sounds, Muzak, are piped into these chicken hutches. One loud noise and the chickens go haywire, killing themselves by flying against the mesh of their cages. Having to spend all their lives stooped over makes an unnatural, crazy, no-good bird. It also makes unnatural, no-good human beings.

That's where you fooled yourselves. You have not only altered, declawed, and malformed your winged and four-legged cousins; you have done it to yourselves. You have changed men into chairmen of boards, into office work-ers, into time-clock punchers. You have changed women into housewives, truly fearful creatures. I was once invited into the home of such a one.

"Watch the ashes, don't smoke, you stain the curtains. Watch the goldfish bowl, don't breathe on the parakeet, don't lean your head against the wallpaper; your hair may be greasy. Don't spill liquor on that table: it has a delicate finish. You should have wiped your boots; the floor was just varnished. Don't, don't, don't . . ." That is crazy. We weren't made to endure this. You live in prisons which you have built for yourselves, calling them "homes," offices, factories. We have a new joke on the reservation: "What is cultural deprivation?" Answer: "Being an upper-middle-class white kid liv-ing in a split-level suburban home with a color TV."

Sometimes I think that even our pitiful tar-paper shacks are better than your luxury homes. Walking a hundred feet to the outhouse on a clear wintry night, through mud or snow, that's one small link with nature. Or in the sum-mer, in the back country, leaving the door of the privy open, taking your time, listening to the humming of the insects, the sun warming your bones through the thin planks of wood; you don't even have that pleasure anymore.

Americans want to have everything sanitized. No smells! Not even the good, natural man and woman smell. Take away the smell from under the armpits, from your skin. Rub it out, and then spray or dab some nonhuman odor on yourself, stuff you can spend a lot of money on, ten dollars an ounce, so you know this has to smell good, "B.O.," bad breath, "Intimate Female Odor Spray" — I see it all on TV. Soon you'll breed people without body openings.

I think white people are so afraid of the world they created that they   10
don't want to see, feel, smell, or hear it. The feeling of rain and snow on your face, being numbed by an icy wind and thawing out before a smoking fire, coming out of a hot sweat bath and plunging into a cold stream, these things make you feel alive, but you don't want them anymore. Living in

boxes which shut out the heat of the summer and the chill of winter, living inside a body that no longer has a scent, hearing the noise from the hi-fi instead of listening to the sounds of nature, watching some actor on TV having a make-believe experience when you no longer experience anything for yourself, eating food without taste — that's your way. It's no good.

The food you eat, you treat it like your bodies, take out all the nature part, the taste, the smell, the roughness, then put the artificial color, the artificial flavor in. Raw liver, raw kidney — that's what we old-fashioned full-bloods like to get our teeth into. In the old days we used to eat the guts of the buffalo, making a contest of it, two fellows getting hold of a long piece of intestines from opposite ends, starting chewing toward the middle, seeing who can get there first; that's eating. Those buffalo guts, full of half-fermented, half-digested grass and herbs, you didn't need any pills and vitamins when you swallowed those. Use the bitterness of gall for flavoring, not refined salt or sugar. *Wasna* — meat, kidney fat, and berries all pounded together — a lump of that sweet *wasna* kept a man going for a whole day. That was food, that had the power. Not the stuff you give us today: powdered milk, dehydrated eggs, pasteurized butter, chickens that are all drumsticks or all breast; there's no bird left there.

You don't want the bird. You don't have the courage to kill honestly — cut off the chicken's head, pluck it and gut it — no, you don't want this anymore. So it all comes in a neat plastic bag, all cut up, ready to eat, with no taste and no guilt. Your mink and seal coats, you don't want to know about the blood and pain which went into making them. Your idea of war — sit in an airplane, way above the clouds, press a button, drop the bombs, and never look below the clouds — that's the odorless, guiltless, sanitized way.

When we killed a buffalo, we knew what we were doing. We apologized to his spirit, tried to make him understand why we did it, honoring with a prayer the bones of those who gave their flesh to keep us alive, praying for their return, praying for the life of our brothers, the buffalo nation, as well as for our own people. You wouldn't understand this and that's why we had the Washita Massacre,[3] the Sand Creek Massacre,[4] the dead women and babies at Wounded Knee.[5] That's why we have Song My and My Lai[6] now.

---

[3]*Washita Massacre:* The U.S. Army, led by Lt. Col. George Custer, attacked a Cheyenne camp at Washita River, now in Oklahoma, on November 27, 1868; the Cheyenne were resisting railroad construction.

[4]*Sand Creek Massacre:* On November 29, 1864, Colorado militiamen attacked an encampment of Southern Cheyenne at Sand Creek in southeastern Colorado, killing about a third of a band of five hundred. Many women and children were killed, mutilated, or tortured.

[5]*Wounded Knee:* At Wounded Knee in South Dakota, Miniconjou Sioux led by Big Foot fought the Seventh U.S. Cavalry in December 1890. This battle, two weeks after Chief Sitting Bull was killed, ended the Ghost Dance War. Wounded Knee was also the site of a 1973 protest by the American Indian Movement.

[6]*Song My, My Lai:* My Lai was a Vietnamese hamlet, part of a village called Song My or Son My. In the most famous of Vietnam atrocities, American soldiers massacred several hundred Vietnamese civilians there on March 16, 1968.

To us life, all life, is sacred. The state of South Dakota has pest-control officers. They go up in a plane and shoot coyotes from the air. They keep track of their kills, put them all down in their little books. The stockmen and sheepowners pay them. Coyotes eat mostly rodents, field mice, and such. Only once in a while will they go after a stray lamb. They are our natural garbage men cleaning up the rotten and stinking things. They make good pets if you give them a chance. But their living could lose some man a few cents, and so the coyotes are killed from the air. They were here before the sheep, but they are in the way; you can't make a profit out of them. More and more animals are dying out. The animals which the Great Spirit put here, they must go. The man-made animals are allowed to stay — at least until they are shipped out to be butchered. That terrible arrogance of the white man, making himself something more than God, more than nature, saying, "I will let this animal live, because it makes money"; saying, "This animal must go, it brings no income, the space it occupies can be used in a better way. The only good coyote is a dead coyote." They are treating coyotes almost as badly as they used to treat Indians.

You are spreading death, buying and selling death. With all your deo-   15
dorants, you smell of it, but you are afraid of its reality; you don't want to face up to it. You have sanitized death, put it under the rug, robbed it of its honor. But we Indians think a lot about death. I do. Today would be a perfect day to die — not too hot, not too cool. A day to leave something of yourself behind, to let it linger. A day for a lucky man to come to the end of his trail. A happy man with many friends. Other days are not so good. They are for selfish, lonesome men, having a hard time leaving this earth. But for whites every day would be considered a bad one, I guess.

Eighty years ago our people danced the Ghost Dance, singing and dancing until they dropped from exhaustion, swooning, fainting, seeing visions. They danced in this way to bring back their dead, to bring back the buffalo. A prophet had told them that through the power of the Ghost Dance the earth would roll up like a carpet, with all the white man's works — the fences and the mining towns with their whorehouses, the factories and the farms with their stinking, unnatural animals, the railroads and the telegraph poles, the whole works. And underneath this rolled-up white man's world we would find again the flowering prairie, unspoiled, with its herds of buffalo and antelope, its clouds of birds, belonging to everyone, enjoyed by all.

I guess it was not time for this to happen, but it is coming back, I feel it warming my bones. Not the old Ghost Dance, not the rolling up — but a new-old spirit, not only among Indians but among whites and blacks, too, especially among young people. It is like raindrops making a tiny brook, many brooks making a stream, many streams making one big river bursting all dams. Us making this book, talking like this — these are some of the raindrops.

Listen, I saw this in my mind not long ago: in my vision the electric light will stop sometime. It is used too much for TV and going to the moon. The

day is coming when nature will stop the electricity. Police without flash-
lights, beer getting hot in the refrigerators, planes dropping from the sky,
even the President can't call up somebody on the phone. A young man will
come, or men, who'll know how to shut off all electricity. It will be painful,
like giving birth. Rapings in the dark, winos breaking into the liquor stores,
a lot of destruction. People are being too smart, too clever; the machine
stops and they are helpless, because they have forgotten how to make do
without the machine. There is a Light Man coming, bringing a new light. It
will happen before this century is over. The man who has the power will do
good things, too — stop all atomic power, stop wars, just by shutting the
white electropower off. I hope to see this, but then I'm also afraid. What
will be will be.

I think we are moving in a circle, or maybe a spiral, going a little higher
every time, but still returning to the same point. We are moving closer to
nature again. I feel it. . . . It won't be bad, doing without many things you
are now used to, things taken out of the earth and wasted foolishly. You
can't replace them and they won't last forever. Then you'll have to live more
according to the Indian way. People won't like that, but their children will.
The machine will stop, I hope, before they make electric corncobs for poor
Indians' privies.

We'll come out of our boxes and rediscover the weather. In the old days   20
you took your weather as it came, following the cranes, moving south with
the herds. Here, in South Dakota, they say, "If you don't like the weather,
wait five minutes." It can be 100 degrees in the shade one afternoon and
suddenly there comes a storm with hailstones as big as golf balls, the prairie
is all white and your teeth chatter. That's good — a reminder that you are
just a small particle of nature, not so powerful as you think. . . .

According to Sioux medicine man Pete Catches: "All animals have power,
because the Great Spirit dwells in all of them, even a tiny ant, a butterfly, a
tree, a flower, a rock. The modern white man's way keeps that power from
us, dilutes it. To come to nature, feel its power, let it help you, one needs
time and patience for that. Time to think, to figure it all out. You have so
little time for contemplation; it's always rush, rush, rush with you. It lessens a
person's life, all that grind, that hurrying and scurrying about. Our old people
say that the Indians of long ago didn't have heart trouble. They didn't have
that cancer. The illnesses they had they knew how to cure. But between
1890 and 1920 most of the medicines, the animal bundles, the pipes, the
ancient, secret things which we had treasured for centuries, were lost and
destroyed by the B.I.A.,[7] by the Government police. They went about tearing down sweat lodges, went into our homes, broke the pipes, tore up the
medicine bags, threw them into the fire, burned them up, completely wiped
out the wisdom of generations. But the Indian, you take away everything
from him, he still has his mouth to pray, to sing the ancient songs. He

---

[7]*the B.I.A.:* Bureau of Indian Affairs.

can still do his *yuwipi* ceremony[8] in a darkened room, beat his small drum, make the power come back, make the wisdom return. He did, but not all of it. The elk medicines are gone. The bear medicine, too. We had a medicine man here, up the creek, who died about fifteen years ago. He was the last bear medicine man that I knew about. And he was good, too. He was really good. . . ."

As for myself, the birds have something to tell me. The eagle, the owl. In an eagle there is all the wisdom of the world; that's why we have an eagle feather at the top of the pole during a *yuwipi* ceremony. If you are planning to kill an eagle, the minute you think of that he knows it, knows what you are planning. The black-tailed deer has this wisdom, too. That's why its tail is tied farther down at the *yuwipi* pole. This deer, if you shoot at him, you won't hit him. He just stands right there and the bullet comes right back and hits you. It is like somebody saying bad things about you and they come back at him.

In one of my great visions I was talking to the birds, the winged creatures. I was saddened by the death of my mother. She had held my hand and said just one word: "pitiful." I don't think she grieved for herself; she was sorry for me, a poor Indian she would leave in a white man's world. I cried up on that vision hill, cried for help, stretched out my hands toward the sky and then put the blanket over myself — that's all I had, the blanket and the pipe, and a little tobacco for an offering. I didn't know what to expect. I wanted to touch the power, feel it. I had the thought to give myself up, even if it would kill me. So I just gave myself to the winds, to nature, not giving a damn about what could happen to me.

All of a sudden I hear a big bird crying, and then quickly he hit me on the back, touched me with his spread wings. I heard the cry of an eagle, loud above the voices of many other birds. It seemed to say, "We have been waiting for you. We knew you would come. Now you are here. Your trail leads from here. Let our voices guide you. We are your friends, the feathered people, the two-legged, the four-legged, we are your friends, the creatures, little tiny ones, eight legs, twelve legs — all those who crawl on the earth. All the little creatures which fly, all those under water. The powers of each one of us we will share with you and you will have a ghost with you always — another self."

That's me, I thought, no other thing than myself, different, but me all the same, unseen, yet very real. I was frightened. I didn't understand it then. It took me a lifetime to find out.   25

And again I heard the voice amid the bird sounds, the clicking of beaks, the squeaking and chirping. "You have love for all that has been placed on this earth, not like the love of a mother for her son, or of a son for his

[8]*yuwipi ceremony:* A sacred ritual of healing, purification, and prayer using tiny sacred rocks gathered by medicine men from anthills for gourds and rattles.

mother, but a bigger love which encompasses the whole earth. You are just a human being, afraid, weeping under that blanket, but there is a great space within you to be filled with that love. All of nature can fit in there." I was shivering, pulling the blanket tighter around myself, but the voices repeated themselves over and over again, calling me "Brother, brother, brother." So this is how it is with me. Sometimes I feel like the first being in one of our Indian legends. This was a giant made of earth, water, the moon and the winds. He had timber instead of hair, a whole forest of trees. He had a huge lake in his stomach and a waterfall in his crotch. I feel like this giant. All of nature is in me, and a bit of myself is in all of nature.

ENGAGING THE TEXT

1. How does Lame Deer view his own personal relationship to nature and animals? How does this relationship compare with yours? Do you think it would be possible in contemporary American society to live the kind of wild life that Lame Deer advocates? How?

2. How, according to Lame Deer, do Native and white Americans differ in their views of life and death? What's wrong, in Lame Deer's view, with white society? Would you agree? How accurate are these portrayals of white or "mainstream" American cultural attitudes?

3. What do you think Lame Deer means when he says that a change is coming and that "A young man will come . . . who'll know how to shut off all electricity" (para. 18)? How would the world change if Lame Deer had his way? Would you want to live in Lame Deer's new world? Why or why not?

EXPLORING CONNECTIONS

4. Compare Lame Deer's views on nature and the wild with those of Henry David Thoreau in *Walking* (p. 646). To what extent does Lame Deer echo Thoreau's views of the wild and wildness?

5. To what extent does Lame Deer confirm Richard Louv's claim (p. 664) that we live in a society suffering from sensory deprivation or "cultural autism"? Does Lame Deer strike you as particularly alive in terms of his sensory experience of the world around him? Why or why not?

6. How might Lame Deer explain why animals are presented so unnaturally in the television programs that Charles Siebert describes (p. 676)? To what extent might Siebert agree with Lame Deer's assessment of white or mainstream American cultural values and attitudes?

EXTENDING THE CRITICAL CONTEXT

7. View the documentary film *Koyaanisqatsi*, which takes its title from the Hopi for "Life Out of Balance," and discuss the critique it offers of modern technology and urban America. To what extent would you agree with Lame Deer that technology has transformed Western civilization into a giant machine?

What, if anything, can be done, in your view, to make contemporary American culture less machine-like?

8. Do some research to learn more about the history of Native American impact on the environment prior to the arrival of Christopher Columbus. To what extent did tribal peoples shape, control, or modify the lands they occupied prior to 1492? How did tribal hunting and farming practices affect animal and plant life? To what extent do your findings support or challenge Lame Deer's claims?

Visual Portfolio

Reading Images of Nature and the Environment

R. CRUMB

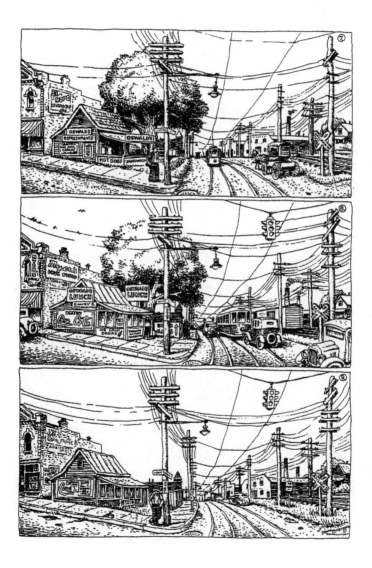

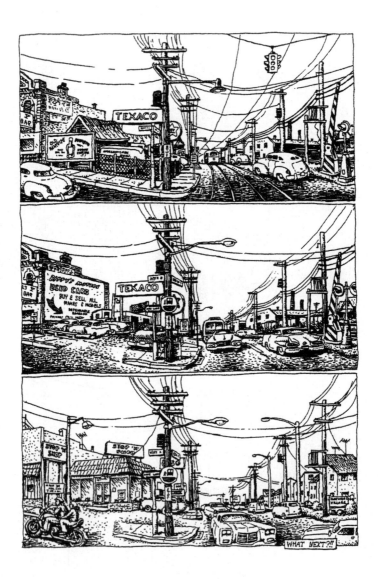

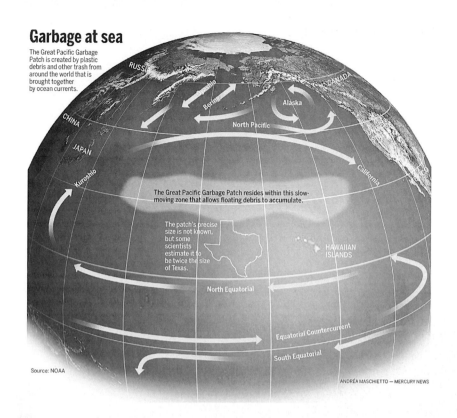

Garbage at sea

The Great Pacific Garbage Patch is created by plastic debris and other trash from around the world that is brought together by ocean currents.

RUSSIA

CHINA

JAPAN

CANADA

Oyashio

Bering

Alaska

North Pacific

Kuroshio

California

The Great Pacific Garbage Patch resides within this slow-moving zone that allows floating debris to accumulate.

The patch's precise size is not known, but some scientists estimate it to be twice the size of Texas.

HAWAIIAN ISLANDS

North Equatorial

Equatorial Countercurrent

South Equatorial

Source: NOAA

ANDRÉA MASCHIETTO — MERCURY NEWS

Visual Portfolio
READING IMAGES OF NATURE
AND THE ENVIRONMENT

1. What does R. Crumb's "A Short History of America" (pp. 695–98) say to you about American attitudes toward nature? Working in groups, discuss how you would design three additional panels showing what will happen to nature in America in the future. Compare your ideas for extending the series in class and discuss which seem most likely to occur. Then, visit this Web site to see how Crumb imagined America's future: http://www.citikin.com/2009/04/r-crumbs-short-history-of-america.html.

2. What do the historical photographs of logging in Minnesota in 1867 and a buffalo skull pile outside the Michigan Carbon Works in 1880 (p. 699) suggest about the reality of America's early relationship with nature? What do these images say in response to idealized renderings of nature like Asher B. Durand's *Kindred Spirits* (p. 639) and the opening panels of R. Crumb's "A Short History of America" (p. 695)?

3. What do the photos of the aftermath of the 2008 coal ash spill that devastated the Emory River in Eastern Tennessee (p. 700) and the "Great Pacific Garbage Patch"—a floating island of plastic trash roughly the size of the state of Texas (p. 701)—suggest about contemporary American attitudes toward nature? Go online to learn more about the coal ash spill incident and the "Great Pacific Garbage Patch." How did these eco-catastrophies happen? How much damage have they done? How might they be prevented or mitigated in the future?

4. How would you describe your reaction to the imaginary global warming photo of New York City underwater on page 702? Do you think this could actually happen in America? Why or why not? Do you think images like this motivate people to make the changes needed to address climate change?

Save the Whales, Screw the Shrimp
JOY WILLIAMS

What happens when American myths collide? Since the founding of the republic, Americans have associated nature with personal freedom. Life in the wilderness and along the Western frontier promised to liberate early Americans from the confines of European culture. Nature offered the individual a sanctuary, a place free of the formalities and constraints of civilization. But today the personal freedoms we cherish threaten to destroy nature itself — at least according to the author of this selection. As Joy Williams sees it, the greatest challenge to nature today is posed by us — and by our self-servingly hip brand of contemporary American culture. Williams is the author of four novels, including State of Grace *(1973) and* The Quick and the Dead, *which was nominated for the Pulitzer Prize in 2002. She has also published three collections of short stories and two works of nonfiction, including* Ill Nature: Rants and Reflections on Humanity and Other Animals *(2001), the source of this selection.*

I don't want to talk about *me*, of course, but it seems as though far too much attention has been lavished on *you* lately — that your greed and vanities and quest for self-fulfillment have been catered to far too much. You just want and want and want. You believe in yourself excessively. You don't believe in Nature anymore. It's too isolated from you. You've abstracted it. It's so messy and damaged and sad. Your eyes glaze as you travel life's highway past all the crushed animals and the Big Gulp cups. You don't even take pleasure in looking at nature photographs these days. Oh, they can be just as pretty as always, but don't they make you feel increasingly . . . anxious? Filled with more trepidation than peace? So what's the point? You see the picture of the baby condor or the panda munching on a bamboo shoot, and your heart just sinks, doesn't it? A picture of a poor old sea turtle with barnacles on her back, all ancient and exhausted, depositing her five gallons of doomed eggs in the sand hardly fills you with joy, because you realize, quite rightly, that just outside the frame falls the shadow of the condo. What's cropped from the shot of ocean waves crashing on a pristine shore is the plastics plant, and just beyond the dunes lies a parking lot. Hidden from immediate view in the butterfly-bright meadow, in the dusky thicket, in the oak and holly wood, are the surveyors' stakes, for someone wants to build a mall exactly there — some gas stations and supermarkets, some pizza and video shops, a health club, maybe a bulimia treatment center. Those lovely pictures of leopards and herons and wild rivers — well, you just know they're going to be accompanied by a text that will serve only to bring you down. You don't want to think about it! It's all so uncool. And you don't want to feel guilty either. Guilt is uncool. Regret maybe you'll consider. *Maybe.* Regret is a possibility, but don't push me, you say. Nature photographs have become something of a problem, along with almost everything else. Even though they leave the bad stuff out — maybe because you *know* they're leaving all the bad stuff out — such pictures are making you increasingly aware that you're a little too late for Nature. Do you feel that? Twenty years too late? Maybe only ten? Not *way* too late, just a little too late? Well, it appears that you are. And since you are, you've decided you're just not going to attend this particular party.

Pascal[1] said that it is easier to endure death without thinking about it than to endure the thought of death without dying. This is how you manage to dance the strange dance with that grim partner, nuclear annihilation. When the U.S. Army notified Winston Churchill[2] that the first A-bomb had been detonated in New Mexico, it chose the code phrase BABIES SATISFAC-TORILY BORN. So you entered the age of irony, and the strange double life you've been leading with the world ever since. Joyce Carol Oates[3] suggests that the reason writers — *real* writers, one assumes — don't write about Nature is that it lacks a sense of humor and registers no irony. It just doesn't seem to be of the times — these slick, sleek, knowing, objective, indulgent times. And the word *environment*. Such a bloodless word. A flat-footed word with a shrunken heart. A word increasingly disengaged from its association with the natural world. Urban planners, industrialists, economists, developers use it. It's a lost word, really. A cold word, mechanistic, suited strangely to the coldness generally felt toward Nature. It's their word now. You don't mind giving it up. As for *environmentalist*, that's one that can really bring on the yawns, for you've tamed and tidied it, neutered it quite nicely. An environmentalist must be calm, rational, reasonable, and willing to compromise; otherwise, you won't listen to him. Still, his beliefs are *opinions* only, for this is the age of radical subjectivism. Some people might prefer a Just for Feet store to open space, and they shouldn't be castigated for it. All beliefs and desires and needs are pretty much equally valid. The speculator has just as much right to that open space as the swallow, and the consumer has the most rights of all. Experts and computer models, to say nothing of lawsuits, can hold up environmental checks and reform for decades. The Environmental Protection Agency protects us by finding "acceptable levels of harm" from pollutants and then issuing rules allowing industry to pollute to those levels. Any other approach would place limits on economic growth. Limits on economic growth! What a witchy notion! The EPA can't keep abreast of progress and its unintended consequences. They're drowning in science. Whenever they do lumber into action and ban a weed killer, say (and you do love your weed killers — you particularly hate to see the more popular ones singled out), they have to pay all disposal costs and compensate the manufacturers for the market value of the chemicals they still have in stock.

That seems . . . that seems only fair, you say. Financial loss is a serious matter. And think of the farmers when a particular effective herbicide or pesticide is banned. They could be driven right out of business.

Farmers grow way too much stuff anyway. Federal farm policy, which subsidizes overproduction, encourages bigger and bigger farms and fewer and fewer farmers. The largest farms don't produce food at all, they grow feed.

[1]*Pascal:* Blaise Pascal (1623–1662), French mathematician, physicist, and philosopher.

[2]*Winston Churchill:* Sir Winston Leonard Spenser Churchill (1874–1965), British politician and prime minister of England from 1940 to 1945 and again from 1951 to 1955.

[3]*Joyce Carol Oates:* American novelist, poet, and short story writer (b. 1938).

One third of the wheat, three quarters of the corn, and almost all of the soybeans are used for feed. You get cheap hamburgers; the agribusiness moguls get immense profits. Subsidized crops are grown with subsidized water created by turning rivers great and small into a plumbing system of dams and irrigation ditches. Rivers have become conduits. Wetlands are increasingly being referred to as *filtering systems* — things deigned *useful* because of their ability to absorb urban runoff, oil from roads, et cetera.

We know that. We've known that for years about farmers. We know a lot these days. We're very well informed. If farmers aren't allowed to make a profit by growing surplus crops, they'll have to sell their land to developers, who'll turn all that arable land into office parks. Arable land isn't Nature anyway, and besides, we like those office parks and shopping plazas, with their monster supermarkets open twenty-four hours a day and aisle after aisle after aisle of products. It's fun. Products are fun. 5

Farmers like their poisons, but ranchers like them even more. There are well-funded federal programs like the Agriculture Department's "Animal Damage Control Unit," which, responding to public discomfort about its agenda, decided recently to change its name to the euphemistic Wildlife Services. Wildlife Services poisons, shoots, and traps thousands of animals each year. Servicing diligently, it kills bobcats, foxes, black bears, mountain lions, rabbits, badgers, countless birds — all to make this great land safe for the string bean and the corn, the sheep and the cow, even though you're not consuming as much cow these days. A burger now and then, but burgers are hardly cows at all, you feel. They're not all *our* cows, in any case, for some burger matter is imported. There's a bit of Central American burger matter in your bun. Which is contributing to the conversion of tropical rain forest into cow pasture. Even so, you're getting away from meat these days. You're eschewing cow. It's seafood you love, shrimp most of all. And when you love something, it had better watch out, because you have a tendency to love it to death. Shrimp, shrimp, shrimp. It's more common on menus than chicken. In the wilds of Ohio, far, far from watery shores, four out of the six entrees on a menu will be shrimp something-or-other, available, for a modest sum. Everywhere, it's all the shrimp you can eat or all you *care* to eat, for sometimes you just don't feel like eating all you *can*. You are intensively *harvesting* shrimp. Soon there won't be any left, and then you can stop. Shrimpers put out these big nets, and in these nets, for each pound of shrimp, they catch more than ten times that amount of fish, turtles, and dolphins. These, quite the worse for wear, are dumped back in. There is an object called TED (Turtle Excluder Device) that would save thousands of turtles and some dolphins from dying in the net, but shrimpers are loath to use TEDs, as they argue it would cut the size of their shrimp catch.

We've heard about TED, you say.

At Kiawah Island, off the coast of South Carolina, visitors go out on Jeep "safaris" through the part of the island that hasn't been developed yet.

("Wherever you see trees," the guide says, "it's actually a lot.") The visitors (i.e., potential buyers) drive their own Jeeps, and the guide talks to them by radio. Kiawah has nice beaches, and the guide talks about turtles. When he mentions the shrimpers' role in the decline of the turtle, the shrimpers, who share the same frequency, scream at him. Shrimpers and most commercial fishermen (many of them working with drift and gill nets anywhere from six to thirty miles long) think of themselves as an *endangered species*. A recent newspaper headline said, "SHRIMPERS SPARED ANTI-TURTLE DEVICES." Even so, with the continuing wanton depletion of shrimp beds, they will undoubtedly have to find some other means of employment soon. They might, for instance, become part of that vast throng laboring in the *tourist industry. . . .*

This is the time of machines and models, hands-on management and master plans. Don't you ever wonder as you pass that billboard advertising another MASTER PLANNED COMMUNITY just what master they are actually talking about? Not the Big Master, certainly. Something brought to you by one of the tiny masters, of which there are many. But you like these tiny masters and have even come to expect and require them. In Florida they're well into building a ten-thousand-acre city in the Everglades. It's a *megaproject*, one of the largest ever in the state. Yes, they must have thought you wanted it. No, what you thought of as the Everglades, the park, is only a little bitty part of the Everglades. Developers have been gnawing at this irreplaceable, strange land for years. It's like they just *hate* this ancient sea of grass. Maybe you could ask them about this sometime. Every tree and bush and inch of sidewalk in the project has been planned, of course. Nevertheless, because the whole thing will take twenty-five years to complete, the plan is going to be constantly changed. You can understand this. The important thing is that there be a blueprint. You trust a blueprint. The tiny masters know what you like. You like *a secure landscape* and *access to services*. You like grass — that is, lawns. The ultimate lawn is the golf course, which you've been told has "some ecological value." You believe this! Not that it really matters — you just like to play golf. These golf courses require a lot of watering. So much that the more inspired of the masters have taken to watering them with effluent, *treated* effluent, but yours, from all the condos and villas built around the stocked artificial lakes you fancy.

I really don't want to think about sewage, you say, but it sounds like progress. 10

It is true that the masters are struggling with the problems of your incessant flushing. Cuisine is also one of their concerns. Great advances have been made in sorbets — sorbet intermezzos — in their clubs and fine restaurants. They know what you want. You want A HAVEN FROM THE ORDINARY WORLD. If you're a NATURE LOVER in the West, you want to live in a WILD ANIMAL HABITAT. If you're eastern and consider yourself more hip, you want to live in a new town — a brand-new reconstructed-from-scratch town — in a house of NINETEENTH-CENTURY DESIGN. But in these new towns the masters are building, getting around can be confusing. There is an abundance of curves and an infrequency of through streets. It's the new wilderness without any trees. You can get lost, even with all the "mental bread crumbs" the masters scatter about as visual landmarks — the windmill, the water views, the various groupings of landscape "material." You *are* lost, you know. But you trust a Realtor will show you the way. There are many more Realtors than tiny masters, and many of them have to make do with less than a loaf — that is, trying to sell stuff that's already been built in an environment already "enhanced" rather than something being planned — but they're everywhere, willing to show you the path. If Dante returned to Hell today, he'd probably be escorted down by a Realtor talking all the while about how it was just another level of Paradise.

> When have you last watched a sunset? Do you remember where you were? With whom? At Loews Ventana Canyon Resort, the Grand Foyer will provide you with that opportunity through lighting that is computerized to diminish with the approaching sunset!

The tiny masters are willing to arrange Nature for you. They will compose it into a picture that you can look at at your leisure, when you're not doing work or something like that. Nature becomes scenery, a prop. At some golf courses in the Southwest, the saguaro cactuses are reported to be repaired with green paste when balls blast into their skin. The saguaro can attempt to heal themselves by growing over the balls, but this takes time, and the effect can be somewhat . . . baroque. It's better to get out the pastepot. Nature has become simply a visual form of entertainment, and it had better look snappy.

Listen, you say, we've been at Ventana Canyon. It's in the desert, right? It's very, very nice, a world-class resort. A totally self-contained environment with everything that a person could possibly want, on more than a thousand acres in the middle of zip. It sprawls but nestles, like. And they've maintained the integrity of as much of the desert ecosystem as possible. Give them credit for that. Great restaurant, too. We had baby bay scallops there. Coming into the lobby there are these two big hand-carved coyotes, mutely howling. And that's the way we like them, mute. God, why do those things howl like that?

Wildlife is a personal matter, you think. The attitude is up to you. You can prefer to see it dead or not dead. You might want to let it mosey about its business or blow it away. Wild things exist only if you have the graciousness to allow them to. Just outside Tucson, Arizona, there is a structure modeled after a French foreign legion outpost. It's the *International Wildlife Museum,* and it's full of dead animals. Three hundred species are there, at least a third of them — the rarest ones — killed and collected by one C. J. McElroy, who enjoyed doing it and now shares what's left with you. The museum claims to be educational because you can watch a taxidermist at work or touch a lion's tooth. You can get real close to these dead animals, closer than you can in a zoo. Some of you prefer zoos, however, which are becoming bigger, better, and bioclimatic. New-age zoo designers want the animals to *flow right out into your space*. In Dallas there's a Wilds of Africa exhibit; in San Diego there's a simulated rain forest, where you can thread your way "down the side of a lush canyon, the air filled with a fine mist from three hundred high-pressure nozzles . . ."; in New Orleans you've constructed a swamp, the real swamp not far away being on the verge of disappearing. Animals in these places are abstractions — wandering relics of their true selves, but that doesn't matter. Animal behavior in a zoo is nothing like natural behavior, but that doesn't matter, either. Zoos are pretty, contained, and accessible. These new habitats can contain one hundred different species — not more than one or two of each thing, of course — on seven acres, three, one. You don't want to see *too much* of anything, certainly. An *example* will suffice. Sort of like a biological Crabtree & Evelyn[4] basket selected with *you* in mind. You like things reduced, simplified. It's easier to take it all in, park it in your mind. You like things inside better than outside anyway. You are increasingly looking at and living in proxy environments created by substitution and simulation. *Resource economists* are a wee branch in the tree of tiny masters, and one, Martin Krieger, wrote, "Artificial prairies and wildernesses have been created, and there is no reason to believe that these artificial environments need be unsatisfactory for those who experience them. . . . We will have to realize that the way in which we experience nature is conditioned by our society — which more and more is seen to be receptive to responsible intervention."

Fiddle, fiddle, fiddle. You support fiddling, as well as meddling. This is   15
how you learn. Though it's quite apparent that the environment has been grossly polluted and the natural world abused and defiled, you seem to prefer to continue pondering effects rather than preventing causes. You want proof, you insist on proof. A Dr. Lave from Carnegie-Mellon — and he's an expert, an economist and an environmental *expert* — says that scientists will have to prove to you that you will suffer if you don't become less of a "throw-away society." *If you really want me to give up my car or my air conditioner, you'd better prove to me first that the earth would otherwise be uninhabitable*, Dr. Lave says. *Me* is *you*, I presume, whereas *you* refers to them. You as in me — that is, *me, me, me* — certainly strike a hard bargain. Uninhabitable the world has to get before you reign in your requirements. You're a consumer after all, *the* consumer upon whom so much attention is lavished, the ultimate user of a commodity that has become, these days, everything. To try to appease your appetite for proof, for example, scientists have been leasing for experimentation forty-six pristine lakes in Canada.

---

[4]*Crabtree & Evelyn:* American retailer of body and home products.

They don't want to *keep* them, they just want to *borrow* them.

They've been intentionally contaminating many of the lakes with a variety of pollutants dribbled into the propeller wash of research boats. It's *one of the boldest experiments in lake ecology ever conducted*. They've turned these remote lakes into huge *real-world test tubes*. They've been doing this since 1976! And what they've found so far in these *preliminary* studies is that pollutants are really destructive. The lakes get gross. Life in them ceases. It took about eight years to make this happen in one of them, everything carefully measured and controlled all the while. Now the scientists are slowly reversing the process. But it will take hundreds of years for the lakes to recover. They think.

Remember when you used to like rain, the sound of it, the feel of it, the way it made the plants and trees all glisten? We needed that rain, you would say. It looked pretty too, you thought, particularly in the movies. Now it rains and you go, Oh-oh. A nice walloping rain these days means *overtaxing our sewage treatment plants*. It means *untreated waste discharged directly into our waterways*. It means . . .

Okay. Okay.

Acid rain! And we all know what this is. Or most of us do. People of   20
power in government and industry still don't seem to know what it is. Whatever it is, they say, they don't want to curb it, but they're willing to study it some more. Economists call air and water pollution "externalities" anyway. Oh, acid rain. You do get so sick of hearing about it. The words have already become a white-noise kind of thing. But you think in terms of *mitigating* it maybe. As for *the greenhouse effect*, you think in terms of *countering* that. One way that's been discussed is the planting of new forests, not for the sake of the forests alone, oh my heavens, no. Not for the sake of majesty and mystery or of Thumper and Bambi,[5] are you kidding me, but because, as every schoolchild knows, trees absorb carbon dioxide. They just soak it up and store it. They just love it. So this is the plan; you can plant millions of acres of trees, and you go on doing pretty much whatever you're doing — driving around, using staggering amounts of energy, keeping those power plants fired to the max. Isn't Nature remarkable? So willing to serve? You wouldn't think it had anything more to offer, but it seems it does. Of course, these "forests" wouldn't exactly be forests. They would be more like trees. *Managed* trees. The Forest Service, which now manages our forests by cutting them down, might be called upon to evolve in its thinking and allow these trees to grow. They would probably be patented trees after a time. Fast-growing, uniform, genetically created toxin-eating *machines*. They would be *new-age* trees, because the problem with planting the old-fashioned variety to *combat* the greenhouse effect, which is caused by pollution, is that they're already dying

---

[5]*Thumper and Bambi:* Woodland characters in the 1942 animated film *Bambi*.

from it. All along the crest of the Appalachians from Maine to Georgia, forests struggle to survive in a toxic soup of poisons. They can't *help* us if we've killed them, now can they?

All right, you say, *wow, lighten up, will you? Relax. Tell about yourself.*
"Well, I say, I live in Florida . . .
Oh my god, you say. Florida! Florida is a joke! How do you expect us to take you seriously if you still live there! Florida is crazy, it's pink concrete. It's paved, it's over. And a little girl just got eaten by an alligator down there. It came out of some swamp next to a subdivision and carried her off, That set your Endangered Species Act back fifty years, you can bet.
  I . . .
Listen, we don't want to hear any more about Florida. We don't want to hear about Phoenix or California's Central Valley. If our wetlands — our vanishing wetlands — are mentioned one more time, we'll scream. And the talk about condors and grizzlies and wolves is becoming too de trop.[6] *We had just managed to get whales out of our minds. Now there are butterflies, frogs even that you want us to worry about. And those manatees. Don't they know what a boat propeller can do to them by now? They're not too smart. And those last condors are* pathetic. *Can't we just get this over with?*   25
Aristotle said that all living beings are ensouled and strive to participate in eternity.
Oh, I just bet he said that, you say. That doesn't sound like Aristotle.[7] He was a humanist. We're all humanists here. This is the age of humanism. Militant humanism. And it has been for a long time.

You are driving with a stranger in the car, and it is the stranger who is behind the wheel. In the backseat are your pals for many years now — DO WHAT YOU LIKE and his swilling sidekick, WHY NOT. A deer, or some emblematic animal — something from that myriad natural world you've come from that you now treat with such indifference and scorn — steps from the dimming woods and tentatively upon the highway. The stranger does not decelerate or brake, not yet, maybe not at all. The feeling is that whatever it is *will get out of the way.* Oh, it's a fine car you've got, a fine machine, and oddly you don't mind the stranger driving it, because in a way, everything has gotten too complicated, way, way out of your control. You've given the wheel to the masters, the managers, the comptrollers. Something is wrong, *maybe,* you feel a little sick, *actually,* but the car is luxurious and fast and you're *moving,* which is the most important thing by far.
  Why make a fuss when you're so comfortable? Don't make a fuss, make a baby. Go out and get something to eat, build something. Make *another* baby. Babies are cute. Babies show you have faith in the future. Although

---

[6]*de trop:* French for "too much" or "too many."
[7]*Aristotle:* Greek philosopher (384–322 B.C.E.).

faith is perhaps too strong a word. They're everywhere these days; in all the crowds and traffic jams, there are the babies too. You don't seem to associate them with the problems of population increase. They're just babies! And you've come to believe in them again. They're a lot more tangible than the afterlife, which, of course, you haven't believed in in ages. At least not for yourself. The afterlife now belongs to plastics and poisons. Yes, plastics and poisons will have a far more extensive afterlife than you, that's known. A disposable diaper, for example, which is all plastic and wood pulp, will take around four centuries to degrade. But you like disposable — so easy to use and toss — and now that marketing is urging you not to rush the potty training by making diapers for four-year-olds available and socially acceptable, there will be more and more dumped diapers around, each taking, like most plastics, centuries and centuries to deteriorate. . . .

You're getting a little shrill here, you say.   30

You're pretty well off. And you expect to become even better off. You do. What does this mean? More software, more scampi, more square footage, more communication towers to keep you in touch and amused and informed? You want to count birds? Go to the bases of communication towers being built all across the country. Three million migratory songbirds perish each year by slamming into towers and their attendant guy wires. The building of thousands of new digital television towers one thousand feet and taller is being expedited by the FCC, which proposes to preempt all local and state environmental laws. You have created an ecological crisis. The earth is infinitely variable and alive, and you are moderating it, simplifying it, killing it. It seems safer this way. But you are not safe. You want to find wholeness and happiness in a land increasingly damaged and betrayed, and you never will. More than material matters. You must change your ways.

What is this? Sinners in the Hands of an Angry God?[8]

The ecological crisis cannot be resolved by politics. It cannot be resolved by science or technology. It is a crisis caused by culture and character, and a deep change in personal consciousness is needed. Your fundamental attitudes toward the earth have become twisted. You have made only brutal contact with Nature; you cannot comprehend its grace. You must change. Have few desires and simple pleasures. Honor nonhuman life. Control yourself, become more authentic. Live lightly upon the earth and treat it with respect. Redefine the word *progress* and dismiss the managers and masters. Grow inwardly and with knowledge become truly wiser. Think differently, behave differently. For this is essentially a moral issue we face, and moral decisions must be made.

A moral issue! Okay, this discussion is now over. A moral issue . . . And who's this we now? Who are you, is what I'd like to know. You're not me, anyway. I admit someone's to blame and something should be done. But I've got to go. It's getting late. Take care of yourself.

---

[8]*Sinners in the Hands of an Angry God:* Title of a famous sermon written by colonial American theologian Jonathan Edwards (1703–1758).

Engaging the Text

1. Who is Williams addressing in this essay? What does she think of her imaginary reader? How effective do you find this approach, and why do you think Williams uses it?

2. Would you agree that we "don't believe in Nature anymore" and that we "don't want to think about it"? What evidence do you see that nature today has become associated with guilt and regret, and that nature itself is regarded by many Americans as "uncool"?

3. Why, according to Williams, has "environment" become "a lost word," and why does she feel that the word "environmentalist" has been "neutered"? Would you agree with these statements? Do you think the way we talk about the environment is as important as what we do to it? Why or why not?

4. Toward the end of her essay, Williams blames the reader for having "created an ecological crisis" (para. 31). What solutions does she offer to rectify this situation? Is she really suggesting, for example, that we ban golf, close shopping malls and zoos, and stop having babies? To what extent would you agree that preserving nature today has become a "moral issue"?

"It saves energy and makes me feel holier."

EXPLORING CONNECTIONS

5. What would Henry David Thoreau (p. 646) probably think of Williams's "reader"? What might Williams's reader think of Thoreau and his view of nature?

6. Write an imaginary dialogue between Richard Louv (p. 664) and Williams about "the know-it-all state of mind" and the importance of direct experience with nature. To what extent do you think America's recent obsession with getting back to nature is actually damaging the environment?

7. How might Charles Siebert's analysis of the way animals are portrayed on television (p. 676) support or complicate Williams's view of our current relationship with nature? Would Siebert agree that pictures of nature make us feel "anxious" today?

EXTENDING THE CRITICAL CONTEXT

8. Write a journal entry about a particularly memorable "artificial environment" you've encountered. It may have been at a mall, museum, zoo or theme park, or at a resort or planned community. How satisfying was your experience of this "proxy environment"? Can you think of any experience you've had with nature that didn't involve human intervention?

9. Go online to research the carbon footprint of a human baby. What can you find out about the environmental impact of having a child? To what extent does the environmental cost of having a baby vary from nation to nation? In light of your findings, would you be in favor of voluntary or government mandated family planning? Why or why not?

From *As the World Burns:*
50 Simple Things You Can Do
to Stay in Denial

DERRICK JENSEN
AND STEPHANIE McMILLAN

We've all seen those cheery eco-self-help books that promise to tell us the "100 Easy Things We Can Do to Save the Planet." Ever since former vice president Al Gore made the project of combating global warming cool by winning both the Academy Award and the Nobel Peace Prize for his film An Inconvenient Truth, *American culture has gone wild about going green. Want to reverse climate change? Try installing compact fluorescent lights! Want to save the polar bears? Buy a hybrid! But as authors of this selection remind us, putting an end to global warming might take more than adjusting individual lifestyles. Derrick Jensen (b. 1960) is an environmental activist and self-described "anarcho-primitivist" who has authored numerous books on nature and modern society, including* Endgame: The Problem of Civilization *(2007). Stephanie McMillan is the creator of the* Minimum Security *cartoon series, which has appeared in magazines and newspapers across the country. Jensen and McMillan collaborated to create the source of this selection:* As the World Burns: 50 Simple Things You Can Do to Stay in Denial *(2007).*

We did it! We saved the planet!

That's if every person in the United States does every one of these things.

But they will! If we just tell them. This isn't so hard! We can do it!

There's just one thing. Total carbon emissions for the United States is 7.1 billion tons.

If every man, woman and child did all of the things on the list from the movie ~ and you know there is precisely zero chance that every man, woman and child in the United States will do this...

I don't like where this is going.

That would only be about a 21 percent reduction in carbon emissions. And since total carbon emissions go up about two percent per year, that whole reduction would disappear in about...

* sigh. *

Oh, I know what you're going to say. You're going to say that in order to have air conditioning and all those other things ~ even if they're solar powered ~ you still have to have mining for the copper wires and the silicon and everything else, and you have to have the whole industrial infrastructure, which means you have to have roads and the whole oil economy to move stuff around, which means you have to have this huge military so you can take the oil from wherever it is, and you have to have this whole system which leads to some people being rich and some people being poor, which means you have to have police to make sure the poor don't take back from the rich, and you have to have prisons and everything else that comes with that.

And then the rich keep getting richer and the poor keep getting poorer.

And it all keeps killing the planet.

I know that's what you'd say.

So then I would say, what about high technology? Can't that work? I really want it to work. I've heard all these great things about how nanotechnology will make production so much easier.

Wouldn't that be a good thing?

But then I know just what you'd say. You'd say that all these technologies follow the same pattern of being hyped and hyped and hyped, and then they always ~always~ cause more pollution and they always ~always~ cause the rich to get richer and the poor to be more exploited, and they always ~ always ~ cause the world to be hurt more and more. Every time.

I know that's what you'd say.

And then after that you'd ask: who controls these technologies? Can I make nanotechnology in my basement? And then you'd say, Of course not. Big corporations will control it just like they control everything else.

And then I'd get really sad because it won't work the way it's promised and I want it to work, and I'll know you're right but I don't want you to be right.

So then I'll ask if we can use biofuels to save us. And you'll say that industrial agriculture is based on natural gas and oil for fertilizers and pesticides, and it's incredibly toxic and it destroys soil and water.

And you'll say it's all controlled by big corporations.

And you'll say that if every single bit of cropland in the United States was used for biofuels it would make up only fifteen percent of this country's demand, but even then it's impossible because growing corn for biofuels actually takes more energy than it makes.

You'd tell me that currently it takes ten calories of dino-fuel to grow one calorie of food in the United States. People have covered croplands with McMansions because they believe they currently have that fuel to waste.

But then you'd tell me that without the ten calories of fuel, they will need way more laborers and way more croplands to feed the people who currently exist.

°Beethoven and The Clash: Ludwig van Beethoven (1770–1827), German composer and
pianist. The Clash: English rock band active in the 1970s and 80s.

ENGAGING THE TEXT

1. Why do the characters in this graphic novel disagree about how to save the world from global warming? How would you describe their positions on the global warming debate? Which one of them do you identify with? Why?

2. What's wrong, according to Jensen and McMillan, with taking personal responsibility for reducing climate change by doing things like conserving natural resources and recycling? Would you agree that lifestyle changes do little more than make us feel better? Why or why not?

3. What solutions do Jensen and McMillan offer to the climate change crisis? Do you agree that to save the environment we need, for example, to recognize that animals are conscious, to "stop the industrial production of everything," and to get rid of "...cities, grocery stores, giant farms, highways... medicines... computers... CDs of Beethoven and The Clash"?

4. What do you think Jensen and McMillan are trying to achieve through this graphic novel? What do you think they want their audience to do as the result of reading it? How realistic is this expectation in your view?

"Can't we just dye the smoke green?"

Exploring Connections

5. How might Richard Louv (p. 664) assess the portrayal of nature in *As the World Burns*? Is nature in this graphic novel just another kind of abstract or artificial version of real nature?

6. How would you expect John (Fire) Lame Deer (p. 686) to respond to Jensen and McMillan's proposal that modern Western civilizations "dismantle the industrial economy" and live in harmony with nature? How likely would this be to happen in Lame Deer's view? Why?

7. Assess the depth of your own ecology using the "Eco Depth Gauge" that appears on page 755. If the characters in *As the World Burns* were to take this test, where do you think they would rate? Where would you? Is it possible that a "quick annihilation" of human life would actually be the best way to save the earth?

Extending the Critical Context

8. View the groundbreaking 2006 environmental film *An Inconvenient Truth* and compare the advice that Vice President Al Gore offers for combating global warming with that offered in *As the World Burns*. What role should personal responsibility play in fighting climate change according to Gore? In general, what do you think individuals should do to fight global warming?

9. Working in groups, research some of the common approaches for mitigating global warming that Jensen and McMillan critique, including, for example, the use of CFLs, recycling, reforestation, and the use of biofuels, solar panels, and wind farming. Based on your research, how accurately does *As the World Burns* portray the effectiveness of these approaches? What other promising techniques for mitigating climate change do Jensen and McMillan omit?

From *The End of Nature*

Bill McKibben

Over the past thirty years, Bill McKibben has emerged as one of the most eloquent leaders of the American environmental movement. A journalist, essayist, and Methodist minister, McKibben (b. 1960) was an early advocate of sustainable living and other measures to fight global warming. First published in 1989, The End of Nature *represents one of the earliest important popular works on the topic of climate change and is still regarded as one of the most powerful explorations of what global warming means for the planet and the human race. In this selection, McKibben reflects on what nature has meant to us — and why we, as a species, will never experience real nature again. McKibben's other publications include* The Age of Missing Information *(1992),* Wandering Home *(2005),* Deep Economy: The Wealth of Communities and the Durable Future *(2007), and, with the members of his "Step It Up" environmental activist team,* Fight Global Warming Now: A Handbook for Taking Action in Your Community *(2007).*

Almost every day, I hike up the hill out my back door. Within a hundred yards the woods swallows me up, and there is nothing to remind me of human society — no trash, no stumps, no fence, not even a real path. Looking out from the high places, you can't see road or house; it is a world apart from man. But once in a while someone will be cutting wood farther down the valley, and the snarl of a chain saw will fill the woods. It is harder on those days to get caught up in the timeless meaning of the forest, for man is nearby. The sound of the chain saw doesn't blot out all the noises of the forest or drive the animals away, but it does drive away the feeling that you are in another, separate, timeless, wild sphere.

Now that we have changed the most basic forces around us, the noise of that chain saw will always be in the woods. We have changed the atmosphere, and that will change the weather. The temperature and rainfall are no longer to be entirely the work of some separate, uncivilizable force, but instead in part a product of our habits, our economies, our ways of life. Even in the most remote wilderness, where the strictest laws forbid the felling of a single tree, the sound of that saw will be clear, and a walk in the woods will be changed — tainted — by its whine. The world outdoors will mean much the same thing as the world indoors, the hill the same thing as the house.

An idea, a relationship, can go extinct, just like an animal or a plant. The idea in this case is "nature," the separate and wild province, the world apart from man to which he adapted, under whose rules he was born and died. In the past, we spoiled and polluted parts of that nature, inflicted environmental "damage." But that was like stabbing a man with toothpicks: though it hurt, annoyed, degraded, it did not touch vital organs, block the path of the lymph or blood. We never thought that we had wrecked nature. Deep down, we never really thought we could: it was too big and too old; its forces — the wind, the rain, the sun — were too strong, too elemental.

But, quite by accident, it turned out that the carbon dioxide and other gases we were producing in our pursuit of a better life — in pursuit of warm houses and eternal economic growth and of agriculture so productive it would free most of us from farming — *could* alter the power of the sun, could increase its heat. And that increase *could* change the patterns of moisture and dryness, breed storms in new places, breed deserts. Those things may or may not have yet begun to happen, but it is too late to altogether prevent them from happening. We have produced the carbon dioxide — we are ending nature.

We have not ended rainfall or sunlight; in fact, rainfall and sunlight may 5
become more important forces in our lives. It is too early to tell exactly how much harder the wind will blow, how much hotter the sun will shine. That is for the future. But the *meaning* of the wind, the sun, the rain — of nature — has already changed. Yes, the wind still blows — but no longer from some other sphere, some inhuman place.

In the summer, my wife and I bike down to the lake nearly every after-noon for a swim. It is a dogleg Adirondack lake, with three beaver lodges, a blue heron, some otter, a family of mergansers, the occasional loon. A few summer houses cluster at one end, but mostly it is surrounded by wild state land. During the week we swim across and back, a trip of maybe forty minutes — plenty of time to forget everything but the feel of the water around your body and the rippling, muscular joy of a hard kick and the pull of your arms.

But on the weekends, more and more often, someone will bring a boat out for waterskiing, and make pass after pass up and down the lake. And then the whole experience changes, changes entirely. Instead of being able to forget everything but yourself, and even yourself except for the muscles and the skin, you must be alert, looking up every dozen strokes to see where the boat is, thinking about what you will do if it comes near. It is not so much the danger — few swimmers, I imagine, ever die by Evinrude.[1] It's not even so much the blue smoke that hangs low over the water. It's that the motor-boat gets in your mind. You're forced to think, not feel — to think of human society and of people. The lake is utterly different on these days, just as the planet is utterly different now. . . .

But still we feel the need for pristine places, places substantially *unal-tered* by man. Even if we do not visit them, they matter to us. We need to know that though we are surrounded by buildings there are vast places where the world goes on as it always has. The Arctic National Wildlife Refuge, on Alaska's northern shore, is reached by just a few hundred people a year, but it has a vivid life in the minds of many more, who are upset that oil compa-nies want to drill there. And upset not only because it may or may not harm the caribou but because here is a vast space free of roads and buildings and antennas, a blank spot if not on the map then on the surface. It sickens us to hear that "improper waste disposal practices" at the American Antarctic research station in McMurdo Sound have likely spread toxic waste on that remote continent, or that an Exxon tanker has foundered off the port of Valdez,[2] tarring the beaches with petroleum.

[1]*Evinrude:* Brand of outboard motor used on recreational boats.
[2]*Exxon tanker . . . port of Valdez:* In 1989, the Exxon *Valdez* ran aground in Prince William Sound, Alaska, spilling an estimated 10.8 million gallons of crude oil.

One proof of the deep-rooted desire for pristine places is the decision that Americans and others have made to legislate "wilderness"—to set aside vast tracts of land where, in the words of the federal statute, "the earth and its community of life are untrammeled by man, where man himself is a visitor who does not remain." Pristine nature, we recognize, has been overwhelmed in many places, even in many of our national parks. But in these few spots it makes a stand. If we can't have places where no man has ever been, we can at least have spots where no man is at the moment.

Segregating such wilderness areas has not been easy. The quiet of the   10
land behind my house, fifty thousand acres of state wilderness, is daily broken by Air Force jets practicing flying beneath radar; they come in pairs, twisting and screeching above the hills, so that for a moment, and a few moments after that, it is no wilderness at all. And often, of course, man invades more insidiously: the synthetic compounds of man's pesticides, for instance, worm their way slowly but inevitably into the fabric of life.

But, even under such stress, it is still wilderness, still pristine in our minds. Most of the day, the sky above my mountain is simply sky, not "airspace." Standing in the middle of a grimy English mill town, George Orwell[3] records this "encouraging" thought: "In spite of hard trying, man has not yet succeeded in doing his dirt everywhere. The earth is so vast and still so empty that even in the filthy heart of civilization you find fields where the grass is green instead of grey; perhaps if you looked for them you might even find streams with live fish in them instead of salmon tins." When Rachel Carson[4] wrote *Silent Spring*, she was able to find some parts of the Arctic still untouched—no DDT[5] in the fish, the beaver, the beluga, the caribou, the moose, the polar bear, the walrus. The cranberries, the strawberries, and the wild rhubarb all tested clean, though two snowy owls, probably as a result of their migrations, carried small amounts of the pesticide, as did the livers of two Eskimos who had been away to the hospital in Anchorage.

In other words, as pervasive a problem as DDT was, and is, one could, and can, always imagine that *somewhere* a place existed free of its taint. (And largely as a result of Carson's book there are more and more such places.) As pervasive and growing as the problem of acid rain surely is, at the moment places still exist with a rainfall of an acceptable, "normal" pH. And if we wished to stop acid rain we could; experimenters have placed tents over groves of trees to demonstrate that if the acid bath ceases, a forest will return to normal. Even the radiation from an event as nearly universal

---

[3]*George Orwell:* Pen name of Eric Arthur Blair (1903–1950), English novelist, essayist, and journalist.

[4]*Rachel Carson:* Rachel Louise Carson (1907–1964), American marine biologist and nature writer. (See p. 644.)

[5]*DDT:* Dichlorodiphenyltrichloroethane, a pesticide used widely from World War II until it was banned in 1972.

as the explosion at the Chernobyl[6] plant has begun to fade, and Scandinavians can once more eat their vegetables.

We can, in other words, still plausibly imagine wild nature — or, at least, the possibility of wild nature in the future — in all sorts of places. . . .

But now the basis of that faith is lost. The idea of nature will not survive the new global pollution — the carbon dioxide and the CFCs[7] and the like. This new rupture with nature is different not only in scope but also in kind from salmon tins in an English stream. We have changed the atmosphere, and thus we are changing the weather. By changing the weather, we make every spot on earth man-made and artificial. We have deprived nature of its independence, and that is fatal to its meaning. Nature's independence *is* its meaning; without it there is nothing but us.

If you travel by plane and dog team and snowshoe to the farthest corner of the Arctic and it is a mild summer day, you will not know whether the temperature is what it is "supposed" to be, or whether, thanks to the extra carbon dioxide, you are standing in the equivalent of a heated room. If it is twenty below and the wind is howling — perhaps absent man it would be forty below. Since most of us get to the North Pole only in our minds, the real situation is more like this: if in July there's a heat wave in London, it won't be a natural phenomenon. It will be a man-made phenomenon — an amplification of what nature intended or a total invention. Or, at the very least, it *might* be a man-made phenomenon, which amounts to the same thing. The storm that might have snapped the hot spell may never form, or may veer off in some other direction, not by the laws of nature but by the laws of nature as they have been rewritten, blindly, crudely, but effectively, by man. If the sun is beating down on you, you will not have the comfort of saying, "Well, that's nature." Or if the sun feels sweet on the back of your neck, that's fine, but it isn't nature. A child born now will never know a natural summer, a natural autumn, winter, or spring. Summer is going extinct, replaced by something else that will be called "summer." This new summer will retain some of its relative characteristics — it will be hotter than the rest of the year, for instance, and the time of year when crops grow — but it will not be summer, just as even the best prosthesis is not a leg.

And, of course, climate determines an enormous amount of the rest of nature — where the forests stop and the prairies or the tundra begins, where the rain falls and where the arid deserts squat, where the wind blows strong and steady, where the glaciers form, how fast the lakes evaporate, where the seas rise. As John Hoffman, of the Environmental Protection Agency, noted

15

[6]*Chernobyl:* In 1986, the Chernobyl Nuclear Power Plant near the city of Pripyat in the Ukraine suffered an explosion leading to the worst nuclear power disaster in history.

[7]*CFCs:* Chlorofluorocarbons are a family of chemical compounds commonly used as flame retardants, refrigerants, and propellants that have been banned due to their destructive effect on the ozone layer, which protects the earth from the sun's ultraviolet radiation.

in the *Journal of Forestry*, "trees planted today will be entering their period of greatest growth when the climate has already changed." A child born today might swim in a stream free of toxic waste, but he won't ever see a natural stream. If the waves crash up against the beach, eroding dunes and destroying homes, it is not the awesome power of Mother Nature. It is the awesome power of Mother Nature as altered by the awesome power of man, who has overpowered in a century the processes that have been slowly evolving and changing of their own accord since the earth was born.

Those "record highs" and "record lows" that the weathermen are always talking about — they're meaningless now. It's like comparing pole vaults between athletes using bamboo and those using fiberglass poles, or dash times between athletes who've been chewing steroids and those who've stuck to Wheaties. They imply a connection between the past and the present which doesn't exist. The comparison is like hanging Rembrandts[8] next to Warhols;[9] we live in a postnatural world. Thoreau once said he could walk for half an hour and come to "some portion of the earth's surface where man does not stand from one year's end to another, and there, consequently, politics are not, for they are but the cigar-smoke of a man." Now you could walk half a year and not reach such a spot. Politics — our particular way of life, our ideas about how we should live — now blows its smoke over[10] every inch of the globe.

About a half mile from my house, right at the head of the lake, the town has installed a streetlight. It is the only one for miles, and it is undeniably useful — without it, a car or two each summer would undoubtedly miss the turn and end up in the drink. Still, it intrudes on the dark. Most of the year, once the summer people have left, there is not another light to be seen. On a starry night the Milky Way stands out like a marquee; on a cloudy night you can walk in utter pitch-black, unable to see even the dog trotting at your side. But then, around the corner, there is the streetlamp, and soon you are in its sodium-vapor circle, a circle robbed of mystery by its illumination. It's true that the bugs love the lamp; on a June night there is more wildlife buzzing around it than in any square acre of virgin forest. But it breaks up the feeling of the night. And now it is as if we had put a huge lamp in the sky, and cast that same prosaic sterile light at all times on all places. . . .

The invention of nuclear weapons may actually have marked the beginning of the end of nature: we possessed, finally, the capacity to overmaster

---

[8]*Rembrandts:* Artworks by Dutch painter Rembrandt Harmenszoon van Rijn (1606–1669).

[9]*Warhols:* Artworks by American painter, visual artist, and filmmaker Andy Warhol (1928–1987).

[10]*Politics . . . now blows its smoke over . . . :* A reference to Henry David Thoreau's 1862 essay "Walking": "In one half-hour I can walk off to some portion of the earth's surface where a man does not stand from one year's end to another, and there, consequently, politics are not, for they are but as the cigar-smoke of a man." (See p. 648.)

nature, to leave an indelible imprint everywhere all at once. "The nuclear peril is usually seen in isolation from the threats to other forms of life and their ecosystems, but in fact it should be seen at the very center of the ecological crisis, as the cloud-covered Everest of which the more immediate, visible kinds of harm to the environment are the mere foothills," wrote Jonathan Schell in *The Fate of the Earth*. And he was correct, for at the time he was writing (less than a decade ago!) it was hard to conceive of any threats of the same magnitude. Global warming was one obscure theory among many. Nuclear weapons were unique (and they remain so, if only for the speed with which they work). But the nuclear dilemma is at least open to human reason — we can decide not to drop the weapons, and indeed to reduce and perhaps eliminate them. And the horrible power of these weapons, which has been amply demonstrated in Japan and on Bikini[11] and under Nevada[12] and many times in our imaginations, has led us fitfully in that hopeful direction.

By contrast, the various processes that lead to the end of nature have   20
been essentially beyond human thought. Only a few people knew that carbon dioxide would warm up the world, for instance, and they were for a long time unsuccessful in their efforts to alert the rest of us. Now it is too late — not too late, as I shall come to explain, to ameliorate some of the changes and so perhaps to avoid the most gruesome of their consequences. But the scientists agree that we have already pumped enough gas into the air so that a significant rise in temperature and a subsequent shift in weather are inevitable. . . .

There are some people, perhaps many, to whom this rupture will mean little. A couple of years ago a group of executives went rafting down a river in British Columbia; after an accident killed five of them, one of the survivors told reporters that the party had regarded the river as "a sort of ersatz roller-coaster." Nature has become a hobby with us. One person enjoys the outdoors, another likes cooking, a third favors breaking into military computers over his phone line. The nature hobby boomed during the 1970s; now it is perhaps in slight decline (the number of people requesting permits to hike and camp in the rugged backcountry of the national parks has dropped by half since 1983, even as the number of drive-through visitors has continued to increase). We have become in rapid order a people whose conscious need for nature is superficial. The seasons don't matter to most of us anymore except as spectacles. In my county and in many places around this part of the nation, the fair that once marked the harvest now takes place in late August, while tourist dollars are still in heavy circulation. Why celebrate the harvest when you harvest every week with a shopping cart? I am a child of the suburbs, and even though I live on the edge of the wild I have only a tenuous

[11]*Bikini:* One of the Micronesian Islands in the South Pacific, Bikini Atoll was the site of more than twenty U.S. nuclear weapons tests between 1946 and 1958.
[12]*Nevada:* Between 1951 and 1992, the Nevada Proving Grounds in southeastern Nevada served as the site for 928 announced nuclear weapons tests.

understanding of the natural world. I can drive past hundreds of miles of fields without ever being able to figure out what's growing in them, unless it's corn. And even farmers have a lessened feel for the world around them. The essayist Wendell Berry[13] quotes from an advertisement for a new tractor: "Outside — dust, noise, heat, storm, fumes. Inside — all is quiet, comfortable, safe. . . . Driver dials 'inside weather' to his liking. . . . He pushbuttons radio or stereo-tape entertainment."

Even this is several steps above the philosophy expressed by a mausoleum director in a full-page newspaper ad that seems to run once a week in my newspaper: "Above-Ground. The Clean Burial. Not Underground with Earth's Disturbing Elements." Four of his "clean, dry, civilized" vaults are already sold out, and a fifth is under construction. While we are still alive, we do sometimes watch a nature program, an account of squid or wildebeest, usually sponsored by Mutual of Omaha. Mostly, however, we watch *L.A. Law*.

Still, the passing of nature as we have known it, like the passing of any large idea, will have its recognizable effects, both immediately and over time. In 1893, when Frederick Jackson Turner[14] announced to the American Historical Association that the frontier was closed, no one was aware that the frontier had been the defining force in American life. But in its absence it was understood. One reason we pay so little close attention to the separate natural world around us is that it has always been there and we presumed it always would. As it disappears, its primal importance will be clearer — in the same way that some people think they have put their parents out of their lives and learn differently only when the day comes to bury them.

How will we feel the end of nature? In many ways, I suspect. If nature means Bartram's great joy at fresh and untrammeled beauty, its loss means sadness at man's footprints everywhere. But, as with the death of a person, there is more than simply loss, a hole opening up. There are also new relationships that develop, and strains and twists in old relationships. And since this loss is peculiar in not having been inevitable, it provokes profound questions that don't arise when a person dies.

The first of these questions, I think, has to do with God. It may seem   25 odd to take a physical event and go straight to the metaphysical for its meaning. But, as we have seen, nature is as much an idea as a fact. And in some way that idea is connected with God. I hesitate to go further than that, for I am no theologian; I am not even certain what I mean by God. (Perhaps some theologians join me in this difficulty.)

It is not a novel observation that religion has been in decline in the modern era. Despite the recent rise of fundamentalism, the crisis of belief continues. Many people, including me, have overcome it to a greater or a

---

[13]*Wendell Berry:* American farmer, environmentalist, and author (b. 1934).
[14]*Frederick Jackson Turner:* American historian (1861–1932), best known for his 1893 essay "The Significance of the Frontier in American History."

lesser degree by locating God in nature. Most of the glimpses of immortality, design, and benevolence that I see come from the natural world — from the seasons, from the beauty, from the intermeshed fabric of decay and life, and so on. Other signs exist as well, such as instances of great and selfless love between people, but these, perhaps, are less reliable. They hint at epiphany,[15] not at the eternity that nature proclaimed. If this seems a banal notion, that is exactly my point. The earliest gods we know about were animals — tigers, birds, fish. Their forms and faces peer out from ancient ruins, and from the totems and wall paintings of our first religions.

And though, as time went on, we began to give our gods human features, much feeling still adheres to the forests and fields and birds and lions — else why should we moan about the "desecration" of our environment? I am a reasonably orthodox Methodist, and I go to church on Sunday because fellowship matters, because I find meaning in the history of the Israelites and in the Gospels, and because I love to sing hymns. But it is not in "God's house" that I feel his presence most — it is in his outdoors, on some sun-warmed slope of pine needles or by the surf. It is there that the numbing categories men have devised to contain this mystery — sin and redemption and incarnation and so on — fall away, leaving the overwhelming sense of the goodness and the sweetness at work in the world.

Perhaps this emotion has dimmed in an urban age, and most people now perceive God through the Christian Broadcasting Network. There is no question, though, that this is one thing nature *has* meant, and meant not just to the ancients but to the great American naturalists who first helped us see the outdoor world as more than a source of raw materials or the home of dangerous animals. "We now use the word Nature very much as our fathers used the word God," John Burroughs[16] wrote at the turn of the century, "and, I suppose, back of it all we mean the power that is everywhere present and active, and in whose lap the visible universe is held and nourished." There are, he added, "no atheists and skeptics in regard to this knowledge." Nature is reality, Thoreau[17] said — distinct from the "Arabian nights entertainments"[18] that humans concoct for themselves. "God himself culminates in the present moment, and will never be more divine in the lapse of all the ages. And we are enabled to apprehend at all what is sublime and noble only by the perpetual instilling and drenching of the reality that surrounds us." That drenching could come in the woods around Walden, but better in true wilderness. On his trip to Mt. Katahdin, Thoreau looked around at the uncut miles and said: "Perhaps where *our* wild pines stand and leaves lie on the forest floor in Concord, there were once reapers, and husbandmen

---

[15]*epiphany:* A sudden realization of the meaning of something.

[16]*John Burroughs:* American naturalist and essayist (1837–1921).

[17]*Thoreau:* American writer, philosopher, and naturalist (1817–1862). (See p. 646.)

[18]*"Arabian Nights Entertainments":* One Thousand and One Nights, or The Arabian Nights, is a collection of ancient and medieval Middle Eastern folktales and stories featuring dramatic situations and supernatural characters; hence, any whimsical entertainment.

planted grain; but here not even the surface had been scarred by man.... It was a specimen of what God saw fit to make this world." The earth is a museum of divine intent.

Simply saying that we apprehend God in nature, however, is just a beginning. It may be true, as a mystic once contended, that most people, sometime in their lives, are moved by natural beauty to a "mood of heightened consciousness" in which "each blade of grass seems fierce with meaning," but the question is: what meaning? "All nature," contended another mystic a century ago, "is the language in which God expresses his thought." Very well, but what thought is that?

The chief lesson is that the world displays a lovely order, an order comforting in its intricacy. And the most appealing part of this harmony, perhaps, is its permanence — the sense that we are part of something with roots stretching back nearly forever, and branches reaching forward just as far. Purely human life provides only a partial fulfillment of this desire for a kind of immortality. As individuals, we can feel desperately alone: we may not have children, or we may not care much for how they have turned out; we may not care to trace ourselves back through our parents; some of us may even be general misanthropes, or feel that our lives are unimportant, brief, and hurried rushes toward a final emptiness. But the earth and all its processes — the sun growing plants, flesh feeding on these plants, flesh decaying to nourish more plants, to name just one cycle — gives us some sense of a more enduring role. The poet Robinson Jeffers,[19] a deeply pessimistic man with regard to the human condition, once wrote, "The parts change and pass, or die, people and races and rocks and stars; none of them seems to me important in itself, but only the whole.... It seems to me that this whole alone is worthy of a deeper sort of love; and that there is peace, freedom, I might say a kind of salvation...."

John Muir[20] expressed this sense of immortality best. Born to a stern Calvinist[21] father who used a belt to help him memorize the Bible, Muir eventually escaped to the woods, traveling to the Yosemite Valley of California's Sierra Nevada. The journal of his first summer there is filled with a breathless joy at the beauty around him. Again and again in that Sierra June, "the greatest of all the months of my life," he uses the word "immortality," and he uses it in a specific way, designed to contrast with his father's grim and selfish religion. Time ceases to have its normal meaning in those hills: "Another glorious Sierra day in which one seems to be dissolved and sent

30

---

[19]*Robinson Jeffers:* John Robinson Jeffers (1887–1962), American poet known for works featuring California's Central Coast.

[20]*John Muir:* American naturalist, author, and early advocate of wilderness preservation (1838–1914).

[21]*Calvinist:* An adherent of the religious doctrine of Calvinism, a variety of Protestantism created by French theologian John Calvin (1509–1564), known for its emphasis on predestination and strict interpretation of the doctrine of original sin.

pulsing onward we know not where. Life seems neither long nor short, and we take no more heed to save time or make haste than do the trees and stars. This is true freedom, a good practical sort of immortality." In a mood like this, space is no more imposing a boundary than time: "We are now in the mountains, and they are now in us, making every nerve quiet, filling every pore and cell of us. Our flesh-and-bone tabernacle seems transparent as glass to the beauty around us, as if truly an inseparable part of it, thrilling with the air and trees, streams and rocks, in the waves of the sun — a part of all nature, neither old nor young, sick nor well, but immortal." . . .

So what will the end of nature as we have known it mean to our understanding of God and of man? The important thing to remember is that the end of nature is not an impersonal event, like an earthquake. It is something we humans have brought about through a series of conscious and unconscious choices: *we* ended the natural atmosphere, and hence the natural climate, and hence the natural boundaries of the forests, and so on. In so doing, we exhibit a kind of power thought in the past to be divine (much as we do by genetically altering life).

We as a race turn out to be stronger than we suspected — much stronger. In a sense we turn out to be God's equal — or, at least, his rival — able to destroy creation. This idea, of course, has been building for a while. "We became less and less capable of seeing ourselves as small within creation, partly because we thought we could comprehend it statistically, but also because we were becoming creators, ourselves, of a mechanical creation by which we felt ourselves greatly magnified," writes the essayist Wendell Berry. "Why, after all, should one get excited about a mountain when one can see almost as far from the top of a building, much farther from an airplane, farther still from a space capsule?" And our atomic weapons obviously created the *possibility* that we could exercise godlike powers.

But the possibility is different from the fact. We actually seem to have recognized the implications of nuclear weapons, and begun to back away from them — an unprecedented act of restraint. In our wholesale alteration of nature, though, we've shown no such timidity. And just as challenging one's parents and getting away with it rocks one's identity, so must this. Barry Lopez[22] reports that the Yupik Eskimos refer to us Westerners "with incredulity and apprehension as 'the people who change nature.' " When changing nature means making a small modification in what we have found — a dam across a river — it presents few philosophical problems. (It presents some, especially when the river is a beautiful one, but they tend not to be ultimate problems.) When changing nature means changing everything, then we have a crisis. We are in charge now, like it or not. As a species we are as gods — our reach global. . . .

---

[22]*Barry Lopez:* American author and environmentalist (b. 1945).

And even if we manage to control the physical effects of our actions — 35
if we come to live in a planet-size park of magnificent scenery — our sense
of the divine will change. It will be, at best, the difference between a zoo and
a wilderness. The Bronx Zoo has done a wonderful job of exchanging cages
for wide, grassy fields, but even though the antelope have room to get up to
speed and the zebra wander as a striped herd, it never crosses your mind
that you are actually in the bush instead of the Bronx. We live, all of a sudden, in an Astroturf world, and though an Astroturf world may have a God,
he can't speak through the grass, or even be silent through it and let us hear.

Engaging the Text

1. In what sense has the idea of nature "gone extinct," according to McKibben?
   Based on your own daily experience, do you agree that the "planet is utterly
   different now" from the way it once was (para. 7)? Why or why not?

2. Do you agree with McKibben that global warming is a greater threat to
   nature than nuclear warfare? Why or why not?

3. What evidence do you see that, in McKibben's words, "Nature has become
   a hobby with us" (para. 21)? What does he mean by this, and why does he
   find this trend troubling?

4. What, according to McKibben, will the end of nature mean? In his view,
   what does the end of nature tell us about ourselves and our relationship with
   divinity? What, after all, is wrong with being capable of controlling nature
   for our own purposes?

Exploring Connections

5. How close are McKibben and Henry David Thoreau (p. 646) in terms of their
   views of nature and the meaning of wilderness? How do you think Thoreau
   might respond to the notion that we have caused the "passing of nature"?

6. To what extent might Richard Louv (p. 664) agree with McKibben's assessment of how the loss of nature will affect future generations? Do you think
   we are already adapting to life in "a postnatural world"? Why or why not?

7. Compare McKibben's views on nature and the sacred with those expressed
   by John (Fire) Lame Deer (p. 686). How likely is it that Lame Deer would
   agree with McKibben's claim that we have "ended" nature? Why or why not?

8. Write an imaginary dialogue between Joy Williams (p. 703) and McKibben
   on what the state of nature today says about us. Would McKibben agree that
   we have been carried away by our own "militant humanism"? Would you?

Extending the Critical Context

9. Go online to learn more about America's wilderness reserves, as mentioned
   by McKibben (para. 8). How did the concept of wilderness reserves develop
   in the United States? How large are these reserves and how much U.S. territory do they protect? To what extent do they continue to be threatened today
   by business interests, development, or the effects of long-distance pollution?

10. Research the concept of ecotourism to find out more about the kinds of excursions that are available in remote wilderness areas. How do ecotourist businesses present themselves? What sorts of people do they target in their ads? What, if anything, can you learn about their impact on the environment? Overall, do you think ecotourism has a positive or negative impact on what remains of the wild?

11. If you haven't already done so, watch the film *Wall-E* and consider what it says about the end of nature. Do you think popular treatments of ecological catastrophe, like *Wall-E*, do any good? Why or why not?

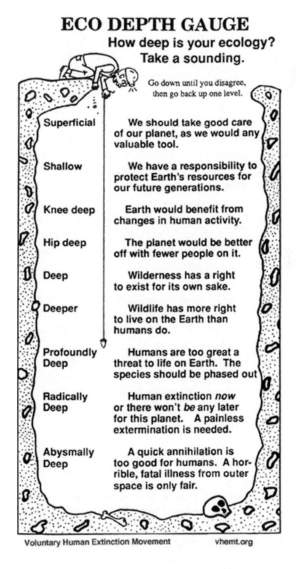

ECO DEPTH GAUGE
How deep is your ecology?
Take a sounding.

Go down until you disagree, then go back up one level.

Superficial — We should take good care of our planet, as we would any valuable tool.

Shallow — We have a responsibility to protect Earth's resources for our future generations.

Knee deep — Earth would benefit from changes in human activity.

Hip deep — The planet would be better off with fewer people on it.

Deep — Wilderness has a right to exist for its own sake.

Deeper — Wildlife has more right to live on the Earth than humans do.

Profoundly Deep — Humans are too great a threat to life on Earth. The species should be phased out

Radically Deep — Human extinction *now* or there won't *be* any later for this planet. A painless extermination is needed.

Abysmally Deep — A quick annihilation is too good for humans. A horrible, fatal illness from outer space is only fair.

Voluntary Human Extinction Movement   vhemt.org

Moving Heaven and Earth

GRAEME WOOD

On March 23, 1989, electrochemists Martin Fleishmann and Stanley Pons shocked the world with the announcement that they'd succeeded in producing "cold fusion" — a safe, "tabletop" form of nuclear power that promised a cheap, limitless supply of energy to meet the world's needs. Unfortunately, the dream of a quick fix to the energy crisis didn't pan out. After scientists around the world failed to replicate Fleishmann and Pons's experiment, cold fusion was dismissed as a hoax. But that hasn't stopped scientists from dreaming about solving the globe's environmental challenges. As Graeme Wood points out in this selection, radical technologies for "reengineering" the earth's climate are taking shape in labs around the world — technologies that may either save the planet or lead to its destruction. Graeme Wood is a journalist and a staff editor for The Atlantic *magazine, the source of this selection.*

If we were transported forward in time, to an Earth ravaged by catastrophic climate change, we might see long, delicate strands of fire hose stretching into the sky, like spaghetti, attached to zeppelins hovering 65,000 feet in the air. Factories on the ground would pump ten kilos of sulfur dioxide up through those hoses every second. And at the top, the hoses would cough a sulfurous pall into the sky. At sunset on some parts of the planet, these puffs of aerosolized pollutant would glow a dramatic red, like the skies in Blade Runner.[1] During the day, they would shield the planet from the sun's full force, keeping temperatures cool — as long as the puffing never ceased.

Technology that could redden the skies and chill the planet is available right now. Within a few years we could cool the Earth to temperatures not regularly seen since James Watt's steam engine[2] belched its first smoky plume in the late eighteenth century. And we could do it cheaply: $100 billion could reverse anthropogenic climate change entirely, and some experts suspect that a hundredth of that sum could suffice. To stop global warming the old-fashioned way, by cutting carbon emissions, would cost on the order of $1 trillion yearly. If this idea sounds unlikely, consider that President Obama's science adviser, John Holdren, said in April that he thought the

---

[1]*Blade Runner:* 1982 American science-fiction film set in an environmentally damaged Los Angeles in the year 2019.

[2]*James Watt's steam engine:* Scottish inventor and mechanical engineer James Watt (1736–1819) created an improved version of the steam engine in the 1770s that made possible its industrial use.

administration would consider it, "if we get desperate enough." And if it sounds dystopian[3] or futuristic, consider that *Blade Runner* was set in 2019, not long after Obama would complete a second term.

Humans have been aggressively transforming the planet for more than two hundred years. The Nobel Prize–winning atmospheric scientist Paul Crutzen — one of the first cheerleaders for investigating the gas-the-planet strategy — recently argued that geologists should refer to the past two centuries as the "anthropocene" period. In that time, humans have reshaped about half of the Earth's surface. We have dictated what plants grow and where. We've pocked and deformed the Earth's crust with mines and wells, and we've commandeered a huge fraction of its freshwater supply for our own purposes. What is new is the idea that we might want to deform the Earth intentionally, as a way to engineer the planet either back into its pre-industrial state, or into some improved third state. Large-scale projects that aim to accomplish this go by the name "geo-engineering," and they constitute some of the most innovative and dangerous ideas being considered today to combat climate change. Some scientists see geo-engineering as a last-ditch option to prevent us from cooking the planet to death. Others fear that it could have unforeseen — and possibly catastrophic — consequences. What many agree on, however, is that the technology necessary to reshape the climate is so powerful, and so easily implemented, that the world must decide how to govern its use before the wrong nation — or even the wrong individual — starts to change the climate all on its own.

If geo-engineers have a natural enemy, it is the sun. Their first impulse is to try to block it out. Stephen Salter, a Scottish engineer, has mocked up a strategy that would cool the planet by painting the skies above the oceans white. Salter's designs — based on an idea developed by John Latham at the National Center for Atmospheric Research — call for a permanent fleet of up to 1,500 ships dragging propellers that churn up seawater and spray it high enough for the wind to carry it into the clouds. The spray would add moisture to the clouds and make them whiter and fluffier, and therefore better at bouncing sunlight back harmlessly into space. Salter, who has investigated the technical feasibility of this idea minutely (down to the question of whether ship owners would mind affixing spray nozzles to their hulls with magnets), estimates the cost to build the first 300 ships — enough to turn back the climatological clock to James Watt's era — to be $600 million, plus another $100 million per year to keep the project going.

Roger Angel, an astronomy and optics professor at the University of Arizona, would block the sun by building a giant visor in space. He proposes constructing twenty electromagnetic guns, each more than a mile long and positioned at high altitudes, that would shoot Frisbee-size ceramic disks. 5

---

[3]*dystopian:* A dystopia is a vision of a grim, dehumanized future.

Each gun would launch 800,000 disks every five minutes — day and night, weekends and holidays — for ten years. The guns would aim at the gravitational midpoint between the Earth and the sun, so that the disks would hang in space, providing a huge array of sunshades that would block and scatter sunlight and put the Earth in a permanent state of annular eclipse. Angel's scheme relies on launch technology that doesn't yet exist (no one has ever wanted to shoot Frisbees at the sun before), and would cost several trillion dollars. "I know it sounds like mad science," he says. "But unfortunately we have a mad planet."

Of all the ideas circulating for blocking solar heat, however, sulfur-aerosol injection — the *Blade Runner* scenario — may actually be the least mad. And it provides an illustrative example of the trade-offs that all geo-engineering projects of its scale must confront. The approach is already known to work. When Mount Tambora erupted in Indonesia in 1815 and spewed sulfur dioxide into the stratosphere, farmers in New England recorded a summer so chilly that their fields frosted over in July. The Mount Pinatubo eruption in the Philippines in 1991 cooled global temperatures by about half a degree Celsius for the next few years. A sulfur-aerosol project could produce a Pinatubo of sulfur dioxide every four years.

The aerosol plan is also cheap — so cheap that it completely overturns conventional analysis of how to mitigate climate change. Thomas C. Schelling, who won the 2005 Nobel Prize in economics, has pointed out how difficult it is to get vast international agreements — such as the Kyoto Protocol — to stick. But a geo-engineering strategy like sulfur aerosol "changes everything," he says. Suddenly, instead of a situation where any one country can foil efforts to curb global warming, any one country can curb global warming all on its own. Pumping sulfur into the atmosphere is a lot easier than trying to orchestrate the actions of 200 countries — or, for that matter, 7 billion individuals — each of whom has strong incentives to cheat.

But, as with nearly every geo-engineering plan, there are substantial drawbacks to the gas-the-planet strategy. Opponents say it might produce acid rain and decimate plant and fish life. Perhaps more disturbing, it's likely to trigger radical shifts in the climate that would hit the globe unevenly. "Plausibly, 6 billion people would benefit and 1 billion would be hurt," says Martin Bunzl, a Rutgers climate-change policy expert. The billion negatively affected would include many in Africa, who would, perversely, live in a climate even hotter and drier than before. In India, rainfall levels might severely decline; the monsoons rely on temperature differences between the Asian landmass and the ocean, and sulfur aerosols could diminish those differences substantially.

Worst of all is what Raymond Pierrehumbert, a geophysicist at the University of Chicago, calls the "Sword of Damocles" scenario. In Greek legend, Dionysius II, the ruler of Syracuse, used a single hair to suspend a sword over Damocles' head, ostensibly to show him how precarious the life of a powerful ruler can be. According to Pierrehumbert, sulfur aerosols would cool the planet, but we'd risk calamity the moment we stopped pumping: the aerosols would rain down and years' worth of accumulated carbon would make temperatures surge. Everything would be fine, in other words, until the hair snapped, and then the world would experience the full force of postponed warming in just a couple of catastrophic years. Pierrehumbert imagines another possibility in which sun-blocking technology works but has unforeseen consequences, such as rapid ozone destruction. If a future generation discovered that a geo-engineering program had such a disastrous side effect, it couldn't easily shut things down. He notes that sulfur-aerosol injection, like many geo-engineering ideas, would be easy to implement. But if it failed, he says, it would fail horribly. "It's scary because it actually could be done," he says. "And it's like taking aspirin for cancer."

In 1977, the physicist Freeman Dyson[4] published the first of a series of   10 articles about how plants affect the planet's carbon-dioxide concentrations. Every summer, plants absorb about a tenth of the carbon dioxide in the atmosphere. In the fall, when they stop growing or shed their leaves, they release most of it back into the air. Dyson proposed creating forests of "carbon-eating trees," engineered to suck carbon more ravenously from the air, and to keep it tied up in thick roots that would decay into topsoil, trapping the carbon. He now estimates that by annually increasing topsoil by just a tenth of an inch over land that supports vegetation, we could offset all human carbon emissions.

Dyson's early geo-engineering vision addressed a central, and still daunting, problem: neither sulfur-aerosol injection nor an armada of cloud whiteners nor an array of space-shades would do much to reduce carbon-dioxide levels. As long as carbon emissions remain constant, the atmosphere will fill with more and more greenhouse gases. Blocking the sun does nothing to stop the buildup. It is not even like fighting obesity with liposuction: it's like fighting obesity with a corset, and a diet of lard and doughnuts. Should the corset ever come off, the flab would burst out as if the corset had never been there at all. For this reason, nearly every climate scientist who spoke with me unhesitatingly advocated cutting carbon emissions over geo-engineering.

But past international efforts to reduce emissions offer little cause for optimism, and time may be quickly running out. That's why a few scientists are following Dyson's lead and attacking global warming at its source. David Keith, an energy-technology expert at the University of Calgary, hopes to capture carbon from the air. He proposes erecting vented building-size structures that contain grids coated with a chemical solution. As air flows through the vents, the solution would bind to the carbon-dioxide molecules and trap them. Capturing carbon in these structures, which might resemble

---

[4]*Freeman Dyson:* American theoretic physicist and mathematician (b. 1923).

industrial cooling towers, would allow us to manage emissions cheaply from central sites, rather than from the dispersed places from which they were emitted, such as cars, planes, and home furnaces. The grids would have to be scrubbed chemically to separate the carbon. If chemists could engineer ways to wash the carbon out that didn't require too much energy, Keith imagines that these structures could effectively make our carbon-spewing conveniences carbon-neutral.

The question then becomes where to put all that carbon once it's captured. Keith has investigated one elegant solution: put it back underground, where much of it originated as oil. The technology for stashing carbon beneath the earth already exists, and is routinely exploited by oil-well drillers. When oil wells stop producing in large quantities, drillers inject carbon dioxide into the ground to push out the last drops. If they inject it into the right kind of geological structure, and deep enough below the surface, it stays there.

We might also store carbon dioxide in the oceans. Already, on the oceans' surface, clouds of blooming plankton ingest amounts of carbon dioxide comparable to those taken in by trees. Climos, a geo-engineering start-up based in San Francisco, is trying to cultivate ever-bigger plankton blooms that would suck in huge supplies of carbon. When the plankton died, the carbon would end up on the sea floor. Climos began with the observation that plankton bloom in the ocean only when they have adequate supplies of iron. In the 1980s, the oceanographer John Martin hypothesized that large amounts of oceanic iron may have produced giant plankton blooms in the past, and therefore chilled the atmosphere by removing carbon dioxide. Spread powdered iron over the surface of the ocean, and in very little time a massive bloom of plankton will grow, he predicted. "Give me half a tanker of iron," Martin said, "and I'll give you the next Ice Age." If Martin's ideas are sound, Climos could in effect become the world's gardener by seeding Antarctic waters with iron and creating vast, rapidly growing offshore forests to replace the ones that no longer exist on land. But this solution, too, could have terrible downsides. Alan Robock, an environmental scientist at Rutgers, notes that when the dead algae degrades, it could emit methane — a greenhouse gas twenty times stronger than carbon dioxide.

Just a decade ago, every one of these schemes was considered outlandish. Some still seem that way. But what sounded crankish only ten years ago is now becoming mainstream thinking. Although using geo-engineering to combat climate change was first considered (and dismissed) by President Johnson's administration,[5] sustained political interest began on the business-friendly right, which remains excited about any solution that doesn't get in

15

---

[5]*President Johnson's administration:* Lyndon Baines Johnson (1908–1973) served as thirty-sixth president of the United States from 1963 to 1969.

the way of the oil companies. The American Enterprise Institute, a conservative think tank historically inimical to emission-reduction measures, has sponsored panels on the sulfur-aerosol plan.

By now, even staunch environmentalists and eminent scientists with long records of climate-change concern are discussing geo-engineering openly. Paul Crutzen, who earned his Nobel Prize by figuring out how human activity punched a hole in the ozone layer, has for years urged research on sulfur-aerosol solutions, bringing vast credibility to geo-engineering as a result.

With that growing acceptance, however, come some grave dangers. If geo-engineering is publicly considered a "solution" to climate change, governments may reduce their efforts to restrict the carbon emissions that caused global warming in the first place. If you promise that in a future emergency you can chill the Earth in a matter of months, cutting emissions today will seem far less urgent. "Geo-engineering needs some government funding, but the most disastrous thing that could happen would be for Barack Obama to stand up tomorrow and announce the creation of a geo-engineering task force with hundreds of millions in funds," says David Keith.

Ken Caldeira, of the Carnegie Institution for Science, thinks we ought to test the technology gradually. He suggests that we imagine the suite of geo-engineering projects like a knob that we can turn. "You can turn it gently or violently. The more gently it gets turned, the less disruptive the changes will be. Environmentally, the least risky thing to do is to slowly scale up small field experiments," he says. "But politically that's the riskiest thing to do."

Such small-scale experimentation, however, could be the first step on a very slippery slope. Raymond Pierrehumbert likens geo-engineering to building strategic nuclear weapons. "It's like the dilemma faced by scientists in the Manhattan Project, who had to decide whether that work was necessary or reprehensible," he says. "Geo-engineering makes the problem of ballistic-missile defense look easy. It has to work the first time, and just right. People quite rightly see it as a scary thing."

The scariest thing about geo-engineering, as it happens, is also the   20
thing that makes it such a game-changer in the global-warming debate: it's incredibly cheap. Many scientists, in fact, prefer not to mention just how cheap it is. Nearly everyone I spoke to agreed that the worst-case scenario would be the rise of what David Victor, a Stanford law professor, calls a "Greenfinger" — a rich madman, as obsessed with the environment as James Bond's nemesis Auric Goldfinger[6] was with gold. There are now thirty-eight people in the world with $10 billion or more in private assets,

[6]*Auric Goldfinger:* Villain in the James Bond film and novel *Goldfinger.*

according to the latest *Forbes* list; theoretically, one of these people could reverse climate change all alone. "I don't think we really want to empower the Richard Bransons[7] of the world to try solutions like this," says Jay Michaelson, an environmental-law expert, who predicted many of these debates ten years ago.

Even if Richard Branson behaves, a single rogue nation could have the resources to change the climate. Most of Bangladesh's population lives in low-elevation coastal zones that would wash away if sea levels rose. For a fraction of its GDP, Bangladesh could refreeze the ice caps using sulfur aerosols (though, in a typical trade-off, this might affect its monsoons). If refreezing them would save the lives of millions of Bangladeshis, who could blame their government for acting? Such a scenario is unlikely; most countries would hesitate to violate international law and become a pariah. But it illustrates the political and regulatory complications that large-scale climate-changing schemes would trigger.

Michaelson — along with many others — has called for public research on some possible legal responses to geo-engineering. "It would be a classic situation where the problem should be handled in an official capacity," he says. In practice, that would likely mean industrialized governments' regulating geo-engineering directly, in a way that lets them monopolize the technology and prevent others from deploying it, through diplomatic and military means, or perhaps by just bribing Bangladesh not to puff out its own aerosols. Such a system might resemble the way the International Atomic Energy Agency now regulates nuclear technology.

And since geo-engineering — like nuclear weapons — would most likely be deployed during a moment of duress, legal experts like Victor have urged establishing preliminary regulations well in advance. "Suppose the U.S. or Brazil decided it needed some combination of emissions-cutting and geo-engineering in a sudden catastrophe," Victor says. "How would the rest of us respond? There's been no serious research on the topic. It has to be done right now, and not in a crisis situation." An outright ban on geo-engineering could lead other countries to try out dangerous ideas on their own, just as a ban on cloning in the United States has sent research to Korea and Singapore; it would constrain all but the least responsible countries.

Victor doesn't believe geo-engineering will solve anything by itself, but he expects that ultimately we will have a cocktail of solutions. Perhaps we could start with a few puffs of sulfur in the atmosphere to buy time, then forests of plankton in the ocean, and then genetically engineered carbon-hungry trees. What isn't an option, Victor says, is refusing to fund more research, in the hope that geo-engineering won't be needed.

---

[7]*Richard Branson:* English industrialist and creator of Virgin Atlantic Airways, Sir Richard Charles Nicholas Branson (b. 1950) is famed for his flamboyant personal style and humanitarian initiatives.

Thomas Schelling, who won his Nobel Prize for using game theory to   25
explain nuclear strategy and the behavior of states in arms races, shares
Victor's frustration about the way geo-engineering has been ignored. Multinational agreements to cut emissions amount to a game of chicken that
tends to end unhappily in Schelling's models. The ideal outcome would be a
technology that changes the game. "We just have to consider that we may
need this kind of project, and might need it in a hurry," he says. "If the president has to go by boat from the White House to the Capitol, we should be
ready scientifically — but also diplomatically — to do something about it."

We should keep such images in mind. And they should remind us
that, one way or another, a prolonged love affair with carbon dioxide will
end disastrously. A pessimist might judge geo-engineering so risky that the
cure would be worse than the disease. But a sober optimist might see it as
the biggest and most terrifying insurance policy humanity might buy —
one that pays out so meagerly, and in such foul currency, that we'd better
ensure we never need it. In other words, we should keep investigating geo-
engineering solutions, but make quite clear to the public that most of them
are so dreadful that they should scare the living daylights out of even a
Greenfinger. In this way, the colossal dangers inherent in geo-engineering
could become its chief advantage. A premonition of a future that looks
like *Blade Runner*, with skies dominated by a ruddy smog that's our only
defense against mass flooding and famine, with sunshades in space and a
frothy bloom of plankton wreathing the Antarctic, could finally horrify the
public into greener living. Perhaps a Prius doesn't sound so bad, when a
zeppelin is the alternative.

ENGAGING THE TEXT

1. What are some of the geo-engineering strategies Wood describes for curbing global warming? What advantages are offered by such technological
   fixes? Which strikes you as the most interesting or promising? Why?

2. Should hybrid and electric cars also be considered forms of eco-engineering?
   What about solar panels and wind farms? What, if anything, sets apart the
   technological innovations Wood describes from any human-made technique
   for curbing greenhouse gases?

3. Why is cutting carbon emissions even more important than directly reducing temperatures worldwide, according to Wood? What approaches does he
   describe for capturing and storing carbon dioxide? What problems might be
   involved in these "carbon sequestration" technologies?

4. What are the drawbacks associated with geo-engineering, and why does
   Wood consider technological solutions to the climate crisis so potentially
   dangerous?

5. Do you agree that geo-engineering should be regulated? How could this be
   done on a worldwide scale? Do you think such regulation would succeed?
   Why or why not?

EXPLORING CONNECTIONS

6. How might Richard Louv's exploration of the "know-it-all state of mind" (p. 664) help explain the attraction of the geo-engineering technologies described by Wood? Do you think that our growing faith in technology will make a hi-tech approach to solving the climate crisis inevitable? Why or why not?

7. Write an imaginary dialogue between John (Fire) Lame Deer (p. 686) and Bill McKibben (p. 743) on the promise and meaning of geo-engineering. How do you think they would view technological solutions to the climate change crisis?

8. What might the final "future" panels of R. Crumb's "A Short History of America" (pp. 695–98) look like if, as Wood suggests, we eventually opt for an eco-engineering solution to the climate crisis?

EXTENDING THE CRITICAL CONTEXT

9. Do some online research to learn more about organized attempts to limit carbon emissions since the signing of the Kyoto Protocol in 1997. Why has it been difficult to get nations to agree on a single approach to reducing greenhouse gases? How likely do you think such an agreement will be in the future?

10. Research these and other promising geo-engineering solutions to the climate crisis to determine how they are currently viewed. How much interest do environmentalists, politicians, and business groups have in geo-technological solutions to the global warming crisis? Do the kinds of solutions described by Wood seem more or less reasonable or attractive than technologies like nuclear power?

In Search of Justice

NYDIA M. VELÁZQUEZ

In 1992, Nydia M. Velázquez made history by becoming the first Puerto Rican woman to be elected to the United States House of Representatives. Serving New York's Twelfth Congressional District — one of the most culturally diverse and economically challenged urban areas in the nation — she has emerged in her ninth Congressional term as a leader on issues of public health and the environment. As Representative Velázquez argues in this selection, ecology isn't just a concern for hikers and survivalists. In urban neighborhoods like those she represents in Brooklyn, Queens, and Manhattan's Lower East Side, pollution and waste disposal have a direct impact on the

lives of millions of low-income American families. As she sees it, sustainabil-
ity is a matter of social justice — not just a matter of good ecological hygiene.
This selection appeared in Sustainable Planet: Solutions for the Twenty-First
Century *(2002), edited by Juliet B. Schor and Betsy Taylor.*

Jacob Riis's[1] groundbreaking 1890 book *How the Other Half Lives*
chronicled the lives of thousands of families living in squalor in New York
City. A horrified public cried out for reform, and the public-housing movement was born. Over the next fifty years, a bold progressive movement
brought extraordinary change in America — an income tax began to bridge
the gap between rich and poor, a social-safety net provided basic protections for workers, and we began to understand that a just society was a
social and moral imperative. What happened?

Today, although we have a much more sophisticated understanding of
what social justice means, low-income families nevertheless find themselves
in more or less the same relative circumstances they were in over a century
ago — struggling to overcome desperate poverty, living in communities that
are tragically unhealthy as the result of pollution and neglect, and laboring
against a culture that considers material possessions the absolute measure
of social value.

The simple fact is that our current unsustainable "more-is-better" culture undermines any hope of achieving justice — at home or abroad. We
often hear about how the United States consumes a vastly disproportionate
amount of resources relative to the rest of the world. Americans are building bigger houses, driving bigger cars, consuming more and more of everything than just about anyone else anywhere.

This is certainly true, and the long-term environmental effects of this
overconsumption may well prove disastrous. But we also forget that the gap
between the rich and the poor in this country is just as severe as, if not
worse than, it is elsewhere. Amazingly, the richest 196 people in America
have more wealth than the poorest 56 *million* Americans.

And one thing is for sure — Americans certainly are not doing all this   5
overconsuming in congressional districts like the one I represent. The residents of Greenpoint / Williamsburg, which makes up the heart of New York's
Twelfth Congressional District, are among the poorest in the country. Forty-
five percent of the households earn less than $12 thousand annually. In some
schools, nearly every child qualifies for the federal school lunch program.

My district is by no means unique. Across America, there are pockets of
dire poverty that are a national disgrace. Perhaps this poverty is not on the

---

[1]*Jacob Riis:* Danish-born Jacob August Riis (1849–1914) was a journalist, photographer,
and social reformer.

scale of some developing-world countries, but it is crushing poverty none-theless. The U.S. Department of Health and Human Services reports that nearly 3 million American children suffer from moderate to severe hunger. More than 9 million children report having difficulty obtaining enough food, suffer from reduced quality of diets, express anxiety about their food supply, and are increasingly resorting to emergency food sources and other coping behaviors. And nearly 7 million Americans are classified by the U.S. Department of Labor as being the "working poor," by spending more than twenty-seven weeks in the labor force, but earning below the official poverty level.

In my district, crime is high, test scores are low, schools are crumbling, and the "American dream" — however you choose to define it — is very, very difficult to attain. For many, hope is represented by a trip to the bodega[2] to buy a lottery ticket. Side by side with the "more is better" dominant culture is an unnoticed "anything is too much" underclass that scrapes for crumbs in the shadows. How can a nation with our riches allow such misery to exist?

An Environmental Catastrophe

One of the first things you are likely to notice when you visit neighborhoods in my district, and others like it, are the trucks. Not trucks heading out, packed with manufactured goods produced in clean, modern, high-tech facilities full of good-paying jobs. No, the trucks are delivering garbage from the rest of the city to waste-transfer facilities located cheek by jowl with schools, apartment buildings, and small businesses struggling to keep afloat. It's illegal to put a cigarette billboard near a child's school. It's perfectly legal to have a garbage dump next to her house.

Amazingly, the waste transfer stations aren't the worst of it. The tour of environmental shame continues on to highly toxic empty lots — so-called "brownfields." Usually, brownfields are the remnants of polluting industries sited in poor communities whose owners have fled, leaving virtually undevelopable property in their wake. Cleanups do occasionally occur, at enormous public expense, while polluters walk away, often to set up shop in another unwitting community. Political opponents may cry "class warfare," but I've personally never seen a waste-transfer station on the upper East Side of Manhattan, or in the Hamptons.[3] In some communities, residents complain about the presence of federal buildings, which generate no real estate tax. We'd take a federal building or two in the twelfth district in a New York minute.

The environmental scorecard in my district is appalling. There are over   10
eighty waste-transfer stations in New York City, and thirty of them are in my district. Greenpoint / Williamsburg has 137 sites that use hazardous

---

[2]*bodega:* A small neighborhood convenience store.
[3]*upper East Side . . . Hamptons:* Affluent areas in or around Manhattan, New York.

substances, called right-to-know sites, fifteen toxic-release inventory sites, twenty-four waste-transfer stations, and one low-level radioactive waste site, all within a five-and-a-half-mile radius. Red Hook has six waste-transfer stations, seven sites that may warrant Superfund[4] designation, and three hazardous waste facilities, all within a one-mile radius. Greenpoint/Williamsburg sits on a 17-million-gallon oil spill. (The Exxon Valdez,[5] by contrast, spilled 10 million gallons of oil. Of course, they at least tried to clean that one up.) The Newtown Creek Sewage Treatment Plant treats the highest volume of hazardous waste and is the biggest producer of hazardous pollutants in the city. The neighborhood is also home to eight coal-burning industrial furnaces and the highly toxic Brooklyn Navy Yard (a federal facility we'd gladly give up).

Hardly a day goes by when we don't hear about how our nation's cities have experienced a renaissance. Although crime rates have dropped in many large cities, people of color are being victimized by toxic polluters and brownfield perpetrators who have managed to escape the wrath of a well-meaning environmental movement that doesn't seem to realize that the "environment" does not begin at the suburb's edge. Believe me, Latinos and African Americans know what the environment is. It's air they can see and water they can't drink. Polling consistently shows that African Americans and Hispanics put a higher priority on protecting the environment than nonminority voters. And no wonder. Study after study has shown that racial minorities disproportionately bear the brunt of this pollution.

- A 1992 EPA study showed that minority populations are disproportionately exposed to air pollutants and hazardous-waste sites.

- A 1990 University of Michigan study showed that minority residents are four times more likely to live within one mile of a commercial waste facility than whites, and that race was a better predictor of proximity to such sites than income.

- A 1994 study by the Center for Policy Alternatives concluded that three out of every five Latinos and African Americans live in a community with one or more toxic-waste site.

The effect of this pollution is a silent national tragedy on a par with Jacob Riis's alarming discoveries. In the predominantly African-American area between New Orleans and Baton Rouge, dubbed "Cancer Alley," where over 130 petrochemical plants, medical waste incinerators, and solid-waste landfills emit highly toxic levels of pollution, people suffer from much higher

---

[4]*Superfund:* Common name for the Comprehensive Environmental Response, Compensation, and Liability Act (CERCLA), a 1980 federal law designed to clean up hazardous waste sites.

[5]*Exxon Valdez:* In 1989, the Exxon Valdez oil tanker ran aground in Prince William Sound, Alaska, spilling an estimated 10.8 million gallons of crude oil.

rates of miscarriage, cancer, tumors, and other chemical-related illnesses. A study by the Louisiana Advisory Committee to the U.S. Commission on Civil Rights found "Cancer Alley" to have disproportionate levels of all cancers. The Latino south side of Tucson is exposed to twenty times the acceptable levels of trichloroethylene,[6] and rates of cancer, birth defects, and genetic mutations in that neighborhood far outpace national averages.

I don't have to walk very far in my district to see a community in the throes of a health crisis. New York City has the second worst air quality in the nation, and the Greenpoint / Williamsburg area has the worst air quality in New York. And it is no surprise that the people who live in this neighborhood are getting sick and dying at an alarming rate.

A 1993 New York Department of Health study showed that in one census tract, childhood cancers are twenty-two times higher than the national expected average. Twenty-three census tracts showed disproportionately higher rates of stomach and lung cancers. Four showed statistically elevated incidences of leukemia. Hundreds of cases of lead poisoning in children have been reported in the past decade. Childhood asthma rates in Brooklyn have tripled in the 1990s. At 13 per 1000, the infant mortality rate rivals that of Estonia, Bulgaria, and the Czech Republic.

I have a constituent whose cousin died of an asthma attack on an Ozone Alert day — at age twenty-two. Her two-year-old daughter now lives with her grandparents. Another constituent's grandchildren suffer regular asthma attacks when they come to visit, only to see the attacks subside when they leave.

It's outrageous that basic environmental-justice protections languish in Congress. There are those in Washington who claim that they want to make sure that "no child is left behind,"[7] yet the hollowness of the claim leaves a deafening echo.

It goes without saying that the communities most adversely affected by the actions of these polluting industries don't have the resources to fight back, and it's little wonder that the many waste-treatment facilities in Williamsburg process garbage from outside the neighborhood.

The residents of Greenpoint / Williamsburg and other poor communities, fighting disease and living in poverty, are no match for wealthy companies who have an unlimited ability to litigate. Unless we bring the full force of the federal government to bear on these polluters, they will continue to poison our air and water and slowly and silently subject our children to a toxic environment with impunity. Where is Jacob Riis when we need him?

---

[6]*trichloroethylene:* A chemical compound commonly used as an industrial solvent that is categorized as a probable carcinogen.

[7]*"no child is left behind":* In 2001 Congress passed the No Child Left Behind Act, which requires states to assess and report on student learning and provides sanctions for schools that fail to increase learning outcome measures. The act has been criticized for not providing adequate funds for its implementation and for school improvement.

We know that protecting the environment is a long-term necessity and that global-climate change puts future generations at risk, but we need to understand that the environment is a matter of life and death right now in our inner-city communities. As our children are slowly poisoned, their ability to learn and to work and to become active, productive participants in this society is being taken away. We are quite simply writing off millions and millions of American children because they happen to be poor.

A Desperate Social Challenge

If the environmental impacts of being poor in today's America are bad,   20
the social effects may be even worse, if that's possible. Those Americans who drew the short straw and live in poverty are systematically shut out of the blessings of American society, Horatio Alger[8] success stories notwithstanding. Talk is cheap in Washington, and talk about "values" is cheaper still. If we really valued work, then the janitors and garbage collectors and sweatshop workers and the rest of the hardworking poor would be able to put food on the table. If we really valued children, we'd make sure that the poorest of our children weren't taught in hallways and broom closets or in shifts and we'd guarantee that they all had textbooks and qualified, well-paid teachers.

A poor child in today's America labors against a dizzying array of social challenges. He lives in a culture that says that what you have is more important than who you are. The message from advertisers and marketers who target kids is quite clear — you gotta have it. And it doesn't really matter what the "it" is. From clothes to computers to cell phones to houses to cars, no American child is immune from the underlying suggestion that owning these *things* defines success. While the message of excess materialism is toxic for all our children, it is especially cruel for the one out of six American children living in poverty. I often wonder how sporting goods executives sleep at night after marketing basketball shoes to low-income children that cost a minimum-wage-earning parent nearly a week's salary to pay for.

Our role models are athletes and movie stars and billionaires. How can we expect our poorest children, malnourished and undereducated, to feel good about themselves when we present these false notions of success? Our real role models should be neighborhood volunteers, nurses, teachers, parents, and small business owners, and all those caring, hardworking people who create jobs, watch over us, and give a community a sense of cohesion, connectedness, and purpose. One of the few good things to be taken from September 11 was the emergence of blue-collar heroes. Let's hope it lasts, but the smart money is still on Michael Jordan and Britney Spears.

---

[8]*Horatio Alger:* American author (1832–1899) best known for novels featuring "rags-to-riches" success stories. (See p. 258.)

Blueprint for a Just Society

People fighting for justice in this country and around the world have every reason to be discouraged, but in fact there are signs of hope that we should be aware of. Anyone familiar with my work in Congress knows that I don't give up easily. If anything, I've just gotten started. Even now, in the face of extraordinary challenges, I am excited about the emerging opportunities in my community and others like it. . . .

Environmental Justice

To its credit, the Clinton administration[9] acknowledged what those of us familiar with such communities knew for years — that people of color have been unfairly treated with regard to the development, implementation, and enforcement of environmental laws, regulations, and policies.

Under former administrator Carol Browner, the Environmental Protection Agency established the Office of Environmental Justice, whose mission is to address the problem of environmental discrimination and set up programs designed to assist what it acknowledges are "disproportionate risks faced by . . . low-income and minority populations." Under the Bush administration,[10] the program saw its already meager budget reduced.

In 1994, President Clinton signed Executive Order 12898, which applies Title VI of the Civil Rights Act to entities receiving federal financial assistance and bars them from using methods or practices that discriminate on the basis of race, color, or national origin. It was a good start to begin to undo generations of wrongs that have been visited upon people of color.

One of the first fights I took up in Congress was to ensure that minority communities receive equitable treatment under environmental law. I did this by introducing legislation to apply this nation's civil rights laws to our environmental regulations. If enacted, my legislation would take the former president's Executive Order an important step further by applying Title VI to actions taken by any company whose pollution disproportionately impacts a particular racial or ethnic group. Title VI is most commonly used in discrimination cases involving public housing and education, but there is no reason that it couldn't be extended to environmental concerns as well.

After all, can anyone say that the health crisis that currently affects people of color in this country is any less important than acts of housing or education discrimination currently protected under Title VI? My proposed legislation targets both potential violators and chronic polluters. Companies would have to show that proposed projects would not pollute in a manner

25

---

[9]*the Clinton administration:* William Jefferson Clinton (b. 1946) served as the forty-second president of the United States from 1993 to 2001.

[10]*the Bush administration:* George Walker Bush (b. 1946) served as the forty-third president of the United States from 2001 to 2009.

that would adversely affect a particular racial group—the burden of proof currently used under Title VI. Existing polluters would be forced to prove that their pollution does not target minority communities.

My sense is that the effect of environmental justice laws could also ripple through the manufacturing sector. Producers might just find themselves dematerializing their production process if they no longer were able to dump waste in the nearest poor neighborhood. They might just start making cleaner products if they were unable to release toxic chemicals with impunity. The nascent green revolution could get a much-needed shot in the arm from an unlikely ally—the justice movement.

While a law to ensure environmental justice would make a tremendous 30 difference for the lives of millions of poor people in this country, it's honestly not enough to just keep polluters out of our communities. To have true environmental justice, we also have to provide safe, open space, parks and community gardens that make neighborhoods worth living in. In my district, there is a desperate struggle underway over the fate of the abandoned Brooklyn waterfront. This was once a highly active shipping and manufacturing center, and if you look past today's rotted piers and disrepair, you can't help but see the promise it holds. With its easy access to transit and a breathtaking view of Manhattan across the East River, the waterfront is perhaps New York City's most potentially valuable real estate. Developed properly, with cooperation from the community and visionary investors, we could create a truly inspired vision of a sustainable community that incorporates open space, creates opportunities for nonpolluting businesses and the jobs that go with them, and that could become a model for urban infill development across the country. This is an opportunity to build an urban development project applying principles of sustainability and combining ecological and economic objectives.

ENGAGING THE TEXT

1. Why, according to Velázquez, are low-income neighborhoods more seriously affected by pollution than more affluent communities? Did you see any evidence in the neighborhood where you grew up of the kinds of disproportionate ecological impacts she describes in her district?

2. To what extent would you agree with Velázquez that America's "more is better" culture undermines efforts to promote social and ecologically safe neighborhoods? Would you agree that American consumer culture is particularly "toxic" or "cruel" for children living in poverty? Why or why not?

3. In your opinion, what would it take to get poor children to see "neighborhood volunteers, nurses, teachers, parents" and other "blue-collar heroes" as role models in place of athletes, movie stars, and billionaires? What good would this do the environment?

4. What does Velázquez mean by "environmental justice"? Do you think environmental justice can or should be legislated? Why or why not?

EXPLORING CONNECTIONS

5. How might Velázquez's observations on the ecology of low-income communities complicate Richard Louv's assessment of the role that nature plays in children's lives (p. 664)? Do you think that children growing up in urban areas like Greenpoint / Williamsburg experience nature in the same way as do children who grow up in the suburbs or rural areas?

6. Working in groups, reconsider R. Crumb's "A Short History of America" (pp. 695–98). Instead of thinking of Crumb's drawings as representing a historical progression, try to label them in terms of different socioeconomic or geographic communities. Where are the Hamptons? Where is Greenpoint / Williamsburg? To what extent does a person's experience of "nature" depend on race and economic status?

EXTENDING THE CRITICAL CONTEXT

7. Working in groups, research and map the location of hazardous waste and toxic industrial sites in different areas of your city or town, including the location of dumps, waste-transfer stations, "brownfields," "right-to-know" sites, and polluting industries. What correlation can you find, if any, between pollution and the socioeconomic status of the various communities you map? (You can find neighborhood environmental mapping tools at the Environmental Protection Agency's "Environmapper" website: www.epa.gov/enviro/html/em/index.html and at the EPA's "Environfacts" site: www.epa.gov/enviro/.)

8. Map the "greenspaces" that are available in various neighborhoods in your town or city. Do you see any correlation between socioeconomic status and the number of parks, playgrounds, public gardens, and other forms of open space available in a given neighborhood?

Our Unhealthy Future Under Environmentalism

JOHN BERLAU

How far would you go to save the earth? That question has troubled environmentalists ever since famed ecological activist Edward Abbey invented the concept of "monkeywrenching" — the use of sabotage to stop industrial development and urban expansion. Inspired by Abbey's writings, a generation of "eco-warriors" has resorted to forms of direct action in the name of environmental defense. But as John Berlau points out in this selection, some feel that organizations like the Earth Liberation Front and the Animal Liberation Front have gone too far. Classified as domestic terrorist threats by the FBI in 2001, these and other eco-anarchist organizations are said to have fire-bombed ski resorts and ranger stations, blown up animal research facilities, and even staged the release of hundreds of wild horses — all in the name of protecting the planet. As Berlau sees it, such "eco-terrorists" are simply criminals, and they don't work alone. In his view, mainstream advocates of sustainability and environmental consciousness also bear responsibility for promoting ecological violence. John Berlau is a fellow in Economic Policy at the Competitive Enterprise Institute and a former correspondent for Investor's Business Daily *and* Insight *magazine. He has also served as a media fellow at the Hoover Institution at Stanford University. This selection comes from his book* Eco-Freaks: Environmentalism Is Hazardous to Your Health! *(2006).*

It was 19 September 2001. A deeply wounded nation was still in shock and on high alert for possible follow-ups to the al Qaeda attacks on the 11th. Of particular concern were any buildings or structures that could be seen as symbols of America and the West. And certainly, hardly anything in the world is seen as a symbol of America more than McDonald's. Some restaurants had already been targets of arson by eco-terrorists.

Still, hardly anyone thought that any kind of terrorist attack would occur at a Ronald McDonald House. Although largely supported by the McDonald's Corporation and local owners of franchised McDonald's restaurants, the nondescript houses are mostly in residential areas. They also serve a noble, noncontroversial purpose: a home-like setting for the families of sick children getting treatment at nearby medical facilities.

But on that September morning at the Ronald McDonald House in Tucson, parents, children, and employees came upon a horrifying sight outside. The four-foot statue of Ronald McDonald, intended to be a welcoming face for the children who love his commercials, had been brutally attacked. Swastikas and obscenities swirled around Ronald from his face to his feet. Given the events that had gone on in New York and Washington and the arsons at McDonald's, those at the house were very frightened. "I became concerned because of the arson and the fact that we've got a full house right now," the House's executive director, Mary Kay Dinsmore, told the *Arizona Daily Star*.[1]

Close to the swastika on Ronald's face appeared sets of three letters that have become all too familiar in the past few years to investigators of domestic terrorism: ELF and ALF.

---

[1]M. Scot Skinner, "McDonald House Statue Is Vandalized with Graffiti," *Arizona Daily Star,* 20 September 2001, 1. [All notes are Berlau's unless otherwise indicated.]

Bad ELFs

The Earth Liberation Front and its sister organization, the Animal Lib-   5
eration Front, are the nation's "number-one domestic terrorism threat,"
according to FBI deputy assistant director John Lewis.[2] The Senate Environment and Public Works Committee estimated that ELF and ALF have
caused more than $110 million in damages.[3] And the acts committed have
grown more sophisticated in recent years, leaving no doubt that eco-terrorism
can be as destructive as full-blown terrorism by any type of group. As the
Christian Science Monitor reports, "somewhere along the way, vandalizing log
trucks and 'liberating' lab rats escalated into firebombs, plots to blow up elec-
trical towers and dams, code names, and anonymous communiqués boast-
ing of destroying millions of dollars in property."[4]

Currently, members of an ELF cell called "The Family" are on trial for
allegedly using "vegan jello," a napalm-like substance made of soap and
petroleum, and homemade time-delayed, fire-setting devices to blow up a
ski resort in Vail, Colorado, in 1998. When the eco-bomb detonated, eight
buildings were left in cinders. "When the timers went off, the entire mountain would go up in smoke," reports Vanessa Grigoriadis in *Rolling Stone.*[5]

The eleven members of The Family (a twelfth committed suicide in
police custody) also stand accused of destroying animal research facilities,
biotech labs, forest ranger stations, a meatpacking plant, and three timber
company headquarters. They have all pleaded innocent, although the US
Justice Department presented mountains of evidence — including some
thirty-five CDs of recorded conversation — in a sixty-five-count indictment
against them.

The Family has shattered other perceptions of eco-terrorism as well.
Namely, through the connection of many of its members to "mainstream"
environmentalism. As Grigoriadis writes in her vivid article in *Rolling Stone,*
which is a magazine not exactly known as hostile to the green movement,
"It's long been assumed that those who counted themselves members of the
ELF . . . were angry suburban boys in their late teens or early twenties who
worked in small cells, performing one or two misdeeds and then disbanding.
In fact, nearly every member of the Family was an adult committed to environmental activism."[6]

ELF, an offshoot of Earth First!, whose activity of spiking trees with
metal rods was mild only by comparison to some of ELF's activities, has

---

[2]Vanessa Grigoriadis, "The Rise & Fall of the Eco-Radical Underground," *Rolling Stone,* 28
July 2006, http://www.rollingstone.com/politics/story/11035255 / the_rise_fall_of_the_ecoradica_
underground/1.

[3]Ibid.

[4]Brad Knickerbocker, "Backstory: Eco-vigilantes; All in 'The Family?'", *Christian Science
Monitor,* 30 January 2006, http://www.csmonitor.com/2006/0130/p20s01-sten.html.

[5]Grigoriadis, "The Rise & Fall of the Eco-Radical Underground."

[6]Ibid.

claimed it always makes sure people are not in the way when it commits its violent acts against property. One set of its and ALF's guidelines claimed that members "take all necessary precautions against harming any animal — human and nonhuman."[7]

But other statements made by the groups and their intermediaries indicate they are willing to countenance physical harm. The North American Animal Liberation Press Office, which acts as a spokesman far ALF, listed as an example of an appropriate activity of a "revolutionary cell" "an animal liberationist shooting a vivisector[8] dead on his doorstep." ALF defines "vivisector" as anyone who engages in medical research. The Press Office lauded what it called "extensional self-defense," a term, it explained, that means "humans who stand up for animals and stop their suffering, using, in the words of Malcolm X,[9] 'any means necessary.'"[10]

Similarly, ELF said in a press release taking credit for setting fire to a Pennsylvania laboratory in 2002: "[W]here it is necessary we will no longer hesitate to pick up the gun to implement justice and provide the needed protection for our planet that decades of legal battles, pleading, protest and economic sabotage have failed so drastically to achieve. The diverse efforts of this revolutionary force cannot be contained, and will only continue to intensify as we are brought face to face with the oppressor in inevitable, violent confrontation."[11]

So far, no one has been killed in the attacks ALF and ELF have claimed credit for. Not, as the FBI seems to realize, for lack of trying. And Tom Randall, a conservative environmental consultant, thinks they may have more direct casualties on their hands than they let on: "My suspicion is if they did kill someone, they wouldn't take credit for it."[12] So while there may have been fatal fires set by ELF members, the national leaders wouldn't take credit for them, leading the public to think the groups are nonviolent.

But that couldn't be further from the truth. ALF and ELF know full well when they set timing devices that research scientists can work anytime during the day, Randall says. And he knows of research scientists who have received life-threatening phone calls.

[7]North American Animal Liberation Press Office, "Frequently Asked Questions about the North American Animal Liberation Press Office," http://www.animalliberationpressoffice.org/faq.htm.

[8]*vivisector:* Someone who practices vivisection — surgery on a live organism, typically done for research or educational purposes. [Eds.]

[9]*Malcolm X:* Born Malcolm Little and also known as El-Hajj Malik El-Shabazz, Malcom X (1925–1965) was an African American Muslim minister and civil rights activist. (See page 210.) [Eds.]

[10]North American Animal Liberation Press Office, "Frequently Asked Questions about the North American Animal Liberation Press Office."

[11]Randall Sullivan, "Hunting America's Most Wanted Eco-Terrorist," *Rolling Stone,* 12 December 2002, http://www.rollingstone.com/politics/story/11034035/hunting_americas_most_wanted_ecoterrorist.

[12]Telephone Interview with Tom Randall, 23 August 2006.

Extremism in the Defense of
Tufted Titmice Is No Vice

Indirectly, eco-terrorists are killing thousands of people, the most vulnerable members of our society. People with debilitating diseases depend on research conducted with animals or with techniques of biotechnology such as gene-splicing, which environmentalists criticize as "unnatural." In the third world, food derived from biotechnology can be fortified with special ingredients to make sure poor children are getting the nutrients they need. When life-saving research is delayed or shut down because of terrorist acts or terrorist threats, the real casualties are the sick and the poor who depend on the ability of scientists to do their work.

Susan Paris, president of Americans for Medical Progress, which represents scientific researchers, detailed the human costs of this type of terrorism: "Because of terrorist acts by animal activists . . . crucial research projects have been delayed or scrapped. More and more of the scarce dollars available to research are spent on heightened security and higher insurance rates. Promising young scientists are rejecting careers in research. Top-notch researchers are getting out of the field."[13]

15

The good news is that people from diverse fields — fields vital to public health and our standard of living — have recognized the threat of eco-terrorism and are coming together to fight it. In Pennsylvania, the state legislature passed a bill toughening penalties for the use or threat of force against facilities involved with animals, plants, and natural resources. According to the regional Ottaway News Service, "The coalition supporting the legislation includes industries, academic institutions and professional associations that ordinarily have little in common." Supporters included the Pennsylvania Farm Bureau, the Pennsylvania Forestry Association, pharmaceutical firms, biotech entrepreneurs, and the academic institutions of Pennsylvania State University, the University of Pittsburgh, and the University of Pennsylvania.[14]

The bill was passed in April 2006 by both houses of the Republican-controlled Pennsylvania legislature and signed by Democratic governor Ed Rendell. "Destroying property, intimidating Pennsylvania residents, or illegally confiscating animals as a way of political protest will not be tolerated in Pennsylvania," Governor Rendell said upon signing the bill.

Rendell emphasized that he and the legislature worked hard to see to it that the bill did not infringe on the right to protest or even punish civil disobedience per se, such as trespassing. "If this legislation imposed additional penalties on persons who were only engaged in peaceful protest that

---

[13]Steven Best, "Behind the Mask: Uncovering the Animal Liberation Front," http://www.drstevebest.org/papers/exerpts/TOFF/Behind_The_Mask_p2.php.

[14]Robert B. Swift, "Unusual Coalition Backs Ecoterrorism Legislation," *Pocono Record*, 12 April 2006, http://www.poconorecord.com/apps/pbcs.dll/article?AID=/20060412/NEWS/604120341/-1/NEWS.

did not involve property damage, I would have vetoed the bill," he remarked. Instead, he noted, the bill only targets acts "against property with the specific intent to intimidate." Rendell concluded that this "type of conduct cannot be countenance in any free society," and — in an encouraging example of bipartisanship for the common good — put his signature to the bill.[15]

Eco-Ties That Bind

Unfortunately, the eco-terrorists have a lot of people in their corner too, even if they're not direct supporters. One would think, for instance, that mainline environmental groups would be the first to want to throw the book at those committing violent acts in the name of protecting the environment, for fear that the whole environmental movement would be tarnished. Yet the state chapter of the Pennsylvania Sierra Club has staunchly opposed any bill that would more harshly punish eco-terrorism. Ottaway News Service paraphrased one of the group's lobbyists as saying, "The Sierra Club[16] bars its own members from engaging in civil disobedience and blockading or trespassing on property, but there is concern about the bill's impact on other environmental groups."[17] Concern over its impact on groups that resort to violence and destruction of property?

Indeed, some mainline environmental leaders have publicly said that   20
eco-terrorism enables the green movement to pursue a good-cop, bad-cop approach to getting what it wants. The late David Brower, longtime head of the Sierra Club and founder of other groups, put it this way to the radical green magazine *E* in 1990: "The Sierra Club made the Nature Conservancy look reasonable. Then I founded Friends of the Earth to make the Sierra Club look reasonable. Then I founded Earth Island Institute to make Friends of the Earth look reasonable. Earth First! now makes us look reasonable. We're still waiting for someone to come along and make Earth First! look reasonable."[18]

The close links between Earth First! founder Dave Foreman and prominent greens gives a chilling look at the place of eco-terrorism in the environmental movement. Foreman has in fact glided back and forth from top-level environmental policy making to "monkeywrenching" and eco-terrorism with relative ease. Foreman had taken a job at a regional chapter of Wilderness Society in the early 1970s, and by the end of the decade was its Washington representative.

---

[15]"Governor Signs Ecoterrorism Bill into Law," Office of the Governor of Pennsylvania, News Release, 14 April 2006, http://www.state.pa.us/papower/cwp/view.asp?Q=451790&A=11.

[16]*Sierra Club:* Founded in 1892, the oldest environmental organization in the United States. [Eds.]

[17]Swift, "Unusual Coalition Backs Ecoterrorism Legislation."

[18]Quoted in David Almasi, "The Radical Spectrum: Environmentalists Push the Envelope to Push Their Cause," *National Policy Analysis,* April 2002, http://www.nationalcenter.org/NPA403.html.

But he lost his patience with politics and decided direct force would be more effective. In the early 1980s, Foreman cofounded Earth First!, which carried as its slogan "No compromise in defense of Mother Earth." In 1985, Foreman published a 350-page how-to guide to eco-sabotage. Entitled *Ecodefense: A Field Guide to Monkeywrenching*, Foreman's book gave its readers useful instructions on how to down power lines, disable heavy equipment, vandalize billboards, and most infamously, "spike" trees. Tree-spiking involves driving a metal rod as deeply as possible into trees that might be logged. "Spike a few trees now and then whenever you enter an area," reads the book's dust jacket.

And readers did.

One man who found out all about tree-spiking was George Alexander. He was a twenty-three-year-old sawmill worker for the Louisiana Pacific paper company. In 1987, Alexander was cutting a section of a redwood log with a saw when all of a sudden the saw hit a metal rod that had been placed there. According to the *San Francisco Chronicle*, Alexander then "incurred severe face lacerations, cuts on both jugular veins and the loss of upper and lower front teeth." As Neal Hrab would later write in a report for the Capital Research Center, "Dave Foreman's response was chilling." Foreman told the *Chronicle*, "It is unfortunate this worker was injured and I wish him the best. But the real destruction and injury is being perpetrated by Louisiana-Pacific and the forest service in liquidating old-growth forests."[19]

As consultant Randall pointed out, it is hard to know how many have been physically harmed or killed by eco-terrorism, because groups will never take credit for incidents in which those injuries occur. In his 1991 memoir, *Confessions of an Eco-Warrior*, Foreman tried to further distance Earth First! and ultimately himself from Alexander's injury. He said it didn't look like an Earth First! sabotage because the "spiked tree was not an old-growth redwood from a sale in a pristine area." He then tried to blame Louisiana-Pacific, because the company may not have put its wood through a metal detector to check for spikes![20]

Foreman said tree-spikers should minimize the chances for harm to workers by warning companies through various methods. Yet he still defended the practice of spiking, even while acknowledging it could lead to more injuries like those of Alexander. "Safety is a relative concept; nothing in life is entirely safe," Foreman wrote. "The record shows, however, that tree spiking is one of the least dangers a logger faces."[21]

If Foreman's was a lone voice on the fringe of the environmental movement — shunned by movement leaders — there would be less cause for concern. Instead, what is most alarming about Foreman's book is its

25

---

[19]Neil Hrab, "Greenpeace, Earth First!, PETA," *Organization Trends*, March 2004, 4, http://www.capitalresearch.org/pubs/pdf/03_04_OT.pdf.

[20]Dave Foreman, *Confessions of an Eco-Warrior* (Harmony Books, 1991), 151–52.

[21]Ibid., 153.

back cover. There, even after the injuries of George Alexander had been widely reported, Foreman is warmly embraced by some of the nation's leading environmental thinkers.

Bill McKibben calls Foreman "[o]ne of the towering figures, the mighty sequoias of American conservation." James Lovelock, developer of the "Gaia hypothesis"[22] widely cited by greens, writes that "Dave Foreman is one who truly understands that the Earth must come first." And Kirkpatrick Sale,[23] author of many influential environmental tracts, gushes that "if anything is to save this imperiled Earth, it is the kind of biocentric ecological vision he [Foreman] here puts so clearly and forcefully."[24]

No, in their statements, the authors do not expressly support tree-spiking and Foreman's other recommended "monkeywrenching" activities. But their words of praise do countenance Foreman and, in turn, the activities he recommends. And showing just how few links separate eco-terrorism from environmentalism's "mainstream," McKibben, Sale, and Lovelock — the writers who praised Foreman — are themselves regularly praised by Al Gore.[25]

Foreman has gone back to a role in formulating environmental policy. He was a founder of the Wildlands Project, which proposes vast swaths of interconnecting land inhabited by wild animals, with human "islands" in-between. It also advocates repopulating many areas with large predators such as wolves, mountain lions, and grizzly bears. Foreman's project lists many academic advisers and claims success in community land-use planning. In fact, the next time you see a cougar in your yard, Foreman may be the guy you want to thank. He has since left the Wildlands Project and is promoting the same ideas at the Rewilding Institute. 30

Reinforcing the notion that the radical and the mainstream are too close for comfort, Foreman was also elected to the board of the Sierra Club in the mid-1990s and stayed there until 1997.

During his Earth First! days, Foreman also had another fan. Theodore Kaczynski, also known as the Unabomber, mailed dozens of letter bombs. He killed three people and wounded twenty-eight before he was arrested in the late 1990s and was sentenced to life in prison after a guilty plea. But even though Kaczynski led a solitary existence in a cabin, he was never exactly alone. FBI agents discovered several volumes of the *Earth First! Journal* when they raided his cabin. Also found was an issue of the publication *Live Wild or Die*, which was financed by an Earth First! cofounder and featured a

---

[22]*Gaia Hypothesis:* Originally proposed by English scientist James Lovelock (b. 1919), the Gaia Hypothesis holds that the earth is a unified "cybernetic system" that acts much like a single living organism. [Eds.]

[23]*Kirkpatrick Sale:* American author, activist, and environmentalist (b. 1937). [Eds.]

[24]Foreman, *Confessions of an Eco-Warrior,* back cover.

[25]*Al Gore:* Albert Arnold "Al" Gore (b. 1948) is an American environmental activist who served as the forty-fifth vice president of the United States from 1993 to 2001. Gore's 2006 documentary on global warming *An Inconvenient Truth* won an Academy Award in 2007. [Eds.]

"hit list" of individuals and corporations it considered most destructive to the environment.[26] Yet one searches in vain in the mainstream media for articles noting the connection of Earth First! to the Unabomber's actions. In fact, there is precious little media asking the question if the harsh rhetoric of mainline environmental groups has anything to do with the spike in eco-terrorism.

A different media situation occurred, however, in another act of domestic terrorism. When Timothy McVeigh blew up the federal Murrah building in Oklahoma City in 1995, pundits rushed in to blame any radio talk show host who had harsh words for big government. Richard Lacayo of *Time* magazine infamously called conservative talk radio hosts "an unindicted co-conspirator" in McVeigh's bombing.[27] This, despite the fact that McVeigh appeared to be more influenced by the white supremacy movement than any arguments about limited government. Nevertheless, conservatives did examine their rhetoric against the government and, in some cases, moderated their tone.

We should always be careful about drawing links between strong words and violent deeds, no matter who the speakers in question are. Those who use violence are solely responsible for their actions. I am a strong believer in the First Amendment and oppose any restrictions on expression, with limited exceptions such as Justice Holmes's[28] example of falsely shouting "fire" in a theater, and speech that directly incites to riot. Strong debate is essential to a free society.

Nevertheless, actions are always preceded by beliefs, and no belief exists in a vacuum. If overstated rhetoric and false information is encouraging violence and terrorism, then society — again, not government — has an obligation to examine that rhetoric and discourage its use. And conservative rhetoric against the government around the time of the bombing in Oklahoma pales in comparison to the attacks on and vilification of those who disagree with environmentalists. And it paints apocalyptic end-of-the-world rhetoric if opponents get their way. Here is a sampling: 35

In fund-raising material for the Natural Resources Defense Council, Robert F. Kennedy Jr.[29] proclaims, "The Bush Administration is quietly putting radical new policies in place that will let its corporate allies poison our air, foul our water, and devastate our wildlands for decades to come."[30] Casting

---

[26]Profile of Earth First!, DiscoverTheNetworks.org. http://www.discoverthenetwork.org/groupProfile.asp?grpid=7229.

[27]Richard Lacayo, "A Moment of Silence," *Time*, 8 May 1995, 42.

[28]*Justice Holmes:* Oliver Wendell Holmes Jr. (1841–1935) served on the U.S. Supreme Court from 1902 to 1932. [Eds.]

[29]*Robert F. Kennedy Jr:* Robert Francis Kennedy Jr. (b. 1954) is an American environmental activist. [Eds.]

[30]Robert F. Kennedy Jr., Natural Resources Defense Council fund-raising mail solicitation, circa spring 2006.

his opponents as "evil," Defenders of Wildlife president Rodger Schlickeisen writes, "The evil special interests are still actively trying to cut major loopholes in the Endangered Species Act."[31] Al Gore said in April 2006, "We have been blind to the fact that the human species is now having a crushing impact on the ecological system of the planet."[32]

Anti-human statements like Gore's are actually the most poisonous kind of environmental rhetoric. Statements about the evil of humanity in general are ultimately more destructive than any verbal attacks on individual humans, such as George W. Bush and Dick Cheney. And this is what binds terrorism advocates like Foreman together with "mainstream" environmentalists like Paul Ehrlich.[33]

In *Confessions of an Eco-Warrior*, Foreman repeatedly refers to what he calls the "humanpox" plague of too many people. He praises the views of Thomas Malthus,[34] whose 1798 treatise that overpopulation would exhaust resources influenced the modern population control movement. But Foreman writes that even if Malthus were wrong about humans running out of resources to sustain themselves, there are still too many darn humans: "Even if inequitable distribution could be solved, six billion human beings converting the natural world to material goods and human food would devastate natural diversity."[35]

Population control guru Ehrlich says much the same thing on the Web site of the Wildlands Project, which, as we have noted, was founded by Foreman. After so many of his doomsaying predictions about humans have been proven wrong, he now speaks of limiting human population and development to solve "the only realistic strategy for enduring the extinction crisis."[36]

Foreman and Ehrlich are Malthusians with a twist. They may no longer   40
believe that humans will starve themselves by exhausting all resources, but that's not really important to them. To them, and to most environmental leaders, population will always be a problem because humans roam on too much habitat that they think belongs exclusively to cougars, wolves, and plants and should be left almost completely undisturbed. That's why environmental groups continue to push population control measures, even as economists and demographers insist that we have an *underpopulation* problem.

---

[31]Rodger Schlickeisen, "Heroes, Villains and the Endangered Species Act," *Defenders*, winter 2006, http://www.defenders.org/defendersmag/issues/winter06/view.html.

[32]Ian Hoffman, "Gore: Will We Destroy Earth? It's a Moral Issue," *Oakland Tribune*, 7 April 2006.

[33]*Paul Ehrlich:* Paul Ralph Ehrlich (b. 1932) is an American entomologist and environmentalist, famous for his 1968 book *The Population Bomb.* [Eds.]

[34]*Thomas Malthus:* The Reverend Thomas Robert Malthus (1766–1834) was a British scholar widely known for his pioneering work on population growth. [Eds.]

[35]Foreman, *Confessions of an Eco-Warrior,* 28.

[36]Wildlands Project, "What We Do," http://www.twp.org/cms/page1090.cfm.

For environmentalists, there will always be too many people and too few species! All statements coming from environmentalists must be evaluated by looking through the anti-human lens that much of them hold.

Eco-Clichés and Berlau's Bumper Stickers

Unfortunately, there are sayings and bumper sticker slogans that many good people who don't share environmentalists' anti-human premises will repeat without further examination. Also as unfortunate, these statements shape public policy in ways that are detrimental, as we have seen, to the health of humans and even wildlife. Let's look at a few, view the problem of their implications, and see if we can come up with our own simple slogans for better ways to conserve resources and solve public health problems.

Sustainable Development

This is a term that has been used for coercive population control policies, blocking development in the name of stopping urban sprawl, and managing forest and fisheries. Jared Diamond[37] uses the term a lot in his popular doomsaying volume *Collapse*. We can buy products that are certified they are made in a "sustainable" way.

But what does the term really mean? For many environmentalists, it means limiting the impact of humans on the planet, and all human impacts are necessarily bad. Not every method of producing things labeled "sustainable" is necessarily bad. But the vagueness of the term and the anti-human implications of it mean that both products and policies labeled "sustainable" merit closer scrutiny. . . .

The Environment

I've talked a lot in this book about environmentalists, and some readers may be left wondering if we can care about clean water and clean air and special animals and trees without subscribing to all the crazy notions of environmentalists? Yes, we can. But one of the most important things is to stop using vague words like "the environment" and "the planet."

It's important to do what we can to protect the *inhabitants* of the environment or the planet. I would say humans first, then animals, and then plant life. If there is a specific pollutant, man-made or natural, affecting human health, we should figure out a way to deal with it. The same goes for feasible solutions for threats to wildlife and plants. But we shouldn't look at these problems from the standpoint that more human impact is necessarily bad. All too frequently these days, a dam or a road is prevented from being built not because it will even reduce the number of the species, but because environmentalists say it will affect that species' ecosystem.

45

---

[37]*Jared Diamond:* Jared Mason Diamond (b. 1937), American scientist and author. [Eds.]

The difference lies in conservation vs. preservation. Teddy Roosevelt was a conservationist. He believed in conserving, as well as using, natural resources and outdoor spots. But unlike John Muir[38] and his disciples at the Sierra Club, Roosevelt was not a preservationist. He knew it was folly to freeze in place the land as it always was. And in truth, we don't know how the land always was. . . . Contrary to myths, Native Americans made great changes to the American landscape. We shouldn't be afraid to do the same.

One thing that has changed since Roosevelt's day is that the folly of government management of natural resources has clearly been shown. When the Soviet Union opened up,[39] scholars were appalled at the rotten treatment of its land.[40] In the United States, by contrast, many private landowners go out of their way to create habitats for animals, and the stiff mandates of the Endangered Species Act[41] actually acts as a disincentive to conservation. The Center for Private Conservation, affiliated with the Competitive Enterprise Institute and run by skilled outdoorsman Robert I. Smith, offers plenty of excellent examples of the private preservation of habitat.[42]

Humans Shouldn't Stand Apart from or Control Nature

Environmentalists often assert that humans arrogantly try to bend nature to their ways, and that they should be more humble. Humans aren't any more special than other parts of nature and should stop acting like they are.

This belief directly conflicts, of course, with many of our religious traditions of Judaism and Christianity. The book of Genesis clearly tells us that God intended us to have "dominion" over and to "subdue" the earth to our needs. We should be wise stewards, but the earth is here for us and for future generations to use.

The ironic thing here is that environmentalists are actually the ones   50 asking us to stand apart from nature. They're asking us not to do the same things as other animals. It's perfectly fine with greens when elephants knock down trees with their trunks and when beavers build dams. It's all right with animal rights proponents when wolves and lions eat other animals, just not when humans do it.

We're animals too. The difference is that we're animals with intelligent minds, capable of restraining our desires. And, of course, we should restrain

[38]*John Muir:* American naturalist, author, and early advocate of wilderness preservation (1838–1914). [Eds.]

[39]*When the Soviet Union opened up:* Following a failed coup attempt in 1991, the Soviet Union dissolved, resulting in the creation of the Russian Republic. [Eds.]

[40]"Health and the Environment in the Former Soviet Union Part I," *Environmental Review,* September 1995, http://www.environmentalreview.org/vol02/feschba.html.

[41]*the Endangered Species Act:* The Endangered Species Act of 1973 protects critically threatened species from the effects of "economic growth and development." [Eds.]

[42]See description at http://prfamerica.org/CEI-CPC.html.

ourselves sometimes. But we shouldn't argue that doing the things we need and want to do for comfort and survival are in any way "unnatural." . . .

Don't Leave a Footprint

The idea here is that humans should leave no lasting trace in nature, that we should have no impact in the ecosystems in which we live. I say, "Leave a Footprint." In fact, leave many footprints. I'd like to put that on a bumper sticker.

The Native Americans left footprints when through their burnings of nature they created the Great Plains. Another who left a big footprint was John Chapman, better known as Johnny Appleseed, when he planted apple trees all over nineteenth-century America.

And leave behind human "footprints" like those that comprise much of the "natural" beauty of Hawaii, as the eminent microbiologist and essayist Renè Dubos points out in his book, *The Wooing of Earth*. Before European settlers arrived, he writes, "the Hawaiian biota was relatively simple and disharmonic. . . . It had no pine trees, no oaks, no maples, no willows, no fig trees, no mangroves [aka wetlands], one single species of palm, and only a few insignificant orchids." The introduced plant species, Dubos writes, "have prospered even better than in their native habitats."[43]

Dubos, the recipient of many awards for his scientific contributions to germ-fighting, concludes his 1980 book with some wise words. There was a character in Voltaire's eighteenth-century novel, *Candide*,[44] called Dr. Pangloss, who always said that whatever situation occurred was "the best of all worlds." To Dubos, "'[n]ature knows best' is the twentieth century equivalent to Pangloss's affirmation." And to Dubos, "[t]he interplay between humankind and the Earth has often generated ecosystems that, from many points of view, are more interesting and more creative than those occurring in the state of wilderness."[45]

So be wise, but don't be afraid to change the landscape and make it better for future generations. The other animals will probably thank you as well. And let's have another homesteading act[46] to privatize the one-third of the land the federal government owns, so that there can be many unique footprints on this land of ours.

Everybody say it loud. We're humans and we're proud!

55

---

[43]René Dubos, *The Wooing of Earth* (Charles Scribner's Sons, 1980), 86.

[44]*Candide: Candide, or Optimism* (1759) by Voltaire, the pen name of French philosopher Francois-Marie Arouet (1694–1778), satirizes irrational optimism. [Eds.]

[45]Dubos, *The Wooing of Earth*, 81.

[46]*another homesteading act:* The 1862 Homestead Act offered citizens free title to 160–640 acres of land in "undeveloped" areas of the United States outside the original thirteen colonies. [Eds.]

ENGAGING THE TEXT

1. Would you agree with Berlau that environmental radicalism is actually terrorism? Do you see any distinction between spray painting graffiti on a Ronald McDonald statue or vandalizing a billboard and the activities of a group like al-Quaeda? What about spiking trees or firebombing tourist resorts?

2. Why do you think Berlau attempts to link the activities of "eco-terrorists" like Unabomber Theodore Kaczynski with mainstream environmentalists like James Lovelock, Bill McKibben, and Al Gore? Would you agree that mainstream environmentalists are somehow enabling "eco-terrorism"?

3. Based on your own experience, do you think that the environmental movement is "anti-human"? Why or why not? To what extent would you agree with Berlau's claim that "we have an *underpopulation problem*" (para. 40)?

4. What's wrong, according to Berlau, with using "eco-clichés" like "sustainable," "the environment," and "the planet"? Would you agree that we'd be better off not using these words? Why or why not?

5. How does Berlau view the relationship between human beings and nature? How does this view compare with your own?

EXPLORING CONNECTIONS

6. How does Berlau's view of nature compare with that of Henry David Thoreau (p. 646)? Which do you find more appealing and why?

7. How might you expect John (Fire) Lame Deer (p. 686) to explain Berlau's view of nature and the relationship between human beings and animals? To what extent do you think Lame Deer would endorse some of the tactics employed by activist groups like Earth First!, the Earth Liberation Front, and the Animal Liberation Front?

8. To what extent do the selections by Joy Williams (p. 703), Derrick Jensen and Stephanie McMillan (p. 715), and Bill McKibben (p. 743) reflect the kind of "anti-human" sentiment that Berlau associates with environmentalism? How might these authors respond to the notion that "God intended us to have 'dominion over' and to 'subdue' the earth" (para. 49)?

EXTENDING THE CRITICAL CONTEXT

9. Research the record and philosophy of one or more of the "eco-terrorist" groups that Berlau cites in this selection. How accurate is Berlau's depiction of groups like Earth First!, the Earth Liberation Front, and the Animal Liberation Front? Do you think "monkeywrenching" and other forms of direct action in the name of the environment are ever justified? Why or why not?

10. Research the Endangered Species Act of 1973 and the Wilderness Act of 1964 to learn more about the history and effectiveness of these attempts to legislate governmental protection. To what extent would you agree with Berlau's claim that government should not be trusted with protecting the environment? Do you agree that it would be a good idea to privatize more federally protected land? Why or why not?

FURTHER CONNECTIONS

1. Research the career of one of the following American scientists, writers, or thinkers to learn more about their contribution to the environmental movement:

George Caitlin	John McPhee
George Perkins Marsh	Wendell Berry
Frederick Law Olmstead	David Brower
Gifford Pinchot	E. O. Wilson
Marjory Stoneman Douglas	Barry Lopez
Loren Eiseley	Terry Tempest Williams
William O. Douglas	Carolyn Merchant
Rachel Carson	Julia Butterfly Hill
Paul Ehrlich	David Quammen
Edward Abbey	Paul Hawkin
Garrett Hardin	Rod Coronado
Gary Snyder	

   In class, share what you learn about your subject's work on behalf of the environment. How would you assess your subject's contribution to the development of the environmental movement?

2. Drawing on the ideas and arguments put forward by Richard Louv (p. 664), Charles Siebert (p. 676), John (Fire) Lame Deer (p. 686), Joy Williams (p. 703), Bill McKibben (p. 743), and Graeme Wood (p. 756), write an essay exploring the notion that twenty-first-century America is entering a "post-natural" era. What evidence do you see in your daily life to suggest that nature is no longer critical — or even very interesting — to us as a nation?

3. Using one of the free tools available online, calculate your personal carbon footprint and that of your household. Compare your results in class and discuss reasons for the differences that you note. What could you do to reduce your personal impact on the environment? (You can find carbon footprint calculators at the Nature Conservancy Web site and at www.carbonfootprint.com.)

4. Survey the "green" organizations on your campus, including those dedicated to combating climate change, recycling, conservation, and animal rights. What are their goals, and how do they seek to achieve them? How many students do they count as active members? How much impact do these groups appear to have on the environment?

5. In addition to the "geo-engineering" solutions to climate change described by Graeme Wood (p. 756), research other high-tech solutions to the energy and global warming crises, including new approaches to ocean and geothermal energy generation, the use of "safe" nuclear and "green hydrogen" power, and "clean carbon" and "carbon sequestration" technologies. What advantages and disadvantages are associated with these approaches to

cutting carbon emissions? Which strike you as the most promising and why?

6. Research the history of and current trends in the animal rights movement. How did the notion of animal rights develop? What are the goals of most contemporary animal rights groups? What arguments do they offer in support of "animal equity"? To what extent would you agree that animals have rights and interests comparable to those of humans? Do you think it is immoral to use animals for display in zoos, for sport in rodeos and horse racing, for scientific research, for food? Why or why not?

7. Do some online research to learn more about population control as a response to the environmental crisis. How did the idea of scientific population control develop? Who are some of the main historical and contemporary figures in the population control movement? What difference is there between population control and eugenics? Hold a debate in class on whether population control should be used to address global environmental issues.

Barbara Ehrenreich. "Serving in Florida" from *Nickel and Dimed* by Barbara Erhenreich. Copyright © 2001 by Barbara Ehrenreich. Reprinted by arrangement with Henry Holt & Company, LLC.

Robert Frank. "Living It: Tim Blixseth." Chapter 4 from *Richistan: A Journey Through the American Wealth Boom and the Lives of the New Rich* by Robert Frank. Copyright © 2007 by Robert L. Frank. Used by permission of Crown Publishers, a division of Random House, Inc.

George M. Fredrickson. "Models of American Ethnic Relations: A Historical Perspective." First published in *Cultural Divides: Understanding and Overcoming Group Conflict*, edited by Deborah A. Prentice and Dale T. Miller. Copyright © 1999 Russell Sage Foundation, 112 E. 64th Street, New York, NY 10021. Reprinted with permission.

John Taylor Gatto. "Against School." Copyright © 2003 by Harper's magazine. All rights reserved. Reproduced from the September issue by special permission.

Naomi Gerstel and Natalia Sarkisian. "The Color of Family Ties: Race, Class, Gender, and Extended Family Involvement." From *American Families: A Multicultural Reader,* 2nd Edition, edited by Stephanie Coontz. Copyright © 1999 Routledge. Reprinted by permission of Naomi Gerstel.

Inés Hernández-Ávila. "Para Teresa." From *Con Razón, Corazón* by Inés Hernández-Ávila. Reprinted by permission of the author.

Hua Hsu. "The End of White America?" First published in the *Atlantic Monthly*. Copyright © 2009 by The Atlantic Monthly. Reproduced with permission of The Atlantic Monthly in the format Textbook via Copyright Clearance Center.

Roger Jack. "An Indian Story." From *Dancing On the Rim of the World: An Anthology of Contemporary Northwest Native American Writing*, edited by Andrea Lerner and published by the University of Arizona Press (1990). "An Indian Story" copyright © Roger Jack. Reprinted by permission of the author.

Derrick Jensen and Stephanie McMillan. Excerpts from *As the World Burns: 50 Simple Things You Can Do to Stay in Denial: A Graphic Novel* by Derrick Jensen and Stephanie McMillan. Copyright © 2007 by Derrick Jensen and Stephanie McMillan. Reprinted with the permission of Seven Stories Press. www.sevenstories.com.

Diana Kendall. "Framing Class, Vicarious Living, and Conspicuous Consumption." From *Framing Class: Media Representations of Wealth and Poverty in America* by Diana Elizabeth Kendall. Copyright © 2005 by Rowman & Littlefield Publishers, Inc. All rights reserved. Reprinted by permission of the publisher.

Jean Kilbourne. "Two Ways a Woman Can Get Hurt." Excerpt from Chapter 12, "Two Ways a Woman Can Get Hurt: Advertising and Violence" in *Can't Buy My Love: How Advertising Changes the Way We Think and Feel* by Jean Kilbourne. Previously published as *Deadly Persuasion*. Copyright © 1999 by Jean Kilbourne. Reprinted with the permission of The Free Press, a Division of Simon & Schuster, Inc. All rights reserved.

Michael Kimmel. "Bros Before Hos." From *The Guyland: The Perilous World Where Boys Become Men* by Michael Kimmel. Copyright © 2008 by Michael Kimmel. Reprinted by permission of HarperCollins Publishers.

Jamaica Kincaid. "Girl." From *At the Bottom of the River* by Jamaica Kincaid. Copyright © 1983 by Jamaica Kincaid. Reprinted by permission of Farrar, Straus & Giroux, LLC.

Dan Kindlon. "The Descent of Men." Excerpts from *Alpha Girls: Understanding the New American Girls* by Dan Kindlon. Copyright © 2006 by Dan Kindlon. Reprinted by permission of Rodale Press.

Jonathan Kozol. "Still Separate, Still Unequal." From *The Shame of the Nation* by Jonathan Kozol. Copyright © 2006 by Jonathan Kozol. Used by permission of Crown Publishers, a division of Random House, Inc.

Maria L. La Ganga. From the *Los Angeles Times*, March 20, 2009. Copyright © 2009 by Los Angeles Times Syndicate. Reproduced with permission of Los Angeles Times Syndicate in the format Textbook via Copyright Clearance Center.

John (Fire) Lame Deer and Richard Erdoes. "Talking to the Owls and Butterflies." From *Lame Deer: Seeker of Visions by John (Fire) Lame Deer and Richard Erdoes*. Copyright © 1994 by Pocket Books. Copyright © 1972 by John (Fire) Lame Deer and Richard Erdoes. Reprinted with the permission of Pocket Books, a Division of Simon & Schuster, Inc. All rights reserved.

Richard Louv. "A Life of the Senses." From *Last Child In the Woods: Saving Our Children from Nature-Deficit Disorder* by Richard Louv. Copyright © 2008 Algonquin Books of Chapel Hill. Reprinted by permission of Algonquin Books of Chapel Hill in the formats Textbook and Other Book via Copyright Clearance Center.

Malcolm X. "Learning to Read." From *The Autobiography of Malcolm X* by Malcolm X and Alex Haley. Copyright © 1964 by Alex Haley and Malcolm X. Copyright © 1965 by Alex Haley and Betty Shabazz. Used by permission of Random House, Inc.

Gregory Mantsios. "Class in America–2006." From *Race, Class, and Gender in the United States*, edited by Paula Rothenberg (New York: Worth Publishers). Copyright © 2007. Reprinted by permission.

Marriage Equality USA. "Prop 8 Hurt My Family—Ask Me How." Courtesy of Marriage Equality USA.

Rubén Martínez. "The Crossing." From *Burning Sand*, to be published by Metropolitan Books, an imprint of Henry Holt & Co. First published in the *Los Angeles Times*, June 27, 2006. By permission of Susan Bergholz Literary Services, New York and Lamy, NM. All rights reserved.

James McBride. "The Boy in the Mirror." From *The Color of Water* by James McBride. Copyright © 1996 by James McBride. Used by permission of Riverhead Books, an imprint of Penguin Group (USA) Inc.

Bill McKibben. "The End of Nature" in *The End of Nature*. Copyright 2006 by Anchor Books, a division of Random House Inc. Reprinted by permission.

Michael Moore. "Idiot Nation." From *Stupid White Men . . . and Other Sorry Excuses For the State of the Nation* by Michael Moore. Copyright © 2002 Michael Moore. Reprinted by permission of HarperCollins Publishers.

Aurora Levins Morales. "Child of the Americas." From *Getting Home Alive* by Aurora Levins Morales and Rosario Morales. Copyright © 1986 by Aurora Levins Morales and Rosario Morales. Reprinted with the permission of Firebrand Books, www.firebrandbooks.com.

Joan Morgan. "From Fly-Girls to Bitches and Hos." From *When Chickenheads Come Home to Roost: My Life as a Hip-Hop Feminist* by Joan Morgan. Copyright © 1999 by Joan Morgan. Portions of the essay originally appeared in *Vibe* magazine. Reprinted with permission of Simon & Schuster, Inc. All rights reserved.

Jennifer Roback Morse. "8 Is Not Hate: The Meaning of a Proposition." First published in NationalReview.com. © 2008 JRM Enterprises. Reprinted by permission of the author.

Katherine S. Newman and Victor Tan Chen. Chapter 3 from *The Missing Class: Portraits of the Near Poor in America* by Katherine S. Newman and Victor Tan Chen. Copyright © 2007 by Katherine Newman and Victor Tan Chen. Reprinted by permission of Beacon Press, Boston.

Vincent N. Parrillo. "Causes of Prejudice." From *Strangers to These Shores: Race and Ethnic Relations in the United States,* 9th edition, pp 74–83. © 1997 Allyn & Bacon. Reproduced by permission of Pearson Education, Inc.

Professor X. "In the Basement of the Ivory Tower." From the *Atlantic Monthly,* June 1, 2008. Copyright © 2008 by The Atlantic Monthly. Reproduced with permission of The Atlantic Monthly in the format Textbook via Copyright Clearance Center.

Richard Rodriguez. "The Achievement of Desire." From *Hunger of Memory: The Education of Richard Rodriguez* by Richard Rodriguez. Reprinted by permission of David R. Godine, Publisher, Inc. Copyright © 1982 by Richard Rodriguez.

Mike Rose. "I Just Wanna Be Average." From *Lives on the Boundary: The Struggles and Achievements of America's Underprepared* by Mike Rose. Copyright © 1989 by Mike Rose. Reprinted with the permission of The Free Press, a Division of Simon & Schuster, Inc. All rights reserved.

Hanna Rosin. "A Boy's Life." First posted on TheAtlantic.com, November, 2008. Copyright © 2008. Reprinted by permission of the author.

Reihan Salam. "The Death of Macho." From *Foreign Policy* by Reihan Salam. Copyright © 2009 by Foreign Policy. Reproduced with permission of Foreign Policy in the formats Textbook via Copyright Clearance Center.

Charles Siebert. "The Artifice of the Natural" by Charles Siebert. Copyright © 1993 by Harper's Magazine. All rights reserved. Reproduced from the February issue by special permission.

Gary Soto. "Looking for Work." From *Living Up the Street: Narrative Recollections* by Gary Soto. Copyright © 1995 by Gary Soto. Used by permission of the author.

Andrew Sullivan. "My Big Fat Straight Wedding." From *The Atlantic.* Copyright © 2008 by Andrew Sullivan. Reprinted with permission of The Wylie Agency LLC.

Studs Terkel. "C. P. Ellis" and "Stephen Cruz." From *American Dream: Lost and Found* by Studs Terkel. Copyright © 1980 Studs Terkel. Reprinted by permission of Donadio & Olson, Inc.

Nydia M. Velázquez. "In Search of Justice." First published in *Sustainable Planet: Solutions for the Twenty-First Century,* edited by Juliet B. Schor and Betsy Taylor. Copyright © 2003 by Beacon Press. Reprinted by permission of Beacon Press in the format Textbook via Copyright Clearance Center.

Joy Williams. "Save the Whales, Screw the Shrimp." From *Ill Nature: Rants and Reflections on Humanity and Other Animals* by Joy Williams. Copyright © by Joy Williams. Originally published in *Esquire* magazine. Used by permission of Random House, Inc.

Evan Wolfson. "What Is Marriage?" From *Why Marriage Matters: America, Equality, and Gay People's Right to Marry* by Evan Wolfson. Copyright © 2004 by Evan Wolfson. Reprinted with the permission of The Free Press, a Division of Simon & Schuster, Inc. All rights reserved.

Graeme Wood. "Moving Heaven and Earth." First published in the *Atlantic Monthly* by Graeme Wood. Copyright © 2009 by The Atlantic Monthly. Reproduced with permission of The Atlantic Monthly in the format Textbook via Copyright Clearance Center.

Art Acknowledgments

CHAPTER 1: HARMONY AT HOME
17, © Hulton Archive/Columbia TriStar/Getty Images.
22, *A Family Tree* © Norman Rockwell Family Agency, Inc.
23, *Freedom from Want* © Norman Rockwell Family Agency, Inc.
24, *Freedom from Fear* © Norman Rockwell Family Agency, Inc.

358, © The New Yorker Collection 2008 Leo Cullum from cartoonbank.com. All Rights Reserved.

CHAPTER 4: CREATED EQUAL
373, © Eli Reed/Magnum Photos.
379, TOLES © 2008 The Washington Post. Reprinted with permission of Universal Press Syndicate. All rights reserved.
388, *Candorville* © Darrin Bell. © 2006 The Washington Post. All rights reserved. Reprinted with permission.
399, Copyright © 2009 Southern Poverty Law Center. Used by permission.
421, © The New Yorker Collection 2000 David Sipress from cartoonbank.com. All Rights Reserved.
423, left, © Dave Martin/AP Photo.
423, right, © Chris Graythen/Getty Images.
439, © Eric Gay/AP Photo.
440, ©Jean-Yves Rebeuf/Image Works.
441, Photo ©Roland Charles 1992. Used by permission of Mrs. Deborah Charles.
442, © The Dallas Morning News/Smiley N. Pool.
443, © The Dallas Morning News/M. Ainsworth.
444, © Todd Bigelow/Aurora Photos.
445, © A. Ramey/PhotoEdit.
446, © Stan Honda/AFP/Getty Images.
447, ©Justin Sullivan/Getty Images.
453, Lalo © 2003 Lalo Alcaraz. Reprinted with permission of Universal Press Syndicate. All rights reserved.
463, *Candorville* © Darrin Bell. © 2006 The Washington Post. All rights reserved. Reprinted with permission.
478, © Christophe Vorlet.
498, © The New Yorker Collection 2000 Alex Gregory from cartoonbank.com. All Rights Reserved.

CHAPTER 5: TRUE WOMEN AND REAL MEN
515, © Carolyn Jones.
535, © The New Yorker Collection 1995 Robert Mankoff from cartoonbank.com. All rights reserved.
548, 549, 551, Photos and drawings of Brandon Simms from the November 2008 *Atlantic*, courtesy of the family.
568, Photo © Michael A. Messner.
569, © Imagestate Media Partners Limited–Impact Photos/Alamy.
570, © Megan Maloy/Getty Images.
571, © Digital Vision/Getty Images.
572, © Hagerty Patrick/Corbis Sygma.
573, © Eli Reed/Magnum Photos.
610, THINK AGAIN (David John Attyah and S.A. Bachman) www.agitart.org.
619, © The New Yorker Collection 2006 David Sipress from cartoonbank.com. All Rights Reserved.
631, © Aaron Goodman Studios, Inc.

CHAPTER 6: AH WILDERNESS!
639, *Kindred Spirits* by Asher Brown Durand. Image © Francis G. Mayer/Corbis.
658, © The New Yorker Collection 1989 Charles Barsotti from cartoonbank.com. All Rights Reserved.
677, Sidewalk Bubblegum © Clay Butler.

695–98, "A Short History of America" copyright © 1979, 2010 by Robert Crumb. Reprinted by permission of Agence Littéraire Lora Fountain & Associates. All Rights Reserved.

699, top, *On the Drive, Pineries of Minnesota* (1867), Library of Congress.

699, bottom, *Buffalo Skulls at Michigan Carbon Works* (1880).

700, © Jerry Greer.

701, top, San Jose Mercury News by Andrea Maschietto. Copyright 2009 by San Jose Mercury News. Reproduced with permission of San Jose Mercury News via Copyright Clearance Center.

701, bottom, Jay Directo/AFP/Getty Images.

702, © John Blackford. Used by permission of AA Reps, Inc.

713, © The New Yorker Collection 2008 Leo Cullum from cartoonbank.com. All Rights Reserved.

742, © The New Yorker Collection 2007 Rob Esmay from cartoonbank.com. All Rights Reserved.

755, *Eco Depth Gauge* by Les U. Knight is licensed under a Creative Commons Attribution 3.0 United States License.

Index of Authors and Titles